THE ELGAR COMPANION TO
POST KEYNESIAN ECONOMICS

The Elgar Companion to Post Keynesian Economics

Edited by

J.E. King

Professor of Economics, Department of Economics and Finance, La Trobe University, Melbourne, Australia

Edward Elgar
Cheltenham, UK • Northampton, MA, USA

© J.E. King 2003

All rights reserved. No part of this publication may be reproduced, stored in a retrieval system or transmitted in any form or by any means, electronic, mechanical or photocopying, recording, or otherwise without the prior permission of the publisher.

Published by
Edward Elgar Publishing Limited
Glensanda House
Montpellier Parade
Cheltenham
Glos GL50 1UA
UK

Edward Elgar Publishing, Inc.
136 West Street
Suite 202
Northampton
Massachusetts 01060
USA

A catalogue record for this book
is available from the British Library

Library of Congress Cataloguing in Publication Data
The Elgar companion to post Keynesian economics / edited by J.E. King.
    p. cm.
  Includes bibliographical references.
    1. Keynesian economics. 1. King, J.E. (John Edward)

HB99.7.E522 2003
330.15–dc21
                                                                    2003044802

ISBN 1 84064 630 6 (cased)

Printed and bound in Great Britain by MPG Books Ltd, Bodmin, Cornwall

Contents

List of figures	viii
List of tables	ix
List of contributors	x
Introduction	xiv

Agency *Edward J. McKenna and Diane C. Zannoni*	1
Austrian School of Economics *Stephen D. Parsons*	5
Babylonian Mode of Thought *Sheila C. Dow*	11
Balance-of-payments-constrained Economic Growth *J.S.L. McCombie*	15
Banking *Gillian Hewitson*	20
Bastard Keynesianism *John Lodewijks*	24
Bretton Woods *Matias Vernengo*	30
Budget Deficits *Julio López G.*	34
Business Cycles *Peter Skott*	38
Cambridge Economic Tradition *G.C. Harcourt*	44
Capital Theory *Ben Fine*	51
Central Banks *Fernando J. Cardim de Carvalho*	57
Circuit Theory *Riccardo Realfonzo*	60
Competition *Nina Shapiro*	65
Consumer Theory *Marc Lavoie*	68
Consumption *David Bunting*	72
Credit Rationing *Martin H. Wolfson*	77
Critical Realism *Andrew Brown*	82
Development Finance *Rogério Studart*	87
Dynamics *J. Barkley Rosser, Jr.*	92
Econometrics *Paul Downward*	96
Economic Policy *Malcolm Sawyer*	101
Effective Demand *Mark Setterfield*	105
Employment *John Hudson*	112
Endogenous Money *Basil Moore*	117
Environmental Economics *Adrian Winnett*	122
Equilibrium and Non-equilibrium *Donald W. Katzner*	126
Exchange Rates *John T. Harvey*	131
Expectations *Éric Tymoigne*	135
Finance Motive *Augusto Graziani*	142
Financial Instability Hypothesis *Louis-Philippe Rochon*	145

vi *Contents*

Fiscal Policy *J.W. Nevile*	149
Full Employment *William Mitchell and Martin Watts*	153
Fundamentalist Keynesians *Bill Gerrard*	159
Globalization *William Milberg*	165
Growth and Income Distribution *Carlo Panico*	170
Growth Theory *Steve Keen*	175
Income Distribution *Thomas I. Palley*	181
Inflation *John Smithin*	186
Innovation *Jerry Courvisanos*	191
Institutionalism *Steven Pressman*	196
International Economics *Robert A. Blecker*	200
Investment *Tracy Mott*	205
Joan Robinson's Economics *Maria Cristina Marcuzzo*	211
Journal of Post Keynesian Economics *Phillip Anthony O'Hara*	215
Kaldorian Economics *A.P. Thirlwall*	221
Kaleckian Economics *Jan Toporowski*	226
Keynes's *General Theory* *Paul Davidson*	229
Keynes's *Treatise on Money* *Giuseppe Fontana*	237
Liquidity Preference *Stephanie Bell*	242
Marginalism *Harry Bloch*	249
Microfoundations *Steven Fazzari*	252
Monetary Policy *Peter Howells*	257
Money *L. Randall Wray*	261
Multiplier *Andrew B. Trigg*	265
New Classical Economics *Athol Fitzgibbons*	271
New Keynesian Economics *Wendy Cornwall*	275
Non-ergodicity *Stephen P. Dunn*	280
Pricing and Prices *Frederic S. Lee*	285
Production *Amitava Krishna Dutt*	289
Profits *Elizabeth Webster*	294
Rate of Interest *Massimo Pivetti*	299
Saving *Robert Pollin*	304
Say's Law *Claudio Sardoni*	309
Socialism *Howard J. Sherman*	313
Sraffian Economics *Gary Mongiovi*	318
Stagflation *John Cornwall*	322
Taxation *Anthony J. Laramie and Douglas Mair*	328
Tax-based Incomes Policy *Laurence S. Seidman*	332
Third Way *Egon Matzner*	337
Time in Economic Theory *John F. Henry*	341
Tobin Tax *Philip Arestis*	346
Transition Economies *Christine Rider*	350

Traverse *Peter Kriesler*	355
Treatise on Probability *Rod O'Donnell*	359
Uncertainty *Murray Glickman*	366
Underconsumption *J.E. King*	370
Unemployment *Mathew Forstater*	374
Wages and Labour Markets *Mario Seccareccia*	380
Walrasian Economics *M.C. Howard*	384
Name index	389
Subject index	395

Figures

1	No reswitching	52
2	Reswitching	53
3	The monetary circuit	61
4	The consumption function	74
5	Wolfson's model of credit rationing	81
6	The principle of effective demand and labour market outcomes	107
7	The special case of Say's Law	109
8	The interaction of expected and actual aggregate demand, and aggregate supply	111
9	Determination of the level of investment	137
10	Determination of the level of employment	137
11	A Say's Law economy	231
12	A Keynesian economy	232
13	The liquidity preference function	244
14	Determination of the rate of interest	245
15	Average annual rates of inflation and standardized unemployment for the G7 countries, 1967–1997	324

Tables

1 Conceptualizations of economic processes 283
2 Saving rates, credit supply and GDP growth for the
   US economy 305

List of contributors

Arestis, Philip: Levy Economics Institute of Bard College, New York, USA

Bell, Stephanie: University of Missouri, Kansas City, MO, USA

Blecker, Robert A.: American University, Washington, DC, USA

Bloch, Harry: Curtin University, Perth, Australia

Brown, Andrew: University of Leeds, Leeds, UK

Bunting, David: Eastern Washington University, USA

Carvalho, Fernando J. Cardim de: Universidade Federal de Rio de Janeiro, Rio de Janeiro, Brazil

Cornwall, John: Dalhousie University, Halifax, Nova Scotia, Canada

Cornwall, Wendy: Mount Saint Vincent University, Halifax, Nova Scotia, Canada

Courvisanos, Jerry: University of Ballarat, Ballarat, Victoria, Australia

Davidson, Paul: University of Tennessee, Knoxville, TN, USA

Dow, Sheila C.: University of Stirling, Stirling, Scotland, UK

Downward, Paul: University of Staffordshire, Stoke on Trent, UK

Dunn, Stephen P.: Department of Health, London, UK

Dutt, Amitava Krishna: University of Notre Dame, Notre Dame, IN, USA

Fazzari, Steven: Washington University, St. Louis, MO, USA

Fine, Ben: School of African and Oriental Studies, University of London, London, UK

Fitzgibbons, Athol: Griffith University, Brisbane, Australia

Fontana, Giuseppe: University of Leeds, Leeds, UK

Forstater, Mathew: University of Missouri, Kansas City, MO, USA

Gerrard, Bill: University of Leeds, Leeds, UK

Glickman, Murray: University of East London, London, UK

Graziani, Augusto: University of Rome 'La Sapienza', Rome, Italy

Harcourt, G.C.: Jesus College, Cambridge, UK

Harvey, John T.: Texas Christian University, Forth Worth, TX, USA

Henry, John F.: California State University, Sacramento, CA, USA

Hewitson, Gillian: La Trobe University, Melbourne, Australia

Howard, M.C.: University of Waterloo, Waterloo, Ontario, Canada

Howells, Peter: University of East London, London, UK

Hudson, John: University of Bath, Bath, UK

Katzner, Donald W.: University of Massachusetts, Amherst, MA, USA

Keen, Steve: University of Western Sydney, Sydney, Australia

King, J.E.: La Trobe University, Melbourne, Australia

Kriesler, Peter: University of New South Wales, Sydney, Australia

Laramie, Anthony J.: Merrimack College, North Andover, MA, USA

Lavoie, Marc: University of Ottawa, Ottawa, Canada

Lee, Frederic S.: University of Missouri, Kansas City, MO, USA

Lodewijks, John: University of New South Wales, Sydney, Australia

López G., Julio: Universidad Autonoma de Mexico, Mexico City, Mexico

Mair, Douglas: Heriot-Watt University, Edinburgh, Scotland, UK

Marcuzzo, Maria Cristina: University of Rome 'La Sapienza', Rome, Italy

Matzner, Egon: University of Technology, Vienna, Austria (retired)

McCombie, J.S.L.: University of Cambridge, Cambridge, UK

McKenna, Edward J.: Connecticut College, New London, CT, USA

Milberg, William: New School University, New York, USA

Mitchell, William: University of Newcastle, Newcastle, Australia

Mongiovi, Gary: St. John's University, Jamaica, NY, USA

Moore, Basil: Wesleyan University, Middletown, CT, USA and University of Stellenbosch, Stellenbosch, South Africa

Mott, Tracy: University of Denver, Denver, CO, USA

Nevile, J.W.: University of New South Wales, Sydney, Australia

O'Donnell, Rod: Macquarie University, Sydney, Australia
O'Hara, Phillip Anthony: Curtin University, Perth, Australia
Palley, Thomas I.: Open Society Institute, Washington, DC, USA
Panico, Carlo: University of Naples, Naples, Italy
Parsons, Stephen D.: De Montfort University, Leicester, UK
Pivetti, Massimo: University of Rome 'La Sapienza', Rome, Italy
Pollin, Robert: University of Massachusetts, Amherst, MA, USA
Pressman, Steven: Monmouth University, West Long Branch, NJ, USA
Realfonzo, Riccardo: University of Sannio, Benevento, Italy
Rider, Christine: St. John's University, Jamaica, NY, USA
Rochon, Louis-Philippe: Kalamazoo College, Kalamazoo, MI, USA
Rosser, J. Barkley, Jr.: James Madison University, Harrisonburg, VA, USA
Sardoni, Claudio: University of Rome 'La Sapienza', Rome, Italy
Sawyer, Malcolm: University of Leeds, Leeds, UK
Seccareccia, Mario: University of Ottawa, Ottawa, Canada
Seidman, Laurence S.: University of Delaware, Newark, DE, USA
Setterfield, Mark: Trinity College, Hartford, CT, USA
Shapiro, Nina: St. Peter's College, Jersey City, NJ, USA
Sherman, Howard J.: University of California, Los Angeles, CA, USA
Skott, Peter: University of Aarhus, Aarhus, Denmark
Smithin, John: York University, Toronto, Canada
Studart, Rogério: UNECLAC, Chile
Thirlwall, A.P.: University of Kent, Canterbury, UK
Toporowski, Jan: South Bank University, London, UK
Trigg, Andrew B.: The Open University, Milton Keynes, UK
Tymoigne, Éric: University of Missouri, Kansas City, MO, USA
Vernengo, Matias: Kalamazoo College, Kalamazoo, MI, USA
Watts, Martin: University of Newcastle, Newcastle, Australia

Webster, Elizabeth: University of Melbourne, Melbourne, Australia
Winnett, Adrian: University of Bath, Bath, UK
Wolfson, Martin H.: University of Notre Dame, Notre Dame, IN, USA
Wray, L. Randall: University of Missouri, Kansas City, MO, USA
Zannoni, Diane C.: Trinity College, Hartford, CT, USA

Introduction

Stripped down to the bare essentials, Post Keynesian economics rests on the principle of effective demand: in capitalist economies, output and employment are normally constrained by aggregate demand, not by individual supply behaviour. Since a decision not to have lunch today – as Keynes famously put it – does not entail a decision to have lunch tomorrow, investment drives saving and not the other way round. Moreover, there exists no automatic or even minimally reliable mechanism that will eliminate excess capacity and involuntary unemployment. Interest rates depend on monetary considerations, not on the so-called 'real' forces of productivity and thrift. There is no 'natural rate of interest' to equilibrate investment and saving, so that an increase in the propensity to save will prove self-defeating, resulting in lower output and reduced employment but not in higher levels of saving.

Thus far Post Keynesians agree with mainstream, neoclassical, 'old' or – less politely put – Bastard Keynesians like J.R. Hicks, Paul Krugman, James Meade and Paul Samuelson. They part company with them, however, in denying the validity of the neoclassical synthesis and in rejecting the IS–LM model, the real balance effect and the notion of the long run as a sort of magic kingdom where the future is knowable (at least probabilistically), expectations are always fulfilled, money has no real significance and all resources are fully employed. In fact Post Keynesianism emerged as a distinct school of thought, in the 1960s, precisely as a reaction against these perversions of Keynes's original vision. In his *General Theory*, as they interpreted it, uncertainty was inescapable, expectations were tentative and unreliable, money affected output as well as prices, and demand-deficient unemployment was the central macroeconomic problem. These issues are discussed below in the entries on effective demand, employment, Keynes's *General Theory*, saving, Say's Law and unemployment. At roughly the same time there emerged a thorough and incisive Post Keynesian critique of the neoclassical theories of capital, growth and distribution, together with an insistence on the importance of cost inflation and the role of incomes policy as an indispensable weapon with which to fight it (see the entries on capital theory, growth and income distribution, growth theory, inflation, stagflation and tax-based incomes policy).

The tendency for Post Keynesians to define themselves through criticism of the mainstream has led many orthodox economists to conclude that they have nothing positive to say. This is quite unwarranted, but it does contain an element of truth: one way of appreciating what Post Keynesians do believe is through understanding what it is that they reject. The entries on Bastard Keynesianism, marginalism, New Classical economics, New Keynesian economics and Walrasian economics can profitably be approached from this perspective. A different but related objection is that Post Keynesianism is incoherent when viewed as a set of positive propositions. In an early survey article Omar Hamouda and Geoff Harcourt (1988) identified three, potentially incompatible, streams of Post Keynesian thinking, which they termed the Fundamentalist Keynesians, the Kaleckians and the Sraffians. There are entries on all three (see fundamentalist Keynesians, Kaleckian economics and Sraffian economics), together with two other heterodox currents often taken to have something in common with them, the Austrians and the institutionalists (see Austrian school of economics and institutionalism).

Post Keynesian economics is certainly a very broad church, and I have tried to reflect this diversity in choosing topics and contributors. The entries on monetary questions provide one example (circuit theory, endogenous money, finance motive, financial instability hypothesis and money) and those on policy issues are another (budget deficits, economic policy, fiscal policy, monetary policy, taxation and tax-based incomes policy). With very few exceptions, Post Keynesians are hostile to neoliberalism and united in their support for active macroeconomic management, nationally and internationally (for the latter dimension, see the entries on Bretton Woods, development finance, globalization, international economics and transition economies).

The focus of this book is predominantly macroeconomic, though Post Keynesians have made important contributions to microeconomic theory and policy (as demonstrated in the entries on agency, competition, consumer theory, environmental economics, and pricing and prices) and on questions of economic philosophy, methodology and research methods (see the entries on Babylonian mode of thought, critical realism, econometrics, non-ergodicity and socialism).

Biographical and autobiographical accounts of many prominent Post Keynesians are readily available elsewhere – see especially Arestis and Sawyer (2000) – and thus with only three exceptions there are no biographical entries here (Joan Robinson's economics, Kaldorian economics and Kaleckian economics). John Maynard Keynes, though, is represented by entries dealing with his three great books (*General Theory*, *Treatise on Money* and *Treatise on Probability*), and his presence throughout the volume is so pervasive that it seemed pointless to provide an entry for him in the name index.

Each entry contains references to the relevant literature. Readers looking for an introductory overview of Post Keynesian economics should begin with the entry on the *Journal of Post Keynesian Economics* in the present volume and then proceed to Holt and Pressman (2001), perhaps in conjunction with the book that it replaced (Eichner 1979). A number of survey articles have appeared, beginning with the previously mentioned paper by Hamouda and Harcourt (1988), and continuing with Arestis (1996) and Arestis and Sawyer (1998), the latter concentrating on policy. Several of the essays in Harcourt (2001) will also be useful. Post Keynesian textbooks include Arestis (1992), Davidson (1994) and – at a more advanced level – Lavoie (1992). A history of Post Keynesian ideas is provided by King (2002), which concentrates on macroeconomics and should be complemented by Lee (1998) on the microeconomic aspects. King (1995) offers a reasonably complete bibliography up to 1994.

I am grateful to Edward Elgar for suggesting this project to me, and indeed for his consistent support for Post Keynesian economics over almost two decades. Philip Arestis and Malcolm Sawyer were extremely helpful at the start, and Fred Lee's assistance was invaluable later on. I must also thank the contributors for tolerating my sometimes savage editorial assaults on their early drafts (which in one case amounted to a 75 per cent cut). It is invidious to single out individuals, but Éric Tymoigne does deserve a special mention for writing lucidly at exceptionally short notice. Subject to the usual disclaimer, Phillip O'Hara wishes to thank Harry Bloch, John King, Peter Kriesler, Marc Lavoie and Douglas Vickers for comments on his entry, and I benefited considerably from the criticism of Marc Lavoie and Michael Schneider on my own.

This volume is dedicated to the memory of Bernard Corry, who sadly died before he could complete the entry that he was working on.

References

Arestis, P. (1992), *The Post Keynesian Approach to Economics: An Alternative Analysis of Economic Theory and Policy*, Aldershot, UK and Brookfield, VT, USA: Edward Elgar.

Arestis, P. (1996), 'Post-Keynesian economics: towards coherence', *Cambridge Journal of Economics*, **20** (1), 111–35.

Arestis, P. and M. Sawyer (1998), 'Keynesian economic policies for the new millennium', *Economic Journal*, **108** (446), 181–95.

Arestis, P. and M. Sawyer (2000), *A Biographical Dictionary of Dissenting Economists*, 2nd edition, Cheltenham, UK and Northampton, MA, USA: Edward Elgar.

Davidson, P. (1994), *Post Keynesian Macroeconomic Theory: A Foundation For Successful Economic Policies For the Twenty-First Century*, Aldershot, UK and Brookfield, VT, USA: Edward Elgar.

Eichner, A.S. (ed.) (1979), *A Guide to Post Keynesian Economics*, London: Macmillan.

Hamouda, O.F. and G.C. Harcourt (1988), 'Post-Keynesianism: from criticism to coherence?', *Bulletin of Economic Research*, **40** (1), 1–33.

Harcourt, G.C. (2001), *Fifty Years a Keynesian and Other Essays*, Basingstoke and New York: Palgrave.

Holt, R.P.F. and S. Pressman (eds) (2001), *A New Guide to Post Keynesian Economics*, London and New York: Routledge.

King, J.E. (1995), *Post Keynesian Economics: An Annotated Bibliography*, Aldershot, UK and Brookfield, VT, USA: Edward Elgar.
King, J.E. (2002), *A History of Post Keynesian Economics Since 1936*, Cheltenham, UK and Northampton, MA, USA: Edward Elgar.
Lavoie, M. (1992), *Foundations of Post Keynesian Economic Analysis*, Aldershot, UK and Brookfield, VT, USA: Edward Elgar.
Lee, F.S. (1998), *Post Keynesian Price Theory*, Cambridge: Cambridge University Press.

Agency

Agents are the sources of choices and decisions. Agency deals with the capacity that enables choices to be made. The provenance of this capacity, its nature, and the factors that enhance or limit it are the main questions of concern. From the point of view of Post Keynesian economics, an additional question arises. As is well known, an essential aspect of Post Keynesian economics is the adoption of the non-ergodicity postulate, which states that probability distributions are not stable over time. As a result, the future is unknown and unknowable. Thus, the Post Keynesian concept of agency is one that must be consistent with the postulate of non-ergodicity.

To speak of 'the Post Keynesian concept of agency' is perhaps too generous, for this is an area of work that is still in development. Indeed, some economists have advanced the claim that important aspects relating to the concept of agency are completely lacking in Post Keynesian economics (Hodgson 2001, p. 22). Still, a perusal of the work in this area clearly reveals a set of factors that will undoubtedly be at the core of any Post Keynesian concept of agency likely to develop in the near future.

Since agents make choices, they must possess a capacity that enables them to accomplish this. The idea of making a choice involves more than just a random or capricious action. To make a choice is to engage in an intentional act based upon reasons and beliefs. Thus, agents must be capable of having reasons and beliefs. Further, to act intentionally implies that one is attempting to bring about some result. An attempt to bring about a certain result is an attempt to structure the world in which the agent lives. To do so, an agent requires the ability to conceptualize the world both as it is, and as the agent would like it to be. Thus, agents must have the capacity to formulate a conception of the world and a conception of what a good life would entail.

Agents equipped with these endowments are then able to make choices. What does the idea of 'making a choice' imply? While not an uncontroversial question, the basic idea is that an agent in a given situation could have selected an action different from that actually undertaken. This, however, does not imply that the agent makes unconstrained choices. A key feature of the Post Keynesian concept of agency is that agents make choices within the context of a social structure, where by social structure we refer to such things as rules, relationships and institutions. The introduction of the idea of the social structure immediately raises a question: what is the

1

relationship between an agent and the social structure? Two traditional answers have been given to this question. The first, the methodological individualist position, advances the claim that structure is entirely the result of individual actions. Thus, the structure is determined by individuals. The second, due to methodological collectivism (or holism), posits that individuals and their actions are entirely determined by the social structure. A hallmark of the Post Keynesian concept of agency is a rejection of both of these views. For Post Keynesians, individual agents are born into a social structure that deeply influences, indeed partly constitutes, the very nature of the agent. However, it is equally true that the actions of agents help to reproduce and transform the social structure. Thus, agent and structure are mutually dependent upon, but not reducible to, each other. The fact that agent and structure are not reducible to each other means that each possesses powers and capabilities that are not solely derived from the other.

Agents, then, make choices in the context of a social structure. The fact that the social structure partly constitutes the individual agent means that the social structure does more than simply constrain the choices available to an agent. Rather, the social structure partly determines who an agent is. At a deep level, an agent is constituted by the meanings of the world he or she both holds and transforms. For Post Keynesians, meaning is not an objective fact about the world. Rather, meaning is both created and transformed as the result of social interaction within a social structure. Differing social structures enable differing types of social interaction that engender different meanings and understandings of the world, hence leading to different individuals. Likewise, different individuals with different understandings of the world will help to bring about different transformations of the social structure. Agents and structure are then engaged in a dynamic process of reproducing and transforming each other. We thus see the context for a frequently heard Post Keynesian expression, 'institutions and history (time) matter'. Moreover, the fact that the actions of agents will bring about a transformation of the social structure also provides an explanation for the existence of non-ergodicity. This follows once we are able to see that the future will be made by people on the basis of meanings that they will freely create, though in the context of the social structure.

The idea of a dynamic interaction between agent and structure helps illuminate another important aspect of Post Keynesian economics. While the world is non-ergodic, it nevertheless often remains fairly stable for significant periods of time. Keynes, and Post Keynesians, partly account for this through the existence of conventions. In explaining how entrepreneurs make investment decisions in a world where the future cannot be known, Keynes expressed the view that agents tend to follow a convention by which they project into the future the present state of things, unless there is some specific reason for believing change likely. For Keynes, conventions are essentially shared rules of behaviour that enable individuals to take actions in situations where the future results of these actions are unknowable. From a Post Keynesian perspective, conventions exist because they are one of the elements agents use to give a coherent meaning to the world in which they live. Thus, conventions actually help create the world, hence the future. Moreover, conventions are formed on the basis of social interaction, which helps us to understand what Keynes meant when he wrote in regard to how expectations of the future are formed: 'We endeavour to fall back on the judgment of the rest of the world which is perhaps better informed' (Keynes 1983, p. 114).

It is one thing to state that individuals and social structure partly constitute each other without being reducible to the other. It is quite another to explain just how this can be. It is clear that we wish to avoid complete reduction of the individual to the social structure, and vice versa. To conflate the individual with the social structure is to remove the possibility of free choice. To reduce the social structure to the individual is to deny the independent existence of physical, chemical and biological forces. Neither of these positions will do. However, to say that individuals and the social structure only partly constitute each other implies that each of these possesses some capabilities that are independent of the other. What, if anything, explains these independent capabilities? Two very different positions can be found in the literature.

The first is known as the Cartesian dualist position. According to this view, it is simply in the nature of things that there exist both material and intentional causes. The material causes deal with the physical, chemical and biological. Intentional causes are the basis of human agency. The existence of intentional causes, founded upon reasons, is what makes free choice possible. Intentional cause, itself, is a bedrock category in the sense that little more can be said concerning what causes intentional cause. As the critics of this position would state, intentional cause is an uncaused cause.

There are a number of difficulties with this position. At the philosophical level, no generally accepted argument has been developed to explain how these two different types of causes can interact and cohere with each other. Perhaps more importantly, at least from the perspective of Post Keynesian economics, is the fact that the Cartesian view is at variance with the idea that individuals and the social structure partly constitute each other. According to the Cartesian position, materialist and intentional causes are independent, bedrock categories, with neither owing its existence to any other factors. Under such a view, individual choices may be constrained by the materialist factors that explain the existence of the social structure, but individuals and the choices they make are not (even partly) constituted by the social structure. This is a view of the world that is more akin to the neoclassical conception rather than the Post Keynesian conception of economics. Finally, the idea of an uncaused cause strikes critics of this position as being unscientific in the sense that the idea rules out from the outset any possibility of further investigation.

The second position found in the literature is newer, and we shall refer to it as the 'evolutionary position' (Bunge 1980). According to this view, materialist and intentional causes are not independent of each other. Rather, intentional causes are 'emergent' properties of the material world. The idea here is that the human capability of intentional choice has evolved over time through the development of materialist (physical, chemical and biological) forces. The term 'emergent' is used in the following, somewhat special, sense. While human intentionality has evolved from materialist forces, it nevertheless possesses irreducible properties of its own. In other words, while intentionality evolves from materialist forces, it cannot be explained solely in terms of these forces.

While the evolutionary position avoids the strict dualism inherent in the Cartesian approach, it too suffers from a number of difficulties. For example, there does not yet exist an adequate explanation as to how intentions actually evolve from materialist forces. More problematic, from the perspective of a social scientist, is the precise meaning of the term 'emergent'. Several questions arise here. First, what exactly does it mean to state that intention is only partly explainable in terms of materialist forces? Does this imply that some aspects of intention are not explicable in terms of anything else? If so, does this not raise the same types of objections that were raised against the Cartesian approach? If, on the other hand, intention can be fully explained by materialist forces, then a serious question is posed as to whether there really exists such a thing as free choice. While the writings of those in the evolutionary camp are clearly sensitive to this issue, it is also the case that the impression is often given that a complete explanation of intention in terms of other causes is what these writers truly seek. How this could be accomplished, in a manner that maintains the possibility of free choice, is unclear. For example Hodgson, in criticizing the idea of an uncaused cause, writes:

> I also noted that chaos theory suggests that even if the world is deterministic, it may appear as entirely spontaneous and free. On recent reflection, I now believe that the admission of the possibility of an uncaused cause is not only unnecessary, for the reasons given in my *Economics and Evolution* book, but also untenable, for the reasons given here. The concept of emergence makes the compatibility of determinism and free will possible, but that does not sustain the notion of an uncaused cause. (Hodgson 2001, p. 39)

While Hodgson here claims that free will and determinism are compatible, many fear that the true import of this claim lies in the analogy with chaos theory. That is, what is really compatible is the appearance of free choice and determinism, not the reality of free choice and determinism.

EDWARD J. MCKENNA
DIANE C. ZANNONI

See also:
Babylonian Mode of Thought; Critical Realism; Expectations; Institutionalism; Non-ergodicity; Time in Economic Theory; Uncertainty.

Bibliography
Bunge, Mario A. (1980), *The Mind–Body Problem: A Psychobiological Approach*, Oxford: Pergamon.
Hodgson, Geoffrey M. (2001), 'Structures and institutions: reflections on institutionalism, structuration theory and critical realism' (mimeo).
Keynes, John Maynard (1983), *The Collected Writings of John Maynard Keynes. Volume XIV: The General Theory and After*, London and New York: Cambridge University Press for the Royal Economic Society.
Lawson, Tony (1997), *Economics and Reality*, London and New York: Routledge.
McKenna, Edward J. and Diane C. Zannoni (1997–98), 'Post Keynesian economics and the philosophy of individualism', *Journal of Post Keynesian Economics*, **20** (2), 235–50.

Austrian School of Economics

The appearance in 1871 of Carl Menger's *Principles of Economics* (*Grundsätze der Volkswirthschaftslehre*) marked the birth of the Austrian School of Economics. After the publication of the book, Menger became embroiled in the famous *Methodenstreit* with Gustav Schmoller, and thus, unfortunately according to some, it was left to others to develop his insights, most notably Eugen von Böhm-Bawerk and Friedrich von Wieser. The development of the Austrian School was further carried on by Ludwig von Mises and Friedrich von Hayek, and later by Ludwig Lachmann and I.M. Kirzner. Other famous economists associated to various degrees with the school include Fritz Machlup, Oskar Morgenstern, Joseph Schumpeter and G.L.S. Shackle.

Mises and Hayek are possibly best known for their respective criticisms of centrally-planned economies. In Hayek's case this took the form of drawing attention to the dispersed, partial, continually changing, and frequently contradictory information possessed by different economic agents in any advanced economy. Hayek argued that the nature of this information made it impossible for governments to direct economic activity with any semblance of economic efficiency. The problem was not merely a collection and computational problem, as information required interpreting and was continually altering. Hayek argued that this problem also raised questions concerning the possibilities for governmental intervention in capitalist economies, thus continuing what has become something of an Austrian tradition of emphasizing the advantages of free markets.

However, as with all schools of economics, homogeneity cannot be assumed. Vaughn (1994) claims that all contemporary Austrian economists subscribe to two views. First, social phenomena are to be explained in terms of the ideas and actions of individuals (methodological individualism). Second, human action takes place in time and under conditions of uncertainty. This leads to an emphasis on individuals possessing different knowledge and expectations, and also on the importance of institutions for the coordination of actions.

Given this, it would seem that the possibility of forging links between Austrian economics and Post Keynesian economics appears very promising, given that the latter also emphasizes the importance of historical time, uncertainty and expectations, and institutions. Further, of the various founding schools of neoclassical economics, Austrian economics would initially appear to be the most congenial to Post Keynesians. Thus Menger drew attention to the importance of 'time and error' in economics (Menger 1976, pp. 67ff.) and, in an article on money, argued that the demand for speculative balances formed a significant component of the demand for money (Streissler 1973). Mises also emphasized 'the uncertainty of the future' (1966, p. 105), argued that the ideas of human action and time are inseparable (pp. 99ff.), and dismissed the 'spurious idea of the supposed neutrality of money' (p. 398).

All this might suggest that any disagreements between the two schools are merely cases of 'disagreements between friends'. However, the history of the relationship between the two schools is one of mutual indifference, incomprehension, and even downright hostility. In part, this is no doubt explicable in terms of historical precedent. Thus Keynes thought Hayek's review of his *Treatise on Money* was carried out with insufficient 'good will', responding by characterizing Hayek's book *Prices and Production* as 'an extraordinary example of how, starting with a mistake, a remorseless logician can end up in Bedlam' (1973, p. 262).

However, the differences between the schools go deeper than lack of good will and the questioning of sanity. In exploring these differences, I shall take Hayek as the spokesperson for the Austrian School, and Davidson for the Post Keynesian School. The main issue I shall focus on is the attempt, by each school, to incorporate uncertainty into their respective economic theories.

As Vaughn (1994) acknowledges, there are two strands in contemporary Austrian economics. The first strand, represented primarily by Kirzner, views Austrian economics as a necessary supplement to mainstream economics. On this account, Austrian economics is not directly concerned with equilibrium states, but with the processes through which equilibrium may be attained, with pride of place given to entrepreneurial discovery and creation. The second strand, represented by Lachmann (who greatly admired the work of Shackle), concentrates on uncertainty and divergent expectations, and is highly suspicious of any reference to the idea of equilibrium.

In a discussion of Austrian economics, Davidson draws attention to the tension between these two strands: 'Austrian subjectivists cannot have it both ways – they cannot argue for the importance of time, uncertainty, and money, and simultaneously presume that plan or pattern coordination must exist and is waiting to be discovered' (Davidson 1989, p. 468). Davidson here correctly recognizes a problem in attempting to fuse the two strands into an 'Austrian view'. If entrepreneurs are formulating plans under conditions of uncertainty, with limited knowledge and divergent expectations, how can it be assumed that somehow these numerous different plans become coordinated? In a recent attempt to resolve this dilemma, Kirzner argues that, given uncertainty, entrepreneurs make mistakes. However, there are 'underlying objective realities' [that] exercise their influence upon entrepreneurial production decisions' (Kirzner 1992, p. 34). Entrepreneurs may make mistakes, but it all comes out in the wash and thus entrepreneurs can still be viewed as successfully steering the economy towards equilibrium.

It is difficult to recognize this as a satisfactory solution, if only because it seems to fall foul of either of the two views that Vaughn claimed all contemporary Austrians subscribe to. Either some mechanism exists which ensures coordination despite ignorance and uncertainty. In this case, rather than explaining how coordination occurs *through* individual ideas and actions, it is explained as occurring *despite* these ideas and actions. Alternatively, coordination occurs through entrepreneurs coming to learn what the 'underlying objective realities' are, in which case there is no ignorance or uncertainty.

Turning to an Austrian perspective, Hayek, in his later works, levelled three main charges against Keynes. First, he argued that Keynes's *General Theory* had been written in response to certain historical events, and was thus not a 'general theory'. Hayek argued that the mistaken view that the theory was 'general' led later economists to apply the theory in inappropriate conditions, leading to inflation. Hayek partially absolved Keynes himself from this mistaken application, as he thought Keynes would have been horrified by the results.

Second, Hayek objected to Keynes's use of a macroeconomic form of analysis, in particular to adoption of aggregate concepts. This objection was in keeping with the Austrian preference for methodological individualism. Thus Hayek argued that the use of aggregate concepts such as 'the level of inflation' or 'the level of unemployment' concealed the fact that different markets could be performing differently, and it was these differences that mattered to individual decision makers. Individuals thus did not think in terms of aggregate concepts, but in terms of the specific features of the markets they were concerned with. It is worth noting that this objection would necessarily entail Hayek rejecting any rational choice model assuming a 'representative individual'.

Third, Hayek objected to what he termed Keynes's 'rationalism'. He thus identified Keynes with the belief that human affairs and problems could be fully known and resolved through the application of reason. I shall suggest that Hayek's objection here still raises questions concerning the Post Keynesian project.

In his initial discussion of Austrian economics, Davidson emphasized that Post Keynesian economics assumes that economic decision makers are operating in a 'non-ergodic environment'. In fleshing this idea out Davidson notes that the Post Keynesian emphasis on uncertainty 'implies that economic decision-makers recognize that today's probabilities (if any) will not govern the future outcome' (Davidson 1989, p. 479). In contrast, economists who believe the world 'is governed entirely by ergodic process' believe that the future is 'merely a statistical reflection of the past' (p. 478). In a subsequent article Davidson draws attention to the fact that reality is transmutable, as 'today's human action can create a new and different reality' (Davidson 1993, p. 430).

The Post Keynesian emphasis on non-ergodicity, coupled with the transmutability of reality, entails uncertainty, where 'no relevant information exists today that can be used as a basis for scientifically predicting future events' (Davidson 1993, p. 430). As entrepreneurs are acting under conditions of uncertainty, market coordination may not occur, and thus there is a role for governments in creating the conditions whereby full employment might occur (Davidson 1989, p. 474). Consequently, 'through institutional and political changes, society can intelligently control and improve the performance of the economy compared with what would occur under laissez-faire' (p. 430). This statement embodies a continued belief in the 'rationalism' that Hayek criticized in Keynes. An enlightened society, through the use of reason and intelligence, can improve on the workings of the economy. However, the problem with this is that the Post Keynesian emphasis on uncertainty appears to leave 'society' bereft of any policy guidelines through which this can be achieved.

If the economy is not at full employment, there seems to be a major problem for any government in trying to ascertain what policies might alleviate this situation. Given uncertainty, the government cannot rely on attempting to implement policies that have worked in the past, as the past is an unreliable guide to the future. Further, as there is no information available today that can allow predictions concerning the future to possess any form of scientific credibility, then governments cannot be sure that any new policy recommendations will not exacerbate, rather than resolve, the problem. These difficulties are compounded with the acknowledgement of a transmutable reality. There will necessarily be a time difference between governments formulating policy, implementing policy, and any results of this policy being achieved. Yet by the time the policy has been implemented and the further time that results can be ascertained, the reality will have changed from what it was (even if known) when policies were formulated.

Post Keynesian economists can, with considerable justification, criticize the view in some Austrian circles that it is possible to emphasize both uncertainty and market coordination. However, it would also seem that the Post Keynesian emphasis on uncertainty raises problems for the argument that governments can resolve coordination problems. This, of course, connects up with Hayek's other point, that Keynes did not advance a 'general theory'. Keynes may well have correctly identified problems of market coordination when he wrote, and correctly identified policy instruments to resolve them. However, given uncertainty, the past is a fickle guide to the future and, given transmutation, the world is now a different place.

In conclusion, Post Keynesians have a valid point when they argue that an emphasis on economic uncertainty raises problems for the assumption that market coordination can occur in the absence of governmental intervention. However, it can also be argued that the emphasis on uncertainty raises problems for the assumption that market coordination can occur through government intervention. An uncertain resolution of the problems raised by uncertainty, perhaps?

STEPHEN D. PARSONS

See also:
Equilibrium and Non-equilibrium; Expectations; Non-ergodicity; Time in Economic Theory; Uncertainty.

References
Davidson, P. (1989), 'The economics of ignorance or the ignorance of economics?', *Critical Review*, **3** (3–4), 467–87.
Davidson, P. (1993), 'Austrians and Post Keynesians on economic reality: a rejoinder to critics', *Critical Review*, **7** (2–3), 371–444.
Keynes, J.M. (1973), *The Collected Writings of John Maynard Keynes. Volume XII: Economic Articles and Correspondence*, London: Macmillan.

Kirzner, I.M. (1992), *The Meaning of Market Process: Essays in the Development of Modern Austrian Economics*, London: Routledge.
Menger, C. [1871] (1976) *Principles of Economics*, trans. J. Dingwall and B.F. Hoselitz, New York: New York University Press.
Mises, L. von (1966), *Human Action: A Treatise on Economics*, 3rd edition, Chicago: Contemporary Books.
Streissler, E.W. (1973) 'Menger's theory of money and uncertainty – a modern interpretation', in J.R. Hicks and W. Weber (eds), *Carl Menger and the Austrian School of Economics*, Oxford: Clarendon Press, pp. 164–89.
Vaughn, K.I. (1994), *Austrian Economics in America: The Migration of a Tradition*, Cambridge: Cambridge University Press.

Babylonian Mode of Thought

The expression 'Babylonian mode of thought' has been used in economics – and particularly in connection with Post Keynesian economics – in an attempt to identify a way of approaching economic analysis which is quite different from the mainstream. We start by tracing the use made of the term, and then discuss in more detail its meaning and significance.

But first we need to consider the term 'mode of thought'. It refers to the principles of knowledge construction and communication which underpin choice of methodology, and indeed daily life: 'As we think, we live' (Whitehead 1938, p. 87). A mode of thought is 'the way in which arguments (or theories) are constructed and presented, how we attempt to convince others of the validity or truth of our arguments' (Dow 1985, p. 11). It is important to dig down to this level, beyond the methodological level, since arguments about the relative merits of different methodologies (such as Post Keynesian and orthodox) can founder through lack of recognition that different modes of thought are also involved.

The term 'Babylonian' was used by Keynes ([1933] 1972) in his biography of Isaac Newton, where he challenged the conventional understanding of Newton as a rationalist, the first of the age of reason. Instead '[h]e was the last of the magicians, the last of the Babylonians and Sumerians, the last great mind which looked out on the visible and intellectual world with the same eyes as those who began to build our intellectual inheritance rather less than 10,000 years ago' (Keynes 1972, p. 364). Keynes contrasted the way in which Newton applied introspection to his knowledge of the history of scientific thought, as well as to experience, in order to arrive at explanations for natural phenomena, on the one hand, with the rational proofs he constructed after the fact, on the other.

The term 'Babylonian' then apparently fell into misuse until introduced to modern economics, as an approach to philosophy of science, in Stohs's (1983) note on the subject of Keynes on uncertainty. He argued that Keynes's ideas on uncertainty could be developed further on Babylonian lines. He had picked up the Babylonian category from Wimsatt's (1981) discussion in terms of the social sciences in general, in juxtaposition to Cartesian/Euclidean thought. According to the Babylonian approach, 'there is no single logical chain from axioms to theorems; but there are several parallel, intertwined, and mutually reinforcing sets of chains, such that no particular axiom is logically basic' (Stohs 1983, p. 87).

Wimsatt in turn had developed the idea from Feynman's (1965) representation of what he called the Babylonian tradition in mathematics, which involved a range of starting-points for arguments, and thus a multiple derivability of physical laws. Feynman contrasted this with the Euclidean approach, which ties all arguments to a set of axioms, and argued that the Babylonian approach was preferable for physics: 'The method of always starting from the axioms is not very efficient in obtaining theorems' (Feynman 1965, p. 47). Indeed the context of this argument is a discussion of the limitations of mathematics for physics: 'The mathematical rigour of great precision is not very useful for physics' (ibid., pp. 56–70).

Following on from Stohs, Dow (1985; 1996) explored the nature and implications of Babylonian thought in order to understand the different underpinnings of mainstream economic methodology from those of the methodologies of other schools of thought. Post Keynesianism being one of those schools of thought, the idea of Babylonian thought came to be one of the ways by which Post Keynesianism has become identified. Further, the specification of Babylonian thought in relation to Cartesian/Euclidean thought has been used in methodological discussion. This represented one of a range of projects over the last decade or so to specify the philosophical and methodological underpinnings of Post Keynesian economics.

Feynman (1965) presented Babylonian mathematics as consisting of an array of chains of reasoning, not tied to any one set of axioms, but governed by the practicalities of the problem at hand. It is thus a realist approach to knowledge. Since no one set of axioms can be relied on as being true, single long chains of reasoning simply serve to compound any inadequacy in the axioms. Rather than constructing a single general formal system, it is seen as preferable to segment reality for the purposes of constructing a range of partial analyses, which are incommensurate; if they were commensurate, the arguments could be formally combined. One chain of reasoning might focus on one segment of reality such that a particular variable is exogenous, which is endogenous to another chain of reasoning. One chain of reasoning might rely on statistical analysis, while another might rely on historical research, for example. Euclidean mathematics, by contrast, is a closed logical system built on one set of axioms using one, mathematical, method; it abstracts from practical problems in order to generate universal solutions within the domain of abstraction. The logical system is thus governed by internal rules rather than reference to reality. This non-realist style of reasoning is also associated with Descartes, hence the term 'Cartesian/Euclidean'.

A Babylonian system of thought is a form of open system of thought, rather than the closed system of Cartesian/Euclidean thought. In an open system, the identity of all the relevant variables and relationships between them is not known, and in any case the meaning of variables and their interrelations is subject to change. There is scope for creativity and discrete shifts, as well as for stability. In a closed system by contrast all variables are pre-specified, and categorized as endogenous or exogenous; what is not known is assumed to be random. (A *model* within a closed system may be open or closed; it is the knowledge of exogenous variables which closes the *system*.) Extrinsic closure rules out anything but random disturbances from outside, while intrinsic closure rules out any change in the variables within the system or in their interrelations.

In order to satisfy these conditions for closure, Cartesian/Euclidean thought is characterized by dualism and atomism. Duals are the all-encompassing, mutually exclusive categories with fixed meaning typical of closed systems. Variables are endogenous or exogenous; values are known with certainty (or within a stochastic distribution whose moments are known with certainty) or are not known at all; relationships are either causal or random; economic agents are rational or irrational, and so on. Atomism involves building up a theoretical system on the basis of the smallest units, which are independent of one another and of the system of which they are a part – rational economic men.

Babylonian thought is neither dualistic nor atomistic. The categories used to account for social life in an evolving environment are not seen as readily falling into duals. Indeed vagueness of categories is seen to have the benefit of adaptability within a changing environment where institutions, understanding and behaviour undergo change. In a system of thought with a variety of incommensurate strands of argument, variables may be exogenous to one strand but endogenous to another. Knowledge is in general held with uncertainty (by economic agents and by economists), so the analysis points to degrees of uncertainty. Further, some strands of argument may refer to individuals, and others to the group level, since causal forces may act in either direction. Indeed individuals are not seen as independent, and their behaviour may change as the environment changes. Institutions and conventions provide the stability to allow decisions to be taken in an uncertain environment. In other words the social structure is understood to be organic.

The concept of Babylonian thought accords well with ideas developed later in the literature which have relevance for Post Keynesian economics. The characterization of Babylonian thought outlined above follows from a particular understanding of the nature of the real world as being organic, that is, itself an open system. Babylonian thought is thus realist, and indeed holds much in common with the critical realist approach to economics (although not its philosophical foundations). While Lawson (1994) argues that critical realism does not in itself provide the basis for identifying schools of thought among those who adopt a critical realist approach, this need not be the case (see Dow 1999). The Babylonian approach suggests a basis for differentiation in the form of realist ontology adopted – whether the economist understands the economic process in terms of production or exchange, class or the rational individual, and so on. The case for the compatibility between Babylonian thought and critical realism was made by Arestis et al. (1999) in response to Walters and Young's (1997) critique; see also Dow (1999).

Similarly, Babylonian thought provides a rationale for pluralism. It justifies both methodological pluralism (methodologists analysing a range of methodologies) and pluralism of method (economists using a range of methods). If the real world is understood as organic, not governed by universal laws, then there is scope for a range of methodologies. Further, Babylonian thought specifically supports the use of a range of different methods for different chains of reasoning. But, to be operational, both forms of pluralism are moderated by the way in which the open system of thought is specified. How the real world is understood will govern the particular choice of methodology, and in turn the range of methods to be used.

The original expression of the Babylonian mode of thought was misunderstood by some as the dual of Cartesian/Euclidean thought – rather than generating a unified methodology, it was seen as encouraging methodological diversity in the extreme sense of eclecticism. Cartesian/Euclidean thought offers a closed axiomatic system, which yields certain conclusions given the axioms. When Babylonian thought was understood as an open system without axioms, with incommensurate methods and with uncertain conclusions, it was taken to imply the absence of methodological principles – an 'anything goes' approach. It was associated with pure pluralism in the sense of a range of methods with no appraisal criteria by which to assess them.

But this is a dualistic interpretation. By avoiding dualism, Babylonian thought is not forced into an 'anything goes' approach. Rather, some criteria are required by which to choose segmentations of the subject matter for analysis, the chains of reasoning to pursue, and the methods employed to pursue them. The subject matter is regarded as too complex to be fully captured in any one analytical system. So a range of choices as to methodology is possible within a Babylonian approach. Since Post Keynesians have a distinctive ontology, a distinctive methodology follows, which differs from the methodology of other schools of thought that also employ an open-systems mode of thought. The corollary is that, while Post Keynesians can (and do) argue for their own methodology and theories, they recognize that others, with different ontologies, will choose different methodologies and theories. While thought progresses within Post Keynesianism, there is also evidence in the extent of Post Keynesian work which crosses boundaries with other schools of thought, that an open thought system fosters creative synthetic developments.

SHEILA C. DOW

See also:

Critical Realism; Econometrics; Non-ergodicity; Uncertainty.

References

Arestis, P., S.P. Dunn and M. Sawyer (1999), 'Post Keynesian economics and its critics', *Journal of Post Keynesian Economics*, **21** (4), 527–49.
Dow, S.C. (1985), *Macroeconomic Thought: A Methodological Approach*, Oxford: Blackwell. Reprinted in a revised and extended version as *The Methodology of Macroeconomic Thought*, Cheltenham, UK and Brookfield, VT, USA: Elgar, 1996.
Dow, S.C. (1999), 'Post Keynesianism and critical realism: what is the connection?', *Journal of Post Keynesian Economics*, **22** (1), 15–33.
Feynman, R.P. (1965), *The Character of Physical Law*, Cambridge, MA: MIT Press. Page references are to the Penguin edition, 1992.
Keynes, J.M. (1933), 'Newton the man', in Keynes, *Essays in Biography*, reprinted in Keynes, *The Collected Writings of John Maynard Keynes*, Vol. X, London: Macmillan for the Royal Economic Society, 1972, pp. 363–74.
Lawson, T. (1994), 'The nature of Post Keynesianism and its links to other traditions: a realist perspective', *Journal of Post Keynesian Economics*, **16** (4), 503–38.
Stohs, M. (1983), '"Uncertainty" in Keynes' *General Theory*: a rejoinder', *History of Political Economy*, **15** (1), 87–91.
Walters, B. and D. Young (1997), 'On the coherence of Post Keynesian economics', *Scottish Journal of Political Economy*, **44** (3), 329–49.
Whitehead, A.N. (1938), *Modes of Thought*, Cambridge: Cambridge University Press.
Wimsatt, W.C. (1981), 'Robustness, reliability and overdetermination', in M.B. Brewer and B.E. Collins (eds), *Scientific Inquiry and the Social Sciences*, San Francisco: Jossey-Bass, pp. 124–63.

Balance-of-payments-constrained Economic Growth

The balance-of-payments-constrained growth model provides a Keynesian demand-oriented explanation of why growth rates differ. This approach stands in marked contrast to the neoclassical growth theory (whether of the Solow–Swan or the endogenous variety), with the latter's emphasis on the role of the supply side. The central tenet of the balance-of-payments-constrained growth model is that a country cannot run a balance-of-payments deficit for any length of time that has to be financed by short-term capital flows and which results in an increasing net foreign debt-to-GDP ratio. If a country attempts to do this, the operation of the international financial markets will lead to increasing downward pressure on the currency, with the danger of a collapse in the exchange rate and the risk of a resulting depreciation/inflation spiral. There is also the possibility that the country's international credit rating will be downgraded. Consequently, in the long run, the basic balance (current account plus long-term capital flows) has to be in equilibrium. An implication of this approach is that there is nothing that guarantees that this rate will be the one consistent with the full employment of resources or the growth of the productive potential.

The main elements of this approach are set out in Thirlwall's (1979) seminal paper. The growth of exports is determined by the growth of world income and the rate of change of relative prices. The growth of imports is specified as a function of the growth of domestic income, together with the rate of change of relative prices. Substituting these into the definitional equation for the balance of payments, expressed in growth rate form, gives the growth of domestic income as a function of the growth of world income, the rate of change of relative prices, and the growth of net international capital flows.

If the impact of the last two on economic growth is quantitatively negligible (as empirically is the case), the growth rate of income consistent with balance-of-payments equilibrium is given by $y_B = \varepsilon z/\pi = x/\pi$, where ε, π, z and x are the world income elasticity of demand for exports, the domestic income elasticity of demand for imports, the growth of world income and the growth of exports. These two equations for y_B are alternative specifications of what has come to be known as 'Thirlwall's law'. It can be seen that the key factor determining the growth of a country is the growth of the exogenous component of demand, that is, exports, which in turn is determined by the growth of world markets. Thus, the model is an extension of the export-led growth hypothesis, but where the balance-of-payments constraint is explicitly incorporated.

There are substantial differences between countries in their values of ε (and of π) and hence in how fast these economies can grow without encountering balance-of-payments problems. The disparities in ε and π are interpreted as reflecting differences in non-price competitiveness (for example, differences in the quality of goods and services, the effectiveness of a country's distribution network, delivery dates and so on). Thus the supply side is important to the extent that these supply characteristics play a crucial role in explaining the growth of exports and, hence, income. This stands in marked contrast to the way in which the neoclassical approach emphasizes the supply side, where technical change and the growth of the labour input are the causal factors in the Solow–Swan growth model and the growth of capital (broadly defined) is the causal factor in the endogenous growth models.

A necessary condition for the balance-of-payments constraint to be binding is that the rate of change of the exchange rate is ineffective in determining the growth of exports and imports. If this were not the case, then real exchange rate adjustments could ensure that the balance of payments was brought into equilibrium at any given rate of the growth of income, including the growth of productive potential. However, it should be emphasized that the balance-of-payments-constrained growth model does not imply that changes in relative prices have *no* effect on the current account.

It may be that changes in these are sufficient to bring a current account deficit back into equilibrium when, for example, the economy is growing at or near its balance-of-payments equilibrium rate, but they are unlikely to be sufficient to raise the balance-of-payments equilibrium growth rate, *per se*. Given the multiplicative nature of the export and import demand functions, to achieve the latter would require a sustained real depreciation.

There are a number of reasons why this is implausible. First, there may be real wage resistance, which makes it difficult for a continuous nominal depreciation to be translated into a corresponding sustained real depreciation. Second, firms may 'price to market' so that imports and exports are unresponsive to any changes in the real exchange rate. Third, the values of the price elasticities of demand may be so low that the Marshall–Lerner condition is barely satisfied. If the absolute value of the price elasticities sum to one, then the rule $y_B = \varepsilon z/\pi$ holds, even if there is a substantial rate of change of relative prices. Goods and services that enter into international trade are for the most part highly differentiated and so their demand curves are relatively inelastic. Firms compete for sales predominantly by attempting to shift outwards the demand curve for their products through increasing their non-price competitiveness, rather than by moving down the demand curve through improving their price competitiveness. (See McCombie and Thirlwall (1994, chapter 4) for a discussion of the empirical evidence.)

Thirlwall's law may be regarded as a dynamic version of Harrod's (1933) foreign trade multiplier. McCombie (1985) demonstrated that in a more complex Keynesian model than Harrod used, Thirlwall's law could be more generally regarded as the workings of the Hicks 'super-multiplier'. An increase in export growth from, for example, a position of current account equilibrium would increase the growth of income directly through the Harrod foreign trade multiplier. Moreover, at the same time, by generating an increasing current account surplus, it allows a further increase in the growth of other domestic components of demand to occur, thereby raising the growth rate even further, until the basic balance is re-established. The combined effect of these two mechanisms represents the operation of the Hicks super-multiplier in dynamic form.

There have been an increasing number of studies that have tested this approach to economic growth. The general methodology is to estimate the value of ε and π for a particular country from export and import demand functions (which include relative price terms) using time-series data. In the original studies, ordinary-least squares was used, but recently more sophisticated econometric techniques have been adopted, for example, those that test for stationarity and cointegration of the data. From the estimates of ε and π, a value for the balance-of-payments equilibrium growth rate can be obtained using the expression for Thirlwall's law, $y_B = \varepsilon z/\pi$. (Alternatively, $y_B = x/\pi$ is sometimes used.) The balance-of-payments equilibrium growth rate, when calculated over a period of a decade or longer, is often found to be very close to the actual growth rate and this has been confirmed by a variety of statistical tests. It is also commonly found that the estimates of the price elasticities in the export and import demand functions are either small or statistically insignificant, or both. This provides further evidence of the unimportance of price competition in international trade. See McCombie and Thirlwall (1994) and the minisymposium in the 1997 edition of the *Journal of Post Keynesian Economics* (Davidson 1997).

Of course, not all countries will necessarily be simultaneously balance-of-payments constrained. At any one time, some countries (or trading blocs) may be 'policy constrained', where demand management policies have resulted in the actual growth of income being below the balance-of-payments equilibrium growth rate. This occurred in the 1970s and 1980s in some advanced countries where governments attempted to curtail the rate of growth of inflation by using deflationary policies. Other countries may be growing so fast that they are 'resource constrained', such as Japan in the early postwar period. The problem is that the balance-of-payments-constrained countries find that their growth rates are effectively limited by the growth of these policy- and resource-constrained countries. If, for example, a particular country curtails its growth for policy reasons, its major trading partners are going to find that their balance-of-payments equilibrium growth rates fall. Their actual rate of growth will then be curtailed, regardless of whether or not the conditions in their domestic market warrant this (McCombie and Thirlwall 1994, chapter 7).

The approach does not just apply to countries with national currencies, but the principle holds also at the regional level (ibid., chapter 8). This suggests that the formation of a monetary union, such as the EMU (European Monetary Union), will not remove the importance of export growth and the balance of payments in determining the overall growth rate of a country.

There have been a number of criticisms of this approach to economic growth. McCombie and Thirlwall (ibid., chapter 5) contains a lively interchange with Peter McGregor and Kim Swales, which first appeared in *Applied Economics*, over such issues as the direction of causation, whether the model captures non-price competitiveness, and whether the law of one price renders the model incoherent. (It is important not to confuse the small variation in relative prices due to the reasons set out above with the neoclassical law of one price. The latter, with its assumptions of competitive markets and that the price elasticity of demand of exports is infinite for a small open economy, does imply that countries cannot be balance-of-payments constrained. However, in practice, prices are determined in oligopolistic markets and are sticky for the reasons noted above.)

Krugman (1989) rediscovered the law, which he termed the 45-degree rule. This is because one country's growth relative to all others will be equiproportional to the ratio of the income elasticity of demand for its exports to the income elasticity of demand for its imports. The relationship between a country's growth rate and the values of ε and π is interpreted in a neoclassical manner and not as reflecting the Harrod foreign trade multiplier. Krugman develops a model based on monopolistic competition and increasing returns to scale. The number of product varieties produced in a country is assumed to be proportional to its effective labour force, where the latter is taken to be a measure of resource availability. As a country's growth rate increases, so does the number of varieties it produces, and this increases both its share in world markets and its value of ε. Hence, the latter is assumed to be determined endogenously. If this were true, it would mean that a faster growth of the UK would suddenly raise the growth of its exports and reduce the income elasticity of demand for imports such as to prevent a deficit from arising, with no downward pressure on the exchange rate. This is implausible and contrary to the historical experience.

Crafts (1988) notes that if, for example, the UK had maintained its share in its overseas markets, the hypothetical or constant-market-share income elasticity of demand for its exports would have been comparable in size with those of the other advanced countries (which all tend to be roughly equal). Consequently, its hypothetical growth rate of exports would have been the same as those of the other countries. Hence, using the constant-market-share estimates of ε, it is argued that the UK's balance-of-payments equilibrium growth rate is approximately the same as those of the other advanced countries, including Japan. But all this shows is that if the UK had matched, say, Japan in terms of its non-price competitiveness, its hypothetical balance-of-payments growth rate would have been the same as Japan's. But the fact is that it did not, and the estimates of the hypothetical income elasticities have no relevance at all as to whether the UK's growth was actually balance-of-payments constrained. All these critiques are assessed in greater detail in McCombie and Thirlwall (1997).

In conclusion, Davidson (1990–91, p. 303) has summarized this approach as a significant contribution to Post Keynesian economic theory in its demonstration that 'international payments imbalances can have severe real growth consequences, i.e., money is not neutral in an open economy'.

J.S.L. McCombie

See also:
Exchange Rates; Globalization; Growth Theory; International Economics; Multiplier.

References
Crafts, N. (1988), 'The assessment: British economic growth over the long run', *Oxford Review of Economic Policy*, **4** (1), Spring, i–xxi.
Davidson, P. (1990–91), 'A Post Keynesian positive contribution to "theory"', *Journal of Post Keynesian Economics*, **13** (2), 298–303.
Davidson, P. (ed.) (1997), 'Minisymposium on Thirlwall's law and economic growth in an open economy context', *Journal of Post Keynesian Economics*, **19** (3), 318–85.
Harrod, R.F. (1933), *International Economics*, Cambridge: Cambridge University Press.
Krugman, P. (1989), 'Differences in income elasticities and trends in real exchange rates', *European Economic Review*, **33** (5), 1031–46.
McCombie, J.S.L. (1985), 'Economic growth, the Harrod foreign trade multiplier and the Hicks super-multiplier', *Applied Economics*, **17** (1), 52–72.
McCombie, J.S.L. and A.P. Thirlwall (1994), *Economic Growth and the Balance-of-Payments Constraint*, Basingstoke: Macmillan.
McCombie, J.S.L. and A.P. Thirlwall (1997), 'The dynamic Harrod foreign trade multiplier and the demand-oriented approach to economic growth', *International Review of Applied Economics*, **11** (1), 5–25.
Thirlwall, A.P. (1979), 'The balance of payments constraint as an explanation of international growth rate differences', *Banca Nazionale del Lavoro Quarterly Review*, **128** (791), 45–53.

Banking

The behaviour of banks in the loan market is of major significance to Post Keynesian analyses of a monetary production economy. When the money supply is endogenous and the central bank sets the cost of wholesale funds (the base rate), and accommodates bankers' demands for liquidity at that rate, the direction of causation between loans and deposits embodied in the traditional exogenous-money/money-multiplier model is reversed. In Post Keynesian models, loans cause deposits and hence bring money into existence as an integral aspect of the operation of the 'real' economy. Thus banks are able to advance the financing for investment without the necessity for saving to have been accumulated beforehand. It follows that investment expenditures can be constrained by credit rationing but not by a shortage of saving. Banks and their ability and willingness to extend loans, then, are a key determinant of increases in the level of employment and output following an *ex ante* increase in the demand for investment goods.

To Post Keynesians, the banking system is in a constant state of innovating and evolving in response to the profit opportunities presented by 'the interaction of economic conditions with regulatory constraints' (Moore 1988, p. 31n; Minsky 1986, chapter 10; Chick 1992, chapter 12). The development of new financing instruments and techniques associated with liability management has been especially significant in the evolution of the banking system. Liability management refers to the ability of banks to vary interest rates to attract both wholesale and retail funds which can be used to finance lending activity. This is in contrast to the asset-management strategy of banks implied by the orthodox account, where banks must either passively await new deposits made available by central bank purchases of government securities, or finance new loans with the proceeds of the sale of other assets. Negotiable certificates of deposit, security repurchase agreements, retail cash management accounts and the interbank market are examples of innovations which have increased the elasticity of the supply of financing relative to regulations intended to limit such responsiveness. However, although these innovations have increased the ability of banks to provide credit on demand, the move to liability management has also increased their exposure to liquidity risk when they do so, since balance sheets are expanded, with potentially volatile sources of funds matching the issuing of new and relatively illiquid commercial loans. Bankers' decision-making processes around these liquidity issues are the subject of some debate among Post Keynesian monetary theorists.

This debate can be framed as disagreement on the extent to which banks are quantity takers in their loan markets. In the case of the horizontalist position, as defined by Moore (1988), banks set the interest rate on loans as a profit-maximizing mark-up over the cost of funds. The mark-up equates the bank's marginal cost of borrowed funds and marginal revenue of lent funds. Bankers provide loans on demand at that rate: 'In their retail loan and deposit markets banks act as price setters and quantity takers' (Moore 1988, p. 55). A shortage of funds is met by borrowing in the wholesale market, using the tools of liability management. As mentioned above, the cost of funds in the short-term wholesale market is determined by the central bank, which, as a market-maker, will typically fully accommodate banks' demands. Should the stance of monetary policy tighten, the central bank's supply of funds will be restricted and the base rate will rise. In this scenario, the credit-money supply function is demand determined and perfectly elastic at the mark-up over the base rate, with the important implication that the liquidity preference theory of the interest rate is thereby invalidated (ibid., pp. 197–204).

Other Post Keynesians agree that the central bank implements monetary policy through its control of the base rate, but disagree that banks are quantity takers to the extent required by the pure horizontalist position. They argue that bankers respond to changes in their liquidity preference by systematically price- and quantity-rationing credit. Thus, liquidity preference theory is essential to an explanation of how and why bankers vary the price and availability of credit for any given base rate (see, for example, Dow 1996). In part, this difference of opinion can be explained as somewhat semantic by pointing out that the horizontalist position is overstated in relation to the issue of the quantity rationing of credit. In fact, in the horizontalist account, banks impose credit limitations on *all* loan applicants and meet unreservedly only the *effective* demand for loans. That is, before banks supply loans 'on demand', applicants have already been subjected to criteria which identify them as applicants to be either fully or partially restricted (see Moore 1988, pp. 55–6). Fully restricted applicants are those who fail to meet the minimum collateral and income and maximum risk requirements set by the bank. Partially restricted applicants are those who are approved for borrowing up to a specified limit. Thus, 'the supply of credit by the banking system is perfectly elastic, *up to borrowers' allotted credit ceilings*' (ibid., p. 337, emphasis added; see also Lavoie 1996). It is therefore a matter of timing – when does credit rationing take place? – which determines whether one argues that banks are or are not unqualified quantity takers.

However, a perfectly elastic credit-money supply function rules out price rationing at any particular base rate. This is justified by the need to clearly distinguish the Post Keynesian exogenous interest rate analysis from the loanable funds, endogenous interest rate, orthodoxy which predicts that an increase in investment necessarily raises the rate of interest (Lavoie 1996, pp. 276–7). Lavoie (p. 279) argues that the base rate is indeed exogenous with respect to the income-generating process, and that it is a separate issue as to how bankers establish mark-ups over that rate. But he further insists that Post Keynesians must argue that there is no compulsion for banks to raise lending rates as economic activity expands. The opposing view is that, at a given base rate, banks will supply more credit to individual borrowers only if accompanied by an increasing loan rate, since borrowers' debt/equity ratios increase and hence lender's risk rises (Dow 1996, pp. 500–503; Minsky 1986, chapter 8). Yet it is certainly plausible that, in a period of optimism and inflated expectations with respect to future stock or flow returns from assets, bankers' perceptions of this increasing risk may be muted to the point of non-existence, at least within the relevant range. Indeed, this point is made by Dow (1996, p. 501, Fig. 1) and similarly by Minsky (1986, p. 193, Fig. 8.4). Moreover, the 'paradox of debt' may apply when considering not a single firm but industrial firms in aggregate.

Specifically, leverage ratios of firms may fall as profits rise with rising investment during the upturn, frustrating firms' plans to finance their expansions with debt rather than equity, and eliminating the increase in lender's risk (Lavoie 1996, pp. 285–6). Furthermore, Lavoie (pp. 292–4) argues that liquidity preference goes by the name of 'animal spirits' in the horizontalist account, and so denies that there is a serious incompatibility between the views of horizontalists and others. Nevertheless, Dow (1996, pp. 502–4) does not agree that the supply of loans is necessarily perfectly elastic and suggests that, even if banks will supply loans to creditworthy borrowers on demand for most of the business cycle, during a downturn the rising liquidity preference of the providers of wholesale funds, as well as the providers of the capital which banks must hold to meet risk-adjusted capital requirements, will cause bankers' liquidity preference, and hence their mark-ups, to rise.

The use of liquidity preference theory is all the more imperative when the business cycle is considered because it allows a cornerstone of Keynes's legacy – the existence of uncertainty – to play a central role in explaining the periodic crises which beset capitalist economies. These crises are characterized by significant increases in loan defaults and interest rate margins, and a collapse in the willingness of bankers to continue to extend credit, entailing a strong desire to move to more liquid balance sheets (a rise in banks' liquidity preference). The upturn which eventually follows the crash is characterized by the reverse of these events. Thus over the cycle, and independently of changes in the base rate, banks revise their views on creditworthiness and appropriate loan rates and, therefore, on quantity and price rationing. Orthodox models of credit rationing due to market failure in the form of asymmetric information between borrowers and lenders miss this key point: there simply is no full-information case, so that default probabilities can only ever be subjectively determined. As Minsky (1986, pp. 239–40) stresses, the 'prudent banker' is faced not by objective probability distributions of returns but by uncertainty and hence the necessity of subjective evaluations of risks. These evaluations are not constrained by depositor monitoring, due to the absorption of risk by the monetary authorities (the classic moral hazard problem). Because the future is unknown and uncertain, rather than probabilistically known and risky, bankers and loan applicants may or may not suffer from asymmetric information but they will typically be making decisions under asymmetric expectations. That is, even if they have the same information (and even if they have the same risk preferences), they evaluate that information differently (Wolfson 1996, pp. 450–51).

A banker's evaluation of information about particular borrowers, their investment projects and their likelihood of repayment involves assessing a number of factors in relation to the bank's established standards or conventions. Factors such as the borrowing history of the applicant, the applicant's debt/equity ratio, the value of collateral, and expected future cash flows given the bank's view of the macroeconomic environment during the period of repayment, are all subjectively assessed. Whether or not these assessments lead to the provision of funds, and at what price, is a function both of conventions – what has happened in the recent past and the extent to which it is expected that the past will be repeated – and of the degree to which a banker is confident in the assessment. When the bank perceives an increase in the default risk of borrowers, due for example to a downturn in the economy, or when its own liquidity preference rises, it raises both the loan price and non-price requirements, so that some borrowers pay higher rates at the same time as other borrowers – those unable to meet the non-price requirements – are rationed (ibid., pp. 452–60). Thus the loan supply function is subject to shifts as bankers' perceptions move between pessimism and optimism, with their liquidity preference correspondingly rising and falling. Banks' extensions of credit are virtually unconstrained in the increasingly optimistic environment of the upturn, which leads them to finance increasingly fragile debt positions (see Minsky 1986, chapter 9). Central banks, as lenders of last resort, play an essential role in mitigating the crises which result from the inevitable reversals of expectations, liquidity preference and cash flows relative to cash commitments which end the growth of the debt pyramid. In short, banks are both destabilizing and indispensable to a monetary-production economy: banking 'is a disruptive force that tends to induce and amplify instability even as it is an essential factor if investment and economic growth are to be financed' (Minsky 1986, p. 229).

GILLIAN HEWITSON

See also:

Central Banks; Credit Rationing; Endogenous Money; Finance Motive; Financial Instability Hypothesis; Liquidity Preference; Monetary Policy; Money; Rate of Interest; Uncertainty.

References

Chick, V. (1992), *On Money, Method and Keynes: Selected Essays*, edited by P. Arestis and S.C. Dow, New York: St. Martin's Press.
Dow, S.C. (1996), 'Horizontalism: a critique', *Cambridge Journal of Economics*, **20**, 497–508.
Lavoie, M. (1996), 'Horizontalism, structuralism, liquidity preference and the principle of increasing risk', *Scottish Journal of Political Economy*, **43** (3), 275–300.
Minsky, H.P. (1986), *Stabilizing an Unstable Economy*, New Haven: Yale University Press.
Moore, B.J. (1988), *Horizontalists and Verticalists: The Macroeconomics of Credit Money*, Cambridge: Cambridge University Press.
Wolfson, M. (1996), 'A Post Keynesian theory of credit rationing', *Journal of Post Keynesian Economics*, **18** (3), 443–70.

Bastard Keynesianism

More has been written about Keynes's *General Theory* than any other work in economics in the twentieth century. It has a reputation of being a difficult book to understand. Some of Keynes's greatest supporters were initially hostile in their reviews. The doyen of American economics, Paul Samuelson found the book so confusing it took him 12 to 18 months to begin to understand it, and then only when it was put in mathematical form. Popularizers had to simplify the book for mass consumption. In the process of simplification and interpretation, the *General Theory* was presented in a way that was comfortable to those brought up on the microeconomic supply and demand apparatus. Again there was a simple graphical presentation (either IS–LM or the Keynesian 'cross') and issues could be discussed in terms of shifts of curves, and slopes and elasticities, and marginal changes of variables. Its pedagogical attractiveness and simplicity soon ruled the textbooks.

However, while economics acquired a new macroeconomic model that was simple, easily grasped and teachable, it was also a model that omitted many important aspects of Keynes's ideas. Joan Robinson in 1962 called this vulgarization of Keynes 'Bastard-Keynesianism' (Robinson 1971, p. 90). Sidney Weintraub called it 'Hicksian Keynesianism' or 'Classical Keynesianism'. 'Hydraulic Keynesianism' is another label used, as is 'Neo-Keynesianism'. The term 'neoclassical synthesis' describes the process through which Keynes's *General Theory* was reconciled with pre-Keynesian thinking. The years from the mid-1950s through to the 1960s were the golden age of the neoclassical synthesis, which in substance was the linking of the Keynesian income–expenditure system with neo-Walrasian general equilibrium analysis. During this period, the terms neo-Keynesian and neoclassical seemed interchangeable. Yet in this context Keynes's contribution was relegated to imposing several price rigidities which, however useful for policy purposes, were nevertheless theoretically trivial. It is this trivialization of Keynes that so offends his true disciples.

The process of simplification and systematization of Keynes began almost immediately. One can see this clearly in the titles of the articles and books published at the time. John Hicks's key article was titled 'Mr. Keynes and the Classics: A Suggested Interpretation'. James Meade's article was 'A Simplified Model of Mr. Keynes' System' and Alvin Hansen's book was *A Guide to Keynes* (1953). Models consisting of a small number of simultaneous equations, presented by Hicks, Hansen, Meade, Brian Reddaway, Roy Harrod, Franco Modigliani and Oscar Lange, came to symbolize the Keynesian revolution. The model was popularly known as the IS–LM model. It seemed to summarize whatever substantive message the interpreters took from Keynes's book in a system of simultaneous equations whose properties were similar to the standard partial-equilibrium supply–demand approach. Once the equations were translated into diagrammatic form (the Hicks–Hansen diagram) many of the apparent obscurities and ambiguities seemed to vanish. Futhermore, it provided a logical basis for activist policy proposals associated with the Keynesian revolution.

Paul Samuelson's response to the *General Theory* is instructive. While he acknowledged that it was a work of genius, it was also (he claimed) obscure, confusing, overly polemical and poorly organized. Keynes, he alleged, had no genuine interest in economic theory, although by intuition he seems to have stumbled on the right path. What was needed was to update and systemize the framework through a system of mathematical equations. Indeed, the IS–LM model was needed to comprehend what the *General Theory* was all about, something even Keynes may not have been sure of. While the IS–LM model was used for advanced students, a truncated version called the Keynesian cross was used for introductory students. Samuelson remarked that 'the intersection $C(Y)+I$ with the 45-degree line gives us our simplest "Keynesian-cross", which logically is exactly like a "Marshallian-cross" of supply and demand' (cited in Weintraub 1977, p. 47).

The Keynesian cross and IS–LM became the two most popular ways through which students 'learned' Keynesian economics. Wide dissemination of the Keynesian cross was achieved through the various editions of Samuelson's introductory text. Relationships between aggregate variables constituted the foundations of the macroeconometric models generated. Aggregate flows of the economy were likely to grind out less than full-employment output levels through various rigidities and imperfections. Keynesians were not concerned with the structure of the economy, as all that was needed was to change a few dials to maintain adequate levels of aggregate demand. The most important dials were those associated with fiscal policy; hence early Keynesians were often called 'fiscalists'. Financial markets and monetary policy were neglected.

As IS–LM and the Keynesian cross became the dominant orthodoxy in macroeconomics, other issues vanished from the mainstream literature. But did these models convey the essential message that Keynes intended to convey in the *General Theory*?

The dissenters from the mainstream interpretation of Keynes all agree that IS–LM and the Keynesian-cross models miss the essence of Keynes, but provide contrasting views as to what that essential message is. Joan Robinson's critique is primarily methodological. She denies the legitimacy of using comparisons of equilibrium positions to analyse processes in actual time, and contrasts models in logical time and those in historical time. The Bastard Keynesians assume microeconomic foundations so that markets behave as if they were Walrasian competitive ones, but agree that an economy can come to rest at an underemployment equilibrium, or move to full-employment equilibrium very slowly, due to deficient aggregate demand. Hence they support demand management policies. Robinson argues that one cannot fit Keynes into a neo-Walrasian framework because it cannot handle historical time. Keynes did not think in terms of simultaneous determination: he was a cause and effect man; investment determined saving, aggregate demand determined output and employment, and so on. Robinson contrasts the Marshallian micro model of Keynes with the Walrasian micro model of the Bastard Keynesians.

The *General Theory* stimulated the construction and testing of aggregative models. These models attempted to replicate the actual economy's behaviour through various systems of mathematical equations, the coefficients of which were derived from historical data. Lawrence Klein played a key role here in pioneering the path for a generation of quantitative research in Keynesian macroeconomics. The economics profession devoted substantial resources to the construction, estimation, testing and manipulation of these large-scale econometric models for forecasting and policy analysis. All the large-scale US models had properties similar to the IS–LM model. While these models were called 'Keynesian' the modellers seemed to have been unaware of Keynes's 1939 critique of Jan Tinbergen's econometric methods and he presumably would not have favoured this development.

Textbook Keynesianism has been subject to frequent attack, with perhaps Sidney Weintraub's (1977) critique being the clearest. Weintraub sees Keynesianism as only tenuously connected to Keynes. The Keynesian-cross income–expenditure analysis uses simple equations relating consumption to income, investment to the interest rate, and an equilibrium balance equation. When solved it leads to an equilibrium income that may or may not correspond to a full-employment level of income. However, in this model, with its inflationary and deflationary gaps, the economy could experience either inflation or unemployment but not both. It could not accommodate stagflation. A Phillips curve was then grafted on to the Keynesian-cross analysis and the Phillips curve became identified as an important part of Keynesianism via Robert Solow and Paul Samuelson. Yet one cannot find the Phillips curve in Keynes, and it would have been inconsistent with his approach to find a sustainable empirical relationship. Keynes would not have supported any stable, dependable, long-term relationship between inflation and unemployment. It was precisely these features of the model that were so successfully attacked by Milton Friedman and the monetarists. Similarly it was the Keynesian macroeconometric models that were attacked by Robert Lucas and the New Classical macro economists. In both cases the attacks related to the Bastard Keynesians; *not Keynes*. Leijonhufvud (1968) highlights this distinction clearly.

Weintraub's alternative Keynesianism, using aggregate demand and aggregate supply analysis, would have avoided these confusions. Stagflation is inconsistent with IS–LM and the Keynesian cross, but not with aggregate demand and aggregate supply. Stagflation is not inconsistent with Keynes's framework. Lorie Tarshis also provided an early text using this framework, but the aggregate supply curve was developed in an imperfectly competitive setting. This allowed an easier incorporation of the 'wage unit' into the analysis. Fiscalism is another concern for Weintraub. Sheila Dow notes that Keynes for most of his life was an endogenous money person and a monetary theorist (Harcourt 2001, p. 48). The neglect of monetary factors in the postwar period would not have been in the spirit of Keynes.

Paul Davidson (1972) and Hyman Minsky (1975) have both emphasized the important role Keynes attributed to the financial sector. For Minsky, Keynesian economics as the economics of disequilibrium is the economics of *permanent* disequilibrium. He contends that the capital-asset valuation process, in conditions of uncertainty, was central to Keynes's argument and that capitalism is inherently unstable due to its financial structure. Davidson, along with George Shackle and others, focuses on fundamental uncertainty. Decision making is undertaken in an uncertain environment, and we need to examine the psychologies of the main players – speculators, investors, consumers, wage-earners. Keynes almost never refers to isolated individuals; he speaks of the psychology of specific social groups. Davidson tries to integrate the monetary detail of Keynes's earlier *A Treatise on Money* with the effective demand features of the *General Theory*. The overriding importance of uncertainty in investment and money markets means that investment expectations are unquantifiable and unpredictable, and their volatility influences the economy's overall instability.

There are other critics of the Bastard Keynesians, like Victoria Chick, who focus on the misapplication of the policy prescriptions of the *General Theory*. Chick argues that fiscal stimulus was designed as shock treatment and not intended to sustain an economy over a long time period. She maintains that Keynes would not have approved of fine-tuning and would have supported the more selective use of fiscal policy, and not continuous budget deficits. The excessive preoccupation with the short run has ignored the long-run tendency to a lack of effective demand with involuntary unemployment. Less concern with fine-tuning and more attention to the long-run expansion of economic activity is required. Keynes's mention of the need for closer scrutiny of the level and composition of investment, or the 'socialization of investment', has also gone unheeded by the mainstream Keynesians.

To sum up the critique of the Bastard Keynesians, the so-called custodians of the real message of the *General Theory* claim that Keynes's vision is too rich to be encapsulated in one graph or a few equations. Wage stickiness or liquidity traps are not essential components of Keynes's message. The 'Economics of Keynes' cannot be analysed in timeless, perfect information, general equilibrium models. A world of fundamental uncertainty moving through historical time is essential to the message of Keynes. Interpreting Keynes through IS–LM is a distortion that forces the *General Theory* into the older neoclassical mould. Mainstream Keynesians such as Paul Samuelson and James Tobin reject these criticisms. Indeed, Robert Solow approves of the Bastard Keynesian label because to him it suggests 'hybrid vigour'!

The debate between the Bastard Keynesians and the true disciples has long been superseded by the attacks on Keynesians of any description by the monetarists and, more powerfully, by the New Classical macro economists. What one finds in the textbooks now is a far greater travesty of Keynes than anything the 'Bastards' did. For example, in Gregory Mankiw's *Principles of Macroeconomics* (1998) one finds a pre-Keynesian loanable funds model; all a budget deficit achieves is higher interest rates, crowding out and lower national saving. Mankiw is presenting the 'Treasury View' that Keynes so devastatingly attacked. In the unemployment chapter there is no mention of aggregate demand; the only causes of unemployment are minimum wage laws, unions, efficiency wages and job search. Unemployment appears to be always at the 'natural' rate, with deviations rare and transitory. A monetarist approach to inflation is provided. This text concentrates on the classical principles of macroeconomics and is a savage departure from the fundamental principles of any kind of Keynesian thought. The 'Treasury View', the quantity theory of money and Say's Law are all found in modern guises. This is all presented as 'New Keynesianism'!

In this modern context, Geoffrey Harcourt (2001) has made a plea for a united front with Keynesians of whatever type, including the Bastard Keynesians, to fight this external challenge. Despite fundamental differences they have enough common cause to draw together to face the monetarist/New Classical assault. At times he says that this is a strategic alliance and everyone is welcome at least at a tactical level, while at other times he thinks that there is enough common ground for the differences to be just 'arguments within the family'. His call for Keynesians of any persuasion to coalesce into a united front seems to have mollified the earlier Post Keynesian antagonism towards the Bastard Keynesians.

JOHN LODEWIJKS

See also:

Econometrics; Effective Demand; Keynes's *General Theory*; Keynes's *Treatise on Money*; New Classical Economics; New Keynesian Economics; Stagflation; Time in Economic Theory; Uncertainty; Walrasian Economics.

Bibliography

Davidson, Paul (1972), *Money and the Real World*, London: Macmillan.
Harcourt, G.C. (2001), *50 Years a Keynesian and Other Essays*, Basingstoke and New York: Palgrave.
Laidler, David (1999), *Fabricating the Keynesian Revolution*, Cambridge and New York: Cambridge University Press
Leijonhufvud, Axel (1968), *On Keynesian Economics and the Economics of Keynes: A Study in Monetary Theory*, London and New York: Oxford University Press.
Minsky, Hyman (1975), *John Maynard Keynes*, London and New York: Macmillan.
Robinson, Joan (1971), *Economic Heresies*, New York: Basic Books.
Weintraub, Sidney (1977), 'Hicksian Keynesianism: dominance and decline', in S. Weintraub, *Modern Economic Thought*, Philadelphia: University of Pennsylvania Press, pp. 45–66.
Young, Warren (1987), *Interpreting Mr. Keynes: The IS–LM Enigma*, Cambridge: Polity Press.

Bretton Woods

The Bretton Woods agreement was part of the reorganization process following the Second World War. The Bretton Woods system, named after the New Hampshire town where the conference was held in July 1944, was relatively short-lived. It extended from late 1946, when the declaration of par values by 32 countries went into effect, to August 1971, if one takes the closure of the gold window in the US as the end of the system, or late 1973, if one takes the breakdown of the Smithsonian agreement. This was a period of great prosperity. The Bretton Woods period exhibited the most rapid growth of output of any monetary regime (Bordo 1993). As a result, this period is usually referred to as the 'golden age' of capitalism.

The Bretton Woods agreement is mostly known for imposing fixed, but adjustable, exchange rates, on the basis of a gold–dollar system. Two main characteristics of the Bretton Woods system should be emphasized, namely the existence of a set of rules, that included fixed exchange rates, but also capital controls and domestic macroeconomic policy autonomy, on the one hand, and the hegemony of the US, on the other.

The Bretton Woods system represented 'the first successful systematic attempt to produce a legal and institutional framework for the world economic system' (James 1996, p. 27). It must be noted that the system worked only because the US, the creditor country, was willing to pay the bill for reconstruction through the Marshall Plan. The Marshall Plan, in turn, was only possible in the environment of the Cold War. Post Keynesian authors have emphasized the importance of creditor countries in expanding demand on a global level (Davidson 1982).

The need for this legal framework was unanimously accepted as a way of avoiding the negative consequences of the inter-war period financial speculation. Ragnar Nurkse forcefully presented the consensus view. According to Nurkse (1944, p. 16), 'the flow of short term funds, especially in the thirties, often became disequilibrating instead of equilibrating, or instead of simply coming to a stop'. This was partially true of the pre-1914 system, but the main difference was the absence of a hegemonic power capable of controlling capital flows through the variation of the interest rate (Kindleberger 1973). Further, according to Nurkse (1944, p. 22), 'in the thirties, there was a gradual but persistent change in economic opinion. The price-level came to be regarded more and more as a secondary criterion of economic stability. The state of employment and national income tended to become the primary criterion.' This change was to a great extent part of the effects of the Keynesian revolution.

John Maynard Keynes was the chief British negotiator at the Bretton Woods conference. It is important to note, given the prominence of Keynes's views during the conference, that he was not an advocate of either fixed or floating exchange rates. His main objective was always the management of the exchanges to achieve domestic policy goals. The development of the principle of effective demand led Keynes to support not only expansionary fiscal policies, but also low interest rate policies, whose ultimate impact would be to reduce the significance of the rentiers' income share, the so-called 'euthanasia of the rentier'.

To guarantee the euthanasia of the rentier, Keynes pointed out that the central bank should be able to set the rate of interest independently from any international pressures. Keynes especially insisted, during the long preparatory works and the negotiations for the Bretton Woods conference, upon the idea that movements of capital could not be left unrestricted. Keynes argued that 'we cannot hope to control rates of interest at home if movements of capital moneys out of the country are unrestricted' (Keynes 1980a, p. 276).

The fact that Keynes accepted, and even defended, the final agreement at Bretton Woods, which diverged in several points from his Bancor proposal, can be attributed to the maintenance of capital controls in the final document (Crotty 1983). Also, it must be noted that, as much as Keynes's Plan, Harry Dexter White's Plan also proposed the use of short-term capital controls (De Cecco 1979). The neoliberal thinking that had come to dominate financial circles in the recent years had little standing at the Bretton Woods conference. Keynes (1980b, p. 17) was categorical in saying 'not merely as a feature of transition, but as a permanent arrangement, the plan accords to every member government the explicit right to control all capital movements. What used to be a heresy is now endorsed as orthodox.'

The control of capital flows means that the central bank does not need to use the bank discount rate to attract inflows of capital, or avoid capital flight. As a result the bank rate can be maintained as low as possible. A reduction of the bank rate leads to a transfer from the finance or rentier sector to the industrial capitalist and working classes, leading to an increase in consumption and investment spending. In addition, low rates of interest reduce the burden of debt servicing, so that active fiscal policies can be pursued by the state without leading to an explosive increase of the debt to GDP ratio. Thus, the prosperity of the golden age period is associated with the euthanasia of the rentier, which was an integral part of the Bretton Woods agreement.

Also, the inter-war period showed that greater capital mobility led to greater exchange rate instability (Nurkse 1944). The fact that increased capital mobility leads to higher volatility of exchange rates should not be read as a one-way relationship. Flexible rates allow the opportunity for speculators to profit from arbitrage; therefore profit-seeking speculation is an inevitable outcome of the abandonment of fixed rates. In that sense, a system of fixed but adjustable exchange rates is more conducive to a situation of reduced capital flows.

However, despite the intense preoccupation with capital controls, capital movements began to play an important role in the late 1960s. A pool of unregulated capital emerged as early as the late 1940s, when the Chinese communist government placed its dollar earnings with a Soviet bank in Paris. This was the origin of the so-called 'Euromarket' (James 1996, p. 179). However, it was not until the late 1950s, with return of the convertibility of the European currencies, and the removal of the current account restrictions, that the transition from a dollar shortage to a dollar surplus took place.

The growth of the Euromarket is also directly connected to the expansion of US multinational firms, and the consequent expansion of US banking abroad. The collapse of Bretton Woods is related to increasing speculative capital flows. According to Triffin (1960) this resulted from the fact that the US economy could not guarantee the convertibility of dollars into gold at the fixed parity. In this view, the collapse of the Bretton Woods system is directly connected to the increasing role of capital movements and the incapacity of the hegemonic country to control them.

Whereas this view is incorporated in the conventional view, the main cause of the demise of Bretton Woods is associated with the inflationary pressures brought about by the expansionary fiscal policies in the US, and the propagation of these inflationary pressures through the international system. The increasingly expansionary fiscal policies of the 1960s – resulting both from the Vietnam War and the Great Society experiment of the Kennedy–Johnson administrations – led to growing balance of payments deficits. The US deficits were initially considered instrumental for the working of an international monetary system that was desperately in need of dollars to obtain the essential imports of capital goods needed for reconstruction. However, by the late 1960s the accumulation of idle dollar balances started to put pressure on the money supply of the rest of world, leading to inflation. That is, according to the neoclassical logic, inflation was caused by the US fiscal and monetary policies, and transmitted to the world as a result of the system of fixed parities.

The collapse of Bretton Woods, then, is related to the unwillingness of foreign countries to import US inflation. That eventually broke the credibility of the fixed exchange rate commitments, and the willingness of the several central banks to cooperate in order to maintain the fixed parities. In other words, the Bretton Woods system failed because the fixed parity commitment was not credible in the face of accelerating inflation.

An alternative explanation for the inflationary pressures of the 1960s is possible, though. This alternative explanation, compatible with the Post Keynesian view, would minimize the effects of the US expansionary fiscal policy in the demise of Bretton Woods. The golden age regime implied a commitment to full employment and the creation of a safety net for unemployed workers. Additionally, the imposition of capital controls and the cheap money policies – which led to low real rates of interest – implied a favourable environment for workers. Parties with strong ties with the labour movement were in power in several Western countries, and this was tolerated, to a great extent, since it was considered a form of reducing the dangers of the Soviet menace. Furthermore, full employment tends to increase the bargaining power of the working class.

In this environment, workers' pressures for higher nominal wages would usually be expected. For a given real rate of interest, and a fixed nominal exchange rate, the only effect of rising wages would be higher prices. In sum, inflation was the result of wage pressures (cost–push) rather than the expansionary fiscal and monetary policies (demand–pull). In that sense, the abandonment of the fixed parities is not connected to the loss of credibility in the face of higher inflation, since the causes of inflation lay somewhere else.

Post Keynesians emphasize the role of financial liberalization in the collapse of the Bretton Woods regime. Paul Davidson (1982) argues that the US dollar represents the asset of ultimate redemption, and hence is used as the measure of international liquidity. As a result the US benefits from a more liberal financial system, since the centrality of US financial market allows it to attract funds to finance persistent current account deficits. For that reason, beginning in the 1960s the US adopted a more self-centred financial policy, promoting financial openness in order to be able to face the growing current account deficits. It is the increasing financial openness of the 1960s, built into the American support for the Euromarket, that ultimately made the Bretton Woods system untenable. Whether the financial disruption and the economic crises caused by the last wave of financial liberalization would lead to an effort to re-regulate financial markets is still an open question. The echoes of Bretton Woods can be still heard in the calls for a new financial architecture.

MATIAS VERNENGO

See also:
Economic Policy; Exchange Rates; Globalization; International Economics; Stagflation.

References

Bordo, Michael D. (1993), 'The Bretton Woods international monetary system: a historical overview', in M. Bordo and B. Eichengreen (eds), *A Retrospective on the Bretton Woods System*, Chicago: University of Chicago Press, pp. 3–108.
Crotty, James (1983), 'On Keynes and capital flight', *Journal of Economic Literature*, **21** (1), 59–65.
Davidson, Paul (1982), *International Money and the Real World*, London: Macmillan.
De Cecco, Marcello (1979), 'Origins of the post-war payments system', *Cambridge Journal of Economics*, **3** (1), 49–61.
James, Harold (1996), *Monetary Cooperation Since Bretton Woods*, New York: Oxford University Press.
Keynes, John Maynard (1980a), *The Collected Writings of John Maynard Keynes. Volume XXV: Activities 1940–1944*, Cambridge: Macmillan and Cambridge University Press for the Royal Economic Society.
Keynes, John Maynard (1980b), *The Collected Writings of John Maynard Keynes. Volume XXVI: Activities 1941–1946*, London: Macmillan and Cambridge University Press for the Royal Economic Society.
Kindleberger, Charles P. (1973), *The World in Depression, 1929–39*, Berkeley: University of California Press.
Nurkse, Ragnar (1944), *International Currency Experience: Lessons from the Interwar Period*, Princeton: League of Nations and Princeton University Press.
Triffin, Robert (1960), *Gold and the Dollar Crisis: The Future of Convertibility*, New Haven: Yale University Press.

Budget Deficits

Although budget deficits have usually been associated with Keynes's economic policy proposals, he was not the first economist to put forward the idea of utilizing deficit financing as a tool to fight unemployment. Moreover, after he had written the *General Theory*, Keynes saw the deficit only as an instrument of last resort. It was rather the Polish economist Michał Kalecki who persistently advocated the use of budget deficits. Keynes's early views on finance can be found in volumes V, VI and IX of his *Collected Writings*, while his more mature outlook can be inferred from volumes XXII and XXVII. Kalecki's writings on finance can be found in volumes I, II and VII of his *Collected Works*.

Already in the 1920s Keynes realized that idle resources normally exist in capitalist economies, and he favoured public works in order to increase aggregate demand. He refined his viewpoint in the *Treatise on Money*, where he argued that in an open economy with a fixed exchange rate regime, variations in the interest rate could not induce simultaneously both internal and external equilibrium. Thus, with wage rigidity and a fixed exchange rate regime, the unemployed would not tend spontaneously to be reabsorbed, while a decrease in the rate of interest to stimulate investment would result in gold outflows and endanger the balance of payments. After completion of the *Treatise* and while working on the *General Theory* he came to utilize Kahn's multiplier as a theoretical underpinning for his proposal, which was now openly related to budget deficits.

However, in the *General Theory* Keynes did not explicitly recommend budget deficits, and in fact the government plays practically no role in that book. The full incorporation of the government into Keynes's mature thought came later, while he was acting as an economic adviser to the British government during the Second World War, and when he reflected on what economic policy should be after the war was over.

Keynes believed that the fundamental role of the government was to ensure conditions where uncertainty, which was the ultimate reason for unemployment, would be minimized, so that enough private investment would be forthcoming to absorb full-employment savings. Within this context, the direct role of fiscal policy would be to smooth out undesired variations in private expenditure (Carvalho 1997).

Keynes recommended separating the budget into two components, a current and a capital budget. He considered unbalancing the current budget as a last resort only, and argued that recourse to deficit would be a sign of a failure of the government's overall economic stance. Moreover, in Keynes's view 'the "capital budget" should be balanced in the long-term but may be adjusted to offset exogenous cyclical changes; the current budget may as a last resort show surpluses or deficits to offset short-term failure of the capital budget but also be balanced over the long term' (Kregel 1985, p. 38). Cyclical fluctuations could be prevented if two-thirds or three-quarters of total investment were under public or semi-public auspices. Nevertheless, Keynes opposed public works to stabilize the cycle because he considered that public works had to be carefully planned. He also opposed the use of taxation to affect consumption because he thought this method unreliable, and he considered it politically infeasible continuously to alter the tax rate.

Michał Kalecki, who independently discovered the theory of effective demand, recognized very early the influence of government expenditure on effective demand. In the early 1930s he showed that, below full employment, deficit financing would raise private profits, and would have a strong expansionary effect. This can be demonstrated by assuming a closed economy where all the productive sectors are vertically integrated and where workers do not save. A rise in government expenditure financed by a deficit will raise sales by an amount equal to the increase in government expenditure plus the increase in workers' consumption. Since the increase in direct costs equals the increase in workers' consumption, private profits, which are equal to sales minus direct costs, will expand by an amount equal to the rise in the budget deficit.

Somewhat later Kalecki added that financing expenditure by taxes levied on private profits would also raise demand, since firms would not (or could not) immediately curtail their investment expenditure after the tax rise had been enacted, because investment was the result of previous investment decisions which require a certain time to be completed and which would be very costly to cancel, and because capitalist consumption is also rather insensitive to expectations. Financing government expenditure with taxes on profits would thus expand aggregate demand, provided that firms did not pass on those higher taxes to consumers via higher prices. However, since under this policy profits would not be raised, the expansionary effect of government expenditure would be smaller than in the case of deficit financing. Thus the notion that a balanced budget can be expansionary also has its roots in Kalecki.

Deficit financing was one of Kalecki's 'Three ways to full employment' (1944), the title of a paper where he showed that, below full employment, deficit financing would raise demand without necessarily entailing inflation, and that an appropriate monetary policy might also prevent the interest rate from rising with the higher output and employment consequent upon the rise in the deficit.

Kalecki argued that in order to maintain full employment in capitalist economies the deficit would probably have to grow continuously, but this need not increase the burden of the national debt. The ratio of debt to output need not rise, provided that the latter grew at a sufficient rate (given by the rate of growth of employment and labour productivity). Moreover, for Kalecki even an increase in interest on the national debt as a percentage of output need not involve any disturbance in output and employment if it were financed by a capital tax, levied on wealth (including ownership of government securities). A similar result could be brought about with a modified income tax, imposed on gross unearned income only (that is, before deduction of depreciation) and where all investment in fixed capital was deducted from the taxable amount.

Yet Kalecki's support for budget deficits was not unqualified. His misgivings, however, had nothing to do with the alleged evils the mainstream view attributes to the deficit: inflation and crowding-out of private investment. Rather, his reservations arose from his concern for social justice: the budget deficit increases profits simultaneously with output and employment. When income distribution is inequitable, and the political situation permits full employment to be coupled with greater social justice, then expanding government expenditure financed by higher taxes on profits and on income of the higher-income brackets should be the preferred policy.

In the early 1930s, Kalecki was probably the first economist to show the positive impact that deficit financing played in the German recovery under the Nazi government. After 1945 he continued with the empirical application of his theory of public finance, and devised a novel and detailed methodology for analysing the effect of government spending on the level of aggregate demand. This enabled him to demonstrate that the growth of government expenditure financed by taxation on profits, not deficit financing, was at the heart of postwar economic recovery.

Deficit spending as a policy tool has recently been revived in the Post Keynesian literature through the proposal to eliminate unemployment by making the government the employer of last resort (ELR). This proposal was originally put forward by Hyman Minsky (1986), who, however, tended to oppose budget deficits. It has been developed more thoroughly by Wray (1998), who recognizes that under an ELR strategy government expenditure will probably grow faster than tax receipts, and a budget deficit will ensue. However, in his view the government can simply create enough new money, or otherwise sell securities, to finance the deficit with an unchanging rate of interest. It has been shown that measures could be taken to minimize the tendencies to inflation and to external disequilibrium that might arise if an ELR policy were implemented (López 2000).

However, Steindl (1990) showed that in the most recent stage of capitalist development the budget deficit has turned from a policy tool to a consequence of the overall evolution of the economy. He utilized the well-known identity:

$$(I - S_B) + (X - M) + (G - T) = (S_H - H)$$

where $(G - T)$ is the budget deficit, $(X - M)$ is borrowing by the outside world, $(I - S_B)$ is borrowing by business, and $(S_H - H)$ is lending by households. Steindl argued:

> The budget deficit ... used to be regarded as an active element, incurred on purpose by the government. In the present circumstances it is more likely to play a passive role, and be dominated by the other sectors. This is due to the large share of taxation in an additional GDP, to the strong and quick reaction of consumers to a change in income and to the fact that the foreign balance is more often dominated by outside influences than by domestic policy (by the GDP)... The budget deficit is predominantly suffered rather than contrived. (Steindl 1990, pp. 217–18)

Nevertheless, as Godley persuasively argues, a budget deficit is still indispensable for long-run growth. He utilizes a single variable termed 'the fiscal stance', which is given by dividing the total flow of government expenditure by the average tax rate. Godley prefers this variable to the budget deficit, which 'measured ex-post facto is a bad measure of the impact of fiscal policy because it notoriously fails to distinguish the effect of the budget on the economy from the effect of the economy on the budget' (Godley and McCarthy 1998, p. 40). Utilizing the fiscal stance, Godley has been able to closely track the evolution of the US economy in recent decades.

JULIO LÓPEZ G.

See also:
Economic Policy; Fiscal Policy; Kaleckian Economics; Keynes's *General Theory*; Money; Profits; Taxation.

References
Carvalho, F. (1997), 'Economic policies for monetary economies. Keynes's economic policy proposals for an unemployment-free economy', *Revista de Economia Politica*, **17** (4), 31–51.
Godley, W. and G. McCarthy (1998), 'Fiscal policy will matter', *Challenge*, **41** (1), 38–54.
Kregel, J. (1985), 'Budget deficits, stabilization policy and liquidity preference: Keynes's postwar policy proposals', in F. Vicarelli (ed.), *Keynes's Relevance Today*, London: Macmillan, pp. 28–50.
López, J. (2000), 'Budget deficit and full employment', *Journal of Post Keynesian Economics*, **22** (4), 549–63.
Minsky, H.P. (1986), *Stabilizing an Unstable Economy*, New Haven: Yale University Press.
Steindl, J. (1990), 'The control of the economy', in J. Steindl, *Economic Papers, 1941–1988*, New York: St. Martin's Press, pp. 216–29.
Wray, L.R. (1998), *Understanding Modern Money. The Key to Full Employment and Price Stability*, Cheltenham, UK and Northampton, MA, USA: Edward Elgar.

Business Cycles

The time path of aggregate output and its main components exhibits significant fluctuations around trend values, as do other important variables, including employment, productivity, prices, wages, interest rates and stock prices. These fluctuations are recurrent but not regular. The pattern of co-movements between the different variables, the amplitudes of the fluctuations and the length of the cycle vary over time. In fact, the delineation of cycle from trend raises many problems, and cycles of different length may coexist in the data; short-run fluctuations may take place with reference to a long-run cycle, rather than around a constant exponential trend. The term 'business cycles' usually refers to relatively short cycles. This entry therefore does not consider 'long waves'. The possible interaction between cyclical characteristics and any long-term trend is also ignored. The main focus will be on fluctuations in output and employment for a closed economy.

Business cycle theories can be categorized in different ways. One common distinction concerns the 'exogeneity' or 'endogeneity' of the cycles. In some theories the fluctuations are caused by external shocks and the cycle, in this sense, is 'exogenous'. The shocks may be completely random and non-cyclical. They constitute the 'impulse', and the cyclical pattern is produced by 'propagation mechanisms' that spread out the effects of the impulse. A positive shock, for instance, may induce firms to increase their investment and, by raising the capital stock, this decision will affect future conditions.

Michał Kalecki (along with Ragnar Frisch and Eugene Slutsky) was a pioneer of the external-shock approach. Most Post Keynesians, however, have followed a different line. According to this alternative approach, external shocks may indeed hit the economy and affect movements in economic activity, but fluctuations would occur even in the absence of shocks. The fluctuations in this sense are created endogenously.

It is sometimes claimed that a reliance on external shocks leaves the cycle unexplained and that endogenous theories are therefore intrinsically superior from a methodological perspective. The claim is not convincing. Unforeseen shocks do hit the economy; some of these shocks must be considered exogenous, and it is easy to set up plausible propagation mechanisms that convert random shocks into irregular cyclical fluctuations.

It should be noted also that the distinction between exogenous and endogenous cycles carries no implications for economic policy. Most neoclassical economists may take an external-shock approach, but policy intervention is both feasible and desirable in some models of exogenous cycles, including some mainstream specifications. External shocks that require policy intervention, moreover, also appear in Post Keynesian analysis, as in the case of the desirability of compensating for autonomous shifts in 'animal spirits'. Conversely, endogenous cycles can be generated in models in which markets clear and outcomes are Pareto optimal, as well as in Post Keynesian models characterized by important market failures. Thus the feasibility and desirability of policy intervention depend on the precise structure of a theory and its cyclical mechanisms.

In general, Post Keynesian theories stress the instability of markets and the need for both regulatory constraints and policy intervention. This emphasis on the inherent problems and limitations of free markets, rather than the exogenous/endogenous distinction, represents the substantive difference *vis-à-vis* most mainstream theories of the business cycle.

Endogenous business cycles can be generated in many ways, and at least four distinct sets of mechanisms have been used in the Post Keynesian literature. The mechanisms are not mutually exclusive, and some contributions combine several mechanisms.

The determination of investment is central to theories that focus on the *goods market*. As a main component of autonomous expenditure, high investment leads to high levels of aggregate demand and output. A high level of output, in turn, will be reflected in high rates of profitability and capital utilization, and this will tend to induce high levels of investment and output in the next period. If investment decisions are relatively insensitive to changes in utilization and profitability, the resulting time path for output will converge to a long-run equilibrium. A high sensitivity, on the other hand, makes this long-run equilibrium (locally asymptotically) unstable: following a slight displacement from the equilibrium position, the economy does not return to the equilibrium but moves further away.

Local instability of this kind can be turned into perpetual fluctuations, rather than cumulative and unbounded divergence, if there are appropriate 'non-linearities' in the investment function and/or in other equations of the model. The existence of 'ceilings' and 'floors' represents a simple example of such 'non-linearities' (gross investment cannot be negative, for instance, and output cannot exceed a full-employment ceiling) but other, less crude non-linearities may also keep the movements bounded and convert local instability into endogenous cyclical movements. Kaldor (1940) is a classic reference for non-linear models in this multiplier–accelerator tradition, but variations on this theme also characterize early contributions by Roy Harrod, Michał Kalecki, Paul Samuelson, John Hicks, Joan Robinson and Richard Goodwin.

Investment needs to be financed, and *financial markets* are given a critical role in some aggregate-demand-based theories of the business cycle. The 'financial instability hypothesis' developed by Hyman Minsky (1982) represents a prominent example. Suppose that, having recovered from past turbulence, the economy now appears to be approaching a smooth equilibrium path. Along this path expectations are largely being met and, using Minsky's terminology, there is 'financial tranquility': firms are able to meet their financial commitments. This very state of tranquility will induce changes in the risk assessments of both lenders and borrowers. Risk premiums fall; lenders start giving loans they would previously have rejected, and borrowers are increasingly prepared to finance their projects in speculative and risky ways. These behavioural changes relax the financial constraints on the rate of investment and a boom ensues. Gradually, the 'fragility' of the financial system increases until a financial crisis causes a rapid rise in interest rates and a contraction of credit and investment. A return to cautious financial practices now follows and the process repeats itself (although the precise financial instruments and institutions may be new and different). The result is perpetual, endogenous fluctuations.

The role of *labour markets and income distribution* has been emphasized by a Marx-inspired literature, with Goodwin's (1967) model of a growth cycle as the most influential example. The model describes the dynamic interaction between the distribution of income and the accumulation of capital. When there is low unemployment – when the reserve army of labour is small, in Marx's terminology – workers are in a strong position and the real wage will be increasing. As real wages increase, however, profit rates suffer and the rate of accumulation declines. With a constant capital–output ratio, the growth rates of output and employment fall, too. Unemployment soon starts to increase, the balance of power starts shifting against workers, and, when the balance has shifted sufficiently, the share of wages stops increasing. Since the *level* of profitability is low, the rate of accumulation will also be low and the rate of unemployment keeps rising at this point. The capitalists now get the upper hand, the wage share starts falling, and profitability and accumulation gradually increase. This increase in accumulation gradually raises the rate of employment, workers once again gain wage increases, and the cycle is complete.

This model formalizes Marx's 'general law of accumulation' and, in Goodwin's original version, the model has no Keynesian features. It presumes that the capital stock is fully utilized at all times; output is determined by the supply side without reference to aggregate demand, and investment adjusts passively to the level of saving. Hybrid models have tried to overcome this weakness by including both Keynesian and Marxian features in the same model (Skott 1989).

Political intervention may itself be a source of fluctuations. This is a position stressed by many free market advocates, but the Post Keynesian argument for a *political business cycle* is different. The classic reference is a short paper by Kalecki (1943). In a technical sense, Kalecki argued, governments may have the ability to control aggregate demand at (near-) full employment, but the maintenance of full employment generates cumulative changes in worker militancy. Increased militancy and inflationary pressures quickly bring together a powerful bloc of business leaders and rentiers and (supported by economists who 'declare that the situation is manifestly unsound') the government allows unemployment to rise. The result, Kalecki argues, is a political business cycle. Although applied by Kalecki to short cycles, the argument is possibly better suited to deal with longer-term fluctuations, and it has been used by a number of writers in relation to the rise in unemployment in the 1970s and 1980s.

Mathematical models have played an important role in the analysis of business cycles in both Post Keynesian and mainstream theory. Not all Post Keynesians are comfortable with the use of these formal techniques. Business cycles, however, involve complex, dynamic interactions and in a purely verbal analysis it is virtually impossible to keep track of these interactions and their implications. Without formalization it may be difficult to decide, for instance, whether a given argument implies that there will be persistent fluctuations, explosive divergence or convergence to a smooth path.

Most formal models of endogenous fluctuations are deterministic. This might seem a serious drawback. The empirical evidence shows irregular cycles and, from a theoretical perspective, it should be easy for both private agents and policy makers to forecast (and to take action to prevent) a cycle that was regular and deterministic.

This objection is not as powerful as it might seem. First, the endogenous view of cycles does not preclude external shocks, and the introduction of shocks (ranging from natural disasters to policy shocks and changes in animal spirits) may remove the regularity without affecting the underlying cyclical mechanism. Second, deterministic, non-linear dynamic models can produce 'chaotic' outcomes that are hard to distinguish from those of a stochastic model. Prediction in these models is virtually impossible, since even the smallest change in initial conditions has dramatic effects on the subsequent movements (for example, Day 1994). Third, the incentives for individuals to try to uncover and take into account aggregate regularities may be small. Most decision makers face specific problems and uncertainties whose effects on the outcome of their decisions dominate the effects of movements in aggregate activity. With limited informational and cognitive resources, these boundedly rational decision makers may choose to ignore the possible influence of aggregate regularities altogether.

Post Keynesians, finally, have always emphasized the historical contingency of economic models. Structural and institutional changes, such as the rise in the size of the public sector, the deregulation of the financial markets, or increased international trade and capital mobility influence the path of the economy and may necessitate a re-specification of the models. The real-wage Phillips curve (a key element in the Goodwin model) may shift, for instance, as a result of changes in labour market legislation.

Interestingly, the historical contingency is sometimes exaggerated in popular writing; only a few years ago, for example, there was a widespread belief that business cycles would disappear in the 'new economy'. While this belief has proved unfounded, the historical contingency and the complexity of business cycles have other implications. Small models, like the ones described above, highlight particular mechanisms. But no single mechanism and no single source of shocks fully explain the diverse patterns of fluctuations that have been observed, and the relative importance of the different mechanisms may vary across both time and place. Thus the different models should be seen as useful tools rather than as complete explanations of the business cycle.

PETER SKOTT

See also:

Dynamics; Equilibrium and Non-equilibrium; Financial Instability Hypothesis; Investment; Kaleckian Economics; Wages and Labour Markets.

References

Day, R. (1994), *Complex Economic Dynamics*, Vol. 1, Cambridge, MA: MIT Press.
Goodwin, R.M. (1967), 'A growth cycle', in C.H. Feinstein (ed.), *Socialism, Capitalism and Economic Growth*, Cambridge: Cambridge University Press, pp. 54–8.
Kaldor, N. (1940), 'A model of the trade cycle', *Economic Journal*, **50** (197), 78–92.
Kalecki, M. (1943), 'Political aspects of full employment', *Political Quarterly*, **14** (4), 322–31. Reprinted in M. Kalecki, *Selected Essays on the Dynamics of the Capitalist Economy, 1933–1970*, Cambridge: Cambridge University Press, 1971, pp. 138–45.
Minsky, H. (1982), *Can 'It' Happen Again? Essays on Instability and Finance,* Armonk, NY: M.E. Sharpe.
Skott, P. (1989), *Conflict and Effective Demand in Economic Growth*, Cambridge: Cambridge University Press.

Cambridge Economic Tradition

The starting-point must be Alfred Marshall (even though Maynard Keynes called T.R. Malthus 'the first of the Cambridge economists' and Keynes's successors were increasingly to draw on classical political economy and Marx for inspiration). Marshall, though, was responsible for the foundation of the Economic Tripos (in 1903) and also, in large measure and at least until very recently, for the approaches to economics in Cambridge even as we know them today. The Marshallian tradition has it that economists should explain how the world works and then, if it does not work well or fairly, do something about it (within well-defined limits). This should be done by theorizing, doing applied work and formulating plausible policies. The approach to applied economics emphasizes the importance of relevance in economics, incorporating the lessons of history, the institutional context and previous social and political conditions, gathered under the rubric of the 'rules of the game'. Theory and measurement are interdependent, feeding back and modifying and expanding one another. This tradition has characterized the contributions of the Faculty's Department of Applied Economics, a research institute which started in 1945 with Richard Stone (one of four Cambridge recipients of the Nobel Prize) as its first director.

Marshall's major contribution was his huge *Principles of Economics*, first published in 1890. It went through eight editions in his lifetime, as volume I for the first five as he initially intended to write two or three more volumes. What would have been the structure of Marshall's ideal *Principles*? In the first volume he wrote about the nitty gritty of economic life – what determines the prices and quantities of commodities produced, what determines the wages, salaries and employment of different sorts of labour, what determines the rates of profit in various industries, that is, a theory of relative prices and quantities. He introduced systematically into economics the use of supply and demand functions and curves in order to analyse the formation of prices and quantities in, principally, freely competitive markets.

His second great contribution was to recognize in a deep way that time is the most elusive, difficult yet relevant concept affecting economic life. To try to capture this insight Marshall used three analytical concepts: the market, the short and the long period. The first deals with existing stocks, the last two with flows. The short period is an analytical device which takes in a period long enough for employment and production but not for the number of firms, or the amounts of machinery available and skilled labour to change; the long period is long enough for firms to enter or exit and for the amount of machinery available and supplies of labour to change (the methods of production known at the start of the long period, however, are not allowed to change). These are not one-to-one descriptions of real life, but analytical devices which exploit the concept of *ceteris paribus*. The economist decides what may or may not vary, in order to get a grip on intricate interconnecting processes and so develop theories of prices and quantities of commodities, and of the services of the factors of production. Money does not get a mention except as a ticket – something in which to measure things; it has little to no analytical role. Everything is done in real, relative terms. Although Marshall understood general equilibrium analysis and had a general equilibrium model in an appendix, he preferred to use partial equilibrium analysis, examining one firm or one industry only, in order to make the analysis manageable and obtain definite results (the limitations of which were explicitly stressed).

Money entered the scene properly when Marshall (in a never fully speltout second volume) developed the quantity theory of money in order to describe what determined the general price level. He argued that, at least in the long period, what was happening in the real sector and what was happening in the monetary sector of the economy – banks and the financial sector generally, the formation of the general price level – were independent of one another. Money was basically a veil. In the short period it was admitted that monetary matters could have real effects, though this was not worked out systematically because of the constraint of the dichotomy between the real and the monetary. The role of monetary institutions, including central banks, was to so control the monetary side of the economy that the underlying real factors operating in a competitive environment were not handicapped in their determination of the allocation of resources, with supplies and demands responding to each other and tending to bring about a sort of social optimum.

This was only a sort of social optimum. The Marshallian tradition did not contain an uncritical defence of *laissez faire* – poverty, unemployment and unsatisfactory working conditions were all recognized, along with a limited role for government to tackle them. Nevertheless, *logically*, it was required to argue that, if there was competition, there were strong forces to ensure the production of goods and services that people wanted by businesspeople who were able to employ their capital as they wanted and workers who could do the jobs they wished to. Only then was it possible to argue that in the long period it was the quantity of money which determined the general price level, as long-period levels of activity and employment could now be regarded as givens along with the long-period value of the velocity of circulation. As to the limitations of the outcome even in these circumstances it was A.C. Pigou, Marshall's successor, who developed the economics of welfare, analysing what happens, and what to do about it, if social costs and benefits were not matched by their private counterparts that the competitive system threw up. His influence is alive and well today under the guise of externalities. Pigou, drawing on his mentor, established another aspect of the Cambridge tradition, that our subject should be, first and foremost, fruit-bearing rather than only light-bearing. This view is to be found in the many editions of *The Economics of Welfare*. An interest in the causes of poverty and inequality, as well as in the distribution of income, reflects this strand. It is especially associated with the writings of James Meade, David Champernowne and Tony Atkinson (who explicitly acknowledges Meade's inspiration and example).

Keynes was Marshall's most distinguished pupil. He dominated Cambridge economics from the 1920s until his death in 1946, and beyond. His work in the late 1920s and in the 1930s significantly extended and radically changed the Marshallian tradition in which he was brought up. He was driven, as were/are all the outstanding Cambridge economists, by an intense seriousness: a desire to understand the world, especially why it malfunctioned, and how to make it a better place.

Trained as a mathematician, Keynes was also a fine philosopher as well as a great economist. He always regarded economics as a branch of moral philosophy. Three strands of his philosophical understanding are especially relevant for the Cambridge economic tradition: first, that in a discipline such as economics there is a spectrum of languages running from intuition and poetry through lawyer-akin arguments to formal logic and mathematics, all of which are relevant for particular issues, or aspects of issues, in the subject; second, that in the workings of complex economic systems, the whole may be more than the sum of the parts; and third, two lessons learned from Marshall: what are the principles which guide sensible (sometimes not so sensible) people doing the best they can in situations of inescapable uncertainty and what are the systemic effects of their behaviour? The significance of these strands was made most explicit in the 1930s when Keynes was writing *The General Theory*. In the 1920s and especially the 1930s he started to rethink drastically how the world worked, initially with his close ally, Dennis Robertson, who is a bridge between Marshall and Keynes, but who, in the end, tragically split with Keynes (a personal tragedy for him and also a professional one for the development of economics).

As Keynes was rethinking Marshall's monetary theory, others at Cambridge were starting to rethink (and in the case of Piero Sraffa ultimately reject) Marshall's theory of the determination of prices and quantities at the level of the firm and industry. Sraffa published two fundamental papers in the mid-1920s, one in Italian and only recently available in an

English translation, the other in the *Economic Journal* (Sraffa 1925 [1999]; Sraffa 1926). Both contained an attack on Marshall's method, that is, the extremely limited practical applications of partial equilibrium analysis (and, he thought then but for different reasons, general equilibrium analysis). But he also suggested that monopoly rather than free competition was the better model of how markets worked, that firms' prices and outputs were constrained by demand rather than by rising supply prices and costs. The appropriate model was therefore one of mini-monopolies surrounded by mini-monopolies so that they had to take account of their actions and other firms' reactions when setting prices. The 1926 paper helped precipitate the imperfect competition revolution developed by Gerald Shove, Richard Kahn and then Austin Robinson and, especially, Joan Robinson. Her 1933 *The Economics of Imperfect Competition*, though still Marshallian/Pigovian in construction, greatly altered the emphasis and details of the results in this tradition. Sraffa had refuted the tradition by 1930 and had started on the long trail which would lead through his edition (with the collaboration of M.H. Dobb) of David Ricardo's works (published between 1951 and 1963) to *Production of Commodities* (Sraffa 1960), both a critique of the foundations of neoclassical theory and simultaneously a rehabilitation of the approach of classical theory including Marx. Joan Robinson only joined him, more or less fully, in the postwar years, Kahn probably never fully and Shove and Austin not at all.

Keynes became more and more dissatisfied with Marshall's way of looking at the economy as a whole, especially the view that we could talk about prices and quantities independently of what was happening in the financial and monetary sectors generally. He also changed the emphasis from the long period, the central core of Marshall's economics, to the short period, including designing policies for other than that '*long run* [in which] we are all dead' (Keynes 1923, p. 65). *A Treatise on Money* (1930), two volumes, was meant to be Keynes's *magnum opus* but it was too constrained by the Marshallian tradition to be successful. So in the 1930s he started again, aided by the remarkable group of young economists in the 'circus', Kahn, James Meade, Austin and Joan Robinson, Sraffa, as well as by Roy Harrod in Oxford.

What did he do in his authentic *magnum opus*, *The General Theory*, published in 1936? The 1920s in the United Kingdom and then in the 1930s in much of the advanced industrialized world was characterized by mass unemployment. Economic theory, though, said that at least in the long term it could not occur if impediments to competition were removed. Keynes, working through his rational reconstruction of the traditional analysis, decided that it was wrong, that there could be a failure of *overall* demand so that people and machines could be involuntarily idle for considerable periods of time and that there were not strong or indeed any forces at work in an unregulated economy that tended to redress these situations. Why? Principally because important expenditure decisions had to be made in situations of inescapable uncertainty about the future. This was especially true of investment decisions, the desire to accumulate, which drove capitalist systems along. Keynes showed that there were no persistent forces at work which, at least on average, could produce enough investment to absorb the resources released by what the community would voluntarily save at the full-employment level of income, where all those willing to work under existing conditions would have jobs. In situations of unemployment there was no way in which those who were willing to work, but who were involuntarily unemployed, could signal to employers that it would be profitable to employ them. And indeed, it would not be profitable unless there were to be a simultaneous, *autonomous* rise in the total demand. It followed therefore that there was a coherent logical case for government intervention; Keynes had provided an explicit theory with which to rationalize the common-sense policies which were being put forward at the time.

A barrier to this being perceived before was the real-monetary dichotomy, with money only a veil. But as it is also a store of value, people could hold it and other financial assets rather than spend. In Keynes's view this second reason for holding money plays an important part in determining the pattern of the rates of interest. The forces concerned may not be such as to give a pattern which induces a rate of accumulation of real things which offsets full-employment saving. We now have an integrated theory of the real and monetary, of a monetary production economy.

All members of the 'circus' influenced Keynes but Kahn, his favourite pupil, was especially influential in the making of *The General Theory*: first, as a remorseless critic of the quantity theory as a causal explanation of the general price level; second, through his work on the short period in the late 1920s, in which he made it a subject worthy of analysis in its own right (though still at the level of the firm and industry); and, third, with James Meade, through his 1931 article on the multiplier, which provided an essential concept for Keynes's new system, showing how investment created saving and not the other way round, as in the traditional view (Kahn 1931).

The General Theory (and a few following articles) were Keynes's great theoretical contribution to economics in the last century and the Cambridge contribution has built on these foundations ever since: developing policies to run a war-time economy including keeping inflation in check, using Keynes's concept of the inflationary gap; designing the required international institutions for the postwar world at Bretton Woods, in order to remove the contractionary, deflationary biases built into the operation of much of the world economy (here Keynes leaves us, dead at the ridiculously early age of 62 in 1946); and, third, in the postwar period developing long-term theories of distribution and growth over time. With this last it was some of Keynes's colleagues in the circus – Kahn, Joan Robinson, Sraffa – together with Nicholas Kaldor (who came to Cambridge from the London School of Economics in the postwar years), Richard Goodwin and Luigi Pasinetti, who were the pioneers.

Within the postwar development of growth theory their work stands out as peculiarly Cambridge in that it draws on insights from the classical political economists, Marx and Keynes, initially in response to Harrod's original and seminal writings just before and after the Second World War (Harrod 1939). One basic question was whether capitalist economies could maintain full employment of labour and capital over time when both the employment-creating and the capacity-creating effects of accumulation were taken into account, together with the classical concern with technical progress, embodied through accumulation itself. In the Cambridge approach (which includes Michał Kalecki's contributions, principally through Joan Robinson) investment led and saving responded, through changes in both output and distribution, taking note of differences in saving propensities at the margin as between wages and profits (and their recipients). (Kaldor flirted with being Jean Baptiste Kaldor for over a decade (Samuelson 1964, p. 345), by assuming that growing economies were fully employed and letting changes in distribution do all the work.) The ultimate goal, probably only reached by Kalecki and Goodwin, was to model descriptively the movement of industrial societies over time.

Joan Robinson and Kahn prefaced this objective with Golden Age analysis, walking before they ran, getting definitions and concepts clear and precise before tackling the much harder task of disequilibrium dynamic analysis. Ever impatient, Kaldor's writings in the 1950s and 1960s were meant to be descriptive analysis, theories to explain his famous 'stylized facts' of economic growth, increasingly in the 1970s and 1980s by means of cumulative causation processes. Neoclassical growth theories, though similarly stimulated (irritated?) by Harrod's writings, tackled his conundrums – the instability of the warranted rate of growth (g_w), the unlikely correspondence of g_w with the natural rate (g_n) – by explicitly concentrating on the supply side and the long-term effects of substitution possibilities in production. Initially aggregate production function as well as multi-sector n commodity models were used. This led to the Cambridge critique of capital and marginal productivity theory generally, associated especially with Kaldor's, Joan Robinson's and Sraffa's writings on value, distribution and capital theory. Also, through Sraffa's contributions and Joan Robinson's writings on Marx and her absorption of Kalecki's approach, the central classical/Marxist organizing concept of the surplus – its creation, extraction, distribution and use

– was integrated into the Cambridge approach and tradition. Pasinetti's (1981) 'theoretical essay on the dynamics of the wealth of nations' is the most systematic and comprehensive development of the classical and Keynesian elements outlined above, thus making him the senior living heir of this strand of the Cambridge tradition.

Finally, the tradition is marked by an interest in the history of our subject and the relevance of our predecessors' writings for current issues. Marshall set the example; Keynes's biographical essays reflect it (though he was not always the most accurate or reliable historian of theory); and Joan Robinson's writings are characterized by references to the insights of past economists, often in order to back up her current interests and interpreted accordingly! The two greats, though, are Kalecki's only two English gentlemen, one a communist and the other an Italian, Maurice Dobb and Piero Sraffa. Sraffa's edition of Ricardo's works and correspondence (with the collaboration of Dobb) and his attempt to rehabilitate the classical approach in *Production of Commodities* are extraordinary examples of scholarship and theory combined. Dobb was the foremost Marxist economist of his era and his writings and influence still diffuse through modern work, even when those affected are not aware of it. Dobb, together with Phyllis Deane and Robin Matthews and their colleagues, also left a distinctive stamp on our understanding of economic history.

I have tried to make clear what I understand to be the Cambridge tradition. I have to say that many of the present decision makers in the Faculty have done their best to suppress this tradition and to replace it with approaches which reflect what they see as the best practice of leading American departments.

G.C. HARCOURT

See also:

Capital Theory; Joan Robinson's Economics; Kaldorian Economics; Keynes's *General Theory*; Keynes's *Treatise on Money*; Sraffian Economics; *Treatise on Probability*.

References

Harrod, R.F. (1939), 'An essay in dynamic theory', *Economic Journal*, **49** (193), 14–33.
Kahn, R.F. (1931), 'The relation of home investment to unemployment', *Economic Journal*, **41** (162), 173–98.
Keynes, J.M. (1923), *A Tract on Monetary Reform*, London: Macmillan (reprinted as volume IV of Keynes's *Collected Writings*, London: Macmillan for the Royal Economic Society, 1971).
Pasinetti, L.L. (1981), *Structural Change and Economic Growth. A Theoretical Essay on the Dynamics of the Wealth of Nations*, Cambridge: Cambridge University Press.
Samuelson, P.A. (1964), 'A brief survey of Post-Keynesian developments [1963]', in R. Lekachman (ed.), *Keynes' General Theory: Reports of Three Decades*, New York: St. Martin's Press, pp. 331–47.
Sraffa, P. (1926), 'The laws of returns under competitive conditions', *Economic Journal*, **36** (144), 535–50.

Sraffa, P. (1960), *Production of Commodities by Means of Commodities. Prelude to a Critique of Economic Theory*, Cambridge: Cambridge University Press.

Sraffa, P. (1925 [1999]), 'On the relations between cost and quantity produced', in L.L. Pasinetti (ed.), *Italian Economic Papers*, Vol. 3, Oxford: Oxford University Press, pp. 323–63.

Capital Theory

'Capital theory' has been used as a shorthand term for the debate known as the Cambridge capital controversies. The reference to Cambridge follows from the dispute having mainly been conducted between prominent figures, or figureheads, attached or aligned to Cambridge, Massachusetts, especially MIT (Massachusetts Institute of Technology), and Cambridge, England. The two Cambridges stood, respectively, as representatives for mainstream neoclassical economics and its critics from radical political economy. A key initiating text was penned by Joan Robinson (1953–54), who was most closely identified with the early phase marking aggressive popularizing of the critique. Sraffa's (1960) classic contribution, long delayed in publication, has served as a basis both for a critique of neoclassical economics – as was its intention – and as an alternative to Marxist value theory. The impact of the capital critique was at its height in the early 1970s, rising and falling with radical political economy. Today, as discussed below, despite the Cambridge critique having won the debate and wrung intellectual concessions from the mainstream, the latter proceeds in practice as if the controversy never occurred, replicating theoretical and empirical errors that were previously exposed and accepted as such.

The Cambridge critique raises a number of inter-connected issues. Here, these will be reduced to, and represented by, three broad aspects. First, in mainstream economics, it has been standard to represent an 'economy' as if it were reducible to an aggregate production function, $F(K, L)$ say, where K is capital and L is labour, with $F()$ exhibiting the standard assumption of decreasing but positive marginal products and overall constant returns to scale. We place 'economy' in inverted commas because it could stand for a country, a sector, a single firm or any producing entity such as a household, with a corresponding production function. In each case, even if imputed for the household, it follows from a knowledge of $F()$ and the capital and labour in use, K and L, respectively, that the rate of profit, r, and the rate of wages, w, can be determined by taking marginal products (with assumptions of full employment and perfect markets for inputs). In particular, $r = f(k)$ where f is the per capita version of F; $f(K/L) = F(K, L)/L$. It follows that the rate of profit falls with an increase in capital per worker as a result of the presumed diminishing marginal product of capital.

52 *Capital theory*

One way of interpreting the Cambridge controversy is in terms of whether this stylized *one-sector* model (there is only one good, with the capital input identical to the output) is capable of being representative of a more complicated economy with more than one good. In other words, it is a discussion about *models* – specifically, are models with more than one good reducible to an 'as if' one-good model? The unambiguous answer is no, unless special assumptions are made about the more complicated economy that essentially make it equivalent to a one-good economy (all outputs are produced with the same input proportions). The presence of more than one good more or less completely undermines the results derived from the one-sector model. First, distribution is not 'determined' by technology alone – what techniques are available and which are in use (by analogy with the one sector, knowledge of F and the technique in use, that is, which particular K/L). I have placed 'determined' in inverted commas because there is only a one-to-one *association* between technology and distribution if there is no double switching or reswitching, briefly elaborated in the next paragraph. If you tell me which technology is use, I can tell you distribution and, it should be added, vice versa. But this says nothing about causation from one to the other or by other factors altogether.

Double or reswitching is difficult to explain briefly so an attempt will be made to do so through use of present value curves that are assumed to be familiar to the reader. Figure 1 shows a number of present value curves, T1,

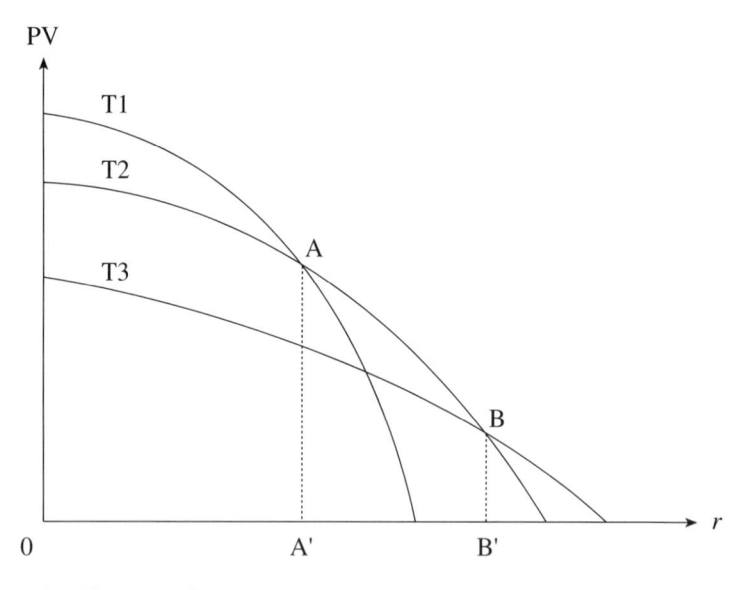

Figure 1   No reswitching

T2 and T3, each representing a technique for producing output. Note, when the rate of profit/interest (the two are treated interchangeably), $r=0$, the corresponding intercept on the present value axis is net output (gross output over and above inputs without discounting). It might be presumed, incorrectly, that higher net output (for T1 over T2 and for T2 over T3) means higher capital intensity. But, even if this sort of one-dimensional statement is to make sense (there are different capital outlays at different points in time), it all depends upon the profile over time of streams of costs and benefits. Even so, at low rates of interest, 0A', technique 1 would be chosen, along A'B', technique 2, and beyond B', technique 3. So a *switch* is made from technique 1 to 2 at A, and from technique 2 to 3 at B. At any rate of interest, there is a corresponding technique and vice versa. We could also add more and more techniques, filling out an envelope, along which there could be continuous switching from one technique to another as the rate of interest changes.

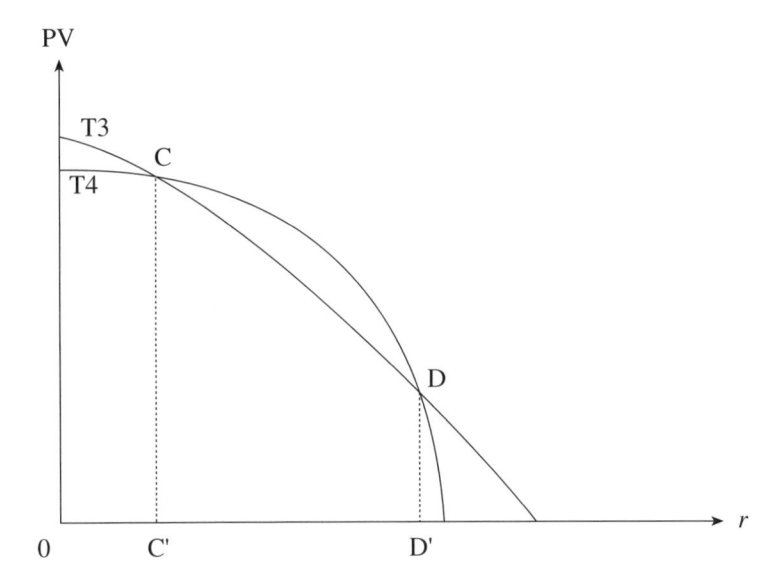

Figure 2   Reswitching

This is fine as far as it goes as long, as previously mentioned, as there is no reswitching. The latter is illustrated in Figure 2. At C, technique 3 switches to technique 4 and, at D, technique 4 switches back to technique 3. There is no necessary one-to-one correspondence between technique in use and the rate of interest. By knowing all techniques available and the actual one in use, we are not able to 'determine' the rate of interest/profit as suggested by reference to the marginal product of capital for the 'as if' one-sector model (with inputs and outputs assessed at different points in time making the present value curves equivalent to having more than one good).

In addition, we cannot write down a sensible production function for the economy as a whole since, even if we can do so for individual sectors in terms of physical quantities of inputs and outputs, aggregating over sectors will require an evaluation of the weight of each sector. This cannot be done in a way that preserves the results of the one-sector model – in particular, that there is an inverse relationship between the measure of capital and the rate of profit. With reswitching, as in Figure 2, it is possible for the same technology to be in use at two different rates of profit. For the results of the 'as if' one-good model to carry over to the more complicated model, the same physical quantities of capital would have to be measured as lower (higher) for the higher (lower) rate of profit. In short, we cannot aggregate capital sensibly to give rise to an 'as if' aggregate production function.

The aspect of the capital controversy just covered is purely technical in content – the one-good model is not representative of a model with more than one good. A second aspect concerns the empirical implications. For, within mainstream neoclassical economics, it has been standard to estimate the economy as if it were represented by a one-sector production function, a practice often also to be found in use in radical political economy. This is most notable in the residual method used to measure the contribution of technical progress to economic growth, as opposed to the contribution made by growth of inputs. In such work, even on the assumption of full employment and perfect competition in all markets, capital is usually aggregated by weighting it at current prices. As the previously reported technical results suggest, this is entirely arbitrary. Indeed, because the economy is being treated as if it only had one good, any change in prices, for whatever reason and in favour of a capital good relative to a consumption good say, will be measured as if the quantity of capital had increased. Accordingly, even though technology will not have changed, it will appear as though output had remained the same despite use of more capital. Technical progress will appear, falsely, to have been negative.

Again this is difficult to explain briefly. But refer to Figure 1 again. As we go round the outside of the curves, the envelope traced by the available techniques including others not shown, there is no technological advance, just switching from one technique to another. But, associated with these, for the 'as if' one-good world, there will be changes in measured output over and above (or below) those attached to technique. This is due to changes in relative prices (which cannot be distinguished from changes in quantities of input and output in the 'as if' one-good world). In short, changes in quantities and prices are treated as if they were purely changes in quantities. It is simply empirical nonsense, as if the changes in the area of a rectangle could be measured by reference to one side (as if it were a circle with that radius, for example).

In short, the standard methods for measuring total factor productivity are invalidated by the Cambridge critique. Further, this can be shown to have nothing to do with reswitching – the conflation of price and quantity effects pertains even if no technique is preferred at two different rates of profit. Despite this, empirical work on the basis of an aggregate production function has proceeded without regard to this totally destructive critique, with only an occasional acknowledgement of the critique, often then with an irrelevant and unexamined appeal to whether reswitching exists in practice.

The third aspect of the capital controversy concerns its wider significance for economic method and the choice between schools of thought. For some, it seemed as if the whole of neoclassical mainstream economics were invalidated by the critique. This is simply false, as the mainstream does not depend upon a one-sector model of the economy. Indeed, the latter is a very special case for, in the absence of more than one good, the model is effectively without demand (unless it be for choice of consumption over time) and utility theory, a central component of the orthodoxy. The results of the Cambridge critique can be accepted and incorporated within a model of general equilibrium, in which there can be no presumption of simple inverse relations between quantities of capital and rates of profit. For, suppose there is an increase in physical quantities of all capital goods, the rate of profit could rise if demand conditions are such that there is an even greater increase in demand for capital-intensive goods or more capital-intensive techniques to produce them. What this does mean, though, is that none of the intuitions attached to the one-sector model hold.

The debate was entirely conducted in terms of choice between linear technologies. Essentially, the last aspect reveals that the debate is about how to close such a model of supply. The mainstream can retreat into general equilibrium and a utility-based demand theory. This, however, leaves it floundering for a notion of capital other than as a physical quantity of inputs, initial endowments, that provides for a stream of utility. The alternative offered by many from within the critique, as well as the critique itself, has been inspired by Sraffa. He showed that there is a trade-off between the rate of profit and the level of wages, as previously posited by David Ricardo. Hence, the terms Sraffian and neo-Ricardianism are often used interchangeably to suggest that technology (and technique in use) alone do not determine distribution, only what is available to redistribute. However, there is a difference between these two closures in method. Sraffa (and Sraffians) model in terms of *physical* conditions of production, input–output matrices and the wage–profit trade-off they sustain (although Sraffa's own preference for closure was via a profit rate related to a distinct rate of interest determined by monetary factors). Neo-Ricardians retain an attachment to the labour theory of value. In either case, with a linear technology, it is possible to close the system by appeal to a trade-off between the rate of profit and the level of real wages, motivated by the idea that capital and labour confront each other over distribution. In addition, the Sraffian approach has been used as a critique of Marxist value theory, arguing that prices diverge from labour values, even if modified by their transformation into prices of production.

As observed, capital theory attained its greatest prominence in the 1970s when radical political economy was considerably stronger than today. Despite the veracity of its empirical and theoretical results, and their acceptance by the mainstream (who conceded that empirical measurement of performance ought to include both supply and demand and not just supply), the mainstream now proceeds as if the Cambridge critique never existed and shamelessly deploys aggregate production functions as if they are without problems. This is particularly notable in the 'new' or endogenous growth theory, where aggregate production functions are used for theoretical and empirical work. It is a particularly appropriate symbol of the analytical weaknesses of mainstream economics, and its ignorance even of its own most recent history as a discipline, since the new growth theory generally proceeds on the assumption that the economy as a whole can be understood as if it were made up of a single sector (apart, occasionally, from a separate sector to generate productivity increase in the 'as if' one-good economy).

BEN FINE

See also:
Cambridge Economic Tradition; Growth and Income Distribution; Income Distribution; Joan Robinson's Economics; Marginalism; Production; Sraffian Economics.

Bibliography
Bliss, C. (1975), *Capital Theory and the Distribution of Income*, Amsterdam: North-Holland.
Fine, B. (1980), *Economic Theory and Ideology*, London: Edward Arnold.
Fine, B. (2000), 'Endogenous growth theory: a critical assessment', *Cambridge Journal of Economics*, **24** (2), 245–65, a shortened and amended version of identically titled School of Oriental and African Studies (SOAS) Working Paper, No. 80, February 1998.
Harcourt, G. (1972), *Some Cambridge Controversies in the Theory of Capital*, Cambridge: Cambridge University Press.
Harcourt, G. (1976), 'The Cambridge controversies: old ways and new horizons – or dead end?', *Oxford Economic Papers*, **28** (1), 25–65.
Hodgson, G. (1997), 'The fate of the Cambridge capital controversy', in P. Arestis, G. Palma and M. Sawyer (eds), *Capital Controversy, Post-Keynesian Economics and the History of Economics: Essays in Honour of Geoff Harcourt*, Vol. I, London: Routledge, pp. 95–110.

Robinson, J. (1953–54), 'The production function and the theory of capital', *Review of Economic Studies*, **21** (1), 81–106.

Sraffa, P. (1960), *Production of Commodities by Means of Commodities: Prelude to a Critique of Economic Theory*, Cambridge: Cambridge University Press.

Central Banks

Central banks are institutions with multiple functions. Existing central banks are, in some cases, a spontaneous product of historical evolution, like the Bank of England, or the result of social engineering, as in the case of central banks created during the twentieth century, like the Federal Reserve in the US. In both cases, central banks were created, or ended up with the power, to manage the supply of national currencies. Orthodox economists tend to see the main (or the sole) responsibility of a central bank as the control of the available *quantity* of money in order to preserve its purchasing power. Keynesian economists, on the other hand, stress the fact that, controlling the ultimate source of liquidity in a modern economy, a central bank is responsible for the smooth operation of the financial system. For Keynesians, thus, a central bank is first and foremost to operate as the *lender of last resort* for the financial system, particularly for the banking system, that creates means of payment under the form of demand deposits.

Post Keynesian economists, in particular, approach a modern market economy as one organized around the existence of forward money contracts (see Davidson 1978). These contracts are essential to allow entrepreneurs to face the uncertainties that plague a market economy. Contracts, however, create obligations to be discharged in the future by the delivery of money from the debtor to the creditor. This simple fact is the foundation of liquidity preference: facing the uncertainty of being able to pay debts when they come due, the possession of money serves to lull one's disquietudes, to borrow Keynes's expression. Money in these economies exists either as currency or as its perfect substitute, demand deposits, private liabilities that have the characteristic of being redeemable on demand, at par. The acceptance of these substitutes, however, depends on confidence that they will actually be redeemable on demand, at par. The only institution that can give this guarantee is the central bank, when it makes known its willingness to trade bank deposits for currency. This makes the central bank the lender of last resort to the banking system.

This view, proposed by Walter Bagehot in his famous *Lombard Street*, was accepted by Keynes and is the foundation of the Post Keynesian approach to central banking. There are some important differences, however, in the way the performance of this function is seen to constrain central banks' behaviour.

Keynes himself believed that central banks, besides performing their defensive function of lender of last resort, could also actively manage the supply of money. In his *Treatise on Money*, Keynes stated that '[t]he first necessity of a central bank, charged with responsibility for the management of the monetary system as a whole, is to make sure that it has an unchallengeable control over the total volume of bank money created by its member banks' (Keynes 1930 [1971], p. 201). He criticized the 'monetary heretics' who maintained that 'in some way the banks can furnish all the real resources which manufacture and trade can reasonably require without cost to anyone' (p. 194). A bank performed a dual function, being 'a provider of money for its depositors, and also as a provider of resources for [its] borrowing customers' (p. 191). This meant that the creation of money by banks had to take into consideration its effects on the value of money. Central banks should use the interest rate as an instrument to control bank reserves, since 'the aggregate volume of the deposits of the member banks of a modern banking system depends on the reserve ratio which the members aim at keeping, and the amount of reserves (in the shape of cash and deposits at the central bank)' (p. 43). Keynes recognized that the central bank could be *forced* to supply reserves to banks, since there were situations in which it had to purchase assets 'in virtue of an obligation, of law or custom, to purchase such an asset if it is tendered on specified conditions' (p. 202). However, a central bank could compensate for these operations and regain the initiative through the investments it could make: '[t]he amount of the central bank's investments, since these are purchased and sold on its own initiative, is entirely within its own control. Action directed towards varying the amount of these is now usually called "open-market policy"' (p. 202).

In sum, for Keynes, a central bank should act as a lender of last resort to the banking system, but this would not necessarily prevent it from also controlling the volume of means of payment available in the economy. The central bank uses the interest rate as an *instrument* to control the volume of reserves of the banking system, but sets its aims both in terms of interest rates and the volume of reserves.

Keynes's approach was emphatically rejected by Kaldor. Kaldor argued that Keynes never completely abandoned the quantity theory of money, which led him to attribute a definiteness to the concept of money that it lacked in modern economies and to give it an importance that it did not have. According to Kaldor, money was not a precise concept, since the public can use many instruments to make payments. Liquidity was a better concept, but liquidity is an attribute shared by many types of vehicles in different degrees. In Kaldor's view, to single out 'money' as a means of payment would falsify the nature and operation of the payment systems, since it would imply confining the attribute of liquidity entirely to an arbitrarily chosen asset (Kaldor 1982). As a result, for Kaldor it was a mistake to assume that a central bank could control the supply of money. It should be concerned exclusively with interest rates, because these affect the actual liquidity premium of the various assets by affecting the supply and demand for each of them. Thus a central bank should set the interest rates over which it had direct control, and freely supply the volume of reserves that were demanded by banks at those rates. As a result, the money supply curve should be represented by a horizontal line, in money/interest rate space, originating at the level of the interest rate set by the central bank.

Kaldor argued that to perform the role of a lender of last resort did not allow the central bank any room for pursuing an active reserve policy. Any attempt to regulate the volume of reserves could threaten the solvency of banks and thus put in jeopardy the supporting role of the central bank. Kaldor's later followers, like Basil Moore, extended Kaldor's argument, which was centred around the use of the discount window, to open-market policies, suggesting, in opposition to Keynes, that central banks were constrained to supply a given amount of reserves also through open-market operations. According to Moore, open-market operations are actually just a way to make the discount window more efficacious: '[o]pen-market operations are used not to affect the quantity of bank cash reserves . . . but rather to compel banking institutions to make use of the central bank's accommodation facilities at the discount window, at the interest rates charged by the central bank' (Moore 1988, p. 89).

The horizontalist approach created by Kaldor represents, however, a more extreme view that is not shared by all Post Keynesians. In fact, authors like Paul Davidson, Hyman Minsky, Jan Kregel and Victoria Chick advance approaches more faithful to Keynes's own views, emphasizing, in different degrees, the capacity a central bank has of taking initiatives in terms of reserve policies, while recognizing that one of its essential functions remains that of a lender of last resort. Davidson, for instance, defines two strategies available for a central bank at any time in terms of creation of reserves: (i) the *income generating method*, by which the central bank accommodates the demand for reserves made by banks in order to satisfy market demands for credit; and (ii) the *portfolio change method*, by which the central bank takes the initiative to use interest rates to induce a desired change in the amount of reserves at the disposal of banks (Davidson 1978). In the first case, the central bank acts in a more passive way, validating the demands coming from the credit market. In the second, though, the central bank tries to implement its own strategies in terms of reserves, through open-market operations, as Keynes suggested.

The debate between Keynesians and Kaldorians within Post Keynesian economics has been evolving for decades now, involving different conceptions of how a central bank should act, but ultimately relating to what each strand believes the role of money in a modern market economy to be, how the financial system works and evolves, and what is the role of monetary policies, among other theoretical and empirical concerns.

FERNANDO J. CARDIM DE CARVALHO

See also:

Banking; Endogenous Money; Financial Instability Hypothesis; Kaldorian Economics; Keynes's *Treatise on Money*; Monetary Policy; Money; Rate of Interest.

References

Davidson, P. (1978), *Money and the Real World*, 2nd edition, London: Macmillan.
Kaldor, N. (1982), *The Scourge of Monetarism*, Oxford: Oxford University Press.
Keynes, J.M. (1930 [1971]), *A Treatise on Money. The Applied Theory of Money,* reprinted as *The Collected Writings of John Maynard Keynes*, Vol. VI, London: St. Martin's Press.
Moore, B. (1988), *Horizontalists and Verticalists. The Macroeconomics of Credit Money*, Cambridge: Cambridge University Press.

Circuit Theory

The debate on Keynes has mainly focused on the principle of aggregate demand and on the analysis of macroeconomic equilibrium with involuntary unemployment. This is in homage to the most widespread interpretation, which holds that Keynes's innovative force exploded with the *General Theory* (1936), the work in which he broke with neoclassical theory and with most of his own earlier work. However, it is also possible to maintain that the *General Theory* should be read as a continuation of the analysis put forward by Keynes in *A Treatise on Money* (1930) and in other works before and after the *General Theory*. According to this interpretation, Keynes's analysis should be considered part of the theory of the monetary circuit (what Keynes called the 'monetary theory of production'), which should also include contributions from the first half of the twentieth century by, among others, Knut Wicksell, Dennis Robertson and Joseph Schumpeter (Realfonzo 1998).

In the second half of the century, starting in particular from the teachings of Keynes and Schumpeter, the theory of the monetary circuit was put forward again and developed mainly by Italian- and French-speaking scholars, such as Augusto Graziani, Marc Lavoie, Alain Parguez and Bernard Schmitt. It has subsequently been supported by François Poulon, Mario Seccareccia, Riccardo Bellofiore, Marcello Messori, Alvaro Cencini, Claude Gnos, Elie Sadigh, Louis-Philippe Rochon, Giuseppe Fontana,

Riccardo Realfonzo and others. The theory of the monetary circuit has aroused growing interest, generating productive debate (for instance, see Deleplace and Nell 1996) and further historical and analytical studies. While significant differences persist on specific points, most of the theoreticians of the monetary circuit follow substantially the same approach, remaining well within the sphere of Post Keynesian theory.

As far as the basic analytical approach is concerned, the theoreticians of the monetary circuit reject the methodological individualism typical of neoclassical doctrine and adopt a socio-historical method. This does not mean that their analyses are necessarily lacking in microfoundations: in their view the study of individual behaviour is always subordinate to the macro approach.

The simplest model of the monetary circuit, with a closed economy and no state sector, can be described in the following way. Let us consider three macro agents: banks, firms and workers. Banks have the task of financing the production process through the creation of money, and of selecting business plans; firms, through access to credit, buy factors of production and direct the production process, making decisions on the quantity and quality of output; workers supply labour services. The working of the economy is described as a sequential process, characterized by successive phases whose links form a circuit of money. A clear understanding of the circuit theory can be obtained from Figure 3.

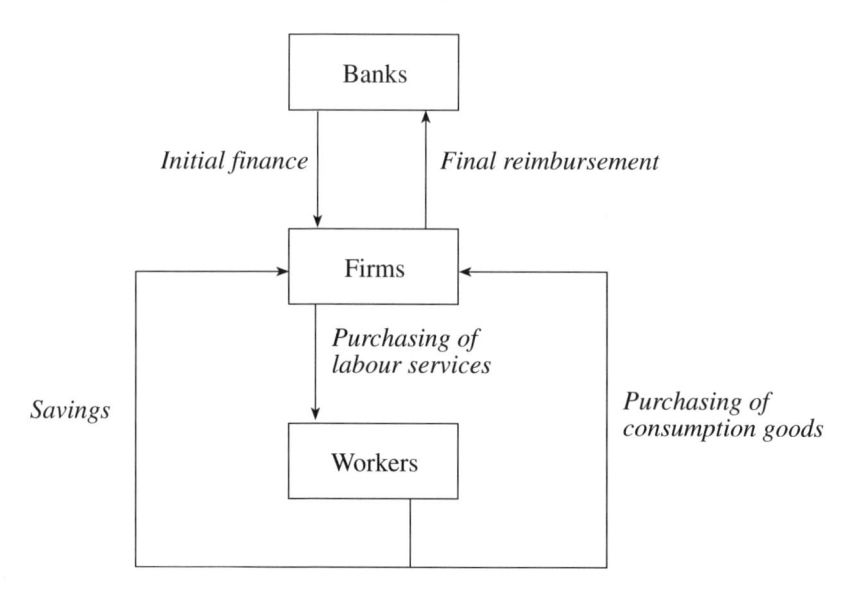

Figure 3 The monetary circuit

62   Circuit theory

The phases in the circuit are as follows:

1. banks grant (totally or in part) the financing requested by firms, creating money (opening of the circuit);
2. once financing has been obtained, firms buy inputs; considering firms in the aggregate, their expenditure coincides with the total wage bill; at this point money passes from firms to workers;
3. once labour services have been purchased, firms carry out production; in the simplest case, firms produce homogeneous goods;
4. at the end of the production process, firms put the goods on the market. It can be envisaged that firms set the sale price following a *mark-up* principle. Supposing workers have a propensity to consume equal to one, firms recover the entire wage bill and maintain ownership of a proportion (corresponding to the mark-up) of the goods produced. If the propensity to consume is less than one, once the workers have purchased consumer goods they must make a further choice about how to use their savings, either hoarding (increase in liquid reserves) or investing (purchase of shares). If all the money savings are invested in shares on the financial market, firms manage to recover the whole wage bill;
5. once goods and shares have been sold, firms repay the banks (closure of the circuit).

Starting from this synthetic description, the remarks below concern the nature and role of monetary variables, the volume of production and employment, the distribution of income and macroeconomic equilibrium (Graziani 1989; Lavoie 1992; Parguez 1996; Realfonzo 1998).

According to the theory of the monetary circuit, money is a pure symbol – merely a bookkeeping entry (or a certificate) – with no intrinsic value, created by the bank in response to a promise of repayment. The bank is defined as the agent that transforms non-monetary activity into activities that are money. This approach therefore holds that it is the decision to grant credit that generates deposits ('loans make deposits'). The money supply is endogenous, in that it is essentially determined by the demand. On a theoretical level, the banking system could create money endlessly. In its turn, the demand for money can be broken down into two distinct parts: the demand for money to finance production (which Keynes called the 'finance motive') and the demand for liquid reserves (dependent on the well-known transactions, precautionary and speculative motives). According to the theory of the monetary circuit, what mainly distinguishes entrepreneurs is their access to bank credit. In fact, money – as Schumpeter said – is the lever through which power over real resources is exercised. From what has been said, it follows that monetary circuit theory rejects traditional principles of the exogenous nature of the money supply and the neutrality of money, as well as the quantity theory of money.

The volume of production is autonomously fixed by firms, based on the expected level of aggregate demand. Naturally, production decisions taken by firms may or may not be supported by banks. If there is credit rationing by banks, firms are unable to translate their production plans into real production processes. To make the matter more complicated, it can be shown that the production decisions taken by firms are also influenced by the possibility of equity rationing. One conclusion drawn by theoreticians of the circuit is that the financial structure of firms is not neutral with respect to production decisions. The employment level depends on firms' production decisions and therefore on the expected aggregate demand. The labour market is thus described, according to Keynes's teaching, as the place where any shortage in aggregate demand is dumped (generating involuntary unemployment). Macroeconomic equilibrium is compatible with the presence of involuntary unemployment.

According to the theory of the monetary circuit, as in Keynes's original work, in the labour market bargaining concerns only money wages. In fact, the price level (and therefore the real wage) is known only at a later phase, when workers spend their money wage in the goods market. This obviously does not mean that, at the time when they bargain for their money wage, workers have no expectations about the price level, but their expectations are not necessarily confirmed by the market. Consequently, there may be a difference between the *ex ante* real wage (expected by workers) and the *ex post* real wage (the actual real wage). If workers' expectations about the price level are confirmed, the expected real wage coincides with the actual real wage. In a model with two types of goods (consumer goods and investment goods) this happens when voluntary saving equals investment. When investment exceed voluntary savings there is a positive gap between the expected real wage and the actual real wage which gives rise to forced saving.

As far as the firm's profit is concerned, monetary circuit theory accepts the thesis that firms as a whole 'earn as much as they spend'. In fact, given the mark-up (which in turn may be made to depend on the industrial concentration ratio), the higher the level of production (and therefore the expenditure on inputs), the higher the firm's real profit. In a model with two types of goods – consumer goods (wage-goods) and investment goods – decisions about the composition of production determine the distribution of income. The higher the demand for and production of investment goods, the higher the profits for firms. Thus scholars of the monetary circuit reject the marginal theory of distribution in favour of a Kaleckian–Post Keynesian approach.

In the theory of the monetary circuit there is a strict distinction between the money market and the financial market, and between the two interest rates that are set there. In the money market, banks and firms negotiate and the interest rate constitutes the price firms have to pay to obtain initial finance. The money interest rate is basically a 'levy' on the gross profit of entrepreneurs. It should be underlined that, in the simple model here described, firms can at the most repay the initial finance to banks but not the interest as well. If there is hoarding, firms will not even be able to repay the initial loan in money. It is possible to envisage that in this case firms may decide either to settle their debt with the banks in goods, or remain indebted to them. It is worth emphasizing, however, that this inability on the firm's part to repay the debt in money terms is not an inevitable feature of monetary circuit models. Indeed, as soon as one moves on to more complex models – with a state sector and/or an open economy, or to models in which firms start production at different times (not simultaneously) – this feature disappears and in theory it is possible that, at the closure of the circuit, firms are able to repay their entire debt (interest included).

In the financial market workers and firms negotiate and the interest rate constitutes the price firms have to pay to raise the money not spent on the goods market. It is, in fact, through the goods market and the financial market working in conjunction that firms try to obtain the final finance, in other words to recover the liquidity initially spent on purchasing inputs. From what we have seen, it can be deduced that for circuit theorists there is a sort of logical hierarchy between the money market and the financial market. In fact, the financial market could not operate at all unless the money market had already been operating. This means that while the individual firm can freely choose whether to get financing through the money market or through the financial market, for firms as a whole no such choice is possible. This is so unless there is a public spending deficit and/or a surplus in the balance of payments such that enough money will flow, through workers' decisions to buy securities, into the financial market.

RICCARDO REALFONZO

See also:
Banking; Endogenous Money; Finance Motive; Keynes's *Treatise on Money*; Money.

References

Deleplace, G. and E.J. Nell (eds) (1996), *Money in Motion: The Post Keynesian and Circulation Approaches*, Basingstoke: Macmillan.

Graziani, A. (1989), 'The theory of the monetary circuit', *Thames Papers in Political Economy*, Spring.

Lavoie, M. (1992), *Foundations of Post-Keynesian Economic Analysis*, Aldershot: Edward Elgar.

Parguez, A. (1996), 'Financial markets, unemployment and inflation within a circuitist framework', *Économies et Sociétés*, **30** (2–3), 163–92.
Realfonzo, R. (1998), *Money and Banking. Theory and Debate (1900–1940)*, Cheltenham, UK and Northampton, MA, USA: Edward Elgar.

Competition

Post Keynesians highlight the shortcomings of markets and the competition that regulates them. For them, as for Keynes, the competition of markets does not make them self-adjusting. It does not keep the demand for their products in line with the supply, or the supply in line with the labour available for its production. Labour can be unemployed, and products in excess supply, under competitive conditions also, and while the competition of firms can bring down their prices, it cannot keep up their production. Indeed, it may in fact 'ruin' them.

The price competition of firms squeezes their profits, and this is the case even if the wages of their workers fall with their prices, for their labour costs are not the only costs of production. Firms have the expense of their plant and equipment, and the service charges on their debt, and when those fixed costs are high, and the investments of the firms irreversible, their price competition can wipe out their profit. It can drive prices down below costs, 'expropriating' the capital invested in their production (Eichner 1969). That capital cannot be taken out of their industries when prices fall, and as long as they stay above the average variable costs of production, the firms will be better off selling products at a loss than not selling them at all.

While ruinous price competition is identified in economics with oligopoly, it is more in keeping with the conditions of perfect competition than those of oligopoly. It is when the products of firms are homogeneous that they must match the price cuts of competitors regardless of the costs, and it is when their numbers are large, and market shares similar, that they cannot effectively 'fix' their prices. There is no dominant firm to enforce their price-fixing agreements, and it makes little sense for the firms to honour them when prices can be undercut and sales lost. And while perfectly competitive firms are small, and their productive capacity limited, they can have fixed costs also. Indeed, their products could not be homogeneous if they were not produced by machinery, and their fixed costs will lock them into a ruinous price war whenever their sales revenue falls short of the amount needed for the recoupment of costs.

The perfect competition idealized in economics is far from ideal – it bankrupts firms and renders prices more volatile. The worst-performing markets of the economy are the ones that come closest to the perfectly competitive markets of the economic texts (Kaldor 1985), and it is because firms cannot operate under the price competition of those commodity markets that they consolidate their industries and differentiate their products (Eichner 1969).

The pricing power of firms is essential to their survival, and their investment depends on it also. They could not generate the revenue that investment requires if they were unable to hold up their prices, for profits would not be high enough for the funding of investment (Eichner 1976). Firms would not be able to finance investment with the profit from their products, or secure (and repay) the loans needed for the external financing of investment projects. And since the profit from their products would be precarious as well as small, their long-run expectations could not be positive (Shapiro 1998). They could not expect to make a profit on a product long enough to recoup the costs of a plant and equipment or product development investment. Those long-lived investments are not profitable when prices are variable and sales insecure, and, in the absence of the 'frictions' and 'restrictions' of markets, there would be little investment in their products (Richardson 1990).

The entry barriers of industries increase and stabilize the investment in products, and while they also lessen competition, they do not end it. Oligopoly changes the competition of firms rather than eliminating it. Their competition shifts from their prices to their products, and the product competition of firms is as beneficial as the price competition. Indeed, it can be more beneficial, for product competition increases the investment in products.

The product changes that update and differentiate the products of firms require investment, as does the advertisement that publicizes the differences in their products. And the firms that compete on the basis of their products must improve them as well as invest in them. They cannot increase market shares without advances in the design or performance of products, and it is only through those product innovations that they can maintain their market dominance. The competition of new entrants is 'pre-empted' not through the prices firms charge for their products, but through the improvements made in them and their technologies.

The product competition of firms develops and improves products, and the product competition of those that manufacture the equipment used in industry improves production processes. Productivity improvements are 'embodied' in the products developed for the purposes of competitive advantage. The productivity growth of modern industry is an outgrowth of its competition, and it is because its firms compete on the basis of their products rather than their prices that their competition advances the course of technical progress. The oligopolization of industry 'endogenizes' the innovation process (Eichner 1976).

This is not to say that the oligopolization of industry is without cost. The profit margins of firms can be too high as well as too low, exceeding the level needed for the funding of their investment. Their investment is not determined by their savings – it also depends on their expectations – and if their profit margins rise without a corresponding rise in their investment, the demand for their products will fall, reducing production and increasing unemployment (Steindl 1976).

But the pricing power of the oligopolist is not 'absolute' (Kalecki 1971). It is limited by the competition of its industry, the substitutes for its products, and the risk of drawing new firms into its market. The substitution and entry effects of its price increases limit the mark-up on its product, and the firm will not increase prices in line with costs unless the prices of competitors also rise. There is no automatic transmission of costs into prices.

The fact that the price competition of oligopolists is tempered by the conditions of their industries does not mean that there is no competitive pressure on their prices. And while this competition may not be strong enough to push prices down, and consumers cannot benefit from the productivity advances of firms unless prices stay in line with costs, mark-ups can be maintained through wage increases as well as price reductions. If money wages increase with the growth of productivity so will real wages, and real wages will rise without the fall in prices that squeezes profits and ruins firms.

The competition of firms does not have to be perfect for their prices to be competitive and mark-ups constant. And while their competition is beneficial, there can be too much competition in industry as well as too little. Perfect competition is not optimal.

NINA SHAPIRO

See also:

Equilibrium and Non-equilibrium; Innovation; Investment; Pricing and Prices.

References

Eichner, A. (1969), *The Emergence of Oligopoly*, Baltimore: Johns Hopkins Press.
Eichner, A. (1976), *The Megacorp and Oligopoly*, Armonk, NY: M.E. Sharpe.
Kaldor, N. (1985), *Economics Without Equilibrium*, Armonk, NY: M.E. Sharpe.
Kalecki, M. (1971), *Selected Essays on the Dynamics of the Capitalist Economy*, Cambridge: Cambridge University Press.
Richardson, G.B. (1990), *Information and Investment*, Oxford: Oxford University Press.
Shapiro, N. (1998), 'Competition and employment', in P. Davidson and J. Kregel (eds), *Full Employment and Price Stability in a Global Economy*, Cheltenham, UK and Northampton, MA, USA: Edward Elgar, pp. 195–201.
Steindl, J. (1976), *Maturity and Stagnation in American Capitalism*, New York: Monthly Review Press.

Consumer Theory

Few efforts have been made by Post Keynesians to explain how consumers make choices. Does that mean that Post Keynesians accept the neoclassical axioms of consumer choice? The answer is no. Although there have been few contributions on consumer behaviour by Post Keynesian authors, there is a certain degree of coherence among them. The few pieces that exist – by well-known Post Keynesians such as Joan Robinson, Luigi Pasinetti, Edward Nell and Alfred Eichner – fit, like a puzzle, with the rest of Post Keynesian theory. These pieces must, however, also be tied to the work of various institutionalists, social economists, marketing specialists and even dissident mainstreamers.

The common ground of Post Keynesian consumer theory can be presented under the form of six principles (Lavoie 1994). They are:

1. the principle of procedural rationality;
2. the principle of satiable needs;
3. the principle of separability of needs;
4. the principle of subordination of needs;
5. the principle of the growth of needs;
6. the principle of non-independence.

The principle of *procedural rationality* asserts that agents lack perfect knowledge and the ability to process a large amount of information. Agents devise means to avoid complex calculations and considerations, and procedures enabling decisions to be taken despite incomplete information. These means and procedures include rules of thumb, the acceptance of social conventions, and reliance on the hopefully better informed opinion of others. Seen from the perspective of neoclassical substantive rationality, procedural rationality may seem to be *ad hoc*, but procedural responses are the only sensible answer to an environment characterized by bounded knowledge and computational capabilities, time constraints and fundamental uncertainty. It could also be called the principle of *reasonable rationality*.

In the case of consumer behaviour, it has long been established by marketing specialists that consumer choice usually involves very simple procedures (Earl 1986, p. 58). Very often there is no decision process to speak of: purchases are made on recommendations, in conformity to social norms, with the consideration of few alternatives, and on the basis of few criteria. Some of the procedures that we follow are conscious – we may then speak of rules or conventions – while others are unconscious; we may refer to them as habits or routines, as in the case of a large part of our repetitive spending on non-durable consumption goods.

The second principle, that of *satiable needs*, can be likened to the neoclassical principle of diminishing marginal utility, but it takes a particular meaning in the Post Keynesian theory of the consumer. Here satiation arises with positive prices and finite income. There are threshold levels of consumption beyond which a good, or its characteristics, brings no satisfaction to its consumer. Beyond the threshold, no more of the good will be purchased, regardless of its price.

One has to carefully distinguish wants from needs, as do Lutz and Lux (1979). There is a hierarchy of needs, where some are more basic than others, which implies that they must be fulfilled in order of priority. In that sense all needs are not equal. Some needs are bound to be satiated much earlier than others. Needs are subject to a hierarchic classification and are the motor of consumer behaviour. By contrast, wants evolve from needs. They can be substituted for each other and constitute 'the various preferences within a common category or level of need' (Lutz and Lux 1979, p. 21). This leads to the next two principles of a Post Keynesian consumer theory.

The principle of the *separability of needs* asserts that categories of needs or of expenditures can be distinguished from each other. In the case discussed by Kelvin Lancaster (1991), with goods described by a matrix of consumption technology with various characteristics, a separate need will be associated with a submatrix of goods and characteristics arising out of a decomposable matrix. The principle of the separability of needs is illustrated by the widely-used econometric models of consumer demand, which assume that broad categories of expenditures enter separately into the overall utility function. In the utility-tree approach, the principle of separability is pushed one step further, since these broad categories of expenditures are further subdivided into several branches.

The separability of needs allows the consumer to divide the decision-making process into a series of smaller multi-stage decisions. The consumer first makes an allocation of his or her budget among needs, and then spends that allocation among the various wants or subgroups of each need, independently of what happens to the other needs. Changes in the relative prices of goods within a given category of wants will have no effect on the budget allocation among various needs, while a fall in the overall price of a group of goods corresponding to a given need will have repercussions on the budget allocation of all needs. The principle of the separability of needs imposes substantial restrictions on the neoclassical principle of price substitution, since separability severely limits the degree of substitutability between goods in different groups. Indeed, a substantial amount of empirical evidence shows that general categories of consumption expenditures have quite negligible own-price elasticities and cross-elasticities.

Further restraints may be added if one goes beyond the principle of separability of needs, by introducing a fourth principle, the principle of the *subordination of needs*. With this principle, utility cannot be represented by a unique catch-all utility measure; it can only be represented by a vector. The principle of the subordination of needs is often associated with the notion of a *pyramid* of needs – a *hierarchy* of needs – as described by the humanistic school of psychology (Lutz and Lux 1979). The integration of the principles of separability and subordination leads to Nicholas Georgescu-Roegen's principle of *irreducibility*. Needs are irreducible.

In the case of utility-tree analysis, the first-stage budgeting problem is resolved by assuming that money is allocated first to necessities and then to discretionary needs. There is no substitution between the budget categories apportioned to necessary needs and discretionary ones. All the principles previously invoked culminate in this hierarchy: needs are separable and the most basic needs are first taken care of in their order of priority, until they are satiated at some threshold level.

There have been some formal representations of the above principles. Hierarchical behaviour is known under the name of lexicographic preference ordering, owing to its similarity with searching for a word in a dictionary. Strict lexicographic ordering, however, is unlikely, and more sophisticated lexicographic approaches have been suggested, with consumers setting targets and thresholds, that is, with the addition of the first principle of Post Keynesian consumer theory, that of satiation (Earl 1986). These noncompensatory ordering schemes are not only reasonable but also compatible with procedural rationality, since a complete utility map is not required. Decisions about the most basic needs can be taken quite independently of the informational requirements of the higher needs. Consumers need know nothing whatsoever about the prices of the goods that are part of the higher needs, and they need not rank alternatives which they cannot attain or which are beyond their satiation levels (Drakopoulos 1994).

Neoclassical authors deny that needs are subject to the principle of subordination. This, it must be presumed, is mainly due to the devastating consequences of the irreducibility of needs for neoclassical theory and its substitution principle. Irreducible needs imply that they are incommensurable and therefore that 'everything does not have a price'. A trade-off is not always possible. The axiom of Archimedes, so popular with choice theorists, does not hold any more (Earl 1986, p. 249), nor does the axiom of gross substitution (Eichner 1987, p. 632), so often invoked among general equilibrium theorists. This reinforces the arguments of Paul Davidson against the use of such an axiom in macroeconomics.

Having assumed that indeed there exists a hierarchy of needs, how do consumers move up the steps of the pyramid? The basic answer is that individuals move upwards in the hierarchy due to income effects. Beyond the principle of satiation, lies the principle of the *growth of needs* – our fifth principle.

When a need has been fulfilled, or more precisely when a threshold level for that need has been attained, individuals start attending to the needs which are situated on a higher plane. There are always new needs to be fulfilled. If they do not yet exist, consumers will create them through innovation, but this may take time (Gualerzi 1998). Needs, however, often require income to be satisfied. To go from one level of need to another dictates an increase in the real income level of the individual. The fulfilment of new needs, and therefore the purchase of new goods or new services, is thus related to income effects. This is the microeconomic counterpart of the Post Keynesian focus on effective demand, that is, on macroeconomic income effects. What is being asserted is that income effects are much more important in explaining the evolution of expenditure on goods than are substitution effects. The latter play only a minor role in a static analysis of consumer behaviour, when similar goods or goods fulfilling the same wants are being considered. Indeed, changes in relative prices have an impact on budget allocation between needs only in so far as they have an impact on real income.

The sixth and last principle is the principle of *non-independence*. The emphasis of traditional theory on substitution effects also has led to the neglect of the learning process in consumption theory. How do consumers rank their new spending opportunities? How do they learn to spend their additional spending power? Consumers watch and copy other consumers. Preferences are not innate, they are acquired by experience and by imitation of the consumption pattern of friends or of people of higher ranks in the consumers' hierarchy. Fads leading to large sales of specific products are thus explained by the informational content of consumption by neighbours, relatives, friends or acquaintances. The impact of socio-economic contact on purchases reinforces the belief that the composition of demand depends on socio-economic classes. Decisions and preferences are not made independently of those of other agents. A household's pattern of consumption will reflect the lifestyle of the other households that constitute its social reference group. Marketing officers, through publicity, will attempt to make sure that households follow the appropriate lifestyle.

Three of the main consequences of this Post Keynesian analysis of consumer choice may now be noted. First, macroeconomic models based on the analysis of income classes and on income effects are a legitimate outgrowth of a Post Keynesian theory of the consumer where price substitution effects are not important or severely constrained to goods which respond to similar characteristics, and where increases or changes in demand are mostly determined by increases in real incomes or changes in consumer preferences. Second, the Post Keynesian theory of consumption, based on the hierarchical nature of needs, is also reminiscent of the classical distinction between necessaries and luxury goods and of the Sraffian distinction between basic and non-basic commodities. Under these circumstances, to ignore substitution effects, based on relative prices, appears to be much less disastrous than to ignore income effects and threshold levels. Third, Post Keynesian consumer theory seems particularly relevant to questions of environment, since environmental issues relative to material wants seem a most obvious application of the principle of subordination of needs (Gowdy and Mayumi, 2001).

MARC LAVOIE

See also:

Agency; Consumption; Institutionalism; Environmental Economics; Non-ergodicity; Sraffian Economics; Uncertainty.

References

Drakopoulos, Stavros A. (1994), 'Hierarchical choice in economics', *Journal of Economic Surveys*, **8** (2), 133–53.
Earl, Peter E. (1986), *Lifestyle Economics: Consumer Behaviour in a Turbulent World*, Brighton, UK: Wheatsheaf.
Eichner, Alfred S. (1987), *The Macrodynamics of Advanced Market Economies*, Armonk, NY: M.E. Sharpe.
Gowdy, John M. and Kozo Mayumi (2001), 'Reformulating the foundations of consumer choice theory and environmental valuation', *Ecological Economics*, **39** (2), 223–37.
Gualerzi, Davide (1998), 'Economic change, choice and innovation in consumption', in Marina Bianchi (ed.), *The Active Consumer: Novelty and Surprise in Consumer Choice*, London: Routledge, pp. 46–63.
Lancaster, Kelvin (1991), 'Hierarchies in goods-characteristics analysis', in Kelvin Lancaster, *Modern Consumer Theory*, Aldershot, UK and Brookfield, VT, US: Edward Elgar, pp. 69–80.
Lavoie, Marc (1994), 'A Post Keynesian theory of consumer choice', *Journal of Post Keynesian Economics*, 16 (4), 539–62.
Lutz, Mark A. and Kenneth Lux (1979), *The Challenge of Humanistic Economics*, Menlo Park: Benjamin/Cumming.

Consumption

Accounting for 70 per cent or more of total spending on final goods and services, consumption is by far the most important component of aggregate demand. The modern theory of aggregate consumption dates from Keynes, who proposed that a 'propensity to consume' governs the functional relationship between a given level of income and expenditures on consumption out of that level of income. Keynes thought the propensity to consume was a 'fairly stable function so that, as a rule, the amount of aggregate consumption mainly depends on the amount of aggregate income'. The propensity to consume itself is largely determined by a 'fundamental psychological law' that consumer units ('men' originally) tend to reduce their rate of consumption (C) as their income (Y) increases; that is, $dC/dY < 1$ with $C = C(Y)$.

Keynes's proposed relationship was quickly subjected to empirical testing, using whatever data were available and whatever specification seemed reasonable. Some anomalies were soon uncovered. First, estimates of marginal propensities using cross-sectional household data ranging from 0.4 to 0.8 could not be reconciled with those derived from time-series aggregate data clustering around 0.9. Second, when transformed into an average consumption model, the linear Keynesian model predicted a long-run declining spending rate not found in the actual data. Third, cross-sectional functions showed shifting or ratcheting spending from one dataset or year to another, behaviour not predicted by cross-sectional specifications or found with time-series data. Although the actual historical development of these anomalies is more complex, they soon became 'a fashionable feature of many macroeconomic textbooks and survey articles' (Thomas 1989, p. 131), generating an enormous literature and motivating many resolutions.

Nearly all these resolutions focused on the 'consumption function paradox', or differences between estimates of cross-sectional and times-series spending behaviour. The best known of these, the life-cycle theory of Franco Modigliani and Richard Brumberg and the permanent income hypothesis of Milton Friedman (reviewed in Deaton 1992; see also Carrroll 2001 and Muellbauer and Lattimore 1995), were essentially similar explanations developed from the neoclassical theory of household behaviour. Like individual consumers, the aggregate or representative consumer unit seeks to maximize the utility from lifetime consumption, an effort constrained by the present value of lifetime income plus any original endowments minus any bequests. Since consumption decisions are motivated by lifetime considerations, the relevant income for these decisions is expected lifetime or 'permanent' income rather than current or 'transitory' income. While these distinctions are nebulous – permanent to one is transitory to another, in the context of aggregate spending – average income was identified as permanent income and any other income as transitory. Thus, in the neoclassical view, in its simplest form, when interest and time discount rates are assumed to be zero, average consumption is a function of average income. Since average data are time-series data, the appropriate marginal propensities are the time-series ones, and since the Keynesian consumption function utilizes current or cross-sectional data, it can be dismissed as reflective of transitory, not permanent, spending behaviour.

While simply a semantic exercise, the neoclassical reformulation of the Keynesian consumption function seemed compelling. It was reasonable, for obviously consumption is determined by more than current income. It was grounded in the microfoundations underlying the education of all economists. Its theoretical, mathematical and econometric complexities, such as determining appropriate or tractable utility functions and measuring permanent income, offered research possibilities for the ambitious. By having consumption determined by long-run considerations, it found favour with anti-Keynesians. But, most importantly, proponents of the Keynesian view offered no effective counter-arguments to the permanent/transitory distinction. As a consequence, macroeconomics shifted away from the implications of current spending behaviour and the Keynesian consumption function was relegated to honorific status, largely serving to motivate extensions of the neoclassical consumption model.

In fact, it is the case for the Keynesian view that is compelling. First, the alleged consumption function paradox simply reflects confusion about the geometric implications of cross-sectional and time-series data. The usual diagrammatic representation of the paradox is shown in Panel A of Figure 4, with the slope of the cross-sectional (CS) function less than that of the time-series (TS) one. The functions cross at Y^*, average income for either. In the neoclassical view, income different from Y^* is transitory. Hence, in the absence of transitory income, all incomes equal average income and fall on the TS function, and the CS function disappears.

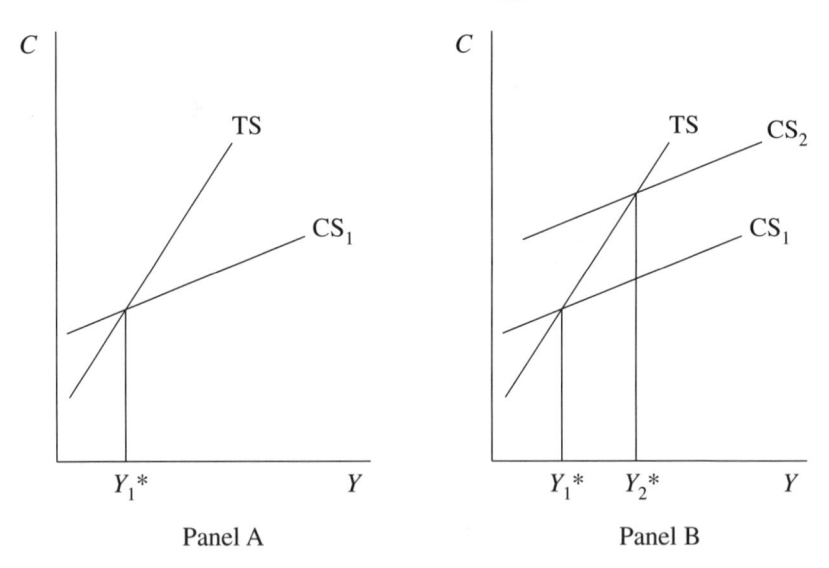

Figure 4   The consumption function

None the less, CS functions still exist for every time period; two are shown in Panel B. Even if the transitory notion is correct, the slopes (marginal propensities) of the CS and TS functions must differ, because the slope of the TS line connecting points on the CS lines cannot equal the slope of either CS line.

Second, the alleged predictive failure of the Keynesian formulation reflects the failure to distinguish carefully between cross-sectional and time-series data. CS functions exist for every time period:

$$c_{ti} = a_t + b_t y_{ti}, \text{ where } i = 1, \ldots, m \text{ consumer units.}$$

When transformed into an average function, the average propensity to consume converges on b_t as CS income increases. Similarly, a TS function exists covering all years:

$$C_t = \alpha + \beta Y_t, \text{ where } t = 1, \ldots, n \text{ years.}$$

When transformed into an average function, the average propensity converges on β as TS income increases. The objection that the Keynesian model produced incorrect predictions about the average propensity is simply the consequence of introducing time-series values into the cross-sectional function. When appropriate income data are used, the CS function predicts a declining average propensity as income increases in any time period while, following the conventional assumption of $\alpha = 0$, the TS function predicts a constant propensity over time. Both these predictions are consistent with the historical record.

Finally, the effects of the definitional relationship between cross-sectional and time-series data have not been realized (Bunting 2001). Like corporations, time-series data are soulless, having no existence beyond the individual consumption and income observations from which they are constructed. But these individual data are the cross-sectional data. Thus, since $C_t = \Sigma c_{ti}$ and $Y_t = \Sigma y_{ti}$, average consumption and income used for TS estimation are also CS averages. This implies that, with average data, the CS function can be stated as:

$$C_t = a_t + b_t Y_t$$

and the TS marginal propensity is:

$$dC/dY = da_t/dY + db_t Y_t/dY.$$

From the TS function, the TS marginal propensity is also:

$$dC/dY = \beta.$$

Assuming constant CS marginal propensities,

$$\beta = da_t/dY + b.$$

In words, the CS and TS marginal propensities differ only because of shifts in the cross-sectional functions.

Time-series coefficients are determined by two factors: an induced component, reflecting cross-sectional consumption behaviour, and an autonomous component, reflecting shifts in that behaviour. The induced component simply indicates that time-series behaviour requires behaviour in every time period, while the autonomous component is necessary for time-series data to exist. With direct estimation, it is not possible to determine whether changes in time-series behaviour are the result of actual behavioural changes or the result of autonomous, unknown influences. Since the time-series coefficient is exactly defined by these two components, time-series behaviour is meaningless – after eliminating autonomous and induced effects, the time-series coefficients are zero.

For their part, Post Keynesians have not shown much interest in expanding or extending Keynes's basic ideas. Since the consumption function is derived from individual data, it actually shows how the distribution of income affects consumption: for example, the rate of spending declines as income rises. This can also be shown by calculating consumption and income shares, $w_i = c_i/\Sigma c_i$ and $v_i = y_i/\Sigma y_i$. Because every consumer unit must have its own consumption function, the CS marginal propensity is an income-weighted average of the individual propensities, $b_t = \Sigma b_i v_i$, implying that changes in the distribution of income produced by alterations in the business cycle or by public policy will change the overall marginal propensity. Autonomous influences are also important, yet these simply indicate that unknown factors influence spending. Determining these factors has obvious merit. Quite possibly they could be demographic and sociological factors, suggesting that the consumption function has a much larger social dimension than is commonly recognized.

The Keynesian view that current income largely determines current consumption is commonly attacked as myopic and unrealistic. Consumer units spend and earn over their lifetimes; most are not fooled by unanticipated changes in current income caused by fortuitous or adverse events. Instead they plan consumption, schedule purchases, set retirement goals, save for rainy days, and the like. It is this focus on individual behaviour that forms the basis of the neoclassical critique of Keynes's theory. As an explicit theory of individual spending behaviour, this perspective is relevant for those able to save, who constitute half or less of all consumer units. For this group, spending could very well be based on lifetime considerations.

However, for the other half or more, those unable to save, annual consumption is simply a question of annual survival and lifetimes are determined year by year.

Unfortunately for the neoclassical critique and for those concerned about myopic spending, regardless of form, Keynes developed a theory of aggregate, not individual, consumption. In macroeconomics (as opposed to microeconomics) individual consumption decisions are revealed in the aggregate data. The motivation for these decisions, or how they fit into some individual lifetime spending plan, is of no consequence. Instead, the aggregate data reveal the annual relationship between consumption and income. While incompletely understood, suffering misrepresentation by its critics and neglect by its adherents, this relationship none the less governs the operation of any aggregate economic system.

DAVID BUNTING

See also:

Effective Demand; Multiplier; Saving.

References

Bunting, D. (2001), 'Keynes' law and its critics', *Journal of Post Keynesian Economics*, **24** (1), 149–63.
Carroll, C.D. (2001), 'A theory of the consumption function, with and without liquidity constraints', *Journal of Economic Perspectives*, **15** (1), 23–46.
Deaton, A. (1992), *Understanding Consumption*, New York: Oxford University Press.
Muellbauer, J. and R. Lattimore (1995), 'The consumption function: a theoretical and empirical overview', in M.H. Pesaran and M.R. Wickens (eds), *Handbook of Applied Econometrics: Macroeconomics*, London: Blackwell, pp. 221–311.
Thomas, J. (1989), 'The early history of the consumption function', in N. de Marchi and C. Gilbert (eds), *History and Methodology of Econometrics*, Oxford: Clarendon Press, pp. 131–49.

Credit Rationing

The theory of credit rationing developed by Stiglitz and Weiss (1981) has received much attention in the economic literature. However, this New Keynesian approach assumes asymmetric information, in which there is a precise probability distribution of returns from potential investment projects known by the borrower but not by the lender. In contrast, the Post Keynesian approach to credit rationing is based on the assumption of Keynesian uncertainty, a non-ergodic future about which both borrower and lender simply 'do not know'. In addition to uncertainty, the Post Keynesian approach builds upon the following concepts:

- *Borrower's risk and lender's risk* In the *General Theory*, Keynes (1936, p. 144) defined borrower's risk as due to doubts about 'actually earning the prospective yield for which he hopes'. Lender's risk was related to either voluntary default by the borrower (moral hazard) or involuntary default 'due to the disappointment of expectation'.
- *Financial fragility* As Hyman Minsky (1986, p. 213) has argued, 'the successful functioning of an economy within an initially robust financial structure will lead to a structure that becomes more fragile as time elapses'. This increase in financial fragility is likely to occur during the expansion phase of the business cycle or over the course of a series of relatively mild business cycles.
- *Endogenous development of expectations* The endogenous development of financial fragility, particularly if accelerated by rising interest rates and falling profit rates (two typical developments near the end of the business cycle peak), leads to a corresponding change in bankers' willingness to lend. This endogenous development of expectations (Crotty 1994) is likely to lead to a reduction in bank lending.

Dow builds upon these concepts to argue for a Post Keynesian theory of credit rationing. She argues that this theory contradicts the horizontalist interpretation of endogenous money: 'a theoretical case is made for amending the horizontalist position to allow for systemic credit rationing, referring particularly to the business cycle' (Dow 1996, p. 498). It would appear that the idea of endogenous money, if interpreted to mean a horizontal supply curve such that bankers accommodate all demands for loans, would indeed be in conflict with a concept of credit rationing in which bankers do not accommodate demands for loans.

Dow argues that, over the course of the business cycle, financial institutions become increasingly less willing to lend. Building upon Minsky's (1975) discussion of borrower's and lender's risk, she asserts that 'the demand for borrowed funds and the supply of borrowed funds are less interest elastic the greater is the perceived borrowers' risk and lenders' risk, respectively' (Dow 1996, p. 500). A more sharply rising supply curve meets a more sharply falling demand curve, with the result being a reduction in the amount of credit extended.

These developments in the economic and financial systems result in a reduced availability of credit, which Dow identifies with credit rationing. She recognizes that there may be an issue in equating these two terms: 'It is a matter of semantics whether or not the resulting availability of credit is termed "rationing"' (p. 499). None the less, she uses this analysis to make her main point, which is that this reduction in credit availability is incompatible with a 'horizontalist' view of endogenous money that assumes accommodating credit behaviour on the part of the banking system.

Wolfson, however, attempts to develop a framework to analyse credit rationing that incorporates a horizontal endogenous money supply curve. He defines credit rationing as 'any situation in which the bank refuses to lend to a particular borrower, despite the borrower's willingness to pay a higher interest rate' (Wolfson 1996, p. 463). In his analysis, he uses the following additional Post Keynesian concepts:

- *The fringe of unsatisfied borrowers* In the *Treatise on Money*, Keynes (1930, vol. I, p. 212) referred to 'an unsatisfied fringe of borrowers' who are refused credit. In this way, Keynes argued, the banks can increase or decrease the volume of their loans (and thus investment) 'without there being necessarily any change in the level of bank-rate [or] in the demand-schedule of borrowers'. Keynes's concept clearly implies a banking system that does not accommodate all demands for credit. Moreover, his reference to changing the volume of loans in the context of both an unchanged interest rate and an unchanged demand schedule would seem to imply a movement *off* the borrowers' demand curve, rather than along it.
- *Asymmetric expectations* Wolfson introduces this term to make the point that the source of credit rationing is the existence of an uncertain future, one in which borrowers and lenders come to different conclusions about future events. It is not necessary to rely on either asymmetric information or even the assumption that lenders are less risk-averse than borrowers. Just different, or asymmetric, expectations will lead to a situation in which borrowers will have some projects that they regard as risky, whereas lenders do not, while borrowers will have other projects that they regard as safe, whereas lenders do not. The first group of projects will never be seen by lenders, while the second group will be rationed (refused credit).

Wolfson draws upon surveys conducted by the Federal Reserve (the Survey on Bank Lending Practices and the Survey on the Terms of Bank Lending) to understand how banks actually ration credit. He concludes (1996, pp. 459–60) that:

1. Banks classify borrowers according to perceived risk, and use these risk classifications to set both price and non-price terms of lending. (Price terms refer to explicit charges, such as the cost of credit lines or the spread of loan rates over a base rate; non-price terms involve other aspects of the loan agreement, such as requirements for collateral, loan covenants, or the size of credit lines.)

2. Higher price terms imply a higher spread over the reference rate, except for borrowers with loan commitments (in the short run).
3. Higher non-price terms raise requirements on existing loans, but also provide the basis for denying credit to those borrowers judged to be insufficiently creditworthy.
4. Banks give preference to borrowers with whom they are familiar.

These observations lead to an important conclusion: since banks increase both price and non-price terms in response to perceptions of higher risk, and since higher non-price terms are the basis for denying a loan, spreads over reference rates and credit rationing move together. This is interesting because, for those borrowers who are rationed, the bank has denied them credit rather than increasing the interest rate charged.

Wolfson builds upon these observations to develop a framework for understanding credit rationing. In doing so, he introduces two additional concepts:

- *Notional demand curve* The notional demand curve expresses the desire for loans by borrowers. It is the traditional demand curve used in most situations to analyse the interaction between supply and demand for a commodity. However, the demand for bank loans is different from the demand for most other commodities. To obtain a bank loan, it is necessary to achieve the consent of the lender. In the situation of credit rationing, it is precisely this consent that is not given. Thus the borrower's demand curve is simply a notional (theoretical, not effective) demand curve for the bank.
- *Creditworthy demand curve* What the bank uses is the creditworthy demand curve. This represents the bank's judgement about the proportion of borrowers desiring loans who are creditworthy. (In the 1996 article, Wolfson used the term 'effective demand curve', rather than 'creditworthy demand curve'. However, as pointed out by Peter Skott and Marc Lavoie, use of the term 'effective demand' is unwise, since it already has a specific meaning within Keynesian economics. 'Creditworthy demand' is a better term (Wolfson 1997; see also Rochon 1999).

Wolfson emphasizes that the judgements made by the bank are those made in the context of uncertainty. Thus they are subject to two concepts discussed by Keynes (1936): a *state of confidence* about any particular forecast of the future, and lending *conventions* that bankers seize upon in the absence of any firm knowledge of the future. Both of these are subject to change. They can change gradually and endogenously over the course of the business cycle, but they can also change dramatically and suddenly during more turbulent times.

Wolfson's ideas can be illustrated with the use of Figure 5. Here L indicates bank loans, r the interest rate charged by the bank, $D^N D^N$ the notional demand curve, $D^C D^C$ the creditworthy demand curve, C the bank's cost of funds, S_A the average spread over the cost of funds charged to the borrower (so that $S_A + C$ represents the interest rate paid by the borrower), and ABD the horizontal 'endogenous money' supply curve. The bank accommodates all creditworthy demands for credit and rations the rest. Thus BD represents the amount of credit rationing, or the 'fringe of unsatisfied borrowers' who would be willing to pay a higher interest rate, but who are refused credit.

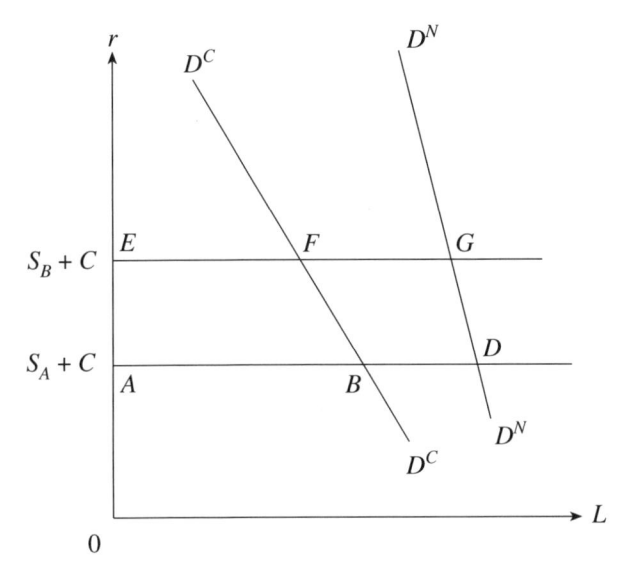

Figure 5 Wolfson's model of credit rationing

If the bank increases its average spread to S_B, then the amount of credit rationing would increase to FG. However, Wolfson indicates that the main 'action' in the model would have less to do with relatively small changes in interest rates at a given point in time, and more to do with factors that affect banks' expectations of the future. He gives three examples: the 'boom and bust' lending in the 1970s and 1980s, the quick collapse of lending that accompanies financial crises, and the typical change from optimism to pessimism (discussed by Minsky and Dow) that occurs as the business cycle expansion nears its peak.

MARTIN H. WOLFSON

See also:
Banking; Endogenous Money; Expectations; Financial Instability Hypothesis; New Keynesian Economics; Non-ergodicity; Uncertainty.

References

Crotty, James (1994), 'Are Keynesian uncertainty and macrotheory compatible? Conventional decision making, institutional structures, and conditional stability in Keynesian macromodels', in G. Dymski and R. Pollin (eds), *New Perspectives in Monetary Macroeconomics*, Ann Arbor: University of Michigan Press, pp. 105–39.
Dow, Sheila (1996), 'Horizontalism: a critique', *Cambridge Journal of Economics*, **20** (4), 497–508.
Keynes, John Maynard (1930), *A Treatise on Money*, New York: Harcourt, Brace.
Keynes, John Maynard (1936), *The General Theory of Employment, Interest and Money*, New York: Harcourt, Brace.
Minsky, Hyman P. (1975), *John Maynard Keynes*, New York: Columbia University Press.
Minsky, Hyman P. (1986), *Stabilizing an Unstable Economy*, New Haven: Yale University Press.
Rochon, Louis-Philippe (1999), *Credit, Money, and Production: An Alternative Post Keynesian Approach*, Cheltenham, UK and Northampton, MA, USA: Edward Elgar.
Stiglitz, Joseph and Andrew Weiss (1981), 'Credit rationing in markets with imperfect information', *American Economic Review*, **71** (3), 393–410.
Wolfson, Martin H. (1996), 'A Post Keynesian theory of credit rationing', *Journal of Post Keynesian Economics*, **18** (3), 443–70.
Wolfson, Martin H. (1997), Letter to Marc Lavoie, 12 March.

Critical Realism

Although known to economists through the work of Tony Lawson and others since the late 1980s, critical realism has a long history and cannot adequately be characterized by the work of any single author or by application within any one discipline. With that caveat key features are presented below: (i) the basic tenets of critical realism, systematized by Roy Bhaskar, which remain definitive of critical realism; (ii) a very brief indication of the development of critical realism since its inception; (iii) the impact of critical realism in (especially Post Keynesian) economics.

Bhaskar (1975) articulates a philosophy of natural science that he terms 'transcendental realism'. This philosophy proposes that objects of science – cells, molecules, atoms, sub-atomic entities, and so on – have an intrinsic structure ('real essence') and associated modes of activity ('mechanisms'). Bhaskar criticizes the received view, enshrined in the 'covering-law' model of scientific explanation, that scientific laws refer to event regularities. He argues, instead, that laws refer to the aforementioned mechanisms and that only under conditions of experimental control does a mechanism necessarily produce an event regularity. Outside of experimental conditions a mechanism acts as an enduring tendency, interacting with other tendencies, to produce the flux of events. In other words reality is an 'open system', whereas the controlled environment of experiment creates a 'closed system'. Furthermore, if laws *did* refer to event regularities, then their application to reality would require that (atomistic) event regularities are ubiquitous *outside* of experiment; that is, it would imply that reality is a closed system such that experiment is unnecessary. Bhaskar opposes such reductionism, which he sees as a legacy of 'positivism'. He proposes, instead, that reality is 'stratified'. Higher strata, such as the molecular level (or, higher still, the cellular level) are causally *irreducible* to the lower strata from which they 'emerge'.

Bhaskar (1979) also offers a philosophy of social science, termed 'critical naturalism'. He argues that social structures and agents are each emergent strata, irreducible to the natural realm, or to each other. On Bhaskar's view social structures, defined as ensembles of social relations, are reproduced (or transformed), often unintentionally, by agents. For example, by getting married a couple unintentionally help to reproduce the institution of marriage; by going to work the worker unintentionally helps to reproduce the social relation of wage labour/capital; by paying rent the tenant unintentionally helps to reproduce the social relation of landlord/tenant. Thus social structures *constrain and enable* the very practices through which they are reproduced. A problem for social science is that experiment is largely impossible. The 'compensator' for this inability to undertake experiment is the social scientists' preconception, gained through their ongoing social activities, of social structures (however distorted it may be). To take one example, agents must, in order to participate in the economy, have concepts of 'money' and 'capital'. The social scientist (who is also an agent within society) uses such preconceptions as premises for hypothesizing the 'deep' social structures that give rise to, or condition, agents' preconceptions. This explanatory move, from preconception to 'deep' social structure, is termed 'retroduction'. Through the 1980s, Bhaskar's ideas gained considerable currency. They were developed and debated by radical philosophers, sociologists and other social scientists, and became known as 'critical realism' (a combination of '*critical* naturalism' and 'transcendental *realism*').

Since the late 1980s, Tony Lawson, followed by a group of economists originally based at Cambridge University, has given voice to critical realism in economics. The most comprehensive statement of their common position (beyond the consolidation of the basic tenets noted above) is found in Lawson (1997). Lawson has added significantly to the critical realist method. Whereas Bhaskar argued simply that 'preconceptions' provide the key to social scientific retroduction, Lawson argues that the social world gives rise to 'partial' or 'demi-' event regularities. It is such 'demi-regs', rather than simple 'preconceptions', that, in general, enable retroduction, according to Lawson. These 'demi-regs' do not presuppose an atomistic reality, as in positivism. Instead, they serve to direct social scientists' attention to where underlying social structures and mechanisms may be located. Lawson gives as an example the 'demi-regularity' of the historically poor comparative productivity performance of the UK. This 'demi-reg' initiates an investigation into the underlying social structures that may account for it; Lawson's previous work argued that one such social structure is the system of industrial relations.

Lawson has used critical realism to criticize mainstream economics. He argues that the essence of mainstream economics is the extensive deployment of a method to which statements of the *form* 'whenever X then Y' (where X and Y refer to events or states of affairs) are central. To explain something is to deduce it from axioms, assumptions and conditions that require statements of the aforementioned form (this is a variant of the 'covering law' model of explanation). Lawson criticizes this 'deductivist' method, and hence mainstream economics, according to Bhaskar's general critique of positivism: the method fails to acknowledge that social science is concerned primarily with 'deep' social structures and agents rather than with event regularities. In attempting to 'close the system', the content of mainstream economics is pushed towards a conceptual world of ubiquitous event conjunctions among atomistic individuals. Yet the real social world is an open system of social structures and agents, not a closed system of atoms. Until deductivism is jettisoned, in favour of methods adequate to open social reality, mainstream economics (both econometrics and economic theory) will remain broken-backed.

Lawson (1994) has contributed to ongoing debate regarding the coherence of Post Keynesian economics. He argues that most, perhaps all, key Post Keynesian 'nominal manifestations', such as opposition to the mainstream; emphasis on making method explicit; focus on uncertainty and history; upholding of genuine human choice; allowance of competing substantive perspectives; and association with certain classical economists, can be rendered 'intelligible' by critical realism. Accordingly, he suggests that Post Keynesian economics is made coherent if grasped as being essentially a critical realist project. Two significant corollaries are: (i) it would appear to be difficult to distinguish Post Keynesian economics from much (old) institutional, Austrian, Marxian and other radical economics, which are likewise redolent of critical realism, in their acknowledgement of open systems; and (ii) the neo-Ricardian commitment to the deductivist method would appear to exclude it from Post Keynesianism (Pratten, not Lawson, makes this claim explicit; see Fleetwood 1999).

Largely as a result of the Cambridge group's efforts (including the weekly Cambridge Realist Workshop, ongoing since 1990, whose list of speakers reads as a 'Who's Who' of the economic methodology discipline), there has been a remarkable rise to prominence of critical realism within: (i) non-mainstream economics, especially within Post Keynesianism; and (ii) the discipline of economic methodology (itself a burgeoning discipline). Taking, firstly, Post Keynesians, there has been a general, though cautious, acceptance of critical realism by leading Post Keynesians. Philip Arestis explicitly characterizes Post Keynesianism as critical realist; Sheila Dow has suggested that her 'Babylonian' method is largely compatible with critical realism. The more critical reactions from within Post Keynesianism, notably Davidson (*JPKE* 1999), have tended to focus on issues of strategy and style (critical realism certainly does contain awkward neologisms). Walters and Young (*JPKE* 1999) argue for a rejection of the marriage of critical realism and Post Keynesian economics but do so from *outside* of Post Keynesianism. Of course, by no means every detail of the Cambridge group's arguments is endorsed, and a major area of controversy concerns econometrics and mathematics, where non-Cambridge-based critical realists have claimed, *contra* the perceived position of the Cambridge group, that critical realism is compatible with econometrics and mathematical modelling.

A number of criticisms have been levelled against critical realism (see, for example, Fleetwood 1999; *JPKE* 1999). Lawson's replies (and the several replies to Stephen Parsons's series of critiques by members of the Cambridge group) have been robust but there is clearly a range of areas that it remains for critical realists to develop. From the above-mentioned collections, and elsewhere, the following criticisms can be noted. Critical realism: (i) does not add much to economic methodology since economics does not posit unobservable entities, beyond those that are trivial; (ii) undertakes a misplaced critique because mainstream modelling does not deal in 'events' at all and hence cannot be deductivist; (iii) misleadingly assimilates very different levels of analysis under the single rubric of 'retroduction'; (iv) employs an unhelpful notion of 'transcendental deduction' in philosophy; (v) falsely states that event regularities of interest to science seldom occur; (vi) employs an opaque notion of social structure; (vii) puts forward a tautological and banal conception of social structure and agency; and (viii) provides little methodological *help* to the social scientist.

From a critical realist perspective, many of these criticisms appear to miss the main point of critical realism in social science: social science should be concerned with ensembles of social relations and with their reproduction or transformation by agents. Many critics do not offer anything like this persuasive description of economic reality, and their criticisms appear myopic as a result. They appear to maintain the philosophical bias against ontology (the theory of being) that critical realism exposes. Indeed, it is not the philosophical justification, but rather the appeal to intuition, that has most likely attracted economists and others to critical realism. While philosophical arguments are important, it is only once they are allied to fruitful methodological and substantive arguments that they are likely to make a real impact. In this vein, Brown (2001) and Brown et al. (2002) reproduce some of the criticisms listed above, and make other criticisms, as part of a positive agenda that embraces the intuitive appeal of critical realism.

Critical realism has made much ground within economics. It seems that it will continue to do so in the future, not only through the efforts of the Cambridge group, but also through the many new converts to critical realism who are now engaged in actively promoting and developing it.

ANDREW BROWN

See also:
Babylonian Mode of Thought; Econometrics; Sraffian Economics; *Treatise on Probability*.

References
Bhaskar, R. (1975), *A Realist Theory of Science*, Leeds: Leeds Books.
Bhaskar, R. (1979), *The Possibility of Naturalism: A Philosophical Critique of the Contemporary Human Sciences*, Brighton: Harvester.
Brown, A. (2001), 'Developing realistic philosophy: from critical realism to materialist dialectics', in A. Brown, S. Fleetwood and J. Roberts (eds), *Critical Realism and Marxism*, London: Routledge, chapter 9, pp. 168–86.
Brown, A., G. Slater and D.A. Spencer (2002), 'Driven to abstraction? Critical realism and the search for the "inner connection" of social phenomena', *Cambridge Journal of Economics*, **26** (6), 773–88.
Fleetwood, S. (ed.) (1999), *Critical Realism in Economics: Development and Debate*, London and New York: Routledge.
JPKE (1999), *Journal of Post Keynesian Economics*, **22** (1), symposium on critical realism.
Lawson, T. (1994), 'The nature of Post Keynesianism and its links to other traditions: a realist perspective', *Journal of Post Keynesian Economics*, **16** (4), 503–38.
Lawson, T. (1997), *Economics and Reality*, London and New York: Routledge.

Development Finance

Two contrasting features often characterize developing economies. On the one hand, economic development is often associated with a significant demand for resources to finance accumulation, technical change and growth. On the other hand, the domestic financial structure, required to channel these resources in appropriate conditions (in terms of maturity structure and costs), is too often underdeveloped (if not non-existent).

In the development economics literature, these issues are addressed from a macroeconomic as well as from an institutional perspective. From the macroeconomic standpoint, the debate often focuses on the determinants and the allocation of saving in developing economies. As usual in macroeconomics, there is a lively debate on the question of causality: some claim that aggregate saving is a requirement for investment and growth, and others argue that the causality is the other way round.

On top of the debate on the causality between aggregate saving and investment, there is an additional issue concerning the relevance of different domestic financial systems in economic development. Even though few economists nowadays doubt that the degree of financial development is an important requirement for economic growth, there is an ongoing debate on the policies required to achieve such a development.

Currently the literature on the issue is dominated by the Shaw–McKinnon and the New Keynesian approaches. In a nutshell, the first one (for a survey see Agénor and Montiel 1996) claims that financial markets in less-developed countries are underdeveloped due to the historical repression of financial systems (through interest rate ceilings, directed credit and so on). Financial repression would cause low saving and low financial deepening, and deter the development of the financial system.

In turn, New Keynesian models focus on the availability and distribution of information between borrowers, lenders and financial institutions. The relaxation of the perfect information hypothesis within a Walrasian framework permits these models to show that, in the context of asymmetric information, credit (and equity) rationing is to be expected in any market economy, and it tends to be more prominent in developing ones. In addition, if informational asymmetries introduce inefficiencies in financial markets, they may have quantitatively significant real effects (Gertler 1988, p. 560). In addition, adverse selection implies that capital is being inefficiently allocated. In other words, in these cases funds for investment will be lower than their potential and the allocation of resources will be distorted.

An alternative view on the issues related to the financing of economic development is based on Keynes's paradigm of the monetary production economy and Minsky's (1982) financial fragility hypothesis. The starting-point of Keynes's analysis is his rejection of Say's Law through his theory of effective demand and his identification of investment as the *causa causans* in the determination of output and employment. This obviously requires that *investment finance* be independent from previous saving (Studart 1995).

In Keynes's story, the aggregate supply of investment finance is mainly determined by the banks' willingness to actively create deposits and credit, and not by savers' preferences. Therefore banks 'hold a key position in the transition from a lower to a higher scale of activity' (Keynes 1937, p. 668) – an assumption that seems to be deeply rooted in his description of the evolution of the banking system in the *Treatise on Money*.

It is noteworthy that in this story the expansion of bank credit is not an anomaly which necessarily leads to Wicksellian cumulative disequilibria (in the form of inflation and forced saving): it is one of *the* most important means by which a monetary economy can grow. A malfunctioning banking system is not one which disrupts the equilibrium between 'true' saving and investment, but one which causes the failure of an important part of the credit system and therefore a reduction in the capacity of the entrepreneur economy to advance purchasing power to investors willing to accumulate.

It is bank credit, not saving, which plays the crucial role in the financing of investment. This would appear to leave no role for savings, but such is far from being the case. The key to understanding such a 'hidden facet' of Keynes's economics has to do with the risks (in a Knightian sense) of financing assets with long-term maturity in inherently uncertain market economies – where the demand for liquidity is always high for a significant proportion of wealth-holders. This is where the issue of *funding* comes into the story.

Funding can be strictly defined as the process of transformation of short-term into long-term liabilities. From a Post Keynesian viewpoint funding is a key concept in the analysis of problems related to the financing of long-lived assets in an economy where finance is mainly provided by the management of short-term liabilities (that is, bank deposits) (Davidson 1986).

Because of the structure of banks' liabilities, such credit is either short term, and borrowers' risk will be rising; or, if the banks agree to finance long-term positions, they will be accepting higher liquidity risks. In one way or another, growth will be followed by an increase of what Minsky termed systemic financial fragility.

In the Keynes–Minsky story, funding takes place through the issuing of long-term securities, that is, in 'primary markets'. The existence of such markets depends on the proper functioning of secondary markets (where old securities are bought and sold), which, in turn, relies on continuous trading to provide the liquidity to otherwise illiquid assets. It is this provision of liquidity that makes long-term bonds and securities attractive to savers – who, as Davidson (1986) has rightly put it, are searching for safe 'liquidity time-machines', and rarely wish to be locked in to holding an asset for a long period of time.

In this sense, funding can be interpreted as a response to a menacing increase in both borrowers' and lenders' risks (Keynes 1936, p. 144). Hence, investment finance in a world of uncertainty is characteristically a twofold process of finance and funding (Keynes 1937, p. 664). Thus the question of funding has interrelated micro- and macroeconomic facets. From the microeconomic perspective, entrepreneurs and bankers desire to fund their long-term commitments on a stable basis because of uncertainty about the prospective conditions of credit and levels of interest rates. From a macroeconomic viewpoint, funding and, therefore, financial markets also play a role, which is seldom spelled out: the role of mitigating the increasing financial fragility inherent in a growing monetary economy. It is important to stress that financial fragility in itself is not a constraint on growth, but it may disrupt the process of expansion. This is especially true if an increase in fragility causes a debt-deflation, an expression of the exhaustion of financial arrangements that may lead to depression.

From the perspective implicit in the Shaw–McKinnon approach, low financial depth and retarded development are direct consequences of financial repression – and therefore the policy to solve such a problem is the liberalization of domestic financial markets in order to increase the availability of domestic saving. In addition, many defenders of this position would argue that opening the capital account would facilitate access to foreign saving.

The New Keynesian approach presents an embarrassing challenge to the view that financial markets are efficient allocators of capital, and makes way for interventionist views that are foreign to the liberal wave that has dominated academe since the 1980s. However, it also leads to the ambiguous view that, were it not for the problems generated by imperfect information or other market failures, that role would be fully restored and the allocative efficiency of capital would prevail. Even if there is room for an analysis of a 'defective' institutional framework (that is, one which is far from the stylized single competitive capital market), the stimulus for saving, especially by maintaining real interest rates, could be prescribed as the means to increase saving and investment. In addition, this ambiguity in the analysis leads to a highly ideological and inevitably inconclusive debate on whether 'government failures' are more prominent than 'market failures' (Jaramillo-Vallejo 1994), and thus whether any policy to mitigate market failures is not likely to make things worse.

In contrast, the Post Keynesian approach rejects the two most important pillars of the conventional approach to development financing: the prior-saving argument and the efficient capital market hypothesis. Financial systems do have a fundamental role in the process of economic development if they are able to transform short-term assets that are demanded by savers as forms of 'liquidity time-machines' into sources of funding with an appropriate maturity structure to finance different economic activities and capital accumulation. This role assumes different possible forms according to the institutional background behind the financial structure.

Appropriate mechanisms to finance and fund growth and accumulation are required for sustainable development. However, nothing can guarantee that development will lead to a capital-market-based financial structure. Indeed, most developing (as well as developed) economies still have a bank-based financial structure, where the capital market is weak and firms depend heavily on credit for raising finance beyond that available from retained earnings.

From a Post Keynesian perspective, the lack or underdevelopment of organized financial markets can have two destabilizing consequences for development. First, if financial markets remain underdeveloped and funding is not available, banks' liquidity preference will be high and they may refrain from expanding their lending activity when the demand for loans is rising rapidly. Second, if finance is forthcoming to sustain growth, the financial position of both firms and banks will become more fragile (how rapidly depends on the rate of growth). Furthermore, even if they do lend more in times of growth, banks will almost certainly prefer short-term loans (to finance consumption, working capital and/or speculation) to longer-term, and hence riskier, investment projects. *Ceteris paribus*, if banks are still prepared to finance expansion despite the lack of appropriate mechanisms to fund investment, the indebtedness of the corporate sector must increase. Growth will only be sustained if some investing firms borrow short, hoping to repay by borrowing until their investment matures and begins to produce additional cash inflows (using Minsky's terminology, more and more investors and financiers will adopt speculative, and even Ponzi, strategies).

Because the weight of speculative finance tends to increase with the acceleration of investment, credit-based systems are thus extremely vulnerable to changes in credit conditions (especially shifts in interest rates) in times of growth. If the financing of long-lived assets is supplied mainly through short-term renewable loans, a change in the rate of interest will represent a significant rise in firms' financial expenditures; if firms try to adjust by cutting other expenditures simultaneously, this may set in motion a vicious circle of financial reactions which could reduce effective demand even further.

The Post Keynesian approach thus leads to distinct policy recommendations for different time horizons. In the long run, market-enhancing policies are required if private mechanisms to finance and fund investment are to evolve – and there are significant experiences in both developed and developing economies of successful market-enhancing economies.

While such mechanisms are not developed, private credit (and equity) rationing is likely to be a pervasive problem of developing economies. This gives support for directed credit policies, especially to developing sectors that, due to their long maturity horizon (for example, long-term fixed capital accumulation) and/or risk characteristics (for example, technology-related investments and small and medium-sized enterprises) are likely to have little access to private financing. Finally, given that most developing countries have a bank-based financial structure, low and stable interest rates are an important requirement to avoid inherent financial fragility associated with resulting maturity mismatches evolving into undesirable processes of financial instability and crises.

ROGÉRIO STUDART

See also:

Credit Rationing; Finance Motive; Financial Instability Hypothesis; Keynes's *Treatise on Money*; Monetary Policy; New Keynesian Economics.

Bibliography

Agénor, P.R. and P.J. Montiel (1996), *Development Macroeconomics*, Princeton, NJ: Princeton University Press.
Davidson, P. (1986), 'Finance, funding, saving and investment', *Journal of Post Keynesian Economics*, **9** (1), 101–10.
Gertler, M. (1988), 'Financial structure and aggregate economic activity: an overview', *Journal of Money, Credit, and Banking*, **20** (3), 559–87.
Jamarillo-Vallejo, J. (1994), 'Comment on "The role of the State in financial markets"', *Proceedings of the World Bank Annual Conference on Development Economics 1993*, Washington, DC: World Bank, pp. 53–8.
Keynes, J.M. (1936), *The General Theory of Employment, Interest and Money*, London: Macmillan.
Keynes, J.M. (1937), 'The "ex-ante" theory of the rate of interest', *Economic Journal*, **47** (188), 663–9.
Minsky, H.P. (1982), 'The financial-instability hypothesis: capitalist processes and the behavior of the economy', in C.P. Kindleberger and J.P. Laffargue (eds), *Financial Crises*, Cambridge: Cambridge University Press, pp. 13–39.
Stiglitz, J. (1994), 'The role of the State in financial markets', *Proceedings of the World Bank Annual Conference on Development Economics 1993*, Washington, DC: World Bank, pp. 19–52.
Studart, R. (1995), *Investment Finance in Economic Development*, London: Routledge.

Dynamics

In analysing growth dynamics, Post Keynesian economics encounters a series of deep contradictions that generate a startling array of alternative models and approaches. These contradictions arise from confronting real contradictions in actual growing economies that are papered over or ignored by standard neoclassical approaches. In variations on the Solow–Swan model, the latter postulate long-run equilibrium growth paths that are set by exogenous factors such as intertemporal time preference rates, population growth, and proclivities for technological change, with these characteristics essentially holding even in the newer, so-called endogenous growth models by Paul Romer and others. The essential contradiction for Post Keynesians arises from Keynes's famous dictum that 'in the long run we are all dead', and from Joan Robinson's equally famous contrasting of logical versus historical time, while at the same time neoclassical growth theory arose out of long-run models by such followers of Keynes as Roy Harrod, Nicholas Kaldor, and even Joan Robinson herself, as well as the neo-Ricardian followers of Piero Sraffa.

Thus more recent Post Keynesians attempt to overcome this contradiction by studying long-run dynamics without positing a long-run solution. They seek to place these outcomes as the consequence of a sequence of short-run solutions. In turn, these short-run solutions attempt to more clearly integrate micro-sectoral outcomes with macrodynamic outcomes. Relative change and transformation over time become important, with the recognition that divergences, both internationally and internally between groups, give rise to outcomes of interest. Furthermore, there is a much greater emphasis on modelling the interaction between cyclical dynamics and complex growth dynamics, with money and disequilibrium outcomes playing much greater roles than in more orthodox approaches. We shall review some of the approaches that have been developed along these lines.

Michał Kalecki was the independent and parallel developer of the Keynesian apparatus who drew on Marxist roots. More influential on many modern Post Keynesians than Keynes himself, Kalecki introduced a more clearly articulated view of microeconomic behaviour and also more clearly focused on longer-run growth issues as well as shorter-run fluctuations questions. All of this makes him in many ways paradigmatic of the more general approach of Post Keynesians to these issues. Some of his more important followers include Josef Steindl, Alfred Eichner, Joseph Halevi, Peter Kriesler, Marc Lavoie, Tracy Mott and Malcolm Sawyer. An overview of Kaleckian models is in King (1996).

At the micro level Kalecki emphasized monopoly power (as did Joan Robinson also) and introduced the idea of mark-up pricing. This contrasts with the usual marginal cost pricing theory of theoretical pure competition, and is also known to correspond more closely with what actually goes on in many real-world industries. This approach also allows for cost-push sources of inflation, in contrast to the usual demand-side factors emphasized by monetarists or New Keynesians.

Growth is driven by capital investment, a view shared with the neoclassicals. But, in contrast to them, investment is endogenous to aggregate demand, with savings endogenously determined by investment, a widely held view among Post Keynesians that has considerable empirical support. But fluctuations in investment, arising from fluctuations of aggregate demand as well as from class struggle that sometimes operates through the political arena, drive shorter-term fluctuations. Thus Kalecki was one of the first to point the way to an integrated Post Keynesian approach.

Piero Sraffa was a close ally of Keynes in his debates with Friedrich Hayek about business cycles in the 1920s and 1930s, and Joan Robinson was a close associate and follower of both men. Nevertheless, in recent decades a deep divide has opened between Post Keynesians who emphasize the monetary short-run equilibrium, such as Paul Davidson, and Sraffians or neo-Ricardians, who emphasize classical long-run supply-side equilibrium models based on input–output matrices. Leaders of the latter school have included Piero Garegnani, Heinz Kurz and Neri Salvadori.

However, several economists have attempted to integrate the two approaches, including Edward Nell and especially Luigi Pasinetti (1993). Pasinetti became well known in the 1960s as a participant in the Cambridge capital theory controversies, along with Garegnani, as one of the analysts of reswitching. He also developed growth models based on capitalist saving behaviour. He extended the Sraffa input–output framework to a growth context in which technical coefficients could change. In the 1970s he altered this by considering vertically integrated units within the input–output framework. This opened the door to a more concentrated analysis of structural transformation over time.

In his more recent formulation, Pasinetti (1993) further decomposes the analysis to a quasi-Marxist model based purely on labour, with no intermediate goods or capital (a logical outcome of the Sraffa critique). This version contains the earlier models, but has now reintegrated Keynesian effective demand as an overall growth determinant. Furthermore, this demand is sectorally specified and evolves through consumer learning. Thus, although it is different in various ways from the Kaleckian formulations, Pasinetti's model also integrates micro with macro in a model with demand-determined growth.

The emphasis on relative sectoral transformation that one finds in Pasinetti and Nell has also been carried forth by others who have brought in the path-dependence dynamics of cumulative causation and hysteresis. Such ideas appeared in Adam Smith and Alfred Marshall to some extent, with Allyn Young restating them in the 1920s, and Nicholas Kaldor emphasizing their significance for the existence of multiple equilibria or no equilibria from the 1930s through the 1980s, and Paul David and Brian Arthur emphasizing path dependence in the 1980s. Some of those following this approach include Mark Setterfield and Rod Cross. But perhaps the most comprehensive integration of these ideas into sectorally specific macro growth models with sectoral and national divergence in specific historical analysis is due to John and Wendy Cornwall (2001).

Uneven growth is more clearly analysed, with economies of scale effects, learning effects and various nonlinearities playing important roles. Transformation is evolutionary, with divergences at the sectoral level ultimately implying divergences at the macro level across nations and over time within nations. The nonlinearities involved are recognized to possibly lead to complex dynamics along the growth path (Rosser 2000). This contrasts with the neoclassical endogenous growth models that remain at the level of aggregate production functions, with all the difficulties this entails, including a distribution theory based on marginal products of aggregated factors of production. The Cornwall and Cornwall analysis, along with related models by Setterfield and Nell, avoids these problems and is more revealing of historical economic dynamics of rising income inequality, both internally and internationally.

An important contribution by Post Keynesians to the analysis of international elements in growth divergence has come from recognizing the role of balance of payments constraints on economic growth. This has been crystallized in what is known as Thirlwall's Law (McCombie and Thirlwall 1994). This posits that over time there must be something like a balance of trade. Thus the growth of imports must be matched by the growth of exports. This implies that a nation's growth will be constrained by global growth along with its import and export elasticities, the variables that enter into the formula that expresses Thirlwall's Law.

Recognition of this has led to much discussion of the role of international finance more broadly in influencing economic growth and development. Post Keynesians who have discussed this at length and made specific proposals include Paul Davidson, Jan Kregel and John Smithin.

Many Post Keynesians have especially stressed the importance of the role of money in economic growth and fluctuations, thereby denying the classical dichotomy, with Paul Davidson and Hyman Minsky particularly important in this regard. However, they have not developed explicit growth models along with their analysis of fluctuations. This has fallen to a more recent group of economists, including Duncan Foley, Peter Skott, Domenico Delli

Gatti and Mauro Gallegatti, Steve Keen, Reiner Franke and Willi Semmler, with Carl Chiarella and Peter Flaschel (2000) providing thorough modelling.

These models are more strictly macro than the ones discussed in earlier sections, and also more clearly lay out the role of the financial sector in investment, with feedbacks from production to finance along Minskyian and Goodwinian lines. Growth interacts with cycles, with the latter becoming dynamically complex. Complex macro cycles have been studied by many, including Richard Day, Alfredo Medio, Tönu Puu, and Rosser (2000).

Finally, extending the analysis of Cornwall and Cornwall, there has developed an essentially neo-Schumpeterian analysis of technical change based on sectors that can lead to structural evolution and transformation over time with complex dynamics, including historical reswitching. Important figures in this analysis have included Richard Day, John Sterman and Gerald Silverberg. A general overview of these models and their complex nonlinear dynamics that links them back to the Cambridge capital theory debates and the historical versus logical time arguments of Joan Robinson can be found in Rosser (2000).

J. Barkley Rosser, Jr.

See also:

Balance-of-payments-constrained Economic Growth; Growth Theory; Innovation; Investment; Kaleckian Economics; Sraffian Economics; Time in Economic Theory.

References

Chiarella, C. and P. Flaschel (2000), *The Dynamics of Keynesian Monetary Growth: Macrofoundations*, Cambridge: Cambridge University Press.
Cornwall, J. and W. Cornwall (2001), *Capitalist Development in the Twentieth Century: An Evolutionary–Keynesian Analysis*, Cambridge: Cambridge University Press.
King, J.E. (ed.) (1996), *An Alternative Macroeconomic Theory: The Kaleckian Model and Post-Keynesian Economics*, Boston: Kluwer Academic Publishers.
McCombie, J.S.L. and A.P. Thirlwall (1994), *Economic Growth and the Balance of Payments Constraint*, London: Macmillan.
Pasinetti, L.L. (1993), *Structural Economic Dynamics. A Theory of the Economic Consequences of Human Learning*, Cambridge: Cambridge University Press.
Rosser, J.B., Jr. (2000), *From Catastrophe to Chaos: A General Theory of Economic Discontinuities, Volume 1: Mathematics, Microeconomics, Macroeconomics, and Finance*, 2nd edition, Boston: Kluwer.

Econometrics

Perhaps emphasizing theoretical rather than methodological differences with neoclassical and new Keynesian economists, from the outset Post Keynesian economists have made use of econometric methods. Thus in the 1980s Alfred Eichner with various research partners presented results associated with estimating 'blocks' of structural equations for a short-period Post Keynesian model of the US economy. Likewise, Philip Arestis undertook a comparable exercise for the UK. In general, casual perusal of the *Journal of Post Keynesian Economics* would suggest that Post Keynesian economists readily use a wide variety of econometric methods. Increasingly, however, while Post Keynesian economics does not draw upon Keynes's ideas only, in the case of econometrics his somewhat ambiguous sentiments are strongly echoed in the literature. Keynes's essentially philosophical argument, that 'the main *prima facie* objection to the application of the method of multiple correlation to complex economic problems lies in the apparent lack of any adequate degree of uniformity in the environment' (Keynes 1939, p. 567) is often cited. This said, Keynes (1973b, p. 300) also stresses the need for 'messy acquaintance with the facts'. So too, in the current Post Keynesian literature, there is a degree of tension between philosophical pronouncements and the practice of economics.

Post Keynesian economics currently presents itself as accepting an 'open-system' philosophical approach from three main perspectives: critical realism associated with Tony Lawson, a 'Babylonian' perspective associated with Sheila Dow, and an 'encompassing' approach associated with Paul Davidson. Critical realism in economics is primarily associated with the work of Lawson (1997), who argues that neoclassical economics has its roots in the philosophical system of positivism – and in particular embraces an ontology – where reality comprises the constant conjunction of atomistic events in a closed system. Here, broadly speaking, the intrinsic condition of closure (ICC) – that each cause produces the same effect – and the extrinsic condition of closure (ECC) – that each effect has the same cause – allow an epistemology based on deduction. Thus theoretical explanation can comprise statements of the form 'whenever event "X" then event "Y"', allowing also for stochastic errors. Consequently the mathematical modelling of individual agency is emphasized in neoclassical economics, coupled with econometric testing. Lawson describes this approach as 'empirical realism'.

In contrast, an open-system approach presents an organic ontological perspective, which implies that human agency is embedded in a social context. Behaviour is thus irreducible to individual action *per se* but, on the contrary, is both conditional on, and results in, multiple modes of the determination of events. Furthermore, critical realists argue that reality is stratified into three domains. These are the level of actual events, the empirical level of experience and sense impression, and the level of the real, where causal relations are located. Accordingly, critical realism maintains that at best there will be a plurality of partial regularities and processes underlying events, and not predictable or universal event-regularities. Econometric inferences are thus inherently problematic.

Davidson's (1996) methodological approach broadly shares these sentiments. He argues that, in general, the neoclassical research programme invokes the axiom of 'ergodicity'. This implies that the world is predetermined and immutable. In the case of probabilistic inferences, therefore, as the past is a good guide to the future, objective or subjective probabilities will ultimately converge on the true values of the parameters of the probability distribution. For Davidson, the ergodicity axiom is the reason why neoclassical economists emphasize probabilities and statistical/econometric inference in their analysis. In contrast Davidson argues that Post Keynesians embrace a non-ergodic and transmutable-reality view of the world in which probabilities, and thus econometric inference, are not reliable guides to the future.

Finally, while echoing the critical realist perspective in stressing the organic nature of society, Dow's (1990) Babylonian approach argues that evidence is validly provided by a variety of sources, such as questionnaire and historical sources. This approach also allows for qualified econometric testing, however, because theories cannot be judged according to the principles of a *particular* theoretical structure and because theoretical and empirical diversity is a logical consequence of open-system thought.

For the purpose of further discussion, though adopting the particular language of critical realism, Post Keynesian philosophical deliberation in general rejects 'empirical realism'. However, the practice of Post Keynesian economics admits of the need for empirical analysis. Herein lies the central tension of this discussion. It is clear that both the estimation of regression coefficients and an emphasis upon drawing statistical inferences require the invocation of the closure conditions noted earlier. The ICC is equivalent to assuming the underlying homogeneity of nature and the atomistic combination of objects. This is required to ensure that the coefficients, or functional form, of a regression are constant over time (or space). The ECC implies that all of the causal factors have been included in an econometric study, or that the effect of external factors on internal factors is constant. This last point is equivalent to assuming that countervailing factors are constant. As noted above, the fact that Post Keynesians, like mainstream economists, regularly employ econometric methods, suggests a possibility of logical inconsistency between the methodological aspirations and the practices of Post Keynesians.

In fact, though not clearly articulated in the literature, the employment of econometrics could also reflect the need for Post Keynesians to adopt an appropriate 'rhetoric' in order to engage in critical discussion with neoclassical economists. It has often been argued that Post Keynesian economics only has coherence in terms of an opposition to neoclassical economics. In a related way econometrics might also act as a vehicle for them to demonstrate comparable technical virtuosity with neoclassical economists.

Yet these are rather unsatisfactory and defensive arguments. Post Keynesians have also sought to present a positive case for employing econometric methods that confronts the issues raised by Post Keynesian philosophical concerns. Summarizing a number of arguments, Downward and Mearman (2002) explore the variety of econometric methods, arguing that not only do a burgeoning set of techniques exist for the researcher to calculate statistics, but that they also form part of various inferential frameworks.

Thus, for example, the 'average economic regression' or textbook approach presents a maintained hypothesis that is assumed to capture a correct specification. Following estimation, the random error terms are analysed and transformations of the model then follow to eliminate any problems. In contrast, the David Hendry/LSE (London School of Economics) approach stems from developments in time-series econometrics. Central to Hendry's research programme is a continual interaction between theory and data; thus knowledge appears to arrive from a complex interaction of deduction and induction. This is demonstrated, for example, in the focus upon error-correction models in the cointegration analysis of time series. Theory describes the long-run relationship, while the data reveal the short-run dynamics of adjustment.

Moreover, in the former case, it can be argued that the 'average economic regression' approach has its roots in Haavelmo's (1944) influential essay. For Haavelmo the essence of econometrics was to build, identify, estimate and assess various models conforming to the optimizing behaviour given by neoclassical precepts. Importantly, he writes, 'the question is not whether probabilities exist or not, but whether – if we proceed as if they existed – we are able to make statements about real phenomena that are correct for "practical purposes"' (Haavelmo 1944, p. 43). On such a basis econometrics can be described as a form of instrumentalist reasoning. In contrast, at times Hendry argues that the literal process that generates data – the data-generating process – can be measured by probabilities as a 'statistical generating mechanism'. However, he also stresses that the 'proof of the pudding lies in the eating' as far as econometric models are concerned.

Other econometric methods draw upon Bayesian inferential logic or 'atheoretical' vector-autoregression analysis. In the former case Ed Leamer's *modus operandi* is to formulate a general family of models, decide what inferences are of importance, which need not be structural relations, express these in terms of parameters, and form prior distributions summarizing any information not in the data set. The sensitivity of inferences to a particular choice of distributions should be analysed to explore their 'fragility'. In the latter case the concept of exogenous variables is rejected and analysis proceeds in terms of simultaneous relationships between jointly endogenous variables. Finally, there exists an eclectic set of broadly cross-sectional methods. For example, Logit and Probit estimators are employed in cases in which the dependent variable is presumed to reflect simple dichotomous categories, or rank-orders. Poisson and negative binomial models are now estimated for models which maintain that dependent variables reflect discrete rather than continuous values (that is, comprise integers or counts). Other developments include allowing for truncated or censored distributions in the dependent variable. The most famous example of this is the Tobit model. Under these circumstances, the assumption is usually that the dependent variable is drawn from a normal distribution but that there is a qualitative break in the measurement of the variable. Interestingly, these latter approaches indicate that econometricians have thought quite deeply about ontological issues. Estimators have been refined in connection with presuppositions about the purported character of phenomena.

Despite these differences, however, Downward and Mearman argue that the underlying inferential logic of most econometric techniques, as typically applied, appeals to measurable probabilities alone. It follows that embracing current philosophical discourse suggests that Post Keynesian inferences cannot simply proceed by appeal to a measurable probability distribution (and by implication a unique set of estimated coefficients).

However, Downward and Mearman also argue that the assumptions involved in estimating coefficients are shared with all (even descriptive) empirical analyses. If this is so, then logically any empirical analysis advocated by Post Keynesians can embrace econometric *estimation*. As far as inferences are concerned, Keynes emphasized the importance of rational belief rather than knowledge as a basis of argument (Keynes 1973a, p. 10). To avoid the problem of induction, Keynes argued that one should examine a particular phenomenon in different contexts, thus engaging in a process of 'negative analogy'. If a phenomenon appears to be a common element between various contexts, then ultimately this can add weight to a particular account of that phenomenon.

From an operational perspective this suggests that various empirical insights should be 'triangulated', that is, compared to insights produced elsewhere. This idea has resonance with, or and can be combined with, the tenets of critical realism. Critical realism strongly argues that analysis should pay explicit attention to ontology and, in particular, explanation should focus, by a process of 'retroduction', on elaborating the underlying causal mechanisms of events. Crucially, these are not likely to be synchronized with empirical statements about the events. Consequently, Downward and Mearman argue that while descriptive and historical analysis might be employed to explore suggested causal mechanisms, it follows that the effects of their action can be assessed, and hence the purported causal mechanism supported, with reference to more quantitative analysis conducted by econometric techniques. Thus econometric methods can potentially perform a very helpful task in codifying events at the empirical level, suggesting issues for further causal investigation and helping to assess the legitimacy of existing causal claims.

It should be clear from this that Post Keynesians do not accept that explanation and prediction are synonymous, as implied by much neoclassical presentation of econometrics. In Post Keynesian thinking, any quantitative prediction becomes merely a scenario whose legitimacy will rest upon the robustness of the claimed causal mechanism that is tentatively identified and/or supported by econometric estimation. Predictions from an econometric model will always be open to revision.

In closing it should be emphasized that philosophy and applied economics need to coexist and to develop from mutual discourse, in terms of both articulating the problems of adequately capturing real elements of economic processes and working towards concrete analysis and policy prescription. Some compromise with a purely philosophical inclination seems inevitable in applying econometric, and indeed other empirical, methods.

PAUL DOWNWARD

See also:

Agency; Babylonian Mode of Thought; Critical Realism; Non-ergodicity; *Treatise on Probability*.

References

Davidson, P. (1996), 'Reality and economic theory', *Journal of Post Keynesian Economics*, **18** (4), 479–508.
Dow, S.C. (1990), 'Post Keynesianism as political economy: a methodological discussion', *Review of Political Economy*, **2** (3), 345–58.
Downward, P.M. and A. Mearman (2002), 'Critical realism and econometrics: constructive dialogue with Post Keynesian economics', *Metroeconomica*, **53** (4), 391–415.
Haavelmo, T. (1944), 'The probability approach in econometrics', *Econometrica* (Supplement), 1–118.

Keynes, J.M. (1939), 'Professor Tinbergen's method', *Economic Journal*, **44** (195), 555–68.
Keynes, J.M. (1973a), *The Collected Writings of John Maynard Keynes. Volume VIII: A Treatise on Probability*, London: Macmillan for the Royal Economic Society.
Keynes, J.M. (1973b) *The Collected Writings of John Maynard Keynes. Volume XIV: The General Theory and After. Part II: Defence and Development*, London: Macmillan for the Royal Economic Society.
Lawson T. (1997), *Economics and Reality*, London and New York: Routledge.

Economic Policy

There is no unique set of economic policies which can be described as Post Keynesian or even closely associated with one of the branches of Post Keynesian economics. Post Keynesian economists have though generally been supportive of certain types of economic policies, notably those to stimulate the level of aggregate demand. Many policy proposals find support from a range of economists of different schools of thought, and there are many differences over policy among Post Keynesian economists (the proposals for a tax on foreign exchange transactions, often labelled the 'Tobin tax', being a current example).

The general approach to policy could be seen to be derived from the basic insight of Kalecki and Keynes for the workings of industrialized market economies, namely that a *laissez-faire* market economy will not usually generate full employment. The essential cause of that failure to create full employment is not some rigidities or 'imperfections' of monopolistic competition, trade unions and so on which could potentially be removed through government action. It is rather that a *laissez-faire* market economy would exhibit elements of instability with booms and busts, and periods of crisis. Further, a market economy would not usually generate a level of aggregate demand consistent with full employment. The achievement of full employment is a widely accepted major policy objective for Post Keynesian economists, and policies and institutional arrangements supportive of high levels of demand are advocated.

The Post Keynesian approach to fiscal policy is informed by the accounting identity of:

$$(\text{Savings} - \text{Investment}) = (\text{Exports} - \text{Imports}) + (\text{Government expenditure} - \text{Taxation}),$$

where (Exports – Imports) is the trade surplus, and equal to the deficit on capital account. There will, in general, be imbalances in the terms of this equation at whatever level of income the economy is operating. The question arises as to what the imbalances would be if income was at a level compatible with full employment. In the case where savings would exceed investment at full employment income, then some combination of trade surplus and government budget deficit would be required to balance the excess of savings over investment to maintain full employment. Running a budget deficit in these circumstances helps to sustain full employment, but it can also be seen that the excess of savings over investment funds the budget deficit. Hence there is no 'crowding out', or upward pressure on interest rates.

Lerner (1943) put the case for what he termed functional finance, which 'rejects completely the traditional doctrines of "sound finance" and the principle of trying to balance the budget over a solar year or any other arbitrary period' (p. 355), and adjustment of total spending to eliminate both unemployment and inflation. 'No matter how much interest has to be paid on the debt, taxation must not be applied unless it is necessary to keep spending down to prevent inflation. The interest can be paid by borrowing still more' (p. 356). Lerner summarized the answers to arguments against deficit spending by saying that the national debt does not have to keep on increasing, and that even if it does the interest does not have to be paid from current taxes. Further, interest payments on bonds are an internal transfer.

From an aggregate demand stance, alternative policy approaches would be the stimulation of investment or the reduction of the propensity to save. For example, Kalecki (1944) in his discussion of 'three ways to full employment' considered the redistribution of income (towards wage earners) as a means of stimulating consumer demand (and thereby reducing savings). He also considered the stimulation of investment, though he saw clear limits to this route. Consider $I/Y = (\Delta K/K).(K/Y)$ where I is net investment equal to the change in the capital stock ΔK, and K/Y is the capital–output ratio. The share of investment in GDP is then given by the multiple of the underlying growth rate (which sets the growth of the capital stock $\Delta K/K$) and the capital–output ratio.

Some Post Keynesian authors (for example, Wray 1998) have advocated the policy of 'employer of last resort' (ELR) whereby the government stands ready to employ anyone at a pre-determined money wage (which may be set to ensure that the wage is sufficient to remove the worker from poverty). It is argued that such a policy would not be inflationary (since the wage paid by the government as ELR remains unchanged) and secures full employment (in that anyone who wishes to work is able to do so, albeit at the ELR wage).

There would be a concern to ensure that the international financial system was conducive to high levels of aggregate demand. In the context of the Bretton Woods fixed exchange rate system, this concern was translated into policy arrangements which sought to ensure that countries which were running trade deficits were not forced into deflationary policies to correct the trade deficit. Keynes (1980, p. 176) sought to design an international payments system which transferred 'the onus of adjustment from the debtor to the creditor position' and aimed 'at the substitution of an expansionist, in place of contractionist, pressure on world trade'. Davidson (1992), building on the work of Keynes, proposed a 'new international payments system' (p. 157) designed 'to resolve payments imbalances while simultaneously promoting full employment economic growth and a long-run stable international standard of value' (p. 153). These proposals included the unit of account and reserve asset for international liquidity being the international money clearing unit (IMCU), with each nation's central bank committed to guarantee one-way convertibility from IMCU deposits at the clearing union to its domestic money. Davidson advocated 'an overdraft system to make available short-term unused creditor balances at the clearing house to finance the productive international transactions of others who need short-term credit', and 'a trigger mechanism to encourage any creditor national to spend . . . "excessive" credit balances accumulated by running current account surpluses' (p. 160). Finally, 'if a country is at *full employment* and still has a tendency toward persistent international deficits on its current account, then this is *prima facie* evidence that it does not possess the productive capacity to maintain its current standard of living' (p. 163, original emphasis).

The era of floating exchange rates has led to a different set of concerns, namely the effects of the large flows across the currency exchanges and the volatility of exchange rates. The volatility of exchange rates (and indeed of prices in financial markets more generally) comes as no surprise to Post Keynesians. In a world of uncertainty, where the equilibrium price in a market is unknowable (and indeed may not exist in any meaningful sense), traders will not (and cannot) hold 'rational expectations' of future prices. They will be influenced by the views of others, and by a variety of information, including recent trends in price. One policy proposal which addresses these concerns is the 'Tobin tax'.

Inflation, or the fear of inflation, may be seen as limiting the achievement of full employment, though many Post Keynesians would cast doubt on the existence of any immutable 'natural rate of unemployment' or deny that any such rate is effectively determined in the labour market. The Post Keynesian views on endogenous money would deny any causal role for money in the inflationary process. Deflation (whether brought through fiscal or monetary policies) is seen as a blunt and inefficient instrument for the control of inflation. Some would envisage that any inflationary problems could be addressed through incomes policy of the social contract form or through tax-based incomes policy, while others would point to the importance of institutional arrangements and the creation of sufficient productive capacity.

The attainment of high levels of productivity requires an appropriate work intensity and commitment on the part of the labour force as well as the provision of sufficient capital equipment, training, skills and management. In many market economies, unemployment (and more particularly the threat of it) serves as a significant mechanism for imposing a high level of work intensity (Kalecki 1943). Unemployment is seen as performing a systemic function (of aiding the disciplining of workers). This is not to argue that unemployment is *necessary* to ensure work effort; indeed unemployment heightens fear and brings demoralization, which serve to undermine it, and different market economies have drawn on mechanisms other than unemployment.

The factors which influence investment and thereby the size of the capital stock (such as profitability and capacity utilization) are generally rather different from the factors which determine the size of the work force (mainly demographic). From that crude observation, we could say that there is no particular reason to think that the capital stock will be adequate for the provision of full employment. There are rather limited opportunities, especially in the short run, for substitution between labour and capital. We would expect that after a period of prolonged slow growth (such as the past two decades) investment may have fallen short of what would be required to sustain full employment.

The pace of growth is generally seen as driven by the growth of demand, with supply (of labour, capital equipment and so on) adjusting to the growth of demand. The effective supply of labour can vary through changes in labour force participation rates, training and skill acquisition and movement of workers from areas of disguised unemployment and low productivity. The amount of capital equipment is determined through the cumulative effect of investment.

The foreign trade position can constrain the rate of growth, in that a growing deficit will emerge if there is a tendency for the growth of imports to exceed the growth of exports. When the (domestic) income elasticity of demand for imports is greater than the (world) income elasticity of demand for the country's exports, then the maintenance of a non-exploding trade deficit requires that the domestic growth rate is sufficiently below the world growth rate so that actual imports and exports grow in line with one another (McCombie and Thirlwall 1997). One policy implication which can be drawn is that continuing growth of output requires growth of exports, and supply-side policies (such as industrial policy) can be required to ensure the production of goods and services for which there is a strong export demand.

The general Post Keynesian approach would be based on the view that the creation of high levels of aggregate demand is necessary for the achievement of full employment. The creation of high levels of aggregate demand can proceed directly through higher government expenditure and/or lower taxation, indirectly through the stimulation of investment and the redistribution of income towards higher spending groups, and through the encouragement of institutional arrangements which are conducive to high levels of demand. But a high level of aggregate demand is a necessary, though not sufficient, condition. Policies to ensure adequate capacity, the creation of a low-inflation environment, an equitable distribution of productive activity and a sustainable balance of trade position are also required (Arestis and Sawyer 1998).

MALCOLM SAWYER

See also:

Balance-of-payments-constrained Economic Growth; Bretton Woods; Budget Deficits; Endogenous Money; Exchange Rates; Fiscal Policy; Full Employment; Monetary Policy; Taxation; Tax-based Incomes Policy; Tobin Tax; Unemployment.

References

Arestis, P. and M. Sawyer (1998), 'Keynesian policies for the new millennium', *Economic Journal*, **108** (446), 181–95.
Davidson, P. (1992), 'Reforming the world's money', *Journal of Post Keynesian Economics*, **15** (2), 153–79.
Kalecki, M. (1943), 'Political aspects of full employment', *Political Quarterly*, **14** (4), 322–31.
Kalecki, M. (1944), 'Three ways to full employment', in Oxford University Institute of Statistics, *The Economics of Full Employment*, Oxford: Blackwell, pp. 39–58.
Keynes, J.M. (1980), *The Collected Writings of John Maynard Keynes. Volume XXVII. Activities 1940–1946. Shaping the Post-War World: Employment and Commodities*, London: Macmillan for the Royal Economic Society.
Lerner, A. (1943), 'Functional finance and the Federal debt', *Social Research*, **10** (1), 38–51 (reprinted in W. Mueller (ed.), *Readings in Macroeconomics*, New York: Holt, Rinehart & Winston, pp. 353–60; citations refer to the reprint).
McCombie, J.S.L. and A.P. Thirlwall (1997), 'The dynamic Harrod foreign trade multiplier and the demand-oriented approach to economic growth: an evaluation', *International Review of Applied Economics*, **11** (1), 5–26.
Wray, L.R. (1998), *Understanding Modern Money: The Key to Full Employment and Price Stability*, Cheltenham, UK and Northampton, MA, USA: Edward Elgar.

Effective Demand

Effective demand is a concept of central importance in Post Keynesian economics. The principle of effective demand states that the level of economic activity – that is, aggregate nominal income and employment – is determined by the level of effective demand, which is, in turn, determined by the

106 *Effective demand*

conjunction of aggregate supply and demand conditions. Aggregate demand conditions are held to play a leading role in this relationship.

The determination of effective demand, and hence the levels of nominal income and employment, results from the interaction of aggregate supply and demand functions that describe relationships between levels of employment and levels of business proceeds. Business proceeds constitute receipts from the sale of final goods and services net of an allowance for the use of capital equipment and thus represent, in the aggregate, the total nominal income of the community. The aggregate supply function describes a relationship between expected proceeds and the levels of employment that firms are willing to offer on the basis of these expectations. The aggregate supply function, then, suggests that firms base their employment offers on the value of goods and services that they think they can sell. Not surprisingly, as expected proceeds rise, so, too, do employment offers (see schedule Z, Figure 6). The aggregate supply function so described can be formulated on the basis of either Marshallian or Kaleckian microfoundations. In the first case, firms equate short-run price expectations with the marginal costs of production in order to determine the profit-maximizing level of output, on which employment offers are then based. In the second case, firms set prices as a mark-up over average costs, with both expected proceeds and consequent employment offers then determined by the volume of output that firms expect to sell at these prices (Asimakopulos 1991, pp. 53–7).

The aggregate demand function, meanwhile, describes a relationship between received proceeds and the levels of employment that generate these receipts. It therefore relates aggregate expenditures in the economy to the level of employment, which is a determinant of household income. According to the aggregate demand function, higher levels of employment are associated with higher household income, and hence higher aggregate expenditures and business proceeds (see schedule D, Figure 6). As this description suggests, some of the components of aggregate demand are endogenous – that is, influenced by the levels of income and employment that they, in turn, help to determine. However, other components of aggregate demand are autonomous – that is, determined independently of the levels of income and employment.

Two important properties of the aggregate demand function mean that it will not, in general, be identical to the aggregate supply function. The first concerns the behaviour of endogenous components of aggregate demand. Although the principle of effective demand associates an increase in employment with both an increase in output and an increase in expenditures, the additional expenditures associated with any increase in employment are understood to constitute only a fraction of the value of the

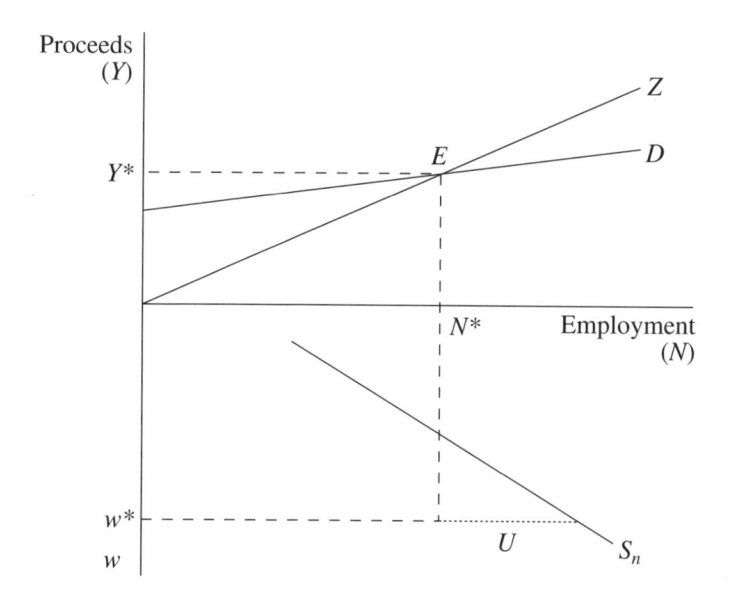

Effective demand 107

Figure 6 The principle of effective demand and labour market outcomes

Key

D = aggregate demand function
Z = aggregate supply function
E = point of effective demand
Y = business proceeds (aggregate income)
N = employment
w = real wage
U = involuntary unemployment
S_n = labour supply

additional output (and hence income) this increase in employment generates. This is due to Keynes's 'fundamental psychological law', according to which the marginal propensity to consume out of additional income is less than one (Keynes 1936, p. 96). Hence the slope of the aggregate demand function differs from (specifically, is smaller than) that of the aggregate supply function, as illustrated in Figure 6.

The second important property of the aggregate demand function concerns the behaviour of autonomous components of aggregate demand. According to the principle of effective demand, autonomous expenditures are genuinely independent of endogenous expenditures, so that there is no automatic tendency for variations in the latter to be offset by changes in the former. This can be understood most simply in the context of a closed economy with no active government sector, in which case it reduces to the proposition that saving does not create investment. This is so for two reasons. First, in a money-using economy, saving does not in and of itself constitute a current demand for goods, as it does in a barter economy. In other words, saving is not identical to investment. (Indeed, saving does not even constitute a demand for consumption goods in some specific future period. In an environment of uncertainty, a decision to avoid commitment to goods and services in the present – that is, to save – represents an indefinite postponement of expenditure.)

Second, saving – considered now as distinct from investment – has no direct impact on the rate of interest, to which investment is, in principle, sensitive. Hence saving cannot automatically create offsetting investment expenditures through variations in the interest rate. An important feature of the principle of effective demand, then, is its treatment of the interest rate as a monetary variable, the determination of which is relatively autonomous from the income determination process. This autonomy is achieved in Keynes (1936) by the liquidity preference theory of the interest rate, and in contemporary Post Keynesian theory by central bank determination of short-term interest rates in an endogenous money environment. Note that the interest rate need not be *absolutely* autonomous from the income generation process. It is quite possible for changes in income to have some impact on the interest rate via changes in liquidity preference or via a central bank reaction function. Neither alters the operation of the principle of effective demand, however. What ultimately emerges from this analysis is a system in which the level of income (and by extension, employment) rather than the interest rate is the key adjustment variable responsible for equating investment and saving, according to a strict causal schema in which changes in investment spending cause (via their impact on the level of income) changes in saving (Amadeo 1989, pp. 1–2).

The level of effective demand is determined by the point of effective demand, at which the aggregate supply and demand functions intersect (point E in Figure 6). The proceeds resulting from this effective demand and the associated volume of employment constitute the economy's equilibrium levels of income and employment. The point of effective demand is an equilibrium in the sense that, at this point, the expected proceeds necessary to encourage firms to offer a particular level of employment (as determined by the aggregate supply function) are exactly equal to received proceeds at this level of employment (as determined by the aggregate demand function). However, the importance attached to historical time and uncertainty in Post Keynesian economics necessitate that care is taken when interpreting the precise nature of this equilibrium relative to equilibrium constructs found in other approaches to economics (Kregel 1976).

Several salient features of the principle of effective demand as described

Effective demand 109

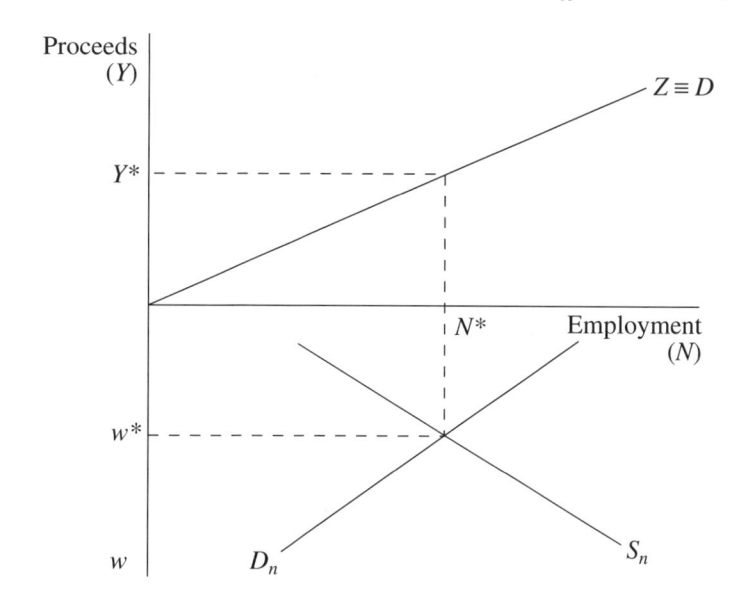

[Figure: diagram showing Proceeds (Y) axis with Y* marked, Z≡D line rising from origin, N* on Employment (N) axis, and below the horizontal axis labour market diagram with w* on w axis, D_n and S_n curves intersecting]

Key

D = aggregate demand function
Z = aggregate supply function
Y = business proceeds (aggregate income)
N = employment
w = real wage
S_n = labour supply
D_n = labour demand

Figure 7   The special case of Say's Law

above are worthy of note. First, because the aggregate supply function will, in general, coincide with the aggregate demand function at only one level of income and employment, the principle of effective demand refutes Say's Law, according to which supply always creates its own demand. Say's Law is, in fact, revealed to be a special case, in which the aggregate demand and supply functions are identical. In this special case, the resulting indeterminacy in the levels of income and employment is resolved by the equation of labour supply and demand – so that variations in the real wage, by establishing a market-clearing level of employment, determine aggregate income (see Figure 7). In general, however, the aggregate supply and demand functions will coincide at only one level of employment, at which point the level of income and the value of the real wage are also determined (the real wage may, in fact, be constant along the aggregate supply function if the latter is based on Kaleckian microfoundations, but will systematically decline as the

110 *Effective demand*

level of employment rises if the aggregate supply function is based on Marshallian microfoundations). Whether or not the level of employment and real wage so established corresponds to a point on the economy's labour supply schedule is an open question; in general it will not, and the resulting deficient demand for labour will give rise to involuntary unemployment (see Figure 6). In the general case, then, variations in effective demand cause changes in income, employment and the real wage (to the extent that this is non-constant), and there is no automatic tendency for the labour market to clear.

Implicit in the contrast above is the observation that, according to the principle of effective demand, the volumes of employment and production depend on firms' anticipations of the value of output that they can sell, rather than on the equation of the marginal physical product and marginal disutility of labour. This draws attention to a number of other salient features of the principle of effective demand: the importance that it attaches to the goods market rather than the labour market as the proximate determinant of the scale of economic activity; the central role it ascribes to firms in actively setting employment and output, rather than passively responding to labour market outcomes; and the epistemological significance of explaining economic activity in terms of *expected* future sales revenues rather than the *known* productive capacities of factors of production.

Several important controversies surround the principle of effective demand. In the first place, and partly as a result of Keynes's original exposition, the terms 'aggregate demand' and 'effective demand' are frequently confused, and there is a long-standing debate as to whether the aggregate demand function describes the proceeds *actually* received by firms at different levels of employment, or the proceeds they *expect* to receive at these various levels of employment. As regards the first of these issues, it should be clear from the foregoing discussion that aggregate demand is a *schedule* (which describes the relationship between levels of employment and received proceeds), whereas effective demand is a *point* (specifically, the point where the aggregate demand and supply functions coincide) (see also Chick 1983, pp. 64–5). As regards the second issue, the aggregate demand function can be thought of as describing either actual or expected magnitudes. Indeed, it is useful to think of two different aggregate demand functions, one describing actual and the other expected proceeds (Amadeo 1989) – although particular microfoundations are required in order to generate an expected aggregate demand function that is upward-sloping (see for example, Asimakopulos, 1991, pp. 43–4). Where the expected aggregate demand function intersects the aggregate supply function determines the level of employment within any production period; where the actual aggregate demand function intersects the aggregate supply function determines the equilibrium position described earlier, at which expected sales proceeds equal proceeds actually received. This equilibrium will actually be achieved when the expected and actual aggregate demand functions and the aggregate supply function all coincide at a single level of employment (see Figure 8).

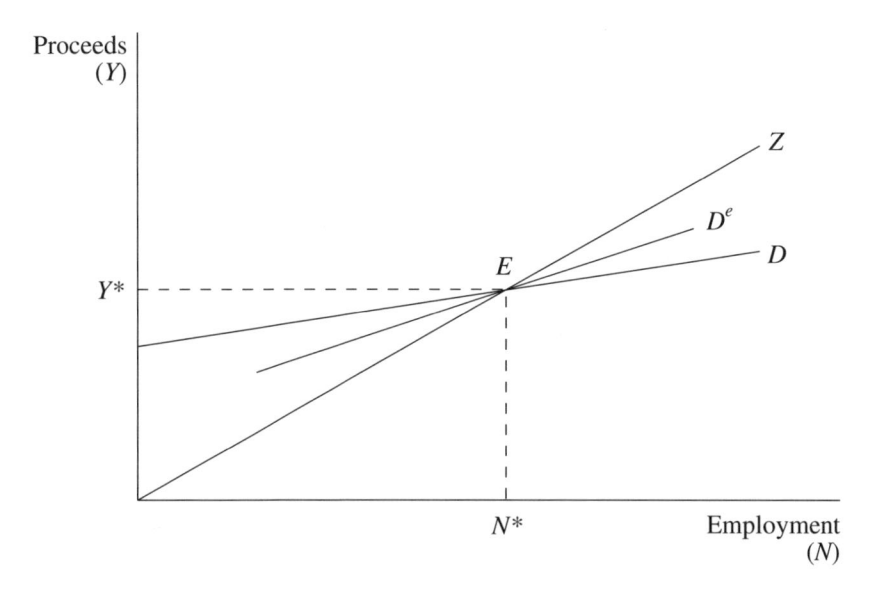

Key

D = actual aggregate demand function
Z = aggregate supply function
E = point of effective demand
Y = business proceeds (aggregate income)
N = employment
D^e = expected aggregate demand funtion

Figure 8   The interaction of expected and actual aggregate demand, and aggregate supply

More recently, Pasinetti has argued that standard expositions of the *principle* of effective demand only succeed in identifying the concept of a *point* of effective demand, rather than anything meriting description as a principle. Pasinetti (1997, pp. 98–100) identifies the *principle* of effective demand with the proposition that changes in demand result in changes in output (at least until full capacity is reached), and argues that this principle operates at a deeper or more fundamental level than is suggested by the behavioural relations commonly used to describe a point of effective demand (Pasinetti 1997, p. 100; 2001, pp. 386–9). That the principle of effective demand is associated with the proposition that macroeconomic activity is demand determined is not controversial. But Pasinetti's suggestion that this principle can be articulated at a 'more fundamental' level of analysis than that associated with specific behavioural relations and a particular institutional context is contentious. It raises the issue of methodological divisions within Post Keynesian economics, between those who favour a long-period method of analysis in which certain 'core' relationships obtain independently of short-term events (in the determination of which institutions *do* play a part), and those who argue that there are no long-period positions defined and reached independently of the sequence of (behaviourally and institutionally specific) short-run outcomes leading up to them. It is not surprising, then, to find critics of Pasinetti's position reasserting the fundamentally behavioural and institutionally specific nature of the principle of effective demand. Davidson (2001, p. 393), for example, defines the *principle* of effective demand as the proposition that the behavioural determinants of the aggregate demand and supply functions differ in the institutionally specific context of a money-using economy.

MARK SETTERFIELD

See also:

Employment; Expectations; Investment; Keynes's *General Theory*; Liquidity Preference; Rate of Interest; Saving; Say's Law; Sraffian Economics; Unemployment.

References

Amadeo, E. (1989), *Keynes's Principle of Effective Demand*, Aldershot: Edward Elgar.
Asimakopulos, A. (1991), *Keynes's General Theory and Accumulation*, Cambridge: Cambridge University Press.
Chick, V. (1983), *Macroeconomics After Keynes*, Cambridge, MA: MIT Press.
Davidson, P. (2001), 'The principle of effective demand: another view', *Journal of Post Keynesian Economics*, **23** (3), 391–409.
Keynes, J.M. (1936), *The General Theory of Employment, Interest and Money*, London: Macmillan.
Kregel, J. (1976), 'Economic methodology in the face of uncertainty: the modelling methods of Keynes and the Post Keynesians', *Economic Journal*, **86** (342), 209–25.
Pasinetti, L. (1997), 'The principle of effective demand', in G.C. Harcourt and P.A. Riach (eds), *A 'Second Edition' of The General Theory, Volume 1*, London: Routledge, pp. 93–104.
Pasinetti, L. (2001), 'The principle of effective demand and its relevance in the long run', *Journal of Post Keynesian Economics*, **23** (3), 383–90.

Employment

Employment is determined by the interaction of demand and supply within the labour market. The Keynesian and Post Keynesian emphasis has by and large been on variations in labour demand as an explanation for variations in employment and more particularly unemployment. Even within the neo-classical model, given an upward-sloping labour supply curve – rather than a vertical one – a shift to the left in the labour demand function will cause a reduction in employment. But it will not necessarily cause an increase in unemployment in excess of the natural rate. In order to explain why there is such a linkage, Post Keynesians appeal to inertia in the wage rate which prevents labour market clearing. This is where much of the research in labour economics has been. Yet it is clear from this brief synopsis that with respect to employment *per se* there are at least two other issues of concern: the magnitude of the slope of the labour supply curve and variations in the labour supply function itself.

Explanations of the failure of the labour market to clear centre around two distinct concepts which differ in the time frame of their impact. First, there are those theories which relate primarily to the stickiness of nominal wages. These theories, such as implicit contracts and menu costs, explain why the labour market is slow to adjust to demand and supply shocks, thus generating 'short-term' unemployment. Second, there are those theories such as insider–outsider, efficiency wages and hysteresis, which predict long-term deviations in the real wage from the market-clearing level. We examine these in turn.

Changing prices, including wages, in response to every change in economic conditions is a costly business and firms find it optimal to limit this process. With wages this is reflected with an annual pay award, which is common in Britain, while in the US a three-year pay agreement is not uncommon. In this case the firm will respond to changes in demand by changing output and employment rather than wages. The work on menu costs is associated with Gregory Mankiw (1985). George Akerlof and Janet Yellen, Michael Parkin, Julio Rotenberg, and Olivier Blanchard and Nobuhiro Kiyotaki have also made significant contributions.

Implicit contract theory involves long-term relationships between firms and workers which it is not optimal to break for short-term considerations. If workers know that they will be employed by the firm for a prolonged period then they are prepared to accept a fixed wage lower than their marginal productivity in return for this guaranteed stability. The reason why workers and firms might prefer implicit contracts with relatively fixed wages is partly a transfer of risk from the more risk-averse individual to the less risk-averse firm. The firm is acting as an insurer against fluctuations in their income attributable to the business cycle. A seminal paper is by Baily (1974). Other important contributions include Costas Azariadis and Edmund Phelps.

A slightly different concept is that of 'efficiency wages' (Solow 1979; see also Carl Shapiro, Akerlof and Yellen). The central assumption is that there is a benefit as well as a cost to a firm of paying a higher wage. There are several reasons why this might be the case. First, a higher wage can lead to a healthier, better-nourished and therefore more productive workforce. Second, a higher wage can increase loyalty among the workforce and hence induce greater effort. Third, higher wages can help in monitoring workers' effort in situations where this is imperfectly observable. Where the wage is equal to the market-clearing wage and where there are relatively abundant job opportunities, workers are indifferent to the possibility of losing their jobs and hence might be tempted to shirk. Paying higher wages will make workers keener to retain their well-paid jobs. A variation on this concept is linked to the difficulties associated with the hiring of workers. Given that not all workers are of equal ability, a firm wishing to hire high-quality labour may find itself frequently disappointed and often faced with the cost of dismissing unsatisfactory workers and rehiring others. To minimize such costs the firm may pay above the market wage, reasoning that workers know their own abilities and poor workers will recognize that this is a job that they will soon be fired from and hence not apply. This is therefore an equilibrium concept; it does not explain sticky wages *per se*, it explains why wages may be set above workers' marginal productivity due to informational asymmetry. It does, however, indicate that employment will be lower than would be the case without this form of market imperfection.

Hysteresis as applied to unemployment is often traced to the influential paper by Blanchard and Summers (1986), although in reality the term 'hysteresis' can be traced all the way back to Joseph Schumpeter at least. Hysteresis challenges the natural rate assumption of neoclassical economics in arguing that even in the long run there are factors which may prevent unemployment returning to its equilibrium level following a (deep) recession. First, a prolonged spell of unemployment might see a deterioration of the workers' skills, thus making re-entry into the labour force more difficult. Second, it may induce a change in attitudes to work and reduce the incentive to find employment. Another possible explanation for 'observed hysteresis' is entry into the hidden economy as the formal economy declines, with entrants reluctant subsequently to exit when given the chance. Thus effectively in economics hysteresis is a supply-side concept; it indicates that following a recession the labour supply curve will shift to the left and will shift back only slowly, if at all. Technically the implication of this is that employment is a random walk with drift, that is, the change in employment is equal to a constant term plus a stochastic, white noise error term. Post Keynesians are sometimes categorized as being non-technical. This is partly a consequence of their belief that theory must be realistic, and mathematical models inevitably involve simplification. Yet the econometric work aimed at determining whether a series is hysteretic, which is possibly linked to its stationarity properties, has made sophisticated use of recent advances in econometrics. This is also evident in other areas of analysis too.

The final approach we shall consider is that related to insiders–outsiders and trade union bargaining (McDonald and Solow 1981). This centres around the concept that those who are already employed (insiders) have more say in wage bargaining than those out of work (outsiders). Often the former are represented by a trade union, which bargains mainly with their interests in mind. The fact that lower wages would help the outsiders does not figure prominently in this decision. This leads to some predictable and testable outcomes, such as the greatest upward impact on wages being in countries with strong trade unions and decentralized bargaining.

In 1960, employment in the US totalled 74 million people. By 2000 this had risen to nearly 140 million. The bulk of this increase came from an increase in the working population aged between 15 and 64 – which increased from 108.4 million to almost 180 million. However, another significant factor was the increase in participation rates, particularly female participation rates. But the market dynamics are complex, and there is a considerable literature which links the decline in the wages of low-skilled men in the 1980s with this rise in female participation – which should generate a reduction in male labour supply. What is beyond dispute is that this rise in female participation rates has been offset to some extent by an even sharper decline in the participation rate of older men, both through a trend to early retirement and a reduction in men working after the retirement age of 65. The impact of these latter changes is mostly to have shifted the labour supply function inwards.

The second point we turn to is the possibility of hysteresis in the demand curve for labour. By this is meant that the relation of this demand function to aggregate demand for goods and services may shift following a recession. In other words it is time dependent. This argument is linked to changes in the level of capital following a recession, through either capital scrapping or the reduction in investment, even in some cases replacement investment. Hence following the recession the aggregate supply curve shifts to the left, and an increase in the aggregate demand for goods will be met by increased inflation and imports rather than increased output and employment (Hudson 1999). In terms of the labour market, the demand function for labour itself becomes sticky. In this respect it has been argued that US bankruptcy laws, which place much more emphasis on the retention of capital and firms as going concerns, are better for long-term employment prospects than European bankruptcy laws.

In approaching this survey I have, in common with most of the textbooks, extended the analysis to include all theorists who reject in part the neoclassical paradigm as applied to the labour market, even though they might not describe themselves as Post Keynesians. This leads us into including in the ambit of this entry theories which Keynes himself would have clearly rejected as irrelevant, and in some cases actually did so. Thus the insider–outsider theory is arguably simply a new bottle for the old wine of labour market clearing being frustrated by union power – a wine which was flowing steadily in the 1920s and 1930s and which Keynes had difficulty swallowing.

Philip Arestis suggests that there are three traditions to Post Keynesian analysis: (i) the importance of effective demand failure, (ii) the role of uncertainty and (iii) the role of institutions, particularly in dealing with the problem of bounded rationality. The principle of effective demand, the concept that demand constraints are the dominant factor in explaining variations in output, is the backbone of the Post Keynesian approach. But to understand why this leads to unemployment – rather than simply to a decline in employment – we need to appeal to the other two concepts. Arestis has also argued that social classes are essential to the second of these approaches, which is essentially Marxian, in adapting Marx's reproduction system to solve the realization problem, and that the third approach is also based upon the dynamic and power/class struggle of economic systems, in which income distribution plays a key role. This may well be so, yet equally concepts such as efficiency wages, implicit contracts, even hysteresis have merits in their own right which appeal and inform beyond Post Keynesians.

It is also noteworthy, perhaps, that in areas where the spirit of the traditions of Karl Marx, Thorstein Veblen and Michał Kalecki might be thought to have particular relevance, for example, labour force participation and the shadow economy, Post Keynesians have largely been absent. Thus, for example, with respect to household production functions the neoclassical school has been given virtually a free run. This is a reflection of the fact that to a considerable extent the Post Keynesian analysis of employment is in fact an analysis of unemployment. This is unfortunate: knowledge is forged in the heat of debate. Post Keynesians should have the confidence and the curiosity to expand their horizons.

JOHN HUDSON

See also:

Effective Demand; Full Employment; Income Distribution; New Keynesian Economics; Wages and Labour Markets.

References

Baily, M.N. (1974), 'Wages and employment under uncertain demand', *Review of Economic Studies*, **41** (1), 7–50.

Blanchard, O.J. and L.H. Summers (1986), 'Hysteresis and the European unemployment problem', *NBER Macroeconomics Annual*, **1**, 15–78.
Hudson, J. (1999), 'A generalized theory of output determination', *Journal of Post Keynesian Economics*, **21** (4), 663–78.
Mankiw, N.G. (1985), 'Small menu costs and large business cycles: a macroeconomic model of monopoly', *Quarterly Journal of Economics*, **100** (2), 529–37.
McDonald, I.M. and R.M. Solow (1981), 'Wage bargaining and employment', *American Economic Review*, **71** (5), 896–908.
Solow, R.M. (1979), 'Another possible source of wage stickiness', *Journal of Macroeconomics*, **1** (1), 79–82.

Endogenous Money

Money may be defined as the asset generally accepted as the means of payment and medium of exchange. The particular asset that is conventionally bestowed with general acceptability has changed enormously over time. For conceptual clarity concerning supply characteristics, it is necessary to distinguish commodity, fiat and credit money.

A wide variety of commodities have been used as money, items as diverse as shells, beads, rice, salt and cattle. The general acceptability in exchange of commodities such as gold and silver evolved gradually over prehistory. Both possessed properties attractive for a money asset, homogeneity, durability, divisibility, a high value to weight ratio, and reproducibility under sharply increasing costs, so their short-run supply was broadly given. 'Money does not grow on trees.' Precious metals are assets to their holders and liabilities to no-one. Commodity money is a physical asset and not a financial claim.

Fiat money is a financial asset, the non-interest-bearing debt of the government. It derives its value because it has been declared legal tender in settlement of debts and taxes, by government fiat. Once the general acceptability of precious metals was established, their main drawback was difficulty in verifying their value. The development of fiat money substituted a difficult to counterfeit certification of value for a full-bodied metal coin.

Since their creation lies completely outside the lending and borrowing process, the quantity of commodity or fiat money denotes nothing about the outstanding volume of credit. As a result the supply of commodity and fiat money can be assumed exogenous, and independent of changes in the demand for money. It appeared reasonable to assume that, in response to a change in the supply of money, prices and incomes would adjust until the exogenous stock was again willingly held. This was the original basis for the 'Quantity Theory of Money', which maintained that changes in the quantity of money were responsible for changes in the level of prices and money income.

Banking originated when Italian goldsmiths first took the strictly illegal step of lending out someone else's gold. The crucial banking innovation was the making of bank IOUs payable to the 'bearer' rather than to a named individual. This led to the discovery that, so long as public confidence in the liquidity of deposits was maintained, a banking house of sufficient repute could dispense with the issue of coin for most transactions, and instead issue its own 'bank notes'.

Credit money is the liability of the issuing bank, and is backed by borrowers' liabilities (IOUs) in the bank's possession. The supply of credit money varies with changes in the demand for bank credit. Deposits are continuously created and destroyed through the granting and repayment of loans. Credit money is never in excess supply, providing the public remains confident that all deposits will be redeemed in fiat money on demand.

Unfortunately the process by which credit money is supplied is somewhat non-transparent. The banking system operates under strict rules imposed by the central bank. In most economies the central bank requires commercial banks to maintain a minimum required ratio of reserves to deposits. This must be complied with. It thus appears that the supply of credit money is controlled by the total volume of bank reserves supplied by the central bank.

Mainstream theory postulates that the total supply of bank deposits is governed by the total quantity of reserves made available by the central bank. The central bank's total liabilities (outstanding notes and coin and bank reserves held with the central bank) are termed the 'high-powered base'. Since the base bears a constant ratio to the stock of money ($m = M/B$) it is believed to support a 'multiple' quantity of deposits. The change in bank loans (ΔL) and in the money supply (ΔM) may be written as a multiple 'm' of the change in the high-powered base (ΔB). 'Reserves cause deposits': $m\Delta B \rightarrow \Delta L \rightarrow \Delta M$.

But this equation does not explain how credit money is supplied. It is simply a rewriting of the identity ($m \equiv \Delta M/\Delta B$). Identities say nothing about the direction of causality. Post Keynesians maintain that causality goes from changes in bank loans (ΔL) to changes in the money supply (ΔM) to changes in the base (ΔB): $\Delta L \rightarrow \Delta M \rightarrow \Delta B$ ('Loans cause deposits').

The mainstream view that central banks control the supply of money hides the fact that banks are essentially retailers of credit, not portfolio managers. Banks sell credit, and create deposits in the act of making loans. Like other retailers, the quantity of credit they sell depends on demand. Post Keynesians substantiate their theory of 'reverse causality', that the direction of causality goes from changes in loans to changes in the base, so that the supply of credit money is endogenous and credit driven, as follows. (For alternative but similar Post Keynesian explanations, see Lavoie 1992; Moore 1988, 2003; Rochon 2001; and Wray 1990.)

Credit money evolved from commodity and fiat money in parallel with the development of capitalism and the private ownership of the means of production. It was no accident that commercial banking first evolved in Renaissance Italy, in response to the demand for working capital by early Italian merchant traders. Business demand for working capital was the major force behind the development of commercial banking.

Production takes time. In market economies production costs must be incurred and paid before the receipt of sales proceeds. Business costs of production constitute business demand for working capital, for which firms must somehow find financing. The owners of firms bear all the risk of production under uncertainty. They must pay out money to purchase productive factors *before* they receive profits from expected future sales.

Credit is demanded by firms to finance increases in the demand for working capital during the production-sales period. Increases in the volume of output require proportional increases in working capital to finance the higher value of inventories of goods in process.

The acceptability of bank deposits as a payments instrument depends on the public's confidence that deposits are always exchangeable for legal tender on demand. Banks volitionally demand cash reserves to maintain the general acceptability of deposits. Required reserve ratios above the ratio of reserves to deposits that banks desire to maintain on liquidity grounds act as a tax on banking, impairing the efficiency of bank intermediation and their international competitiveness.

Banks are price setters and quantity takers in their lending and deposit markets. So long as they remain within their assigned overdraft ceiling, the amount of loans taken out is the decision of the borrower, not the bank. Firms borrow primarily to finance their demand for working capital, of which the largest component is the wage bill. Loans are repaid after firms receive their sales proceeds, the notion of the 'monetary circuit' (see Deleplace and Nell 1996 and Graziani 1989). An increase in the wage bill has a greater than unitary effect on total bank lending. Banks lend to households in addition to firms, and household borrowing is positively related to wage income.

The supply of credit money is endogenously credit driven. Banks only lend to borrowers whom they believe can repay their debts. Bank lending officers make a discretionary judgement of the maximum amount an individual borrower will be able to repay, based on their estimates of the borrower's three 'C's': collateral (liquid wealth), credit (pecuniary income) and character (borrowing history). They provide overdraft facilities (credit lines) up to this ceiling or limit.

When a banker makes a loan he or she credits the borrower's account. The supply of credit money responds to changes in the demand for bank credit. Bank loans operate like credit cards. Modern banks provide creditworthy borrowers with substantial overdraft facilities, and then make credit available on demand up to their credit limit. (The credit-utilization rate in developed economies fluctuates around 50 per cent; see Moore 1988, chapter 2.) Most poor households and small firms, and in developing economies the entire 'informal sector', are credit constrained. They form Keynes's 'perpetual fringe' of unsatisfied borrowers. Banks regard lending to them as too risky, so they receive no credit. Quantity rationing is inherent in credit markets.

For the banking system as a whole, total loans equal total deposits. But individual banks must match their supply of funds to their loan demand. Since the innovation of certificates of deposit (CDs), deficit banks are able to borrow funds directly from surplus banks in wholesale markets, reducing their demand to hold liquid reserves.

The conclusion that the money supply is credit driven is strongly supported empirically for many countries over different periods (see Moore 1988, chapter 9).

Mainstream theory regards the level of interest rates as determined by the real forces of supply and demand for loanable funds, and by wealth-holders' liquidity preferences. But in all modern economies the level of short-term interest rates is *exogenously* set by the central bank.

Cash reserves are supplied to the banking system as demanded by the central bank, in its role of residual supplier of system liquidity. It sets the interest rate at which it lends reserves to the banking system to realize its stabilization objectives. Central banks have great discretion over the level of interest rates they set, even in highly open economies. Only when the central bank adopts a fixed exchange rate regime does it lose its ability to set the short-term rate; the domestic rate then becomes equal to the foreign rate, set by the central bank of the largest foreign economy.

Central bank open-market operations provide the banking system with slightly less reserves than they are required to hold. In this manner it keeps banks 'in the Bank', and forces them to borrow reserves at the margin from the central bank. This enables the central bank to ensure that the overnight rate it charges the banking system for the loan of reserves, termed 'bank rate' in most countries, becomes the short-term market interest rate (in the US it is termed the 'federal funds' rate).

Banks administer their lending and deposit rates, and attempt to meet all loan demand that results, so long as borrowers remain within their assigned overdraft ceiling. Lending rates are set as a mark-up over the central bank's lending rate. The size of the mark-up depends on their market power in different markets, reflecting their estimate of the interest elasticity of the demand for credit. Administered lending and deposit rates are changed infrequently, and price leadership is common. Over the period between changes in bank rate, the supply of bank credit is horizontal, at the interest rate set exogenously by the central bank.

Changes in the short-term interest rate have become the central bank's chief exogenous policy instrument to achieve its stabilization goals. Short-term rates are varied procyclically over the business cycle, by an amount depending on the authorities' 'policy reaction function' (see Moore 2003), recently termed a 'Taylor Rule'.

Thus the supply of credit money is endogenously demand determined and credit driven. Loans create deposits, banks decide who is creditworthy, creditworthy borrowers decide on the amounts they wish to borrow, and in so doing determine the supply of credit money, and the central bank sets the short-term interest rate as its policy instrument. Purchasing goods and services with deposits transfers the ownership distribution of deposits among economic units, but does not change the quantity. Once created, deposits are always accepted, so long as they retain their general acceptability. Deposits are reduced only by encashment into currency, by the repayment of bank loans and by the scale of securities by the banking system. The volume of lending *by* the banking system determines the volume of lending *to* the banking system.

BASIL MOORE

See also:

Banking; Central Banks; Circuit Theory; Credit Rationing; Development Finance; Monetary Policy; Money; Rate of Interest.

References

Deleplace, G. and E. Nell (eds) (1996), *Money in Motion: The Post Keynesian and Circulation Approaches*, London: Macmillan.
Graziani, A. (1989), *The Theory of the Monetary Circuit*, London: Thames Papers in Political Economy.
Lavoie, M. (1992), *Foundations of Post-Keynesian Economic Analysis*, Aldershot, UK: Edward Elgar.
Moore, B.J. (1988), *Horizontalists and Verticalists: The Macro-economics of Credit Money*, New York: Cambridge University Press.
Moore, B.J. (2003), *Shaking the Invisible Hand: Complexity, Endogenous Money and Exogenous Interest Rates*, Cheltenham, UK, and Northampton, MA, USA: Edward Elgar.
Rochon, L.-P. (2001), *Credit, Interest Rates and the Open Economy: Essays on Horizontalism*, Cheltenham, UK, and Northampton, MA, USA: Edward Elgar.
Taylor, J. (1999), *Monetary Policy Rules*, Chicago: University of Chicago Press.
Wray, L.R. (1990), *Money and Credit in Capitalist Economies: The Endogenous Money Approach*, Aldershot, UK: Edward Elgar.

Environmental Economics

Over the past twenty years or so environmental economics from being a fringe activity has become one of the most active areas of economic research. (In this entry the term 'environmental economics' is used broadly, to include the closely related area of natural resource economics.) It has become a major, even dominating, influence within significant areas of policy debate, including momentous global issues such as climate change and biodiversity loss. Mainstream environmental economics is currently dominated by the neoclassical paradigm in the ways in which it formulates and analyses the two key areas with which it is concerned: the valuation of environmental assets and the design of policy instruments to manage those assets. These are bought together in the study of sustainable development: how is it to be defined and achieved, if, indeed it is desirable? Thus environmental economics is essentially a branch of applied welfare economics. In some respects, environmental economics represents a rather extreme interpretation of the neoclassical paradigm, with its belief in the possibility of extending, with reasonable reliability, individual valuations to all sorts of non-marketed 'commodities', with its definition of environmental problems as essentially flowing from market 'failures', and with its advocacy of the efficacy and desirability of incentive-based policy instruments to correct for these failures.

Partly due to its somewhat extravagant faith in the neoclassical paradigm and partly, also, because of the necessary interface between environmental economics and the natural sciences, mainstream environmental economics has not been without its critics. Some of this criticism is simply misplaced (for example, that environmental economics cannot properly account for the life cycle of products), and easily rebutted by any well-trained neoclassical economist. But some is fundamental. This is especially true of those criticisms which challenge the foundations of neoclassical approaches to the environment, and which thence seek alternative accounts of sustainability based on physical or natural processes intrinsic to the environment, such as energy usage (Georgescu-Roegen 1971) or biological resilience (Common and Perrings 1992). Some of these accounts aspire to create an entirely new form of economics based, for example, on a redefinition of the concept of scarcity or value.

Leaving this aside, for the moment, what is conspicuously lacking in the debate is a serious attempt to draw ideas from heterodox schools of thought *within* economics, broadly defined, in order to criticize and reformulate environmental economics. The only significant exceptions are as follows. First, some moves have been made to extend neo-Ricardian models of production and growth to incorporate some process-related natural resource and environmental components (Kurz and Salvadori 1995, chapter 12). Second, richer, psychologically-based or socially-embedded accounts of human behaviour have been drawn on to criticize the appropriateness of attempts to extend neoclassical valuation processes over non-market domains (Kahneman and Knetsch 1992; Sagoff 1988). However, beyond these, it seems obvious that Post Keynesian economics can provide insights which have the potential to provide a powerful critique of neoclassical environmental economics and pointers to a reformulation of the subject. This entry attempts to outline a few of these insights. It uses the term Post Keynesian economics in a comprehensive sense, so as to include and develop both the steps just mentioned, along with others. All this is tentative and very much represents work in progress.

In the neoclassical view, environmental problems are just one species of externality and are to be costed at the price which an efficient market would impute to them: they would not exist if markets were complete and in equilibrium. This seems to many to fail, in some sense, to grasp the real existence of environmental problems independent of their specification in an economic model. It might be a reason for adopting one of the alternative accounts, mentioned above, of what might be called environmentally-embedded sustainability in order to define the nature of environmental problems, with all the foundational issues thus entailed. The present entry proceeds more pragmatically, and attempts in part to formulate a debate between neoclassical and possible Post Keynesian perspectives on the environment.

Does the Post Keynesian approach encompass the concept of externalities? Presumably not. To use two (or three) arguments, which may or not be consistent with each other: what sense would the neoclassical notion of allocative efficiency make in, first, a (non-trivial) monetary economy where markets were necessarily incomplete or in continuous disequilibrium, or, second, in an economy where prices were (re)production prices, Sraffian or Kaleckian, and not indices of scarcity? To this it might be objected that neoclassical general equilibrium is an ideal-type construct which specifies the necessary conditions for allocative efficiency, and this normative status is untouched by Post Keynesian arguments. This raises deep questions about the nature of economic models, which are not pursued further here.

A Post Keynesian argument which appears more secure against this sort of objection might run as follows. The Post Keynesian perspective on the nature of prices would apply to the attempt to use supposedly allocatively efficient prices to value environmental assets and damage to them. In many, perhaps most, of the cases which are of most interest to environmental economists, there are no observable or even imputable prices of any sort to use in such valuations. One widely used procedure in such cases is to use the so-called 'contingent valuation method', eliciting prices by questioning people about their willingness to pay for environmental benefits or to accept losses. As noted above, this has provoked a variety of criticisms, partly because of what appear to be irreducible anomalies, but a Post Keynesian one might run along these lines. The answers given in contingent valuation surveys could represent an attempt by respondents to formulate a response based on the prices that people know in their everyday economic lives. So what if these prices are not, for one or other of the reasons given above, to be interpreted as meaningful indicators of underlying preferences and relative scarcities? We might ask: where does a person's notion of an appropriate price come from if not from social practice?

It is indisputable that many environmental problems, however defined, involve extended time horizons and extreme uncertainty, and that these are closely related. This is fertile territory for Post Keynesians. In mainstream environmental economics, time is routinely dealt with by discounting. This is a source of much criticism from environmentalists, for familiar practical and ethical reasons (Broome 1992). For Post Keynesians, similar arguments might be made as in the case of prices in general. In what sense can an efficient interest rate be defined bearing in mind, say, the capital controversies or the concept of the interest rate as an essentially monetary phenomenon? Here, an attempted neoclassical rebuttal would not be so convincing: the notion of an interest rate which somehow encapsulates intertemporal efficiency would be regarded by many Post Keynesians as simply meaningless. Needless to say, this is contentious.

In dealing with risk, standard environmental economics generally assumes a world of calculable probabilities. Post Keynesians would, of course, reject this in favour of radical uncertainty, which undoubtedly characterizes many environmental problems. Not only does this undermine the specifics of much environmental modelling, forecasting and management, but it also links with the foregoing questions to do with the nature of interest rates and prices so as to lend additional support to a more comprehensive critique of neoclassical environmental economics.

More positively, there is a need for a proper integration of natural resources and environmental assets into a well-formulated model of a monetary economy. Here Post Keynesians have a real chance to develop an innovative approach, perhaps building on an own-rates analysis.

The standard neoclassical model of efficient resource extraction relies on asset valuations based on arbitrage across asset returns. Financial instruments are introduced as simple comparator assets. A Post Keynesian would regard this as a quite inappropriate way to capture the essential characteristics of a monetary economy.

Sustainability is a highly debatable concept. Its status within neoclassical environmental economics is not entirely clear: it is essentially a side condition, rather than intrinsic to the logic of the model. At all events, the core of the concept is that some measure of welfare is bounded from below over time. This is often expressed in terms of maintaining an appropriate aggregate capital stock. Welfare is ultimately dependent on the return to this stock. The capital stock is very broadly defined, to include natural resource and environmental assets, alongside physical, human and even social capital. It should be noted that this framework is very widely used, even by those who are dismissive of neoclassical environmental economics. Indeed, one of the more common *mistaken* criticisms of environmental economics is that it does not use a comprehensive enough definition of capital. (This needs to be distinguished from the criticism that the market-based values used in aggregation are inappropriate.) A Post Keynesian would argue, instead, that such aggregation procedures are inherently flawed. There is a need, however, to explicitly extend the so-called 'Cambridge critique' to encompass natural resources and environmental capitals. In addition, the problems, already discussed, with assigning allocatively efficient prices to the components of such capital stocks, and uncertainties in future stocks, would be further ingredients in a comprehensive critique.

Many of the mainstream accounts of sustainability-as-maintaining-aggregate-capital strengthen the criterion by requiring some individual components of the aggregate to be maintained as well, on the grounds that the weaker criterion overestimates the possibilities of substitution within the economy, though others are more sanguine. A Post Keynesian would presumably have no problem with models of production that assume limited substitutability. But introducing it as an assumption does raise questions about the coherence of the neoclassical model of sustainability, which do not seem to be very clearly appreciated.

In understanding the possibilities for long-run sustainability, an area which needs further exploration is the integration of natural resource and environmental assets into growth models, especially those with endogenous innovation (Aghion and Howitt 1998, chapter 5). Some of the newer work on endogenous innovation and growth has strong similarities, in some respects, with Kaldorian models, but otherwise relies on questionable neoclassical modelling of representative agents. One particular aspect that has barely been investigated, which again has a strong Kaldorian flavour, is the relationship between environmental performance and the sectoral and spatial structure of the economy. What are the relative natural resource and pollution intensities of production and consumption processes in the primary sector, in manufacturing and in services, and at various population densities? Both innovation and structure have acquired crucial significance in evaluating the sustainability of the new information economy, and Post Keynesian, and especially Kaldorian, approaches would seem to have much potential here.

ADRIAN WINNETT

See also:

Capital Theory; Kaldorian Economics; Production; Rate of Interest; Time in Economic Theory; Uncertainty.

References

Aghion, P. and P. Howitt (1998), *Endogenous Growth Theory*, Cambridge, MA: MIT Press.
Broome, J. (1992), *Counting the Cost of Global Warming*, Cambridge, UK: White Horse Press.
Common, M.S. and S.C. Perrings (1992), 'Towards an ecological economics of sustainability', *Ecological Economics*, **6** (1), 7–31.
Georgescu-Roegen, N. (1971), *The Entropy Law and the Economic Process*, Cambridge: MA: Harvard University Press.
Kahneman, D and J.L. Knetsch (1992), 'Valuing public goods: the purchase of moral satisfaction', *Journal of Environmental Economics and Management*, **22** (1), 57–70.
Kurz, H.D. and N. Salvadori (1995), *Theory of Production: A Long-period Analysis*, Cambridge, UK: Cambridge University Press.
Sagoff, M. (1988), *The Economy of the Earth*, Cambridge, UK: Cambridge University Press.

Equilibrium and Non-equilibrium

Three facts relating to economic analysis in general are relevant in understanding equilibrium and non-equilibrium. First, the primary purpose of economic analysis is to explain real economic phenomena (prediction, of course, may be a byproduct). Second, one common method by which economic explanation proceeds is through the construction of economic models. And third, model building necessitates abstracting from reality and concentrating on the 'smallest' number of forces that adequately represent what is actually happening. In this context, consider the notion of equilibrium first.

Equilibrium is a feature of a model. A collection of variables is in equilibrium if they are 'at rest'. That is, all forces or laws in operation that might influence the values those variables take on balance each other out and there is no tendency for the variable values to change. The idea of equilibrium was imported from the physical sciences where it was (and is) applied with respect to the properties of physical, nonsentient objects. In the economic context, the focus of equilibrium has been, and continues to be, on human action derived from mental decision processes. Thus equilibrium obtains when no decision maker, to the extent that his or her action has been appropriately captured in the model, has even the slightest motivation to change any plan or action.

Traditionally, the notion of equilibrium has been one of the most, if not the most important organizing feature of economic analysis. In many instances, either equilibrium in a model is thought to prevail, or it is taken to be the end towards which everything is moving. Explanation based on the former often interprets observations of the real economic world as equilibria. Thus, for example, each price–quantity data point arising in an isolated market may be construed as located at the intersection of the demand and supply curves assumed to be in play at the moment it was observed, and may therefore be explained as the outcome of the interaction of the forces of demand and supply. Explanation founded on the latter frequently interprets observations as lying on a time path that converges to equilibrium, as is the case when, say, cobweb models with stable equilibria are taken as the representation of reality. From either perspective the end result (here, the equilibrium), is independent of the movement towards it (should that movement be relevant).

Since the presence of equilibrium requires no change in the variable values at equilibrium, and since change, or a lack thereof, can only be discerned over time, the idea of time is fundamental to that of equilibrium. Moreover, the nature of the concept of time employed has to be such as to make it possible to recognize circumstances in which change in the relevant variable values is absent. The notion of time usually invoked for this purpose is called 'logical time'. Logical time merely provides a way of ordering events without reference to the actual passing of time. Although, in this manner of representing reality, past events come before present events and present events come before future events, the different possibilities and significance for the spacing of those events, along with the fact that past, present and future events all have different qualities in relation to human abilities to know and experience them, are ignored. All events (past, present and future) are assumed to be completely knowable at least probabilistically. This means that plans can be assumed to be carried out on the basis of correct knowledge and expectations that will, on average, turn out to be correct. As a consequence, it is possible to envisage behavioural and expectational variable values that reflect realized plans and hence do not require alteration as the system represented by the model moves across past, present and future states. Logical time, then, along with the requirement of full knowledge that goes with it, is essential to the traditional concept of equilibrium as described above. In this form, equilibrium has been invoked by economists independently of time (though time, as just described, is implicit), as existing through time, as temporary or changing as time passes, in terms of unchanging growth rates and full-employment growth paths, and in reference to the short and long runs and to both microeconomic and macroeconomic phenomenon.

But in spite of its usefulness in, and widespread appearance over almost two centuries of economic discourse, the concept of equilibrium has little place in Post Keynesian economics. This is because Post Keynesian economics, in part, views the workings of the real economic system as a 'process of continuous and organic change' (Galbraith 1978, p. 8) that is so fundamental, pervasive and dynamic that that system cannot be corralled by any notion of equilibrium. The vehicle for the expression of this change, in addition to a more sensitive regard for the institutional structures in relation to which the actual economy operates, is the vision of historical, as opposed to logical, time that informs virtually all Post Keynesian analytical constructions.

By the phrase 'historical time' is meant time that is actually experienced by human beings, in which each moment in history is unique, in which knowledge of past events is necessarily fragmentary and variable depending on each person's perception of them, and in which the occurrence of future events and their properties is not only unknown even probabilistically, but is also unknowable. As time passes, individuals change not only with respect to the knowledge in their possession or in their epistemic status, but they also experience unforeseeable modifications in their economic endowments and in their perceptions of external institutional structures, environments and the possibilities of action taken by others. Because planned behaviour continually changes with these variations, it is not possible for behavioural variables to remain constant through time. Hence the concept of equilibrium, at least in its conventional connotation, is both irrelevant and meaningless.

The organizing feature that replaces the notion of equilibrium in Post Keynesian economics may be referred to as 'non-equilibrium'. An analysis is organized in reference to non-equilibrium if the notion of time upon which it rests is historical. Because of the changing nature of the subjects of inquiry, because of the fluidity of economic endowments and expectations that market processes generate, and because of the continually evolving character of institutional structures, such an analysis constructed for any moment or period is different from that constructed for any other. Moreover, non-equilibrium analyses permit the end result of a process (not an equilibrium) to be influenced by the means of achieving it. They also allow for the presence of non-probabilistic uncertainty and are capable of including in their explanatory reach phenomena that are subject to that uncertainty. Thus, for example, in the context of decision making that accounts for (non-probabilistic) ignorance of the future, a richer complex of forces can be incorporated into the analysis and description of economic phenomena. And the recognition of money as a historical time and non-probabilistic uncertainty phenomenon, in which actual time passes between the receipt and disposal of funds, permits addressing the reality that the set of forces obtaining at the time of the funds' receipt might be different from those at the time of their disposal. The latter, in turn, may give rise to changes in liquidity preference and in the level and stability of expenditure streams, and macroeconomic problems in which labour markets do not clear may result. Like traditional economics, explanation from the Post Keynesian perspective may also proceed by constructing models. But, as this discussion suggests, these models are rather different in character from those of traditional economics. (For a more complete discussion, see Katzner 1998.)

At first, in the construction of an explanation of a phenomenon for, say, the period between moments t^0 and t^1, where $t^0 < t^1$, Post Keynesian or 'non-equilibrium analysis' may be conceived of as proceeding analogously to that which would arise under the equilibrium alternative: a model may be built up, its solutions or time paths studied, and one time path identified with observed reality between t^0 and t^1. Then, by pursuing the latter time path beyond t^1, one possible description of what could happen next may be provided. It is important to understand, however, that although non-equilibrium-analytic models constructed in this way might seem similar to their equilibrium-analytic counterparts, the difference between them remains significant and far-reaching. For unlike the models of 'equilibrium analysis', a non-equilibrium-analytic model itself, that is, the variables, parameters and relations of which it is composed, would be thought of as time dependent. Once t^0 or t^1 changes, one could not, for the reasons described above, expect the same model to be appropriate. Hence the 'fixed' parameters do not remain fixed, and the structural relations themselves dissolve: if t^1 were to increase, then the history of reality is modified by the passage of time and explanations of occurrences after t^0 undergo such profound change (due to the unforeseen and unpredictable novelty at t^1 that enters the fabric of real life after t^1) that the analytical structures of those explanations are unlikely to hold up in its wake. Shackle (1974, p. 42) has referred to this process in general as 'kaleidics'. Clearly the methodology of non-equilibrium analysis does not allow formal prediction as permitted by the methodology of equilibrium analysis.

Still, stretches of time may unfold during which real-world newness does not appear to impinge substantively on the particular phenomena under investigation. The lack of impact could be reflected in at least two ways. First, it may be that the equations of a model seem to be roughly stable over time in the sense that for a while, as t^1 expands, a single time path (stationary or otherwise) generated by the model continues to approximate observations of reality reasonably well. Here traditional equilibrium analysis, though coming from a different methodological perspective while using the same variables, parameters and relations, provides a formal picture of the real world identical to that furnished by Post Keynesian or non-equilibrium analysis. Furthermore, it is only in unusual cases like these that the possibilities, exposed by the model, of what could happen in the future actually transpire.

Second, and perhaps even less likely, stability over time could also arise with respect to the solution values of the variables even as the equations of the model modify. Thus it may happen that all observed values between t^0 and t^1 are 'essentially' similar. Hence reality between t^0 and t^1 could be viewed as in a pseudo-stationary state: novelty occurs, but either not to a sufficient extent or not in ways that significantly affect the values of the variables in the analysis. Bausor (1982–83, pp. 173–7) calls this 'historical equilibrium'. In such a case, what is seen can be explained either in terms of a traditional equilibrium analysis with a single model containing a unique stationary state and with all of the assumptions that that entails or, in the language of non-equilibrium analysis, with a 'model' whose equations might modulate but whose solutions remain essentially the same over time.

During periods of transformation, the two approaches clearly supply quite distinct explanations of real-world phenomena. On the one hand, traditional equilibrium analysis can only explain unforeseen change by asserting, after the fact, that 'outside' forces caused alteration in functions or parameter values. But the idea of a continually modulating equilibrium responding to, say, repeated parametric variation is not a very satisfying way of conceptualizing the effects of novelty. Non-equilibrium analysis, on the other hand, cannot provide much of an understanding of unforeseen change either. Yet the acknowledgement of such change is part of the internal structure of its methodological tissue. Non-equilibrium analysis expects change and leaves room for it. Its emphasis is on process and the present state, and on what might happen subsequently. By comparison, equilibrium analysis, with its focus on the end result towards which time paths, if not already there, converge, makes room for change only after it has been observed.

DONALD W. KATZNER

See also:

Dynamics; Expectations; Non-ergodicity; Time in Economic Theory; Uncertainty; Walrasian Economics.

References

Bausor, Randall (1982–83), 'Time and the structure of economic analysis', *Journal of Post Keynesian Economics*, **5** (2), 163–79.
Galbraith, John Kenneth (1978), 'On Post Keynesian economics', *Journal of Post Keynesian Economics*, **1** (1), Fall, 8–11.

Katzner, Donald W. (1998), *Time, Ignorance, and Uncertainty in Economic Models*, Ann Arbor: University of Michigan Press.
Shackle, G.L.S. (1974), *Keynesian Kaleidics*, Edinburgh: Edinburgh University Press.

Exchange Rates

The central feature of the Post Keynesian approach to exchange rates is the belief that capital flows play an active, autonomous role in the economy. This view is key in terms of both their explanation of currency price determination and their policy prescriptions; it is also what most distinguishes Post Keynesian scholarship from orthodox. This entry begins with a review of the latter.

Mainstream theories of exchange rates, though there are several, ultimately agree that the underlying forces driving foreign currency prices are the *fundamentals*. Unfortunately, little effort is expended in explaining these determinants (see Harvey 2001). Definitions range from simple lists of potential candidates to circular references to them as 'those variables suggested by economic theory'. In reviewing this literature it becomes apparent that the unifying theme among the seemingly disparate approaches is that the fundamentals represent *that set of variables guaranteeing the efficient operation of the foreign currency market*. Orthodoxy is therefore assuming the optimality of the outcomes created by real-life foreign exchange operations; to them the task at hand is to identify these undiscovered variables.

A second feature of the mainstream approach is their acceptance of Say's Law and consequent relegation of monetary factors to irrelevance. No orthodox exchange rate model treats portfolio capital flows as anything but transitory factors, serving merely to finance trade flows. If short-term investment moves a currency price, this is merely a reflection of the fundamental factors in the economies in question. Thus, though capital is undeniably the largest factor in the balance of payments today, it can be safely ignored. It is no more responsible for *determining* prices than the mechanism which affixes stickers to cans of soup at the grocery store (or, to offer a more modern analogy, resets the register's interpretation of the universal price code symbol).

As a result of these dispositions, orthodox exchange rate theory focuses almost exclusively on trade flows as the determinant of currency prices. Note that if currency prices are indeed driven by trade flows, trade imbalances must represent an excess demand for the money of the surplus nation. A corollary to the orthodox approach is therefore that balanced trade can be expected to prevail over the long run.

Empirical tests of mainstream exchange rate models have fared very poorly, even by the admission of supporters. Trade does not tend towards balance, capital flows appear to have enormous influence on currency markets, and exchange rates have been far too volatile for their only determinants to have been fundamental in origin. This has led to considerable questioning within the orthodox school, the basic result of which has been the conclusion that short-term currency movements may be irrational and therefore 'non-economic'; economists' time, they conclude, is best spent focusing on long-term movements. Note the striking similarity of this position to that of the classicals criticized by Keynes in *The General Theory*.

The Post Keynesian view is driven by their rejection of Say's Law (due to Keynesian uncertainty) and the consequent belief that finance plays a substantive role in determining output and employment. Within this context, Post Keynesians argue that currency prices are a function of international investors' portfolio decisions. Moneys of nations whose assets are in greatest demand will tend to appreciate; those in least demand will depreciate. While the value of international assets may be related to trade flows in some indirect manner (which would tend to return us to the orthodox position), it is primarily financial considerations that underlie agents' decision making. Greatest among these is the potential for capital gain from selling an asset in the future. Expectations therefore play a central role in the Post Keynesian explanation. However, unlike the 'rational expectations' employed by the orthodox school, which simply passively observe and predict outcomes (the latter being generated by the fundamentals), those posited in the Post Keynesian view *create* the objective variable. If market participants expect (in aggregate) that European assets will become more valuable, investors will enter the market to purchase those assets and thus cause their (and the euro's) appreciation. The trick to earning profits becomes guessing the behaviour of the rest of the market.

How do agents form their expectations? That, of course, is the key question. It is also a very difficult one. In their search for a realistic formulation of agents' expectation-formation processes Post Keynesians have turned in part to other disciplines. The work of the psychologists Daniel Kahneman and Amos Tversky has provided an excellent starting-point. In their view, people make decisions on the basis of simple heuristics, the most important of which are availability, representativeness and anchoring. Availability is used to estimate frequency or likelihood. In general, the more available something is in memory (either through imagination or recalling past instances), the more frequent or likely that event is deemed to be. Representativeness is most useful when the decision maker is concerned with the probability that object A belongs to class B (for example, the likelihood that event A is the result of process B, or that process B will create event A). The simple rule of thumb is, the more A resembles B, the more likely it is that it belongs to class B. Anchoring occurs when the individual must make an estimate. Psychologists have discovered that, regardless of the procedure used to arrive at an initial estimate, people tend to anchor any subsequent revisions to it.

Among the many implications of these rules of thumb are that agents overemphasize the importance of events that are more recent or dramatic (leading to overreaction in financial markets); they tend to place undue confidence in making decisions based on scant information (which, combined with the Post Keynesian characterization of decision making in an environment of uncertainty, tends to create volatility); and they will tend to accept the current rate as the standard against which to consider future movements (as in Keynes's concept of convention). There is furthermore a great deal of support from the psychological literature for the existence of bandwagon effects in financial markets. This is key because it helps to explain what appear to be self-sustaining trends and the existence and popularity of technical analysis (which is generally based on the premise that emerging trends will continue). Orthodoxy, in relying on the fundamentals approach, has discounted the importance of both bandwagons and trading rules. However, empirical analysis has found them to be important in explaining short-term currency movements (the time horizon that orthodoxy has all but abandoned). The multi-disciplinary approach of Post Keynesian economics also provides theoretical underpinnings for other observed phenomena, such as cash-in effects (the tendency of agents to sell appreciating assets) and currency-desk mandated trading limits for dealers (as a defence against risk-taking behaviour in the face of losses).

In summary, the Post Keynesian view of exchange rates is based on the empirical fact that currency prices are driven by short-term capital flows. Those flows are in turn a function of agents' expectations, which are best modelled using a combination of standard Post Keynesian tools (Keynes's concepts of convention, uncertainty and so on) and some borrowed from psychology. The picture that emerges is not one of a market characterized by stability, efficiency and optimality (all benevolently guided by the invisible hand of the fundamentals), but of an institution where agents' imperfectly considered actions create currency prices. Those actions may be marked by stability for long periods of time (though with whipsaw patterns created by the interactions of the cash-in and bandwagon effects) as agents rely on convention to anchor to stable levels or rates of change; but because they are subject to availability and bandwagon effects they are apt to rapid revision in the face of salient events (even when those events may seem inconsequential to cooler heads).

Currency markets affect world welfare in a number of ways. First, international commerce (especially trade) is discouraged by the volatility of exchange rates. Although one could correctly argue that this instability has hardly brought import and export activity to a halt, it has at the very least caused a shift of world resources away from productive activities and into pecuniary ones. Ironically, the change in focus entailed by that shift has no doubt exacerbated the problem by increasing the size and importance of international capital.

Second, if one of the goals of an international monetary system is a tendency to balanced trade, then our current arrangements do not and cannot deliver. Simply put, one price cannot except by coincidence clear two markets. Were there no capital flows in the world then (assuming minimal government intervention) trade imbalances would represent market disequilibria. Current account deficits and surpluses would soon be eliminated. Alternatively, were capital flows very small as compared to trade flows, then agents in the former would have a vested interest in tracking the latter; they would operate to anticipate current account activities and to offer liquidity on a timely basis. However, given that the overwhelming majority of international commercial activity takes the form of portfolio investment, there is no reason to believe that events in the world's current account are of more than minor interest to the agents acting in the capital account. Even when a nation is heavily indebted and one might expect a massive depreciation/devaluation to take place to correct an accompanying trade deficit, investors have rightly come to anticipate that the more normal course of action will be emergency loans and grants that allow a continuation of the status quo. There is no automatic stabilizer operating in the post-Bretton Woods world.

As a consequence of their understanding of the foreign exchange market, the most common recommendation of Post Keynesian economists with respect to the organization of the international economy is that we control the flow of capital. This notion is hardly new. Keynes argued at the Bretton Woods conference that nations must reserve the right to control all capital movements. His recommendation was not entirely ignored, but the efforts made were half-hearted and, in the end, easily circumvented by investors. Of course, addressing this shortcoming has now been complicated by the *laissez-faire* attitude that prevails among policy makers and academics.

But reforming the international monetary system will require more than simply slowing the rate of international portfolio investment flows. In recognition of this fact, Paul Davidson has recommended a comprehensive plan that addresses both currency and broader macro issues. At its core is a recognition that Say's Law does not operate in the real world and that we must therefore undertake policy to generate full employment. The system would feature a fixed exchange rate (as a means of making international transactions prices more predictable) and provisions to control capital flows (so that those fixed rates could be defended). Furthermore, it would place the burden of resolving trade imbalances on the *surplus* country and not the deficit country. This is logical, according to Davidson, because in a less-than-full-employment world where Say's Law does not hold, surplus nations are antisocial drains on world employment. This proposed system will thereby avoid the inherent deflationary biases of those based on orthodox understandings of the currency market.

JOHN T. HARVEY

See also:

Bretton Woods; Economic Policy; Expectations; Globalization; International Economics; Say's Law; Tobin Tax.

Bibliography

Davidson, Paul (1972), *Money and the Real World*, London: Macmillan.
Davidson, Paul (1998), 'Volatile financial markets and the speculator', *Economic Issues*, **3** (2), 1–18.
Harvey, John T. (1993), 'Daily exchange rate variance', *Journal of Post Keynesian Economics*, **15** (4), 515–40.
Harvey, John T. (1999), 'Exchange rates: volatility and misalignment in the post-Bretton Woods era', in Johan Deprez and John T. Harvey (eds), *Foundations of International Economics: Post Keynesian Perspectives*, London: Routledge, pp. 200–211.
Harvey, John T. (2001), 'Exchange rate theory and "The fundamentals"', *Journal of Post Keynesian Economics*, **23** (1), 3–15.
Schulmeister, Stephan (1987), 'An essay on exchange rate dynamics', *Research Unit Labour Market and Employment Discussion Paper 87–8*, Berlin: Wissenschaftzentrum Berlin für Sozialforschung.

Expectations

One of the intrinsic properties of our world is that the future is uncertain. This uncertainty affects the way decisions are made because economic actors (entrepreneurs, bankers, employees, government) have to define their priorities by relying on their expectations about the future so as to anticipate it (that is, to act in advance of what they think will happen). In *The General Theory*, Keynes explains how and why expectations influence the current and future states of the economic system and how expectations are formed. He was followed by many different authors, including Joan V. Robinson, Nicholas Kaldor, Roy F. Harrod, George L.S. Shackle, Evsey D. Domar, Hyman P. Minsky, Paul Davidson and Jan A. Kregel, who have clarified and developed Keynes's analysis.

The first problem when dealing with expectations is to look at how and why they matter. Because we live in a monetary production economy, the most influential expectations are those of entrepreneurs and of the banking and financial communities. Keynes distinguishes between short-term expectations, long-term expectations and confidence in these expectations. The first consist of expectations of costs and sale proceeds induced by a certain level of production, for a given level of capital equipment (new capital assets are not available for production yet). The aim of this calculation is to find progressively the point of effective demand, that is to say, the point at which production is expected to give the highest reasonable profits (the highest profits possible without jeopardizing the long-term viability of the firm). This point represents the current equilibrium position (by which Post Keynesians mean state of rest and not market clearing) induced by a given state of *long*-term expectation. The short term refers here to the 'shortest interval after which the firm is free to reverse its decision as to how much employment to offer' (Keynes 1936, p. 47). These short-term expectations are gradually revised in the light of current economic results. However, to simplify the analysis, Keynes considers that 'the theory of effective demand is substantially the same if we assume that short-term expectations are always fulfilled' (Keynes 1937b, p. 181). Thus, one can consider that entrepreneurs 'do not, as a rule, make wildly wrong forecasts of the equilibrium position' (p. 182) so that 'if we suppose a state of expectation to continue for a sufficient length of time for the effect on employment to have worked itself out . . . completely . . . the steady level of employment thus attained may be called the long-period employment corresponding to that state of expectation' (Keynes 1936, p. 48). Then, with this simplification, the point of effective demand is the actual level of production.

What really matters for the economic system are the past and current states of long-term expectations (Kregel 1976). These concern the future net cash flows provided by old and new capital assets. The past states of long-term expectation are reflected in the current amount and composition of the capital equipment. In the simple Keynesian economic model, the current state of long-term expectation (named E in a draft of *The General Theory*) determines the expected level of expenditures for investment (I) and consumption (C). Indeed, E is a key variable for the marginal propensity to consume (and so C), but also, and mainly, for the marginal efficiency of capital and the interest rate (and so I). Therefore, the aggregate demand curve (D) and aggregate supply curve (Z) are drawn for a given E.

Minsky (1975) elegantly showed how the state of long-term expectation affects the level of investment (that is, the production of new capital assets) and, via the multiplier, the level of employment. Thus, for two different states of long-term expectation with short-term expectations realized, see Figures 9 and 10.

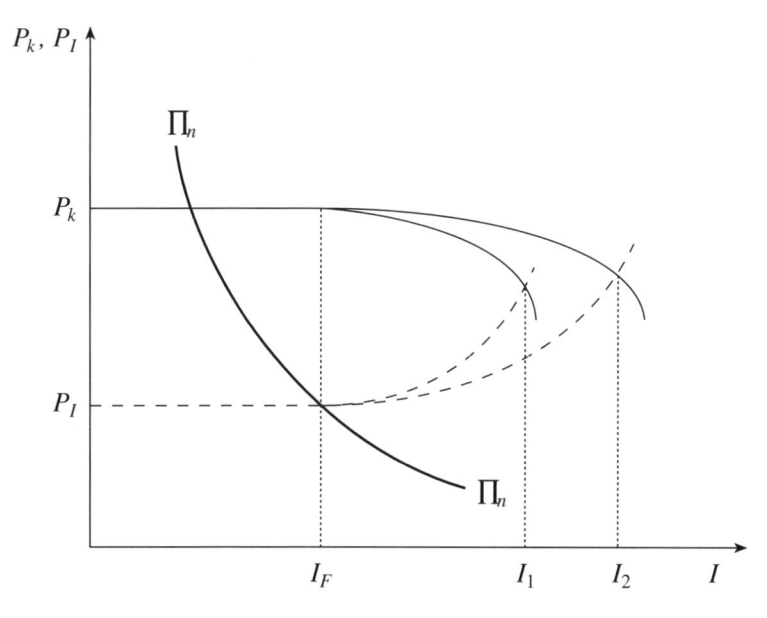

Figure 9 Determination of the level of investment

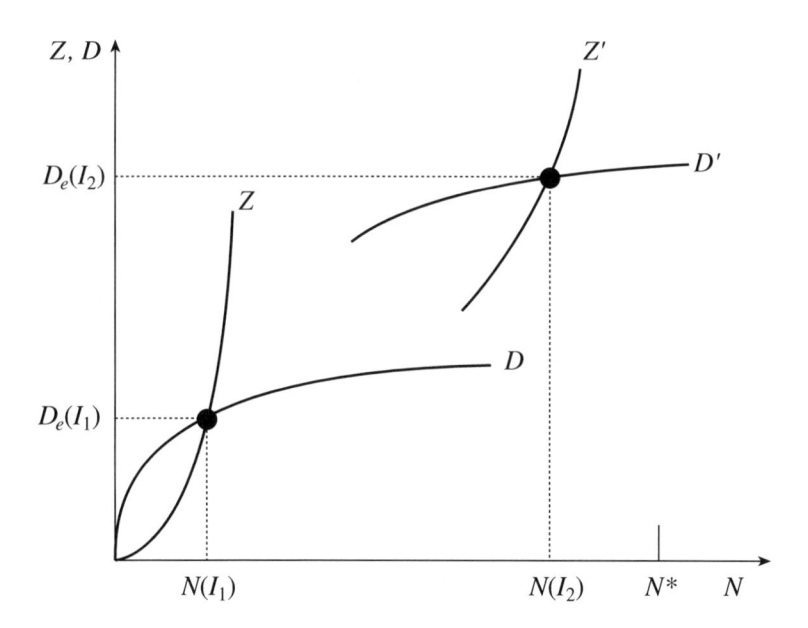

Figure 10 Determination of the level of employment

138   *Expectations*

P_k is the demand price of capital assets. It is the marketable price of existing capital assets. This price depends on the entrepreneur's (or borrower's) risk, which is the entrepreneur's sentiment about the viability of his project (or, at the macroeconomic level, entrepreneurs' opinion about the current and future states of the economy). Thus, P_k is determined by the expectations entrepreneur's make about the future net cash flows (Π_n) generated by a certain level of investment. P_I is the supply price of capital assets; the price to pay to get new capital assets. This price is fixed by the producers of capital assets out of a mark-up over costs. When investment is not completely self-financed ($I > I_F$), the supply price depends on the lender's risk, which is the lender's opinion about the creditworthiness of a borrower. Then P_I is influenced by the expectations of lending institutions concerning the future net cash flows provided by capital assets. Indeed, these expectations greatly influence the cost of external financing (interest rates; prices of stocks).

As long as economic conditions are favourable ($P_k > P_I$), the equalization of the two prices determines I. The more optimistic *both* entrepreneurs and lending institutions are, the higher the level of investment is, leading to a higher level of effective demand (and so of production). However, it is sufficient for the state of long-term expectation of one community (entrepreneurs, financial analysts or banks) to be degraded to decrease the level of investment. This depressive effect may grow because entrepreneurs and lending institutions are influenced by each other while determining their long-term expectations. Thus, more pessimistic (optimistic) expectations from one community can lead to more pessimistic (optimistic) in the other one: P_k and P_I are related (Keynes 1936, p. 145).

Actually the reality is worse than that because the two prices do not depend only on the lending institutions' expectations (for P_I) and entrepreneurs' expectations (for P_k). Indeed, the expectations of speculators are also very important. Kaldor (1939) shows in great detail how speculation may generate economic instability. Speculators make portfolio arbitrages to earn short-term capital gains, so they are not interested in future rents provided by a capital asset during its entire life. For speculators, buying, for example, financial assets is a game that consists in trying to anticipate what the main opinion of the financial community will be in the short term. This is the famous beauty contest situation described by Keynes in chapter 12 of *The General Theory*. Each judge of the contest is asked not to try to find the most beautiful woman (that is, the most economically viable capital assets), but the woman that other judges consider the most beautiful (that is, assets that others will buy in the near future). The problem is that this kind of behaviour has a tendency to become generalized in financial markets; it is possible to make quick capital gains and, by not adopting this behaviour, one may make capital losses. Thus, speculators can lead both lending institutions and entrepreneurs to adopt a speculative behaviour (forecasting the psychology of the market) instead of an enterprise behaviour (that is, act in expectation of future income streams provided by the productive use of capital assets). Therefore, the state of long-term expectation, which is already very fragile because it depends on forecasts of economic variables in the long run about which we know very little (wages, interest rates, tastes of consumers, degree of competition and other variables), is still more precarious because it depends on fads and fashions in the financial markets. This, however, does not mean that the state of long-term expectation is completely unstable. It means only that this state can change very abruptly for insignificant or purely cyclical reasons. These changes are largely independent of the realization or not of short-term expectations, because 'it is of the nature of long-term expectations that they cannot be checked at short intervals in the light of realized results' (Keynes 1936, p. 51).

However, for Keynes and Post Keynesians the real problem is elsewhere (Kregel 1976). What really matters for employment is neither the fulfilment or not of short-term expectations, nor the instability of long-term expectations. It is, instead, the level of the latter that is important: high unemployment ($N^* - N_j$) results from an insufficient level of effective demand (D_e). Stated alternatively, because economic actors are too pessimistic, their spending is too low to implement a level of production that is consistent with full employment. This shows that the conditions of equilibrium are endogenously determined by economic actors' actions, which are based on their expectations. There is no predefined state that the economy can reach; this state is created and modified by economic actors' anticipations (Kregel 1986). At the macroeconomic level, economic actors are responsible for their own economic situation. Then, pessimism may be so high that economic actors cannot solve their problems by themselves, or, economic actors can be too optimistic and indulge in dangerous behaviours leading to doubtful investments and financial weakness. Indeed, during 'a boom the popular estimation of the magnitude of both . . . borrower's risk and lender's risk, is apt to become unusually and imprudently low' (Keynes 1936, p. 145). The government should thus do everything to limit and to regulate the economic impact of pessimism and optimism. Indeed, this economic actor has the financial and technical ability to anticipate the macroeconomic consequences of the current anticipations of private agents. Entrepreneurs are only concerned with expectations of profits of their own activities; and it is not their job to take into account the macroeconomic consequences of their own decisions.

The preceding has shown how expectations influence the current state of the economy (determination of the level of production and of the current level of capital equipment) and why they are important (insufficient effective demand or unsustainable economic patterns). It is now necessary to look at how the state of expectation is formed to better understand how it evolves. Here 'the *confidence* with which we make this forecast' (Keynes 1936, p. 148) becomes important.

Once again it is necessary to make a distinction between short-term expectations and long-term expectations. Concerning the former, Keynes agrees that they can quite easily be formed by using probability calculus. To find the effective scale of production, an entrepreneur will make 'several hypothetical expectations held with varying degrees of probability and definiteness' (p. 24 n. 3). The constant overlapping between short-term expectations and current results (p. 50) makes this probabilistic calculation quite easy because it is based on a routine process.

If probabilities can be used more or less easily for short-term expectations, long-term expectations cannot be based mainly on this kind of method of decision. The mathematical expectation is, at best, an element among others in the process of decision. Indeed, to apply probability calculus with confidence and to base his or her actions only on this method of decision, an economic actor has to assume that the economic system is ergodic. This means that the properties of the system in which decisions are made are not modified by these decisions (Davidson 1991). However, investment spending is a crucial decision (Shackle 1955) because it leads to irreversible qualitative changes in the economic system. Thus, future possibilities and properties of the economic system evolve as new technologies and methods of production are introduced. There is another important reason why long-term expectations cannot rely essentially on probabilities: these expectations depend on factors that we know little about, so that the state of confidence plays a dominant role in the formation and change of long-term expectations. This implies that, contrary to probability calculus, probability and confidence do not necessarily move in the same way and have to be clearly separated. It is not because more information is available that confidence is increased; 'events, such as crises, can radically diminish the confidence with which views of the world are held' (Minsky 1975, p. 65).

Thus, 'the *state of confidence*, as they term it, is a matter to which practical men always pay the closest and most anxious attention' (Keynes 1936, p. 148). To evaluate this state of confidence, economic actors refer to the prevailing convention concerning the present and future states of the economy. This means that, to take crucial decisions, they rely heavily on the past and current economic situations, and that they judge the current opinion of the majority as the best (Keynes 1937a). However, entrepreneurs can also go against the convention in place and let their instinct dominate their decisions. Long-term expectations then depend on different elements that are related but have little to do with probability (Dequesh, 1999): animal spirits, creativity and uncertainty perception are three of them. It follows from this that conventions are fragile and subject to sudden changes. However, they are usually stable enough for entrepreneurs whose optimism and animal spirits push them to invest. Moreover, this uncertainty about the future is less an obstacle than a stimulus to investment. Uncertainty leaves the system open to the imagination of entrepreneurs regarding profit opportunities. If investment depended on 'nothing but a mathematical expectation, enterprise [would] fade and die' (Keynes 1936, p. 162).

ÉRIC TYMOIGNE

See also:

Non-ergodicity; *Treatise on Probability*; Uncertainty.

References

Davidson, Paul (1991), 'Is probability theory relevant for uncertainty?', *Journal of Economic Perspectives*, **5** (1), 129–43.
Dequesh, David (1999), 'Expectations and confidence under uncertainty', *Journal of Post Keynesian Economics*, **21** (3), 415–29.
Kaldor, Nicholas (1939), 'Speculation and economic activity', *Review of Economic Studies*, **7** (1), 1–27. Reprinted and revised in N. Kaldor, *Essays on Economic Stability and Growth*, London: Duckworth, 1960, pp. 17–58.
Keynes, John M. (1936 [1973]), *The General Theory of Employment, Interest and Money*. Reprinted in *The Collected Writings of John Maynard Keynes*, Vol. 7, London: Macmillan for the Royal Economic Society.
Keynes, John M. (1937a) [1973]), 'The general theory of employment', *Quarterly Journal of Economics*, **51** (2), 209–23. Reprinted in *The Collected Writings of John Maynard Keynes*, Vol. 14, London: Macmillan for the Royal Economic Society, pp. 109–23.
Keynes, John M. (1937b [1973]), 'Ex post and ex ante', 1937 lecture notes. Reprinted in *The Collected Writings of John Maynard Keynes*, Vol. 14, London: Macmillan for the Royal Economic Society, pp. 179–83.
Kregel, Jan A. (1976), 'Economic methodology in the face of uncertainty: the modeling methods of Keynes and the Post-Keynesians', *Economic Journal*, **85** (342), 209–25.
Kregel, Jan A. (1986), 'Conceptions of equilibrium: the logic of choice and the logic of production', in I. Kirzner (ed.), *Subjectivism, Intelligibility, and Economic Understanding*, New York: New York University Press, pp. 157–70. Reprinted in P. Boettke and D. Prychitko (eds.), *Market Process Theories, Volume 2: Heterodox Approaches*, Cheltenham, UK and Northampton, MA, USA, Edward Elgar, 1998, pp. 89–102.
Minsky, Hyman P. (1975), *John Maynard Keynes*, London: Macmillan.
Shackle, George L.S. (1955), *Uncertainty in Economics*, Cambridge: Cambridge University Press.

Finance Motive

The finance motive for holding money was introduced by J.M. Keynes (1937a, 1937b, 1939) one year after the publication of the *General Theory* (1936) and has been since then the object of a long and lively debate. However, the concept and the term have remained strictly related to Keynes's writings and never became a part of the common economic language.

In the *General Theory*, Keynes had concentrated his attention on money as a store of wealth, neglecting the analysis of money as an intermediary of exchanges. The reason for so doing was in part a purely analytical one. Only if considered as a stock does money become an observable and measurable variable; on the other hand, in any single instant of time, the whole of the money stock must be present in the liquid holdings of some agent or other. A second reason, possibly the main one for concentrating on money as a stock, was that Keynes considered the demand for liquid stocks to be at the origin of prolonged failures of aggregate demand, the main phenomenon he wanted to explain.

Severe criticisms of the Keynesian treatment of money in the *General Theory* were put forward by as authoritative an economist as D.H. Robertson, who accused Keynes of being 'so taken up with the fact that people sometimes acquire money in order to *hold* it, that he had apparently all but entirely forgotten the more familiar fact that they often acquire it in order to *use* it' (1940, p. 12). Robertson's remarks convinced Keynes that his model had to allow not only for money lying idle in somebody's holdings but also for money moving from the holdings of one agent to the holdings of another one, thus allowing the exchange of goods and services to take place.

In three articles published between 1937 and 1939, Keynes answered his critics and completed his model by a simple construction containing a description of the whole process of money creation. Any agent wanting finance for his business will ask for credit, usually (but not necessarily) from a bank. If liquidity is supplied by a bank, the money stock is increased. If it is supplied by some other agent in possession of idle money and being willing to lend it, the money stock does not change and the velocity of circulation is increased. As soon as the bank (or some other agent) has granted him the required credit, the agent is in possession of a liquid sum. It is clear that the agent is now holding money not for the sake of keeping it idle but in order to spend it. In fact he will only hold his money balance for the short time covering, in Keynes's own words, 'the interval between planning and execution [of expenditure]' (1937b, p. 663 [1973, p. 216]). In this case, according to Keynes, the motive behind the demand for money is not a transaction, or a precautionary, or a speculative motive, but a fourth motive, named by Keynes the *finance motive for holding money*. As soon as it is spent, money initially held as finance enters the money holdings of some other agent (wage-earners, suppliers of intermediate goods) and becomes, as the case may be, one of the more familiar transactions, precautionary, or speculative balances.

By his analytical construction, Keynes was trying to reconcile the demand for money as an intermediary of exchange, historically the first and more intuitive concept of money, and the demand for money as a demand for a store of wealth, the basic definition around which he had built the analysis of the *General Theory*.

Simple as the Keynesian construction may be, it has given rise to a number of misunderstandings. Most interpreters of Keynes believe that finance is only required when firms are facing an increase in output and that a stationary level of output is somehow self-financed (Chick 1983, pp. 198–200). In their view, the finance motive for holding money is strictly connected to the transactions motive, the only difference between the two being that while the first one defines the demand for liquid balances as a function of current income, the second one defines an increase in the demand for money as a function of an increase in the expected level of income.

Keynes himself may have induced a similar interpretation by his insisting on the fact that the use of finance is what makes possible an increase in production (1937a, p. 247 [1973, p. 209]; 1937b, p. 668 [1973, p. 222]). However this is clearly wrong. What is true is that, in a stationary economy, a constant level of output may require a constant volume of finance (if the velocity of circulation is constant). In that case, finance, as Keynes himself said, may become a constant *revolving fund*, used again and again. However, in a monetary economy, where money is the only means of payment and the banks are the only producers of money, no level of output can be obtained if it is not duly financed by the banks, and the revolving fund itself has to be supplied by the banks.

The same idea that the finance motive should be assimilated to the transactions motive for holding money has given rise to the suggestion that finance, being an advance provision of cash for investment, might have nothing to do with speculation. If this were true, introducing the finance motive might mean neglecting the conflict between finance and industry, a fundamental feature of the *General Theory*. However, this does not seem to be strictly correct. Keynes himself, when describing the demand for finance, explicitly mentions the fact that finance 'covers equally the use of the revolving pool of funds to finance . . . (e.g.) an increased turnover on the stock exchange' (1939, p. 573 [1973, p. 283]). The presence of finance in the model in no way rules out conflict between finance and industry. It rather introduces into the model a new, and possibly more interesting, kind of conflict, namely the one between bankers and entrepreneurs. In the *General Theory* Keynes had given space to the conflict between entrepreneurs and rentiers. In his later articles his purpose is to introduce what he names 'the power of the banks' (1937a, p. 248 [1973, p. 211]).

A second misinterpretation, common to most authors dealing with finance, is to consider finance as only needed when investment expenditure is involved (Asimakopulos 1983). In fact, finance is required for any kind of output, and no distinction can be made between production of consumer goods and production of capital goods. Keynes's statements in this direction are as repeated as they are clear: 'The production of consumption goods requires the prior provision of funds just as much as does the production of capital goods' (Keynes 1939, p. 572 [1973, p. 282]; see also Keynes 1937a, p. 247 [1973, p. 208]; 1937b, p. 667 [1973, p. 221]; 1939, p. 573 [1973, p. 283]).

The prevailing confusion between finance and investment is responsible for the peculiar statement that, whenever the level of investment is increased, firms can repay their bank debt only after the multiplier process has fully worked itself out (Cesaroni 2001). It is of course quite true that it is only when the multiplier process has come to an end that *ex ante* (or voluntary) savings are again equal to investment. But this has nothing to do with finance. Once investment is executed, an increase in income equal to it is created. If liquidity preference is stable and government securities are absent, the new income will be entirely spent either on the commodity market or on securities issued by private firms. Therefore, even after the very first round of expenditure, the firms will be fully able to repay their bank debt.

The debate on Keynes's finance motive shows that 65 years after the publication of the *General Theory*, confusion still persists between prior finance, needed for any kind of production (the problem Keynes was trying to analyse), and the totally different problem of how an adequate supply of saving is generated in order to bring saving and investment to equality. The first one is a problem concerning the credit market; the second one is the problem of ensuring equilibrium in the commodity market. The fundamental distinction between finance and saving that Keynes was trying to make does not seem to have been absorbed, and his conclusion that 'the investment market can become congested through a shortage of cash. It can never become congested through a shortage of saving' (1937b, p. 669 [1973, p. 222]) seems to be still ignored.

AUGUSTO GRAZIANI

See also:
Banking; Circuit Theory; Investment; Liquidity Preference; Money; Multiplier.

Bibliography

Asimakopulos, A. (1983), 'Kalecki and Keynes on finance, investment, and saving', *Cambridge Journal of Economics*, **7** (3–4), 221–33.
Cesaroni, G. (2001), 'The finance motive, the Keynesian theory of the rate of interest and the investment multiplier', *European Journal of the History of Economic Thought*, **8** (1), 58–74.
Chick, V. (1983), *Macroeconomics after Keynes*, Oxford: Philip Allan.
Keynes, J.M. (1936), *The General Theory of Employment, Interest and Money*, London: Macmillan.
Keynes, J.M. (1937a), 'Alternative theories of the rate of interest', *Economic Journal*, **47** (186), 241–52 (reprinted in Keynes 1973, pp. 201–15).
Keynes, J.M. (1937b), 'The ex-ante theory of the rate of interest', *Economic Journal*, **47** (188), 663–9 (reprinted in Keynes 1973, pp. 215–23).
Keynes, J.M. (1939), 'The process of capital formation', *Economic Journal*, **49** (195), 569–74 (reprinted in Keynes 1973, pp. 278–85).
Keynes, J.M. (1973), *The Collected Writings of John Maynard Keynes. Volume XIV: The General Theory and After. Part II: Defence and Development*, London: Macmillan for the Royal Economic Society.
Kregel, J. (1986), 'Keynes and finance. From the *Treatise* to the *General Theory*', (mimeographed) (printed in Italian: 'Il finanziamento in Keynes. Dal *Trattato* alla *Teoria Generale*', in M. Messori (ed.), *Moneta e produzione*, Turin: Einaudi, 1988, pp. 59–71).
Robertson, D.H. (1940), 'Mr Keynes and the rate of interest', in D.H. Robertson, *Essays in Monetary Theory*, London: P.S. King & Son, pp. 1–38.

Financial Instability Hypothesis

Hyman Minsky had a long and distinguished career that spanned almost four decades, during which he developed a number of key insights into the workings of modern financial economies. Minsky's work is complex and rich, and attempts to model the real world in which financial institutions play a key role. Minsky's work has had a definite influence, not only on Post Keynesians, but also on institutionalists and Marxists. Recently, however, New Keynesians have also showed a keen interest in his work.

For Minsky, orthodox theory is best described as a 'village market' where bartering one good for another is the principal economic activity. A capitalist economy, in contradistinction, is much closer to a 'Wall Street' system where agents, businesspeople and bankers deal with investment financing and capital assets. It is within this setting that Minsky's financial instability hypothesis is developed. It deals with a capitalist economy of production, in Keynes's sense, where finance and financial institutions play a key and decisive role.

Among Minsky's many important contributions, the financial instability hypothesis remains his most important. It explains the inherent cyclical nature of modern financial economies, and how economic booms can sow the seeds for an eventual downturn, that is, how stability breeds instability. Capitalist economies cannot be studied without referring to their monetary and financial nature.

Minsky's work on financial instability incorporates aspects of Keynes, Michał Kalecki and Irving Fisher. First, Minsky's work is set within an environment of Keynesian uncertainty. Businesses and banks operate in an uncertain environment in Keynes's sense, and hence their expectations and decisions are made in a world devoid of reliable knowledge. Second, Kalecki's principle of increasing risk is another central component of Minsky's work, according to which firms and the macro economy become more fragile as their level of debt increases. As it expands, the economy becomes increasingly fragile. In this sense, financial cycles are endogenous. Finally, as the economy collapses, deflation may ensue, implying that debt incurred during the expansionary phase of the cycle may not be reimbursed. This may then lead to debt-induced bankruptcies and a deepening recession. However, expansionary fiscal policy and a central bank acting as a lender of last resort may help in limiting the scope of the recession.

For Minsky, the early stages of an economic cycle are best described as periods of caution, as agents remember the last phases of the previous cycle. Coming out of a recession, firms tend to undertake safe investment projects where the expected revenues exceed the necessary debt repayments. Agents' liability structures are very liquid and the debt/equity ratio of firms is relatively low, or at least within respectable or acceptable levels. Firms expect good returns and expectations are generally fulfilled. In this stage, the economy is in a tranquil phase of 'hedge finance'. Firms tend to finance their investment initially through retained earnings, or at least internal financing is much greater than external financing.

As the boom continues, however, firms decide to undertake additional investment. Minsky (1982, pp. 120–24) refers to this phase as 'economic euphoria'. The optimism is fuelled by growth, and is shared by banks (p. 121). This is a key element. As firms invest more than their retained earnings allow, they will seek access to bank credit. Provided banks are as optimistic as firms, they will finance new investment. Simultaneously, asset prices start rising as speculators enter the market. These 'Ponzi financiers' tend to borrow heavily to purchase assets in the hope of selling them at higher prices.

As both firms and speculators become more indebted and less liquid, interest rates start to rise, as rates are positively correlated with debt/equity ratios. It is the illiquidity of both banks and firms that fuels the rise in interest rates. This rise of interest rates places the economy at risk, as firms may not be able to meet their debt commitments. Refinancing existing debt is made at a higher rate of interest, implying that cash outflows are greater than cash inflows. Debt burdens are increasing. Higher interest rates and less-liquid balance sheets also imply growing fragility of the banking system. This is when the economy moves into a situation of 'Ponzi finance'. Financial euphoria slowly leads to financial panic, and a crisis may be at hand. At this point, asset prices and gross profits collapse; investment falls or even stops. The economic boom is now replaced by an economic downturn.

The degree to which the economy spirals downward will depend largely on the role of prices, but also on fiscal and monetary policy. If price inflation is high, firms' revenues may be sufficient to permit them to honour part of their debt commitments. If price inflation is low, however, accumulated debt will be too much of a burden, and the economy will continue to spiral downward.

Minsky's work on financial instability carries important policy implications in the Keynesian tradition. Since it discusses the inherent tendency for economies to go from booms to busts, it addresses the specific roles of fiscal and monetary policies in constraining the dynamic nature of capitalist economies. In fact, since Minsky's work relies on developed modern institutions, it can be used to explain why large-scale depressions have not occurred since the 1930s. Since the public sector was small, fiscal policy could not have prevented the Great Depression. It is in this sense that Minsky's work is institutionally sensitive.

Today, however, the story is much different and governments are active and important players in the real world. Fiscal policy can have an important role in preventing further economic malaise, as fiscal deficits can translate into larger gross profits, enabling firms to honour their cash commitments on outstanding debt. Moreover, fiscal deficits may also limit the extent to which debt deflation occurs. According to Minsky (1982, p. xx): 'A cumulative debt deflation process that depends on a fall of profits for its realization is quickly halted when government is so big that the deficit explodes when income falls'. Furthermore, the central bank can have an important role in preventing runs on banks. It does so by expanding the monetary base to allow sufficient liquidity. It can also relax certain regulatory rules, like reserve requirements. By doing so, a liquidity crisis can be avoided. Both policies can help in preventing continued deterioration of money profits, which are important for debt validation and asset prices. Minsky's reliance on modern institutions explains in fact why 'It' has not happened again.

In Minsky's world, capitalism is not a system that tends naturally to stability. It is fraught with chaotic episodes and tendencies to periodic booms and slumps. This is characteristic of financial and monetary economies in an uncertain world. This does not mean that a depression cannot happen again. Governments and central banks may choose not to act.

Moreover, sound fiscal and monetary policies do not eliminate the financial phases of economic cycles, as these are endogenous to the cycle. Policy cannot avert the existence of Ponzi speculators.

Minsky's financial instability hypothesis has raised some concern among Post Keynesians. Key to this criticism is the fact that Minsky's analysis of financial fragility is essentially based on the microeconomic behaviour of the bank and the firm and is devoid of macroeconomic significance. This has led Lavoie and Seccareccia (2001) to question the 'missing macroeconomic link'.

Minsky's analysis of the notion that economic expansion leads to higher debt/equity ratios that translate automatically into higher interest rates may be applicable to the individual firm or bank. As their debt/equity ratios increase, banks may perceive them as riskier and may charge a higher rate of interest to cover the higher risk. His analysis, however, may not necessarily hold for the macro economy. In other words, as the economy expands, it may not necessarily become more fragile or riskier, and there is no reason why rates of interest need to increase, especially in an environment of endogenous money with exogenous rates of interest. These are set by the central bank.

Minsky, in fact, provides only one example of his financial fragility hypothesis in a macroeconomic setting. It can be found in an early article in the *American Economic Review* (Minsky 1957). The only problem is that the argument is set within the loanable funds approach (Lavoie 1996; Lavoie and Seccareccia 2001; Rochon 1999), which would explain why interest rates automatically increase during expansions.

Furthermore, Minsky's early analysis is silent on Kalecki's profit equations (although they figure in his later writings: see Minsky 1977). Had Minsky taken note of these equations, he would perhaps have realized that debt/equity ratios might not rise during expansions, which would then imply that the economy does not necessarily become increasingly fragile. As Lavoie and Seccareccia (2001, p. 84) argue, 'There is a missing link. Minsky does not provide any rationale to justify his rising leverage ratio thesis at the macroeconomic level.'

LOUIS-PHILIPPE ROCHON

See also:

Banking; Business Cycles; Central Banks; Fiscal Policy; Kaleckian Economics; Liquidity Preference; Monetary Policy; Rate of Interest; Uncertainty.

Bibliography

Bellofiore, R. and P. Ferri (eds) (2001), *Financial Keynesianism and Market Instability: The Economic Legacy of Hyman Minsky*, two vols, Cheltenham, UK and Northampton, MA, USA: Edward Elgar.

Lavoie, M. (1996), 'Horizontalism, structuralism, liquidity preference and the principle of increasing risk', *Scottish Journal of Political Economy*, **43** (3), 275–300.
Lavoie, M. and M. Seccareccia (2001), 'Minsky's financial fragility hypothesis: a missing macroeconomic link?', in R. Bellofiore and P. Ferri (eds), *Financial Fragility and Investment in the Capitalist Economy: The Economic Legacy of Hyman Minsky, Volume II*, Cheltenham,UK and Northampton, MA, USA: Edward Elgar, pp. 76–96.
Minsky, H. (1957), 'Monetary systems and accelerator models', *American Economic Review*, **47** (6), 859–83.
Minsky, H. (1977), 'The financial instability hypothesis: an interpretation of Keynes and an alternative to "standard" theory', *Nebraska Journal of Economics and Business*, **16** (1), 5–16.
Minsky, H. (1982), *Can 'It' Happen Again? Essays on Instability and Finance*, Armonk, NY: M.E. Sharpe.
Minsky, H. (1986), *Stabilizing an Unstable Economy*, New Haven: Yale University Press.
Nasika, E. (2000), *Finance, Investment and Economic Fluctuation: An Analysis in the Tradition of Hyman P. Minsky*, Cheltenham,UK and Northampton, MA, USA: Edward Elgar.
Rochon, L.-P. (1999), *Credit, Money and Production: An Alternative Post-Keynesian Approach*, Cheltenham, UK and Northampton, MA, USA: Edward Elgar.

Fiscal Policy

Fiscal policy is concerned with the economy-wide effects of government expenditure and revenue raising. Post Keynesians believe that there is no endogenous mechanism in a capitalist economy which will ensure that economic activity tends to full employment, even in the long run. Hence, fiscal policy is important as a major way in which the government can raise aggregate demand to the full-employment level. In a justly celebrated article, Lerner (1943) argued that fiscal policy should not be based on 'sound finance' in which expenditure was balanced by revenue over a year or some other arbitrary period. Instead fiscal policy should be based on 'functional finance'. Government expenditure and revenue should be determined so that total expenditure in an economy is at the rate which will produce full employment without inflation. This is to be done without any concern about whether the resulting budget is in surplus or deficit.

With the neoclassical resurgence in the 1970s and succeeding decades, 'sound finance' was again adopted by many economists and policy makers as the overriding guide to good fiscal policy. While Post Keynesian economists generally have a more complex theory of inflation than that implied by Lerner in 1943, they share his rejection of 'sound finance'. Much of the Post Keynesian writing on fiscal policy is designed to counter neoclassical arguments against budget deficits. Nevile (2000) contains a survey of these neoclassical arguments and the counters to them.

Among the neoclassical arguments, crowding-out theory and the twin deficits hypothesis are of particular importance, as each has had a substantial impact on actual policy making. Crowding-out theory maintains that an increase in the deficit will cause a fall in private investment expenditure of (almost) the same size as the rise in the deficit. If the government borrows to finance the deficit this, it is argued, will force up interest rates, reducing private investment. Moreover, even if the various multiplier effects are such that economic activity increases, more money will be demanded by the public to carry out this increased economic activity. They will try to borrow this extra money, forcing up interest rates further until the increase in gross domestic product is reversed.

An assumption underlying this crowding-out thesis is that the monetary authorities are successful in maintaining a constant stock of money. Even if the monetary authorities were successful in doing this, the analysis that shows increased government expenditure leading to higher interest rates also shows that any increase in private expenditure will lead to a rise in interest rates. In this respect, expansionary fiscal policy is no different from any other stimulus that might lift the economy out of recession. However, even before financial deregulation the monetary authorities in developed economies did not maintain a constant volume of money. Since financial deregulation, the volume of money is endogenous. In effect those supporting crowding out in today's world of deregulated financial markets are arguing that, whenever government expenditure increases, the central bank actively tightens monetary policy to the extent necessary to reduce private investment by an amount equal to all, or most of, the increase in public expenditure.

There is one qualification that should be made to this conclusion: short-term interest rates are the monetary policy instrument, but long-term interest rates may be more relevant to investment decisions in the private sector. It is possible that large budget deficits might increase the spread between short- and long-term interest rates, for example because they increase expectations of inflation, so even if short-term interest rates were held constant long-term rates could rise, crowding out private investment. However, there is no evidence that this happens, and more generally empirical studies have found little evidence of a relationship between budget deficits and interest rates. (See, for example, Nevile 2000, pp. 160–61 and endnote 11.) In addition, many Post Keynesians would deny that the link between interest rates and private sector investment is strong.

The second influential argument, the twin deficits hypothesis, maintains that if a budget deficit is created or increased, the balance of payments current account deficit will increase by a very similar amount so that all the expansionary impact will go overseas through increased imports. The social accounting identities ensure that this will happen if other things do not change, but this proves nothing unless one has a theory to support the implied *ceteris paribus* assumption. Supporters of the twin deficits hypothesis usually have no theoretical foundations for their arguments and those that have been put forward hold only in very long-run equilibrium situations, making them largely irrelevant to anti-cyclical policy making. Moreover, empirical evidence does not support the twin deficits hypothesis. For example, from 1990 to 1993 in G7 countries on average budget deficits more than doubled and the current account deficit fell to zero. This was not an isolated incident. A similar story applies to the years 1980 to 1983.

Post Keynesian writing on fiscal policy has not all been defensive. Lerner's arguments of 1943 have been developed and qualified in important ways that relate to inflation, external balance and the public debt. Much has been done on indicators of the stance of fiscal policy and the mistake of trying to use fiscal policy to solve structural problems has been pointed out. For a while after the Second World War it did seem possible that there was a narrow zone of economic activity compatible with both full employment and a very low rate of inflation. However, as more and more workers were younger, with no memories of the depression of the 1930s, the situation predicted by Michał Kalecki emerged. Full employment reduced substantially employers' power to discipline workers, leading to declining efficiency and inflationary wage demands. Most Post Keynesian economists argued that, if fiscal policy was to be successful in maintaining the economy at, or close to, full employment, it had to be supplemented with an incomes policy. (See, for example, Cornwall 1983, chapters 11 and 12.) As well as specific incentives or penalties in tax-based incomes policies (see ibid., pp. 272–5), fiscal policy can support incomes policies at the macro level, for example, through a general trade-off between wage rises and tax cuts or increased expenditure on the 'social wage'. Experience with incomes policies suggests that even successful ones are only effective for a limited period of time, which can usually be measured in years rather than decades. Ongoing innovation in designing incomes policies is important if fiscal policy, together with other policies, is to maintain full employment without inflation.

Inflation also interacts with balance of payment problems. Continuing large budget deficits, especially if accompanied by large current account deficits, may lead financial markets to fear an increase in the rate of inflation in a country and to withdraw financial investment, leading to a decline in the value of the country's currency on the foreign exchange market. The resulting inflationary pressure can put stress on any incomes policy and could lead to a depreciation/inflation vicious circle. Whether or not the concerns about budget deficits are well founded, the actions of financial markets cannot be shrugged off. If more than one equilibrium position is possible they may result in an economy reaching an equilibrium with a high rate of unemployment. This is particularly the case where equilibrium is path determined. While most Post Keynesians focus on the disequilibrium path in the short to medium run, rather than some longer-term equilibrium position, the conclusion is the same: namely that fiscal policy may have to be modified to meet the fears of financial markets, for example, by ensuring that the budget is balanced or in surplus when the level of economic activity is high. Financial market fears may be greater if a country has persistent large current account deficits, and many would agree that this is justified if the current account deficit is used to finance increasing consumption rather than increasing investment. Post Keynesian economists have pointed out that this situation is a sign of structural imbalance and structural change is necessary before fiscal policy can be effective in maintaining full employment.

If a country's public debt is held by its own citizens, the liability (to taxpayers) is balanced by the assets of those who hold the debt. Nevertheless, the consequences for income distribution may be important. In theory these could be overcome through tax and other fiscal measures for redistribution. In practice, if the interest bill is large, this may not be feasible for political and even administrative reasons. A large public debt relative to GDP reduces the freedom of action with respect to fiscal policy and may impose other burdens. A quasi 'sound finance' argument, that the budget should be balanced not over a year but over the business cycle, is too strict as it ignores the effects of inflation and economic growth. If nominal gross domestic product is growing there can be a positive budget deficit on average over the business cycle without any upward trend in the ratio of public debt to gross domestic product. Most Post Keynesians argue that a deficit on average is usually necessary for the health of an economy (see, for example, Bougrine 2000, various chapters).

Since Post Keynesian economists believe that fiscal policy is a major tool in the very important task of managing aggregate demand, they are particularly interested in measuring the effects of fiscal policy. The discussion has centred on the construction of a single-number indicator of the stance of fiscal policy. Most would agree that single-number indicators are very inadequate given the varying multipliers that are attached to different categories of government expenditure and taxation. However, it seems impossible to move media discussion and political arguments past a single-number indicator, with the nominal budget deficit the most often used despite its manifest flaws (see Eisner 1986). Attention has therefore focused on alternative measures of the budget deficit. It is well known that, while fiscal policy affects the level of economic activity, the level of economic activity affects the outcome of fiscal policy, with tax revenues falling during recessions and government expenditure on transfer payments automatically increasing. An alternative measure of the stance of fiscal policy is the structural deficit, or the size the deficit would be at a benchmark level of high employment, but with the current expenditure and taxation laws. Most commentators agree that the sale of public assets should be excluded when calculating the structural deficit. Post Keynesians argue that the decline in the value of the government debt (including currency) due to inflation should be subtracted from the deficit. Eisner adds an additional point, arguing that not only must one correct for inflation, but it is also necessary to look at the market value of the public debt, not its face value. The former fluctuates with changes in the interest rate. Most ignore this point, which strictly speaking relates to monetary policy, not fiscal policy. Any calculation of structural deficits involves making a judgement about what level of economic activity should be taken as a benchmark. While this may not affect year to year changes in the structural deficit, it will certainly determine the size of this deficit and often will determine whether fiscal policy is judged to be expansionary or contractionary. The selection of the benchmark is affected by the relative weight one gives to the dangers of inflation and unemployment. Hence, no calculation of the structural deficit is completely objective.

J.W. NEVILE

See also:

Budget Deficits; Economic Policy; Full Employment; International Economics; Investment; Monetary Policy; Taxation; Tax-based Incomes Policy.

References

Bougrine, Hassan (ed.) (2000), *The Economics of Public Spending: Debts, Deficits and Economic Performance*, Cheltenham, UK and Northampton, MA, USA: Edward Elgar.
Cornwall, John (1983), *The Conditions for Economic Recovery: A Post-Keynesian Analysis*, Oxford: Martin Robinson.
Eisner, Robert (1986), *How Real is the Federal Deficit?*, New York: Free Press, Macmillan.
Lerner, Abba P. (1943), 'Functional finance and the federal debt', *Social Research*, **10** (1), February, 38–51.
Nevile, J.W. (2000), 'Can Keynesian policies stimulate growth in output and employment?', in Stephen Bell (ed.), *The Unemployment Crisis in Australia: Which Way Out?*, Cambridge: Cambridge University Press, pp. 149–74.

Full Employment

> Blessed are the extravagant, for theirs shall be full employment.
> (Lekachman 1966, p. 94)

The term 'full employment' can be traced back to William Petty's 1662 work, *A Treatise on Taxes and Contributions*, in which he argued that non-productive labour could be supported as a consequence of the capacity of producers of consumption goods to generate a surplus over and above their own subsistence. The classical economists did not consider full employment specifically but J.-B. Say (1803) denied that a production economy could ever suffer a general glut which would otherwise have led to unemployment. Say's Law that 'supply creates demand' became the epithet of classical and neoclassical theory and its underlying reasoning still dominates orthodox macroeconomics today. There was not a denial that unemployment could occur but it was considered to be a manifestation of a temporary disruption, rather than being a generalized tendency of a capitalist production system. A lack of consumption would become by definition an act of investment. Moreover, it was argued that there was a strict separation between output and price theory – the so-called 'classical dichotomy'. So the existence of money posed no special problems. While J.C.L. Simonde de Sismondi and Thomas Malthus demurred and argued that generalized gluts could occur even if the savings–investment identity held, their analyses were flawed. It was Karl Marx, in his critique of Malthus, who provided a modern Post Keynesian rationale for generalized gluts. Marx understood that money could be held as a store of value and this behaviour interrupted the sequence of sale and purchase. He also laid the foundations of multiplier theory by arguing, in *Theories of Surplus Value*, that, once this unity of sale and purchase was disturbed, the chain of contractual relationships between suppliers became threatened and overproduction, and then bankruptcies and unemployment, became widespread.

So, by 1900, there were two broad views about the possibility of full employment: (a) Marxian views of crisis and the reserve army of unemployed, which saw capitalism as being incompatible with a fully employed working class; and (b) the dominant (marginalist) view that unfettered market operations would ensure that all those who wanted to work at the equilibrium real wage could find it because Say's Law held. Full employment became equivalent to the equilibrium intersection between the demand for and supply of labour, which in turn reflected the productive state of the economy driven by technology and the unconstrained preferences of the population. By definition, any workers who were idle were voluntarily enjoying leisure and could not reasonably be considered unemployed. Mass unemployment was considered to be a transitory disturbance.

The advent of the Great Depression made it hard to justify the view that the persistently high unemployment was due to changing preferences of workers (increased quits in search of leisure), excessive real wages (in the face of money-wage cuts), and/or a temporary interruption to market efficiency. For the first time, notwithstanding Marx's inspiring insights, Western economists articulated a macroeconomics that could define a coherent concept of full employment and also explain mass unemployment in terms of the inherent tendencies of monetary capitalism. The clue lay in recognizing the unique role that money could play in resolving the tensions that uncertainty created in the decision-making calculus of decentralized agents, but also in realizing that the fallacy of composition was endemic in the prevailing (micro) explanations of unemployment.

Whether the 1930s marked the birth of Post Keynesian notions of full employment is debatable. Post Keynesian theory has fractured origins, with some practitioners seeing the labour market in Marxian, then Kaleckian terms and others tracing their ancestry to Keynes and his *General Theory*. Certainly, the attack against the marginalist faith in self-equilibration mounted by Keynes (1936) and his monetary analysis was path-breaking. It also more clearly outlined what we now mean by the term 'full employment'.

Keynes linked full employment to national income levels, such that full employment occurred at the level of output when all who want to work at the going money-wage rates can find a job. Full employment was the absence of involuntary unemployment. This was defined by the following thought experiment: if a rise in nominal demand with constant money wages increased the price level (of wage-goods) but also resulted in both the demand for and supply of labour increasing beyond the existing volume of employment then those who gained the new jobs were involuntary unemployed. Involuntary unemployment was to be expected in a monetary economy subject to uncertainty, because the act of holding money as a source of liquidity provided the type of interruption to the output–spending balance that Marx had clearly envisaged.

Consequently, the maintenance of full employment required government policies to maintain levels of aggregate demand sufficient to achieve output levels consistent with all available labour being employed. Significantly, a departure from full employment was construed as a systemic failure, rather than an outcome related to the ascriptive characteristics of the unemployed and/or the prevailing wage levels. Consistent with this notion was the coexistence of unfilled vacancies and unemployed workers as part of the normal daily resolution of hiring and quits. Accordingly, full employment arose when all unemployment was frictional. Beveridge (1944) defined full employment as an excess of vacancies at living wages over unemployed persons. The emphasis was on jobs.

Macroeconomic policy in the postwar period was designed to promote full employment. Beveridge (1944, pp. 123–35) argued that 'The ultimate responsibility for seeing that outlay as a whole, taking public and private outlay together, is sufficient to set up a demand for all the labour seeking employment, must be taken by the State'. In the following years, a number of Western governments, including those in Britain, Australia and Canada, made a commitment to at least 'high and stable' employment, if not full employment. The US government was more circumspect, with its 1946

Employment Act aiming only to ensure that employment opportunities were maintained. From 1945 to the mid-1970s, most governments used counter-cyclical budget deficits and appropriately designed monetary policy to maintain levels of demand sufficient to maintain full employment. Unemployment rates in Western economies were at historical lows throughout this period.

In the 1950s, however, the emphasis on jobs was replaced by a concern for inflation. Although only a subtle change, the redefinition of full employment in the early 1950s in terms of an irreducible minimum unemployment rate (see Mitchell 2001) gave way soon after to the Phillips curve revolution. The Keynesian orthodoxy considered real output (income) and employment as being demand determined in the short run, with price inflation explained by a negatively sloped Phillips curve (in both the short run and the long run). Policy makers believed they could manipulate demand and exploit this trade-off to achieve socially optimal levels of unemployment and inflation. The concept of full employment had been redefined to be the rate of unemployment that was politically acceptable, given the accompanying inflation rate.

Milton Friedman's 1968 American Economic Association address and the supporting work from Phelps (1967) provided the basis for the expectations-augmented Phillips curve, which spearheaded the resurgence of pre-Keynesian macroeconomic thinking in the form of monetarism. Underpinning the natural rate hypothesis (NRH) was a unique cyclically-invariant natural rate of unemployment (NRU), which was consistent with stable inflation. There was no long-run, stable trade-off between inflation and unemployment. The concept was broadened in the 1970s to incorporate a number of structural labour market impediments, and the term non-accelerating inflation rate of unemployment (NAIRU) become popular.

The acceptance of these new ideas was aided by the empirical instability of the Phillips curve in most OECD (Organization for Economic Cooperation and Development) economies in the 1970s following the OPEC (Organization for Petroleum Exporting Countries) price rises. Unemployment was considered to be voluntary and the outcome of optimizing choices by individuals between income and leisure. Full employment was assumed to prevail (with unemployment at the natural rate), given the operation of market forces, unless there were errors in interpreting price signals. The NAIRU was now viewed as synonymous with full employment. There was no discretionary role for aggregate demand management; only microeconomic reform would cause the NRU to change. Accordingly, the policy debate became increasingly concentrated on deregulation, privatization and reductions in the provisions of the welfare state, while the monetarist 'fight inflation first' strategies ensured that unemployment persisted at high levels. The NAIRU proponents responded by claiming that the steady-state unemployment rate must have risen due to worsening structural impediments, although they failed empirically to substantiate their argument. The fact that quits were strongly pro-cyclical undermined the NRH, but the orthodoxy managed to avoid the damaging empirical evidence. Full employment as conceived by Beveridge had been abandoned.

With Post Keynesian economics dependent on the use of aggregate demand management as a means of attenuating the fluctuating spending patterns of the private sector (in particular, investment), the NAIRU approach to inflation control presented a fundamental quandary.

The earlier approach to improving the Phillips curve trade-off was to complement demand management policy with incomes policy, the latter being designed to batten down the supply (cost) side. Some Post Keynesians (principally the Marxian strain) had inflation models based on incompatible real income claims by workers and capital that delivered analytical findings observationally equivalent to the NAIRU approach. They also saw a role for incomes policy although, following Marx and Michał Kalecki, they did not think that full employment (in the Keynesian sense) and capitalism were compatible.

The modern Post Keynesian approach to the NAIRU challenge is best represented by the hysteresis and persistence literature, although some of the developments in this regard are strictly Neo-Keynesian. Hysteresis or path-dependence was traced to various cyclical adjustments that occurred in the labour market, which could be reversed in a growing economy. So while the steady-state unemployment rate rose after a long downturn, aggregate demand expansions could bring it down again. Once again full employment could be achieved at relatively low unemployment rates without ever-accelerating inflation. More recent empirical work has cast doubt on the robustness of the NAIRU story and provided strong support for a hysteretic–asymmetric interpretation of the inflation–unemployment relationship (Mitchell 2001).

Despite these developments, Post Keynesians cannot agree on the way to pursue full employment. The predominant view assumes that the economy is still amenable to a broad Keynesian spending expansion. Some Post Keynesians eschew this approach, arguing that it will be inflationary and/or environmentally damaging. They observe that the economies which avoided the plunge into high unemployment in the 1970s all maintained a sector that provided an employer of the last resort capacity to redress the flux and uncertainty of private sector spending. In most countries, throughout the 1950s and 1960s, the public sector played this role, which ceased when the monetarists began attacking the public sector on (orthodox) efficiency grounds. Accordingly, these Post Keynesians propose a job guarantee (Mitchell 2001) or an employer of last resort (Wray 1998), where the public sector maintains a constant fixed-wage job offer to anyone who cannot find employment elsewhere.

These models present a serious challenge to the conventional wisdom that budget deficits are unsustainable, which is accepted by many Post Keynesians. Wray and Mitchell argue that the issue of government securities is designed to sustain the target interest rate, set by monetary policy, rather than being required *ex ante* to finance expenditure. They argue that deflationary fiscal and monetary policy which drives employees out of the private sector into lower-paid job guarantee jobs provides an adequate counter-inflation policy if required.

Other Post Keynesians, including Arestis and Sawyer (1998), disagree. They point to the possibility of higher inflation and an unsustainable balance of trade leading to a growing ratio of debt to GDP. However, these are problems associated with the pursuit of full employment *per se*, and not the policies adopted to achieve it. A higher current account deficit as a ratio of GDP may promote a depreciation, which would reduce the overall real incomes of residents, but it may also be the price that must paid for increased employment opportunities. In addition, Arestis and Sawyer remain uncertain about the relationship between interest rates and budget deficits and note the potential adverse reaction of the financial markets to fiscal expansion.

Over the past 30 years the NAIRU concept has obfuscated the debate over the capacity of capitalist economies to achieve and maintain full employment, as traditionally understood. Somewhat belatedly this debate is now occurring, but it remains unresolved within the deeply divided Post Keynesian literature.

WILLIAM MITCHELL
MARTIN WATTS

See also:

Budget Deficits; Economic Policy; Effective Demand; Employment; Fiscal Policy; New Classical Economics; Say's Law; Tax-based Incomes Policy; Unemployment; Wages and Labour Markets.

Bibliography

Arestis, P. and M. Sawyer (1998), 'Keynesian economic policies for the new millennium', *Economic Journal*, **108** (446), 181–95.
Beveridge, W. (1944), *Full Employment in a Free Society*, London: Allen & Unwin.
Keynes, J.M. (1936), *The General Theory of Employment, Interest and Money*, London: Macmillan.
Lekachman, R. (1966), *The Age of Keynes*, Harmondsworth: Penguin.
Mitchell, W.F. (2001), 'The Job Guarantee and inflation control', in E. Carlson and W.F.

Mitchell (eds), *Achieving Full Employment*, Supplement to the *Economic and Labour Relations Review*, **12**, 10–26.

Phelps, E.S. (1967), 'Phillips curves, expectations of inflation and optimal unemployment over time', *Economica*, **34**, 254–81.

Say, J.-B. (1803), *A Treatise on Political Economy*, Library of Economics and Liberty. Retrieved 30 June 2002 from the World Wide Web: http://www.econlib.org/library/Say/sayT0.html.

Vickrey, W.S. (1993), 'Today's task for economists (full-employment policy)', *American Economic Review*, **83** (1), 4–14.

Wray, L.R. (1998), *Understanding Modern Money: The Key to Full Employment*, Cheltenham, UK and Northampton, MA, USA: Edward Elgar.

Fundamentalist Keynesians

The term 'fundamentalist Keynesians' originates with Coddington (1976) to describe 'those who have seen Keynes's work as a frontal assault on the whole reductionist programme' (p. 1259). The fundamentalist Keynesians are those radical/Post Keynesians who see Keynes's *General Theory* as a rejection not only of the theories and policy prescriptions of neoclassical economics but also of its analytical (reductionist) methods. In particular, the fundamentalist Keynesians interpret Keynes as emphasizing the importance of uncertainty in economic behaviour and, as a consequence, rejecting the usefulness of both the optimization calculus and equilibrium analysis.

Coddington associated the fundamentalist strand of Keynesianism primarily with George Shackle and Joan Robinson. Both Shackle and Robinson believed the essence of Keynes's revolutionary contribution to be his analysis of the effects of uncertainty on investment in chapter 12 of the *General Theory*, a theme that Keynes highlighted in his subsequent (1937) *Quarterly Journal of Economics* article. Both also argued that Keynes's analysis implies the need for a fundamental change in the analytical methods employed by economists. Robinson (1979) summarized the methodological argument very succinctly: 'As soon as the uncertainty of the expectations that guide economic behaviour is admitted, equilibrium drops out of the argument and history takes its place' (p. 126). Shackle (1967) considered Keynes to have invented a scheme of thought for dealing with the effects of uncertainty on economic behaviour. Shackle called this scheme of thought 'the *kaleidic* analysis of a development through time in which one situation or event grows out of another' (p. 151, emphasis in original). More recently, Davidson (1991) has restated the methodological argument as the rejection of the ergodic axiom that allows uncertainty to be modelled as a well-defined probability distribution. From Davidson's perspective, Keynes's concept of uncertainty represents a non-ergodic process in which economic behaviour consists of crucial decisions and unique events such that individuals cannot specify a complete set of possible future outcomes and associated probabilities.

Coddington dismissed the fundamentalist Keynesians as purely nihilistic as regards the development and practical application of economic theory. He argued that the fundamentalists give too much emphasis to those parts of Keynes's thought that are merely a ground-clearing exercise. For Coddington, fundamentalist Keynesians are on the slippery slope towards subjectivism, driving a wedge between behaviour and circumstance that negates analysis and renders economic theorizing impossible.

There is some validity in the criticism of early fundamentalist Keynesians as rather nihilistic, emphasizing mainly the negative aspect of Keynes's work. But Coddington himself was guilty of an excessive emphasis on the negative aspect of Keynesian fundamentalism. He ignored, for example, Shackle's attempts to construct an alternative theory of decision making under uncertainty using the concept of potential surprise. Coddington also wrongly implied that Keynes's concern with uncertainty was a transitional phase. Keynes had a long-standing interest in probability theory dating back to his undergraduate days. He published *A Treatise on Probability* in 1921 and explicitly referred back to this work in his discussion of uncertainty in chapter 12 of the *General Theory*.

The recognition of the centrality of probability and uncertainty throughout Keynes's thought led to the emergence of a 'new' Keynesian fundamentalism that sought to ground Keynes's later economic analysis in his early philosophical thought, especially *A Treatise on Probability*. This new Keynesian fundamentalism originated with Lawson (1985) and the subsequent books by Carabelli (1988), Fitzgibbons (1988) and O'Donnell (1989). A central theme of the new fundamentalists is the relationship between Keynes's analysis of uncertainty in the *General Theory* and the logical theory of probability that Keynes developed in *A Treatise on Probability*. Although the emphasis of the new fundamentalists is on the task of interpretation, there is a clear implication that Keynes's logical theory of probability may provide the basis for the development of an alternative economic theory of behaviour under uncertainty.

Keynes's logical theory of probability was an attempt to generalize beyond the frequency theory of probability. Keynes defined probability as the rational degree of belief in a proposition given the available evidence. A probability is a rational degree of belief in the sense of being objectively derived by logic rather than a matter of individual subjective evaluation. Keynes's concept of probability is epistemic in the sense of pertaining to the nature of knowledge. In contrast, frequency theory treats probability as an aleatory concept relating to the nature of the world. For Keynes, relative frequencies are a special type of quantitative data from which a numerical degree of belief in a proposition can be derived. Indeed, Keynes argued that numerical probabilities are a special case that had been overemphasized because of their amenability to mathematical manipulation. Keynes considered probabilities to be typically non-numerical and, in some cases, non-comparable.

As well as the notion of probability as a rational degree of belief, Keynes also introduced the concept of the weight of an argument. The weight of an argument is a measure of the amount of evidence on which a proposition is based. For the most part, Keynes considered the weight of an argument to be the amount of relevant evidence. The weight of an argument is independent of its probability. As additional relevant evidence is acquired, the weight of an argument increases but the rational degree of belief in the proposition may increase, decrease or remain unchanged. However, Keynes is not entirely consistent in his definition of the weight of an argument. He also referred to the weight of argument as the degree of completeness of evidence, as well as the balance of absolute amounts of relevant knowledge and relevant ignorance. These two alternative definitions of the weight of argument imply the possibility that additional relevant evidence may reduce weight if the assessment of relative ignorance is revised upwards. Despite the conceptual difficulties in formalizing the definition of the weight of an argument, Keynes stressed that weight as well as probability is relevant to practical decision making.

Keynes's emphasis on the importance of the weight of an argument is a key element in his critique of the doctrine of mathematical expectation as a theory of human behaviour under uncertainty. The doctrine of mathematical expectation implies that alternative courses of action are evaluated by weighting the value of the outcome with its probability. Keynes considered this approach to be too limited as a theory of human behaviour under uncertainty. He argued that any such theory must incorporate not only the value of the outcome and its probability as determinants of human behaviour, but also the weight of the available evidence and the risk attached (that is, the possible losses associated with any course of action). Keynes considered the possibility of amending the doctrine of mathematical expectation by weighting the value of the outcome with what he termed the 'conventional coefficient' instead of the probability. The conventional coefficient depends not only on the probability of the outcome but also on weight and risk. The conventional coefficient would tend towards the probability as weight tends towards unity and risk tends towards zero. However, Keynes concluded that the conventional coefficient is too restrictive in its formalization of the effects of probability, weight and risk on uncertain choices between alternative courses of action.

In attempting to interpret Keynes's later economic writings as grounded in his earlier philosophical thought, a crucial issue is the extent to which his philosophical position remained unchanged in any fundamental way between *A Treatise on Probability* and the *General Theory*. The 'continuity-or-change?' debate has focused on four principal pieces of textual evidence: a biographical essay on F.Y. Edgeworth published in 1926; a letter to F.M. Urban, the German translator of the *Treatise*, also written in 1926; a review of Frank Ramsey's *Foundation of Mathematics* in 1931; and Keynes's autobiographical essay, 'My Early Beliefs' that was read to the Bloomsbury Group in 1938. These texts are ambiguous and subject to radically different interpretations. There remains considerable controversy regarding whether Keynes retained both the logical theory of probability and the belief that the inductive method is only applicable to atomistic (as opposed to organicist) systems. Disputes over interpretation such as these cannot be resolved in any definitive way by textual evidence, since ultimately they represent differences over the appropriate frame of reference. The only closure possible to the question 'what did Keynes really mean?' is to recognize the possibility of multiple answers and to move on to another question. From the perspective of constructing an alternative non-neoclassical theory of economic behaviour under uncertainty, the relevant question is whether or not Keynes's analysis in the *General Theory* can be developed by reference back to *A Treatise on Probability*. In this case the emphasis shifts to the possibility of theoretical continuity rather than its actuality in Keynes's own intellectual development.

Keynes's analysis of economic behaviour under uncertainty is fundamental to the logic of the *General Theory*. Keynes rejected the two foundations of neoclassical theory, namely, the aggregate labour market and Say's Law that supply creates its own demand, the latter justified theoretically by the loanable funds theory of the rate of interest as the equilibrating mechanism ensuring that planned savings and investment are equated. Keynes proposed the principle of effective demand in which the level of income (and, in turn, output and employment) would adjust via the multiplier process to bring savings automatically into line with the volume of investment. Hence, ultimately, the level of employment depends on the determinants of the volume of investment, *ceteris paribus*. Keynes argued that the investment decision depends on prospective monetary yields (that is, the marginal efficiency of capital) exceeding the rate of interest. But prospective yields on investment depend on the state of long-term expectations. There is, therefore, an essential link between uncertainty and involuntary unemployment. If business is highly uncertain about future investment prospects, the volume of employment will fall, leading to downward multiplier effects on income, output and employment. It is this essential link that is emphasized by the fundamentalist Keynesians.

Keynes drew a crucial distinction in the *General Theory* between short- and long-term expectations. Short-term expectations relate to day-to-day production decisions. These expectations are subject to continual revision in the light of market outcomes. Mistaken short-term expectations can cause temporary departures from the full-employment equilibrium, as had been recognized by neoclassical economists prior to Keynes. In particular, underestimation of current market demand is one of the causes of frictional unemployment. Mistaken short-term expectations do not cause involuntary unemployment.

In contrast, long-term expectations relate to the estimation of the prospective monetary yields from investment projects. Keynes conceived of the state of long-term expectations as consisting of two components: the most probable forecast and the state of confidence. The latter refers to the degree of uncertainty attached to the most probable forecast. It is at this point that Keynes explicitly referred back to *A Treatise on Probability* and the concept of the weight of an argument to clarify the meaning of uncertainty. It is also consistent with his earlier criticism of the doctrine of mathematical expectation as too limited. The investment decision depends not only on the probability of alternative outcomes but also on the degree of confidence attached to these probability estimates, based on an assessment of the amount of relevant evidence. This insight provides the basis for the construction of an alternative theory of economic behaviour under uncertainty. Keynes argued further that business recognizes the precariousness of its estimates of prospective yields and, as a consequence, investment decisions are not based purely on mathematical calculations. He recognized that there are crucial non-rational elements in investment behaviour, namely, an innate urge to action over inaction (that is, animal spirits) as well as falling back on the conventional belief that the existing state of affairs will continue unless there are specific reasons to expect particular changes.

Keynes's analysis of economic behaviour under uncertainty in the *General Theory* required a change in the method of equilibrium analysis. Keynes retained the notion of equilibrium in the general sense of a position of rest but rejected the specific neoclassical definition of equilibrium as a market-clearing allocative outcome. Keynes set out a three-stage 'shifting equilibrium' analysis (see Gerrard 1997). The first stage is to determine the point of long-period equilibrium given a particular state of long-term expectations. The second stage is the logical-time analysis of the process of transition from one long-period equilibrium to another consequent on a shift in the state of long-term expectations. The final stage is the dynamic analysis of historical time consisting of a complex of overlapping transitional processes arising from a multitude of changes in long-term expectations.

To conclude: fundamental Keynesians have been critical, and rightly so, of neoclassical methods of analysis. To the extent that this criticism is grounded on Keynes's detailed analysis of probability, long-term expectations and equilibrium, the fundamentalists are not nihilistic but rather should be seen as providing the foundations for the construction of a truly radical Keynesian alternative.

BILL GERRARD

See also:

Equilibrium and Non-equilibrium; Expectations; Keynes's *General Theory*; Non-ergodicity; Time in Economic Theory; *Treatise on Probability*; Uncertainty.

References

Carabelli, A. (1988), *On Keynes's Method*, London: Macmillan.
Coddington, A. (1976), 'Keynesian economics: the search for first principles', *Journal of Economic Literature*, **14** (1), 1258–73.
Davidson, P. (1991), 'Is probability theory relevant for uncertainty? A Post-Keynesian perspective', *Journal of Economic Perspectives*, **5** (1), 129–44.
Fitzgibbons, A. (1988), *Keynes's Vision: A New Political Economy*, Oxford: Clarendon Press.
Gerrard, B. (1997), 'Method and methodology in Keynes's General Theory', in G.C. Harcourt and P.A. Riach (eds), *A 'Second Edition' of The General Theory. Volume 2*, London: Routledge, pp. 166–202.
Lawson, T. (1985), 'Uncertainty and economic analysis', *Economic Journal*, **95** (380), 909–27.
O'Donnell, R.M. (1989), *Keynes: Philosophy, Economics and Politics*, London: Macmillan.
Robinson, J. (1979), 'History versus equilibrium', in J. Robinson, *Contributions to Modern Economics*, Oxford: Basil Blackwell, pp. 126–36. (First published in *Thames Papers in Political Economy*, London, 1974.)
Shackle, G.L.S. (1967), *The Years of High Theory: Invention and Tradition in Economic Thought 1926–1939*, Cambridge: Cambridge University Press.

Globalization

Globalization is not a term invented by economists, and thus it is one of which all economists – Post Keynesian and mainstream alike – are suspicious, despite (or, in some cases, because of) the fact that it is at the centre of many contemporary economic policy debates. To the extent that globalization is considered synonymous with liberalization, Post Keynesians have been outspoken sceptics. In the face of the dominant neoliberal economic model with its call for financial market deregulation and fiscal and monetary austerity, Post Keynesians have insisted instead on expansionary macroeconomic policies and controls on international capital movements.

Globalization can be seen as a two-part process – the globalization of production and the globalization of finance. While both parts are the result of heightened international capital mobility, the globalization of finance is understood through the Post Keynesian theory of markets, while the analysis of the globalization of production requires the Post Keynesian theory of the firm and oligopoly. The globalization of production comprises international trade and foreign direct investment, and while the Post Keynesian theory is less well developed in these areas than in the area of finance, it none the less provides the building blocks for a rich description and policy-relevant theory of globalized production. Below we consider each of the aspects of globalization in turn.

Post Keynesians are generally sceptical of the global benefits of international financial market liberalization for two basic reasons. The first follows from the general Post Keynesian view that market flexibility does not bring optimality (for example, full employment) since the problem of unemployment is the result neither of market rigidities nor of information distortions resulting from government intervention or imperfect competition. Failures of effective demand can exist in the absence of either of these conditions. Moreover, price movements alone (through wages or exchange rates) are unlikely to bring about large adjustments in international payments imbalances and are swamped by the effect of changes in income and demand. Accordingly, international differences in the rate of economic growth – and thus international divergence of incomes – are explained in Post Keynesian theory by international differences in the income propensities to export and import.

The second is related to the risk of capital flight that comes with capital market liberalization. Post Keynesians have relied on Keynes's distinction between 'speculation' and 'enterprise', the former referring to 'the activity of forecasting the psychology of the market' and the latter 'the activity of forecasting the prospective yield of assets over their whole life' (Keynes 1936 [1964], p. 158). Keynes noted that capital markets – national or international – can at times be dominated by speculative behaviour that can move the economy away from full employment. In an oft-cited passage, he wrote:

> Speculators may do no harm as bubbles on a steady stream of enterprise. But the position is serious when enterprise becomes the bubble on a whirlpool of speculation. When the capital development of a country becomes a by-product of the activities of a casino, the job is likely to be ill-done. (Keynes 1936 [1964], p. 159)

Keynes saw the effects of speculation to be particularly detrimental in an open economy context when there is a risk of capital flight. In his 1933 essay, 'National self-sufficiency', Keynes argued that the ability of the state to pursue full employment (monetary and fiscal) policy may be jeopardized by international capital mobility. Thus, Keynes wrote, '[L]et goods be homespun wherever it is reasonably and conveniently possible, and, above all, let finance be primarily national' (Keynes 1933 [1982], p. 236).

For these two reasons, Post Keynesians have been sceptical of flexible exchange regimes and of capital market liberalization generally. Price inelasticity of trade explains the inefficiency of exchange rate adjustment, while the volatility of liberalized capital markets gives support to the policy of capital controls. Post Keynesians make the empirical argument that the rapid rates of economic growth experienced during the era of Bretton Woods resulted, in part, from the *limits* on the international mobility of capital and the relative fixity of exchange rates. Post Keynesians have typically found the source of Asian economic crises of the 1990s in the excessive (or too rapid) liberalization of foreign capital markets and have supported the use of bank-based rather than equity-based financing for economic development on the grounds that the latter encourages excessive speculation (and capital flight) rather than entrepreneurship.

Scepticism towards capital market liberalization has led to a variety of proposals for the regulation of international capital flows, including a transactions tax on international capital flows, an international reserve and capital adequacy requirement on all financial corporations, international procedures for the orderly sorting out of competing claims in the case of default on sovereign debt, or the establishment of a new central bank clearing unit to promote expansionary payments adjustment rather than the contraction that occurs in the current system.

The starting-point of the Post Keynesian theory of the globalization of production is the recognition that, in a market economy, unemployment, excess capacity and international payments imbalances have no natural tendency to reverse themselves. For a country operating at full employment, a payments imbalance can be expected to bring pressure for a change in the price level, as posited by the price-specie-flow mechanism. In the presence of persistent unemployment, trade imbalances will bring about movements in the rate of interest rather than in the price level. Trade imbalance results not in a change in the price level but in a potential liquidity problem for the deficit country by reducing the monetary base. This, in turn, will alter the interest rate. A surplus on current account will, by similar logic, reduce the rate of interest. Interest rate increases might, of course, move the economy further from full employment. Keynes himself argued that under certain conditions the balance of payments is the main determinant of the rate of interest, in which case improving the balance of payments is essential for the attainment of full employment.

Three important implications emerge for the understanding of globalization. First, without a well-functioning price-specie-flow mechanism, trade imbalances may persist over long periods of time. The balanced trade implication of the principle of comparative advantage is, in this way, equivalent to Say's Law in an open economy, whereby export growth automatically generates an equivalent increase in imports, or vice versa. Second, the direction of international trade, and thus the international division of labour, will be determined by *absolute* rather than comparative advantage since the mechanisms which would otherwise transform a situation of differential comparative costs into one of differences in absolute money costs and prices no longer operate. That is, the adjustment is simply not adequate to guarantee that the principle of comparative advantage will determine the direction of trade and a zero payments balance for all countries (Milberg 2002). According to Robinson (1973, p. 16), 'The comforting doctrine that a country cannot be "undersold all round" was derived from the postulate of universal full employment. The argument consists merely in assuming what it hopes to prove.' Finally, if trade is determined by absolute advantage and countries can indeed be 'undersold all round', then free trade is not necessarily the first-best policy, since infant industry protection may be needed to spur technical change needed for international competition.

The other aspect of globalized production is foreign direct investment, and Post Keynesian pricing theory provides some relatively untapped insights. Hymer, building on Ronald Coase's emphasis on transactions costs and Alfred Chandler's focus on the historical evolution of corporate capitalism, was the first to understand that the phenomenon of foreign direct investment was necessarily driven by oligopolistic firms. The high volume of 'cross-hauling' (that is, simultaneous inward and outward foreign direct investment in one country) implies that the process is not driven simply by arbitrage of temporarily high profit opportunities in one location compared to another. Hymer, and later others, argued that the transnational firm is a non-market institution, and its desire to *internalize* international operations constitutes a market failure, but is the prime reason for firms to invest abroad rather than serve foreign markets in other ways, such as exports. In oligopoly, firms are large and few, or as Hymer puts it, 'the size of the market is limited by the size of the firm' (Hymer 1970, p. 443).

The oligopoly corporation emerged in the late nineteenth century as the organizational form that best captured economies of scale, best avoided the otherwise destructiveness of price-based, 'perfect' competition, and insulated investment from cyclical downturns. Transnational corporate investment began as oligopolies matured in the 1920s. Over time, foreign direct investment became 'a new weapon in the arsenal of oligopolistic rivalry' (Hymer 1972, p. 444) as firms sought new markets, and the control of resources and cheap labour – all the while conserving their transactions cost advantage over market-based operations such as through exports.

Post Keynesians have long recognized the ruinous nature of price competition and thus the necessity of oligopoly over the long run (Eichner 1976, p. 11). More important, such a recognition has led to an alternative theory of price determination in capitalism, in which the firm, rather than market forces of supply and demand, plays the dominant role. According to Shapiro and Mott (1995, p. 38), 'The prices derived in the mark-up models of the [Post Keynesian] theory are not the prices that serve the unconscious ends of the market (the allocative efficiency of the neoclassical theory or the systemic reproduction of the Ricardian conception) but the ones that serve the conscious ends of the enterprise.' In Eichner's (1976, chapter 2) theory of the 'megacorp', firms use pricing as a means to generate finance for future investment. From the perspective of the transnational corporation, international investment allows the internalization not only of firm-specific advantages related to technology, management, marketing and so on, but also the internalization of the pricing decision on international (intra-firm) transactions.

Does the recent trend towards outsourcing and subcontracting constitute a reversal of the oligopolistic trend identified by Chandler, Hymer, Eichner and others? The process has become so prevalent that the contemporary manufacturing firm often does no manufacturing at all. Most outsourcing relations today are 'arm's length' in a formal sense only. The rise in outsourcing and subcontracting constitutes a sharpening of the hierarchical structure that Hymer identified with the modern corporation, due to the added flexibility that outsourcing provides and the selective competition (among suppliers) that it promotes. Subcontracting is driven by the desire of firms to increase flexibility and lower unit labour costs. Cost reduction can come with increased productivity or lower wages. In this sense, the rise of international outsourcing reintroduces the ruinous competition from which capitalism escaped in the late 1800s. The expansion of sweatshop labour is thus an integral part of the globalization of production, and is another source of rising income inequality in developing countries.

The insights of Hymer and Eichner can form the foundation of a Post Keynesian theory of international production, but the full theory remains undeveloped and untested. Moreover, a truly Post Keynesian theory will make a connection between the finance and production processes in the global economy. This becomes especially important as firms outsource production operations and focus increasingly on financial management. Investment location decisions may themselves be influenced by foreign exchange portfolio considerations, for example. That is, the manufacturing firm is increasingly a financial unit. Keynes's distinction between speculation and enterprise is being blurred further as foreign direct investment can increasingly be hedged with the build-up of domestic liabilities.

In the conclusion of *The General Theory*, Keynes wote that 'The outstanding faults of the economic society in which we live are its failure to provide for full employment and its arbitrary and inequitable distribution of wealth and incomes' (Keynes 1964, p. 372). These faults are arguably worse today than they were 25 years ago, when the current wave of globalization began. The global economy suffers chronic unemployment, excess capacity in most manufacturing sectors and growing income inequality. Real wage suppression and lax social standards in poor countries has not brought them a degree of international competitiveness sufficient to generate economic development; financial liberalization has hastened economic crises in East Asia, Russia and Central and South America; and austerity imposed by the International Monetary Fund has tended to worsen these problems. The economic logic of a policy of sustained global demand expansion with regulated international capital mobility is reasonably well established, but the political obstacles to its implementation remain large.

WILLIAM MILBERG

See also:

Bretton Woods; Competition; Economic Policy; Exchange Rates; International Economics; Pricing and Prices; Tobin Tax.

References

Eichner, A.S. (1976), *The Megacorp and Oligopoly*, Cambridge: Cambridge University Press.
Hymer, S. (1970), 'The efficiency (contradictions) of multinational corporations', *American Economic Review*, **60** (2), 441–8.
Hymer, S. (1972), 'The multinational corporation and the law of uneven development', in J.

Bhagwati (ed.), *Economics and the World Order: From the 1970s to the 1990s*, New York: Free Press, pp. 436–63.

Keynes, J.M. (1933 [1982]), 'National self-sufficiency', *Yale Review*, Summer. Reprinted in *The Collected Writings of John Maynard Keynes. Volume XXI: Activities 1931–1939*, London: Macmillan for the Royal Economic Society, pp. 233–46.

Keynes, J.M. (1936 [1964]), *The General Theory of Employment, Interest and Money*, New York: Harcourt, Brace & Jovanovich.

Milberg, W. (2002), 'Say's Law in the open economy: Keynes's rejection of the theory of comparative advantage', in S. Dow and J. Hillard (eds), *Keynes, Uncertainty and the Global Economy*, Cheltenham, UK and Northampton, MA, USA: Edward Elgar, pp. 239–53.

Robinson, J. (1973), 'The need for a reconsideration of the theory of international trade', in R. Swoboda (ed.), *Current Issues in International Economics*, London: Macmillan, pp. 15–25.

Shapiro, N. and T. Mott (1995), 'Firm-determined prices: the Post-Keynesian conception', in Paul Wells (ed.), *Post-Keynesian Economic Theory*, Boston: Kluwer Academic Publishers, pp. 35–48.

Growth and Income Distribution

The determinants of growth were a major concern of the classical economists, who related growth to income distribution. The latter affects the saving decisions of the different classes and, according to some classical economists, their investment decisions too. Adam Smith and Karl Marx also underlined the role of technical progress, presenting a broad analysis of this subject, which can be considered an antecedent of the modern cumulative causation and evolutionary approaches.

The rise of the neoclassical school in the second half of the nineteenth century brought about a change of perspective in economic theory. Allocation of resources became the major concern and the problem of distribution was seen as one aspect of the general pricing and allocation process. Neoclassical economists argued that competitive forces, operating through variations in relative prices and factor substitution, generate a tendency to full employment and to the exploitation of the growth potential of the economy. These market mechanisms were examined in what Keynes called the 'real department of economics'. The 'monetary department' dealt instead with business fluctuations, arguing that the working of the credit system cause or amplify them.

The severity of the Great Depression changed the course of these events. As Roy Harrod pointed out (see Young 1989, pp. 30–38), previous recessions had not led the economy too far from full employment, nor had they cast doubt on the belief that the economy is able to return to it. The Great Depression, however, endangered political stability and raised the problem of a new political approach and of a new economic theory able to clarify whether market forces can lead the economy towards full employment or government intervention is required to restore it.

Moving along these lines, in 1932 Keynes introduced the concept of a 'monetary theory of production' to attack the neoclassical separation between the real and the monetary departments of economics and the idea of a tendency to full employment. Harrod, on the other hand, began in 1933 to develop economic dynamics. His work was stimulated by the will to extend Keynes's ideas to the dynamic context. The seminal 'An essay in dynamic theory' thus conceived modern growth theory as a Keynesian theory: it developed the views that the economic system does not tend necessarily to full employment and that the rate of growth may be affected by the autonomous components of aggregate demand, coming from the government, the private and the foreign sectors.

In opposition to Harrod's views, Robert Solow presented in 1956 a dynamic version of neoclassical theory. He argued that variations in relative prices and factor substitution led the economy to a full-employment steady growth path. The debate on capital theory, enhanced by the publication in 1960 of Piero Sraffa's *Production of Commodities by Means of Commodities*, scrutinized Solow's conclusions. Some outstanding neoclassical economists acknowledged the validity of some criticisms raised against their theory. Paul Samuelson recognized, in the summing up of the 1966 Symposium in the *Quarterly Journal of Economics*, that in the long-period analysis of an economy where more than one commodity is produced, the occurrence of 'reverse capital deepening' is the general case. This conclusion undercut the neoclassical 'parables' that extended to a multi-commodity economy the conclusions from the analysis of a one-commodity world and challenged the view that price variations and factor substitution lead the economy to full employment.

During the same years, Kaldor (1955–56) and Pasinetti (1962) developed the Post Keynesian theory of growth and distribution by assuming that market forces operate along lines that are different from those envisaged by neoclassical authors and similar to those described by the classical economists. Like the latter, Kaldor and Pasinetti assumed that the propensities to save of different income earners (or classes, or sectors of the economy) are not equal, and argued that variations in income distribution bring about variations in total saving and aggregate demand, leading the economy to steady growth. The Post Keynesian theory of growth and distribution introduced the 'Cambridge equation' and the 'Pasinetti theorem', which state that in steady growth the rate of profit is equal to the ratio between the rate of growth and the capitalists' propensity to save, and does not depend on technology or on the workers' propensity to save. In 1966 Samuelson and Franco Modigliani challenged this conclusion and proposed an 'anti-Pasinetti' or 'dual' theorem. They argued that in steady growth, if the capital owned by the capitalist class is zero, the capital–output ratio is equal to the ratio between the workers' propensity to save and the rate of growth, while the rate of profit depends on the technological relation connecting this variable to the capital–output ratio. Whether the 'Pasinetti' or the 'dual' theorem applies depends on this technological relationship too.

By focusing on the role of income distribution in the growth process, and underlining the links with the classical economists and the differences with neoclassical authors, the theory proposed by Kaldor and Pasinetti failed to emphasize that there is no automatic tendency to full employment. However, developments in the Kaldor–Pasinetti theory, which have examined the role of the demand coming from the government sector, atone for this failure.

Kaldor's 1958 Memorandum to the Radcliffe Commission shows many similarities with the views on the role of government policy proposed by Harrod and other Keynesian authors. Kaldor considered government policies to be necessary to pursue stability and growth. For him, monetary policy is the appropriate tool against economic fluctuations, while fiscal policy is relevant to the long-range objective of sustained growth. He proposed to use the Cambridge equation to determine the tax rate compatible with both the full-employment rate of growth and the rate of interest fixed by the monetary authority. In doing so he showed awareness of the complexity of the growth process, when he anticipated the view, developed some years later, that an expansionary fiscal policy may cause problems for the international competitiveness of the economy and for the maintenance of sustained growth in the future.

Kaldor did not present his conclusions on the role of government policy in a formalized way. The first formal presentation of the Post Keynesian theory of growth and distribution, which explicitly introduces the government sector, was provided by Ian Steedman in 1972. He assumed a balanced budget to show that the Cambridge equation – in a revised form that takes into account the existence of taxation – holds in a larger number of cases than the dual theorem of Samuelson and Modigliani. By the late 1980s, Fleck and Domenghino and Pasinetti started a debate on the validity of the Cambridge equation when the budget is *not* balanced. The debate examined a large number of cases, showing when the Cambridge equation holds and confirming the conclusions previously reached by Steedman (see Panico 1997). Its results describe how the views presented by Kaldor to the Radcliffe Commission can be formally developed, clarifying some features of his proposals. Moreover, they show the existence of some other common elements between the classical and the Post Keynesian traditions, allowing the reconciliation of two approaches to distribution, which had previously been considered alternative. These are the approach proposed by Kaldor and Pasinetti in their theory of growth and distribution and that implied by

Sraffa's hint in *Production of Commodities* to take the rate of profit, rather than the wage rate, as the independent variable (determined, in turn, by the money interest rates) in the classical theory of prices and distribution.

Another line of development in the Keynesian literature on growth focuses on the demand coming from the private sector in the form of autonomous investment. This literature presents several investment-driven growth theories based on different specifications of the investment function.

The neo-Keynesian theory, proposed by Joan Robinson and Kaldor, assumes a direct functional relationship between investment and the rate of profit. This theory, which determines growth and distribution simultaneously, extends to long-period analysis the 'paradox of thrift', according to which an increase in the propensity to save causes a reduction in the rate of profit and in the rate of growth. Moreover, it underlines the existence of an inverse relationship between the real wage rate and the rate of growth.

The Kaleckian theory, inspired by Michał Kalecki and Josef Steindl, assumes that (i) productive capacity is not utilized at its 'normal' level, (ii) the profit margin is an exogenous variable depending on the degree of monopoly enjoyed by oligopolistic firms, (iii) prices are determined through a mark-up procedure, and (iv) investment is positively related to the rate of profit, which is a proxy for the state of expected profitability and the availability of internal finance, and the degree of capacity utilization, which reflects the state of aggregate demand. This theory confirms the neo-Keynesian conclusion on the paradox of thrift and argues, in opposition to the neo-Keynesian theory, for the existence of a positive relationship between the real wage rate and the rate of growth in the presence of long-run underutilization of capacity. This result, known as the 'paradox of costs', is due to the fact that the rise in the real wage rate brings about an increase in demand and capacity utilization, which has a positive effect on the rate of profit and on investment.

The Kaleckian theory has been recently amended by work inspired by Bhaduri and Marglin (1990), which takes into account the different effects on investment of the rate of profit, the profit margin and capacity utilization. By introducing an investment function positively related to the profit margin and to capacity utilization, these works identify a wage-led and a profit-led growth regime. In both cases, a rise in the real wage rate reduces the profit margin and increases capacity utilization. However, in the wage-led regime the overall effect of an increase in the real wage rate on growth is positive, as in the Kaleckian paradox of costs, because the positive effect on growth generated by the increase in capacity utilization is assumed to be greater than the negative effect on growth generated by the decrease in the profit margin. In the profit-led regime the opposite result holds, because the positive effect on growth generated by the increase in capacity utilization is assumed to be lower than the negative effect generated by the decrease in the profit margin.

Finally, an attempt has been made in recent literature to develop a neo-Ricardian theory of growth, which starts from a classical theory of prices and distribution. This theory, in opposition to the neo-Keynesian and Kaleckian theories, assumes that the investment function depends on the discrepancies between actual and normal capacity utilization and underlines the need to develop the analysis of growth through the comparison of long-period positions. Moreover, it makes the rate of profit depend on the money rate of interest, as suggested by Sraffa in *Production of Commodities*.

The last line of development of Keynesian literature focuses on the influence on growth of demand coming from the foreign sector, a problem already considered by Harrod in the 1930s. This literature plays down the role of distributive variables and is intertwined with the analysis of growth as a 'cumulative process'.

In a series of essays written between 1966 and 1972, Kaldor used the notion of 'cumulative causation' to describe the actual performance of economies. He attributed to the demand coming from the foreign sector the primary role in setting in motion the growth process. The domestic sources of demand mainly influence, instead, the competitiveness of the economy and the intensity with which an external stimulus is transmitted to the rate of growth. According to Kaldor, the composition of output and demand has an important influence on the rate of change of productivity, owing to the presence of variable returns in the different sectors of the economy and to the fact that increasing returns occur mainly in the capital-goods sector. For Kaldor, high ratios of investment to aggregate demand and of the capital-goods sector in the productive structure enhance productivity changes, which, in turn, improve the international performance of the economy, setting up and intensifying cumulative processes. He distinguished between the concepts of 'consumption-led' and 'export-led' growth. The latter, he argued, is more desirable than the former, which tends to have negative long-run effects on productivity and international competitiveness, since it increases the weight of non-increasing returns sectors in the productive structure of the economy. This distinction was at the basis of Kaldor's claim, noted above, that the maintenance of sustained growth in the future may be endangered by the use of fiscal policy, which, according to him, tends to increase the share of consumption in aggregate demand.

In 1975, Robert Dixon and Anthony Thirlwall presented an 'export-led growth model', which formalized some aspects of Kaldor's views. Thirlwall (1979), on the other hand, worked out a dynamic analysis showing how growth may be constrained by the equilibrium of the balance of payments, disregarding the operation of cumulative processes. In spite of this simplification, the empirical applications of the new analysis, which are able to account for differences in the rates of growth among countries and the cumulative divergence in their GDP levels, have produced more satisfactory results than those of the 1975 export-led model. Recently Moreno Brid (1998–99) and McCombie and Thirlwall (1999) have extended Thirlwall's new analysis to take into account the impact of the persistent accumulation of external debt on the economy's long-term rate of expansion. These extensions have opened new areas of research into the financial restrictions imposed by international credit institutions on the long-term economic growth of countries with persistent trade balance deficits.

CARLO PANICO

See also:

Cambridge Economic Tradition; Capital Theory; Growth Theory; Income Distribution; Investment; Kaldorian Economics; Kaleckian Economics; Sraffian Economics.

References

Bhaduri, A. and S. Marglin (1990), 'Unemployment and the real wage: the economic basis for contesting political ideologies', *Cambridge Journal of Economics*, **14** (4), 375–93.
Kaldor, N. (1955–56), 'Alternative theories of distribution', *Review of Economic Studies*, **23** (2), 83–100.
McCombie, J. and A.P. Thirlwall (1999), 'Growth in an international context: a post Keynesian view', in J. Deprez and J.T. Harvey (eds), *Foundations of International Economics: Post Keynesian Perspectives*, London: Routledge, pp. 35–90.
Moreno Brid, J.C. (1998–99), 'On capital flows and the balance-of-payments constrained growth model', *Journal of Post Keynesian Economics*, **21** (2), 283–98.
Panico, C. (1997), 'Government deficits in the Post Keynesian theories of growth and distribution', *Contributions to Political Economy*, **16**, 61–86.
Pasinetti, L.L. (1962), 'Rate of profit and income distribution in relation to the rate of economic growth', *Review of Economic Studies*, **29** (4), 103–20.
Thirlwall, A.P. (1979), 'The balance of payments constraint as an explanation of international growth rate differences', *Banca Nazionale del Lavoro Quarterly Review*, 128, pp. 45–53
Young, W. (1989), *Harrod and His Trade Cycle Group*, London: Macmillan.

Growth Theory

Sustained but irregular and unevenly distributed growth in output has been a defining aspect of capitalism. An equally defining aspect of Post Keynesian economic analysis has been its desire to realistically confront this complex phenomenon. The undeniable difficulty of this task in part explains why the Post Keynesian literature on growth is as irregular and uneven as its subject matter.

Post Keynesian growth models range from those that focus solely on the phenomenon of growth and eschew the analysis of cycles, to others in which cycles and growth are inseparable. However, most if not all Post Keynesian growth models are distinguishable from neoclassical models by considering at least two of the factors of growth, cyclicality and distribution (where the last factor concerns social classes, or different sectors of industry, or both). There is therefore a strong overlap between Post Keynesian treatments of growth, cycles, distribution and industrial structure. All are intrinsically entwined in Post Keynesian analysis and the real world.

Harrod set the tone for subsequent work by Post Keynesians when, in criticizing the neoclassical proclivity to treat growth and cycles as independent phenomena, he stated that 'the trend of growth may itself generate forces making for oscillation' (Harrod 1939, pp. 14–15). His single-sector model of unstable growth was driven by a savings function that depended upon the level of output, and an investment function that depended upon the rate of change of output. From this he derived a formula that equated the savings to output ratio to the product of the rate of growth, and the ratio of investment to change in output (the latter is known as the incremental capital to output ratio, or ICOR). This equality applied both to the actual recorded rate of growth and ICOR, and the desired rate of growth and desired ICOR that together fulfilled capitalist expectations. If the actual rate of growth exceeded the desired rate, then the actual level of investment would be below the desired level – which then led to an increase in investment that accelerated the rate of growth even further; the reverse mechanism applied if actual growth was below the desired rate.

Joan Robinson, Nicholas Kaldor, Luigi Pasinetti, Richard Goodwin and Edward Nell set off different analytic streams subsequent to Harrod's seminal contribution. Each stream involved some compromise forced by the difficulty of modelling the dynamic process of growth, though none compromised realism as completely as was commonplace in neoclassical theory. Today a substantial new band of nonlinear modellers are slowly blending these historic roots with modern nonlinear mathematical methods and computational analysis.

Robinson overcame the pre-computer inability to model growth processes out of equilibrium with the mental device of comparative 'golden age' economies. The structure of an economy was clearly specified in terms of classes (workers, capitalists, rentiers), sources of income (wages, profits, rent/interest), expenditures (consumption, investment, placement), industry sectors (consumption, investment), and fundamental rates of change (population growth, technical progress). The proportions between these variables that would be needed to ensure the highly unlikely outcome of stable growth were then worked out, and two economies were assumed to be in this golden age (sometimes with differing key values, such as the level of real wages). A change in behaviour could then be postulated in one economy (for example, an increase in birth rates leading to a rise in unemployment, or an increase in technical progress in investment goods) that would move it off its golden path, and the change in systemic behaviour was evaluated with respect to the economy that continued in its golden state. Kregel (1975) gives a very accessible overview of Robinson's method, and provides a useful survey of the rival approaches of Kaldor and Pasinetti.

Kaldor extended Harrod's model by incorporating the topic of income distribution between workers and capitalists, where capitalists had a higher propensity to save than workers. Using the extreme assumption that workers do not save and capitalists do not consume, he linked the rate of profit to the rate of growth. Kaldor eschewed the concept of an aggregate measure of capital, and argued that since technical progress was embodied in new machines, capital in use would have a profile from the most profitable new machinery to the near-obsolete that would earn a zero rate of profit.

However, while Robinson's approach emphasized the extreme improbability of any economy ever being on a 'golden path', and Harrod's model had an unstable equilibrium, Kaldor made the opposing assumptions that long-run growth had to involve the full employment of labour, and that the long-run equilibrium was stable. His reason for these assumptions – that growth concerns long-period analysis and only a full-employment equilibrium could prevail in the long term – would not be accepted today, since it is well known that models of complex systems do not have to converge to an equilibrium but can remain indefinitely in a 'far-from-equilibrium' state. This assumption also drove a wedge between Kaldor's short-run Keynesianism and his long-run analysis.

Pasinetti corrected Kaldor's model to allow for workers owning a proportion of profits, but concluded that the rate of growth was nevertheless determined by the accumulation decisions of capitalists alone.

Kaldor also contributed a 'weather vane' to economic analysis by arguing that there were a number of 'stylized facts' that any theory of growth had to explain if it were to be regarded as prima facie tenable. These included the primacy of the rate of growth of the manufacturing sector in determining overall growth via the technological progress and increasing returns to scale that emanate from this growth, the decline in agricultural employment over time, and the relative constancy of income shares over time. Subsequent Post Keynesians have added effective demand growth as a key constraint on overall growth, a secular decline in manufacturing and rise of service employment in advanced economies, and the need for models of growth in which the monetary and financial system plays a crucial role.

Goodwin's growth cycle, published in the centenary year of Marx's *Capital*, gave a mathematical rendition of Marx's chapter 25 verbal model of a growth cycle driven by a struggle over the distribution of income between workers and capitalists in which the rate of unemployment acted as a check upon workers' wage demands. Technically the model was a descendant of the 'predator–prey' model first developed in biology by Alfred Lotka and Vito Volterra, while economically it included the complete panoply of growth, cycles and income distribution. Although criticized in some quarters for structural instability and a lack of empirical verification, it has been used as a basis for many more general models and is still a fruitful basis for further research. Blatt (1983) provides a clearer explanation of this model than can be found in Goodwin's original writings.

Kaldor aside, most Post Keynesian work on growth has presumed that the main constraint on the rate of economic growth comes not from supply-side issues as in neoclassical theory, but from effective demand constraints and the non-neutrality of money.

Post Keynesians have also been interested in explaining why growth occurs, as well as finding means to model it.

Kornai (1990) argues that firms in capitalist economies are constrained not by resources and productivity, as in the neoclassical model, but by limits to effective demand. This demand constraint means that firms operate with significant excess capacity, since without this they can neither respond to changes in the structure of demand, nor take advantage of problems that might beset competitors. As a result, production costs do not vary with output, and firms compete by product innovation rather than via price: price competition is the exception rather than the norm.

Product innovation in turn requires research, development and investment, which both generates growth and gives rise to waves of Schumpeterian 'creative destruction' that give growth in capitalist economies its cyclical nature. This analysis thus grounds technical progress and growth in productive capacity in the competitive interactions of firms vying for profit and market share.

Nell (1998) emphasizes the transformational nature of growth in a capitalist economy – growth involves not merely quantitative increase, but also qualitative change in the composition of output, the nature of economic institutions, and the state of economic expectations. Like Kornai, Nell stresses the role of real, historical markets in promoting increased productivity, social change and growth. He also attempts to integrate Sraffa's appreciation of the multi-sectoral nature of output into a dynamic model of the economy.

Failures in growth also attract Post Keynesian attention, with the most notable failure being the Great Depression. The most cogent explanation here has come from Hyman Minsky's blending of Irving Fisher's 'debt deflation' hypothesis with Keynes's analysis of the formation of expectations under uncertainty. Minsky developed the hypothesis that a period of stable economic growth will lead to capitalists and bankers revising their risk aversions, leading to an increased willingness to take on debt to finance expansions that will inevitably result in a period of financial stress and a collapse in the growth rate. This hypothesis that 'stability is destabilizing' neatly returns us to the Harrodian foundations of Post Keynesian growth theory, by providing a link between the rate of growth and the development of capitalist expectations – and hence their rate of investment.

Nonlinearity and 'chaos theory' (or more properly complexity theory) are playing an increasing role in modern Post Keynesian work on growth. Nonlinear relations arise naturally in economics out of interactions between variables (for example, by the multiplication of the wage rate times the level of employment to determine the wage bill) and obvious nonlinear social relations (such as the relationship between the rate of growth of the economy and profits and the willingness of capitalists to invest). When put into mathematical models of growth – using differerence or differential rather than simultaneous equations – these nonlinearities in turn generate the stylized fact that distinguishes the Post Keynesian approach to growth theory from the neoclassical: unstable, cyclical growth. It is thus possible to have models of the long run in which the system continues to fluctuate, and in which the system never converges to an equilibrium. Chiarella and Flaschel (2000) is a very sophisticated example of this approach, using building blocks that would be acknowledged by traditional Keynesians as well as Post Keynesians.

These models can be partially characterized by the mathematical properties of their equations, but modern computer technology has also added the possibility of numerically simulating the behaviour of complex, high-dimensional models with far-from-equilibrium dynamics. This technology obviates the need to make simplifying assumptions, such as constancy of income shares, which were previously used to make dynamic reasoning tractable.

A comprehensive Post Keynesian theory of growth would clearly involve the following elements: a treatment of the causes of innovation in a market economy, where competition is primarily in product differentiation rather than price; multiple industry sectors rather than the abstraction of homogeneous output, so that the disproportional growth of the real economy is mirrored by the model, and the impossibility of producing an aggregate measure of capital is explicitly acknowledged; a relationship between the rate of technical progress and the income distribution and effective demand constraints inherent in a capitalist economy; a key role for non-neutral monetary factors, with the possibility that debt accumulation dynamics may on occasions retard and even reverse the process of growth; and a resulting model that generates both endogenous cycles and endogenous growth, with a significant possibility of economic breakdown under the weight of financial factors. While the many strands of Post Keynesian thought to date have provided most of the necessary strands, it remains true that blending an overall tapestry remains a research project for future Post Keynesians.

STEVE KEEN

See also:

Business Cycles; Dynamics; Financial Instability Hypothesis; Growth and Income Distribution; Innovation; Kaldorian Economics.

References

Blatt, J. (1983), *Dynamic Economic Systems: A Post Keynesian Approach*, Armonk, NY: M.E. Sharpe.
Chiarella, C. and P. Flaschel (2000), *The Dynamics of Keynesian Monetary Growth*, New York: Cambridge University Press.
Harrod, R.F. (1939), 'An essay in dynamic theory', *Economic Journal*, **49** (193), 14–33.
Kornai, J. (1990), *Vision and Reality, Market and State: Contradictions and Dilemmas Revisited*, New York: Routledge.
Kregel, J.A. (1975), *The Reconstruction of Political Economy: An Introduction to Post-Keynesian Economics*, London: Macmillan.
Nell, E.J. (1998), *The General Theory of Transformational Growth*, New York: Cambridge University Press.

Income Distribution

The dominant theory of distribution in modern economics is the neoclassical marginal productivity approach, also known as the 'supply and demand' approach. Marginal productivity theory conceives capital as a productive factor, and it argues for the existence of an inverse monotonic relation between the rate of profit and the quantity of capital employed in the production process. This relation constitutes the demand for capital schedule. The supply of capital is determined by households' portfolio demands for capital, and the equilibrium rate of profit and quantity of capital are then determined by the intersection of the supply and demand curves for capital.

The process of wage determination is entirely analogous to that determining the rate of profit. Labour is also viewed as a productive factor, and there exists an inverse monotonic relation between the wage rate and the quantity of labour employed. This relation constitutes the demand for labour schedule. The supply of labour is determined by households' utility-maximizing choice over leisure and market income, and the equilibrium wage rate and employment level are determined by the intersection of the supply and demand curves for labour.

Perfect competition is the hallmark of the marginal productivity theory of income distribution. Departures from perfect competition can be introduced to explain such phenomena as discrimination in labour markets. This introduces 'economic' and 'monopoly' rents, with some factors being paid more than they would in a competitive market. This is also the neoclassical approach to trade unions. However, these modifications retain the basic marginalist approach to income distribution, interpreted as the outcome of an exchange process based on choices at the margin in a world in which production is described by a continuous concave function that is homogeneous of degree one.

The concept of a production function is crucial to neoclassical theory, providing the basis for marginal products from which are derived the demand for labour and capital schedules. The logical foundations of this concept formed the initial focus of a debate that was to become known as the Cambridge capital controversies. The controversy was launched by Joan Robinson's (1953–54) article challenging the existence of an aggregate production function on the grounds that it is impossible to aggregate heterogeneous capital. The Robinson critique has now been largely accepted, but is generally ignored by neoclassical economists in practice.

Another criticism of neoclassical marginal productivity theory, which is post-modernist in character, emphasizes the social construction of marginal products (Palley 1996a, pp. 64–7). Within existing accounts of marginal productivity theory, factors are paid their marginal products, which are objectively measurable. Such a position assumes that objective measurement is possible. Yet measurement is intrinsically social, being an act of interpretation based upon socially negotiated rules. These rules attribute value and are derived from understandings that are themselves socially derived. As knowledge, beliefs and social arrangements change, so too will measurements. Who does the measuring affects the measurement outcome. Such considerations introduce a radical subjectivism into neoclassical production theory that parallels ordinal utility theory, which introduced radical subjectivism into neoclassical consumer theory in the 1930s. As a result, even if well-defined production functions exist, income distribution can never be the result of a purely technical process and is always inevitably tainted by social forces.

A key feature of the neoclassical supply and demand approach is that it is a joint theory of employment and factor price determination. Supply and demand schedules determine both prices and quantities, and the downward-sloping labour demand schedule imposes a binding trade-off whereby real wages can only increase if employment falls. The neo-Ricardian framework, developed by Piero Sraffa, aims to sunder the link between wages and employment. The Sraffian system has a number of appealing properties. The determination of the normal wage reflects social and historical forces, opening the way for the introduction of bargaining power concerns. It also breaks with the labour demand curve notion that the level of real wages constrains the level of employment. Instead, in the Sraffian system the real wage constrains the profit rate, and the binding trade-off is between the profit rate and wages. Since the model does not use aggregate capital, but instead only requires a competitively maintained common rate of profit on the value of inputs, it is not subject to Robinson's (1953–54) capital critique.

The traditional Marxian approach to income distribution is constructed through the lens of the labour theory of value, and the focus is on the extraction of surplus value. In this framework, concern lies with the rate of surplus value, which measures the degree of exploitation of labour. Over the last 25 years, a distinctive American neoclassical school of Marxism has developed, leading figures of which are Samuel Bowles, Herbert Gintis and John Roemer. These economists accept the existence of a well-defined neoclassical production function, but they break with the neoclassical assumption that technology is exogenous. Instead, they argue that it is endogenously selected. The significance of this argument is that choice of technology now involves human agency, social context and control.

The importance of control for distributional outcomes signals the importance of power. This brings into play the issue of perfect competition, which is another assumption embedded in neoclassical marginal productivity theory. Perfect competition ensures that both capital and labour have no power. It is not that the two are equally powerful, but rather that neither has any power. Removing the perfect competition assumptions of costless mobility and perfect free information restores power to centre stage.

The above neoclassical Marxian concerns link with the macroeconomics of Michał Kalecki (1942). A central component of Kalecki's macroeconomics is the mark-up, and its determination constitutes a key element of the Kaleckian research programme. In the standard Kaleckian model output is produced through a linear production function involving labour, and prices are a mark-up over average cost. The mark-up determines the wage and profit shares, bringing to the fore the question of what determines the mark-up. A modern neoclassical industrial organization perspective would focus on the degree of monopoly in product markets. Neoclassical Marxism focuses on control and bargaining power issues.

Keynesian economics emphasizes the significance of aggregate demand, and aggregate demand considerations figure centrally in the Post Keynesian approach to income distribution. The Post Keynesian approach was developed by Kaldor (1956), and has its roots in another side of Kalecki's (1942) macroeconomics. Rather than the mark-up, the pivotal point is different propensities to consume out of wage and profit income. Given exogenous propensities to save out of profit and wage income, the profit share is determined exclusively by the investment share of output. If the propensity to save out of wage income is zero, which is Kalecki's assumption, then the profit share depends on just the investment share and the propensity to save out of profits. Higher investment spending raises the profit share, while a higher propensity to save out of profits lowers it. This leads to the Kaleckian dictum that 'capitalists earn what they spend, while workers spend what they earn'. The logic behind this Post Keynesian result is that investment needs to be financed by saving, and income distribution must therefore be appropriate to support the right level of saving. If investment spending goes up, a higher profit share is needed to generate additional saving. If the propensity to save goes up, a lower profit share is needed to reduce total saving.

In Kaldor's (1956) Post Keynesian model there is an implicit class structure consisting of workers and capitalists. Pasinetti (1962) explicitly models this class structure, using the assumptions that (i) workers have a lower propensity to save than capitalists, (ii) capitalists' only source of income is profit income, (iii) workers receive both wage and profit income – wage income for supplying labour and profit income on their saving, and (iv) the rate of interest is equal to the rate of profit. The assumption that workers have a lower propensity to save ensures that their saving out of wage and profit income does not drive down the capitalists' ownership share of the capital stock to zero. Given these conditions, Pasinetti shows that steady-state income distribution is unaffected by workers' saving behaviour. The economic logic is simple. In a steady state the capitalist share of the capital stock is constant, and they must save sufficient to maintain this ownership share. Consequently, the profit share must be such that it can support a share of saving appropriate to maintaining the capitalists' ownership share. Viewed in this light, the Post Keynesian theory of income distribution might better be thought of as a theory of wealth ownership.

Pasinetti's theorem regarding the irrelevance of worker saving behaviour has been remarkably robust with regard to introduction of other sources of saving. It holds when government saving is introduced via the government budget constraint and also in the presence of life-cycle saving behaviour. However, there are a number of limitations to the Post Keynesian approach to income distribution. First, it is an exclusively real theory of the interest rate, which is determined by the profit rate, and this is at odds with Keynesian theory, which emphasizes liquidity preference. Introducing monetary factors into the analysis invalidates Pasinetti's theorem regarding the irrelevance of the workers' propensity to save for steady-state distributional outcomes. To the extent that money balances are disproportionately held by workers, they must save more to maintain their share of the money stock, which influences steady-state income distribution. Palley (1996b) introduces financial intermediation and inside debt, and demonstrates that Pasinetti's theorem holds if lending is done via a loanable funds market, but is invalidated if done through a banking system with endogenous credit money.

In sum, the Post Keynesian approach to distribution, with its focus on the dynamics of capital accumulation within classes, makes a valuable contribution. Yet, despite introducing class, it makes no mention of class conflict in the form of labour market struggle. Nor is there any mention of product demand conditions, in the form of the rate of capacity utilization. These considerations suggest that is an incomplete account of the determination of income distribution.

The above reflections on the Post Keynesian approach point to the fact that income distribution is likely determined by a complex of factors, suggesting the need for a synthetic approach. The neo-Marxian approach to income distribution can be synthesized with Keynesian demand considerations. Palley (1998) presents a short-run neo-Marxian model in which labour market bargaining conditions determine the distribution of income, and aggregate demand conditions determine the state of labour market conditions. Because aggregate demand is affected by income distribution, owing to Kaleckian differences in the propensity to consume out of wage and profit income, there is a feedback loop between aggregate demand (the goods market) and income distribution (the goods market). The canonical long-run version of the neo-Marxian–Keynesian model is attributable to Goodwin (1967), who constructs a model in which labour market conditions drive profit rates, profit rates drive the rate of accumulation, and the rate of accumulation feeds back to affect labour market conditions. When placed in a multiplier–accelerator framework, this generates cyclical growth, with a full-employment profit rate squeeze sending the economy into a phase of slower growth with rising unemployment that lasts until the profit rate has recovered.

The theory of distribution is more than just a matter of social and ethical interest. It also profoundly affects the way in which we view the economy. The neoclassical marginal product of labour is interpreted as the labour demand curve, and this enforces an inexorable trade-off between wages and employment. This trade-off drives opposition to minimum wages and unions, and it also drives macroeconomic policy recommendations that aim to lower unemployment by weakening employee protection and making wages downwardly more flexible. Yet all of these policy stances are predicated on a theory whose microeconomic foundations are deeply controversial. Moreover the validity of these policies is also questioned by macroeconomic monetary analyses that show why lower real and nominal wages may not increase employment.

The theory of distribution lies at the core of theories of output and employment determination. Seen in this light, it provides a window on the range of theories explaining the operation of modern capitalist economies. That being so, it is startling that marginal productivity theory is the only theory taught in most university classrooms. It is sometimes suggested that neoclassical theory represents the culmination of grand theory in economics, and from here on in it is a matter of making small advances at the margin. However, if economic theory is viewed as an exercise in story-telling, then the stories economists tell will be influenced by the social and political environment. A change of environment could easily give rise to a burst of new story-telling, and the grandest theory of all – the theory of income distribution – could then be subject to a wave of re-telling.

THOMAS I. PALLEY

See also:

Capital Theory; Growth and Income Distribution; Kaldorian Economics; Marginalism; Sraffian Economics; Wages and Labour Markets.

References

Goodwin, R.M. (1967), 'A growth cycle', in C.H. Feinstein (ed.), *Socialism, Capitalism, and Economic Growth*, Cambridge: Cambridge University Press, pp. 54–8.
Kaldor, N. (1956), 'Alternative theories of distribution', *Review of Economic Studies*, **23** (2), 83–100.
Kalecki, M. (1942), 'A theory of profits', *Economic Journal*, **52** (206–7), 258–67.
Palley, T.I. (1996a), 'Out of the closet: the political economy of neo-classical distribution theory', *Review of Radical Political Economics*, **28** (3), 57–67.
Palley, T.I. (1996b), 'Inside debt, aggregate demand, and the Cambridge theory of distribution', *Cambridge Journal of Economics*, **20** (4), 465–74.
Palley, T.I. (1998), 'Macroeconomics with conflict and income distribution', *Review of Political Economy*, **10** (3), 329–42.
Pasinetti, L. (1962), 'Rate of profit and income distribution in relation to the rate of economic growth', *Review of Economic Studies*, **29** (4), 267–79.
Robinson, J. (1953–54), 'The production function and the theory of capital', *Review of Economic Studies*, **21** (2), 81–106.

Inflation

The Post Keynesian theory of inflation is eclectic in a way that the neoclassical or orthodox theory is not. It allows for multiple causes of, and explanations for, inflationary phenomena, as opposed to the typically mono-causal nature of orthodox theory. The main reason for this is a more realistic view of the credit-creation process, namely the theory of endogenous money (Moore 1979, Wray 2001). This implies that any factor tending to raise money costs has the potential to cause an increase in the general price level, as firms/entrepreneurs incurring the costs will have access to newly-created financial resources to pay for them. Orthodox theory, with an exogenous money supply, only allows for changes in relative prices as long as the money supply remains fixed. If one element of costs increases, this must be offset by a fall elsewhere.

The backbone of orthodox theory is one version or another of the quantity theory of money, illustrated by the equation of exchange, $MV = PY$. This is an identity in principle, but if it is assumed that the money supply (M) is exogenous (controlled by the central bank), the velocity of circulation (V) is roughly a constant, and that money is neutral and superneutral (so that changes in money-supply growth will not affect the growth rate of real GDP (Y)), it also provides a simple theory of the aggregate price level (P). Letting lower-case letters represent proportional rates of change, we have:

$$p = m - y \qquad (1)$$

The inflation rate (p) will be determined by the rate of growth of the money supply (m) minus the rate of growth of GDP (y). Although the theory of monetarism, associated with the work of Milton Friedman in the mid-twentieth century, was more sophisticated than this (allowing for variable velocity and short-run output effects), this statement captures the basic idea. It is a mono-causal theory of inflation in the sense that almost all variation in inflation is attributed to variation in monetary growth. There are some obvious problems, however, such as how precisely to define the money supply in an era of rapid financial innovation, and whether or not it can sensibly be regarded as exogenous in any reasonably sophisticated banking system. One such problem, clear to 'Fed-watchers' in financial markets, is that in practice the monetary policy instrument is usually a short-term interest rate (the Federal Funds rate in the United States), rather than any quantitative measure of the money supply or monetary base.

Contemporary central bankers, therefore, seem to have a practical theory of inflation owing more to Knut Wicksell than to Irving Fisher or Milton Friedman, such as:

$$p = \alpha(r^n - i) \qquad (2)$$

where α is a positive coefficient. Here the nominal interest rate i has the connotation of the policy-determined rate set by the central bank, and r^n is Wickell's 'natural rate', a real interest rate supposedly determined in the market for 'real capital', independently of any monetary influence. If the policy-determined rate is set 'too low' this creates an incentive for bank borrowing as long as the discrepancy exists, hence an endogenous increase in the rate of money growth, and ultimately inflation. The reverse occurs if the rate is set 'too high'. Wisdom in monetary policy entails searching for the 'correct' setting of the policy-determined rate, to precisely match the natural rate. Then, supposedly, there would be no inflation, and the unemployment rate, GDP growth rate, and the interest rate would all be at their 'natural' levels. The contemporary 'Taylor rule' for monetary policy, for example, can plausibly be interpreted in these terms. As with the original Wicksellian model, this approach provides a twist on the quantity theory in the sense of a more realistic conception of how money is introduced into the economy. However, it does not depart too far from orthodoxy, due to the underlying assumption that the economy always tends to a non-monetary market equilibrium. Inflation/deflation is caused by the gap between the natural and policy-determined interest rates, which can be created either by deliberate monetary policy, or by a change in the natural rate itself, not matched by the monetary authority. If this is not precisely a 'mono-causal' view of inflation, there are still only a limited number of possible inflation sources.

Contrary to the above, according to Joan Robinson (1979, p. xix) 'one of the most important insights of the Keynesian revolution was . . . that the general level of prices in an industrial economy is determined by the general level of *costs*, and . . . the main influence upon costs is to be found in the relation between money-wage rates and output per unit of employment' (emphasis added). This can be illustrated by the formula, $P = kW/A$, a rival to the orthodox equation of exchange, associated with the work of Sidney Weintraub (Davidson 1994). Here W is the average nominal wage rate, A is average labour productivity, and k is the 'mark-up' or profit share. According to this, prices will rise if the money wage rises, if the mark-up rises, or if productivity falls. If, further, the profit share stays roughly constant, this gives the theory of inflation alluded to by Robinson, that inflation is caused mainly by a rate of increase of money wages faster than productivity growth. This can be written:

$$p = w - a \qquad (3)$$

where w is wage inflation, and a is productivity growth. The remedy for inflation, then, would not be changes in the rate of money supply growth or the interest rate, as suggested by monetarists or Wicksellians, but specifically an *incomes policy* of some kind. In other words, regulations or agreements restricting the rate of growth of money incomes. Such policies, of course, have their own problems of implementation, including the need to gain public support for the restrictions. In particular, a concern of labour unions where incomes policies have been suggested is that 'wage and price controls' should not turn out to be wage controls only. There should be a measure of equity in controlling the receipts of other income groups also. Some Post Keynesians have therefore responded with various 'clever' proposals (Davidson 1994, p. 149) to meet these concerns, such as the tax-based incomes policy (TIP) suggested by Weintraub and Henry Wallich, the market anti-inflation plan (MAP) of Abba Lerner and David Colander, and, more recently, employer of last resort (ELR) proposals advocated by members of the contemporary neo-Chartalist school, whereby government employment at a fixed wage creates a 'buffer stock' programme for labour (Wray 2001).

As mentioned, in the orthodox view of the world cost-based inflation would be ruled out by the idea that the money supply is fixed, or at least under the control of the central bank. In Post Keynesian theory the assumption is that the 'money supply' will normally increase endogenously via credit creation to accommodate or validate any underlying increase in costs. This point can be illustrated by combining the expressions $MV = PY$ and $P = kW/A$, noting that $Y = AN$. If both velocity and the mark-up are held constant we obtain:

$$m = w + n \qquad (4)$$

where $w+n$ is the growth rate of the nominal wage bill. So from this, what seems to be mainly at issue is the question of causality. Reading equation (4) from right to left the inference is that an increase in the growth of the wage bill causes the money supply to grow (and hence causes inflation). The monetarists might put this the other way around, arguing that an exogenous increase in money-supply growth first causes price inflation, and only later causes wage inflation in a 'catching-up' process. The debate comes down to which is the more realistic description of banking practices in the contemporary credit economy. One item on the Post Keynesian side of the ledger is that, if money supply growth is just a link in the chain, as opposed to a primary causal factor, it becomes much less urgent to have a precise statistical measurement of this magnitude, which in any event seems to be increasingly difficult in current conditions.

Note that the Post Keynesian approach lays much stress on the influence of income shares on the overall price level. In the simple example looked at above there are just two shares, the wage share and a generic profit share. For other purposes, it may also be useful to distinguish, for example, the rentier share from that of entrepreneurial capital, or to introduce other types of income classification. Hence, an important development in the Post Keynesian literature has been the notion of *conflict inflation*, put forward by such authors as R.E. Rowthorn and A.K. Dutt (Lavoie 1992), which generalizes the notion of conflict over income shares. Each of the different income-earning groups tries to improve its real share by increasing nominal claims on output, and these claims are facilitated by the possibility of credit creation. Inflation results because this is the only way to reconcile the competing real and nominal claims. Note that in an open system, changes in the terms of trade will also be highly relevant if (for example) labour's target for its 'real wage' includes a substantial proportion of foreign goods. Again, some sort of consensus over income distribution would be needed to reduce inflationary pressures.

If we were to briefly summarize the differences between the orthodox and Post Keynesian approaches to inflation sketched out above, this might revolve around the old distinction between *demand–pull* and *cost–push* inflation. At one time this was a staple of the textbooks, but it is now neglected. From this perspective, orthodox theory basically has output determined on the supply side, with money prices (and hence inflation) determined by demand. The simplest version of Post Keynesian theory, however, reverses this, and has prices determined on the supply side by costs (compare the quotation from Robinson above), with output/employment determined on the demand side, via the principle of effective demand. There is obviously some truth to this characterization of the debate, and the 'Phillips curve' explanation of inflation, postulating a trade-off between inflation and unemployment to be exploited by demand-side policy, has always had an ambiguous status among Post Keynesians (Davidson 1994; Palley 1996).

However, it would be going too far to say that the Post Keynesian school neglects the concept of demand–pull inflation. The key underlying assumption of endogenous money allows for an eclectic view in this respect. The Post Keynesian model does allow for what Keynes called 'true inflation', that is, inflation caused by continued increases in demand after some putative situation of full employment has been reached. Here the analysis of the 'inflationary gap' from the old-fashioned textbooks would apply, with a caveat perhaps as to how frequently such situations occur in practice, and also that full employment in this sense must be interpreted as a genuine measure of capacity utilization, rather than the market-determined 'natural rate' (of unemployment) of the neoclassicals. In addition, as in some versions of conflict inflation theory, it can be recognized that feedback does exist between demand pressures and the market power of different groups competing for income share. Some of this may well be operative before overall full employment is reached, due to bottlenecks of various types. Hence, it should be possible for Post Keynesian theory not only to stress the cost–push aspect neglected by orthodox theory, but also to 'reclaim the demand–pull approach' (Palley 1996, p. 166).

Inflation is a complex social process, and it seems unlikely that there is any one explanation of the phenomenon valid for all times and all places. For any theory which asserts, for example, that higher growth is always associated with higher inflation, it is always possible to point to empirical instances of the opposite, either stagflation (low growth with high inflation) or, more benignly, non-inflationary growth. The Post Keynesian approach may therefore ultimately have an advantage over more orthodox explanations of inflation, precisely because of its open-ended and eclectic nature. The key features are money-supply endogeneity and the rejection of natural rate concepts (either of the interest rate or of unemployment). These allow for coherent explanations of most of the empirical possibilities. At a minimum, the potential for cost–push inflation is recognized, which in itself must provide for a richer description of real-world events than a view in which such things are ruled out by assumption.

JOHN SMITHIN

See also:

Endogenous Money; Full Employment; Money; Rate of Interest; Tax-based Incomes Policy; Wages and Labour Markets.

References

Davidson, P. (1994), *Post Keynesian Macroeconomic Theory: A Foundation for Successful Economic Policies for the Twenty-First Century*, Aldershot: Edward Elgar.
Lavoie, M. (1992), *Foundations of Post-Keynesian Economic Analysis*, Aldershot: Edward Elgar.
Moore, B.J. (1979), 'Monetary factors', in A.S. Eichner (ed.), *A Guide to Post Keynesian Economics*, White Plains, NY: M.E. Sharpe, pp. 120–38.
Palley T.I. (1996), *Post Keynesian Economics: Debt, Distribution and the Macro Economy*, London: Macmillan.
Robinson, J. (1979), 'Foreword', in A.S. Eichner (ed.), *A Guide to Post Keynesian Economics*, White Plains, NY: M.E. Sharpe, pp. xi–xxi.
Wray, L.R. (2001), 'Money and inflation', in R.P.F. Holt and S. Pressman (eds), *A New Guide to Post Keynesian Economics*, London: Routledge, pp. 79–91.

Innovation

As the research field of economics deepened over more than two centuries since the Industrial Revolution, the linkage between innovation and economic development, which early classical writers emphasized, has become more tenuous. Only economists examining the economy as a vast interconnected 'open systems' canvas continued to maintain this link, notably Karl Marx, Rosa Luxemburg, Michał Kalecki and Joseph Schumpeter. In the 1990s this situation altered dramatically, with an enormous expansion of research into innovation from many perspectives. Post Keynesian economics, after some early efforts in this area, has tended to neglect this issue.

Innovation can be defined as the application of knowledge in a new form to increase the set of techniques and products commercially available in the economy. These techniques can be technological or organizational. The forms that innovation can take are (i) continuous incremental (or 'Kaizen'); (ii) radical discontinuous based on research and development (R&D); (iii) technological systems change based on a cluster of innovations; and (iv) techno-economic paradigm shift due to major structural change (for example, the steam engine, information technology). Forms of innovation can dovetail into higher-order innovation, thus becoming increasingly more important to society.

Contemporary research into innovation has taken two approaches. One is the study of broad-based evolutionary change in the long-term structure of capitalism, while the other is narrow-based entrepreneurship studies at the firm and industry levels. Post Keynesian analysis links innovation to investment decision making, so that the elements of effective demand and cyclical volatility at the broad base are related to the cumulative processes in all forms of innovation at the firm/industry level. This entry focuses on analysis of innovation that is based on this Post Keynesian perspective and incorporates research from both approaches.

Attempts to incorporate investment into the theoretical analysis of innovation have been limited. Two major exceptions to this are Salter (1960) from the neoclassical perspective, and Freeman and Perez (1988) from the evolutionary perspective. Both innovation studies set up economic 'snapshots' which provide case study patterns to show the plausibility of the theoretical relations they derive with respect to investment.

Salter examines technical change and its implications for means of production (MOP) increments at the margin in different industry sectors. In an exceptionally insightful manner, Salter recognizes the gap between available innovation and its application via investment. He uses market signals to indicate possible postponements in the use or introduction of more innovative MOP and consequent delays in scrapping old MOP; thus the capital stock becomes 'fossilised' (Salter 1960, p. 154). This exposes technical change to different rates of productivity growth between industries. The leading Post Keynesian, Geoffrey Harcourt, used Salter's approach to technical change in a number of significant articles in the 1965–75 decade, culminating in Harcourt and Kenyon (1976) on the impact of investment decisions incorporating technical change on pricing behaviour.

Freeman and Perez (1988) take a dynamic structural adjustment view of the economy with respect to innovation, and note the mismatch of current investment to new available technology. Rather than market signals, they emphasize variations in the climate of confidence related to the type of innovation and the life cycle of the industries which account for this mismatch, leading to intensified investment instability. Courvisanos (1996) has extended this work in an effort to incorporate life-cycle innovation into investment instability.

The classic proposition of an investment model with innovation comes from Joseph Schumpeter, who recognized that the investment function responds to waves of optimism and pessimism that create clusters of innovation, and thus 'bunching' of investment. This produces susceptibility to unstable investment cycles and the development of a trigger mechanism to initiate fundamentally new innovation systems with long-wave implications. Kalecki endorses and reinforces this cycle-trend effect that innovation has on the investment function. The intensity of innovation both affects the amplitude of investment cycles and shifts the trend path of investment growth, by flows of vicious and virtuous circles. Virtuous circle effects occur as innovation intensity rises, increasing the amplitude of the upper turning-point of the investment cycle and shifting the trend path upwards. Vicious circle effects increase the amplitude of the lower turning-point, shifting the trend downwards. The pace of innovation is a shift parameter in the Kaleckian investment function.

The cause of clustering of innovation and subsequent bunching of investment ('clust-bun') is in debate. The Kaleckian feature of expanded reproduction has not been recognized by the protagonists in this debate. The prerequisite for clustering is deep depressions or breakthroughs in technology, both reflecting reactions by the private and public sectors to deep problems in the downswing of the previous business cycle. Then, the bunching requires effective demand stimulus through widespread diffusion of the cluster effect that can only be achieved through the availability of a surplus for investment (private profits and public deficit spending). Impediments to this 'clust-bun' effect reside in the institutional frameworks of nations, particularly those with still dominant mature industries with older technologies (Freeman and Perez 1988, pp. 58–65). Increased uncertainty arising from large investment in the new technology systems also adds a further impediment through increased macroeconomic volatility, slowing down the diffusion process.

The causal sequencing of innovation and investment is reversed in work done by Nicholas Kaldor and Joseph Schmookler, with the rate of investment determining the rate of innovation. Kalecki also recognizes this sequence, despite having identified the innovation-driven process. Kalecki places this investment-driven process clearly into an appropriate context by viewing the innovation process as 'part and parcel of "ordinary" investment' (Kalecki 1954, p. 158), or endogenous innovation.

Instead of unidirectional causality, the discussion above clearly implies a circular flow, where one innovation process feeds into the other. Kaldor's principle of cumulative causation is the 'self-reinforcing dynamic' in the circular process of investment demand leading to innovation that then stimulates further investment. The distinction between exogenous and endogenous innovation specifies how innovation enters this cumulative causation process. In this context, R&D expenditure is central to the endogenous innovation process, with large firms with strong profit results having the ability to undertake large R&D spending, while registration of patents from R&D efforts reflects the clustering of innovations.

Gomulka et al. (1990, p. 535) attempt to provide ergodic closure to the Kalecki trend and cycle theory. They argue that Kalecki's central role of innovations in preventing the trend rate of unemployment from increasing is unsupportable, as 'the balanced growth rate which Kalecki took to be stable is, in fact, unstable, rendering it unsuitable to serve as the trend growth rate'. Lavoie (1992, pp. 297–327) examines Kalecki's innovation and investment analysis at the theoretical level and rejects the ergodic closure assumption which ties this theory back to the neoclassical mainstream. Kalecki clearly assumes that the rate of capacity utilization may diverge from its full-capacity rate even in the long run, with the 'reserve army of the unemployed' as a typical feature of capitalism for a considerable part of the

194 *Innovation*

cycle. This asserts instability, as the dynamic non-ergodic business cycle has innovation-creating conditions that move the trend growth away from any analytical 'stability'.

In Kalecki's view of innovation, endogenous innovation is of secondary importance from the scientific standpoint, coming as it does from: (i) slight adaptations of previous capital equipment; (ii) cosmetic improvement in old products; and (iii) extension of previous raw material sources. Such innovation is called endogenous because it is the cycle itself that induces the innovation and, with it, higher levels of investment orders. With endogenous innovation occurring in a Kaleckian macro economy, the analysis can focus on how such innovation is developed at the firm/industry level and consequently affects the economy.

The firm's R&D expenditure is a form of intangible investment to be incorporated in the long-term business investment plan. This enables the firm to hold a stock of innovations that are ready to be applied when susceptibility to investment risk is relatively low. In this way endogenous innovation can be generated and directed by a process of investment. When a firm decides to increase investment at relatively low susceptibility under competitive pressures and higher costs of postponement, its R&D investment in the past makes these innovations ready to implement. R&D investment effectively increases the strategic productive capacity of the firm. In an industry where innovation is a regular competitive strategy, R&D expenditure would be large and would vary under the same susceptibility pressures as capital expenditure. In an industry where innovation is only occasionally implemented, R&D expenditure would be small and relatively constant over the investment cycle.

The endogenous creation of innovations out of low susceptibility makes some MOP obsolete and thus not part of excess capacity calculation. Also, oligopolistic firms (and industries) lobby for the assistance of governments in reducing private costs of production (through subsidies, tax concessions or protection) when these firms attempt to expand their market by innovations in order to utilize new, and decommission old, idle productive capacity. Such innovation and underwriting of the related risks reduces the rate of increase in susceptibility and encourages an investment recovery.

R&D amounts in aggregate to a large body of investigation going on continuously (at different rates of intensity). This large R&D spending and related innovation effects are bound to lead to some major new 'discovery' or 'invention' which is related to the total aggregate R&D, rather than to any particular R&D project. This discovery is linked to possible small developments in various laboratories and informal networks between firms and industries, eventually coming to fruition in some way divorced from any specific competitive behaviour. New technological paradigms come out of such aggregate developments and are the basis of structural change to a new long wave of boom and prosperity (Freeman and Perez 1988, pp. 47–58). Changes in technological systems and paradigms arise only after all the minor improvements (endogenous innovation) are squeezed out of the old systems and paradigms by 'monopoly capital' entrepreneurs who want to protect existing MOP and delay the new paradigm taking over. There is also a 'log jam' in endogenous innovations based on the new paradigm, which compounds the latter's slow initial adoption. This occurs when established powerful entrepreneurs, with much old MOP, cannot justify the entire shake-up of industries, since not enough interrelated clusters have been formed.

Technological paradigm shift leads to exogenous innovation input affecting the investment cycle. Introduction of a new paradigm produces a large exogenous boost to industry investment at low susceptibility points. This investment boom relates to paradigm changes in large important industry sectors that adopt new technology systems (for example, petrochemical innovations), or in the whole economy (for example, steam engine innovations). Either way, the investment boom is strong and resilient over a series of future cycles in susceptibility.

As the institutional framework slowly adapts to the new technological system, entrepreneurs' reactions to uncertainty of profits result from competitive pressures and growing inefficiencies of old MOP. This induces adaptation (by industries) and imitation (within industries) of technological trajectories that are totally new, establishing, at very low susceptibility, the new investment upturn. This creates a new investment boom and at the same time re-establishes the conditions for a new phase of steady development. A paradigm shift occurs when the newly-adapted technological systems pervade the whole economy. Many from the evolutionary school identify such a shift with the beginning of a new long wave in the economy's development.

This analysis links together the two types of innovations described by Paul Baran and Paul Sweezy, namely 'normal' (or endogenous) and 'epoch-making' (or exogenous). A period of secular decline in economic development can now be associated with the limitations of scale production in oligopolistic competition, as the old technology systems are running out of possible new adaptations. Diffusion of the old systems through endogenous innovation slows down, and imitators become considerably fewer. The large powerful corporations attempt to protect existing capital values and ignore the new technological systems that are being developed on the fringes of the corporate world. This tends to exacerbate the mismatch between new technologies and a powerful institutional framework based around monopoly capital. It was Steindl, back in 1952, who recognized this secular decline as the incentive to reduce surplus capacity and invest in established monopoly capital sectors. In his 1976 introduction to the 1952 book reprint, Steindl stated that he was 'ready to admit a possibility which I denied in my book: that it might be the result of exhaustion of a long technological wave' (1976 p. xv). In this way, the conclusions of the Kaleckian and evolutionary traditions can be integrated.

JERRY COURVISANOS

See also:
Business Cycles; Growth Theory; Institutionalism; Investment; Kaldorian Economics; Kaleckian Economics.

References
Courvisanos, J. (1996), *Investment Cycles in Capitalist Economies: A Kaleckian Behavioural Contribution*, Cheltenham, UK and Brookfield, VT, USA: Edward Elgar.
Freeman, C. and Perez, C. (1988), 'Structural crises of adjustment, business cycles and investment behaviour', in G. Dosi, C. Freeman, R. Nelson, G. Silverberg and L. Soete (eds), *Technical Change and Economic Theory*, London: Pinter, pp. 38–66.
Gomulka, S., A. Ostaszewski and R.O. Davies (1990), 'The innovation rate and Kalecki's theory of trend, unemployment and the business cycle', *Economica*, **57** (228), 525–40.
Harcourt, G.C. and P. Kenyon (1976), 'Pricing and the investment decision', *Kyklos*, **29** (3), 449–77.
Kalecki, M. (1954), *Theory of Economic Dynamics*, London: George Allen & Unwin.
Lavoie, M. (1992), *Foundations of Post-Keynesian Economic Analysis*, Aldershot: Edward Elgar.
Salter, W.E.G. (1960), *Productivity and Technical Change*, Cambridge: Cambridge University Press.
Steindl, J. (1976), *Maturity and Stagnation in American Capitalism*, 2nd edition, New York: Monthly Review Press.

Institutionalism

Institutionalism is an approach to economics that sees economic life as taking place within a social context. In contrast to neoclassical economists, institutionalists see human behaviour as determined more by social factors than by deliberative individual thought.

Behaviour depends on the habits, the routines, and the customs of economic actors. These actors are households, workers and business firms, as well as the government and its policies and regulations. Their habits, routines and customs are the rules they use to make decisions. They are matters of law or tradition; and they get passed along by example, by society's expectations, and by the power of the state. People tend to follow these rules because they see everyone else doing so. People also follow these rules because they provide a simple way to deal with the uncertainty and the complexity of everyday life (Hodgson 1988).

When most people follow institutional rules, behaviour becomes more certain and individuals are less likely to feel foolish by acting differently or by being wrong when they make important choices. Institutional rules thus provide for stability in a world of uncertainty.

Post Keynesians believe that methodological individualism prevents economists from seeing the impact of social phenomena on individual choice and also keeps them from providing useful guidance to society. By adopting an institutionalist or social perspective on individual choice, Post Keynesians can analyse how the perceptions of economic agents are moulded by institutions and habits. It also lets them address important economic and social issues that are assumed away by neoclassical theory.

Institutions appear at several key places in Post Keynesian economic analysis. First, institutional factors help explain the consumption behaviour of households. Second, institutions help us understand the investment decisions of business firms. Third, institutional considerations lead to the creation of money in capitalist economies and are responsible for the unique role of money. Finally, they help us understand the stability of capitalism, and how and why economic policy can improve economic outcomes. We consider these items in turn.

Institutionalists see consumer preferences and consumer spending stemming from learned social behaviour rather than from any innate utility functions. Consumer spending is determined by what is necessary to maintain a lifestyle similar to one's friends and neighbours, and possibly a lifestyle that is a bit more lavish than that of one's friends and neighbours. This argument goes back to the work of Veblen (1899 [1908]), regarded as one of the founding fathers of institutionalist thought.

These behavioural dispositions help explain why consumption is stable and also why fiscal policy is able to expand or contract the economy. Consumption is stable because it depends on spending habits. For most middle-class households, this means spending most, if not all, of one's regular pay-packet. As a result, the propensity to consume additional income will be stable over time and also have a relatively high value.

A stable and high propensity to spend means that consumers will usually spend a large fraction of any extra money that they receive. This has important policy implications. Tax cuts, even temporary tax cuts enacted during a recession, will increase individual spending nearly dollar for dollar; likewise government spending will increase income (and therefore spending) by some large fraction of any additional state expenditures. For this reason, fiscal policy can be counted on to affect the overall macro economy in a fairly predictable manner.

On the neoclassical approach, business investment is a rational and maximizing decision. Firms compare the costs of investing (interest lost due to borrowing or employing retained earnings) with the benefits (future earnings discounted for the time value of money). If benefits exceed costs, the firm will undertake the new investment project; otherwise there will be no new investment.

For Keynes, business investment was *not* undertaken on this basis, because firms are unable to make the calculations required of them. Future earnings are inherently uncertain. Post Keynesian economists also stress the uncertainty of the investment decision; such decisions must be made on the basis of educated guesses, gut feelings, or 'animal spirits'. These decisions arise not out of individual contemplation, but rather from a collective process where everyone watches what everyone else is doing.

Firms will invest if and only if a lot of other firms are investing and greater investment seems to be a safe choice. In contrast, when 'animal spirits' are pessimistic, few firms will invest. Under these circumstances, any single firm that invests will experience sluggish sales and low or non-existent profits. Here, the investment decision will turn out to have been a mistake. For this reason, negative expectations by some firms quickly translate into negative expectations by most firms, and little investment takes place. With little investment there will be high unemployment, expectations will remain poor, and the economy will remain mired in recession.

Money, for Post Keynesians, is an institutional construct that helps reduce uncertainty. Holding money reduces uncertainty for the firm because workers must be paid with money and debts must be repaid with money; it reduces uncertainty for people because households know that they will be able to pay for necessities in the future with the hoarded money. In addition, money (unlike stocks and other assets) does not change much in value from day to day and from month to month. By holding money, households will not be subject to sharp declines in net worth in the future.

Because it is a refuge from uncertainty, people and business firms will want to hold or hoard money in difficult economic times rather than spend it. But this demand for money creates macroeconomic problems that lead to even greater uncertainty and greater demand for money.

According to Davidson (1994, p. 18), money has two essential characteristics that lead to unemployment in a world with an unpredictable and unknowable future. Money helps create unemployment because it has zero elasticity of production and because there are no substitutes for money. The former characteristic refers to the fact that no one is hired to produce money when people want money rather than goods. The second property refers to the fact that there is no substitute for money to pay off debts; even if the return to holding money falls to zero, people still need money. When people fear for the future, they desire to hold money. But because no one is hired to produce money, workers get laid off, businesses cannot sell goods, and everyone is more fearful about the future.

In Post Keynesian analysis, the state serves as an important institution that can counteract other forces undermining spending and leading to unemployment. It does this by employing fiscal and monetary policies to help control unemployment. The state can also help by creating institutional structures that tend to stabilize the economy – property rights, a central bank which operates as a lender of the last resort, and stable international economic relationships.

In addition, and in contrast to more traditional views of the state, Keynes argued that the state was itself an important economic institution. As Skidelsky (1989) has argued, Keynes saw the state as a set of institutions that would provide for public goods and benefits, the prime benefits of which would be full employment and important public goods and services that business firms were unwilling or unable to provide. It fills in for other social institutions when these institutions fail.

There are several mechanisms by which the state can fulfil these institutional functions. First, the state helps convert uncertainty and discontinuity into calculable risk. It gives economic actors confidence that the future will be like the past. The state provides the laws and regulations that are necessary for capitalist production to take place. It also provides for stability and security in life. This includes monetary stability, exchange rate stability, welfare benefits, old-age pensions and deposit insurance. For example, deposit insurance, in conjunction with central banks operating as a lender of last resort, reduces the likelihood of bank runs and financial collapse. State welfare systems are institutions which recognize that the market, the family and social networks sometimes are not enough to generate individual security. People may not spend if fearful of the personal consequences of becoming unemployed. A viable social safety net alleviates this concern (Larson 2002).

Second, the state also provides an anchor for decision making. Firms can have more confidence in their own investment decisions when they know that the government will help maintain aggregate investment and full employment. This greater confidence will, in turn, generate more private business investment.

For Keynes, it did not matter how the state spent its money; what mattered was that the money got spent. In a much-quoted passage, Keynes writes about the need for more houses, hospitals, schools and roads. But, he notes, many people are likely to object to such 'wasteful' government expenditures. Another approach was therefore necessary. 'If the Treasury were to fill old bottles with banknotes, bury them at suitable depths in disused coal-mines which are then filled up to the surface with town rubbish . . . private enterprise [would] dig the notes up again [and] . . . there need be no more unemployment' (Keynes 1936 [1964], p. 129).

Keynes (ibid., p. 378) preferred, however, 'a somewhat comprehensive socialization of investment'. What he was advancing here was government spending policies to stabilize the aggregate level of investment in the national economy. For Keynes, the state needed to run deficits and invest in education, infrastructure, health care and so on during times of high unemployment. And during boom times, the government would need to reduce its investment spending and run budget surpluses. By following these budgetary rules, the economy would be more stable, businesses and consumers would face less uncertainty, and both groups would spend more (Pressman 1987, 1995).

In brief, employed correctly, monetary policy and fiscal policy function as uncertainty-reducing institutions. They give business firms the confidence to invest, knowing the chances are good that production from any new plants will be sold at a profit. They also give consumers confidence in the future, and keep them from hoarding money in fear of bad economic times. Other institutional arrangements created by the state that tend to stabilize the economy will have similar beneficial effects.

STEVEN PRESSMAN

See also:

Agency; Consumer Theory; Economic Policy; Investment; Money; Uncertainty.

References

Davidson, P. (1994), *Post Keynesian Macroeconomic Theory*, Aldershot: Edward Elgar.
Hodgson, G. (1988), *Economics and Institutions: A Manifesto for a Modern Institutional Economics*, Philadelphia: University of Pennsylvania Press.
Keynes, J.M. (1936 [1964]), *The General Theory of Employment, Interest and Money*, New York: Harcourt Brace.
Larson, S. (2002), *Uncertainty, Macroeconomic Stability and the Welfare State*, Aldershot: Ashgate.
Pressman, S. (1987), 'The policy relevance of *The General Theory*', *Journal of Economic Studies*, **14** (4), 13–23.
Pressman, S. (1995), 'Deficits, full employment and the use of fiscal policy', *Review of Political Economy*, **7** (2), 212–26.
Skidelsky, R. (1989), 'Keynes and the state', in D. Helm (ed.), *The Economic Borders of the State*, Oxford: Oxford University Press, pp. 144–52.
Veblen, T. (1899 [1908]), *Theory of the Leisure Class*, New York: Macmillan.

International Economics

The conventional approach to international economics divides the subject into two separate branches. The 'micro' part, called *international trade*, analyses the determinants of countries' exports and imports, and the effects of alternative trade policies on economic welfare (including income distribution), using purely 'real' or barter models. The 'macro' part, called *international finance*, analyses balance of payments adjustment and exchange rate determination using aggregative models that emphasize monetary and financial factors. The 'pure' trade theory assumes that automatic financial and macroeconomic adjustment mechanisms effectively ensure the conditions (balanced trade with full employment) under which trade follows comparative advantage and all nations gain from free trade.

Post Keynesians reject this bifurcated approach to international economics, and especially the implied neutrality of monetary and financial factors with regard to 'real' trade. Although Post Keynesian analyses may focus on either the trade or financial side of the subject, the Post Keynesian approach emphasizes how international trade and financial relations impact on each other (see Deprez and Harvey 1999). Especially, in line with the general view of a 'monetary production economy' in which the financing of economic activity has non-neutral, real effects, Post Keynesians deny the existence of automatic adjustment mechanisms that maintain balanced trade and full employment as assumed in the standard pure trade theory. This opens up the door to theories that emphasize the causes and consequences of trade imbalances, and the real adjustments in income and employment required to offset them.

These theoretical distinctions are of vital importance because of their implications for trade and financial policies. The conventional argument for mutual benefits to all countries from free trade, based on the theory of comparative advantage, is rooted in 'pure' trade models that assume balanced trade and full employment as well as capital immobility. If any of these assumptions are dropped, the theory of comparative advantage breaks down, and it can no longer be presumed that free trade policies are always in a nation's best interest (although positive Post Keynesian analyses of trade policies are poorly developed to date). On the financial side, the absence of automatic monetary adjustment mechanisms implies the need for activist government policies and international cooperative arrangements (such as managed exchange rates and/or capital flow restrictions) in order to foster more balanced and mutually beneficial trade and to promote global full employment.

One core Post Keynesian idea that links international trade and finance is Joan Robinson's theory of international conflict over limited global markets, which she called 'the new mercantilism' (see Robinson 1978, pp. 190–222). In a world with inadequate aggregate demand and involuntary unemployment, countries often seek to run trade surpluses in order to boost their own output and employment. Since not all countries can run surpluses at the same time, the countries that succeed in obtaining them effectively compel other countries to run deficits, which saddle the latter countries with lower national incomes and higher unemployment rates than they would otherwise have. Thus, export-led expansion in some countries comes at the expense of import-imposed contraction in others, or – in Robinson's colourful adaptation of Adam Smith's famous remark – export-led growth is a 'beggar-my-neighbour' policy. This analysis of conflictive trade relations stands in marked contrast to the conventional view of largely harmonious trade relationships – a view which ignores the existence of demand-side limits to global exports (and which allows for conflict only over the barter terms of trade).

The Post Keynesian approach necessarily includes critiques of conventional theories of automatic balance of payments adjustment. For example, in the 'specie-flow' mechanism of David Hume and David Ricardo, which applies to a fixed exchange rate system, a trade surplus (deficit) leads to an inflow (outflow) of monetary reserves (gold or hard currencies), which in turn raises (lowers) the money supply and causes a rise (fall) in the price level that makes a country's products less (more) competitive, and hence reverses the trade imbalance. Post Keynesians criticize this theory because (among other things) they deny that the supply of money determines the price level in a modern industrial economy, as well as because this theory ignores the role of capital flows in financing trade imbalances. As long as countries with trade surpluses run offsetting capital account deficits (that is, become net lenders) and countries with trade deficits run offsetting capital account surpluses (that is, become net borrowers), overall balance of payments equilibrium can be sustained without eliminating *trade* imbalances.

Another type of automatic stabilization mechanism involves flexible exchange rates. Traditional analyses developed before the 1973 collapse of Bretton Woods presumed that countries with trade surpluses would have appreciating currencies and countries with deficits would have depreciating currencies, leading to the restoration of balanced trade. However, Post Keynesians argue that flexible exchange rates are monetary variables that are driven primarily by financial capital flows and asset market speculation, and hence need not move in the 'right' direction for balancing trade – and, even when they do adjust, exchange rate changes may not generate the desired improvements in the trade balance due to low price elasticities or offsetting price changes. While these points are recognized by some mainstream economists, the implication that imbalanced trade will not follow comparative advantages is emphasized only by Post Keynesians.

Post Keynesians who follow in the Kaleckian tradition emphasize the feedback effects of international competition on domestic profit mark-up rates, and hence on the distribution of income between profits and wages (see the chapter by Blecker in Deprez and Harvey 1999). When a currency appreciates (or domestic costs rise relative to foreign), oligopolistic firms squeeze price–cost margins in order to 'price-to-market', which in turn leads to a fall in the profit share with possible negative repercussions for investment and growth (although this may be offset by a boost to domestic consumption arising from higher real wages and labour income). When a currency depreciates (or domestic costs fall relative to foreign), the opposite happens as domestic oligopolies are enabled to raise their price–cost margins without losing market share, income is redistributed from wages to profits, and the potential repercussions for investment and growth as well as for consumption are all reversed. Outcomes in which a redistribution of income towards profits is contractionary are known as 'stagnationist', while outcomes in which such a redistribution is expansionary are known as 'exhilarationist'. Mainstream economists have recognized the flexibility of profit margins in response to exchange rate fluctuations – what they call 'partial pass-through' – but they have not analysed the effects on income distribution, aggregate demand and economic growth.

At the microeconomic level, Post Keynesians argue that trade generally follows absolute rather than comparative advantages (see Milberg 1994). There are two different versions of this approach. For trade in standardized products, which can be manufactured in similar processes with comparable quality in a large number of countries, exports are based on *competitive advantages* in unit costs of production, principally unit labour costs (that is, wages adjusted for productivity, or 'wages in efficiency units'). Thus, the countries with the lowest unit costs in a certain product, taking into account current wages and other direct input costs (for example, raw materials and energy), relative to the productivity of labour and other inputs, and adjusted for prevailing exchange rates, will export that product, regardless of whether they have a 'true' comparative advantage in it. In labour-intensive industries where technology is standardized and productivity is fairly uniform, only low-wage countries will export the products, especially when capital is mobile and firms can locate production wherever production costs are lowest (see Brewer 1985). Thus, there is some truth to the popular notion of low-wage competition, but only if it is understood in the proper context (that is, wages are adjusted for productivity, products are standardized and capital is internationally mobile).

However, there are many internationally traded goods for which neither production processes nor product qualities are standardized. For these goods, a few technological leaders have either absolutely superior (lower cost) technologies, or else produce absolutely higher qualities of the goods, than any other countries. In these industries, which include important sectors such as aerospace, industrial machinery, computer software and medical equipment, trade is determined by *technological gaps* – that is, the countries with the superior technology or product are the exporters, and all other countries are importers (see Dosi et al. 1990). Relative cost factors (such as wages or exchange rates) are not important in these sectors and product lines. Of course, individual products can shift over time from being innovative products traded according to technological gaps to standardized products traded according to competitive advantages, in line with Raymond Vernon's (1966) 'product cycle' theory. As a result, the small club of innovating countries (led by the United States in the postwar period, and joined more recently by Japan and others) needs to keep inventing newer innovative goods (for example, supercomputers or biotechnology) in order to stay ahead of the competitive curve (since such countries typically have high wages, and therefore cannot compete in standardized manufactures). The technology gap theory of trade in innovative products thus complements the absolute competitive advantages theory for standardized goods, allowing for a fairly complete explanation of most international trade especially in manufactures.

Other Post Keynesian views can be covered more briefly since they are discussed elsewhere in this volume. To deal with the volatility of flexible exchange rates as well as the deflationary biases in traditional adjustment mechanisms for deficit countries, some Post Keynesians have advocated a return to a Bretton Woods-like system of adjustable pegs, but accompanied by a mechanism to shift the burden of adjustment to the surplus countries. Paul Davidson (1992–93) calls for the establishment of an international monetary clearing house, which not only would create an international reserve asset (international monetary clearing unit, or IMCU), but also would require surplus countries to spend their surpluses and thus impart an expansionary bias to the global adjustment process. In addition, many Post Keynesians have advocated policies to discourage destabilizing flows of short-term capital and to prevent speculative attacks on currencies. However, Post Keynesian views on such policies vary, with some advocating Tobin taxes on foreign exchange transactions while others call for more direct forms of capital controls or financial regulations.

Finally, the theory of 'balance-of-payments-constrained growth' focuses on the long-term consequences if trade imbalances cannot be sustained indefinitely and countries are eventually forced to balance their trade (or at least, to restrict trade imbalances to levels that can be financed through sustainable net capital flows). This view, which is elaborated by McCombie and Thirlwall (1994), assumes that the long-run adjustment to balanced trade is effectuated mainly through changes in output quantities (income levels or growth rates), not by changes in relative prices (real exchange rates). The implication is that countries with slow export growth and high income elasticities of import demand are condemned to grow more slowly than their trading partners if they are forced to balance their trade in the long run.

Note that, while the basic version of this model does assume balanced trade in the long run, it does not assume full employment or that the adjustment mechanisms that restore balanced trade are neutral or painless, and the model can be adapted to allow for capital flows.

ROBERT A. BLECKER

See also:

Balance-of-payments-constrained Economic Growth; Bretton Woods; Exchange Rates; Globalization; Tobin Tax.

References

Brewer, A. (1985), 'Trade with fixed real wages and mobile capital', *Journal of International Economics*, **18** (1/2), 177–86.
Davidson, P. (1992–93), 'Reforming the world's money', *Journal of Post Keynesian Economics*, **15** (2), 153–79.
Deprez, J. and J.T. Harvey (eds) (1999), *Foundations of International Economics: Post Keynesian Perspectives*, London and New York: Routledge.
Dosi, G., K. Pavitt and L. Soete (1990), *The Economics of Technical Change and International Trade*, New York: New York University Press.
McCombie, J.S.L. and A.P. Thirlwall (1994), *Economic Growth and the Balance-of-Payments Constraint*, New York: St. Martin's Press.
Milberg, W. (1994), 'Is absolute advantage passé? Towards a Post Keynesian/Marxian theory of international trade', in M. Glick (ed.), *Competition, Technology and Money: Classical and Post-Keynesian Perspectives*, Aldershot: Edward Elgar, pp. 220–236.
Robinson, J. (1978), *Contributions to Modern Economics*, New York: Academic Press.
Vernon, R. (1966), 'International trade and international investment in the product cycle', *Quarterly Journal of Economics*, **80** (2), 190–207.

Investment

The Post Keynesian theory of investment begins with the work of John Maynard Keynes and Michał Kalecki in the 1930s. Keynes's ideas about the determinants of investment in *A Treatise on Money* (1930 [1971]) and *The General Theory of Employment, Interest, and Money* (1936 [1964]) depart from the neoclassical theory mainly by emphasizing expectations of the profitability of investment spending and the expectations involved in the determination of financial market prices. The fundamental formulation of investment in neoclassical theory is that it is determined by the intersection of a downward-sloping schedule of the marginal productivity of increasing quantities of capital equipment relative to a given amount of the other factors of production, with an upward-sloping schedule of the community's willingness to abstain from consumption to supply quantities of capital at different rates of return.

In the *Treatise* Keynes argued that the value of new investment goods would rise and fall relative to the cost of production of new investment, spurring changes in the level of investment, as the public and the banking system changed their opinions about the desirability of moving wealth between deposits and securities. A change in the willingness of the community to supply capital, that is, to save, would thus only change the level of physical investment if it also changed the level of financial investment in securities. The level of investment could change in turn, relative to the willingness to save, as the desirability of holding securities changed.

In the *General Theory* Keynes described the investment demand schedule as a schedule of the 'marginal efficiency' of capital. Although Keynes held that his marginal efficiency of capital schedule was equivalent to Irving Fisher's derivation of the 'rate of return over cost' from neoclassical optimizing behaviour, he was clear that his schedule stood for the expected profitability of additions to the capital stock and explicitly rejected the idea that the value of capital was determined by the productivity of capital. This schedule slopes downwards, Keynes wrote, since increased demand for capital goods raises the cost of producing them and an increased supply of any type of capital reduces its prospective yield. Later theorists were to say that as these factors influencing the profitability of additional capital were affected by the time period in which the capital is to be produced and installed, the schedule should instead be called the marginal efficiency of *investment*, or additions to the capital stock per unit of time.

Keynes saw the supply of finance for investment as coming from the willingness of the public and the banks to give up liquidity, which determined the relevant interest rate. The 'degree of excess bearishness', which determined the value of investment in the *Treatise*, became divided into the expectations of profitability of the marginal efficiency of capital schedule and the degree of liquidity preference for holding 'money' versus long-term debts, given the quantity of money supplied by the central bank.

Kalecki (1990, 1991) criticized Keynes's theory of investment on the grounds that it was insufficiently dynamic. That is, Kalecki questioned the idea of having investment determined by the intersection of a given marginal efficiency of capital schedule and the relevant mix of interest rates, because he held that changes in the level of investment so determined would feed back upon the marginal efficiency of capital schedule itself, first as, for example, increased investment increased aggregate demand and so the profitability of investment, and later as the new capital produced by the investment became available and so depressed the profitability of further investment.

Kalecki's depiction of how investment spending is determined thus requires a dynamic process in which investment interacts with output, profits and the level of the capital stock, as in the flexible accelerator or capital-stock adjustment model, though his own models were specified in terms of investment, capital and profits, rather than output. Kalecki's theory of the financing of investment comes from his 'principle of increasing risk'. Addressing the question of what limits the size of the capital investment of any firm, Kalecki allowed that a firm which is large relative to the size of its market would be limited by this, but he held that there is another factor limiting firm expansion, which is the proportion of the owner's capital that is invested in the firm. For, Kalecki argued, the more of the wealth of any individual unit of capital that is sunk into one business, the more at risk is the individual's entire wealth position. This financial limit on investment means that there is a quantity constraint, as well as a price of funds constraint, on investment spending.

Keynes's ideas about 'borrowers' risk' and 'lenders' risk' in the *General Theory* make a similar point, but Keynes tended to place more emphasis on the psychological conventions governing the determination of financial market prices. That is, he argued that speculative activity directed towards the prices of long-term debt and corporate shares could significantly affect investment spending. In the face of the radical uncertainty of our knowledge of the future prospects of business, Keynes reasoned that stock market valuations of the marginal efficiency of capital would often represent the results of speculation about the psychology of the market rather than sensible forecasts of the long-term profitability of corporate capital. He discussed the ability of central bank policy to move long-term interest rates to achieve the desired level of investment, and he feared conditions under which monetary policy would not be able to overcome speculators' liquidity preference sufficiently. He thus called for the state to take responsibility for ensuring an adequate level of investment through its direct actions.

James Duesenberry (1958 [1977]) combined the flexible accelerator, in which the level of investment is explained by the level of output relative to the level of existing productive capacity, with the financing effects on investment arising from current profit flows and a measure of the existing debt burden, based on Kalecki's ideas on the determination of investment finance, into a dynamic marginal efficiency of investment and marginal cost of funds determination of investment. Empirical work in the 1950s and early 1960s on this approach to investment demonstrated support for Kalecki's and Keynes's ideas.

Theoretical developments of the Post Keynesian theory of investment were made in the 1970s by Paul Davidson and Hyman Minsky. Davidson (1972 [1978]) specified the schedule of the demand price of capital goods as a function of entrepreneurial capitalists' subjective rate of discount, expectations of growth in product demand, their ability to raise the necessary financing, and their calculations of depreciation. His supply price schedule is given by the size of the existing capital stock and the increasing cost of production of new capital goods. Davidson's model is thus able to trace the effects of financial considerations and product market demand more clearly than Keynes's *General Theory* formulation, which appears to emphasize only the level of interest rates as the cost of finance, and stock market prices as the measure of the value of investment projects.

Minsky's (1975) formulation takes the cost of production of new capital to any one firm as given. It then takes the demand price to be the capitalized value of the expected cash flows from investment, which decreases as the level of investment rises into the range where use of external financing increases borrower's risk. In the region of external financing, Minsky depicted increasing lender's risk as a schedule raising supply price at an increasing rate above the cost of production of new capital. The intersection of the demand and supply price schedules gives the level of investment spending. Minsky's graphical exposition is somewhat similar to Duesenberry's, but he describes the details of financial concerns, in terms of both interest rate and debt burden effects, much more thoroughly and insightfully than anyone else. Minsky's dynamic treatment of the interactions among investment, profits and debt provides a financial counterpart to Kalecki's portrayal of investment, profits and capital interactions.

In the 1960s, interest in estimating a version of the neoclassical model of investment determination revived. Neoclassical economists claimed that profits or other flow measures of the availability of funds only appeared successful in investment regressions because they were highly correlated with, and thus were acting as a proxy for, the level of output, which all theories agreed to be a significant determinant of investment. In the 1980s, however, work by Steven Fazzari and several different co-authors offered empirical support to Post Keynesian ideas on investment. Fazzari and Tracy Mott (1986–87) was the earliest of these to demonstrate support for the role of output demand, internal finance and debt burden measures in explaining investment. In later studies, Fazzari and others showed further the importance of internal financing constraints, following the work of Kalecki, Minsky and some more recent work based on asymmetric information, in explaining investment.

Most of the theoretical and empirical work discussed above is concerned with the determinants of business fixed investment. Both Kalecki and Keynes also wrote about the factors governing inventory investment, arguing that inventory investment should be influenced by factors similar to those which determined fixed investment but also be affected by shorter-term movements in the availability of finance and in expectations of sales relative to current stocks. Fazzari's empirical work on inventory investment has supported this.

Keynes and Kalecki also both tended to consider the question of the level of current investment apart from any questions of changes in technique, or capital intensity, which was arguably the main concern of marginal productivity theory. The 'Cambridge capital critique' has questioned the notion of 'capital intensity' as a measurable concept, and the claim that investment should be analysed as a process of changes in the ratio of 'capital' to labour in long-run equilibrium is something that no Post Keynesian would accept.

Of course, changes in the type of capital must be taken into account in any long-run analysis of investment. In the Post Keynesian literature these have been treated mainly under the heading of 'innovations'. Josef Steindl's (1952 [1976]) work on long-run growth within a Kaleckian perspective argues that in young industries investment is stimulated by the ability of 'progressive' firms to lower costs through expansion and innovation, and then to lower prices further in order to drive out higher-cost firms. This price-cutting maintains capacity utilization at high rates until only a small group of producers with similar cost structures remain. Price cutting now offers no advantage to the remaining oligopolists, who thus abandon it. This in turn decreases the level of investment spending, unless new products or methods of production emerge. In this way Steindl developed his ideas about 'absolute concentration' into a theory of a long-run tendency towards macroeconomic stagnation.

Post Keynesians have always acknowledged to some extent the importance of what Keynes called 'animal spirits' as a key influence on the level of investment spending. Some Post Keynesians have objected that this makes investment depend too heavily on the subjective reactions of managers to fundamental uncertainty, and therefore underestimates the objective determinants of investment. Kalecki's explanation of investment seems clearly to rest much more on objective factors, though he did allow that psychological matters might influence investment activity.

TRACY MOTT

See also:

Capital Theory; Expectations; Innovation; Kaleckian Economics; Keynes's *General Theory*; Keynes's *Treatise on Money*.

References

Davidson, Paul (1972 [1978]), *Money and the Real World*, London: Macmillan.
Duesenberry, James (1958 [1977]), *Business Cycles and Economic Growth*, Westport, CT: Greenwood Press.
Fazzari, Steven and Tracy Mott (1986–87), 'The investment theories of Kalecki and Keynes: an empirical study of firm data, 1970–1982', *Journal of Post Keynesian Economics*, **9** (2), 171–87.

Kalecki, Michał (1990, 1991), *Collected Works of Michał Kalecki*, Vols I and II, Oxford: Clarendon Press.
Keynes, John Maynard (1930 [1971]), *A Treatise on Money*, London: Macmillan.
Keynes, John Maynard (1936 [1964]), *The General Theory of Employment, Interest and Money*, New York: Harcourt Brace.
Minsky, Hyman (1975), *John Maynard Keynes*, New York: Columbia University Press.
Steindl, Josef (1952 [1976]), *Maturity and Stagnation in American Capitalism*, New York: Monthly Review Press.

Joan Robinson's Economics

When Joan Robinson began to study economics in 1922, Marshallian theory, in the form of the version taught by Pigou, was economics in Cambridge (*CEP* I, p. vii; *CEP*, followed by the Roman number, stands for J.V. Robinson, *Collected Economic Papers*, volumes I–V, Oxford, Blackwell, 1951–79. Starred items indicate the 2nd edition). In 1928–29, she attended the course 'Advanced Theory of Value', given by Piero Sraffa, who was 'calmly committing the sacrilege of pointing out inconsistencies in Marshall' (*CEP* I, p. vii), and met Richard Kahn, who was preparing his fellowship dissertation on the *Economics of the Short Period*; it was the beginning of a life-long collaboration.

Robinson's first publication, *Economics is a Serious Subject. The Apologia of an Economist to the Mathematician, the Scientist and the Plain Man*, was dedicated to Sraffa. By that time the book that was going to give her fame and academic respectability, *The Economics of Imperfect Competition*, was finished. Its starting point was Sraffa's proposal 'to re-write the theory of value, starting from the conception of the firm as a monopolist' (Robinson 1969, p. 6); its aim was to extend the marginal technique to all market forms. By this means she hoped to provide an answer to the challenge posed by Sraffa. However, twenty years later she repudiated the book as 'a blind alley' (Robinson 1978, p. x).

At the same time she was involved in the developments of Keynes's new ideas with the activity of the Cambridge 'Circus', which met between January and June 1931, writing two papers on issues being debated there. In 'A parable on saving and investment' she attacked Keynes's argument on the 'widow's cruse' in the *Treatise* because 'he was tacitly assuming that output was unchanged' (Robinson 1933, p. 82). In *The Theory of Money and the Analysis of Output* she urged Keynes to take the analysis of the *Treatise* to its logical conclusion, that is, that 'output may be in equilibrium at any number of different levels' (*CEP* I, p. 56). Finally, she was one of the recipients of the first proofs of the *General Theory*, which she commented on in June 1935.

Shortly afterwards, she wrote some essays drawing 'a number of riders' from the *General Theory* (*CEP* V, pp. 185–6), which were published in 1937 with the title *Essays in the Theory of Employment*; in the same year she embarked on the project of writing a version of the *General Theory* suitable for teaching to first-year students, which became her *Introduction to the Theory of Employment*.

One of the articles collected in the *Essays* occasioned her encounter with Michał Kalecki (*CEP* V, p. 186). Robinson very soon realized that Kalecki's analysis was indeed as important as Keynes's, and took upon herself the task of 'blowing the trumpet for him' (ibid.); she later claimed that it was Kalecki, rather than she herself, who 'brought imperfect competition in touch with the theory of employment' (Robinson 1969, p. viii).

Kalecki, who had drawn his inspiration from Marx's reproduction schemes, aroused her interest in them. She began to read Marx in 1940, with Maurice Dobb as her 'tutor'. Her most substantial work on the subject, *An Essay on Marxian Economics*, came out in 1942. The main conclusion of the book, while revaluating many points of Marxian analysis, was the rejection of Marx's value theory, and over the years she maintained a negative view of any attempt 'to solve the problem of transformation' (*CEP* I, p. 148).

The lesson drawn from the study of Marx in those years was later summed up by her with the sentence: 'For me, the main message of Marx was the need to think in terms of history, not of equilibrium' (Robinson 1973, p. x). The influence of Marx appears very clearly in her 1949 review of Harrod's *Towards a Dynamic Economics*, a book which threw in 'the challenge to develop a Keynesian analysis of accumulation in the long run' (*CEP* II*, p. iii).

The main programme of the 1950s in Cambridge was to develop a long-run analysis of accumulation, that is, to develop an analysis 'which has freed itself from the need to assume conditions of static equilibrium' (*CEP* II*, p. iii). The stumbling-block to the dynamic analysis was given, according to her later recollection, by 'the lack of an adequate conception of the rate of profit' (*CEP* II*, p. vi). In fact, on the basis of Keynes's and Kalecki's theory of effective demand, the level of total profits can be determined, while to determine the rate of profit it is necessary to define the value of the stock of capital, but at the time 'no one seemed able to do so' (Robinson 1978, p. xvi). She recorded having 'innumerable discussions with Piero Sraffa but they always consisted in his heading off from errors; he would never say anything positive. Thus it was not till I found the "corn economy" in his *Introduction* to Ricardo's *Principles* that I saw a gleam of light on the question of the rate of profit on capital' (ibid., p. xvii).

The attempt to extend Keynes's short-period analysis to the theory of long-run development was thus conceived as a return to the 'classical' analysis of accumulation. Her famous books of the late 1950s and early 1960s, *Accumulation of Capital* (1956), *Exercises in Economic Analysis* (1960) and *Essays in the Theory of Economic Growth* (1962a), are directed against models of growth 'according as they exhibit some kind of inbuilt propensity to maintain full employment over the long run' (Robinson 1962a,

p. 87). The 'golden-age method', using steady growth models with full employment, was provided to examine the relation between accumulation and the rate of profit (*CEP* V, p. 21). The difference between the equilibrium method and the 'historical' method was seen as a different treatment of time: 'To make a comparison between two situations, each with its own future and its own past, is not the same thing as to trace a movement from one to the other' (Robinson 1960, p. v).

The 'long struggle to escape' (*CEP* III*, p. 52) from a conception in which accumulation is seen as a substitution of labour for capital 'in a given state of technical knowledge' meant reinstating the possibility of the analysis of innovations and technical progress, as Smith, Ricardo and Marx had done.

In her attempt to analyse the relationship between the rate of profit and the choice of techniques, Robinson was faced with the question of the meaning to be given to the expression 'quantity of capital'. In her 1953–54 article on the production function, and then in the *Accumulation of Capital*, she had invented a 'pseudo-production function', as Robert Solow later called it (*CEP* V, p. 82), in order to be able to list the techniques specified in a supposed 'book of blueprints', which represented the state of technical knowledge at a given point of time. The pseudo-production function was meant to show the possible equilibrium positions corresponding to different values of the rate of profit. So she encountered the phenomenon of reswitching, namely that:

> [O]ver certain ranges of a pseudo-production function the technique that becomes eligible at a higher rate of profit (with a correspondingly lower real-wage rate) may be less labour intensive (that is, may have a higher output per man employed) than that chosen at a higher wage rate, contrary to the rule of a 'well-behaved production function' in which a lower wage rate is always associated with a more intensive technique. (*CEP* IV, pp. 144–5)

With the publication in 1960 of Sraffa's *Production of Commodities by Means of Commodities* the basic tenets of his criticism of neoclassical theory could be seen more clearly. Sraffa's message has a twofold significance, according to Robinson: 'to knock out the marginal productivity theory' and to re-establish 'the classical doctrine that the rate of profit on capital depends upon the technical structure of production and the share of wages in net output' (*CEP* V, p. 95).

The conviction that it is possible to keep the scientific and ideological levels of analysis separate is at the core of Robinson's attitude to economics. In 1962 she presented her methodological ideas in *Economic Philosophy*, where she argued that in scientific discourse it is possible to distinguish empirical propositions from metaphysical propositions, as Karl Popper had maintained (Robinson 1962b, p. 3). Unfortunately, as she commented in her *Exercises in Economic Analysis*: 'Economics does not offer, like the well-developed natural sciences, a body of knowledge which the lay public can accept as established' (Robinson 1960, p. xv).

When she became Professor of Economics at Cambridge in 1965, she chose as the topic of her inaugural lecture, 'The new mercantilism', a denunciation of the mystique of free trade in historical practice and in the theoretical tradition since the time of Adam Smith (*CEP* IV, p. 4). She argued that contemporary neo-mercantilist philosophies and policies are always followed and theorized when the benefits of free trade are in danger (*CEP* IV, pp. 12–13).

In the early 1970s Robinson came insistently to the question of identifying the *pars construens* of her thought 'in the classical tradition, revived by Sraffa, which flows from Ricardo through Marx, diluted by Marshall and enriched by the analysis of effective demand of Keynes and Kalecki' (Robinson 1973, p. xii). However, in the work of reconstruction she found herself in disagreement with some of her allies in the battle against neoclassical economics. One point in particular became central in the discussion, that is, the maintenance of a concept of a long-run equilibrium in the context of historical analysis (Robinson 1980, p. 128).

It is the criticism of the concept of equilibrium, not only of neoclassical equilibrium, which she sees as the legacy of Keynes; therefore the main instrument with which to attack the neoclassical theory should be the distinction between historical time and logical time. In this respect she found Sraffa's language in *Production of Commodities* limited, because what it is offered is 'a purely logical structure – an elaborate thought experiment. There is no causation and no change' (Robinson 1980, p. 132). This is why she sees it as more promising to begin again with Keynes, who discusses events 'in terms of processes taking place in actual history' (Robinson 1979, p. xiv).

At the end of her life Robinson became increasingly dissatisfied with economics and more and more disillusioned with it as a body of knowledge which could be used to solve problems in the real world. She was increasingly concerned with those fundamental issues which are obscured rather than clarified by contemporary economic theory. Her last paper, published posthumously, originally had a telling title, 'Spring cleaning': 'We should throw out all self-contradictory propositions, unmeasurable quantities and indefinable concepts and reconstruct a logical basis for analysis with what, if anything, remains' (Robinson 1985, p. 160).

This is the legacy that Robinson has handed down to us. (See Marcuzzo 1996, 2001.)

MARIA CRISTINA MARCUZZO

See also:
Cambridge Economic Tradition; Capital Theory; Growth and Income Distribution; Growth Theory; Kaleckian Economics; Sraffian Economics; Time in Economic Theory.

References

Marcuzzo, M.C. (1996), 'The writings of Joan Robinson', in M.C. Marcuzzo, L.L. Pasinetti and A. Roncaglia (eds), *The Economics of Joan Robinson*, London: Routledge, pp. 330–63.
Marcuzzo, M.C. (2001), 'Joan Robinson: une quête passionnée de la rationalité', in G. Harcourt (ed.), *L'économie rebelle de Joan Robinson*, Paris: L'Harmattan, pp. 27–58.
Robinson, J. (1933), 'A parable on saving and investment', *Economica*, **13** (39), 75–84.
Robinson, J. (1956), *The Accumulation of Capital*, London: Macmillan.
Robinson, J. (1960), *Exercises in Economic Analysis*, London: Macmillan.
Robinson, J. (1962a), *Essays in the Theory of Economic Growth*, London: Macmillan.
Robinson, J. (1962b), *Economic Philosophy*, London: Watts.
Robinson, J. (1969), *The Economics of Imperfect Competition*, London: Macmillan, second edition.
Robinson, J. (1973), 'Preface' to J.A. Kregel, *The Reconstruction of Political Economy: An Introduction to Post-Keynesian Economics*, London: Macmillan, pp. ix–xiii.
Robinson, J. (1978), *Contributions to Modern Economics*, Oxford: Blackwell.
Robinson, J. (1979), *The Generalization of the General Theory and Other Essays*, London: Macmillan.
Robinson, J. (1980), *Further Contributions to Modern Economics*, Oxford: Blackwell.
Robinson, J. (1985), 'The theory of normal prices and reconstruction of economic theory', in G.R. Feiwel (ed.), *The Theory of Normal Prices and Reconstruction of Economic Theory*, London: Macmillan, pp. 157–65.

Journal of Post Keynesian Economics

Political economy experienced a revival in the 1960s in many nations of the world, leading to the inception of many associations with journals to support a growing number of adherents and fellow travellers. Post Keynesians never developed their own formal (multinational) association, and it was not until the late 1970s that specifically Post Keynesian journals emerged, starting in the UK with the *Cambridge Journal of Economics* in 1977. In the same year, the father of Post Keynesian economics in the United States, Sidney Weintraub (1914–83), along with a former student, Paul Davidson, sent out invitations to potential subscribers to another new journal. To their 'shock' and 'amazement', they received cheques from more than 400 subscribers within a month of the mailout (see Davidson, *JPKE*, Fall 1998, p. 3). The first issue of the *Journal of Post Keynesian Economics* (*JPKE*) thus emerged in the Fall of 1978, published by M.E. Sharpe of New York, with a pre-eminent international Honorary Board of Editors, and the editors Davidson and Weintraub overseeing the journal through the usual four issues a year.

The first issue of the journal included an editorial 'Statement of Purposes' (*JPKE*, Fall 1978, pp. 3–7), which made it clear that the journal was to be concerned with 'innovative theoretical work that can shed fresh light on contemporary economic problems' while 'contest[ing the] orthodoxy' that dominates journals in the US. The editors believed that 'Innovative ideas on inflation and unemployment have been routinely suppressed by prominent journals'. Such ideas have tried to 'explain the real world' as well as provide a 'reliable guide to public policy'. They cite some of the greats from the distant past – Adam Smith, David Ricardo, Karl Marx, J.S. Mill, W.S. Jevons, Alfred Marshall and J.M. Keynes – as well as some from the late 1970s – Joan Robinson, Nicholas Kaldor, Richard Kahn, Michał Kalecki, Abba Lerner, J.K. Galbraith and Hyman Minsky – as forging the central intellectual spirit of Post Keynesian economics. This spirit incorporates a monetary theory of production, where financial relationships influence economic processes in the short and long runs ('money matters'), due to hysteresis, path dependency and fundamental uncertainty. Money matters because the financial system generates credit for productive and financial activities, and the holding of money and credit influences velocity, money supply and thus GDP. Special reference is given in the journal to the problems of uncertainty, credit and demand in affecting inflation, unemployment, corporate power, capital–labour relations, demand management tools and 'strategies to enhance the general welfare – in the elemental, benign sense of that elliptical concept'. Significantly, the editors added that: 'It is not a new sect that we seek to foster; it is instead a reasoned debate with a fair shake for innovative, unorthodox attitudes. The term "post Keynesian" [sic] will thus be broadly interpreted, spotlighting new problems and revealing new theoretical perspectives.'

Apart from general articles, the journal has included many interesting symposia, comments, book reviews, an editorial corner and a series of lively and humanistic academic biographies (written mainly by board member Geoffrey Harcourt). Since the death of Weintraub in 1983, Paul Davidson has been the sole editor and main force behind the journal. His views have some bearing on its content and trend. For instance, he has never been too impressed by Sraffian themes, and has sought to differentiate Keynes's message from that of Kalecki (although both have impacted on the *JPKE*). Through its 25-year history the journal has concentrated on relating the core theory of Post Keynesian economics – concerning money, uncertainty and demand – to new developments, trends or problems in the world. For instance, in the 1970s and 1980s it paid special attention to the problems associated with stagflation, while during the 1990s and early 2000s it gave more attention to financial crises, global imbalances and conflicts.

The principal themes of the core theory encouraged by Davidson seem to be, wittingly or unwittingly, a symbolic reflection of the composition of the Honorary Board of Editors. A core theme running through the journal, as

Philip Arestis says (ironically quoting Michał Kalecki (1899–1970)), is that 'Post Keynesian analysis firmly embraces the view that "the institutional framework of a social system is a basic element of its economic dynamics"' (*JPKE*, Summer 1989, p. 611). This reflects the concerns of (especially) board members Arestis, Galbraith (chair), Gunnar Myrdal (1898–1987), Daniel Fusfeld, Robert Heilbroner, Hyman Minsky (1919–96), Wallace Peterson and Warren Samuels. Of prime importance in this respect is an understanding of capitalism as a system, comprising a mixed economy – state and corporation; a heterogeneous series of social classes – workers, capitalists and salaried professionals; a corporate system of big and small firms; a complex system of finance – including banks, institutional investors and central authority; and a series of nation-states, global institutions and networks.

The main institutional themes of the journal link, directly or indirectly, to the theory of circular and cumulative causation (CCC), emanating especially from board members Myrdal, Nicholas Kaldor (1908–86) and A.P. Thirlwall. According to CCC, the main institutions and sectors of the economic system link together in a complex circuit of cybernetic feedback and interaction. Supply and demand are interdependent. For instance, households are not only consumers but also investors in durable structures. This requires a detailed analysis of habits, social conventions, bounded rationality, and a hierarchy of needs from basics to luxuries (including Veblen goods and conspicuous consumption). Investment demand is associated with economies of scale/scope, new technology, complex dynamics, changes in capacity utilization and structural change. A proper system of government spending enhances infrastructure, knowledge and organization. And the 'balance of payments constraint' recognizes the impact of import elasticities, world income and non-price competition on economic growth. Demand is the prime mover of the CCC circuit, since it links to the creation of new needs and changes to the systems of production and distribution, and hence links productivity and exports through economies of scale, learning by doing and structural modifications to needs and technologies. (See the debate on 'Effective demand', *JPKE*, Spring 2001, pp. 375–440; and the 'Symposium' on 'Thirlwall's Law and the BOPC', *JPKE*, Spring 1997, pp. 311–86.)

A primary source of change in a Post Keynesian world that is copiously developed in the journal is fundamental uncertainty, or non-ergodic dynamics, a theme expounded by Davidson as well as *JPKE* board members Donald Katzner, Minsky, G.L.S. Shackle (1903–92) and Douglas Vickers. In their view, investment is largely affected by the prevailing business climate and demand, especially the degree of confidence in the future, and hence expected profits, *à la* chapter 12 of Keynes's *General Theory of Employment,*

Interest and Money (1936). The future, however, is unknown and therefore uncertain (rather than strictly probabilistic): the greater the level of uncertainty, the lower the expected rate of profit and rate of investment. Firms engage in routines, organizations and institutions, such as accounting notions of cash flow, net worth and mark-up pricing, to provide stability and structured activity in a world of uncertainty. This enables firms to invest in capital goods and consumer goods production – based largely on credit – with some degree of confidence that profits will flow from such activities. But, despite all this, fundamental uncertainty and ignorance about the future still prevail, which periodically lead to booms and recessions of varying magnitudes. (See the 'Symposium' on 'Investment', *JPKE*, Summer 1992, pp. 423–96; the issue mainly on 'Uncertainty', Fall 1993, pp. 3–54; and the Spring 1996 issue.)

Editor Davidson has published a lot on demand and supply equations and conditions that are interdependent. The supply side links to work on non-price competition, 'degree of monopoly', mark-up pricing principles and the megacorp, especially by board members Alfred Eichner (1937–88), Fred Lee, J. Barkley Rosser Jr, Malcolm Sawyer and Nina Shapiro. National income, equating price level (p) times output (q), from the supply side (Y_s), equals:

$$Y_s = pq = (\kappa w/A)q.$$

Weintraub explained inflation through a wage–cost mark-up equation, $p = \kappa w/A$, where κ is the average mark-up of prices over unit wage (variable) costs, w/A, w the average money-wage rate and A the average product per worker. The mark-up by firms, κ, is said to be remarkably stable, dependent mainly on the relationship between wages and labour productivity (*JPKE*, Winter 1981–82, pp. 291–300). Inflation has thus been linked in the *JPKE* to wages upwardly deviating from productivity, leading firms to adjust their prices accordingly.

National income in nominal terms, from the demand side (Y_d), includes workers' wages (W) and capitalists' profit (Π), which equals consumption (C) plus investment (I) plus the government budget deficit (GD) and the trade surplus (TS):

$$Y_d = W + \Pi = C + I + GD + TS.$$

In Kaleckian models, workers spend all of their income, and capitalists spend what they receive (adjustments have been made for workers and capitalists saving some of their income and so on). Under these conditions, aggregate profit equals the consumption of capitalists plus investment plus the budget deficit plus the trade surplus. Workers press for wage claims in the industrial relations arena, while firms seek claims through their target price mark-ups (*JPKE*, Fall 1991, pp. 93–110). The *JPKE* has published papers supporting the 'conflicting claims' theory, where inflation is due to aggregate nominal income claims – wages and profits – exceeding the total available income.

The *JPKE* specializes in developing endogenous explanations for economic phenomena, such as the creation of credit, business cycles, financial crises and exchange rates. This material reveals that during business cycle upswings – such as 1984–87 or 1996–2000 (1992–97 in parts of Asia) – the generation of euphoria leads to a high rate of investment, as well as a stock market boom, financed largely by endogenous credit. According to Hyman Minsky's 'distance memory hypothesis', firms typically forget about previous financial crises and recessions and get caught up in the euphoric environment. Traders speculated in the late 1990s–2000 period, for instance, about 'new rules to the game', and technology stocks not needing fundamentals in the 'new business environment', which supposedly 'justified' further credit expansion. The journal has explored endogenous money and credit responding to higher demand through instruments such as bank bills, certificates of deposit, capital inflow, financial innovations and reserve bank 'accommodation'. Forces endogenous to the upswing – such as higher oil and energy prices, interest rate pressures, speculative bubbles and heightened global conflict – bring about a collapse of prospective yields, greater uncertainty, a speculative bubble crash, a declining rate of investment demand and further financial crises, for instance during 2000–2002 as euphoria turned to global and national pessimism and recession (*JPKE*, Spring 1990 and Winter 2000–2001).

This leads the journal to concentrate on policies that moderate the instabilities of the business cycle, such as incomes policies, global institutions, basic income schemes, prudential financial policies and organizational arrangements (see *JPKE* Winter 1997–98, Spring 2000 and Summer 2000). A recurring global policy proposal is monetary reform, where the onus is on (current account) surplus nations increasing their effective demand, thereby restoring some degree of world balance. A cooperative global approach to balance of payments problems is seen to be better than one where deficit nations bear the brunt of adjustment through fiscal and monetary deflation. The cooperative policy could thus help to moderate various conflicts, including terrorism, war, crime and industrial instability, through the provision of global stability, trust, agreement and income.

Over the past quarter of a century the *Journal of Post Keynesian Economics* has been instrumental in promoting theoretical and policy insights that enhance the democratic and participatory workings of the economy in the pursuit of full employment and price stability. It has tracked and critically analysed the contemporary economic performance of the US and world economies. The journal has done well to propagate a coherent alternative analysis of economic theory and policy in a difficult 'era of neoliberalism'. Advances in knowledge have been made in relation to a monetary theory of production, set in an environment of fundamental uncertainty, circular and cumulative causation, and interdependencies between supply and demand. The editor has encouraged the building of empirical evidence, the linking of theory and practice, and the development of policy prescriptions that are innovative yet relatively pragmatic, but always inspired by the need for fundamental reforms of capitalism. The ability of the journal to withstand editorial, systemic and disciplinary instabilities and progress further will influence the future of Post Keynesian economics in the United States and elsewhere.

PHILLIP ANTHONY O'HARA

Kaldorian Economics

Nicholas (Miklos) Kaldor (1908–86) was one of the most original and controversial economists of the twentieth century. *The Economist* newspaper once described him as 'the best known economist in the world not to have received the Nobel Prize'. In the 1930s and 1940s he made fundamental contributions to the theory of the firm; welfare economics; trade cycle theory; capital theory and Keynesian economics. In the 1950s, he turned his fertile mind to public finance and to growth and distribution theory, and was the joint architect with Joan Robinson and Richard Kahn of the Post Keynesian school of economics which extended Keynesian modes of thinking to the long run. Then in the 1960s he turned his attention to the applied economics of growth and initiated an enormous secondary literature related to the idea of manufacturing industry as the engine of growth based on static and dynamic increasing returns to scale. In the 1970s he led world-wide the assault on the doctrine of monetarism which, as he described it, spread with the virulence of a plague from North America under the influence of Milton Friedman to infect academic thinking and policy making in several parts of the world, including most notably the United Kingdom during the government of Margaret Thatcher in the 1980s. He lost the battle but won the war because monetarism as a coherent intellectual doctrine is now dead.

It is clear from the above that Kaldor led several lives as an economist; his range of interests was wide, but he also had a vision of how capitalist economies function and a strong intuition concerning what is important and what is unimportant, what is cause and what is effect. There is a Kaldorian economics and an interesting story to tell.

Kaldor was Hungarian by birth. As a boy he attended the famous Minta school in Budapest, and then at the age of 17 attended the Humboldt University in Berlin to study economics for eighteen months before coming to the London School of Economics (LSE) in 1927, where he fell under the influence of Allyn Young (who tragically died in 1929, aged 53) and then of Lionel Robbins and (later) Friedrich von Hayek. In 1930 he graduated with first-class honours and stayed on at the LSE first as a research assistant and then as an assistant lecturer. The Keynesian revolution was still six years off, and his early research work was in the Austrian tradition – an analysis, for example, of the overcommitment of Austrian industry and the problem of the Danubian states. It was not long, however, before Kaldor crossed swords with Robbins and Hayek and became one of the first converts at the

LSE to the thinking in Keynes's *General Theory*, along with Abba Lerner and Ursula Hicks. While Kaldor disagreed with some of the details of the *General Theory*, and made important contributions himself to its understanding, he never wavered from the thrust of its central message that monetary production economies are fundamentally different from barter economies, and that unemployment can exist for long periods of time even in the presence of wage and price flexibility, because of uncertainty associated with the peculiar properties of money.

Kaldor's first major theoretical contributions came in 1934–35 with four papers: 'A classificatory note on the determinateness of equilibrium', in which he was the first to coin the term 'cob-web theorem' to describe oscillations around an equilibrium; 'The equilibrium of the firm'; 'Mrs. Robinson's *Economics of Imperfect Competition*'; and 'Market imperfections and excess capacity'. In the next five years, including the first year of the war, there appeared a further spate of papers in diverse fields (Thirlwall 1987 and Targetti 1992 contain a full bibliography). There was his major survey of capital theory; his attack on Arthur Pigou's theory of how wage cuts affect unemployment – it must be through a reduction in the rate of interest; his critique of Edward Chamberlin and the distinction between monopolistic and imperfect competition; his debate with Hayek over capital intensity and the trade cycle; his introduction of compensation tests into welfare economies; his classic paper 'Speculation and economic stability' which John Hicks described in personal correspondence as 'the culmination of the Keynesian revolution in theory – you ought to have got more honour for it' (Thirlwall 1987, p. 75, n. 46); and his 1940 nonlinear model of the trade cycle.

During the Second World War the LSE was evacuated to Cambridge, and Kaldor became more acquainted with the Cambridge economists, particularly Joan Robinson, Richard Kahn, Piero Sraffa, Pigou and Keynes himself. He spent most of the war years working on aspects of public policy, both national and international, related both to the war and preparations for the peace. In particular, he played a major role in the analysis and thinking behind the two Beveridge reports on *Social Insurance* (in 1942) and *Full Employment in a Free Society* (in 1944), and also the construction of national income accounts, then in their infancy. He emerged from the war with a high reputation as an incisive applied economist, which led to his appointment on several international commissions, and then in 1947 as research director of the Economic Commission for Europe in Geneva headed by Gunnar Myrdal. In 1949 he returned to Cambridge as a Fellow of King's College and a member of the Economics Faculty, where he remained for the rest of his life.

His interest in public finance, and particularly tax matters, deepened when he was appointed in 1951, along with John Hicks, to the Royal Commission on the Taxation of Profits and Income. Kaldor was the author of a trenchant Minority Report and also a classic book entitled *An Expenditure Tax* arguing the case for taxing expenditure rather than income, both on grounds of equity and as a means of promoting growth. His tax expertise was later sought in several developing countries, and led to his appointment in the United Kingdom as a special tax adviser to the Chancellor of the Exchequer in two Labour governments (1964–69 and 1974–76).

Despite his multifarious contributions to economic theory and policy, Kaldor will be remembered in the history of economic thought largely for his work in growth economics and his challenge to equilibrium theory. In the mid-1950s and early 1960s there was his pioneering work on growth and distribution theory. In the mid-1960s there was his innovative thinking on the applied economics of growth, and then from the 1970s to his death there was his constant assault on the assumptions, predictions and usefulness of the Walrasian, general equilibrium framework of analysis for an understanding of the dynamics of capitalism in the real world. What are the mainsprings of growth in developed and developing countries? Does it make sense to separate capital accumulation and technical progress as in mainstream neoclassical growth theory? Why does the capital–output ratio remain roughly constant despite an ever-increasing ratio of capital to labour? Why does fast growth seem to be associated with industrialization? What determines the growth of industry in a closed economy (including the world) and in an open economy? Why is there a tendency for levels of development between regions and countries to become polarized, contrary to the predictions of neoclassical growth theory? These are the major questions that Kaldor attempted to answer in a series of profound and provocative papers over 30 years (for example, Kaldor 1956, 1957, 1961, 1966, 1970, 1972, 1996).

In 1956 Kaldor revolutionized the theory of the functional distribution of income by showing that the share of profits in national income must be related to the share of investment in national income and the propensity to save out of wages and profits, and that the orthodox neoclassical theory of distribution based on relative factor prices and quantities is not only theoretically fraught with problems, but, in any case, unnecessary. The Kaldor theory of distribution is beautiful in its simplicity. Let full-employment income (Y) be divided between consumption (C) and investment (I), with consumption out of wages equal to $c_w W$ and consumption out of profits equal to $c_p P$ (where W is wages, P is profits and c_w and c_p are the propensities to consume out of wages and profits, respectively). Therefore, $Y = c_w W + c_p P + I$. But $P = Y - W$. Therefore $P = c_p P + I - s_w W$, where s_w is the propensity to save out of wages. The share of profits in income is therefore equal to $P/Y = (I/Y)/(s_p - s_w) - s_w/(s_p - s_w)$, where s_p is the propensity to save out of profits. Profits must be the dependent variable and investment the independent variable because capitalists can decide what to invest but they cannot decide what they earn.

Kaldor's 1957 and 1961 growth models introduce the innovation of the technical progress function (TPF) to replace the neoclassical production function, which makes what is an artificial distinction between movements along a function and shifts in the whole function. Kaldor was adamant that capital accumulation and technical progress go together; most technical progress requires capital accumulation for its embodiment and there is unlikely to be much new capital accumulation without technical progress. The TPF relates the rate of growth of output per worker (r) to the rate of growth of capital per worker (k). In linear form: $r = a + b(k)$. The position of the function (a) depends on 'autonomous' productivity growth (for example, learning by doing) and the slope of the function (b) depends on the technical dynamism of the economy. Equilibrium growth at a constant capital–output ratio is given by $r = a/(1-b)$. Countries grow at different rates with the same capital–output ratio because of differences in the parameters of the technical progress function. The TPF is important not only because it provides a more realistic representation of the growth process, but also because it provides an explanation of why the capital–output ratio is no higher in rich countries than in poor countries, contrary to the prediction of orthodox neoclassical growth theory; countries are simply on different TPFs. Kaldor's TPF is thus the precursor, and true progenitor, of 'new' growth theory (or endogenous growth theory), which also seeks to explain why the marginal product of capital apparently does not fall as countries get richer and invest more. There are 'technological forces' that keep the capital–output ratio from rising, such as human capital formation, research and development and technological spillovers from trade.

Kaldor was not made a professor at Cambridge until 1966, aged 58, but in his famous Inaugural Lecture (Kaldor 1966) he turned his attention to the applied economics of growth and presented a series of growth laws which have subsequently been widely tested in different contexts. Kaldor's thesis was that manufacturing industry is the engine of growth for two major reasons. First, manufacturing industry is subject to increasing returns which other sectors are not (at least to the same extent, and certainly not agriculture). This hypothesis is also known as Verdoorn's Law (see McCombie et al. 2002), which Kaldor revived, it having lain effectively dormant for 17 years. Second, manufacturing industry generates fast growth because it draws resources in from sectors where the marginal product is less than the average, so that productivity growth is induced outside of the manufacturing sector. Today, the evidence for Kaldor's laws is most clearly seen in the newly industrializing countries of South-East Asia, where GDP growth is rapid and the share of manufacturing industry in GDP is also rising fast.

But what determines the growth of industry? In the open economy it is the growth of exports in a circular and cumulative process (Kaldor 1970), although subject to a balance of payments constraint. In the closed economy, such as the world economy, it is land-saving innovations in agriculture that are crucial for industrial growth (and the performance of developed countries) as an offset to diminishing returns. In his 1986 Hicks Lecture on 'Limits to growth' (and elsewhere, for example, Kaldor 1996), he emphasizes the importance of an equilibrium terms of trade between the two sectors of agriculture and industry (developing and developed countries) for maximizing the growth rate of the economy as a whole.

In all these fields of theoretical and empirical enquiry mentioned above, Kaldor attracted many disciples, but also many adversaries. Academic hostility came from asking awkward questions about neoclassical economics in general and equilibrium theory in particular, and was understandably most prevalent in the US. Kaldor's legacy to the profession is nearly 200 articles, pamphlets and books, many of the former being collected in his nine volumes of *Collected Essays*. Although he wrote no grand treatise, these volumes will provide a lasting testimony and monument to the energy, creativity and endeavour of one of the greatest economists of the twentieth century.

A.P. THIRLWALL

See also:

Balance-of-payments-constrained Economic Growth; Cambridge Economic Tradition; Equilibrium and Non-equilibrium; Growth and Income Distribution; Growth Theory; Income Distribution.

References

Kaldor, N. (1956), 'Alternative theories of distribution', *Review of Economic Studies*, **23** (2), 83–100.
Kaldor, N. (1957), 'A model of economic growth', *Economic Journal*, **67** (268), 591–624.
Kaldor, N. (1961), 'Capital accumulation and economic growth', in F. Lutz (ed.), *The Theory of Capital*, London: Macmillan, pp. 177–222.
Kaldor, N. (1966), *Causes of the Slow Rate of Economic Growth of the United Kingdom*, Cambridge: Cambridge University Press.
Kaldor, N. (1970), 'The case for regional policies', *Scottish Journal of Political Economy*, **17** (3), 337–48.
Kaldor, N. (1972), 'The irrelevance of equilibrium economics', *Economic Journal*, **82** (328), 1237–55.
Kaldor, N. (1996), *Causes of Growth and Stagnation in the World Economy* (Mattioli Lectures), Cambridge: Cambridge University Press.

McCombie, J., M. Pugno and B. Soro (2002), *Productivity Growth and Economic Performance: Essays on Verdoorn's Law*, London: Palgrave.
Targetti, F. (1992), *Nicholas Kaldor*, Oxford: Clarendon Press.
Thirlwall, A.P. (1987), *Nicholas Kaldor*, Brighton: Harvester Wheatsheaf.

Kaleckian Economics

Kaleckian economics may be broadly defined as the economic theories enunciated by Michał Kalecki (1899–1970), and the extensions of those theories by economists who were influenced by him. Kalecki was a Polish engineer and mathematician who taught himself economics in a left-wing political milieu during the 1920s, where the main intellectual influences were Austro-Marxism, Rosa Luxemburg, Mikhail Tugan-Baranovsky and Henryk Grossmann. From 1929 to 1936 he was employed at the Business Cycle and Prices Institute in Warsaw, where the first national income statistics for Poland were constructed. In 1933 he published his first analysis of the business cycle under capitalism, arguing that it was due to the instability of investment, which in turn was caused by fluctuations in capitalists' profits. Investment was crucial. Under capitalism, in Kalecki's view, investment is the main determinant of aggregate demand as well as, in its turn, determining profits, where capitalists' costs are mainly accounted for by wages, which are by and large consumed. This was summarized in an aphoristic precis of Kalecki's theory (attributed by some to Joan Robinson, and by others to Nicholas Kaldor): 'Workers spend what they earn, capitalists earn what they spend'. This can easily be derived from the well-known Keynesian savings identity, in which saving (S) is by definition equal to gross investment (I), plus the fiscal deficit (government expenditure minus taxation, $G - T$), plus the trade surplus (exports minus imports, $X - M$). Assume that there are only two classes in society, capitalists and workers, earning profits and wages respectively, which can be saved or consumed. The saving identity therefore represents workers' and capitalists' saving (S_w and S_c):

$$S = I + (G - T) + (X - M) = S_w + S_c.$$

If workers' saving is deducted from both sides of the equation, then the saving identity shows only capitalists' saving:

$$S_c = I + (G - T) + (X - M) - S_w.$$

Since profits can only be saved or consumed, adding capitalists' consumption (C_c) to the right-hand side of the equation gives an expression for profits (P):

$$P = C_c + S_c = I + (G - T) + (X - M) + C_c - S_w.$$

Profits are therefore equal to gross investment, plus the fiscal deficit, plus the trade surplus, plus capitalists' consumption, minus workers' saving. The greater is capitalists' expenditure on investment or their own consumption, or the fiscal surplus, or the expenditure of foreign residents on exports, the greater will profits be. Higher profits will tend to result in higher investment until excess capacity emerges and investment is reduced, causing profits to fall and a decline in economic activity to continue until excess capacity is eliminated and investment starts to rise. Higher profits then finance higher investment and stimulate a boom in economic activity.

In 1936 Kalecki left Poland for Stockholm and eventually for London, where Joan Robinson recruited him to Keynes's circle. While critical of Keynes's equilibrium reasoning, he readily participated in Cambridge and later Oxford discussions on the possibilities of full employment under capitalism. At this time he developed his pricing analysis, in which the markup over prime costs is determined by imperfect competition, and an analysis of corporate finance in which external finance is a liability that enhances financial risks, as well as providing liquidity. After the Second World War, Kalecki worked for nearly ten years for the United Nations, where he studied in detail the problems of developing countries. Out of this, in later years, came an analysis of economic development focusing on financial bottlenecks to capital accumulation in the developing countries, in a context of socio-economic 'structural' obstacles, poverty, rural backwardness and food supply, to capitalist primary accumulation. In 1955 Kalecki returned to Poland. In the dislocation caused by Stalinist overinvestment, he emphasized the limited effectiveness of investment because of the need to maintain adequate levels of consumption and avoid excessive imports. He was a strong critic of market socialism, arguing that market mechanisms are less efficient than an effectively adjusted and centralized investment programme. Kalecki and his associates were subjected to political attacks and an anti-Semitic purge in 1968.

In the years after Keynes's death, Joan Robinson championed Kalecki's work for its radical criticism of capitalism, namely that capitalism is unstable (the business cycle), tends to regressive distributional values (cost-minimization holds down wages, while high profits are necessary to maintain investment), and is hostile to full employment (because it undermines labour discipline) (Robinson 1966). Kalecki's exposition of his analysis in the form of mathematical models based on national income identities made his work attractive to the first generation of Keynesian model-builders, in particular Lawrence Klein and David Worswick. They were attracted by models which gave a more systematic account of business cycles than Keynes's (Klein 1947).

During the 1950s Kalecki was influential in the monopoly capitalism school of Marxists, through the work of Paul Sweezy and Josef Steindl. Kalecki's analysis shows how the problem of realizing surplus value as profits, in twentieth-century capitalism, was alleviated by corporate investment and deficit spending by governments. At the same time, the absence of competition gives capitalists monopoly profits, which make excess capacity more tolerable. Such excess capacity in turn reduces the capitalists' inclination to invest, causing a tendency to economic stagnation (Baran and Sweezy 1966; Steindl 1952).

Kalecki's ideas were at the forefront of the emergence of Post Keynesian economics during the 1970s. Here Kaleckian economics provided a clear and consistent alternative to the neoclassical synthesis of Keynesian ideas with Walrasian general equilibrium. Kalecki could provide not only a theory of the business cycle (an essential element of any economic analysis after the return of economic instability to capitalism in the 1970s), but also microeconomic foundations, which are largely absent in Keynes's *General Theory*. (Their absence had facilitated the neoclassical and monetarist interpretation of Keynesian unemployment as being due to wage inflexibility.) Kalecki provided a more radical microeconomic explanation, in terms of monopoly and excess capacity reducing the propensity to invest out of profits (King 1996; Sawyer 1985). In this way Post Keynesian analysis spliced Kalecki's price and business cycle theory on to more orthodox Keynesian concerns about aggregate demand and full employment.

However, Post Keynesians have, by and large, preferred to overlook two aspects in which the work of Kalecki and Keynes is less than compatible. The first of these arises out of their respective treatment of expectations and uncertainty. Expectations play a central role in Keynes's explanation of the instability of investment, to which both theorists attributed the business cycle. In Kalecki's view, business confidence is largely determined by current profits, so that further analysis of the subjective elements entering into businesspeople's expectations is unnecessary. Uncertainty then plays a crucial role in Keynes's liquidity preference theory of money. Coming from outside the Marshallian tradition, Kalecki did not find it necessary to postulate any aggregate demand for and supply of money, outside the wholesale money markets, and he took it to be a central feature of capitalism that the banking system accommodates business demand for credit. Money is therefore endogenous to the system, and uncertainty is less important in portfolio demand for money (Keynes's 'speculative' demand) than changes in short-term interest rates, relative to the long-term rate of interest.

Kalecki was also critical of Keynes's emphasis on the long-term rate of interest (the yield on long-term bonds) as a determinant of investment. That rate of interest was shown to be relatively stable, and therefore was of little use in explaining the instability of investment. Keynes resolved this problem by arguing that the expected return on investment that is in excess of the long-term rate of interest (his marginal efficiency of capital) is volatile, and therefore accounts for the instability of investment. Kalecki argued instead that investment is volatile because the internal liquidity of the corporate sector that is free of external financial liabilities (and is therefore available for investment without imposing potentially ruinous financial overheads on companies) fluctuates with profits and the degree of external financing. This is Kalecki's 'principle of increasing risk'. W.H. Locke Anderson made a pioneering study of this in the early 1960s. The chief exponent of Post Keynesianism as a theory of finance capital, Hyman Minsky, used Kalecki's theory of the business cycle, but developed his own analysis of investment financing based on Keynesian expectations and Irving Fisher's debt deflation theory of economic depressions (Minsky 1986).

While Post Keynesians have tended to use Kalecki's analysis selectively to fill the lacunae in Keynes's economics, and the collapse of Communism has seriously limited the interest in Kalecki's economics of socialism, recurrent economic crises in developing and newly-industrialized countries, and volatile financial conditions in the older capitalist countries, offer scope for new developments in, and applications of, Kalecki's economics.

JAN TOPOROWSKI

See also:

Business Cycles; Development Finance; Expectations; Financial Instability Hypothesis; Pricing and Prices; Profits; Socialism; Uncertainty; Underconsumption.

References

Baran, P. A. and P.M. Sweezy (1966), *Monopoly Capital: An Essay on the American Economic and Social Order*, New York: Monthly Review Press.
Kalecki, M. (1990–97) *Collected Works of Michał Kalecki*, edited by Jerzy Osiatyński, Oxford: Clarendon Press.
King, J.E. (ed.) (1996), *An Alternative Macroeconomic Theory: The Kaleckian Model and Post-Keynesian Economics*, Boston: Kluwer.
Klein, L.R. (1947), *The Keynesian Revolution*, New York: Macmillan.
Minsky, H.P. (1986), *Stabilizing an Unstable Economy*, New Haven: Yale University Press.
Robinson, J. (1966), 'Kalecki and Keynes', in *Economic Dynamics and Planning: Essays in Honour of Michał Kalecki*, Oxford: Pergamon Press, pp. 335–41.
Sawyer, M.C. (1985) *The Economics of Michał Kalecki*, London: Macmillan.
Steindl, J. (1952), *Maturity and Stagnation in American Capitalism*, Oxford: Blackwell.

Keynes's *General Theory*

Most economists recognize that Keynes's 1936 book *The General Theory of Employment, Interest and Money* was revolutionary. Unfortunately there is not a consensus as to what was revolutionary about this volume.

Some economists have argued that the aggregate accounting scheme used by Keynes was the revolutionary aspect. But Kuznets had developed a system of aggregate income accounts by 1929, long before Keynes was even thinking about a general theory of employment, interest and money.

Many Old and New Keynesians believe that the Keynesian revolution is nested in supply-side market imperfections that result in the rigidity of money wages and prices, asymmetric information and lack of transparency. But throughout the nineteenth century classical economists had argued that monopoly elements in the market were the cause of unemployment and Keynes (1936, chapter 19) specifically denies that such supply-side elements are the fundamental cause of unemployment. Keynes claimed that it was on the demand side and not on the supply side that his revolution was embedded. Surely, then, price inflexibility was not a revolutionary idea in 1936.

Many scholars, for example, Don Patinkin and Axel Leijonhufvud, have argued that Keynes's revolution was centred on the multiplier concept. Post Keynesians believe that there is a much more fundamental foundation for Keynes's revolution. After all, if the revolutionary essence was the multiplier, then the proper name would have been the Kahnian revolution, for Keynes merely transformed Richard Kahn's employment multiplier measured in terms of employment units into an expenditure multiplier measured in either nominal or money-wage unit terms (Keynes 1936, p. 115). It would be hard to justify the canonization of Keynes in the economic literature if all he had done was to focus attention on a concept that a former student had developed and published years earlier.

Keynes (1936, p. 192) was convinced that the assumption of less than perfect price flexibility made by the 'weaker [classical] spirits' was not necessary to explain persistent unemployment and that this assumption caused 'injury to . . . logical consistency'. Instead, Keynes developed an expanded demand classification system to demonstrate that Say's Law 'is not the true law relating the aggregate demand and supply functions . . . [and hence] there is a vitally important chapter of economic theory which remains to be written and *without which all discussions concerning the volume of aggregate employment are futile*' (ibid., p. 26; italics added).

Say's Law specifies that all expenditure (aggregate demand) on the products of industry is always exactly equal to the total costs of aggregate production (aggregate supply including gross profits). Letting D^w symbolize aggregate demand and Z^w aggregate supply (both measured in wage units, that is, nominal values deflated by the money-wage rate), then:

$$D^w = f_d(N) \tag{1}$$

and

$$Z^w = f_z(N). \qquad (2)$$

Say's Law asserts that:

$$f_d(N) = f_z(N) \qquad (3)$$

'for *all* values of N, i.e., for all values of output and employment' (ibid., pp. 25–6). In other words, in an economy subject to Say's Law, the total costs (including profits and rents) of the aggregate production of firms (whether in perfect competition or not) are recouped by the sale of output. There is never a lack of effective demand. The aggregate demand and aggregate supply curves coincide (see Figure 11). In a Say's Law economy, there is never an obstacle to full employment, no matter what the degree of price flexibility in the system.

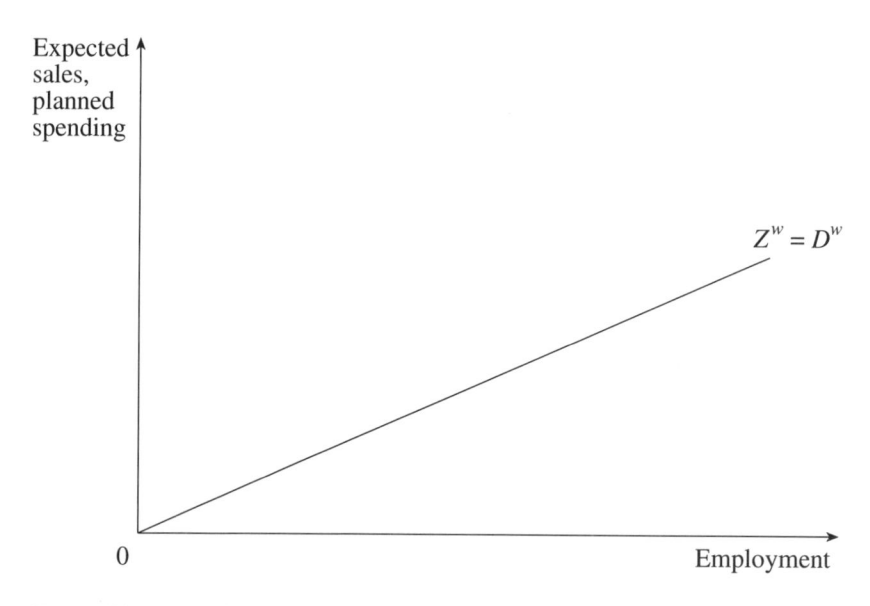

Figure 11   A Say's Law economy

To develop the 'true law' relating D^w and Z^w for a monetary economy, Keynes produced a model where the aggregate demand and aggregate supply functions, $f_d(N)$ and $f_z(N)$, need not be coincident (see Figure 12); as the general case, there is no necessity for the determinants of the aggregate demand function to be identical with the determinants of aggregate supply.

232 Keynes's General Theory

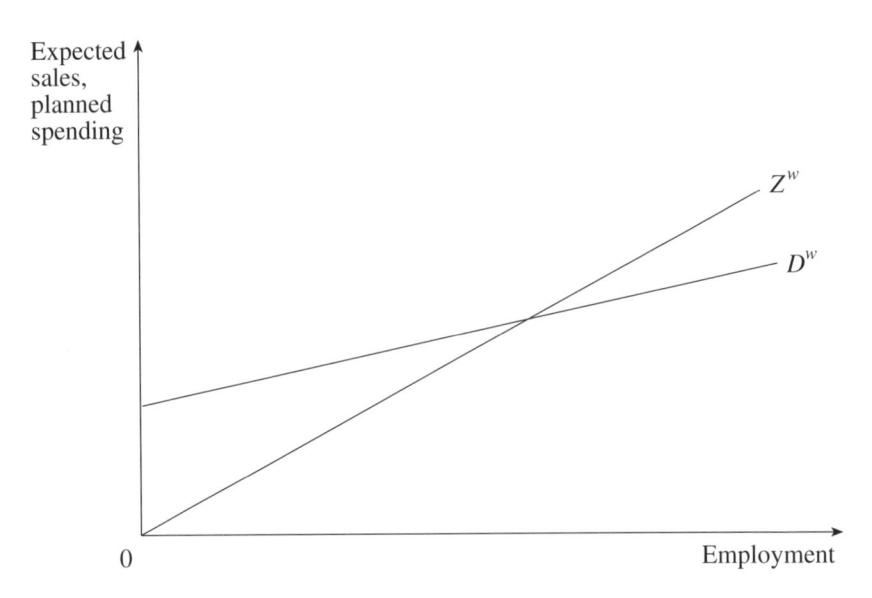

Figure 12 A Keynesian economy

Keynes differentiated his theory from classical economics by a taxonomic analysis of aggregate demand. As equation (1) suggests, classical theory fitted all expenditures into a single category, D^w, aggregate demand (which is created entirely by supply). Keynes, on the other hand, divided all types of expenditures into two demand classes, that is,

$$D^w = D_1^w + D_2^w = f_d(N) \tag{4}$$

where D_1^w represented *all* expenditures which 'depend on the level of [current] aggregate income and, therefore, on the level of employment N' (Keynes 1936, p. 28). Thus:

$$D_1^w = f_1(N). \tag{5}$$

Logically, therefore, D_2^w represents *all* expenditures *not* related to current income and employment:

$$D_2^w \neq f(N). \tag{6}$$

Classical theory is a special case of Keynes's general analytical system that can occur only if additional axioms are imposed to force the aggregate demand function to consist solely of expenditures *equal* to current income at all levels of N. Demand will then have the same determinants as supply. The necessary additional classical postulates for Say's Law are:

1. the *axiom of ergodicity* which asserts that the future can be reliably calculated from past and present market data. In Old Classical theory ergodicity was usually subsumed when it was assumed that decision makers possessed foreknowledge of the future. In New Classical theory it is presumed that agents have rational expectations about a statistically reliably predictable future;
2. the *axiom of gross substitution*, so that flexible relative prices ensure that all markets clear; and
3. *the neutral money axiom*, which ensures that changes in the nominal money supply have no real effects.

Unfortunately, while Keynes was developing his principle of effective demand the modern axiomatic theory of value had not yet been developed, so that Keynes could not explicitly label the equivalents of the 'axiom of parallels' that had to be 'overthrown' (Keynes 1936, p. 16) to produce a general theory. Nevertheless, in 1937, Keynes (1937 [1973], pp. 408–9) specifically noted that in the new 'monetary theory of production' that he was developing, the neutral money axiom was not applicable in either the short run or the long run. Yet even today, Blanchard (1990, p. 828) proclaims that all macroeconomic New Classical and New Keynesian models 'impose the long-run neutrality of money as a maintained assumption. This is very much a matter of faith, based on theoretical considerations [that is, axiom based], rather than on empirical science'.

Keynes's specification of the 'essential properties of money' in his general theory requires rejecting the classical postulate that money (and all other liquid assets) are *gross substitutes* for the products of industry. Money (and all other liquid) assets possess two essential properties (Keynes 1936, pp. 230–31). These are:

1. The elasticity of production of money is zero; in essence, money is nonproducible by the use of labour in the private sector. *Money does not grow on trees*. Money (and all liquid assets) therefore cannot be harvested by hiring otherwise unemployed workers to harvest money trees whenever people demand to hold additional liquid assets as a store of value.
2. The elasticity of substitution between money (that is, liquid assets) and producible goods is zero. Accordingly, any increase in demand for liquidity (nonproducibles to be held as a store of value), and resulting changes in relative prices between nonproducible liquid assets and the

products of industry, will not divert the demand for liquidity into a demand for goods and services. Keynes (ibid., p. 241) insisted that 'the attribute of "liquidity" is by no means independent of these two [elasticity] characteristics' and therefore as long as savers store their wealth in assets whose 'elasticities of production and substitution may be very low', unemployment equilibrium can exist no matter what the supply-side conditions are.

Since classical theory assumes that only producibles provide utility, then, in the long run, only a 'lunatic' would want to hold a nonproducible good as a liquid store of value. Keynes (1936, chapter 12; 1937 [1973], pp. 112–15), on the other hand, used the concept of uncertainty to explain why, even in the long run, people would reveal a preference to hold nonproducibles such as money as a store of value no matter how high its relative price rose *vis-à-vis* the products of industry. (The future is uncertain rather than merely risky in the probabilistic sense.) If nonproducibility is an essential attribute of all assets that possess the characteristic of liquidity and the holding of liquid assets can provide a long-run security blanket against uncertainty, then liquid assets can provide utility in a way that producibles cannot.

Hahn demonstrated that unemployment occurs when 'there are in this economy resting places for savings other than reproducible assets' (1977, p. 31) and the existence of 'any non-reproducible asset allows for a choice between employment-inducing and non-employment inducing demand' (ibid., p. 39). In an uncertain world, he who hesitates to spend on producibles and holds liquid assets instead is free to make a decision another day. By jettisoning the classical axioms of ergodicity and gross substitution, Keynes could demonstrate that, as a general case, unemployment is possible and money is not neutral.

The axiomatic microfoundations of classical economic theory, on the other hand, ensure that all income is always spent on the products of industry. In the simplest case all current expenditures are equal to current income, as utility-maximizers are constrained by their income (budget-line constraint) in their choice between good A and all other producibles. To spend less than one's income is to reveal a preference below the budget line and thereby to engage in non-utility-maximizing behaviour. The aggregate of all this microfoundational spending would be classified under D_1^w. The marginal propensity to spend out of current income is unity, and any additional supply (the micro-equivalent is an upward shift in budget constraint lines) creates its own additional demand. (In an intertemporal setting with gross substitutability over time, agents plan to spend lifetime income on the products of industry over their life cycle. The long-run marginal propensity to spend is unity.) Consequently, in either the short run or the long run, $f_d(N) = f_z(N)$ for all values of N and Figure 11 is relevant.

Keynes's taxonomy was a general analysis that could lead to non-classical results. Keynes's second expenditure category, D_2^w, was not equal to 'planned' savings (which can be defined as $f_z(N) - f_1(N)$). Only if D_2^w is assumed to be equal to planned savings is:

$$D_2^w = f_z(N) - f_1(N) \tag{7}$$

and

$$D^w = D_1^w + D_2^w = f_1(N) + f_z(N) - f_1(N) = f_z(N). \tag{8}$$

A comparison of equation (8) and equation (2) shows that if D_2^w is assumed equal to planned savings, then aggregate demand and supply are identical and Say's Law holds.

To ensure that equations (7) and (8) did not represent a general case, Keynes asserted that the future is uncertain in the sense that it cannot be either foreknown or statistically predicted by analysing past and current market price signals. If the future is uncertain, then expected future profits, the basis for current D_2^w investment spending, can neither be reliably forecasted from existing market information, nor endogenously determined from today's 'planned' savings function, $f_z(N) - f_1(N)$ (Keynes 1936, p. 210). Instead investment expenditures depend on the exogenous (and therefore by definition, sensible but not rational) expectations of entrepreneurs, or what Keynes called 'animal spirits'. Thus:

$$D_2^w \neq f(N) \tag{9}$$

in either the short or long run.

Explicit recognition of the possibility of more classes of current demand for producible goods and services based on a smaller axiomatic foundation makes Keynes's analysis a more general theory than classical theory. The latter becomes 'a special case and not ... the general case' (ibid., p. 3), where the category of 'all expenditures *not* related to current employment' is empty. In terms of equation (4), classical theory asserts that:

$$D_2^w = 0 \tag{10}$$

and therefore

$$D^w = D_1^w = f_1(N) = f_z(N) = Z \tag{11}$$

for all values of N.

The next logical task for Keynes was to demonstrate that 'the characteristics of the special case assumed by classical theory happen not to be those of the economic society in which we actually live' (ibid., p. 3). In other words, Keynes had to demonstrate that even if $D_2^w=0$, the D_1^w function would not be coincident with his macro-analogue of the age-old supply function for all values of N. To do this Keynes had 'to throw over' the classical axioms of neutral money (that is, the possession of money *per se* provides no utility) and gross substitution.

If these restrictive axioms are jettisoned, then some portion of a utility-maximizing agent's income might be withheld from the purchase of producible goods and diverted into purchasing nonproducible money and/or other nonproducible liquid assets. The marginal propensity to spend out of current income on the products of industry would then be less than unity. In an uncertain world, the possession of money and other nonproducible liquid assets provides utility by protecting the holder from fear of being unable to meet future liabilities. As long as producible goods are not gross substitutes for holding nonproducible liquid assets (including money) for liquidity purposes, then no change in relative prices can induce income earners to buy producibles with that portion of income they wish to use to purchase additional long-run security (against non-ergodic economic conditions) by holding liquid assets.

In sum, Keynes's general theory of employment must be applicable to an uncertain (non-ergodic) world. When money and all other liquid assets possess certain essential properties, then agents can obtain utility (by being free of fear of possible future insolvency or even bankruptcy) only by holding a portion of their income in the form of nonproducible liquid assets. If the gross substitutability between nonproducible liquid assets (including money) and producible goods is approximately zero (Keynes 1936, chapter 17; Davidson 1982–83, 2002), then when agents want to save (in the form of nonproducible liquid assets) money is not neutral, even with perfectly flexible prices. Thus, the general case underlying the principle of effective demand is:

$$D_1^w = f_1(N) \neq f_z(N) \tag{12}$$

while planned savings, $f_z(N) - f_d(N)$, are equal to the amount out of current income that utility-maximizing agents use to increase their holdings of nonproducible liquid assets. The decision to save today means 'a decision not to have dinner today. But it does not necessitate a decision to have dinner or to buy a pair of boots a week hence or a year hence or to consume any specified thing at any specified date' (Keynes 1936, p. 210).

By proclaiming a 'fundamental psychological law' associated with 'the detailed facts of experience', where the marginal propensity to consume is always less than unity, Keynes (ibid., p. 96) finessed the possibility that equation (9) is ever applicable. If the marginal propensity to consume is always less than unity, then $f_1(N)$ would never coincide with $f_2(N)$, even if $D_2^w = 0$, and the special classical case is not applicable to 'the economic society in which we actually live' (ibid., p. 3).

In sum, Keynes's principle of effective demand demonstrates that, in a non-ergodic world, it is the existence of nonproducible assets that are held for liquidity purposes and for which the products of industry are not gross substitutes that is the fundamental cause of involuntary unemployment. The lack of perfect price flexibility is neither a necessary nor a sufficient condition for demonstrating the existence of unemployment equilibrium.

PAUL DAVIDSON

See also:

Bastard Keynesianism; Effective Demand; Liquidity Preference; Microfoundations; Money; Non-ergodicity; Uncertainty; Unemployment.

References

Blanchard, O.J. (1990), 'Why does money affect output?', in B.M. Friedman and F.H. Hahn (eds), *Handbook of Monetary Economics*, Vol. 2, New York: North-Holland, pp. 779–835.
Davidson, P. (1982–83), 'Rational expectations: a fallacious foundation for studying crucial decision making', *Journal of Post Keynesian Economics*, 5, Winter, pp. 182–96. Reprinted in P. Davidson, *Inflation, Open Economies, and Resources*, edited by Louise Davidson, Macmillan: London, 1991, pp. 123–38.
Davidson P. (2002), *Financial Markets, Money and the Real World*, Cheltenham, UK and Northampton, MA, USA: Edward Elgar.
Hahn, F.H. (1977), 'Keynesian economics and general equilibrium theory', in G.C. Harcourt (ed.), *Microfoundations of Macroeconomics*, London: Macmillan, pp. 25–40.
Keynes, J.M. (1936), *The General Theory of Employment, Interest and Money*, New York: Harcourt Brace.
Keynes, J.M. (1937), 'The general theory of employment', *Quarterly Journal of Economics*, 51 (2), 209–23. Reprinted in *The Collected Writings of John Maynard Keynes*, Vol. XIII, edited by D. Moggridge, London: Macmillan for the Royal Economic Society, 1973, pp. 109–23. All references are to the reprint.

Keynes's *Treatise on Money*

A Treatise on Money by John Maynard Keynes was published on 24 October 1930, after six years of deep thinking and practical work on, for example, the economic policies of the Liberal Party and the decline of the cotton industry. In the mind of Keynes, at that time already a well-known figure in world politics, the *Treatise* was designed to provide the most comprehensive and systematic analysis of monetary matters ever produced (Harrod 1951, chapter 10). It was to do for his academic reputation what political and cultural activities had already done in the public arena (Patinkin 1976). But the *Treatise* has had bad luck in a way that explains the fortunes and misfortunes of Keynesian economics more generally.

To modern students and most scholars, Keynes means *The General Theory of Employment, Interest and Money* (1936). Keynes is the analyst of unemployment and the depression. He is the theorist of aggregate demand and equilibrium unemployment as well as the promoter of public expenditure. The *Treatise* is then at the best a prelude, in the words of Schumpeter, a collection of 'imperfect and embarrassed first statements of *General Theory* propositions' (Schumpeter 1952, p. 278). According to this orthodox interpretation of Keynes's work what is new and important in the *Treatise* is absorbed and developed in the *General Theory*, and the permanent value of the latter is the explanation of short-run unemployment. An alternative view starts with a more balanced reading of the *Treatise*. It defends the originality of that work but it also emphasizes the continuous evolution of what Keynes was later to call a monetary theory of production, that is, the search for a sound analytical framework based on the principle of non-neutrality of money (and non-neutrality of choice). This alternative view is also supported by early interpretations of the *Treatise*:

> The latter [the *General Theory*] was written somewhat in haste after Keynes had achieved in his own mind a wide theoretical synthesis . . . he was anxious to get this before the public quickly. The *Treatise*, by contrast, contains all his gathered wisdom about monetary matters . . . It is, I would submit, impossible to have an understanding of Keynes in depth, if one has not read the *Treatise*. (Harrod 1969, p. 163)

The *Treatise* consists of seven Books organized in two volumes, namely *The Pure Theory of Money* (vol. 1, Books I–IV) and *The Applied Theory of Money* (vol. 2, Books V–VII). Book I is concerned with the definition of the nature of money and the description of its historical origins. Book II deals with the laborious and complex description of various index numbers. An important outcome of those two books is the idea that aggregate concepts like the price level or the quantity of money are not adequate for explaining the behaviour of the main economic variables (Skidelsky 1992, chapter 10). Next follows the core of the *Treatise*, Books III–IV. There Keynes offers a formal and rigorous discussion of the static and dynamic problems of monetary theory, including the presentation of his 'fundamental equations'. Book V considers the empirical magnitudes of his key variables, and Book VI deals with the institutional features of the banking system. Finally, Book VII lays out the implications of the analysis for both national and international stabilization policies.

The basic problem that Keynes sets out to analyse in the *Treatise* is the instability of market economies. The analysis is very clear: the initial and most influential cause of output fluctuations in modern economies is the change in the level of investment. Since profit is the 'mainspring' of those changes, a theory of profit is then essential for the explanation of economic fluctuations. Thus capital accumulation and income distribution are the main themes of the *Treatise* (Graziani 1981). At the same time Keynes argues that changes in the level of prices are the primary mechanism of reconciliation between the investment decisions of entrepreneurs and the distribution of income between wages and profit. These price movements are explained by means of the fundamental equations.

The analytical framework of the *Treatise* is grounded on the distinction between wage-earners and entrepreneurs, together with the related separation between expenditure on consumption goods and on capital goods:

> Saving is the act of the individual consumer and consists in the negative act of refraining from spending the whole of his current income on consumption. Investment, on the other hand, is the act of the entrepreneur whose function it is to make the decisions which determine the amount of the non-available output, and consists in the positive act of starting or maintaining some process of production or withholding liquid goods. . . . The vital point to appreciate is this . . . the performance of the act of saving is in itself no guarantee that the stock of capital goods will be correspondingly increased. (Book III, pp. 155–8)

Saving and investment are made by two different groups of people, and for Keynes there is no spontaneous market mechanism that necessarily reconciles them. It is indeed in this divergence and the consequent disequilibrium process that Keynes envisages the source of profit creation. The story unfolds as follows. If investment runs ahead of (below) saving it means that entrepreneurs have decided to produce less (more) consumption goods than the amount wage-earners have decided to purchase. The price of those goods increases (decreases), as does the remuneration of entrepreneurs. Abnormal (or subnormal) profit – as Keynes called it – is then due to the divergence between investment and saving (equation (viii), Book III, p. 124).

The price of consumption goods plays a key role in Keynes's theory of income distribution. In equilibrium it is equal to average (long-period normal) cost but when, as in the case above, investment differs from saving, 'the price level, as determined by the first term [that is, cost], is upset by the fact that the division of the output between investment and goods for consumption is not necessarily the same as the division of the income between savings and expenditure on consumption' (Book III, p. 123). Changes in the price level of consumption goods have the role of reconciling, via the mechanism of forced saving ('involuntary abstention'), the production decisions of entrepreneurs with the expenditure plans of wage-earners. For instance, with investment running ahead of saving and under the assumption that abnormal profit is entirely saved, a redistribution of income from entrepreneurs to wage-earners takes place and equilibrium is again restored (Kahn 1984, pp. 67–8). Keynes formally derived these results from his definition of the price level of consumption goods as equal to the monetary cost of production per unit of output (what Keynes called 'the rate of efficiency earnings') plus any element of abnormal (or subnormal) profit per unit of output. This is the meaning of the first fundamental equation; the second fundamental equation extends this idea to the price level of output as a whole (Book III, pp. 122–4).

Thus booms and slumps derive from the difference between saving and investment. More importantly for what would later be argued in the *General Theory*, Keynes argues that 'voluntary abstinence' is no guarantee of prosperity. This idea is well illustrated in the famous banana parable describing a community in a state of equilibrium that is disturbed by a thrift campaign (Book III, chapter 12, sec. ii). With an increase in saving entrepreneurs are now forced to reduce the price of bananas (otherwise they will rot). The unexpected (abnormal) loss causes entrepreneurs to reduce their wage bills by laying off workers and/or cutting wages. But this does not help as long as the community continues to save more than it invests. Output declines until either 'the thrift campaign is called off or peters out as a result of the growing poverty; or . . . investment is stimulated by some means or another so that its cost no longer lags behind the rate of saving' (p. 160). A similar case, of course, could be argued for an increase of investment in, for example, new banana plantations. The crux of the whole parable is that saving can be made identical to investment as a result of a change in output though, as Robinson argued, Keynes may have failed fully to realize that he had actually elaborated a long-period analysis of output (Robinson 1960, p. 56).

In terms of the policy implications of the analysis, Keynes suggests that the banking system should try to eliminate economic fluctuations and in consequence to stabilize the purchasing power of money. By keeping the market rate of interest equal to the natural rate of interest, that is, to the notional rate 'at which saving and the value of investment are exactly balanced' (Book III, p. 139), the banking system would preserve the condition of zero (abnormal) profit. Keynes believed that in general the banking system could do the job. However, he also warned that the natural rate of interest relies on profit expectations of entrepreneurs, and hence it is independent of the objective technical conditions of production. A potential conflict may then arise between domestic and external equilibrium. In a severe slump, with profit expectations running very low, the banking system may not be able to afford effective reductions in the market rate without causing a large outflow of domestic currency. In this case Keynes suggested that 'the Government must itself promote a programme of domestic investment' (Book VII, p. 337).

Several authors have argued that the *Treatise* and the *General Theory* embody the same vision, the same appreciation of empirical observation and the same analytical structure (for example, Amadeo 1989, chapters 3–4). What really differentiates the *Treatise* from the *General Theory* is the formal method and the specific purpose of the analysis. Keynes had always in mind a close connection between theory and practice, but under the pressure of historical events his thought about the form of that connection went on changing. In 1930 Keynes was mainly concerned with the instability of market economies, the ups and downs that characterize the credit cycle. Output and employment were seen as moving around some norm, and he aimed to explain the causal mechanism behind those movements. But by 1936 he felt that the problem was now not with fluctuations around a norm but with the norm itself. Persisting mass unemployment was the practical interest, and for the sake of getting his solution across, he was content to set aside some of his most brilliant though highly heterodox ideas. This is the ultimate link between his two major books and the main reason for reverting to the *Treatise*.

GIUSEPPE FONTANA

See also:
Business Cycles; Growth and Income Distribution; Monetary Policy; Money; Saving.

Bibliography
Amadeo, E.J. (1989), *Keynes's Principle of Effective Demand*, Aldershot, UK: Edward Elgar.
Graziani, A. (1981), 'Keynes e il Trattato sulla Moneta [Keynes and the Treatise on Money]', in A. Graziani, C. Imbriani and B. Jossa (eds), *Studi di Economia Keynesiana [Studies in Keynesian Economics]*, Naples: Liguori, pp. 211–34.
Harrod, R.F. (1951), *The Life of John Maynard Keynes*, London: Macmillan.
Harrod, R.F. (1969), *Money*, London: Macmillan.
Kahn, R.F. (1984), *The Making of Keynes's General Theory*, Raffaele Mattioli Lectures, Cambridge: Cambridge University Press.
Moggridge, D.E. (1992), *Maynard Keynes: An Economist's Biography*, London: Routledge.
Patinkin, D. (1976), *Keynes's Monetary Thought. A Study of Its Development*, Durham, NC: Duke University Press.
Robinson, J. (1933 [1960]), 'The theory of money and the analysis of output', in J. Robinson, *Collected Economic Papers*, Vol. I, Oxford: Basil Blackwell, pp. 52–8.
Schumpeter, J.A. (1946 [1952]), 'John Maynard. Keynes', in J.A. Schumpeter, *Ten Great Economists*, London: Allen & Unwin, pp. 260–91.
Skidelsky, R. (1992), *John Maynard Keynes: The Economist as Saviour 1920–1937*, London, Macmillan.

Liquidity Preference

The idea that 'the' rate of interest adjusts until the supply of savings is brought into equality with the demand for savings dates back at least as far as Henry Thornton. The proposition is exemplified by the loanable funds theory of the rate of interest, which Keynes attempted to overthrow in *The General Theory*. Ralph Hawtrey, Bertil Ohlin and Dennis Robertson were Keynes's primary adversaries, each subscribing to the idea that the rate of interest would settle at the point where the (flow) supply of savings and the (flow) demand for investible funds would be equal. According to the theory, an increase in savings (given the level of income) would bring 'the' rate of interest down just enough to stimulate capital production to the point where the additional saving would be exactly exhausted by the additional demand for new investment. Accordingly, an increase in aggregate saving could alter the *composition* of aggregate demand (that is, less consumption and more investment), but it could not cause a reduction in the *level* of aggregate demand. Thus, full employment could not be undermined by the preference of households to save rather than spend money.

The experience of the Great Depression in the 1930s made it impossible to sustain the notion that capitalist economies were self-regulating. Moreover, it caused many economists to become dissatisfied with the quantity theory of money – the theory that holds that changes in the quantity of money are primarily responsible for causing changes in national income. By the logic of the quantity theory, it should have been possible for the central bank to stop the downward spiral by increasing the money supply. Keynes's liquidity preference theory offered a new perspective on these problems.

The difference between Keynes's analysis and the traditional theory of interest, which he considered 'a nonsense theory' (Keynes 1936 [1964], p. 177) essentially amounts to a distinction between the economics of full employment and the economics of unemployment. In Keynes's view, the traditional analysis was flawed because it treated saving and investment as the determin*ants* of the system and the rate of interest as a determin*ate* when, in fact, savings and investment are the determin*ates* of the system, and the rate of interest is a determin*ant*. Moreover, he emphasized that because saving depends upon income and income depends upon investment, it was impossible to conceive of an independent shift in either schedule. According to Keynes, a shift in the savings schedule would, in general, cause a change in income, 'with the result that the whole schematism based on the assumption of a given income breaks down' (ibid., p. 179).

An equally crucial blow to the traditional theory followed from Keynes's recognition that money, held in its barren form, yields no monetary reward. According to the loanable funds theory, interest was the reward for parting (today) with command over goods and services. But, as Keynes pointed out, the act of saving, by itself, generates no necessary reward in the form of interest. Wealth can be stored in various forms (for example, idle balances, short- or long-term financial instruments, capital assets, or other forms of income-earning property), but interest will be forthcoming only if individuals agree to part with idle cash in favour of short- or long-term financial instruments. With this in mind, Keynes set out to discover why anyone, outside of a lunatic asylum, would ever choose to hold money in its barren form.

Initially, he offered three reasons: (i) the transactions motive, (ii) the precautionary motive and (iii) the speculative motive. The transactions motive refers to a desire to hold money for the purpose of meeting anticipated expenditures (that is, bridging the time gap between known receipts and known expenditures). The precautionary motive, in contrast, has to do with the desire to hold cash for the purpose of meeting unanticipated expenditures. According to Keynes, increases (decreases) in the level of income would be associated with increases (decreases) in the size of the cash balances held to satisfy the transactions and precautionary motives. Like the precautionary motive, the speculative motive arises as a consequence of uncertainty. However, unlike the transactions and precautionary motives, an individual's desire to hold money to satisfy the speculative motive is a function of anticipated movements in a range of asset prices rather than changes in the level of income. Here, the idea is that individuals hold money in order to hedge against a declining securities market. If, for example, bond prices are expected to rise, individuals will prefer to become less liquid today (that is, to transform idle money balances into bonds) in order to take advantage of anticipated capital gains. In contrast, if speculators expect bond prices to fall to a point where interest gains are outweighed by capital losses, they will prefer to become more liquid today (that is, to hold idle money balances instead of less liquid financial instruments). The money balances that are held to satisfy these three motives reflect the individual's degree of liquidity preference.

The desire to hold liquid assets (that is, coins, paper currency and bank deposits) can be analysed graphically by means of a liquidity preference function. Leaving aside the desire to hold money to satisfy the transactions and precautionary motives, Keynes proposed that the liquidity preference function could be envisaged as 'a continuous curve relating changes in the demand for money to satisfy the speculative motive and changes in the rate of interest as given by changes in the prices of bonds and debts of various maturities' (ibid., p. 197). Figure 13 depicts this relation. The liquidity function L_a reflects the desire to hold money as an asset (that is, the desire to hold idle cash balances to satisfy the speculative motive). The curve shows the quantities of money that individuals, in the aggregate, will wish to hold at various rates of interest.

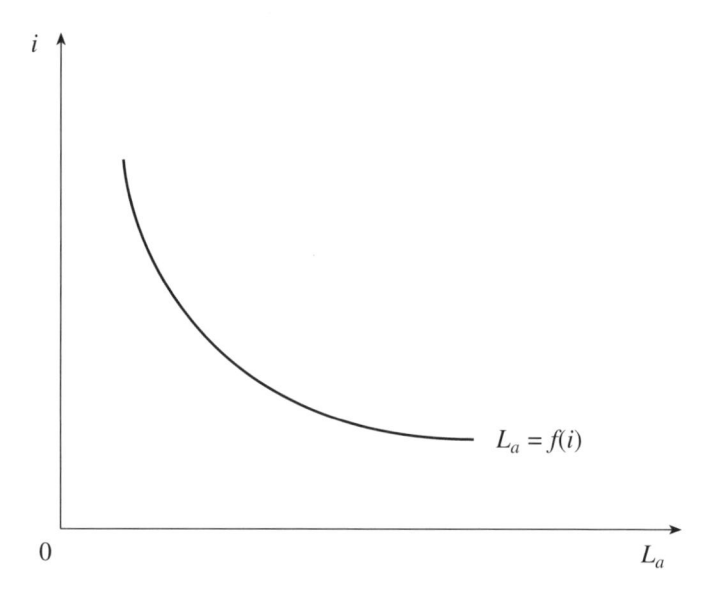

$$L_a = f(i)$$

Figure 13   The liquidity preference function

Keynes gave two reasons for the downward-sloping nature of the liquidity function. First, he explained that a fall (rise) in the rate of interest will be associated with an increase (decrease) in the demand for money as an asset, since the penalty for being liquid (that is, the forgone interest) has been reduced. Second, he suggested that a decline (rise) in the rate of interest will be associated with an increased (decreased) demand for cash balances to satisfy the speculative motive because some market participants will anticipate a future rise (fall) in the rate of interest.

As Keynes explained, both the position and the shape of the liquidity preference function depend upon the state of long-term expectations. What matters most are expectations regarding the future path of asset prices. Thus if speculators, who are constantly forming expectations about the future course of interest rates, believe that the market's estimate of future interest rates (as implied by current prices) is mistaken, they will attempt to profit from knowing better what the future will bring. If they believe that future rates will lie below those currently assumed by the market, they will have an incentive to reduce their liquidity by borrowing money today in order to purchase longer-term bonds. In contrast, if they expect future rates to lie above those assumed by the market, they will have an incentive to increase the liquidity of their portfolios by selling bonds today.

Only when the expected return on every financial asset in every portfolio is equal will market participants be satisfied with their existing holdings. Thus, in order for the money market to be in equilibrium, expectations must be such that investors are willing to hold the current mix of money and bonds, given the current structure of interest rates. In contrast to the loanable funds theory of the rate of interest, which treats 'the' rate of interest as the outcome of the forces equilibrating the flow supply of loanable funds with the flow demand for investible resources, this complex of rates will be determined by the stock demand for money relative to its stock supply.

Given the aggregate money supply, only the portion not desired to satisfy the transactions and precautionary motives is available to satisfy the speculative motive (that is, the stock demand for money). Figure 14 incorporates this constraint into the analysis. M_a is drawn as a vertical schedule, indicating the quantity of money available to satisfy the speculative motive. The interaction of these schedules determines not just the rate of interest on money but also the complex of rates on assets of various maturities. These rates can change either because the supply of money available to satisfy the speculative motive has been altered (that is, M_a shifts) or because

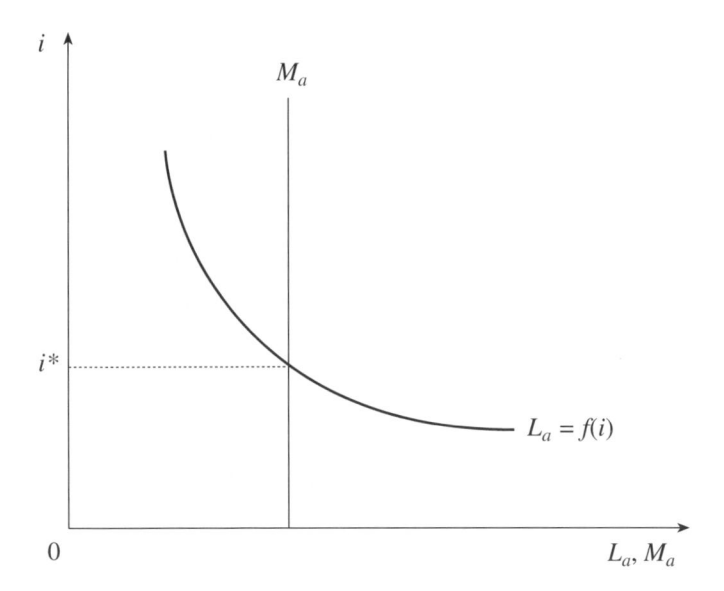

Figure 14 Determination of the rate of interest

the expectations that determine the position and shape of the liquidity preference function have changed (that is, L_a shifts).

At any interest rate above i^*, the stock of money available to be held as an asset exceeds the amount of money that individuals, in the aggregate, wish to hold to satisfy the speculative motive. In this situation, the rate of interest will have to fall until all of the money that is not desired for transactions or precautionary balances is willingly held to satisfy the speculative motive. Similarly, at any rate of interest below i^*, the quantity of money that market participants wish to hold as an asset exceeds the amount of money available to be held as an asset. Assuming the banking system and the monetary authority do not respond by increasing the money supply, the rate of interest will have to rise to the point where the public is willing to hold the existing stock of money (or, more appropriately, the stock of existing securities). Thus the rate of interest is the premium required to induce market participants to hold less-liquid assets.

Two important conclusions distinguish Keynes's analysis from the (neo)classical approach, which incorporated both loanable funds theory and the quantity theory of money. First, there is no reason to suppose that the rate of interest will settle at a price that is consistent with full employment. According to Keynes, saving and investment determine not the rate of interest but the aggregate level of employment. Moreover, an increase in the propensity to save (for example, a rise in liquidity preference) should be expected to increase interest rates, discourage investment and reduce employment – not reduce the interest rate and induce enough investment to maintain full employment. Second, changes in the money supply have a direct effect on interest rates (through portfolio adjustments) and only an indirect effect on national income. This does not imply that the monetary authority can simply manipulate the money supply until an interest rate consistent with full employment is achieved; changes in the state of long-term expectations can always override any desired policy outcome. Keynes makes this clear in his attack on the quantity theory argument, cautioning that 'if . . . we are tempted to assert that money is the drink which stimulates the system to activity, we must remind ourselves that there may be several slips between the cup and the lip' (ibid., p. 173).

Generally speaking, Keynes's theory of liquidity preference remains an integral part of the Post Keynesian approach. But there are some notable exceptions. Basil Moore (1988), for example, argues that the liquidity preference theory actually undermines the rationale of *The General Theory*. According to Moore, liquidity preference theory is incompatible with endogenous monetary theory. Lavoie (1985) agrees, arguing that Post Keynesians must reject liquidity preference theory because it is relevant only in the context of an exogenously determined money supply.

The criticisms of Moore and Lavoie appear to follow from the manner in which Keynes treated the determination of the money supply in *The General Theory*. According to Moore, Keynes should have retained the endogenous treatment of the money supply he adopted in his *Treatise on Money* and designated the interest rate as an exogenously determined variable. If the interest rate is exogenously determined (by the monetary authority) and the supply of money is perfectly elastic at this rate, then an outward shift of the liquidity preference function cannot increase the rate of interest. Thus, for Moore and Lavoie, the problem appears to be this: if the supply of money always fully accommodates the demand for money (that is, the money supply is endogenous), then it cannot be true that an increase in the demand for money will increase the rate of interest.

Wray (1990) argues that liquidity preference and endogenous money are indeed compatible and that the criticisms of Moore and Lavoie are based on a failure to distinguish between the (stock) demand for money and the (flow) demand for credit. He, Kregel (1986), Davidson (1978) and Dow and Dow (1989) emphasize the finance motive, which Keynes introduced in 1937 as a fourth motive for holding money. In this 1937 article, Keynes reasserts his commitment to the endogenous theory of money, explaining that as long as banks are willing to accommodate an increase in the demand for credit, there is no reason why the interest rate should rise with an increase in the level of planned activity. Thus, while changes in the (stock) demand for money can affect the rate of interest, changes in the (flow) demand for credit (that is, bank borrowing) need not.

When the concept of liquidity preference is extended to banks and other financial institutions, the rate of interest will be determined by the supply of money (as determined by the banking system) and the liquidity preference of both commercial banks and the non-bank public. Wray (1990) makes an excellent case for the compatibility of liquidity preference and endogenous money and provides a thorough review of the role of liquidity preference in the general theories of both Keynes and the Post Keynesians.

STEPHANIE BELL

See also:

Banking; Endogenous Money; Expectations; Money; Uncertainty.

References

Davidson, Paul (1978), *Money and the Real World*, London: Macmillan.
Dow, Alexander C. and Sheila C. Dow (1989), 'Endogenous money creation and idle balances', in John Pheby (ed.), *New Directions in Post-Keynesian Economics*, Aldershot: Edward Elgar, pp. 147–64.
Keynes, J.M. (1936 [1964]), *The General Theory of Employment, Interest and Money*, New York: Harcourt Brace.

Keynes, J.M. (1937), 'Alternative theories of the rate of interest,' *Economic Journal*, **47** (186), 241–52.
Kregel, Jan (1986), 'A note on finance, liquidity, saving, and investment', *Journal of Post Keynesian Economics*, **9** (1), 91.
Lavoie, Marc (1985), 'Credit and money: the dynamic circuit, overdraft economics, and Post Keynesian economics', in Marc Jarsulic (ed.), *Money and Macro Policy*, Boston, Dordrecht and Lancaster: Kluwer-Nijhoff Publishing, pp. 63–84.
Moore, Basil (1988), *Horizontalists and Verticalists: The Macroeconomics of Credit Money*, Cambridge: Cambridge University Press.
Wray, L. Randall (1990), *Money and Credit in Capitalist Economies: The Endogenous Money Approach*, Aldershot: Edward Elgar.

Marginalism

Marginalism is a term used to refer to the process of developing theoretical propositions from the imposition of conditions on the marginal values of variables. In modern neoclassical economics these conditions are derived from the assumption that economic agents engage in optimizing behaviour. In particular, the conditions are expressed as first-order conditions for optimization of the agents' objective function, along with the corresponding second-order conditions to ensure a maximum or minimum as appropriate to the problem. A standard example is derivation of the proposition that product supply curves are upward sloping in perfectly competitive markets. This proposition follows from finding that product price equal to marginal cost is the solution to the first-order condition for profit maximization by individual producers, while rising marginal cost with output is required to satisfy the corresponding second-order condition assuming a horizontal demand curve facing the producer.

The use of marginal conditions to develop theoretical propositions has a long tradition in economics. An early example is David Ricardo's analysis of the distribution of income between workers, capitalists and landowners in *The Principles of Political Economy and Taxation* (1817). Here, Ricardo determines the rent of land of varying quality by imposing the marginal condition that the rent of land at the extensive (or intensive) margin equal zero. He then imposes the conditions that capital accumulates until profits equal zero and that the wage of workers is driven to the subsistence level by the growth of population. In modern parlance, the growth of capital and population are each governed by a marginal condition.

Marginalism was established as an all-encompassing method of theoretical analysis in economics with the 'marginalist revolution' of the early neoclassical economists in the late nineteenth century. In the writings of Carl Menger, W.S. Jevons, Léon Walras and Vilfredo Pareto, Ricardo's analysis of production and supply based on conditions at the margin was extended by an analysis of demand conditions based on marginal utility. Alfred Marshall consolidated the revolution in his *Principles of Economics* (1890), providing a short-period marginal analysis of supply and demand to complement Ricardo's long-period supply analysis.

Modern neoclassical economics extends marginalism from its primary use in theoretical analysis to encompass also empirical analysis. Machlup (1946) argues that the lack of realism in the assumptions of marginalism does not undermine its usefulness as a technique for predicting behaviour.

To Machlup, decision makers can, and do, act 'as if' they are equating marginal conditions, even though they do not have the information necessary to calculate exact values. Errors in optimization are to be expected, but the 'way in which changes in the essential variables will affect the probable decisions and action of the business man is not much different if the curves which the theorist draws to depict their conjectures are a little higher or lower, steeper or flatter' (ibid., p. 536).

Today, marginal analysis dominates mainstream economics in both theory and practice. Students around the world are taught that marginal analysis constitutes the principles of economics. Applications of economics to business decisions and public policy are primarily based on evaluating changes in marginal conditions associated with hypothesized behaviour. Finally, estimation of economic relationships is generally based on assuming that economic agents optimize according to the solution of marginal conditions, but that they make errors that are normally distributed with zero mean.

Criticism of marginalism is fundamental to Post Keynesian economics. Indeed, the Keynesian revolution began with Keynes's critique of the application of marginal conditions for equilibrium in the labour market in *The General Theory of Employment, Interest and Money*. Keynes accepts the application of marginal analysis to the employment decisions of individual businesses and the labour supply decisions of workers, but argues persuasively that the marginal condition of wage equal to the value of the marginal product of labour is not sufficient to guarantee full employment in a capitalist economy. The problem noted by Keynes is that when wages and prices move together, a reduction in the money wage cannot be relied on to remove excess supply of labour. What is required is an increase in effective demand, which is most readily accomplished by government expenditure programmes.

Keynes's followers at Cambridge extended the critique of marginalism to other notions of equilibrium based on marginal conditions. Roy Harrod pointed to the fragility of full employment in a growing economy due to the knife-edge requirements for a balance between the growth in supply and growth in effective demand. Joan Robinson attacked the neoclassical parable of accumulation, noting that it ignores changes in relative prices required to maintain the marginal conditions for equilibrium in input markets with a change in the ratio of interest rate to wage rate. According to Robinson, these changes in relative prices destroy our ability meaningfully to measure a quantity of capital from the collection of heterogeneous productive equipment and structures used in the production process.

The attack on marginalism by Keynes and his followers emphasizes problems with its internal coherence, particularly problems encountered once marginal conditions for individual optimization decisions are aggregated to examine the behaviour of an economic system in either a static context or through time. Other Post Keynesians go further and reject the usefulness of marginalism in its entirety. A seminal contribution to this strand of critique is the pioneering study of business pricing behaviour by Hall and Hitch (1939). Hall and Hitch surveyed business executives responsible for price setting and concluded that prices are predominantly set by reference to average cost, suggesting the need for a pricing theory based on the full-cost principle rather than a theory based on the marginal conditions required for profit maximization. Machlup's (1946) argument about economic agents acting 'as if' they are engaged in optimizing behaviour was aimed directly at refuting the survey evidence provided by Hall and Hitch.

Both marginalists and followers of the full-cost principle now understand that there can be formal equivalence between a profit-maximizing price and a full-cost price. Indeed, there is recognition that many influences, such as increases in prices of variable inputs, have a similar impact on prices in both approaches. However, as Lee (1990–91, p. 263) notes, 'it is clear that the Post Keynesian full cost pricing equation is radically different from its marginalist counterpart'. Particularly important to Lee as distinctive features of Post Keynesian pricing are (i) the absence of an influence of demand on prices, (ii) a role for social conventions in determining prices and (iii) the evolving nature of the firm such 'that prices and quantities have a historical/temporal dimension that effectively precludes a determinant relationship between price and quantity, and price-quantity and maximizing objectives' (ibid., p. 259).

In spite of the general hostility towards marginalism, some concepts with origins in marginal analysis have survived and prospered in Post Keynesian literature. A good example is the degree of monopoly. Lerner (1934) develops the degree of monopoly as the difference between price and marginal cost divided by price as a way of measuring the impact of monopoly on the efficiency of resource allocation, thereby providing a clear application of marginalism in economics. Lerner's definition is adopted in Kalecki's (1938) analysis of the distribution of income. Further, Kalecki (1940) subsequently provides his own derivation based on satisfying the marginal conditions for profit maximization under conditions of imperfect competition. However, Kriesler (1987) suggests that Kalecki's disenchantment with aspects of the marginalist derivation eventually led him to substitute a distinctly non-marginalist pricing equation as the basis for the degree of monopoly in his analysis of income distribution.

In summary, marginalism has not been banished completely from Post Keynesian economics, in spite of strong criticism by some Post Keynesians and outright rejection by others. This diversity of treatment is consistent with the open systems ontology espoused by Post Keynesian methodologists. Rather than seek sole allegiance to a single method of analysis, as is the case with marginalism for our neoclassical colleagues, Post Keynesians recognize the virtue of using a variety of analytical methods in furthering our understanding of a complex and continually evolving economic system. In this context, Downward's (1999, chapter 6) assessment of the debate between marginalists and advocates of the full-cost pricing principle is particularly revealing.

HARRY BLOCH

See also:

Capital Theory; Employment; Income Distribution; Pricing and Prices; Walrasian Economics.

References

Downward, Paul (1999), *Pricing Theory in Post Keynesian Economics*, Cheltenham, UK and Northampton, MA, USA: Edward Elgar.
Hall, R.L. and C.J. Hitch (1939), 'Price theory and business behaviour', *Oxford Economic Papers*, **2**, 12–45.
Kalecki, Michał (1938), 'The determinants of the distribution of national income', *Econometrica*, **6** (2), 97–112.
Kalecki, Michał (1940), 'The supply curve of an industry under imperfect competition', *Review of Economic Studies*, **7**, 91–112.
Kriesler, Peter (1987), *Kalecki's Microanalysis*, Cambridge: Cambridge University Press.
Lee, Frederic S. (1990–91), 'Marginalist controversy and Post Keynesian price theory', *Journal of Post Keynesian Economics*, **13** (2), 249–63.
Lerner, Abba P. (1934), 'The degree of monopoly', *Review of Economic Studies*, **1**, 157–75.
Machlup, Fritz (1946), 'Marginal analysis and empirical research', *American Economic Review*, **36** (4:1), 519–54.

Microfoundations

The term 'microfoundations' has entered discussions of Post Keynesian theory from neoclassical analysis. In its broadest sense, the term refers simply to the behavioural specification for individual economic agents within macroeconomic models. With this definition, all behavioural theories of individual behaviour within macroeconomic models constitute microfoundations.

The practical meaning of the term in neoclassical analysis, however, is more narrow. In common mainstream usage, the term microfoundations refers to the linkage between macroeconomic models and the maximization of utility and profit by individual agents. While this procedure dates back at least to the life-cycle model of consumption (Franco Modigliani) and the neoclassical model of investment (Dale Jorgenson), the new classical macroeconomic revolution of the 1970s placed much greater emphasis on microfoundations in this narrow sense. The reason for this methodological shift is the famous 'Lucas critique'. This idea arose initially from models that explore the neutrality of money with 'rational' expectations, but its implications have spread far beyond this context. The Lucas critique questions the usefulness of the predictions from any economic model that is not specified in terms of so-called deep, structural parameters of taste and technology, for only these parameters are invariant to different policy regimes. This dictum has been used in much of neoclassical macroeconomics to dismiss a priori any analysis, theoretical or empirical, without microfoundations that explicitly link results to parameters of tastes through utility maximization and parameters of technology through profit maximization.

The interface between this approach and results in Post Keynesian economics is very large. With respect to methodology, two issues are salient: the role of optimization and the specification of expectations. Post Keynesian writers have an eclectic approach to optimization. There are numerous examples of the use of optimization as the foundation for behavioural theory in Keynesian and Post Keynesian research. In discussing the classical 'postulates' in chapter 2, section V of the *General Theory*, Keynes accepted the view that the marginal productivity of labour equals the real wage. Davidson (1998) describes the point of effective demand in terms of the behaviour of 'profit maximizing entrepreneurs'. Fazzari et al. (1998) use maximization for a representative firm to explore the impact of imperfect competition on firms' employment and pricing decisions in a Keynesian macroeconomic model. Keynes's analysis of the marginal efficiency of capital in chapter 11 of the *General Theory* concludes that investment will equate the marginal efficiency of the capital stock to the market rate of interest, consistent with the results of a maximization model. Unlike the new classical approach, however, there is no methodological restriction in Post Keynesian analysis that dictates the use of optimization as a behavioural axiom. Many relations are motivated by behaviour that does not rely solely on optimization. For example, Keynes's 'fundamental psychological law' links consumption to income without reference to any explicit optimization conditions. However, as the examples above show, the use of optimization to explore microfoundations need not be inconsistent with the Post Keynesian research programme.

A more significant difference between neoclassical and Post Keynesian microfoundations arises in the specification of expectation formation. The neoclassical rational expectations approach specifies expectations from the actual statistical predictions of the model. Expectations therefore have no independent existence in such models; they are determined fully by the structural microfoundations, usually preferences and technology. This modelling approach contrasts sharply with the great emphasis put on the significant and independent role for expectations in Keynesian and Post Keynesian research. In these models, changes in expectations can occur without any change in technology or preferences, and such independent changes in expectations significantly affect the predictions of the model. This approach allows phenomena such as 'convention', 'confidence' and 'animal spirits' to affect macroeconomic outcomes. Although long-standing work on 'bounded rationality' has received some recent attention among neoclassical macro economists, there remains a great gulf in the microfoundations of expectations between the modern neoclassical tradition, which usually strives to make expectations entirely subordinate to technology and preferences, and the Post Keynesian approach, in which expectation formation is itself an independent and fundamental influence on the path of the economy. (Crotty 1994 makes a similar point and links it insightfully to an assessment of the logic of grounding neoclassical models in the microfoundations of individual agent choices.)

This gulf in the conception of expectation formation reflects more than a difference in modelling strategy. It is linked inherently to the significant difference between orthodox and Post Keynesian conceptions of uncertainty. Uncertainty in neoclassical macroeconomic models is represented by probability distributions over ergodic stochastic processes. Most Post Keynesian writers reject this conception in favour of 'fundamental', 'true' or 'Keynesian' uncertainty, which implies that stable, objective probability distributions do not exist for key variables that affect microeconomic decisions. The microfoundations question for expectations therefore is not whether real-world agents do or do not behave in accordance with the rational expectations hypothesis. In the Post Keynesian perspective, there is no logical basis for rational expectations because the statistical information required for rational expectations simply does not exist.

Clearly, the choice of microfoundations plays a key role in understanding the difference between Post Keynesian and other forms of economic analysis. The remainder of this entry considers how these differences appear in three different contexts of central significance for macroeconomics: labour demand, the financing of investment and the role of nominal rigidity.

The first of Keynes's 'classical postulates' (*General Theory*, chapter 2) presents a classical theory of labour demand that appears consistent with the modern neoclassical microfoundations approach. That is, firms maximize profits constrained by their technology. Labour demand arises from the solution to the first-order condition for maximization that equates the physical marginal product of labour to the real wage. Because Keynes maintains the first classical postulate, it appears on the surface that his theory is consistent with at least this aspect of neoclassical microfoundations. Such a conclusion, however, is misleading. While the Keynesian theory is consistent with the result that the real wage equals the marginal product of labour at an effective demand equilibrium, this result differs from the conclusion that the technologically-determined marginal product of labour is the labour demand schedule. For as Davidson (1998, p. 825) and Fazzari et al. (1998, p. 534) argue, one cannot define the effective demand for labour in a Keynesian model without knowledge of the state of aggregate demand and its impact on firms' output markets. In a Keynesian model, the effective demand for labour is a single point on the marginal product of labour schedule, the point consistent with constraints on firm sales imposed by the state of aggregate demand. Fazzari et al. generalize this result to the empirically relevant case of imperfect competition. They argue that the presence of market power at the micro level makes the aggregate sales constraints arising from insufficient aggregate demand evident in the microfoundations of firm behaviour. Furthermore, the importance of sales constraints for microeconomic production and employment decisions need not come from price or wage rigidities. These results contrast strongly with the neoclassical analysis of labour demand and production, for which aggregate demand is irrelevant, at least in the absence of nominal rigidities. These differences do not stem from differences in the behavioural postulates in the microfoundations, such as profit maximization. Rather, the distinction arises from a different conception of how microeconomic agents are embedded in the macroeconomic environment.

The study of the link between finance and investment provides another example of an active research area in which the distinction between Post Keynesian and neoclassical microfoundations plays an important role. Keynes and many Post Keynesian authors, perhaps most prominently Hyman Minsky, have emphasized the connection between financial markets, the availability of financing, and investment spending. When Jorgenson and others developed neoclassical microfoundations for investment, however, any consideration of financial constraints disappeared. Jorgenson explicitly linked this approach to the Modigliani–Miller theorem that gives conditions under which real firm investment decisions are independent of financial structure. This research effectively eliminated financial considerations from most mainstream investment research for two decades. In the 1980s, however, a deeper analysis of the microfoundations of investment decisions with asymmetric information between firms and lenders led to reconsideration of the independence of investment from finance. The result has been a large mainstream literature that supports the importance of financing constraints for investment. This analysis of the microfoundations of investment with asymmetric information appears to bring mainstream investment theory closer to the Post Keynesian perspective of Minsky and others.

The extent of convergence between neoclassical and Post Keynesian microfoundations for financial effects on investment has generated controversy. There is little doubt that the large body of mainstream empirical research that supports the importance of financial conditions for investment also supports Post Keynesian views. There is more debate on the theoretical side, regarding the importance of asymmetric information for the microfoundations of financing constraints. Fazzari and Variato (1994, pp. 359–61) point out that meaningful financing constraints on firm investment require that potential lenders refuse to fund investment projects that firms wish to undertake. They conclude that this outcome implies a systematic asymmetry in the information lenders and firms have about investment projects. Furthermore, they argue that asymmetric information is not a minor 'imperfection' in real-world capital markets. Rather it is a pervasive characteristic of decentralized market economies and it therefore must be part of the microfoundations of investment theory. Along similar lines, Dymski (1993) discusses the complementarity of asymmetric information and Post Keynesian microfoundations based on a Keynesian conception of uncertainty. In contrast, however, Van Ees and Garretsen (1993) argue that microfoundations based on asymmetric information, at least the kind of asymmetric information models that have been pursued in mainstream analysis, cannot be reconciled with Post Keynesian theory because the mainstream models require an ergodic stochastic environment which is inconsistent with fundamental uncertainty. Crotty (1996) also explores the importance of expectations for investment with fundamental uncertainty. He argues that many important aspects of Keynesian investment theory and the linkages between investment and finance cannot be understood from microfoundations of asymmetric information models.

Finally, the mainstream literature known as 'New' Keynesian is largely motivated by the exploration of microfoundations that are of little relevance to Post Keynesians. The New Keynesian approach emphasizes nominal rigidity of either wages or prices. Following the elevation of optimizing microfoundations after the Lucas critique, simply assuming nominal rigidity was considered *ad hoc*. New Keynesian macroeconomics therefore strives to explain nominal rigidity with optimizing models. This class of microfoundations has little relevance for Post Keynesian macroeconomics because the Post Keynesian approach does not require nominal rigidity to obtain effects of aggregate demand on output and employment (see Fazzari et al. 1998 for discussion and further references).

STEVEN FAZZARI

See also:

Agency; Credit Rationing; Effective Demand; Employment; Expectations; Financial Instability Hypothesis; Investment; Marginalism; New Classical Economics; New Keynesian Economics; Non-ergodicity; Uncertainty; Wages and Labour Markets.

References

Crotty, James R. (1994), 'Are Keynesian uncertainty and macrotheory incompatible? Conventional decision making, institutional structures and conditional stability in Keynesian macromodels', in G. Dymski and R. Pollin (eds), *New Perspectives in Monetary Macroeconomics: Explorations in the Tradition of Hyman Minsky*, Ann Arbor: University of Michigan Press, pp. 105–42.

Crotty, James R. (1996), 'Is New Keynesian investment theory really "Keynesian"? Reflections on Fazzari and Variato', *Journal of Post Keynesian Economics*, **18** (3), 333–57.

Davidson, Paul (1998), 'Post Keynesian employment analysis and the macroeconomics of OECD unemployment', *Economic Journal*, **108** (440), 817–31.

Dymski, Gary (1993), 'Keynesian uncertainty and asymmetric information: complementary or contradictory?', *Journal of Post Keynesian Economics*, **16** (1), 49–54.

Fazzari, Steven M., Piero Ferri and Edward Greenberg (1998), 'Aggregate demand and firm behavior: a new perspective on Keynesian microfoundations', *Journal of Post Keynesian Economics*, **20** (4), 527–58.

Fazzari, Steven M. and Anna Maria Variato (1994), 'Asymmetric information and Keynesian theories of investment', *Journal of Post Keynesian Economics*, **16** (3), 351–69.

Van Ees, Hans and Harry Garretsen (1993), 'Financial markets and the complementarity of asymmetric information and fundamental uncertainty', *Journal of Post Keynesian Economics*, **16** (1), 37–48.

Monetary Policy

Whatever its detailed variants, Post Keynesian monetary policy is unified by four characteristics, three of which stem directly from Keynes's *General Theory*. Of the three, the first is the dominant role given to aggregate demand in determining the level of economic activity; the second is the lack of any automatic tendency for that level of economic activity to coincide with the full-employment level of output; the third is the desire for a more equal distribution of income and wealth. The fourth characteristic, not present in the *General Theory* itself, is the acceptance of an endogenous money supply where the role of the central bank consists of setting the price at which it will make available the reserves required to validate the lending which banks wish to undertake, given the demand for loans. This 'price' is the central bank's official dealing rate and it provides the foundation for the level and structure of market rates. In the light of these interest rates and what is often called the 'state of trade' borrowers decide on the (flow) of new bank lending that they require and the resulting new loans create additional deposits, that is, 'money'. Thus monetary policy in Post Keynesian economics is interest rate policy (see, for example, Moore 1988).

In the Post Keynesian view, monetary policy affects *both* output and prices. Moreover, the effect upon prices runs *through* output. This is quite different from the more extreme versions of neoclassical economics where monetary policy is seen to affect only prices, and differs also from the more moderate versions where output may also be affected in the short run but as an unfortunate, simultaneous, byproduct of interest changes.

The immediate effect of a rise in interest rates falls upon demand, through five channels: a wealth effect as a result of falling asset prices; an increase in the price of consuming now as opposed to saving; a rise in the cost of credit; an increase in the external value of the currency and a redistribution of spending power from the relatively poor to the better-off with higher propensities to save. Since firms are largely price-setting, quantity adjusters, the effect of the monetary tightening has its immediate effect upon output and eventually upon unemployment. Any downward pressure on prices occurs only subsequently as the result of prolonged underutilization of resources. And the slowing of monetary growth, so often misidentified in the orthodox literature as the *cause* of falling inflation, occurs only because firms' falling production requires less working capital in the form of bank loans.

Interestingly, the Post Keynesian definition of monetary policy and its analysis of the transmission mechanism is not far removed from that adopted by 'mainstream' economists with experience of the realities of central banking (Goodhart 1994) or from the statements of central banks themselves (Bank of England 1999). There are, though, major differences on the *goals* of monetary policy.

Given the belief that there are no automatic mechanisms for ensuring full employment and their tendency to support Keynes's proposition that it is more important to disappoint the rentier than the worker, there is a natural preference among Post Keynesians for a monetary (interest rate) policy that takes full employment as its primary objective. This is flatly at odds with the objectives of monetary policy as conducted by governments and central banks in developed countries for the last twenty years or so. In practice, the emphasis has been upon price stability (or at least low inflation) as the main or even only goal of monetary policy, achieved by sustained high real interest rates accompanied by chronically depressed output. Intellectually, this has drawn support from the 'rational expectations' and 'policy irrelevance' work of the 1970s, which argued that there is no sacrifice involved (in output or employment) since monetary policy *can* only affect prices. Minimizing inflation is a 'free lunch'. Such arguments amount to a restatement of the 'classical dichotomy' wherein money is a 'veil' whose quantity determines the overall level of prices but has no effect upon quantities which are determined by 'real' forces. In its modern incarnation, this commitment to the classical dichotomy takes the form of inflation targeting wherein interest rate policy is assigned the sole function of minimizing medium-term inflation and real magnitudes enter the picture only as indicators of likely future movements in inflation. This can be seen most clearly where central banks adopt a 'Taylor-type' rule for the setting of interest rates. Measurements of the output gap are important, but only because they provide *information* which can be used in the choice of interest rate whose sole purpose remains to minimize inflation. If central banks adhere rigidly to a Taylor rule and the object of monetary policy is solely the minimizing of inflation, then we are not far removed from the rule-governed monetary policy of the kind advocated by Milton Friedman and others in the 1960s. The interest rate replaces the stock of money as the instrument of policy and the instrument is set according to a rule which features output and real interest rates rather than the long-run growth of output.

To their credit, some mainstream economists (Laidler 1990; Blanchard et al. 1997) have consistently rejected this view, faced with clear evidence that the tightening of monetary policy in the early 1980s and 1990s clearly played a part in the accompanying recessions. More importantly, the general public has always been sceptical of any argument that monetary policy does not affect their jobs and incomes. This has forced governments to recognize the danger that operating a tight monetary policy was likely to lead to electoral defeat if they were seen as authors of a policy in which the public perceived real costs. From this was born the belief that monetary policy was 'best' operated by an independent central bank which did not have to confront democratic preferences. The result has been a creeping privatization of monetary policy in which central banks have been reconstituted with charters giving them at least instrument independence (for example, the Bank of England in 1997) and in some cases the freedom to set the inflation target as well (the European Central Bank in 1999).

In the Post Keynesian view, therefore, monetary policy as operated has helped sustain an unwarrantedly high level of unemployment and loss of output. Furthermore, because monetary policy has become a 'one-club', interest rate, policy it also has distributional effects which work against broadly the same groups as are disadvantaged by chronic restrictions of output. The distributional effects of interest rates operate most obviously through agents' portfolios, in particular through their net holdings of floating rate assets. Where these holdings are positive, a rise in interest rates redistributes income in their favour (abstracting from any effects of the local tax regime). By the same mechanism, those with net floating rate liabilities lose. Thorbecke (1999) has shown that in periods of disinflationary policy the burden of adjustment is unequal between production sectors (construction and durables suffer most) and between social groups (low-income workers and minorities pay the highest price).

At the heart of Post Keynesian monetary policy, therefore, is not so much a body of technical analysis which cuts it off from the mainstream (or at least from its more realistic practitioners) but a desire to rid the *practice* of policy from its deflationary biases, to reassert the value of discretion in responding to monetary shocks and to restore accountability in the conduct of monetary policy. At the heart of Post Keynesian policy is lower interest rates. But it is widely recognized that such a policy will face severe constraints, especially in the form of reactions from global financial markets. Much discussion of what a Post Keynesian monetary policy might look like in practice is thus taken up with suggestions for intervention in and regulation of the financial system. For countries with independent central banks enjoying goal and instrument independence, legislation may be required to force a change in targets towards less-deflationary policy. For central banks with only instrument independence, governments have retained the power to set less-disinflationary targets. Any unilateral moves of this kind, however, especially if accompanied by a public commitment to a permanent shift in policy goals, would immediately bring an adverse reaction from foreign exchange markets. Post Keynesian monetary policy recognizes therefore the need for the redesign of the international monetary system aimed at reducing the scale and volatility of foreign exchange flows and creating a means whereby deficit countries can adjust without necessarily reducing demand. Some form of 'adjustable peg' system seems most appropriate, and suggestions have been made by Davidson (1992). Lowering interest rates has the inevitable consequence of giving an immediate boost to the present value of all (including financial) assets as well as increasing the demand for credit, much of which may later find its way into asset-price inflation rather than productive use. Such dangers could be overcome by a willingness to consider lending ratios imposed either upon financial institutions who could be encouraged by the appropriate use of such ratios to favour certain types of lending, or by ratios (of loan to spending) imposed upon borrowers in the way that hire-purchase agreements once used to specify minimum deposits (Arestis and Sawyer 1998).

Peter Howells

See also:

Central Banks; Economic Policy; Endogenous Money; Inflation; New Classical Economics; Rate of Interest.

References

Arestis, P. and M.C. Sawyer (1998), 'Keynesian economic policies for the new millennium', *Economic Journal*, **108** (446), 181–95.
Bank of England (1999), 'The transmission mechanism of monetary policy', *Bank of England Quarterly Bulletin*, May, 161–70.

Blanchard, O., A. Blinder, M. Eichenbaum, R. Solow and J.B. Taylor (1997), 'Is there a core of practical macroeconomics that we should all believe?', *American Economic Review*, **87** (2), 230–46
Davidson, P. (1992), 'Reforming the world's money', *Journal of Post Keynesian Economics*, **15** (2), 153–79.
Goodhart, C.A.E. (1994), 'What should central banks do? What should be their macroeconomic objectives and operations?', *Economic Journal*, **104** (427), 1424–36.
Laidler, D.E.W. (1990), *Taking Money Seriously*, Hemel Hempstead: Philip Allan.
Moore, B.J. (1988), *Horizontalists and Verticalists*, Cambridge: Cambridge University Press.
Thorbecke, W. (1999), 'Further evidence on the distributional effects of disinflationary monetary policy', Levy Institute Working Paper No. 264.

Money

Defining money is a vexing problem for monetary theorists. Readers are familiar with the two usual approaches – defining money by its functions, or simply and arbitrarily choosing some empirical definition (as Keynes did in the *General Theory*: 'we can draw the line between "money" and "debts" at whatever point is most convenient' (Keynes 1936 [1964], p. 167). However in the Post Keynesian approach, the critical distinction is between a unit of account and a thing that is denominated in a unit of account (following Keynes of the *Treatise*: 'the money-of-account is the description or title and the money is the thing which answers to the description' (Keynes 1930 [1976], p. 3). Many theorists make no such distinction, as they use the term to sometimes refer to the 'thing' (the medium of exchange) and other times to refer to the 'title'. To avoid confusion, I shall carefully distinguish among money (the 'title', or dollar in the US), high-powered money (a particular money-thing – reserves and currency), and bank money (another money-thing – demand deposits or private bank notes).

In the Post Keynesian view, money is not simply a handy *numéraire* in which prices, debts and contracts happen to be denominated. This contrasts with a general equilibrium approach, in which we may choose any one good to serve as *numéraire*, converting relative values to nominal values in terms of the *numéraire*. Indeed, the typical story of the origin of money is really based on a *numéraire* approach, in which Robinson Crusoe decides to use 'tobacco, leather and furs, olive oil, beer or spirits, slaves or wives . . . huge rocks and landmarks, and cigarette butts' as 'money' (Samuelson 1973, pp. 275–6). When, say, seashells are chosen as money by Crusoe, he has simultaneously chosen a *numéraire* and designated which 'commodity money' will serve as the money-thing. Eventually, Crusoe discovers that gold – again, both a *numéraire* and a money-thing – has superior properties.

The conjectural history propagated by Samuelson (and many others) is dismissed by all serious historians and anthropologists. Interested readers are referred to numerous accounts that emphasize the social nature of the origins of money (see Wray 1998 for extensive references to the literature). In any case, our primary purpose for examining history and pseudo-history is to illuminate the nature of modern money. In my view, a system based on a commodity or *numéraire* money is not a 'money economy' as Keynes defined it. Rather, an economy in which money serves as nothing more than a *numéraire* is what Keynes called a barter or real wage economy. Even if there really has been a historical stage in which there was a commodity money, I would argue that it sheds no light on the operation of our modern money system, in which both the unit of account and the money-things denominated in that account arise from social practices (Ingham 2000).

Thus Post Keynesians emphasize the difference between two approaches – what Goodhart (1998) has called C-form (Chartalist) and M-form (Metallist, or commodity money) – that is to say, between a theory in which money is a social unit of account or that in which money is nothing more than a *numéraire* commodity adopted for convenience. The C-form approach (or what has also been called the state money, or taxes-drive-money, theory) insists, as did Keynes, that the state 'writes the dictionary' (decides what will be the money of account – for example, the dollar in the US) in all modern economies. This goes a long way towards explaining what would appear to be an otherwise extraordinary coincidence: the one-nation-one-currency rule. As Nobel laureate Robert Mundell's work makes clear, if money is simply a *numéraire* chosen to facilitate exchange, then one would expect use of a particular *numéraire* within an 'optimal currency area' (Goodhart 1998). There is no reason to expect such to be coincident with nation states. In fact, however, the one-nation-one-currency rule is violated so rarely that exceptions border on insignificance, and those few cases are easily explained away as special cases, as Goodhart demonstrates. The European Union thus represents a substantial and perhaps risky exception.

This leads us to an explanation of the use of money: why is money used? The orthodox story begins, as we have seen, with Crusoe and Friday who grow tired of the inconveniences of barter. In any case, money comes out of the market. An alternative view that is consistent with a social approach to money argues that money derived from the pre-civilized practice of *wergeld*; or to put it more simply, money originated not from a pre-money market system but rather from the penal system (Goodhart 1998; Wray 1998). An elaborate system of fines for transgressions was developed and, over time, authorities transformed this system of fines paid to victims for crimes to a system that generated payments to the state. Until recently, fines made up a large part of the revenues of all states. Gradually, fees and taxes as well as rents and interest were added to the list of payments that had to be made to authority.

According to the C-form or taxes-drive-money approach, the 'state' (or any other authority able to impose an obligation – whether that authority is autocratic, democratic or divine) – imposes an obligation in the form of a generalized, social unit of account: a money. This does not require the pre-existence of markets, or of a *numéraire*, or of prices of any sort. Once the authorities can levy such an obligation, they can then name exactly what can be delivered to fulfil this obligation. They do this by denominating those things that can be delivered, in other words, by pricing them in the money unit.

Thus far we have only explained the money of account (the description). Once the state has named the unit of account, and imposed an obligation in that account, it is free to choose 'the thing' that 'answers to the description'. The state-money stage reaches full development when the state actually issues the money-thing answering to the description it has provided – that is, high-powered money. Economists often distinguish between a 'commodity money' (say, a full-bodied gold coin) and a fiat paper money. However, regardless of the material from which the money-thing issued by the state is produced, the state must announce its value.

Indeed, in spite of the amount of ink spilled about the Gold Standard, it was actually in place for only a relatively brief instant. Throughout most of history, the money-thing issued by the authorities was not gold-money nor was there any promise to convert the money-thing to gold (or any other valuable commodity). It should be noted that for most of Europe's history, the money-thing issued by the state was the hazelwood tally stick. Other government-issued money-things included clay tablets, leather and base metal coins, and paper notes. Why would the population accept otherwise 'worthless' sticks, clay, base metal, leather or paper? Because the state agreed to accept the same 'worthless' items in payment of obligations (fees, fines and taxes) to the state.

Georg Friedrich Knapp (1842–1926) distinguished between 'definitive' money accepted *by* the state in ('epicentric') payments of obligations *to* the state, and 'valuta' money used *by* the state in its own payments ('apocentric') (Wray 1998). In today's modern money systems, high-powered money fulfils both functions. Of course, it appears that the US government accepts bank money in payment of taxes, but in reality payment of taxes by bank cheque leads to a reserve drain from the banking system. Government spending, of course, takes the form of a Treasury cheque, which when deposited in a private bank leads to a reserve credit. Note that, so long as government does accept bank money in epicentric payments at par with high-powered money, from the point of view of the non-bank public there is no essential difference between bank money and high-powered money. This is not true for banks, which lose reserves when taxes are paid by bank cheque and gain reserves whenever Treasury cheques clear.

Finally, Knapp defined as 'paracentric' those payments made between non-government entities. In all modern economies, these mostly involve use of bank money and other money-things issued by the non-government sector (what can be called 'inside' or 'credit' money). There is a hierarchy or pyramid of money-things, with non-banks mostly using bank moneys for net clearing and with banks using high-powered money for net clearing with other banks and with the government. Note that all these money-things are denominated in the unit of account, that is, the account in which obligations to the state are enumerated, and all credit money-things also represent a social relation – that between creditor and debtor.

Post Keynesians are best known for their work on credit money and the endogenous money approach. Because there is a separate entry on endogenous money in this volume, we need only briefly summarize the endogenous money approach, while explaining the relation between credit money and state money.

The evolving Post Keynesian endogenous approach to money offers a clear alternative to the orthodox neoclassical approach that is based on central bank control of an exogenous money supply through provision of reserves. Early Post Keynesian work emphasized uncertainty and was generally most concerned with hoards of money-things held to reduce 'disquietude', rather than with money-things 'on the wing' (the relation with spending). However, Post Keynesians always recognized the important role played by money in the 'monetary theory of production' that Keynes adopted from Marx. Circuit theory, mostly developed in France, focused on the role money plays in financing spending. The next major development came in the 1970s, with Basil Moore's horizontalism (somewhat anticipated by Nicholas Kaldor), which emphasized that central banks cannot control bank reserves in a discretionary manner. Reserves must be 'horizontal', supplied on demand at the overnight bank rate (fed funds rate) administered by the central bank. This also turns the textbook deposit multiplier on its head, as causation must run from loans to deposits and then to reserves.

This led directly to development of the 'endogenous money' approach that was already apparent in the circuit and Marxist literature. When the demand for loans increases, banks normally make more loans and create more banking deposits (money-things), without worrying about the quantity of reserves on hand. Privately-created credit can thus be thought of as a horizontal 'leveraging' of reserves, although there is no fixed leverage ratio.

Like Keynes, Post Keynesians have long emphasized that unemployment in capitalist economies has to do with the fact that these are *monetary* economies. Keynes had argued that the 'fetish' for liquidity (the desire to hoard) causes unemployment because it keeps the relevant interest rates too high to permit sufficient investment. While it would appear that monetary policy could eliminate unemployment, either by reducing overnight interest rates or by expanding the quantity of reserves, neither avenue will actually work. When liquidity preference is high, there may be no rate of interest that will induce investment in illiquid capital – and even if the overnight interest rate falls, this may not lower the long-term rate. Further, as the horizontalists make clear, the central bank cannot simply increase reserves in a discretionary manner as this would only result in excess reserve holdings, pushing the overnight interest rate to zero without actually increasing the supply of private money-things. Indeed, when liquidity preference is high, the demand for, as well as the supply of, loans collapses. Hence there is no way for the central bank to simply 'increase the supply of money' in order to raise aggregate demand. This is why those who adopt the endogenous money approach reject IS–LM analysis in which the authorities can eliminate recession simply by expanding the 'money supply' and shifting the LM curve out.

L. RANDALL WRAY

See also:

Banking; Central Banks; Circuit Theory; Endogenous Money; Liquidity Preference; Monetary Policy.

References

Goodhart, C. (1998), 'The two concepts of money: implications for the analysis of optimal currency areas', *European Journal of Political Economy*, **14** (3), 407–32.
Ingham, G. (2000), '"Babylonian madness": on the historical and sociological origins of money', in J. Smithin (ed.), *What is Money?*, London and New York: Routledge, pp. 16–41.
Keynes, J.M. (1930 [1976]), *A Treatise on Money. Volume 1: The Pure Theory of Money*, New York: Harcourt Brace Jovanovich.
Keynes, J.M. (1936 [1964]), *The General Theory of Employment, Interest and Money*, New York: Harcourt Brace Jovanovich.
Samuelson, Paul (1973), *Economics*, 9th edition, New York: McGraw-Hill.
Wray, L. Randall (1998), *Understanding Modern Money: The Key to Full Employment and Price Stability*, Cheltenham, UK and Northampton, MA, USA: Edward Elgar.

Multiplier

A key aspect of Keynes's impact upon political economy has been the role of the multiplier in justifying injections of government expenditure into an unemployment-prone capitalist economy. For Keynes, writing in the depression of the 1930s, the possibility that each pound of Treasury expenditure could generate a multiplied effect on total income represented a valuable political argument. Borrowing from the work of his student, R.F. Kahn, Keynes was able to argue that each newly employed worker would carry out expenditure that resulted in a ripple effect of additional employment and income, the multiplier measuring the size of the total expansion. Moreover, this impact on total income would even generate sufficient savings to fund the initial injection of expenditure, with no cost to the Treasury.

To illustrate this argument, consider an initial injection of investment (ΔI) by firms. This injection generates new income in a series of rounds. In the first round there is an increase in income (ΔI), out of which expenditure increases according to the propensity to consume b. Hence in the second round income increases by $b\Delta I$. In the third round this newly generated income generates a further bout of expenditure resulting in an increment $b(bI)$. This process will continue until eventually the impacts peter out. The overall impact upon income is:

$$\Delta Y = (1 + b + b^2 + b^3 + \ldots)\Delta I. \tag{1}$$

Taking the sum of the polynomial contained in the brackets:

$$\Delta Y = \frac{1}{1-b}\Delta I. \tag{2}$$

This is the multiplier relationship between increments in investment and income. So long as the propensity to consume b is less than 1, the multiplier takes a value more than 1. More income is generated than the initial injection in investment; the impact upon the economy is multiplied, hence the term multiplier.

Since the propensity to consume defines the proportion of income that is spent on goods and services, $1 - b$ is the propensity to save. It follows that $(1 - b)\Delta Y$ represents the total volume of savings (ΔS) generated by the injection of investment. Taking the denominator of the multiplier equation to the left-hand side we have the identity:

$$\Delta S = \Delta I. \tag{3}$$

This is the second politically attractive feature of the multiplier model: the injection of investment is financed out of savings generated by the income-generating process. Not only does investment generate more income than the initial outlay; it is also self-financing. There is a compelling argument, under circumstances of high unemployment, for the state to intervene to ensure that income is stimulated by new investment.

For Post Keynesians this analysis is fraught with difficulties because of the time that it takes for new savings to be generated by the multiplier process. New savings only match the initial injection of investment after a series of rounds in which consumer spending reacts to changes in income. Indeed, it has been argued that firms must borrow money in order to finance investment in the hope that savings will be forthcoming that can be used to pay off their debts, as the multiplier process works itself out. Since the multiplier process is not instantaneous, it is necessary to consider the way in which investment is financed.

The main source of finance is the banking system. Consider what happens when a bank agrees to make a loan for a new investment project. A remarkable institutional observation, which is now central to much of Post Keynesian thought, is that this loan is both an asset and a liability. After the loan is granted it is used by the firm to pay the supplier of new equipment and to hire new workers. The recipients now hold this outlay as deposits in the banking system. The initial loan therefore represents an asset (a promise by the firm to pay) and a liability (a promise by the banking system to pay).

For some Post Keynesians, this institutional observation has led to the conclusion that the multiplier process is not required as an explanation of how investment is financed. Since each loan is a deposit, the banking system is capable of financing investment without relying on a multiplier process to generate more income and savings. Indeed, for Moore (1994) an injection of investment is *instantaneously* equal to savings because of the deposits generated by each new loan.

A similar position is adopted in the French circulation approach. Money is viewed as changing hands in a closed circuit, from banks to firms and households, and back to the banking system. The problem with the multiplier process is that changes in investment generate changes in income, but implicitly there is a dead weight of total income that remains unchanged. For Schmitt: 'If some incomes are "created" how can we explain that other incomes are simply maintained in "inertia" through time, where they are deemed to be neither created nor destroyed?' (Deleplace and Nell 1996, p. 125). In the circulation approach all income is generated by injections from the banking system that return back to the banking system as part of the money circuit. The multiplier is an obstacle to seeing clearly the conditions under which circuits are completed.

The importance of the multiplier can be defended, however, by arguing that even though the multiplier process is not a required condition for the finance of investment, its impacts should still be taken into account. A change in investment will still result in more workers being employed, and those workers will spend additional income on additional goods and services. Indeed by ignoring the multiplier it is possible to overestimate the amount of money that needs to be advanced by the banking sector in order to enable a complete circuit of money. Without multiplier effects that ripple between firms and households, banks are required to advance all of the money required for both consumption and investment purposes at the start of the circuit. In circuit theory the web of debt may appear larger and hence more prone to instability than is actually the case once the multiplier process is taken into account.

Although the multiplier has been considered thus far as a dynamic process, Chick (1983) demonstrates that in Keynes's *General Theory* this dynamic approach is defined alongside a comparative static interpretation. In the static variant there is a precise focus comparing different points of static equilibrium. Consider a closed economy in which income (Y) is made up of consumption (C) and investment (I):

$$Y = C + I. \tag{4}$$

Assuming that consumption is dependent upon income such that $C = bY$, with b representing the propensity to consume:

$$Y = bY + I \tag{5}$$

which by manipulation can be written as

$$Y = \frac{1}{1-b} I. \tag{6}$$

As before, the term $1/1-b$ is the multiplier, but here the relationship between aggregate income and investment is specified instead of the relationship between changes in these magnitudes. Paul Davidson argues that in comparative statics the multiplier should be used to compare two economic systems, each with identical propensities to consume, but different volumes of investment. Following an earlier insight provided by Joan Robinson, this can be viewed as a controlled experiment in which two systems are compared holding everything else constant (Davidson 1994, pp. 40–41).

To some extent this interpretation limits the use that can be made of the multiplier. The multiplier is not used here as a method of explaining the actual course taken by a capitalist economy over time. The points of equilibrium can be compared but, in contrast to multiplier process analysis, there is no attempt to explain how an economy moves between two positions of equilibrium. As a consequence, Davidson contends that the multiplier is marginal to Keynes's system.

Moreover, Davidson argues that in the early 1930s Keynes had worked out the substance of the *General Theory* without the multiplier, only adding it in for political reasons. This contrasts directly with Patinkin's revealing quotation of Keynes: 'The essential role that the multiplier plays in the *General Theory* is attested to by Keynes' declaration to Beveridge, shortly after its publication, that "about half the book is really about it"' (Patinkin 1982, p. 199). Patinkin (ibid., p. 19) also relies on the multiplier to dismiss Michał Kalecki's claim to have discovered the substance of the *General Theory* prior to Keynes, arguing that this would be impossible as Kalecki did not discover the role of the multiplier in his system until 1943.

Aside from discussion about the origins of the *General Theory*, a case can be made for the analytical power provided by the multiplier in establishing the conditions that are required for full employment. Stated simply, the principle of effective demand shows that firms will not in general produce at full employment because of the leakage of savings from the economic system. As Chick (1983, p. 253) makes clear, the multiplier equation (6) 'says exactly what the Principle of Effective Demand says: that for a given level of income to be sustainable, the gap between income and consumption must be filled with investment'. Since consumers have positive savings, only a part of income is realized by consumer demand. The shortfall must be taken up by investment, and Keynes shows that in general private investment cannot be expected to do this job.

The importance of the multiplier in specifying the conditions required for full employment is testified by its relevance to long-run analysis. On the boundaries of Post Keynesian theory it has been argued that the principle of effective demand is only truly general in its applicability when extended to the long run. The key problem with Keynes's short-run period of analysis is that investment is viewed only as a component of aggregate demand. There is virtually no attention paid to the increase in productive capacity that will result in the next period. In the Harrod–Domar growth model the multiplier has a key role in identifying the necessary conditions for matching aggregate demand with productive capacity in the long run. Domar (1957) develops a dual approach to investment, one side of which is its capacity-generating role, the other its impact on demand via the multiplier. The requirements on aggregate demand to match this growth in capacity render the maintenance of full employment even more unlikely than is perceived in a short-run framework.

Long-run analysis also provides the basis for interaction with corresponding traditions in economic thought. Domar identified the close relationship between his growth model and Marx's reproduction schema, with the multiplier taking centre stage (Trigg 2002). Similarly, the multiplier is central to an emerging Sraffian literature on the relationship between effective demand

and long-run capacity utilization (Serrano 1995). Common to both this and the Marxian approach is the observation that a monetary production economy must necessarily also be a surplus-producing economy. Investment goods that allow an expansion of productive capacity are by definition surplus goods. It should be noted, however, that in order to facilitate a simple macroeconomic exposition, this literature is limited to the narrow assumption that only one commodity is produced. Since monetary economies are necessarily multisectoral, with money providing the mechanism for exchanging heterogeneous commodities, the issue of aggregation requires close methodological attention – a challenge that applies with equal force to the models of circuit theory and multiplier process analysis.

ANDREW B. TRIGG

See also:
Circuit Theory; Consumption; Effective Demand; Endogenous Money; Finance Motive; Fiscal Policy; Growth Theory; Keynes's *General Theory*.

References

Chick, V. (1983), *Macroeconomics After Keynes*, Oxford: Philip Allan.
Davidson, P. (1994), *Post Keynesian Macroeconomic Theory*, Aldershot, UK: Edward Elgar.
Deleplace, G. and E.J. Nell (eds) (1996), *Money in Motion: The Post Keynesian and Circulation Approaches*, Basingstoke: Macmillan.
Domar, E.S. (1957), 'Expansion and employment', in Domar, *Essays in the Theory of Economic Growth*, New York: Oxford University Press, pp. 83–108.
Moore, B.J. (1994), 'The demise of the Keynesian multiplier: a reply to Cottrell', *Journal of Post Keynesian Economics*, **17** (1), 121–34.
Patinkin, D. (1982), *Anticipations of the General Theory?*, Oxford: Basil Blackwell.
Serrano, F. (1995), 'Long period effective demand and the Sraffian supermultiplier', *Contributions to Political Economy*, **14**, 67–90.
Trigg, A.B. (2002), 'Surplus value and the Keynesian multiplier', *Review of Radical Political Economics*, **34** (1), 57–67.

New Classical Economics

New Classical economics is a macroeconomic doctrine designed to oppose Keynesian policies and theories, and demonstrate the self-regulating powers of the capitalist system. Its leaders included Robert Lucas, Thomas Sargent, Neil Wallace and Robert Barro. The doctrine flourished especially in the US and during the 1975–85 decade when most of its notable works were written. It has since sunk into decline because the circumstances that gave rise to the doctrine have changed, but it is fair speculation to say that it may manifest itself again, at some appropriate time and in another form.

The classical economists in the early nineteenth century had argued that capitalism was a self-regulating system which would not, by itself, generate recessions and a business cycle. A century later J.M. Keynes replied that the classical economists had forgotten uncertainty, which could cause a drive for liquid assets at the expense of commodity demand. Keynes therefore found inherent fault in the capitalist system, and argued that the economy needed regulation at the macro level. The New Classical economists replied that, since microeconomic theory did not recognize uncertainty, nor should macro theory. They believed that rational behaviour – meaning maximization – should be the dominant theme of both micro and macro theory, from which they concluded that Keynesian macroeconomic policies were ineffective.

Keynes had said that classical theory did not explain the economy, and the New Classical economists replied with a point about what constituted an acceptable theory. The New Classical innovations were primarily of a methodological nature, but their formulators were theoreticians rather than philosophers, and their innovations were presented in sophisticated mathematical terms and as scientific discoveries.

New Classical references to the old classical predecessors are rare and sparse, and it is obvious that they were more directly influenced by Monetarism, except on one particular point where that doctrine seemed inconsistent with reason and experience. In 1968 Milton Friedman had distinguished between anticipated and unanticipated monetary changes, in order to argue that countercyclical policy would normally have no lasting beneficial effects. His argument was that if the financial markets thought in real terms, and took prospective inflation into account, then nominal changes (in the money supply) would lead only to nominal changes (in the price level). Keynesians had argued that an increase in the money supply would have real effects, in that it would reduce the rate of interest; Friedman replied that in a rational economy the real rate of interest would remain unchanged, because monetary increases would simply lead to inflation. Friedman concluded that the Phillips curve operated only in the short run, and that there was a natural rate of unemployment that could not be changed by Keynesian policy.

Friedman's attack on Keynesian demand management precipitated the widespread liberalization and deregulation of markets during the last quarter of the twentieth century. Many of these changes were liberating, but some were potentially destabilizing, and required a high degree of confidence in the self-regulating powers of the macro economy. Yet Friedman's rebuttal of Keynes depended on a particular and dubious assumption. Specifically Friedman assumed that the velocity of money would remain constant regardless of other economic change. For if monetary velocity did remain constant then increases in the money supply would have only inflationary effects, and tendencies to hoard would have only deflationary effects, without changing the level of unemployment.

Yet the evidence seemed to show that monetary velocity increased during booms and decreased during recessions, in response to changes in the precautionary demand for money. There also seemed to be a long-run tendency to economize on the use of money, in accordance with the growing sophistication of the capital markets. Finally, the constant velocity of money proposition seemed arbitrary because it did not follow from microeconomic theory. Friedman advanced econometric evidence for the constant velocity proposition, and he also argued that what mattered was the results and not the theory and its assumptions. Nevertheless, a whole philosophy of government could hardly be based on an empirical relationship that was inexplicable and at best difficult to discern.

New Classical theory rose to prominence by arguing that the refutation of Keynes did not require a constant velocity of money, because the self-equilibrating quality of the capitalist system followed from pure microeconomic theory. The only assumption required was that individuals would act rationally as elementary microeconomic theory assumes. The stability of capitalism, and the inefficacy of countercyclical policy, could then be demonstrated as a matter of mathematics.

This theme of rational behaviour was the major innovation of New Classical economics; and most of Friedman's conceptual innovations, including the natural rate of unemployment and the distinction between anticipated and unanticipated changes in the money supply, became corollaries that followed from it. If decision makers rationally maximized then Say's Law would hold, markets would clear, and capitalist stability would follow.

Rationality also meant that Keynesian policies would have no effect. (For some mysterious reason the following argument is known as the 'Ricardian equivalence theorem'.) Keynesian theory postulated that government budget deficits would stimulate the economy and increase employment. The New Classicals conceded that government spending, by itself, was stimulatory. However, government budget deficits also carried the prospect of future tax rises; and rational markets would understand that the capitalized value of the implied future taxes would approximately equal the value of the additional government spending. The prospect of these future taxes would reduce spending, by just as much as the government had increased it. Therefore what the Keynesians had thought was an expansionary fiscal policy was not expansionary at all.

Keynesian theory had assumed – only implicitly but nevertheless crucially – that the financial markets were subject to money illusion. As a matter of fact, basic Keynesian theory demonstrated that there would be inflation after the money supply increased. However, Keynesian theory implicitly assumed that market agents did not know the theory – because if the markets were rational, nominal changes would have only nominal effects. The Keynesian theory of knowledge made no sense, because it assumed that the policy makers knew the theory and that the agents did not. Yet it was impossible to modify the theory, because dual knowledge – rational policy makers but money illusion in the markets – was fundamental.

The main question was, what did the markets really know? The New Classical answer, which had been given by John Muth, was that the markets would economize information while making maximizing choices. They would learn over time, using the available information in the most efficient way. Rational markets would learn how to respond most effectively to Keynesian policies or any other exogenous changes that would disturb the system. Thus, if a central bank adjusted the money supply, the adjustment would have no real effect on a rational market system – unless the change was a signal that the bank knew something that the markets did not. Thus Muth writes:

> I would like to suggest that expectations, since they are inferred predictions of future events, are essentially the same as the predictions of the relevant economic theory ... The [rational expectations] hypothesis asserts three things: (i) information is scarce, and the economic system generally does not waste it; (ii) the way expectations are formed depends specifically on the structure of the relevant system describing the economy; (iii) a 'public prediction' will have no substantial effect on the operation of the economic system unless it is based on insider information. (Muth 1961, p. 316)

A discernible air of excitement permeates many of the New Classical writers, who must have felt that they were at the very conjunction of transforming ideas. There was a new macroeconomic doctrine that flowed elegantly from microeconomics, and for the first time integrated micro and macro theories. The social and political implications included justification for a greater degree of economic freedom. And their system seemed to 'work', because from 1975 to 1985 most national economies were troubled primarily on the supply side, and the demand-side problems that the Keynesians had addressed were not on the horizon.

One major theoretical problem was not addressed. The theory was that (except for a random variable) the market would be able to predict future prices. This followed from elementary microeconomics, because rationality – maximization – is only meaningful if there is full knowledge, or some stochastic version of full knowledge. Then, if the market can predict the future, countercyclical policies will have no effect for the reasons given above. However maximization implies that economic behaviour is consistent and in principle predictable.

If there is uncertainty about the future, then, microeconomic theory notwithstanding, market behaviour will not be predictable and consistent. When Muth noted that rational people do not waste information, he should also have said that people *cannot* act 'rationally' in the sense of New Classical economics unless they have a high degree of information. Maximization is impossible unless the constraint is understood, or in other words it is necessary to know the opportunity line as well as the indifference curve. For, when information is poor, and economic agents do not understand their economic constraints, the animal spirits and states of confidence that are emphasized by the Keynesians can dominate the macroeconomic picture. Economic agents may advance their self-interests in an intelligent way, using what information they have as fluidly as possible, but there is no reason why their actions should be consistent over time. Uncertainty does not cancel out, but renders economic behaviour fluid and indeterminate.

If there were a small increase in the money supply in a stable economy then it would be reasonable to expect that prices would increase in proportion to the increase in the money supply. In such circumstances, where there is a high degree of information, the Keynesians were wrong and New Classical theory comes into its own. But in more general conditions, when people do not more or less know what the future will bring, and economic agents cannot optimize, Keynesian policies constitute effective 'signals'. The effectiveness of Keynesian policies is the norm, and 'rationality' in the New Classical sense is the exception, because macroeconomic instability arises in circumstances of imperfect information.

New Classical economics became irrelevant when it was overtaken by the course of events. From the mid-1980s to the early years of the twenty-first century, the global economy went from boom to recession to boom again and recession again. There is nothing in New Classical theory to explain this sequence of destabilizing swings in aggregate demand, nor is there anything that would suggest a remedy. The main ideas of Monetarism and New Classical theory now live on in New Keynesian economics, which is another supply-side doctrine that recognizes 'rational' behaviour and the natural rate of unemployment. The difference is that New Keynesian economics does concede that there are faults and difficulties in the economy, and it also recognizes the possible mismatch of aggregate demand and supply. However it is a compromise doctrine that lacks the logical rigour of New Classical theory.

The New Classical economists raised important issues of method and theory. They demonstrated some important faults and errors in the Keynesian system, and their ideas encouraged the process of economic deregulation at a time when Monetarism seemed to be failing its own empirical tests.

ATHOL FITZGIBBONS

See also:

Agency; Economic Policy; Expectations; Fiscal Policy; Inflation; Monetary Policy; Non-ergodicity; Say's Law; Uncertainty; Walrasian Economics.

Bibliography

Fitzgibbons, A. (2000), *The Nature of Macroeconomics: Instability and Change in the Capitalist System*, Cheltenham, UK and Northampton, MA, USA: Edward Elgar.
Friedman, M. (1968), 'The role of monetary policy', *American Economic Review*, **58** (1), 1–17.
Hoover, K. (ed.) (1992), *The New Classical Macroeconomics*, two vols, Aldershot: Edward Elgar.
Lucas, R. and T. Sargent (1981), *Rational Expectations and Econometric Practice*, Minnesota: University of Minnesota Press.
Muth, J. (1961) 'Rational expectations and the theory of price movements, *Econometrica*, **29** (3), 315–35.

New Keynesian Economics

Central to New Keynesian theory is the notion that wages and prices do not adjust rapidly enough to achieve the 'self-regulation' of classical and neoclassical economics. The latter theories assume frictionless markets, which ensure rapid correction whenever the economy deviates from its long-run equilibrium. New Keynesian theorists believe that market failures amplify and lengthen such deviations, accounting for business cycles. Although it is alleged to be a macroeconomic theory, its practitioners concentrate on establishing the microeconomic foundations of the price and wage stickiness that is generated by market failures. The absence of market clearing is supported by the argument that quantity rather than price adjustments are in the interest of both workers and firms, that is, that market participants behave rationally. In this way, New Keynesian economics purports to show that decisions at the microeconomic level are optimal while capable of generating adverse effects at the macroeconomic level.

The claim that economic agents' rational behaviour not merely prevents the economy from absorbing shocks but amplifies and extends their effects is in stark contrast to the New Classical view that rational behaviour ensures a rapid return to equilibrium. Not surprisingly, the New Keynesian interventionist policy prescription creates a similar contrast. While agreeing that in some cases private actions will offset public policy, they argue that this is by no means always the case. They endorse built-in stabilizers and discretionary policy to reduce macroeconomic fluctuations, but are less optimistic about the power of policy than are Keynesians and Post Keynesians. New Keynesians warn against discretionary policy that initiates offsetting private action, and reject 'fine-tuning' as unrealistic. However, within these parameters, they view government action as a remedy, rather than as a cause of problems.

The beginning of New Keynesian theory is usually traced to work by Fischer (1977) and Phelps and Taylor (1977), but studies of wage and price inflexibilities as the result of rational behaviour substantially predate these works and the use of the New Keynesian label. For example, J.R. Hicks published work in the 1930s that stressed downward rigidity of nominal wages as a key factor contributing to 'fair' labour–employer relations that enhance efficiency. Okun (1975) considers 'fairness' in cementing firms' relations with customers to explain price rigidities. Buyers regard price increases in response to rising costs to be fair, but as 'gouging' if they are a response to rising demand. Other explanations of wage rigidity viewed labour as a long-term investment in human capital (Doeringer and Piore 1971). Lastly, Keynes himself stressed the importance of relative wages in explaining inflexibility. In all these examples, price and wage rigidities result from rational behaviour.

New Keynesians distinguish between nominal and real rigidities. A nominal rigidity prevents money prices from adjusting proportionately to changes in nominal output. Real rigidities, such as the stickiness of a real wage or of a relative wage or price, can be traced to firms acting to increase efficiency. Early New Keynesian efforts concentrated on discovering why nominal wages are inflexible. Explanations included overlapping staggered wage contracts and efficiency wages. Overlapping contracts refers to the real-world practice of labour and employers agreeing to wage contracts that commonly cover periods ranging from one to three years. Moreover, these contracts end at various times throughout the year. Consequently, even though expectations may be revised as economic conditions change, nominal wages are fixed in contracts that are due for renegotiation at intervals during the ensuing three years, delaying the adjustment indicated by the revised expectations. Then, if demand falls, wage cuts are not possible, leaving layoffs as the only option.

The macroeconomic costs of these quantity adjustments can be very large, causing sometimes lengthy recessions while the wage adjustments occur. Nevertheless, the long-term wage contracts that impose quantity adjustments are preferred by both firms and workers. In the case of long-term contracts, the primary advantage is to reduce the high costs of negotiation borne by both firms and unions. These involve cash outlays as well as time, not only for the negotiations, but also to conduct the necessary research into existing wages and working conditions in comparable firms, and into assessing the economic conditions – inflation, employment, profits – likely to prevail over the life of the contract. A second advantage is the reduced opportunity for strikes, which are also costly to both labour and employers.

A second explanation of nominal wage rigidities attributes slow adjustment to the practice of paying efficiency wages. Efficiency wages involve the payment of a premium over the nominal wage predicted by traditional labour market analysis. The premium arises from the claimed dependence of productivity on the wage paid. The higher wage is expected to reduce slacking and absenteeism because workers believe they are treated well by their employer, and enables firms to attract better-quality workers. In addition, it increases workers' attachment to the firm, reducing costs associated with high turnover. The result is an improvement in productivity sufficient to justify the higher wage. For example, faced with an adverse demand shock, firms will not reduce the efficiency wage, since this would lower productivity and increase costs. Instead, the rational firm will cut employment.

This emphasis on the labour market was a natural first step for research in the Keynesian tradition. However, as long as profits are flexible, nominal wage stickiness is not sufficient to explain fluctuations of real output. For example, if profits are allowed to fall, nominal prices could fall, reducing or eliminating output fluctuations. The next phase of work emphasized price stickiness as a necessary condition for changes in real output, and dealt with the question of why nominal prices are not flexible enough to mirror changes in nominal output. In contrast to the competitive model used by New Classical theory, most New Keynesian analyses use a model of monopolistic competition, giving firms some control over price. The essential feature of this model is that price is always above marginal cost, so that firms are willing to sell more at the existing price when demand increases, while a perfect competitor would not sell more unless the price rose. However, following a change in demand, the model predicts adjustment of both price and quantity by the rational, profit-maximizing firm. Clearly, monopolistic competition alone cannot account for sticky prices. Some modification is needed to reconcile rationality and price stickiness.

One such modification has been the development of models of staggered price contracts (for example, Blanchard 1986) with strong parallels to the staggered wage models referred to above. These investigate the effects of staggered price setting for overlapping periods, starting from the premise that the length of the period during which the price remains fixed depends on the costs of adjustment. The staggering of price adjustments is attributed to firm-specific shocks occurring at different times. As with overlapping wage contracts, adjustment to changing demand conditions is achieved slowly and in a piecemeal fashion.

A core contribution to New Keynesian theory is the menu cost approach. Menu costs are associated with changing prices in response to changing demand, such as the cost of publishing new price lists and catalogues, and changing price tags. Broader definitions of menu costs also include managerial time taken as well as cash expenditures made to establish the need for change and to renegotiate contracts with suppliers. Faced with a drop in demand for its product, conventional analysis simply predicts that the profit-maximizing firm will reduce price. New Keynesian analysis suggests that reducing price will incur high menu costs, so that profit may well be maximized by keeping price constant (Akerlof and Yellen 1985). The rational firm will therefore cut output, not price. It is claimed that even small menu costs can cause severe recessions (Mankiw 1985).

The different explanations of the absence of market clearing have each been subjected to particular criticism, usually by critics who implicitly accept the general framework of analysis. One such criticism of the menu cost approach is that while it stresses the costs incurred when prices are adjusted, it fails to address the costs attendant upon quantity adjustment. These would include costs of shutting down equipment, storing or scrapping semi-finished products, renegotiating contracts with input suppliers (or paying contractually agreed penalties) and, ultimately, reversing these to restore output levels later. In short, they bear great similarity to the menu costs of price adjustment. A second problem with this approach concerns the failure to consider menu costs in a dynamic context. The menu costs of a price reduction might wipe out profit for a period of time, after which profit would recover. The implicit assumption is that the time period equals or exceeds the period of depressed demand.

These are relatively minor criticisms compared with the general shortcomings of New Keynesian economics. Indeed, it can be criticized as being very narrow in its focus, and neither Keynesian nor new. First, the analyses of rigidity are typically framed in terms of a shock to a 'representative' firm, without regard for the variability of non-market-clearing responses and their causes. However, empirical observation shows that periods of price rigidity are of extremely variable length, with prices changing frequently in some industries, and seldom in others (Carlton 1986). Carlton also found that small price changes (for example, less than 1 per cent) are not uncommon, suggesting very low menu costs. His paper also considers industry structure, the type of product and the nature of relations between firms and customers, all of which have implications for pricing behaviour, and none of which is addressed by New Keynesian economics. Second, virtually no effort is made to incorporate the propagation mechanisms that are central to what are usually accepted as macrodynamic models. This neglect is clearly consistent with the underlying assumption of New Keynesian literature that, imperfections notwithstanding, the economy is self-regulating in the broader sense that it hovers round a macroeconomic equilibrium at the NAIRU (non-accelerating inflation rate of unemployment). Given this characteristic, New Keynesian models cannot be regarded as Keynesian; they are special cases of the neoclassical model. Finally, as suggested above, these ideas are not new, but reprise an older literature that treats wage and price rigidities. The earlier literature is richer in content, if less rigorously presented.

New Keynesian economics as a distinct school of thought was short-lived. Although much of the recent research in asymmetric information, credit rationing and coordination problems might be classified as New Keynesian, the term is rarely encountered in literature published since the early 1990s. Instead New Keynesian thought has become part of the broader field of research and has been reabsorbed into the current mainstream concern with the economics of imperfections.

WENDY CORNWALL

See also:

Credit Rationing; Economic Policy; Microfoundations; New Clasical Economics; Pricing and Prices; Unemployment; Wages and Labour Markets.

References

Akerlof, George and Janet Yellen (1985), 'A near-rational model of the business cycle with wage and price inertia', *Quarterly Journal of Economics*, **100** (5), Supplement, 823–38.
Blanchard, Olivier J. (1986), 'The wage-price spiral', *Quarterly Journal of Economics*, **101** (3), 543–65.
Carlton, Dennis W. (1986), 'The rigidity of prices', *American Economic Review*, **76** (4), 637–58.
Doeringer, P. and M. Piore (1971), *Internal Labor Markets and Manpower Analysis*, Lexington, MA: D.C. Heath.
Fischer, Stanley (1977), 'Long-term contracts, rational expectations, and the optimal money supply rule', *Journal of Political Economy*, **85** (1), 191–205.
Mankiw, N. Gregory (1985), 'Small menu costs and large business cycles: a macroeconomic model of monopoly', *Quarterly Journal of Economics*, **100** (2), 529–38.

Okun, A. (1975), 'Inflation: its mechanics and welfare cost', *Brookings Papers on Economic Activity*, **2**, 351–401.

Phelps, Edmund S. and John B. Taylor (1977), 'Stabilizing powers of monetary policy under rational expectations', *Journal of Political Economy*, **85** (1), 163–90.

Non-ergodicity

In response to the growing hegemony of the rational expectations revolution and the increasing complaint levelled against Post Keynesian economics that its concept of uncertainty had not been formalized or empirically evaluated, Paul Davidson introduced the notion that the Post Keynesian conception of uncertainty could be articulated with reference to a technical distinction between ergodic and non-ergodic processes. Building on Samuelson's suggestion that economic knowledge about the future rested on the axiom of ergodicity, Davidson (1982–83) argued that the Post Keynesian conception of 'unknowledge' was predicated on the rejection of the universality of the ergodic axiom. He suggested that the Post Keynesian view of time and discussion of the salience of uncertainty could be defined with respect to the absence of governing ergodic processes – what he labelled 'non-ergodicity'.

Ergodic theory has been explicitly developed in the theory of stochastic processes although the term itself arises from statistical mechanics (see Parry 1987 for a technical discussion). It refers to the property by which the time and space averages that originate and are computed from any data-generating process either coincide for a series of infinite observations, or converge as the number of observations increases (with a probability of one) for a finite number. That is to say, averages from past realizations collapse on the objective probability distribution that governs current and future outcomes. Under such conditions the past reveals the future, and the rational expectations hypothesis that the process of competition forces agents to use all the amount of available information in forming expectations about the future which are efficient, unbiased and without persistent errors, appears reasonable – in the long run at least (see Table 1, below).

In Davidson's (1982–83) seminal paper he argued that the rational expectations hypothesis was a misleading caricature of Keynes's recognition of the importance of uncertainty and expectations, because the ergodic assumption implies that the past reveals the future – that over time agents can predict the future with actuarial certainty-equivalence. On the ergodic hypothesis, the passage of time does not affect the joint probability laws governing processes; history ultimately does not matter. In contrast, Davidson argued that agents would be truly uncertain under conditions of non-ergodicity, that is, in the absence of governing ergodic processes. This is not to deny a priori that some economic processes may be ergodic, at least for short periods of calendar time. But, under non-ergodic conditions, sampling from the past in the manner implied by the rational expectations theorists is not sensible since, *even if* agents have the ability to assemble and process all the relevant information pertaining to past and present outcomes, the future course of events will still not reveal itself. There are no governing social or economic laws to learn, and sensible agents will come to recognize their capacity to make their own history in the context of contemporaneous institutions.

The fact that most macroeconomic time series are non-stationary provides empirical evidence for this view. Indeed, Solow (1985, p. 328) recognized as much when he wrote 'much of what we observe cannot be treated as a stationary stochastic process without straining credulity'. What is more, while the existence of co-integration or unit roots may be suggestive of an underlying ergodic relationship it may also be misleading, not least for the introduction of spurious stationarity. As Klein (1994, p. 37) argues,

> Stationarity means that in a time distribution of data, one could get the same moments of the distribution no matter what block of time. It is a mathematical property of a time series or other kind of collection of sample data. I do not think economic data are necessarily stationary or that economic processes are stationary. The technique of co-integration, to keep differencing data until stationarity is obtained and then relate the stationary series, I think can do damage ... [as it] may introduce new relationships, some of which we do not want to have in our analysis.

Nevertheless the concepts of stationarity and non-stationarity should not be conflated with the ergodic–non-ergodic distinction. If the estimates of the time averages do not vary with the period under observation then a stochastic process can be said to be stationary. However, as some stationary stochastic processes are non-ergodic, that is, limit cycles, non-stationarity is not a necessary condition for the existence for non-ergodic processes. But all non-stationary processes are non-ergodic. Non-stationarity is thus a sufficient condition for non-ergodicity and provides an empirical foundation for Post Keynesian claims about the relevance of history and uncertainty.

Nevertheless Davidson's discussion seeks to go beneath purely stochastic considerations, identifying the underlying causal mechanisms and emergent properties and structures that generate non-ergodic time series. In a much-neglected aspect of his discussion of non-ergodicity, Davidson (1982–83, p. 192) emphasizes the link to G.L.S Shackle's concept of creative, crucial decision making, arguing that the existence of crucial decision making represents a sufficient condition for the existence of non-ergodic processes. Situations where purely processing information from the past provides insufficient information about the course of future events is suggestive of a creative role for human agency. Here crucial decisions refer to non-routine decisions that take place in historical time. A crucial decision involves large transaction and sunk costs and cannot be unmade without loss; it calls attention to the fact that one is irrevocably tied (married) to one's decisions. Moreover, as this conceptualization relates to both consumption and production decisions that involve calendar time and large transaction costs, it moves beyond Keynes's apparently arbitrary distinction between 'autonomous' investment and 'non-autonomous' consumption decisions. It provides a more appropriate framework within which to elaborate Keynes's principle of effective demand and to outline the relevance of liquidity considerations and their nexus to the non-neutrality of money.

In linking non-ergodicity to Shackle's concept of crucial decision making, Davidson advocates a broader, creative view of agency than that contained within mainstream models of human behaviour. Accordingly he has expanded the concept to incorporate non-stochastic processes (Davidson 1991). Deterministic models of decision making which are elaborated in logical time require Leonard Savage's ordering axiom – the presumption, at least in principle, that agents can make a transitive ordering over all possible outcomes. This involves a pre-programmed future and invokes a substantive rationality that is inconsistent with the fecundity which Post Keynesians impute *a posteriori* to agents. Post Keynesians recognize that it is impossible to form a transitive ordering over a yet-to-be created future in which circumstances inconceivable at the point of origination emerge.

Subsequently, and in response to the numerous meanings that could be imputed to non-ergodicity, as well as to encompass developments in complexity and chaos theory, Davidson (1996) has reformulated his discussion in terms of a distinction between immutable and transmutable economic processes. Immutability encompasses the ergodic and ordering axioms and embodies 'the presumption of a programmed stable, conservative system where the past, present and future reality are predetermined whether the system is stochastic or not' (ibid., pp. 480–81). In immutable models, history is predetermined and choice is neither genuine nor matters. Under such a reformulation immutability refers to attempts to elaborate (real or imagined) universal event regularities and to develop theoretical structures of the general form 'whenever event (type) X then event (type) Y'. Thus it closely parallels Lawson's discussion of closed systems. In contrast, the broader notion of transmutability encompasses the stochastic discussion of non-ergodicity within a creative and emergent conceptualization of history in which choice is genuine, matters, and can make a difference in the long run – not least in affecting liquidity considerations and influencing the employment path of an economy over time. On this view of economic processes, sensible agents recognize that the environment in which they make decisions is characterized by the absence of programmed and predetermined processes and is creative, open, emergent and uncertain.

This transmutable conception of economic processes provides for a delineation between the Post Keynesian approach to modelling and theorizing about economic processes and that of many Austrians, New Classicals, New Keynesian and New Institutionalist economists (see Table 1). It also underscores some of the methodological affinities between Post Keynesianism and the German historical school, the older institutionalists and critical

Table 1 Conceptualizations of economic processes

A. IMMUTABLE REALITY (AN ERGODIC SYSTEM)

Type 1 In the short run, the future is known or at least knowable. Examples of theories using this postulate are:

(a) Classical perfect certainty models
(b) Actuarial certainty equivalents, such as rational expectations models
(c) New Classical models
(d) Some New Keynesian theories

Type 2 In the short run, the future is not completely known due to some limitation in human information processing and computing power. Examples of theories using this postulate are:

(a) Bounded rationality theory
(b) Frank Knight's theory of uncertainty
(c) Savage's expected utility theory
(d) Some Austrian theories
(e) Some New Keynesian models (e.g., coordination failure)
(f) Chaos, sunspot and bubble theories

B TRANSMUTABLE OR CREATIVE REALITY – (A NON-ERGODIC SYSTEM)

Some aspects of the economic future will be created by human action today and/or in the future. Examples of theories using this postulate are:

(a) Keynes's *General Theory* and Post Keynesian monetary theory
(b) Post-1974 writings of Sir John Hicks
(c) G.L.S. Shackle's crucial experiment analysis
(d) Old Institutionalist theory

Source: Reproduced from Davidson (1996, p. 485).

realists, and provides for a renewed exchange of ideas with other potentially compatible approaches (Dunn 2000).

This broader discussion of non-ergodicity underscores the Post Keynesian view of economic time and its nexus to the macroeconomics of modern credit-money production economies. It provides for a strong critique of the rational expectations hypothesis, not rejecting it on the basis that it provides an unrealistic model of actual decision making, but rather advancing a distinctive view of human agency that is broader than that contained within models of bounded rationality or complexity and provides a challenge to the conventional wisdom that markets work best without government intervention (Davidson 1996). Moreover it can be used in theorizing in a positive fashion to clarify the informational foundations of monetary non-neutrality and transaction cost theory, as well as providing for a strategic conceptualization of the modern corporation (see Dunn 2001 and the references contained therein).

As Sir John Hicks conceded in personal correspondence with Davidson (12 February 1983): 'I have missed a chance, of labelling my own point of view as *non-ergodic*. One needs a name like that to ram a point home. I had tried to read a book on stochastic processes, but I was not sharp enough to see the connections' (italics added).

STEPHEN P. DUNN

See also:

Agency; Austrian School of Economics; Critical Realism; Expectations; Liquidity Preference; Money; Time in Economic Theory; Uncertainty.

References

Davidson, P. (1982–83), 'Rational expectations, a fallacious foundation for studying crucial decision-making processes', *Journal of Post Keynesian Economics*, **5** (2), 182–97.
Davidson, P. (1991), 'Is probability theory relevant for uncertainty? A Post Keynesian perspective', *Journal of Economic Perspectives*, **5** (1), 129–43.
Davidson, P. (1996), 'Reality and economic theory', *Journal of Post Keynesian Economics*, **18** (4), 479–508.
Dunn, S.P. (2000), 'Wither Post Keynesianism?', *Journal of Post Keynesian Economics*, **22** (3), 343–64.
Dunn, S.P. (2001), 'Uncertainty, strategic decision-making and the essence of the modern corporation: extending Cowling and Sugden', *Manchester School*, **69** (1), 31–41.
Klein, L. (1994), 'Problems with modern economics', *Atlantic Economic Journal*, **22** (1), 34–8.
Parry, W. (1987), 'Ergodic theory', in J. Eatwell, M. Milgate and P. Newman (eds), *The New Palgrave: A Dictionary of Economics*, Vol. 2, London: Macmillan, pp. 184–8.
Solow, R.M. (1985), 'Economic history and economics', *American Economic Review*, **75** (2), 328–31.

Pricing and Prices

Post Keynesians see the discipline of economics as being concerned with explaining the process that provides the flow of goods and services required by society to meet the needs of those who participate in its activities. Consequently, Post Keynesian economic theory is the theoretical explanation of this social provisioning process in a capitalist economy. Hence Post Keynesian theory is concerned with explaining those factors that are part of the process, including the setting of prices by business enterprises.

The business enterprise is a specific social organization for coordinating and carrying out activities associated with the provisioning process. It consists of an organizational component, a production and cost component, a series of routines that transmit information (such as costs, sales and prices) which enables workers and management to coordinate and carry out their activities, and a management that makes strategic decisions about prices (as well as investment). When making decisions, management is motivated by different goals, such as growth of sales, developing new products, entering new geographical regions or markets, generating dividends for shareholders, and/or attaining political power. Hence, management views price setting, or pricing, as strategic decisions designed to meet these goals (Eichner 1976; Lee 1998; Downward 1999).

To set a price of a product, the pricing administrators of the business enterprise first determine its cost base. Utilizing costing procedures derived from the management accounting procedures used by the enterprise, the pricing administrators determine the product's average direct costs (ADC), average overhead costs (AOC) and average total costs (ATC) at normal output. The relevance of normal output is that it enables the pricing administrators to determine the product's normal costs. That is, since ADC, AOC and ATC vary as output changes, it is necessary to select a particular amount of output if costs for pricing are to be determined before production takes place and the actual costs of production are known. With the normal costs administratively determined, the pricing administrators select a profit mark-up to be applied to the normal costs to set the price. This pricing procedure means that the price of the good is set before the good is produced and exchange takes place. The pricing administrators then take the administratively-determined price (which is determined outside the market) and administer it to (or impose it on) the market.

At the centre of the pricing process are the administratively-determined mark-up, normal cost and target rate of return pricing procedures. Mark-up pricing procedures consist of marking up average direct costs based on normal output to set the price, with the mark-up being sufficient to cover overhead costs and produce a profit:

labour and material-based mark-up pricing: price $= (\text{NADC})(1+k)$ (1)

where NADC is normal average direct material and labour costs of the product and k is the mark-up for overhead costs and profits.

Normal cost pricing procedures come in two forms. The most basic consists of marking up NADC to cover overhead costs, which gives normal average total costs (NATC), and then applying the profit mark-up to NATC to set the price:

normal cost pricing: price $= [(\text{NADC})(1+g)](1+r)$ (2)

where g is the mark-up for overhead costs and r is the mark-up for profit.

A more detailed normal cost pricing procedure consists of applying the profit mark-up to a completely delineated NATC to set the price:

normal cost pricing: price $= (\text{NATC})(1+r)$.   (3)

Lastly, the target rate of return pricing procedure consists of marking up NATC by a certain percentage to generate a volume of profits at normal output that will produce a specific rate of return with respect to the value of the enterprise's capital assets connected with the production of the product. That is, given the value of the capital assets (VCA) associated with the production of the product, the pricing administrators want to obtain a specific target rate of return (TRR) on those assets. Therefore, the amount of profits required to meet the target rate of return is TRR $\times$ VCA = target profits, P_t. To incorporate the target profit figure into the price, P_t is first divided by normal output (*no*) to get the targeted costing margin, cm_t, and then divided by NATC to get the targeted profit mark-up (t):

target rate of return pricing: price $= (\text{NATC})(1+t)$
$= (\text{NATC})[1 + \text{TRR} \times \text{VCA}/(no)\text{NATC}]$.   (4)

Given the targeted profit mark-up, if the business enterprise produces at normal output, enough profits will be generated to attain the desired target rate of return on the capital assets (Eichner 1976; Lavoie 1992; Lee 1998; Downward 1999).

Because actual output can differ from the normal output, the actual costs of production can differ from normal costs, so that the actual profit or target mark-up can differ from the profit or target mark-up used to set the price. Consequently, in the context of the ebbs and flows of business activity and especially the business cycle, the business enterprise will not always achieve its target rate of return or desired profits, sometimes being above it and other times being below it.

The prices set by pricing administrators using normal cost-based pricing procedures have five properties. The first property is that the price is not based on or related to actual costs, and immediate or current market forces do not affect the profit mark-up. That is, irrespective of the pricing procedures used by pricing administrators, the shape of the enterprise's average direct cost curve or its average total cost curve is immaterial for pricing purposes. The costs used for pricing are determined prior to production and are based on normal output. Consequently, the shape of the ADC cost curve or ATC curve is not important for price-setting purposes. Instead the price is based on normal costs, while actual costs vary around it as actual output varies around normal output. As for the profit mark-up, the evidence strongly suggests that it remains stable for significant periods of time so that in some cases it is considered customary by pricing administrators; it is based on long-term competitive forces and will change when those forces change; and it is unaffected by momentary fluctuations in sales. To explain theoretically the magnitude and the relative stability of the profit mark-up, Post Keynesians have utilized either market structure arguments or investment-determining mark-up arguments. However, neither argument has much empirical support. Thus the profit mark-up remains theoretically underexplained in Post Keynesian theory (Wood 1975; Eichner 1976; Čapoğlu 1991; Lavoie 1992; Sawyer 1995; Downward 1999).

Given normal costs and the stability of the profit mark-up, it follows that the second property of administered prices is that they are stable in that they remain unchanged for extended periods of time and for many sequential transactions. Consequently, administered prices are neither exchange-specific prices nor prices that reflect the impact of immediate variations in sales. This implies that markets that have stable, normal cost-based prices are not organized like auction markets or oriental bazaars where the retailer engages in individual price negotiation for each transaction. Rather, an enterprise that desires to enter these unorganized markets must first announce a price for its product and then enter into direct buyer–seller interaction to obtain sales. Since buyer–seller interactions take place both simultaneously and through time, business enterprises find that stable prices are cost-efficient in terms of selling costs, reduce the threat of price wars, and facilitate the establishment of goodwill relationships with customers (Lee 1998; Downward 1999).

A third property of administered prices is that they are set largely without reference to an inverse price–sales relationship and are not set to achieve a specific amount of sales. In studies of price determination, business enterprises have stated that variations of their prices within practical limits, given the prices of their competitors, produced virtually no change in their sales and that variations in the market price, especially downward, produced little if any changes in market sales in the short term. Moreover, when the price change is significant enough to result in a significant change in sales, the impact on profits has been negative enough to persuade enterprises not to try the experiment again. Consequently administered prices are maintained for a variety of different outputs over time. The fourth property of administered prices is that they change over time. The pricing administrators of business enterprises maintain pricing periods of three months to a year in which their administered prices remained unchanged; and then, at the end of the period, they decide on whether to alter them. The factors which are most important to the enterprises in this regard are changes in labour and material costs, changes in the mark-up for profit and changes in normal output. Factors prompting the enterprises to alter their profit mark-ups include short- and long-term competitive pressures, the stage that the product has reached in its life cycle, and the need for profit. Moreover, since normal output is administratively determined, it is possible for pricing administrators to alter it perversely over the business cycle, resulting in the NATC increasing in the downturn and decreasing in the upturn. If the mark-ups for profit remain constant, then the pricing administrators would be setting countercyclical or perverse prices. Consequently, administered prices can change from one pricing period to the next in any direction, irrespective of the state of the business cycle. However, evidence does suggest that within short periods of time (such as two-year intervals), changes in costs will dominate price changes, whereas over longer periods of time changes in the mark-up will play a more important role (Lee 1998; Downward 1999).

The fifth and final feature of administered prices is its role in the reproduction of the business enterprise. That is, pricing administrators use cost-based pricing procedures to set prices that would enable the enterprise to engage in sequential acts of production over time and thereby reproduce itself and grow. More specifically, because market conditions facing the enterprise's many products are not uniform and change over time, its pricing administrators utilize a variety of multi-temporal, open-ended pricing strategies designed to achieve time-specific and temporally undefined goals. The compendium of pricing strategies is known as the enterprise's pricing policy, and the prices that the pricing administrator administers to the various markets, are based on one or more of these strategies. Thus, the administered prices of a business enterprise are strategic prices whose common and overriding goals are reproduction and growth (Eichner 1976; Lavioe 1992; Lee 1998; Downward 1999).

FREDERIC S. LEE

See also:

Competition; Income Distribution; Kaleckian Economics; Production.

References

Čapoğlu, G. (1991), *Prices, Profits and Financial Structures*, Aldershot: Edward Elgar.
Downward, P. (1999), *Pricing Theory in Post Keynesian Economics*, Cheltenham, UK and Northampton, MA, USA: Edward Elgar.
Eichner, A.S. (1976), *The Megacorp and Oligopoly*, Cambridge: Cambridge University Press.
Lavoie, M. (1992), *Foundations of Post-Keynesian Economic Analysis*, Aldershot: Edward Elgar.
Lee, F. (1998), *Post Keynesian Price Theory*, Cambridge: Cambridge University Press.
Sawyer, M.C. (1995), *Unemployment, Imperfect Competition and Macroeconomics*, Aldershot: Edward Elgar.
Wood, A. (1975), *A Theory of Profits*, Cambridge: Cambridge University Press.

Production

It can be argued that, in the mainstream neoclassical or marginalist theoretical apparatus, the role of production is subsidiary to that of exchange. The core of that approach, which explores how scarce commodities are allocated among alternative uses through the price mechanism, can be represented using a model of exchange with given endowments of non-produced commodities. Production can be introduced into this model at a later stage to show how resources are transformed into goods through the production function, without fundamentally altering the basic insights to be drawn from the approach. In contrast, in Post Keynesian economics, as in the classical political economy and Marxian/radical approaches, production takes a more central role.

The centrality of production in Post Keynesian economics can in turn be related to some of its main concepts, such as effective demand, historical time and uncertainty (see Dutt and Amadeo 1990). Perhaps the key concept common to all varieties of Post Keynesianism is that of effective demand, and its role in determining employment and unemployment in the short run and the rate of accumulation and growth in the long run. Since effective demand determines these by determining the level and rate of change of production, production naturally takes a central place in the Post

Keynesian approach. Another important idea stressed in Post Keynesian economics is the concept of historical time, as opposed to logical time in which historical processes and irreversibilities are not adequately captured. Chick (1983, pp. 16–21) discusses how major economic decisions such as consumption, saving, investment and especially production can be portrayed as being made over historical time. In this sequence, production decisions have to be made prior to sales, but with the expectation of sales affecting how much firms produce. These expectations have been referred to in the literature as short-period expectations, which are different from the long-period expectations which govern investment decisions, following Keynes's Marshallian approach of the *General Theory*. A related concept, stressed more in some varieties of Post Keynesianism than in others, is that of uncertainty, which is distinguished from risk because objective probabilities cannot be assigned to the consequences of many kinds of economic decisions as is assumed in the analysis of risk. While the concept of uncertainty is stressed in discussions of investment and asset-holding decisions, it has also been invoked in discussion of production. In uncertain situations firms and other economic agents are often seen as following conventions and rules of thumb, behaviour which may be much more rational than doing detailed cost–benefit calculations of their actions.

An examination of the theory of production at the level of individual producers illustrates the importance of some of these ideas. Since Post Keynesian economics does not comprise a unified body of theory, but rather several different approaches, it is useful to consider two different approaches to such a theory, one derived from the Marshallian tradition of Keynes's *General Theory* presentation, and the other the Kaleckian approach which stresses imperfect competition. Although hybrid forms which combine features from these two approaches exist, it is instructive to consider the two separately.

In the Keynesian approach the firm is assumed to operate in a purely competitive environment, in the sense that it expects to sell any amount at the going price. But since the firm has to make its production decision without knowing the price which will prevail when its produce will be brought to the market it is assumed to form short-period expectations, which take the form of an expected price. With the money wage assumed to be given, the firm is then taken to maximize its profit by equating its marginal product of labour (assuming diminishing returns and a given stock of capital) to the ratio of the wage to the expected price. This determines the firm's market-period or 'day' equilibrium level of employment and output. Once each firm makes its production and employment plans and carries them out, income flows are generated in the form of wages and profits, and these determine the level of consumption, while firms make investment plans depending on their long-period expectations, which are taken to be exogenous. Assuming that aggregate effective demand depends on the price level (perhaps because of its effect on the real wage, and hence on consumption demand with differential propensities to consume out of wage and profit income), the price is assumed to vary to equate demand to total market-period equilibrium. There is no guarantee that the expected price of firms (for simplicity assumed to be the same for all firms) will be equal to the market-period equilibrium price. If they are different, firms will adapt by adjusting their expectations, and thereby (under certain conditions) arrive at the short-period equilibrium level of production, at which not only does the market clear but the firms' short-period expectations are also fulfilled, although long-period expectations are still taken as given. The short-period equilibrium level of output depends on the level of investment spending, among other things, and may well be below the full-employment level of output. This approach can be seen as providing a simple formalization of the role of effective demand in determining output, of historical time in which different periods are carefully distinguished, and of uncertainty, through its invocation of short- and long-period expectations. Moreover, the approach can be used as a basis for examining changes in long-period expectations and its relation to short-period expectations, which can be shown to lead to various kinds of path-dependencies in the determination of the aggregate level of production (see Dutt 1997). However, some Post Keynesians exhibit some hostility to it and to the aggregate demand–aggregate supply analysis related to it, given its closeness to marginalist traditions following from its assumptions of pure competition and production functions that exhibit diminishing returns.

These Post Keynesians prefer the Kaleckian approach, in which firms in oligopolistic situations enjoy some degree of monopoly power. In this approach, given the uncertainty concerning the level of aggregate demand and the behaviour of other firms, firms use the rule of thumb of setting their price as a mark-up on their unit prime or variable costs. The assumption of a fixed unit labour requirement, a fixed money wage, that labour is the only variable factor, and a fixed mark-up (which depends on factors such as the level of industrial concentration), the price becomes constant, and the firms adjust their level of output to the level of demand for their product, while maintaining excess capacity given their stock of capital. In this approach the level of production for each firm is determined by the demand for the firm's product. The aggregate level of production in the economy is therefore determined by aggregate effective demand, and will in general be consistent with excess capacity and unemployed labour. This approach represents a more radical departure from neoclassical economics, because of its assumption of fixed unit labour requirements, which can be allowed to vary due to changes in technology and in the social relations of production as in Marxian and radical presentations, rather than due to factor substitution.

The feature common to both approaches is the role of aggregate effective demand. There cannot be a self-contained microeconomic theory of production: the level of output depends on the demand for each firm, which depends on macroeconomic factors (and some rule according to which total demand is apportioned between firms). This essentially macroeconomic theory of output determination makes output depend on aggregate levels of consumption, investment and other sources of demand.

However, the discussion presented so far leaves open the possibility that, although unemployment equilibrium can occur in the short run, there may be forces in the economy which change the level of production of firms in a direction which will drive aggregate production to fully employ all the economy's resources in the longer run. For instance, this may occur in the first model if unemployment leads to a fall in the money wage which will induce firms to employ more workers and to produce more. In both models unemployment can lead to a fall in the wage or the price level, which increases the real supply of money, which through wealth effects on demand or through a reduction of the interest rate can induce firms to invest more, and thereby increase the demand for goods. These forces can take the economy to positions of full employment, as suggested by the 'neoclassical synthesis' or 'Bastard' Keynesian approach. The demonstration that there are no such necessary tendencies is therefore an important concern of Post Keynesian economics.

Post Keynesians argue that the money wage is determined by institutional factors rather than by the automatic forces of supply and demand. Thus, the importance given to relative wages by workers in the wage bargaining process may prevent wage reductions, as argued by Keynes (1936) himself, or issues such as efficiency wages or insider–outsider considerations may explain wage rigidity. While this wage rigidity interpretation of Keynesian macroeoconomics is common in mainstream circles, especially in neoclassical synthesis and New Keynesian quarters, this interpretation would make Keynesian economics little different from that of the pre-Keynesians, who were quite aware that wage rigidity could result in unemployment.

Post Keynesians have also emphasized that wage reductions need not take the economy to full employment, following Keynes's own lead in chapter 19 of the *General Theory*. Thus, they argue that money supply in a credit-money economy is demand determined, so that a fall in the wage and price level, rather than automatically reducing the interest rate because of an excess supply of money, will simply reduce the supply of money endogenously. Moreover, even if the interest rate does fall, when the wage and price levels fall, firms – caught in an uncertain situation – may not increase investment, and asset-holders may simply wish to hold more money. Thus, standard mechanisms of expansion relying on asset market considerations are short-circuited. A fall in wages and prices may actually reduce the cash receipts of firms from the sale of goods and, given precommitted costs, might lead them to cut back investment, and even worse, declare bankruptcy in extreme cases. More generally, deflation will redistribute wealth from debtors to creditors, thereby possibly reducing aggregate demand. A fall in the money wage, if it results in a fall in the real wage, can also redistribute income from wage-earners to profit recipients with a lower marginal propensity to consume, which also reduces aggregate demand. Moreover, neo-Ricardian Keynesians argue that a fall in the interest rate may not increase aggregate investment if one takes into account the fact that capital goods are produced inputs, and that changes in the interest rate or profit rate can cause changes in the relative prices of capital goods and lead to 'perverse' changes in aggregate investment demand. In the absence of automatic tendencies which take output to full employment, it may be supposed that this will be achieved by governments, especially through fiscal and monetary policies. However, such policies can be ineffective or slow to take effect, and there may be political constraints on full-employment policies as discussed by Kalecki (1971), which imply that even in the longer run, production is determined by aggregate demand considerations rather than supply-side factors.

AMITAVA KRISHNA DUTT

See also:

Effective Demand; Employment; Expectations; Kaleckian Economics; Marginalism; Sraffian Economics; Time in Economic Theory; Uncertainty.

References

Chick, Victoria (1983), *Macroeconomics After Keynes. A Reconsideration of the 'General Theory'*, Cambridge, MA: MIT Press.
Dutt, Amitava Krishna (1997), 'Equilibrium, path dependence and hysteresis in post-Keynesian models', in P. Arestis and M. Sawyer (eds), *Markets, Unemployment and Economic Policy: Essays in Honour of G.C. Harcourt*, Vol. 2, London: Routledge, pp. 238–53.
Dutt, Amitava Krishna and Edward J. Amadeo (1990), *Keynes's Third Alternative? The Neo-Ricardian Keynesians and the Post Keynesians*, Aldershot: Edward Elgar.
Kalecki, Michał (1971), *Selected Essays on the Dynamics of the Capitalist Economy*, Cambridge: Cambridge University Press.
Keynes, John Maynard (1936), *The General Theory of Employment, Interest and Money*, London: Macmillan.

Profits

While profits are literally the difference between the revenue from sales and the costs of production, the scope of the term varies according to what is admitted as a cost. If one believes that all value is produced by labour (aside from natural non-reproducible resources), then only labour incomes are costs and all non-labour incomes accrue as profits. If, on the other hand, tangible capital is thought to contribute towards the production process, then dividends and other returns to the owners of plant and machinery are netted out of profits.

Profit, under any economic definition, represents a return from financing acts which produce a good or service. It does not, in economics, include winnings from zero-sum activities such as gambling or arbitrage. Nor would most economists accept that it includes net capital gains, although the difference between current profits and capital gains is temporal (higher profit expectations raise the current value of an asset) and may be irrelevant to the firm if the asset is realized. Profits are a flow arising from current production. Lack of clarity among authors about what they include in the term 'profits', as well as lack of recognition of the non-uniqueness of the definition, can be a source of confusion for readers and remains a barrier to inter-school-of-thought discussions.

Profits are received for advances of money or resources made in the expectation of future benefits, whether these moneys are used to buy the services of current or intermediate inputs into the production process, as exemplified by David Ricardo's corn model, or so-called investment goods whose use may last beyond a single production cycle. However, a convention used often in economic analysis (but not accounting), is to regard profits earned on working capital as secondary details, in order to focus on the more complex relationship between investment goods and profits. This convention was probably established because expenditures made with respect to longer time horizons exhibit greater volatility and uncertainty. Accordingly investments which are expected to furnish returns beyond a year will, in general, be more important determinants of other economic phenomena than investments that repay themselves within a week.

From a single firm's perspective, funds advanced in each time period equal the amount of working capital advanced to cover the costs of producing the good or service: payments to labour, leasing costs (direct or implicit owner costs) of using reproducible plant, equipment or intangible assets, and rents on non-reproducible inputs. From the point of view of the whole economy, however, rents are not true costs but transfer payments (as there are no opportunity costs), and the costs of producing the reproducible assets can be decomposed in a similar way according to the costs of the respective investment-goods businesses. Taken to its limit, each production process can be reduced to labour and non-reproducible inputs, with the only true cost of production being a dated series of labour inputs, as revealed by Sraffa's (1960) scheme of prices. However, in each stage of production, a surplus exists after the firm has paid for the costs of labour and non-labour inputs. And this, summed over all firms, is gross aggregate profit.

If the costs (Alfred Marshall's quasi-rents) of using capital goods, that is, capital consumption or depreciation, are essentially released flows of stored labour, what then accounts for the existence and size of profits? Why isn't all income paid to labour? In order to understand the determinants of profits it is important to recognize the importance of the ownership of financial capital and the power of finance over economic resources. Rentiers and firms will not invest in production, or any given project, unless they expect it to return a minimum or normal rate of profit (the ratio of profits accrued per funds advanced). Rentiers and firms are not compelled to invest and they can, when they desire, keep their finances as secure financial assets. Furthermore, economic resources cannot be mobilized without financial backing. Borrowing can supplement collateral but cannot replace this backing (see Kalecki 1939). Hence, profits form the incentive for rentiers to invest.

The two components of *ex ante* normal profits include default-free interest payments and returns to compensate for the 'normal' uncertainty associated with doing business. The default-free interest rate is set by central banks and represents a totally secure alternative way for capital owners to place their funds. Owners of financial assets, or their banking intermediaries, will not lend to businesses for investment unless they are assured of a greater return than what they would receive from these default-free bill rates. To the extent that these central banks offer an elastic supply of these bills, the rate of interest becomes the minimum supply price for rentiers of financial capital. However, non-zero default-free banking rates constitute a net injection of funds into the economy and the cost to the public of this convention or policy action may be a redirection of funds from the central government's normal budgetary policies. That is, the higher are the interest payments governments need to make to meet their interest obligations, the more funds are diverted, in the first instance, from their appropriations to portfolios.

Even if the default-free rate was set at zero, businesses would still require a positive return in order to commit themselves to production. There are substantial uncertainties associated with investments, and unless some compensation is forthcoming a rational rentier would place funds in a sequence of government bills instead. While the premium for uncertainty is undoubtedly positive (to the extent that business people are economically rational), there are few theories to explain how much is required to compensate the rentier for his/her risk of investing in a business, as the evaluation of *uncertainty* is subjective. Knight (1921) recognized that, at the limit, profits are not required to compensate for *risk* (actuarial-based risk), for if people have complete information about the probabilities of all possible contingencies, then they can objectively estimate an expected value. The greater the frequency of repeated instances of the risky situation, the more certain will be the expected outcome. Accordingly, at the limit, no premium is required to compensate for actuarial risk, only non-actuarial uncertainty.

Clearly if the business expects a project to return greater than normal profits it will proceed with the project and consider the windfall (pure) above-normal profits as a reward for recognizing an overlooked and unexploited opportunity. In this way, expected profits attract the attention of entrepreneurs who will shift resources into or out of markets with a speed determined by the magnitude of the difference between demand and supply.

However, the distinction between monopoly profit and 'normal' returns is not as clear as it sounds. Where does the 'normal' premium for uncertainty end and above-normal profits begin? Some industries are more inherently risky than others, and firms which aggressively pursue monopoly profits by investing in uncertain and unpredictable intangible capital, would expect to be compensated by a higher premium for uncertainty. Until this issue has been resolved, no explanation can exist for the level of normal profits and it would be difficult in practice to identify whether firms or industries are receiving monopoly profits.

While positive *ex ante* profits are required for *ex ante* investment, these profits do not always materialize. *Ex post* profits can vary for reasons related more to macroeconomic factors than the behaviour or expectations of the specific firm. For example, as recognized by Kalecki, while firms can set their profit mark-up on unit costs, they cannot determine how much they will sell and consequently how much total profit they will make.

There are relatively few theories which seek to explain the size of *ex post* aggregate profits and thus the extent to which *ex ante* expectations can be simultaneously realized (long-run equilibrium). Neoclasssical aggregate production function theories, such as Robert Solow's 1956 model, have been used in conjunction with J.B. Clark's marginal productivity theory to show that the normal rate of profits is simply the value of the marginal product of (aggregate) capital. As such, at long-run equilibrium the level of profits reflects the innate productivity of aggregate tangible plant and equipment. However, all measures of aggregate capital (needed to calculate the value of the marginal product of capital) use the prices of capital goods and thus an embedded rate of profit. This endogenous value measure of aggregate capital does not therefore constitute an *independent* explanation of the rate of profit.

The nineteenth-century theory of Ricardo defined the level of profits per unit of output to be the difference between the subsistence wage for labourers per unit of output and the average product of labour on the most marginal land in the economy. The level of production was consistent with full employment. However, this theory is less relevant where the average wage rate can and does vary over time and where subsistence is culturally defined.

Kalecki (1939) has one of the most comprehensive theories of the determination of profits. Using a simple two-sector macroeconomic model (with no government or foreign sectors) he uses the two identities:

$$Y \equiv C_w + C_K + I$$
$$Y \equiv W + P$$

where Y is output, C_w is workers' consumption, C_K is capitalists' consumption, I is investment demand, W is the wage bill and P is total profits. If it is assumed that workers do not save, such that $C_W = W$ but capitalists consume a small portion of their income, such that $C_k = A + \lambda P$ (where A is a given constant and λ is the marginal propensity to consume) this gives $P = (A + I)/(1 - \lambda)$. Since I can be determined by the deliberate decisions of businesses (and A and λ by rentiers) but P cannot, the direction of causation must run from I, A and λ to P. Introducing workers' saving obscures, but does not destroy, this basic conclusion. Kalecki also had a microeconomic theory of the minimum *ex ante* rate of profit (which he took as exogenous to the economy) and average profit per unit of output (which depended on the rate of competition). However, the *ex post* rate and level of profits for each firm depend on the aggregation of all microeconomic investment decisions, and accordingly are out of the hands of any individual business.

Finally, a word about how entrepreneurs or business managers actively seek to make profits. Classical and neoclassical theories commonly portray the flow of profit-seeking funds as action like water passively seeking an even level. In contrast to this, contemporary Post Keynesian, Austrian and evolutionary theories, which have a genesis in Joseph Schumpeter and G.L.S. Shackle, endow the entrepreneur with a more aggressive and less mechanical role. These theories begin with the postulate that any activity, which aims to maximize profits, implicitly aims to maximize monopoly profits. Monopoly or above-normal profits are received through exploiting some special demand or cost advantage that creates economic distance between the firm and its nearest market rivals. Thus a profit-seeking firm is ultimately aiming to develop endogenous barriers to entry.

This assertive profit-seeking behaviour by firms involves intangible investments in the development of marketing and distribution channels, R&D, workforce training and management strategies (see Webster 1999). Investing in tangible plant and equipment *per se* will not create above-normal profits, as there is nothing unique or difficult to copy about such activities and they do not therefore result in the creation of endogenous barriers to entry. Tangible capital can be bought off the shelf and reproduced *ad infinitum* at a constant cost. Intangible assets, by contrast, are heterogeneous and difficult to copy primarily because they are heavily embodied in diverse human beings. It is investment in intangible capital that creates monopoly profits and endogenous barriers to entry and thus monopoly profits.

Essentially, this brings the discussion of the source of profits back to the original point that profits are incomes accruing to non-labour inputs. If, on the one hand, profits are received by owners of financial wealth but, on the other, their size depends on the behaviour of other human beings, then an incongruity may exist within the incentive structure between the creators of monopoly profits and their beneficiaries.

ELIZABETH WEBSTER

See also:

Capital Theory; Competition; Income Distribution; Innovation; Investment; Kaleckian Economics; Sraffian Economics; Uncertainty.

References

Kalecki, M. (1939), *Essays in the Theory of Economic Fluctuations*, Oxford: Clarendon Press.
Knight, F.H. (1921), *Risk, Uncertainty and Profit*, Boston: Houghton Mifflin.
Sraffa, P. (1960), *Production of Commodities by Means of Commodities*, Cambridge: Cambridge University Press.
Webster, E.M. (1999), *The Economics of Intangible Investment*, Cheltenham, UK and Northampton, MA, USA: Edward Elgar.

Rate of Interest

Interest is the price for the use of capital – the 'pure' remuneration of capital whatever the form of its employment, whether financial or real. If production is carried on with the firm's own capital, interest constitutes its opportunity cost and as such will enter into that normal cost which in the long run tends to be equated with the unit price. Firms would not continue to replace plant which is wearing out unless the prices for their commodities were such that they could not do better for themselves by investing their depreciation funds in gilt-edged securities; conversely, commodity prices could not permanently involve rates of return on the firms' funds exceeding the relevant rates of interest – those to be earned in the market on long-term fixed-interest securities in which there is no element of risk – by more than a normal remuneration for the 'risk and trouble' of productively employing capital. The case of share capital does not alter the fundamentals of this picture. It may be presumed that the nearest competing alternative to shares is long-term bonds, and that ordinary shares will be held only if the expected yield on them exceeds the yield on long-term bonds. As there is a significant section of the investing public ready to switch from one kind of investment to the other, this tends to maintain their respective yields at a steady level. That is to say, at any given time there will be a certain relationship between the prices of the various classes of securities: a shift in the price of one large class must be followed by a general shift in the whole range of prices. Thus a rise in prices for long-term government bonds – a fall in the long-term rate of interest resulting from the pursuing of a cheap-money policy – will be followed by a rise in prices of securities generally. But a higher quotation for existing equities implies that companies can raise capital by issuing shares on more favourable terms; in the words of Keynes, a high quotation for existing equities has 'the same effect as if (companies) could borrow at a low rate of interest' (1936, p. 151 n. 1). So the issue of common stock, as a method of financing investment available to joint-stock companies, will also become cheaper (or dearer) in the face of a persistent fall (or rise) in interest rates. We may conclude, therefore, that quite irrespective of the kind of capital employed in production a lasting lowering (or raising) of interest rates tends to make normal costs stand lower (or higher) than they would otherwise have done, and thus, by the competition among firms within each industry, to affect prices correspondingly. Given the level of money wages, any such change in the price level brought about by a lasting change in interest rates would then be accompanied by a change in the same direction in the level of prices in relation to the level of money wages, thereby causing changes in income distribution. A prolonged fall in interest rates should cause a fall in prices relative to the wage level and thereby bring about a lower rate of profit and a higher real wage, while a prolonged rise in interest rates should raise the rate of profits, and thus reduce the real wage.

Although economic theory has always looked at interest as the price for the use of capital in production, it has however also generally regarded it as a subordinate phenomenon. In the words of Joan Robinson: '[o]ver the long run, the interest rate rentiers can exact is dominated by the profits that entrepreneurs can earn, not the other way around' (1979, p. xxii). In fact, according to both classical and marginalist economists there is, between the normal rate of profit and the money rate of interest, a long-run causal relationship going from the former to the latter, so that the rate of interest is ultimately determined by those real forces which explain the course of the normal rate of profit: the real wage rate and production techniques, in the classical theory of distribution up to David Ricardo; the 'fundamental phenomena' of productivity and thrift, as far as marginalism is concerned. An important implication of this way of conceiving the relation between interest and profit is the denial of any substantial power on the part of the monetary authorities. Given the state of the real forces governing normal profit – the 'natural real rate' – the impact on the price level or on real output and accumulation of any lasting discrepancy between the courses of the two rates would force the monetary authorities to act so as to make the rate of interest move in sympathy with the rate of profit. An autonomous lowering of the lending rate by the monetary authorities would drive the price level *up*, contrary to what has been outlined in the previous paragraph; this is because overall monetary expenditure would expand as a consequence of the difference which would be created between the lending rate and the 'natural real rate'. In actual experience, however, rising prices very rarely coincide with low or falling interest rates and the opposite is the general rule (the so-called 'Gibson Paradox'). Instead of assuming a lowering of interest rates by the monetary authorities, other things being equal, one would then simply have to make the alternative assumption that a difference between the rate of profit and the rate of interest generally arises because it is *the former* which rises or falls, while the latter remains unchanged and only belatedly follows (see Wicksell 1906 [1962], pp. 204–5).

An unprejudiced observation of concrete reality clearly played a significant part in Keynes's interpretation of the rate of interest as a 'monetary phenomenon'. The fact that Keynes was far from being entirely happy with his monetary explanation of interest (Keynes 1937 [1973], p. 213), did not shake his conviction that the rate of interest is *not* determined by the real forces envisaged by the neoclassical theory. Unfortunately, the persistence in Keynes's analysis of some traditional neoclassical premises seriously weakens his concept of the rate of interest as a magnitude determined by monetary factors. In particular, the idea of an investment demand schedule constitutes an obstacle which a monetary theory of interest cannot easily overcome. Notwithstanding the statement in the *General Theory* that he 'no longer' regards Wicksell's concept of a 'natural real rate' as 'a most promising idea' (Keynes 1936, p. 243), the natural rate is still there, as the rate that would ensure equality between full-employment saving and investment decisions. Keynes's underemployment equilibrium is ultimately the result of the presence in the economic system of factors that hinder the possibility of bringing the actual rate of interest down to its 'natural' or full-employment level. It is, in other words, the result of a limited flexibility of the money rate of interest. This limited flexibility is actually all that Keynes has to offer as a basis for his non-orthodox concept of interest as a monetary phenomenon. But if one takes into account the fact that even in Wicksell there is no automatic gravitation of the money rate towards the level of the natural real rate (banking policy having to perform the task), then the difference between the two authors will not appear that marked. They both share the idea of an inverse relation between the rate of interest and investment decisions, while the conflict of opinions is essentially centred upon the degree of the (non-automatic) flexibility of the rate of interest, in the face of discrepancies between full-employment savings and investment decisions. One can say that it was largely in the light of this comparison that the neoclassical synthesis could argue, successfully and with foundation, that the determination of the current rate of interest by the intersection of the supply schedule of money and the demand schedule for money, while adequate for showing that the flexibility of the rate of interest is not of an automatic nature, is, however, insufficient to sustain the thesis of a *limited* flexibility of the rate of interest. And if current money interest can normally be brought to, and kept at, its 'natural' level – provided the monetary authority applies to its action 'a modest measure of persistence and consistency of purpose' (Keynes 1936, p. 204) – then the neoclassical real forces of productivity and thrift may still be regarded as the ultimate determinants of the equilibrium rate of interest.

Things are quite different if there is no such thing as a 'natural' rate of interest – a normal rate of profit, that is to say, determined independently by real forces and which can be taken as the *primum movens*. We would be back in this case to the picture outlined at the beginning of this entry, that is, it would be difficult not to acknowledge that, given money wages and production techniques, a lowering (raising) of interest rates by the monetary authorities would actually drive the price level *down* (up), owing to the adaptation of prices to normal costs caused by competition. There would thus be nothing 'paradoxical' in the positive correlation between interest and prices one generally finds in actual experience. And at a given level of real output, the rate of interest would also regulate the quantity of money in active circulation – a quantity that adapts itself to the needs of trade – via its influence on the price level: interest, prices and the quantity of money would all move in the same direction, with the policy-determined interest rate acting as the *primum movens* of the process.

The 'monetary' explanation of distribution that I started to develop a few years ago (see Pivetti 1991) is precisely an attempt to emancipate us from any real explanation of the rate of interest – an attempt prompted by Sraffa's suggestion that in the necessary long-run connection between normal profit and money interest it is the latter which is susceptible to setting the pace (see Sraffa 1960, p. 33). By focusing on the actual mechanism whereby the rate of interest is likely to set the pace in its connection with normal profit, eventually I got hold of the notion of money interest as an autonomous determinant of normal money production costs which governs the ratio of prices to money wages. As pointed out earlier, this interpretation of interest does not require any particular assumption as to the kind of capital employed in production: borrowed, in the form of shares or a firm's own capital. For any given situation of technique, there is a price level that depends on the money wage and on the money rate of interest, with the latter acting as the regulator of the ratio of the price level to the money wage. This ratio is thus seen as the connecting link between the rate of interest and the rate of profit: by the competition among firms within each industry, a persistent change in the rate of interest causes a change in the same direction in the level of prices in relation to the level of money wages, thereby generating a corresponding change in the rate of profits and an inverse change in the real wage. Wage bargaining and monetary policy come out of this analysis as the main channels through which class relations act in determining distribution. Class relations are seen as tending to act primarily upon the profit rate, via the money rate of interest, rather than upon the real wage as maintained by both the English classical economists and Marx. Indeed, the level of real wage prevailing in any given situation is viewed as the *final result* of the whole process by which distribution of income between workers and capitalists is actually derived. Interest rate determination is thus not seen as constrained by a normal profitability of capital which is predetermined by some natural, technical or accidental circumstances – be they the relative scarcity of capital and labour, a 'subsistence' real wage, or the rate of growth of the economic system. Rather the rate of interest is regarded as a policy-determined variable, a conventional monetary phenomenon 'determined from outside the system of production' (Sraffa 1960, p. 33) and not subject to any general law. One can describe interest rate determination in terms of sets of objectives and constraints, on the action of the monetary authorities, which have different weights both among the various countries and for a particular country at different times (see Pivetti 1991, pp. 11–17, 33–6), and with which, to a very large extent, the parties' relative strength is ultimately intertwined.

MASSIMO PIVETTI

See also:

Bastard Keynesianism; Endogenous Money; Income Distribution; Liquidity Preference; Monetary Policy; Sraffian Economics.

References

Keynes, J.M. (1936), *The General Theory of Employment, Interest and Money*, London: Macmillan, 1964.
Keynes, J.M. (1937), 'Alternative theories of the rate of interest', *Economic Journal*, **47** (186), 241–52. Reprinted in *The Collected Writings of John Maynard Keynes. Volume XIV: The General Theory and After. Defence and Development*, D. Moggridge (ed.), London: Macmillan and Cambridge University Press for the Royal Economic Society, 1973, pp. 201–15.
Pivetti, M. (1991), *An Essay on Money and Distribution*, London: Macmillan.
Robinson, J. (1979), *The Generalisation of the General Theory and Other Essays*, London: Macmillan.
Sraffa, P. (1960), *Production of Commodities by Means of Commodities*, Cambridge: Cambridge University Press.
Wicksell, K. (1906 [1962]), *Lectures on Political Economy. Volume II: Money and Credit*, London: Routledge & Kegan Paul.

Saving

What is the relationship between saving behaviour in capitalist economies and their macroeconomic performance? This question is a hardy perennial in the history of economics, and one that has carried great theoretical and practical significance through its many revivals. It is easy to see why this is so, since any economy that aspires to long-term increases in productivity and average living standards must devise effective means of raising the quantity and quality of its capital stock. The role of saving is central to this process, though how exactly it exerts influence has long been a matter of contention.

Debates on how saving behaviour affects long-term growth and business cycles stretch back to those between David Ricardo and Thomas Malthus on whether Say's Law of markets that 'supply creates its own demand' can be violated, thereby creating the possibility for 'general gluts' or depressions. The Keynesian revolution, of course, was also focused on this issue, as Keynes rebelled against the 1934 'Treasury View' that higher saving rates were a necessary precondition for stimulating investment and lifting the British economy out of depression. Arguing against the intuitively appealing notion that an adequate pool of saving must exist before the funds for investment can be drawn, Keynes and Richard Kahn developed the concept of the multiplier to demonstrate the counterintuitive point that higher levels of investment will generate higher saving as well. Many of the most pressing policy concerns of today remain centred on the relationship between saving and macroeconomic performance.

What is saving? The answer is not obvious. Moreover, answering the most basic questions about the impact of saving on macroeconomic activity – including whether saving rates are rising or falling – depends on how one defines and measures the term (this discussion follows Pollin 1997b). Two standard approaches to measuring saving are as an increase in net worth and as the residual of income after consumption. As accounting categories, these two saving measures should be equal in value. But making this distinction raises a major question: when one considers the category of asset-specific saving, should the value of assets be measured at historical costs or market values? Only the historical cost measure is equivalent conceptually to residual saving. Measured at market values, asset-specific saving will of course fluctuate along with fluctuations in asset prices themselves.

Another major issue is distinguishing *gross* saving, including depreciation allowances, and *net* saving, which excludes depreciation. In principle, net saving measures the funds available to finance economic growth, while gross saving would also include funds set aside for replacing worn-out capital stock. In practice, however, depreciation allowances do not simply finance replacement. Rather, they are primarily used to finance investment in capital stock that represents some advance over previous vintages. As such, depreciation funds are also utilized to promote economic growth.

What is the most appropriate definition of saving? In fact, for the purposes of economic analysis, there are legitimate reasons to examine each concept. There are three basic reasons for considering saving patterns by any measure. The first is to observe households' portfolio choices, in which case asset-specific saving is obviously the only option. The second purpose would be to understand consumer behaviour. Here we would want to measure consumption directly relative to income, making saving a residual. However, asset-specific saving at market values would also be important here in so far as it contributes to understanding consumer behaviour. The third reason for measuring saving is with respect to examining its role in determining credit supply, that is, the source of funds available to finance investment and other uses of funds. This role for saving is clearly the primary consideration among analysts seeking to understand the relationship between saving and macroeconomic performance. In fact, however, the connections between any given measures of saving, the provision of credit, and overall rates of economic activity are quite loose. We can see some indication of such loose connections through Table 2, on the US economy.

Table 2 Saving rates, credit supply and GDP growth for the US economy (in percentages)

	1960–69	1970–79	1980–90	1991–2000
Net private saving/GDP	9.6	9.8	8.9	6.3
Gross private saving/GDP	17.1	18.4	19.1	16.4
Net worth private saving/GDP	25.2	35.2	32.4	30.5
Total lending/gross private saving	60.5	86.9	106.1	106.4
Real GDP growth	4.4	3.3	2.9	3.2

Note: For brevity, two sets of cycles (1970–73/1974–79 and 1980–81/1982–90) have been merged.

Sources: US National Income and Product Accounts; US Flow of Funds Accounts.

The first three rows of the table show annual figures on net, gross and net worth saving in the US relative to nominal GDP between 1960 and 2000. The data are grouped on a peak-to-peak basis according to National Bureau of Economic Analysis business cycles. The last two rows of the table show, respectively, measures of credit supply and overall activity: first the ratio of total lending in the US economy relative to gross private saving, then the average annual growth rate of real GDP.

To begin with, the table shows substantial differences in the cycle-to-cycle behaviour of the three saving ratios. For example, between the 1970s and 1980s cycles, the net saving ratio fell from 9.8 to 8.9 per cent, the gross saving ratio rose from 18.4 to 19.1 per cent, and the net worth ratio fell from 39.5 to 32.4 per cent. Meanwhile, between these same two cycles, the lending/saving ratio rose sharply from 86.9 to 106.1 per cent, while the rate of GDP growth fell from 3.3 to 2.9 per cent.

At the very least, one can conclude from these patterns that we cannot take for granted any analytic foundation through which we assume a simple one-way pre-Keynesian causal connection whereby, as James Meade (1975, p. 82) put it, 'a dog called saving wagged its tail labelled investment' instead of the Keynesian connection in which 'a dog called investment wagged its tail labelled saving'.

The pre-Keynesian orthodox view held that the saving rate is the fundamental determinant of the rate of capital accumulation, because the saving rate determines the interest rate at which funds will be advanced to finance investment. Keynes's challenge to this position constituted the core of the ensuing Keynesian revolution in economic theory. Nevertheless, what we may call the 'causal saving' view was nevertheless restored fairly quickly to its central role in the mainstream macroeconomic literature.

Despite neglect among mainstream economists, the 'causal investment' perspective has advanced substantially since the publication of Keynes's *General Theory* (1936). One major development has been precisely to establish a fuller understanding of the interrelationship among saving, financial structures and real activity. This has brought recognition that the logic of the causal investment position rests on the analysis of the financial system as well as the real-sector multiplier–accelerator model.

Of course, the multiplier–accelerator analysis is the basis for the 'paradox of thrift', that is, low saving *rates* (saving as a proportion of income) can yield high *levels* of saving and vice versa when real resources are not fully employed. However, considered by itself, the multiplier–accelerator analysis neglects a crucial prior consideration: that the initial increment of autonomous investment must be financed, and the rate at which financing is available will influence the size of this investment increment and the subsequent expansion of output, income and saving.

Kaldor (1960) was an early critic of the multiplier–accelerator causal investment position, and his argument was revived by Asimakopulos (1983). Their critique focuses on the interregnum between an autonomous investment increase and the attainment, through the multiplier–accelerator process, of a new level of saving–investment equilibrium. The Kaldor–Asimakopulos position is that, as a general case during such interregnum periods, intermediaries could not be expected to accept a reduction in liquidity without receiving an interest rate inducement to do so. Rather, for intermediaries to supply an increased demand for credit would require either a rise in interest rates or a prior increase in saving. As such, low rates of saving again yield high interest rates and a dampening of investment – an argument, in other words, that returns us to the causal saving position.

In fact, Keynes himself addressed this issue, working from his theory of liquidity preference and interest rate determination. But this dimension of his argument is far less well known than the consumption function and multiplier analysis, at least in part because it is less fully developed in the *General Theory* itself.

Holding the level of saving constant, Keynes argued that the banking system – private institutions as well as the central bank – was capable of financing investment growth during the interregnum without necessarily inducing a rise in interest rates. That is, as he put it, 'In general, the banks hold the key position in the transition from a lower to a higher scale of activity' (1973, p. 222). Keynes based his position on a central institutional fact, that private banks and other intermediaries, not ultimate savers, are responsible for channelling the supply of credit to non-financial investors. The central bank can also substantially encourage credit growth by increasing the supply of reserves to the private banking system, thereby raising the banks' liquidity. But, even without central bank initiative, the private intermediaries could still increase their lending if they were willing to accept a temporary decline in their own liquidity. The reason that the fall in the intermediaries' liquidity would be only temporary is that liquidity would rise again, even before the completion of the multiplier, when the recipients of the autonomous investment funds deposited those funds with an intermediary. Moreover, the completion of the multiplier process would mean that an increase in saving equal to the investment increment had been generated. Overall, then, it is through this chain of reasoning that Keynes reached what he called 'the most fundamental of my conclusions within this field', that 'the investment market can become congested through a shortage of cash. It can never become congested through a shortage of saving' (1973, p. 222).

This more fully developed Keynesian position emphasizes clearly the central role of financial institutions in establishing the relationship between saving and macroeconomic activity. More recent literature has developed this idea in several directions (see the contributions in Pollin 1997a). Other researchers have broadened further this investigation as to the relationship among saving, institutional structures and macro activity. Indeed, in the

1990s a substantial literature developed arguing that financial systems that channelled savings within a tighter regulatory structure tended to outperform economies in which capital markets operated more freely (Pollin 1995 reviews this literature). Countries categorized as having more tightly regulated 'bank-based' financial systems were Germany, France, Japan and, among the less-developed Asian countries, South Korea. The US and the UK represented the less-regulated 'capital marked-based' system. But, by the mid-1990s, the debate over the relative merits of these systems was short-circuited by two factors: first the stock market bubble in the United States, which lent temporary credence to the idea that capital market-based systems could operate more effectively; and, second, the global ascendance of neoliberal economic policies in economies such as Japan, France and Korea, contributing, in turn, to greater economic instability in these economies in the late 1990s. But a restoration of this line of research on alternative financial institutional environments will be critical for developing new policy regimes that can promote more stable as well as more egalitarian growth prospects.

More broadly within the realm of policy, there always have been clear important normative issues at play in the debates over saving behaviour. The agenda following from a causal saving perspective consists of seeking to raise national saving rates through measures such as providing preferential tax treatment to capital income, eliminating government deficit spending, or even paying off completely outstanding government debts. These will normally also generate a less equal distribution of income. Building from a causal investment analytic framework points to policy approaches that directly encourage higher investment while also promoting egalitarian distributional outcomes. Such measures would include increasing aggregate demand and employment through fiscal and monetary interventions or more equal income redistribution, or, through various institutional reforms, giving preferential access to credit for productive private investment relative to unproductive speculative expenditures. The policy ideas that flow from a causal investment perspective are committed to utilizing most effectively the interconnections observed in research among growth, stability and distributional equity.

ROBERT POLLIN

See also:

Consumption; Keynes's *General Theory*; Multiplier; Say's Law.

References

Asimakopulos, A. (1983), 'Kalecki and Keynes on finance, investment and saving', *Cambridge Journal of Economics*, **7** (3–4), 221–33.

Kaldor, Nicholas (1960 [1939]), 'Speculation and economic activity', in N. Kaldor, *Essays on Economic Stability and Growth*, London: Duckworth, pp. 17–58.
Keynes, John Maynard (1936), *The General Theory of Employment, Interest and Money*, New York: Harcourt Brace.
Keynes, John Maynard (1973 [1938]), 'The "ex ante" theory of the interest rate', in *The Collected Writings of John Maynard Keynes, Volume XIV: The General Theory and After: Defence and Development*, London: Macmillan for the Royal Economic Society, pp. 215–23.
Meade, James (1975), 'The Keynesian revolution', in M. Keynes (ed.), *Essays on John Maynard Keynes*, Cambridge: Cambridge University Press, pp. 82–8.
Pollin, Robert (1995), 'Financial structure and egalitarian economic policy', *New Left Review*, **214**, November–December, 26–61.
Pollin, Robert (ed.) (1997a), *The Macroeconomics of Saving, Finance and Investment*, Ann Arbor: University of Michigan Press.
Pollin, Robert (1997b), 'Financial intermediation and the variability of the saving constraint', in Pollin (ed.), pp. 309–66.

Say's Law

Say's Law, also known as the 'law of markets', is a set of ideas and propositions that were originally formulated during the classical period in the history of economics. Despite the name, Jean-Baptiste Say was neither the inventor of the law nor was he its clearest and most coherent advocate. Important contributions to the development of the law were made by Adam Smith, James Mill, David Ricardo and John Stuart Mill. After the demise of classical political economy and the rise to dominance of neoclassical economics, Say's Law remained essentially unchallenged, even though economists paid much less attention to it. Say's Law has always generated opponents. During the classical period, Thomas Robert Malthus, J.C.L. Simonde de Sismondi and Karl Marx were some of the most important critics; in modern times, John Maynard Keynes undoubtedly provided the most radical and clearly articulated critique of Say's Law. Only Keynes, however, succeeded in convincing a significant part of the profession that the law was incorrect and had to be rejected (for a thorough historical reconstruction of the debate on Say's Law, see Sowell 1972, but also Baumol 1977).

The basic idea underlying the 'law of markets' is that there cannot be any obstacle to economic growth deriving from an insufficient level of aggregate demand. Whatever the level of aggregate supply, it will give rise to an equal level of aggregate demand. If there are obstacles to growth, they depend on other factors, such as, for Ricardo, decreasing returns in agriculture. In the analyses of markets carried out by classical adherents to Say's Law, the production and sale of goods generates an income which is either spent for consumption or saved. What is saved, however, is also spent, as it is devoted to investment. Thus production gives rise to purchasing power of equal value that is entirely spent to buy the current production itself.

Situations in which aggregate supply exceeds aggregate demand are therefore impossible.

The analysis was based on the assumption that the exchange of goods through money is conceptually the same as barter, in which it is impossible that any divergence between demand and supply arises because sellers are necessarily at the same time buyers. Money was regarded merely as a device to facilitate exchanges, which was therefore demanded only for this function. It was assumed that people do not draw any utility from holding money in a larger amount than that required to exchange commodities. The law in its classical formulation also implied that the existing productive capacity of the economy is always fully utilized, even though this does not mean that labour is fully employed: the existing productive capacity might be insufficient to employ the entire labour force. In other words, if there is unemployment, it does not result from an insufficient level of demand but from an insufficient growth of capital.

It is hard to find Say's Law expressed in these terms by any post-classical economist. None the less, neoclassical economics left the law of markets essentially unchallenged. Its basic aspects were accepted: money was still regarded essentially as a mere device to make exchanges more efficient, and it was held that saving is necessarily transformed into investment. However, there were some significant differences between the classical and neoclassical versions of the law. First of all, classical economists simply assumed that saving *is* investment, so that any discrepancy between the two variables is impossible; neoclassical economists, instead, admitted the possibility that saving and investment diverge. Such a divergence, however, would be eliminated by some equilibrating mechanism. Second, for the classics, the law only implied the full employment of capital; whereas, for neoclassical economics, the validity of the law also implied the full employment of labour. Also in this case, unemployment of labour would be eliminated by an equilibrating mechanism.

For Smith, Ricardo and so on, the transformation of saving into investment was essentially a direct process, in the sense that savers themselves were those who invested. For the neoclassicals, the process was essentially indirect: saving and investment decisions are not necessarily made simultaneously and by the same people. For this reason saving and investment may diverge; but market mechanisms take care of this by ensuring that the equality is restored. The variable that plays this equilibrating role is the rate of interest. Abstaining from present consumption (saving, that is, the supply of capital) is a direct function of the interest rate, and investment (the demand for capital) is an inverse function, so that any divergence between the two variables is eliminated by variations in the interest rate. For the classics, the possible existence of unemployment did not give rise to any adjusting mechanism that would bring the economy to the full employment of labour; for neoclassical economists, variations of the (real) wage rate bring the economy to full employment. If there is an excess supply of labour, a decrease in the real wage rate would induce firms to increase their demand for labour and eliminate unemployment.

These analytical differences between classical and neoclassical economists can also be pointed out by expressing Say's Law in two different ways: as an *identity* and as an *equality*. Classical economists, by assuming that saving is investment, accepted the law as an identity (the equality between aggregate supply and demand is always true); neoclassical economists, by concentrating on equilibrating mechanisms, accepted the law as an equality, which is true only in equilibrium (see, for example, Sowell 1972, pp. 34–8).

Keynes held that, before him, Malthus went closest to a satisfactory criticism of Say's Law, but he was probably far too generous to Malthus's critique of Say and Ricardo. Malthus did not provide a coherent alternative analytical framework, as he maintained the assumption that saving is investment. It was Marx who developed a more satisfactory critique of the law of markets, which resembles Keynes's own criticism in several respects (Sardoni 1991). In Marx, as well as in Keynes, the rejection of Say's Law is based on the idea that the analysis of the working of the economy must be carried out by taking account of money, which plays a more crucial role than merely being a device to facilitate exchange. For Marx, the existence of money breaks the unity between selling and buying; the exchange of commodities through money is not conceptually the same as barter. Those who own money can always decide not to convert it into commodities and, hence, break the unity of exchange. In particular, capitalists can decide to keep money 'idle' instead of investing, whenever they expect that producing commodities will not be profitable.

Turning now to consider Keynes, it is useful to distinguish between two different analytical levels at which he developed his critique of Say's Law. On the one hand, he carried out a critique of the law that is addressed to the essential theoretical foundations on which it rests; on the other hand, especially in *The General Theory*, he also developed a criticism that is more complex and articulated, as it takes into account analytical aspects that are typical of the neoclassical version of the law.

Keynes's essential critique hinges on the idea that what makes the law untenable is that the economy of the world in which we live is a *monetary economy*, that is, an economy in which money plays a much more fundamental role than the advocates of the law implied. The income of the factors of production, which is generated by production, is not necessarily spent entirely on current output; income not spent on consumption goods can be kept in the form of money rather than being transformed into goods.

The explanation of why individuals may wish to hold money as a store of value is one of the key elements of Keynes's theory. He was deeply convinced that the economic and social environment is dominated by uncertainty, which cannot be reduced to risk and treated with the traditional tools of probability theory. But, notwithstanding uncertainty, individuals have to make decisions and to act. They do so by 'pretending' that the calculation of the probabilities of a series of prospective advantages and disadvantages is possible. In order to behave in such a way, some techniques are devised, which essentially are conventions like assuming that the present is a reliable guide to the future despite the past evidence to the contrary, or trying to conform to the behaviour of the majority.

These are, for Keynes, 'flimsy' foundations for decision making, and they are subject to sudden and violent changes. It is in this context that money plays a crucial role, different from its function as a medium of exchange. Money demanded as a store of value is, for Keynes, an indicator of people's distrust of their conventions concerning the future. When conventions break down and expectations become more uncertain, demanding money is a sort of 'insurance' against uncertainty. The demand for money, however, is in no way similar to the demand for any other good or service: an increase in the demand for it, which means a decrease in the demand for some other goods or services, does not give rise to a corresponding increase in its production. Money has a zero elasticity of production (Keynes 1936, p. 230). Thus, as in Marx's analysis, money can be demanded and kept idle rather than being spent on goods or services. This is the basic reason why Say's Law does not hold.

Keynes, however, criticized the law in its neoclassical version; therefore, he also had to consider those specific aspects on which neoclassical economists concentrated. In particular, he had to reject the idea that there is an equilibrating mechanism that brings aggregate supply and demand to equality by ensuring the equality between saving and investment. For Keynes, saving is not necessarily transformed into investment. The act of saving does not imply the supply of a corresponding amount of funds to those who wish to invest. Once the amount of saving has been decided, the individual has to decide whether to keep it in the form of money or to part with it for a certain time, that is, to lend it. Such a decision depends on the individual's liquidity preference. This vision of saving decisions implies that the interest rate is not a return to saving on waiting as such. In fact, 'if a man hoards his saving in cash, he earns no interest though he saves as much as before'. The interest rate, instead, is 'the reward for parting with liquidity' (Keynes 1936, p. 167). Therefore, the rate of interest cannot play the equilibrating role that is given to it in neoclassical analysis. There can be situations in which liquidity preference is so high that the interest rate is at too high a level to allow investment to reach its full-employment level, that is, that level that ensures the level of aggregate demand associated with the full employment of labour and capacity. In other words, it is not true that any level of supply whatsoever generates an equal level of demand.

Keynesian economists of the neoclassical synthesis accepted Keynes's rejection of Say's Law but in their analyses, based on the IS–LM model, they concentrated on the more technical aspects of the reasons why the interest rate cannot guarantee the full-employment level of investment (for example, the so-called 'liquidity trap'), while Keynes's deeper critique of market economies and his notion of uncertainty were essentially neglected. Post Keynesian economists, by emphasizing the importance of decision making under uncertainty, more clearly link the rejection of Say's Law to an alternative notion of the essential features of market economies. Contemporary mainstream economics, having rejected Keynes's theory altogether, has returned to the full acceptance of Say's Law, even though macro economists hardly ever mention it in their analyses.

CLAUDIO SARDONI

See also:

Bastard Keynesianism; Keynes's *General Theory*; Liquidity Preference; Rate of Interest; Uncertainty; Unemployment; Walrasian Economics.

References

Baumol, W.J. (1977), 'Say's (at least) eight laws, or what Say and James Mill may really have meant', *Economica*, **44** (174), 145–62.
Keynes, J.M. (1936), *The General Theory of Employment, Interest and Money*, London: Macmillan.
Sardoni, C. (1991), 'Marx and Keynes: the critique of Say's Law', in G.A. Caravale (ed.), *Marx and Modern Economic Analysis*, Vol. II, Aldershot: Edward Elgar, pp. 219–39.
Sowell, T. (1972), *Say's Law. An Historical Analysis*, Princeton: Princeton University Press.

Socialism

Most Post Keynesians are not socialists. But almost all are reformers, who advocate major reforms of capitalism, designed not only to help stability, but also to increase equality. There is nothing incompatible between advocating major reforms in the short run and advocating a complete change to socialism in the long run. So a minority of Post Keynesians are also socialists.

What is meant by socialism? Fortunately, the Soviet Union is dead and buried. So we can ask what a Post Keynesian approach to socialism may be. If one wants to consider something called socialism, there are three questions to be asked: the role of democracy in socialism, the plan versus the market in socialism, and the degree of equality in socialism.

All Post Keynesian socialists are agreed that any socialist society must be democratic. To understand the issue fully, however, the long and convoluted history of this issue must be briefly mentioned. Karl Marx and Friedrich Engels fought in the 1848 revolution for democracy in Germany and they supported every movement for democracy in their lifetime. European socialist parties, from the German Social Democrats to the British Labour party grew up in a struggle for the extension of democracy, including suffrage rights for male workers and for women.

After the Bolshevik revolution of 1917 in Russia, however, the embattled Bolsheviks became less and less democratic, with 60 years of one-party dictatorship. Their defence was a parody of Marxism: they argued that the Soviet Union had only one class, the working class, so it needed only one party to be democratic. In truth, it was a dictatorship over workers and everyone else – and the horrors of that dictatorship set back the cause of anything called socialism by many decades.

Socialism means that the people rule over the economy, not a small group of capitalists or a small group of bureaucrats appointed by a dictator. A precise definition would be that socialism means the extension of democracy from the political sphere into the economic sphere. Some of the procedural necessities and safeguards in the political sphere under socialism are spelled out in detail by Ralph Miliband (1994). In the economic sphere, two types of democratic procedures have been advocated. One is to have local, state and national ownership by a democratically elected government. The other procedure is to have corporate boards democratically elected by the employees of each enterprise. Of course, there may be any mix of these two forms – even a role for a democratic government representative and regulations within an employee-run enterprise. This poses the question of the manner of control of the economy.

Post Keynesian socialists are divided on what would be the best way to coordinate a socialist economy. Some – probably a minority at present – favour some form of democratic central planning. Others – perhaps a majority – favour a market type of socialism (for a good introduction to the debate among socialists, see Ollman 1998).

The Soviet Union had extreme central planning with dictatorship. In that model, almost all industry and about half of agriculture was directly owned and run by the government. A group of planners, appointed by the ruling party, drew up a plan for the whole economy. To do this, they had to know (i) the available resources, including all known raw materials, every type and quality of labour, and every type and quality of capital. They also had to know (ii) the preferences of the government and all consumers. Finally, they had to know (iii) all the technological coefficients telling them what could be produced with a given amount of resources. Of course, even with the best presently available information network, collecting all such information down to the enterprise level would be impossible in any limited amount of time, such as six months to a year. So they dealt instead with broad aggregates of each industry, divided at most into about 500 categories. With that general information, they calculated several variants of a national plan. It was then up to the government dictatorship to decide on which variant would be used, depending on its time preferences between present production and investment for future expansion. The plan which was adopted was then handed down as law to the managers appointed by the dictatorship. Although some discussion was allowed in the early stages, criticism of the final plan was not allowed, nor was it healthy for employees to criticize the managers.

Such excessive planning in a dictatorial setting nevertheless managed to transform the economy from an underdeveloped, mainly rural and agricultural one, to the second largest industrialized economy in the world. From 1928 to 1989 – excluding the Second World War – the Soviet economy never suffered a decline in aggregate output. Moreover, it had full employment that entire time. So it has been argued that, whatever its other problems, central planning can provide for full employment, development out of underdevelopment, and rapid growth rates for at least a time. On the other side, it was clear that the Soviet economy suffered from a high level of inefficiency. That inefficiency grew worse as the economy became more complex and the problems of central planning grew. So it has been argued that central planning always leads to enormous inefficiency – though whether it is worse than the crises of capitalism is another question. The truth, however, is that the Soviet experience gave us very limited lessons. It was not democratic planning, but planning under a one-party dictatorship. Dictatorships must lead to vast inefficiency in government-owned enterprises. There can be no criticism of cabinet decisions on the plan, there can be no criticisms of the details of planning at the lower levels, and there can be no criticism of management (until after they are fired). There can be no freedom for scientists to choose the direction of scientific research because the ultimate decisions on the direction and funding of research will be under political control. Thus one cannot say whether Soviet inefficiency resulted from excessive planning, from dictatorship, or from their combination. If it was the combination, how should the blame and the praise be allocated?

Those who argue that central planning always leads to unacceptable inefficiency argue that socialism would be better with a market form. Managers could be told to maximize profit, rather than follow a plan. But most advocates of market socialism would argue for employee-controlled enterprises, since this would provide a high level of direct democracy. Of course, government could control some functions, such as environmental regulations, while employees controlled the rest. The only extensive experience known of a form of market socialism with employee control of enterprises was in Yugoslavia – but that again was conditioned by a one-party dictatorship that affected the results. Yugoslavia did seem to have considerable enterprise efficiency, such as better quality control than the Soviet Union. But as Yugoslavia moved from central planning to independent enterprises, it also witnessed all the problems of capitalism, including monopoly profits, inflation, and cycles of boom and bust with cyclical unemployment. It also moved towards a society with great emphasis on consumerism, and with feelings of helplessness by unemployed or employees in firms doing poorly or going bankrupt. There was plenty of food and other goods in the stores, but an unequal income distribution which meant that many people could not buy an adequate basket of goods. Many people began to work in more than one job. So market socialism has been attacked as leading to instability and alienation.

Many Post Keynesian socialists conclude that, under present technological and social circumstances, a feasible socialism must combine market and plan. The smallest businesses could remain private. Medium-sized businesses could all be employee controlled so as to provide incentives and efficiency and internal democracy. To stabilize the economy, the giant conglomerates require direct public control and planning. Even the largest, government-owned firms would leave many functions, such as safety, hours and forms of the production process, to internal democracy. This is not a vision of utopia, but it would mean the end of extraction of profits from employees by a small elite and it would mean a large degree of economic democracy through planning by democratic governments at local, state, national and world levels, as well as a large measure of internal democracy for firms with the most employees.

There is vast inequality under capitalism. John Maynard Keynes advocated greater equality of income distribution, both to increase the stability of capitalism and for ethical reasons. All Post Keynesians advocate more equality under capitalism and would surely endorse more equality under socialism.

Socialism by itself does not necessarily mean equality. If all capitalist ownership and profits are eliminated, then the single largest source of inequality will be eliminated. In addition, democratic control of the economy may bring a decision for greater equality, but it could mean a decision to retain wide disparities of income. Under centrally planned socialism, where all income is determined by planners and politicians, it is possible for a democratically elected government to reduce drastically the inequality of wages and salaries, but it is also possible to increase wage and salary inequality. In a market socialist economy, the market decides; so one person might earn $5,000 a year, while another earns $1,000,000 a month,

In the old Soviet Union, Stalin decided that the conservative argument, that great income inequalities are necessary to provide great incentives, was correct. Therefore, for much of Soviet history, the degree of inequality of wage and salary income was about the same as in the United States. It is true that private profit income was outlawed, but the elite did receive secret income and very important non-monetary privileges, including villas, chauffeured cars and medical specialists.

At the other extreme, in the utopia described by Edward Bellamy (1887) there was central planning with equal wages for everyone – with only a few medals or fewer hours for the most dirty, dangerous and difficult jobs. But, given the present psychology of employees under capitalism, it is true that equal wages would enormously reduce incentives to work. Perhaps decades of new experience and propaganda would change that psychology, but that is speculation.

Still more utopian is the world described by Ursula Le Guin (1974), in which there is central planning, but there is no money or prices, so everyone can take what they need – with only peer pressure as a goad – to work or a limit on demand. With present psychology, that would mean almost no work and unlimited demand – an impossible situation. In addition, aside from incentive and demand problems, central planning with no explicit prices or money would be very difficult in any complex economy.

Most Post Keynesians would urge fiscal means to reduce inequality. They advocate highly progressive taxes together with government spending to provide certain free goods and services to everyone with negligible effect on incentives. If the items are necessities, such as health care, then there will be only a limited increase in demand.

Health care is provided to some extent by every industrialized country other than the United States. In the United States, over 40 million people have no guaranteed health care. If a socialist society provided free health care to all, that would reduce inequality, provide for a basic need and increase productivity. Another area of struggle in many capitalist countries is the provision of free higher education. If a socialist society wished to go further, it could ensure that everyone has a minimum necessary amount of food to eat, a certain minimum level of housing, and free public transportation, with no economic disruption if this is done gradually.

HOWARD J. SHERMAN

See also:
Kaleckian Economics; Transition Economies.

References

Bellamy, Edward (1887 [1987]), *Looking Backward*, New York: Modern Library.
Le Guin, Ursula (1974), *The Dispossessed*, New York: Harper Prism.
Miliband, Ralph (1994), *Socialism*, New York: Verso.
Ollman, Bertell (1998), *Market Socialism: The Debate among Socialists*, New York and London: Routledge.

Sraffian Economics

Among the many unsettled issues within Post Keynesian economics, one of the most divisive concerns the relationship between Keynes's theoretical framework and the analytical tradition associated with Piero Sraffa (1898–1983). In the 1970s, Sraffian economics was generally regarded not only as compatible with Post Keynesianism, but as an important branch of it. (The essays in Nell 1980, for example were the culmination of a project to integrate Keynesian, Kaleckian, Sraffian and Marxian insights into a unified Post Keynesian account of postwar capitalism.) By the end of the 1980s, however, this view had largely given way to the presumption that the two frameworks are distinct and, in at least some key respects, incompatible.

Sraffa is best known as the author of *Production of Commodities by Means of Commodities* (1960), which provided the basis for a capital-theoretic critique of the neoclassical theory of distribution. Orthodox theory explains income distribution in terms of the interaction of the demand for and supply of scarce factors of production. The theory requires (i) that the endowment of each factor of production be known *prior* to the determination of prices and distribution; and (ii) that the demand for any factor declines as the price of its productive services increases. Sraffa's analysis suggested that in a long-period setting neither of these conditions can be presumed to hold for the factor called 'capital'. Since capital is composed of many different kinds of produced means of production, whose prices themselves depend upon the real wage and the profit rate, the endowment of capital, specified as a value magnitude, cannot be known prior to distribution. Moreover, changes in distribution can cause the prices of capital goods to vary in highly complex ways, so that no systematic relation can be established between the profit rate and the capital intensity of production. The upshot of all this is that the substitution mechanisms that underpin the price-elastic factor demand functions of neoclassical theory lack solid foundations. But these substitution mechanisms are precisely what justify the orthodox claim that, in the absence of impediments to the adjustment of prices, market forces will push the economy towards full employment.

The capital critique was part of a larger constructive agenda that motivated Sraffa's scientific work from the late 1920s. His objective was to lay a foundation for the reconstruction of the classical political economy approach pioneered by Adam Smith, David Ricardo and Karl Marx that had been, as Sraffa (1960, p. v) put it, 'submerged and forgotten' with the rise of neoclassical economics. A distinctive feature of the classical theory is its treatment of income distribution not in terms of the equilibrating interaction of price-elastic supply and demand functions, but as the outcome of the interplay of class interests in a historically conditioned institutional setting. Profits are conceived as a residual, or surplus, appropriated by the owners of capital after the replacement of the material inputs – including the wage goods consumed by workers – used up in the production of aggregate output; for this reason the classical theory is sometimes called the surplus approach.

In their analysis of value and distribution the classicals treated the following variables as parametric: (i) the size and composition of the social product; (ii) the technical conditions of production; and (iii) the real wages of workers. The equation systems of Parts I and II of *Production of Commodities* establish that these data are sufficient to determine relative prices and the profit rate. (Sraffa's formulation fixes the profit rate and determines the real wage as a residual; but it makes no difference to the logic of the theory which distribution variable is taken as parametric.) From the same equations Sraffa derived a trade-off between the real wage and the profit rate, which corresponds to the classical–Marxian conception of distribution as grounded in the opposition of class interests.

Sraffa's analysis and Keynes's theory of effective demand intersect at several junctures. First, by knocking out the foundations of neoclassical distribution theory the capital critique buttresses Keynes's contention that there is no mechanism within capitalism capable of ensuring that the labour market will tend to clear. Second, the classical theory of value and distribution – including Sraffa's modern formulation of it – is open-ended with regard to the determination of the level and composition of the social product. Some variation on the Keynes–Kalecki effective demand mechanism could therefore provide an explanation of outputs that is compatible with the classical surplus framework.

Third, Sraffa's analysis calls into question some aspects of Keynes's articulation of the theory of effective demand, and helps to account for the theory's assimilation, in weakened form, into mainstream economics. Keynes incorporated into *The General Theory* two elements of Marshallian orthodoxy: the proposition that in equilibrium the real wage must equal the marginal product of labour; and the notion that investment demand is a decreasing function of the interest rate. The capital critique undermines both of these claims. The Sraffian literature on Keynes maintains, furthermore, that by adopting them he opened the way for the interpretation of

The General Theory in terms of the neoclassical synthesis, according to which, under conditions of wage and price flexibility, the Keynes effect and the real balance effect ensure that the labour market tends to clear in the long run. On this interpretation Keynes's argument applies to the short period or to circumstances in which persistent market imperfections prevent the price adjustments that would otherwise bring about full employment. In failing to detach himself fully from his Marshallian roots, Keynes produced 'an inherently unstable compromise' that in the end fell short of its revolutionary promise (Garegnani 1978–79; see also Milgate 1982).

Sraffa appears to have harboured reservations about *The General Theory*. His manuscripts at Trinity College, Cambridge, indicate that he disliked the liquidity preference theory of interest, but this by itself seems inadequate to account for his scepticism. It is possible that Sraffa recognized earlier and more clearly than other members of Keynes's circle that the book's argument was susceptible to assimilation into the orthodox framework Keynes wanted to scuttle. The way past this difficulty, most Sraffian writers would contend, lies in jettisoning the Trojan horses Keynes incorporated into *The General Theory* – the Marshallian elements that are anyway vulnerable to the capital critique.

Throughout most of the formative period of Post Keynesian economics, from 1960 until the mid-1980s, the affinities between the Keynes–Kalecki effective demand mechanism and Sraffa's work were not a matter of dispute. Since then, however, the Post Keynesian project of integrating Keynes, Michał Kalecki and Sraffa has lost momentum, and something of a rift appears to have developed between the Sraffian camp and many of those who identify themselves as Post Keynesians. The history of this rift remains to be sorted out, though it appears to be connected, no doubt as both cause and effect, to the failure of the Trieste summer school to achieve one its principal goals – the forging of a unified methodological and analytical foundation for the Post Keynesian project. The tensions are largely unnecessary, and at least some Post Keynesian resistance to the Sraffian view is based on a misunderstanding of it. There are of course genuine differences of perspective, but these do not render the two traditions incompatible with each other.

Much of the Post Keynesian literature exhibits a strong antipathy towards attempts to explain economic phenomena in terms of equilibrating forces, and the classical surplus approach has come in for some criticism because of its utilization of models of long-period gravitation to explain aspects of income distribution and price determination. There is no disputing the practical importance of the themes emphasized by Post Keynesians – uncertainty, expectations, disequilibrium; what is at issue is how to incorporate these phenomena into a coherent account of social processes. Uncertainty, technical change and coordination failure account for much of the complexity of economic life. A Sraffian would argue that it is the very complexity of these issues that justifies the indispensability of a long-period theory of value and distribution: disequilibrium processes can best be understood by reference to the gravitational forces they disrupt. There is no necessary incompatibility on methodological grounds between the Post Keynesian and Sraffian frameworks; the two complement each other, each providing a different set of tools for different sorts of analytical problems.

Similarly, the Sraffian approach to money is not incompatible with a broad Post Keynesian perspective. The Sraffian framework allows for the non-neutrality of money via the effect of the money rate of interest on distribution. Pivetti (1985) and Panico (1985), developing a hint from Sraffa (1960, p. 33), have argued that the rate of interest fixed by the monetary authorities regulates the rate of return on non-financial capital. The argument starts from the familiar stylized fact that central banks can regulate interest rates but cannot generally control the money supply; the reasoning is therefore consistent with the endogeneity of money, a defining Post Keynesian premise. In the models developed along this line, money is not neutral at all: the monetary authorities, by setting the interest rate, influence distribution, and this has consequences for the composition, level and growth of aggregate output, and for employment. The forces that regulate distribution are no doubt more complicated than the mechanism described in these models, but the approach nevertheless clarifies important aspects of the distributional role of finance. The question is not *whether* money is non-neutral – on this, the Sraffian and Post Keynesian positions are not in conflict – but *how* it is non-neutral.

Underlying the Sraffian argument is a presumption that what we can say about money depends on how we conceive value and distribution. One of the reasons the Post Keynesian literature relies so heavily on the pervasiveness of uncertainty is that it is not solidly grounded in a theory of value and distribution; this deficiency is partly a byproduct of the rift with the Sraffians. Post Keynesian arguments about uncertainty are not so much wrong as extremely limited in what they can explain. Long before the publication of *The General Theory*, Keynes's neoclassical predecessors understood that uncertainty and fluctuations in business confidence could disrupt the market's coordinating mechanisms. If, as many Post Keynesians contend, the monetary nature of capitalist production is what accounts for unemployment, it would appear to follow that in a non-monetary economy the postulates of neoclassical theory hold, and that such an economy would tend towards full employment. But the capital critique undermines the neoclassical theory of distribution, and hence its theory of employment, *whether the economy utilizes money or not*. The Sraffian analysis of money and interest suggests furthermore that the non-neutrality of money does not reside – or at any rate does not reside exclusively – in the uncertainty inherent in monetary exchange regimes. Non-neutrality is indeed incompatible with the neoclassical theory of distribution; but there is no evident incompatibility between the non-neutrality of money and the classical surplus approach of Sraffa.

Fuller discussions of these issues can be found in the essays contained in Eatwell and Milgate (1983). For a general overview of Sraffa's scientific legacy, see Mongiovi (2002).

GARY MONGIOVI

See also:

Cambridge Economic Tradition; Capital Theory; Equilibrium and Non-equilibrium; Income Distribution; Rate of Interest; Uncertainty.

References

Eatwell, J. and M. Milgate (eds) (1983), *Keynes's Economics and the Theory of Value and Distribution*, Oxford: Duckworth.
Garegnani, P. (1978–79), 'Notes on consumption, investment and effective demand, Parts I & II', *Cambridge Journal of Economics*, **2** (4) and **3** (1), 335–53 and 63–82.
Milgate, M. (1982), *Capital and Employment*, London: Academic Press.
Mongiovi, G. (2002), 'Classics and moderns: Sraffa's legacy in economics', *Metroeconomica*, **53** (3), 223–41.
Nell, E.J. (ed.) (1980), *Growth, Profits and Property*, Cambridge: Cambridge University Press.
Panico, C. (1985), 'Market forces and the relation between the rates of interest and profit,' *Contributions to Political Economy*, **4**, 37–60.
Pivetti, M. (1985), 'On the monetary explanation of distribution', *Political Economy: Studies in the Surplus Approach*, **1**, 73–103.
Sraffa, P. (1960), *Production of Commodities by Means of Commodities*, Cambridge: Cambridge University Press.

Stagflation

The term 'stagflation' describes the simultaneous occurrence of inflation and stagnation, the latter defined by the existence of high unemployment. The term gained popularity in the early 1970s with the simultaneous increase in rates of inflation and unemployment throughout the developed capitalist economies. Hitherto in the post-Second World War period, the behaviour of inflation and unemployment rates traced out a negative relation between inflation and unemployment rates, a relation formalized in the Phillips curve, which was to become an integral part of Post Keynesian macroeconomics.

Two related impacts of the events following the Great Inflation of the early 1970s were a serious challenge to the dominance of Keynesian macroeconomics and the emergence of a radically different set of beliefs. Supposedly the simultaneous occurrence of rising unemployment and inflation rates constituted definite proof of fundamental flaws in Keynesian theory and its application as a tool for forecasting (Lucas and Sargent 1978). To Post Keynesians, and indeed to macro economists mindful of the complexity of the economic world, this response was but another example of the dangers of relying on gross correlations to substantiate or refute a theory. In fact, by simply taking account of additional influences on inflation rates that were prominent during the stagflation period, the negative relationship assumed in the original Phillips curve remains unchallenged. In isolating the critical historical events responsible for stagflation, it is necessary to give a more precise definition of stagflation. Here the term will refer to the simultaneous occurrence of high unemployment rates and high rates of inflation compared to those of the 'golden age'.

Figure 15 shows average annual rates of inflation $\dot{p}$ and unemployment U of the seven large OECD (Organization for Economic Cooperation and Development) economies from the closing years of the golden age to the closing years of the last century. An outstanding feature throughout the period in the G7 (and in other OECD economies) is the pronounced upward trend in unemployment rates beginning in the late 1960s until 1983. A second notable feature is the upward trend in inflation rates from 1967 until 1980, covering most of the same period in which unemployment rates doubled their golden-age rates and resulting in over a decade of stagflation. Furthermore, during the first half of the 1980s unemployment rates rose to triple their golden-age rates, and not until the mid-1980s did inflation rates fall to their golden-age rates. Finally, Figure 15 reveals that, from the mid-1980s until the recession of the early 1990s, the small decline in unemployment rates from historic highs was sufficient to double inflation rates by 1990. Only in the 1990s, with the return of unemployment rates to approximately 2½ times their golden-age rates, did inflation fall back to its golden-age rates.

Events of the times raised several questions whose answers are still a matter of dispute. First, why were unemployment rates not only high but also trending upwards since the early 1970s? Second, if, as Post Keynesians maintain, stimulative aggregate demand (AD) policies are effective in reducing unemployment when unemployment is involuntary, why were such policies not implemented? Third, what were the causes of a more than decade-long period of stagflation? And, fourth, why did it require a period of high unemployment of over three decades, culminating in almost two decades of unemployment rates nearly 2½ times their golden-age levels, to rid the system of high inflation?

324 *Stagflation*

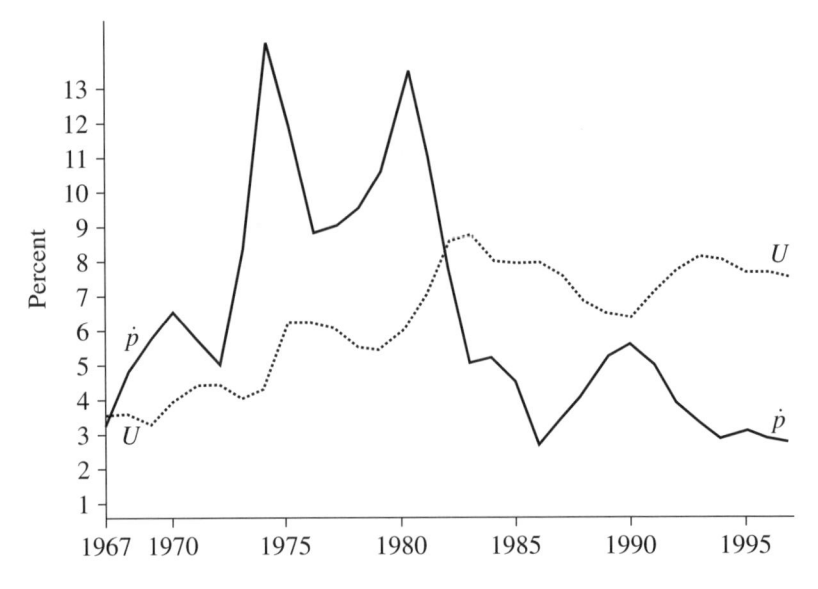

Note: Data include West Germany prior to 1993, after which data for the unified Germany are used.

Sources: OECD, *Historical Statistics*, various issues; OECD, *Economic Outlook*, **44**, December 1988, Table R11; OECD, *Economic Outlook*, **65**, June 1999, Annex Tables 16 and 22.

Figure 15   Average annual rates of inflation ($\dot{p}$) and standardized unemployment (U) for the G7 countries, 1967–1997

To those of a neoclassical persuasion, capitalism is a self-regulating system. The core of their explanation of the long-run upward trend in unemployment rates was a rising 'equilibrium' rate of unemployment, alternatively referred to as the NAIRU (non-accelerating inflation rate of unemployment) or natural rate of unemployment. This is a rate of unemployment determined solely by supply forces, which AD policies can alter permanently only by accepting ever accelerating or decelerating rates of inflation. Hence no other rate of unemployment was 'natural'. To Post Keynesians, much if not most of the pronounced upward trend in unemployment since the early 1970s could be explained in terms of deficient aggregate demand. A sustained policy-induced increase in aggregate demand could have led to a permanent reduction in unemployment without an acceleration of inflation rates, because the unemployment was largely involuntary. In other words the long-run Phillips curve was downward sloping. Why, then, did the authorities allow the unemployment rate to remain so high?

The opinion of governments and central bankers was that if stimulative policies strong enough to maintain the economy at golden-age unemployment rates had been introduced any time before the late 1990s, inflation would have risen to politically unacceptable, although not necessarily accelerating, rates. Unlike the golden-age period, when the goals of full employment and acceptable rates of inflation could be realized simultaneously, the early 1970s saw the emergence of an inflationary bias, that is, an inability of the economy to reach full-employment rates of unemployment without experiencing unacceptable rates of inflation. A shift in the Phillips curve outward to the right had taken place. Recovery in unemployment required more than a stimulation of aggregate demand; it required measures to contain inflation at full employment. When these proved unavailable, the full-employment goal was sacrificed in the interests of restraining inflation. This leads to the third question – what initiated the episode of stagflation?

Figure 15 reveals a sharp rise in inflation in the late 1960s to rates well above their previous golden-age rates, followed by a smaller decline in the early 1970s and then, in 1973–74, the first of two explosions in inflation rates. Underlying these price movements was a series of 'shocks', beginning with the 'wage explosion' of the second half of the 1960s, continuing with the breakdown of the Bretton Woods agreement, the rapid run-up of commodity prices and prices of foodstuffs in the early 1970s and finally the explosion in oil prices in 1973–74. In each case the impacts of the shocks were then magnified by the activation of wage–wage and wage–price inflationary mechanisms and propagated throughout the economies. By themselves the disturbances provide a plausible explanation of the Great Inflation up to the mid-1970s and, when account is taken of a second oil shock in 1979–80, of the strong inflationary trend until 1980. Thus, even without taking further account of the wage explosion, the episode of stagflation could be explained as large price disturbances dominating the effects of policy-induced unemployment increases on inflation outcomes.

Without denying the influence of shocks on inflation, such an interpretation ignores the lasting impact of developments leading up to the explosion in money wages that had preceded the other shocks just cited. While the increase in unemployment rates worked to restrain money and thereby price increases, influences other than shocks and rising unemployment rates had a major impact on wage settlements and therefore on price movements throughout the period covered in Figure 15. These influences were trends in underlying income and employment expectations and aspirations of the average citizen and worker, generated by the prolonged period of low unemployment and rising living standards of the golden age. During the period leading up to the Great Inflation, living standards had risen steadily and were expected to continue to rise indefinitely. Furthermore, a growing proportion of the labour force had never experienced long spells of unemployment, if any, and were convinced that full employment would be guaranteed by government. These growing expectations and aspirations generated growing demands upon the system that would carry over beyond the golden age. Thus the so-called 'wage explosion' of the late 1960s was a symptom of a profound institutional change that had a lasting effect on inflation and unemployment.

Evidence supporting the lasting effects of rising income and employment expectations and aspirations can be seen in the behaviour of wage and price inflation in the mid-1970s. In 1975–76, wage and price inflation rates fell in response to restrictive policies and a decline in commodity prices, including oil. However, only a slight reduction in unemployment rates in 1977–78 led to an increase in inflation rates once again. Events of the 1980s provided further evidence of the short-lived effects of earlier restrictive policies on wage and price inflation. Restrictive policies successfully reduced inflation in the first half of the 1980s to levels little different from those of the golden age, but at a large unemployment cost. However, beginning in 1987 with a rather moderate fall in unemployment rates from existing historically high rates, inflation rates rose until the recession of 1990.

This leads to the fourth question. Since the overriding concern of the authorities over the period covered in Figure 15 was to reduce inflation through restricting AD policies, eventually permitting a reduction in unemployment ('short-term pain for long-term gain'), why did the reduction of inflation rates to their golden-age levels take so long and why was it so costly in terms of unemployment? The mainstream explanation stressed the lasting effects of the 'inflationary psychology' that had built up over the many earlier years of high inflation. Reversing the deeply ingrained expectations of continued high inflation would require an equally long period of time and persistent restrictive policies.

An alternative explanation adhered to by Post Keynesians (Cornwall and Cornwall 2001) and others (Phelps Brown 1971, 1975 and Salvati 1983) focused on developments in the labour market, most of which have just been discussed. As outlined, the transitory effect of restrictive policies and the underlying strength of the average worker's expectations and aspirations are related. In addition, the restrictive policies initiated to fight the Great Inflation confirmed labour's suspicion that they were made the victims of the fight against inflation. This prolonged the period during which labour would continue to demand high wage increases.

However, the impact of prolonged high unemployment and the stagnation of real earnings on income and job expectations and aspirations eventually worked to reduce wage demands. The high unemployment cost of reducing inflation rates in the pre-1990s period can be attributed to the job and income expectations and aspirations formed in the golden age, and continued into the earlier phases of the high-unemployment episode. The ability eventually to bring down and to maintain low rates of inflation in the 1990s can be attributed to an eventual reversal of expectations and aspirations. By the recession of the early 1990s, after 13 years of unemployment rates averaging more than $2\frac{1}{2}$ times their golden-age rates, inflation rates fell below their golden-age levels and remained so throughout the balance of the decade. Unemployment rates fell in the second half of the 1990s, for example in the United States, but on average the recovery in employment in the G7 (and in the OECD) was modest. Stagflation had ended as inflation had been 'conquered' but stagnation continued through the remaining years of the 1990s (not shown in Figure 15).

No-one can predict the future but, barring the occurrence of unpredictable serious shocks or endogenous structural changes in the economy, there seems no reason to expect these trends to be reversed in the near future. The income and employment expectations and aspirations of the average citizen are likely to remain subdued.

JOHN CORNWALL

See also:

Bretton Woods; Economic Policy; Inflation; Unemployment; Wages and Labour Markets.

References

Cornwall, J. and W. Cornwall (2001), *Capitalist Development in the Twentieth Century; An Evolutionary–Keynesian Analysis*, Cambridge: Cambridge University Press.
Lucas, R. and T. Sargent (1978), 'After the Phillips curve: persistence of high inflation and high unemployment', in *After Keynesian Economics*, Federal Reserve Bank of Boston, pp. 49–72.
Phelps Brown, E.H. (1971), 'The analysis of wage movements under full employment', *Scottish Journal of Political Economy*, **18** (3), 233–43.
Phelps Brown, E.H. (1975), 'A non-monetarist view of the pay explosion', *Three Banks Review*, **105**, 3–24.
Salvati, M. (1983), 'Political business cycles and long waves in industrial relations: notes on Kalecki and Phelps Brown', in C. Freeman (ed.), *Long Waves in the World Economy*, London: Butterworths, pp. 202–24.

Taxation

It is difficult to find an explanation for the failure until recently of Post Keynesian economics to develop its own approach to taxation. Afer all, Kalecki had realized as early as 1937 that the publication of Keynes's *General Theory* required a whole new approach to taxation. His response was a short paper in the *Economic Journal* entitled 'A theory of commodity, income and capital taxation' (Kalecki 1937). But Kalecki never developed his thinking beyond the simple short-period model of his 1937 paper. In correspondence between Keynes and Kalecki at the time, Keynes indicated that he was also thinking along similar lines to Kalecki, but had not developed his ideas as far as Kalecki's. While a possible explanation for Keynes was that he never completely broke free from the strictures of neoclassical theory, particularly income distribution theory, this clearly does not explain Kalecki's failure. The only significant postwar advance in the development of a Post Keynesian approach has been by A. (Tom) Asimakopulos and J. Burbidge (1974). However, theirs was still a short-period model that also suffers from some other limitations.

In recent years, perceptive public finance economists such as A.B. Atkinson, J.E. Stiglitz, L. Kotlikoff, L. Summers and R.A. Musgrave have recognized that there are serious problems with the mainstream approach to taxation. Their concerns have centred principally on the incompatibility of the micro and macro elements of the orthodox approach. However, because they have constrained themselves to working within the neoclassical paradigm, they have been unable to find a solution. If the incidence and macroeconomic effects of taxation are to be better understood, they will have to be approached from outside the orthodox framework.

Taking a Post Keynesian approach requires us to go back to Kalecki's path-breaking paper of 1937 and show how the introduction of taxation modifies the various elements of his theoretical schema – his theories of income determination, income distribution, investment, business cycles and growth. In the event, the introduction of taxation into Kalecki's theory does not fundamentally alter the micro–macro relationships that characterize his entire approach. At the macroeconomic level, the aggregate flows in the economy determine the level of profits. At the microeconomic level, the degree of monopoly, as reflected in price/prime cost mark-ups, determines the distribution of income. Tax policy can affect the aggregate flows of spending and profits, but firms' pricing decisions, as reflected in their mark-ups of price over prime cost, determine the intra-industry and inter-industry and class distributions of income. Ultimately, the confluence of these factors determines the short-period incidence of taxes. It is this incidence, through its impact on firms' investment decisions, that generates a long-period effect. This critical interdependence between the microeconomic and macroeconomic forces in Kaleckian theory in general, and tax theory in particular, provides a framework that is lacking in mainstream public finance theory.

In his original 1937 paper, Kalecki analysed the short-period effects of the taxation of commodities, income and capital on employment, the level of national income and its distribution. There is an important interdependence in Kalecki between the level and the distribution of national income. As he stated (Kalecki 1968, p. 61): 'Gross income . . . is pushed up to a point at which profits out of it are determined by the "distribution factors".' Kalecki used the term 'degree of monopoly' to describe these factors that determine the income shares of profits and wages such as industrial concentration, product differentiation, entry barriers or trade union power. Using Kalecki's famous profit equation (where aggregate profits are defined as the sum of investment, the government budget deficit, net exports and the difference between capitalist consumption and worker savings), the short-period macroeconomic effects of taxes on profits or wages depend on three things: (i) the relative marginal propensities to spend out of wages and profits; (ii) whether or not there are compensating changes in the level of government expenditure; and (iii) the extent to which a tax change is shifted through a change in business mark-ups.

Post Keynesian/Kaleckian tax analysis becomes more complex when we move out of the short period. The first step is to integrate Kalecki's theory of taxation with his theory of the business cycle (Laramie and Mair 2000). This shows that the taxation of wages and profits can have short-period effects on profits and that the short-period effects of the taxation of profits can have long-period effects on investment. These long-period effects of the taxation of wages and profits can affect the amplitude of the business cycle and the trend rate of investment. The impact of the tax system on the business cycle and the trend is derived from Kalecki's investment function. The two channels through which the tax system operates are the rate of depreciation and the level of profits. The depreciation channel operates by affecting the real tax bill associated with old equipment. As this equipment becomes physically and financially less productive as a result of technological change, an increase in the rate of tax on profits will increase the rate of depreciation, accelerate its obsolescence and encourage its replacement by newer, more efficient and more profitable plant. The effect on the level of profits of a change in taxation operates directly through a change in tax rates and indirectly through a change in the wage share of national income on the flows of spending that comprise aggregate profits.

These two effects can then be analysed at various stages in the recovery and downswing of the business cycle. The effects of tax policy on the amplitude of the business cycle depend critically on whether or not the wage tax and the profit tax are shifted. In the simplest scenario, we assume: (i) no shifting of either a wage tax or a profit tax; and (ii) that the effect of a tax change on the level of profits is greater than its effect on the rate of depreciation. Then an increase in a tax on profits will reduce profits and dampen the amplitude of the cycle, and an increase in a tax on wages will increase profits and attenuate the cycle. This example is only one of a large number of possible permutations of tax change and tax shifting but it illustrates the potential offered by a Post Keynesian/Kaleckian model for a stabilization role for fiscal policy.

The effects of taxation on the long-period growth of the economy are even more difficult to establish. In the first place, there must be a theory of growth to provide a framework of analysis. The problem is that the form in which Kalecki left his growth theory when he died was unsatisfactory, with undue emphasis on 'cautious capitalism'. A more balanced version of Kalecki's growth theory has been developed by Gomulka et al. (1990). Introducing taxation into this revised version allows us to examine the effects of balanced changes in the structure of taxation on long-term growth, stability and employment (Laramie and Mair 2000). As with the effects of taxation on the business cycle, the results are complex and heavily dependent on whether or not the taxes are shifted via changes in business price/cost mark-ups. Nevertheless, it can be shown that there are circumstances under which balanced changes in the structure of taxation as between wages and profits will achieve greater stability, promote faster long-term growth and reduce unemployment.

It is not only at the aggregate level of the economy as a whole that Post Keynesian/Kaleckian tax theory can be applied. Typically, in discussions of fiscal policy, it is the role of central or federal government that is emphasized, while that of states or local governments is ignored. But in many countries, state and local government receipts and expenditures represent a significant share of GDP and thus affect aggregate spending and economic growth. Also, much of the provision of government goods and services is done at the state or local level and is likely to have aggregate demand and aggregate supply effects. A Post Keynesian/Kaleckian approach to state and local taxes seeks to identify their effects on post-tax profits. This is done by separating out state, local and federal budget deficits and examining the institutional and political factors that have determined the budget stances of state and local governments. Laramie and Mair (2000) have shown that in the United States, for example, because of institutional and political factors, the macroeconomic effects and incidence of state and local taxes are remarkably different from the incidence of similar federal taxes on corporate profits.

Post Keynesian/Kaleckian analysis also provides a framework within which to consider the macroeconomic effects of fiscal policy in the European Union. The establishment of the European Central Bank and the introduction of the euro have resulted in a loss of national monetary autonomy that requires adherence to new fiscal constraints. Post Keynesian/Kaleckian tax theory suggests that stabilization need no longer depend on the application of the orthodox Keynesian policy of running budget surpluses or deficits. Stabilization objectives can be achieved within given volumes of government revenue and spending by altering the structure of taxation. Thus compliance by a member state of the eurozone with the budgetary constraints of membership need not act as a constraint on its ability to use fiscal policy as an instrument of stabilization. This is an implication of Post Keynesian/Kaleckian tax analysis which would enable member governments of the European Monetary Union (EMU) to retain a significant degree of autonomy over fiscal policy without violating the rules of the Maastricht Treaty.

A significant feature of Kaleckian tax analysis is that it provides a challenge to the supply-side argument that economic growth can be stimulated only by cutting government spending and taxation. The theoretical and empirical arguments that underpin supply-side economics are rather weak. In particular, this line of argument is based on the marginal productivity theory of income distribution, where the economy is constrained by supply-side determinants. In contrast to the orthodox approach in which the real wage rate is assumed to be determined in the labour market, a Kaleckian approach argues that the real wage is determined in the product market. This underlines the fundamental difference between the Kaleckian and the orthodox (including early Keynesian) approaches to taxation. Post Keynesians have to recognize the political and economic constraints on the ability of demand management policy by itself to bring an economy to the level of full employment and keep it there. Chief among the political constraints is the one that Kalecki recognized as early as 1943, namely the political power of rentiers and capitalists (Kalecki, 1943). The macroeconomic incidence and effects of taxation in a Post Keynesian/Kaleckian model depend critically on whether or not tax shifting occurs. Tax shifting occurs when either workers or capitalists are able to engineer a favourable shift in business mark-ups in response to an increase in the taxation of wages or profits, in order to maintain or increase their share of national income. Business mark-ups and Kalecki's underlying degree of monopoly theory of income distribution play a pivotal role in determining the macroeconomic outcomes of fiscal policy.

This issue poses a serious dilemma for governments in the twenty-first century. If governments seek to pursue fiscal objectives of stimulating investment and growth within a balanced budget framework by reducing the taxation of profits, they run the risk of achieving the exact opposite, depending on how the factors that determine the degree of monopoly, and hence the distribution of income, pan out. Governments may find themselves increasingly having to try to resolve contradictory demands from different groups in society over what may be considered a socially equitable distribution of income. Post Keynesian/Kaleckian tax theory identifies profound implications for the future of capitalism, implying that fiscal policy can either counter or reinforce the very nature of capitalism. The ultimate effect of fiscal policy on stability and growth depends on how aggregate spending flows and business mark-ups react to tax changes, in other words on how the level of profits and distribution of income are modified.

ANTHONY J. LARAMIE
DOUGLAS MAIR

See also:
Budget Deficits; Fiscal Policy; Kaleckian Economics; Tax-based Incomes Policy.

References
Asimakopulos, A. and J. Burbidge (1974), 'The short-period incidence of taxation', *Economic Journal*, **84** (334), 267–88.
Gomulka, S., A. Ostaszewski and R.O. Davies (1990), 'The innovation rate and Kalecki's theory of trend, unemployment and the business cycle', *Economica*, **57** (228), 525–40.
Kalecki, M. (1937), 'A theory of commodity, income and capital taxation', *Economic Journal*, **47** (187), 444–50.
Kalecki, M. (1943), 'Political aspects of full employment', *Political Quarterly*, **14** (4), 322–31.
Kalecki, M. (1968), *Theory of Economic Dynamics*, New York: Monthly Review Press.
Laramie, A.J. and D. Mair (2000), *A Dynamic Theory of Taxation: Integrating Kalecki into Modern Public Finance*, Cheltenham, UK and Northampton, MA, USA: Edward Elgar.

Tax-based Incomes Policy

The tax-based incomes policy (TIP) was an innovative proposal that received serious consideration in the United States from leading economists and policy makers in the 1970s in response to the severe bouts of stagflation – simultaneous inflation and recession. 'Incomes policies', as they were called then, tried to bring governmental pressure on leading firms to hold down their price and wage increases, thereby reducing inflation without utilizing the painful pressure of a deep recession. TIP was intermediate between voluntary wage-price guidelines and wage-price controls. TIP used financial incentives to try to induce firms to hold down price and wage increases. Advocates of TIP felt voluntary guidelines were too weak, controls too strong, but that TIP was just right and compatible with a market economy that ran on financial incentives.

TIP was advocated as an alternative to unleashing central banks to subdue inflation by a draconian tight monetary policy that 'worked' by generating a deep recession and high unemployment, forcing desperate workers to accept small wage increases, which led to small cost increases and small price increases. In the early 1980s, central banks in many countries, including the United States, took this painful course. Inflation was indeed subdued at a high social cost, and the TIP proposal receded from debate and discussion. The past two decades have been fortunate in generally avoiding stagflation shocks in most countries, inflation has remained generally low, and TIP has remained dormant. It is possible, however, that some day another upward supply shock, such as the one administered by OPEC (Organization of Petroleum Exporting Countries) in the 1970s, will once again inflict economies with another serious dose of stagflation. If that day comes, there may once again be renewed interest in the tax-based incomes policy.

Although TIP came to win the support of several mainstream Keynesian economists in the 1970s, such as Arthur Okun of the Brookings Institution and James Tobin of Yale University, and even the co-authorship of a mainstream conservative economist, Henry Wallich, a member of the Board of Governors of the Federal Reserve, the original proponent and most spirited advocate for TIP was the distinguished Post Keynesian economist, Sidney Weintraub of the University of Pennsylvania (Seidman 1983).

Although Weintraub's articles proposing TIP first appeared in 1971, the Post Keynesian theory that led him to the proposal began in the late 1950s. In 1959 he published *A General Theory of the Price Level*, presenting theory and evidence linking the money (nominal) wage to the price level, and challenging the quantity (of money) theory of inflation with an alternative wage-cost mark-up theory of inflation. He proposed 'watch-tower control', a voluntary wage guideline equal to average productivity growth. As inflation heated up in the second half of the 1960s, Weintraub continued his work on the key role of the money wage in the inflation process, and the need for a 'wage policy' ('incomes policy'). He gradually became convinced that voluntary guideposts were too weak. He was passionately opposed to the use of unemployment to restrain wage inflation, but he was also averse to wage and price controls as too rigid for a sustained solution during peacetime. So what was left? In 1970, Weintraub proposed a method he believed would be stronger than voluntary guidelines, but more flexible than controls: a tax incentive. His suggestion appeared as a short piece in the *New York Times* entitled, 'A proposal to halt the spiral of wages and prices'. Conservative Henry Wallich had offered a similar idea in a *Newsweek* column in 1966. Weintraub then published a full-length discussion of the proposal in the British journal *Lloyds Bank Review* in January 1971 entitled 'An incomes policy to stop inflation'.

Leonard Silk, economics columnist for the *New York Times*, brought Weintraub and Wallich together for a luncheon. The result was the joint article, 'A tax-based incomes policy', which appeared in the *Journal of Economic Issues* in June 1971. By the end of the decade, after two bouts of stagflation, TIP began to make its way into policy discussions and into the textbooks. By the early 1980s, virtually every macroeconomics textbook presented a brief description of the TIP proposal, citing Weintraub and Wallich as its authors.

How did Weintraub arrive at TIP? In his 1959 book, Weintraub asserted that price is roughly a constant mark-up, to which he gave the letter k, on unit labour cost, which in turn equals the money wage divided by productivity. If the mark-up k stays roughly constant over time in an economy, it follows that price will remain stable if the wage grows at the same rate as productivity. He presented empirical evidence supporting the relative constancy of k. Weintraub went further and asserted that the wage-cost mark-up equation is a more useful and reliable way to analyse inflation than the famous quantity of money hypothesis, which states that the product of money and velocity equals the product of the price level and real output, and that velocity V is relatively constant. Weintraub presented empirical evidence showing that whereas the mark-up k is relatively constant, velocity V is erratic and volatile. Hence, he concluded that the money wage is a more reliable cause of the price level than the money supply.

But what, in turn, causes the money wage to change? Most economists believed then and now that the money wage is an endogenous variable determined by the unemployment rate and expected inflation (the augmented Phillips curve hypothesis), or even somehow determined directly by the money supply. Here Weintraub sets out perhaps the most controversial part of this theory: the hypothesis that the money wage is largely 'exogenous'. Here is a quotation from his 1961 book, *Classical Keynesianism* (p. 51):

> The money wage partakes of the character of a rather fully exogenous variable. It was this view that commended itself to Keynes, who felt that the money wage that emerged from collective bargaining did not lend itself to description in terms of neat and determinable demand and supply curves with their implicit recognition of the 'market forces'.

In his 1978 book, *Capitalism's Inflation and Unemployment Crisis*, Weintraub responds directly to the conventional view of what determines the money wage, the augmented Phillips curve hypothesis (p. 107):

According to the new disciples, W can be most anything, depending on 'expectations.' This is a curious theory indeed to be promulgated by endogenous proponents, for the exogeneity aspect is simply demoted from money wages and promoted in 'expectations'.

Weintraub's focus on the money wage in the inflation process, his conviction that the wage is largely exogenous, and his opposition to the use of unemployment to restrain wage inflation, led him in 1970 to propose TIP. Perhaps his most complete exposition of TIP is in his 1978 book, *Capitalism's Inflation and Unemployment Crisis*, where he devotes chapters 6–8 to its theory, design and practical implementation.

Weintraub regarded TIP as fundamentally different from mandatory controls. It is important to quote from his 1978 book on this point, because some analysts, especially critics, have characterized TIP as essentially the same as controls. Weintraub introduces TIP as follows (pp. 122–3):

> Rather than emulating the methods of the collectivist societies which issue commands to 'do it or else,' free societies must combat inflation by replicating the incentives and deterrents of the price mechanism. An effective instrument is already at hand in the traditional tax powers; they need not be exercised in an onerous way, especially since revenue is not the objective. As in most good law, the tax regulations must allow legal circumvention to impart flexibility; evasion can be permitted – but at a price, in the manner of a traffic fine for conscious speeding, maybe under emergency contingencies... An Incomes Policy enforced through the tax mechanism can thus be compatible with a market economy and the broader attributes of freedom.

Clearly, Weintraub is a Post Keynesian, not a Post-Marxian. His aim is to fix the market system, not supplant it.

Like Keynes, Weintraub generally accepts the pattern of relative wages and prices, and the resulting allocation of resources, generated by the market economy. He simply wants to induce smaller wage and price increases – less inflation – without interfering with the pattern of relative wages and prices and the resulting allocation of resources. His highest priority is to avoid fighting inflation through tight money and high unemployment.

Weintraub devotes more than two pages to the shortcomings of permanent wage-price controls, beginning the discussion as follows (p. 154):

> Pervasive and meticulous price and wage controls are inimical to the functioning of the market economy. At best, they are a form of shock therapy to force a healthier frame of mind on 'inflationary expectations' as a temporary remission interlude. Unless innocuously applied as a toothless bark, they must end up diverting innumerable – and mostly trivial – private decisions into public forums for tedious hearings before committees under political aegis.

In these three chapters, Weintraub devotes substantial space to practical administration. He emphasizes that TIP should be limited to the largest corporations – perhaps 1,000 – that set the wage-price pattern in the economy; and that a stiff tax penalty on the corporation is the key to TIP's strength. He opposes some recent suggestions that TIP apply to most firms in the economy and that a tax reward be used instead of a tax penalty.

One problem that has plagued the original Weintraub–Wallich version of TIP is that it appears anti-labour, because it contains a wage standard but no price standard. In their 1971 article, Wallich and Weintraub explain that a price standard should be unnecessary according to the wage-cost mark-up equation, and may prove difficult to administer. In *Capitalism's Inflation and Unemployment Crisis*, Weintraub offers several suggestions for a more balanced TIP package. It is possible that a balanced price-wage TIP, limited to large corporations, may prove able to win greater political support than the original wage-only version, yet still prove administratively feasible. Work on making TIP appear more balanced took place in the late 1970s (Seidman 1978). Should stagflation return, and a revival of interest in TIP occur, some of this work may prove useful.

Although Weintraub's work appears to focus on inflation, it is his passion for preventing high unemployment that reveals the Post Keynesian spirit of his work. What alarms him is the apparent willingness of many economists and policy makers to use high unemployment as the main weapon against inflation. In his 1961 book, *Classical Keynesianism*, he wrote (pp. 39–40):

> If unemployment is the answer to the inflation problem, then Keynesianism as a social philosophy is dead, literally interred by Keynesians and, curiously, all in the name of the mentor . . . The only alternative to conscious and deliberate creation of unemployment in which the forces of aggregate demand are running strong, and one which could still preserve the analytical and philosophical system fashioned by Lord Keynes, would be some deliberate design and control of the money wage level, just as we have learned to use fiscal and monetary policy to control aggregate demand . . . How to contain the money wage level while maintaining full employment, and without breeding unacceptable interferences in labor markets, comes close to being the most important policy issue of our day.

One decade later Weintraub (1971) published his *Lloyds Bank Review* article proposing in detail a tax-based incomes policy.

LAURENCE S. SEIDMAN

See also:
Inflation; Stagflation; Wages and Labour Markets.

References
Seidman, L. (1978), 'Tax-based incomes policies', *Brookings Papers on Economic Activity*, **2**, 301–48.

Seidman, L. (1983), 'Sidney Weintraub, the man and his ideas', *Challenge*, **26** (5), 22–8.
Wallich, H. and S. Weintraub (1971), 'A tax-based incomes policy', *Journal of Economic Issues*, **5** (2), 1–19.
Weintraub, S. (1959), *A General Theory of the Price Level*, Philadelphia: Chilton.
Weintraub, S. (1961), *Classical Keynesianism*, Westport, CT: Greenwood Press.
Weintraub, S. (1971), 'An incomes policy to stop inflation', *Lloyds Bank Review*, **99**, 1–12.
Weintraub, S. (1978), *Capitalism's Inflation and Unemployment Crisis*, Reading, MA: Addison-Wesley.

Third Way

In the 1980s, parties of the left found themselves in a severe political crisis, for an obvious reason: people's expectations of the basic institutions those political forces had helped to establish were increasingly disappointed. The historical achievement of social democracy (the term includes similar parties around the world), that is, the welfare state, began to show signs of financial crisis due to overexpansion, rising unemployment and tax revolt, as well as inefficiencies reflected in rising costs of services combined with decreasing quality of delivery. The Soviet model based on collective property and central planning had disappointed expectations of steady improvement in individual and collective consumption. Both the communist and the social democratic establishment had discredited themselves by legal and illegal enrichment, though on differing scales.

The implosion of the Soviet system intensified the need for a new strategy by the democratic left. It put an end to the momentum of systems competition. The capitalist system of market economies thus permanently lost its constraining pole. The monopolar world order of US dominance soon became manifest. It is based on a *military–technological*, a *monetary–industrial* and a *media–ideology* core and is decisively supported by a web of alliances ranging from the North Atlantic Treaty Organization (NATO), the European Union and the Organization for Economic Cooperation and Development (OECD) to the International Monetary Fund (IMF) and the World Trade Organization (WTO), but also includes Microsoft, CNN, Moody's and certain foundations. Neoliberal thought has become the paramount hegemonic ideology, the only one with global reach. The answer to any political question, be it economic, social or scientific, will tend to comply with this dominant world-view. It is very difficult, sometimes risky and mostly in vain to argue for other possible answers. The response, in most cases, is clear: priority is to be given to the 'market', particularly to monetary stability, deregulation and the privatization of previously public tasks and public property. Those favouring the privatization of anything public have adequately named this the 'Washington Consensus'.

The modernization of social democracy and the identification of a post-communist perspective was attempted under several labels such as 'Third Way', 'New Labour', '*Neue Mitte*' or 'Modern Governance'. In this entry, in order to avoid futile terminological exercises, the expression 'Third Way' is used to cover all major projects for modernizing the moderate left. The first such attempt was initiated in the US by the Democratic Leadership Council, a group supporting Bill Clinton's presidential candidacy. For quite some time, at least in Europe, political and intellectual initiatives by Tony Blair (Blair 1998) and Anthony Giddens (Giddens 2000) received considerable attention. To further the integration of varying modernization currents, the term 'Multiple Third Ways' was introduced. (A book with this title (Cuperus et al. 2001) gives an account of all shades, including dissenting opinions in French and Italian centre-left parties.) In this entry, preference is given to the expression 'Thirdwayism'.

In *political practice*, Thirdwayism may be characterized by three basic elements: (i) acceptance of monetary stabilization, deregulation and privatization as top priorities in economic and social policy; (ii) a changed role for the state, from caretaker to empowering agency; and (iii) acceptance of US dominance in technology and military fields. Thus due attention is given to the core areas of US dominance. In actual policy making, the supply side receives top priority in programmes promoting technology, innovation and research, as well as education at all levels, including forms of lifelong learning. Full-employment Keynesianism has thus been replaced by labour market policy. The emphasis is now put on flexibility, which is promoted by deregulation and training in certain skills, as well as a reduction of unemployment benefits. Responsibility for finding a job is individualized. Everybody becomes a manager of his or her own human resources, individually responsible for his or her own upkeep. It is the modernized welfare state's task to empower people and restrict public support to those 'objectively' disabled. Abuse of public welfare is to be minimized, over-ruling the principle of free choice of employment. Inequality in income and wealth, even if growing dramatically, is accepted as a way of promoting economic growth, following the assumption that such growth will eventually 'trickle down' to benefit all. Equality is a political concern only with respect to provision of educational opportunities and mitigation of social exclusion.

In order to justify this change in political practice one employs *stylized facts*. Top on the list are 'necessities' imposed on all economic subjects and political actors by *globalization*. This is claimed to be engendered by the technological revolution, which demands a *knowledge-based society* and a *New Economy*. According to this world-view, claimed to be superior to old theories like Keynesianism, the 'new' economy was, until the economic downturn of 2001, regarded as invulnerable to business cycles.

At the *theoretical level*, Thirdwayism constitutes a radical break with the past. In the economic sphere 'markets' are conceived as self-regulating. In the political sphere, the left–right divide is declared to be inadequate for describing modern society. The centre is defined as 'radical' and the establishment of consensus is declared to be the essence of politics.

Thirdwayism may be criticized regarding both practice and theory. Practical performance, evaluated by the voter, is ultimately decisive. As there are positive elements in any political project, in the case of Thirdwayism this mainly applies to the envisaged reform of the state bureaucracy and of public institutions. A turn away from a more authoritarian to a more cooperative mode of functioning is a topical problem in all modern societies. This reform perspective is reinforced by the need to cope with financial crises in the various public domains. A whole range of supply-side goods, such as education, research and development must also be included in any up-to-date reform programme. No doubt, Third Way parties are on the right track in a number of issues. Thirdwayism, however, lacks a theoretical basis of its own. Most of its theoretical arguments are borrowed from mainstream social thought. This lack of theoretical backing seriously impedes it from regaining the intellectual initiative over hegemonic neoliberalism and reintroducing social and economic reform.

Globalization, based on technology, is also perceived in a rather pervasive way by Thirdwayism. Due to inevitable global competition, this phenomenon is seen as permeating investment, production, trade and finance, as well as information and research. It is regarded as a natural process, selecting the fittest modes in an evolutionary sense. The obvious fact that globalization proceeds along a manmade path and is defined by manmade rules remains completely out of the picture. A closer look would reveal those rules to be construed by US players, in alliance with other global actors. The Washington Consensus is the dominant prescription for solving almost all economic and social problems on this globe. For example, this set of recipes is mandatory for countries with structural payments deficits that need to qualify for loans by the IMF and related institutions. Thirdwayism does not even mention the Washington Consensus or 'IMF conditionality'. In short, Thirdwayism boils down to an attempt to adapt the reasoning and action of former left-wing and centre-left parties to the ideological hegemony of neoliberalism.

Markets are by no means self-regulating, but in a systematic way unstable and open to failure. Performance which is socially acceptable, therefore, requires regulation and active policy intervention. In its radical version, Thirdwayism accepts that states are embedded in markets. In a similar vein, there is no proof that private property is generally preferable to other forms of ownership. Given this, economic policy inspired by J.M. Keynes and

Michał Kalecki or Post Keynesian economics cannot be dismissed as theoretically outdated and politically impracticable. Thirdwayism's anti-Keynesianism results from submission to the dominant microeconomic approach, which considers macroeconomics in general, and an active fiscal and monetary policy in particular, as being erroneous and futile. This judgement, however, is based on insufficient analysis. Thirdwayism rejects Keynesian methods of increasing private consumption through redistribution of income and increasing government expenditure on social consumption goods, in particular if they are financed by budget deficits. In line with the Washington Consensus, only boosting investment through tax reduction and expenditure in infrastructure is admissible, even if this in fact is also one of the main ways to increase employment in Keynesianism. By depicting that school of thought as outdated, circular flow reasoning is also removed from the analytical arsenal. (This is comparable to abolishing double-entry accounting as an analytical tool in business!) The political consequences are severe. First, it is no longer possible to assess whether the promotion of private investment and exports is based on sufficient aggregate demand. Second, effective demand shortages, for example, those due to petrol-price inflation or the asymmetric adaptation mechanism, which limit effective demand in both debtor and creditor countries, are overlooked. Third, asset-price inflation (or deflation), so important for understanding global stock exchange movements during the years preceding and following 2000, becomes inexplicable. Last but not least, economic instability and ensuing avoidable damage can no longer be analysed in terms of institutional deficiencies, as they are instead primarily attributed to individual misbehaviour, such as 'inflexibility' or 'welfare dependency'.

If the left–right divide is correlated with more or less equality in income and wealth, or access to opportunities and power, it is hard to see why this distinction should be regarded as outdated. Given the dramatic increase in inequality in recent decades, it is equally difficult to comprehend how consensus as a primary virtue can play such an overwhelming role in any important up-to-date political project. Indeed, in advanced political theory the 'difference' between 'us' and 'them' is being reactivated as a centre-piece of politics. It allows one to define the dividing line between political adversaries and to mobilize supporting interests.

Thirdwayism can, finally, be characterized by its neglect of three major issues:

1. What is the modern *public* purpose? A redefinition of the *public purpose* is pertinent at the local, regional, national, continental and the global levels. It is a precondition for defining the adversary and for mobilizing supporting interests.

2. Which new role should be ascribed to *public* property? The redefinition of property, perceived as a bundle of rights, reflecting (a role for) the *private* and the *public* interest, is an inevitable *theoretical* task. Its urgency is exemplified by at least two phenomena: first, by the public-good quality of old and new knowledge; second, by WTO regulations allowing the privatization of intellectual property, such as scientific discoveries.
3. What role should institutional diversity play and what forms might it take? Institutional diversity and awareness of cultural legacies have been found to constitute a comparative advantage in economic development. Their neglect was one of the reasons for the Soviet Union's inferiority in systems competition. By elaborating on those issues, strangely ignored by Thirdwayism, an agenda for the future could take shape.

This is, however, not achievable without overcoming the ideological hegemony of neoliberalism. This endeavour, if successful, opens up the path to a post-Washington Consensus, or, formulated positively, to an agenda for a future global *res publica*.

EGON MATZNER

See also:
Economic Policy; Globalization; Transition Economies.

References
Blair, Tony (1998), 'The Third Way: new politics for the new century', London: *Fabian Pamphlets*, 588.
Cuperus, René, Karl Duffek and Josef Kandel (2001), *Multiple Third Ways. European Social Democracy Facing the Twin Revolution of Globalisation and the Knowledge Society*, Amsterdam, Berlin and Vienna: Wiardi Beckman Stichting et al.
Faux, Jeff (1999), 'Lost on the Third Way', *Dissent,* Spring, 67–76.
Giddens, Anthony (2000), *The Third Way and Its Critics*, Oxford: Polity Press.
Laclau, Ernesto and Chantal Mouffe (2001), 'Preface to the second edition', in Ernesto Laclau and Chantal Mouffe, *Hegemony and Socialist Strategy. Toward a Radical Democratic Politics*, London: Verso, pp. xii–xix.
Matzner, Egon (2000), *Monopolar World Order. On the Socioeconomics of US Dominance*, Szombathely: Savaria University Press.

Time in Economic Theory

Conventional (neoclassical) economics allows no place for time in the sense of a historical, uni-directional process. While Alfred Marshall observed that time was 'the source of many of the greatest difficulties in economics' (*Principles of Economics*, 8th edn, p. 92), neither he nor his descendants were able to incorporate meaningful time into their theory. Equilibrium analysis, whether of a partial or a Walrasian form, cannot manage time in its historic context. Contrary to textbook authorities, the short and long runs of neoclassical theory do not refer to the passage of historic (calendar) time, but are mere analytic concepts that allow 'time enough' for whatever logically needs to happen to permit the equilibrium outcomes intrinsic to the argument to unfold. In the general equilibrium world, time is essentially excluded from the theory because everything happens simultaneously – there is no process or sequence of events taking place over real time.

Various attempts have been made to deal with time in a more realistic fashion, but still retain the notion of equilibrium states to which the economy is always tending. Such efforts, since they are contained within an equilibrium framework based on a Cartesian deductive method, must reduce time to some non-historic meaning: economic processes must be reversible and the future must be knowable if equilibrium outcomes are to have any meaning. As the neoclassical equilibrium argument is of a mechanical nature, similar to the inner workings of a clock-like machine, one can trace the sequence of events through a system of interconnected variables (gears) in any direction: a deterministic outcome will always obtain and no 'arrow of time' is permitted by the argument. Hicks's 'weeks' are not to be confused with the passage of real time (Hicks 1939). Week 2 does not historically follow week 1, because the equilibrium adjustment process undergone in week 1 could just as logically follow that of week 2: 'weeks' are interchangeable. And, if processes are reversible and the future knowable, any expectations admitted in this theory (if the assumption of full information is dropped) must also be reversible. There can be no uncertainty in the sense that we simply do not know what the future state(s) will be (Dow 1996, chapter 6).

The notion of equilibrium is further constrained by the requirement that economic laws be of a universal nature, applicable to all places and all times. This connotes that, although superficial appearances seem to indicate that the world undergoes change, no fundamental change is possible. Since change can take place only through the passage of time, the neoclassical theory cannot incorporate history.

For mainstream theorists, time is simply an intellectual construct developed to conform to the equilibrium requirements of the theory itself. Assumptions of perfect knowledge of past, present and future states – where there are no disappointed expectations in the past and where the future is known – 'emasculate the very concepts of time and uncertainty in economics' (Davidson 1978, p. 14). In the 'bounded rationality' version of the argument, the precise future is not known, but all possible future states are knowable. Economic agents can still behave rationally on the basis of quantifiable probability estimates of the future, though suboptimal (satisficing rather than optimizing) results will prevail. This is not because the future is yet to be created (implying the passage of historical time), but because decision makers are constrained by their own cognitive limitations. Agents intend to behave rationally in the sense of optimizing some variable (utility), but cannot because they are incapable of acquiring the knowledge to do so and do not have the necessary computational skills that would allow them to use such knowledge in an optimizing calculation. The fundamental problem, then, lies not with an uncertain future, and thus with time, but with the cognitive limitations of the economic agent. Were it not for these limitations, agents *could* optimize because they *could* be certain. But they must be content with a limited rationality as they can only assign a probability to the success of any particular decision. This approach could be termed 'probabilistic determinism' rather than the certain determinism of the more traditional theory (Dunn 2001).

For Keynes, and those economists who follow his lead, time is of crucial importance in understanding the workings of a monetary (capitalist) economy, and is inextricably linked to *fundamental* uncertainty and to money itself. Economic processes occur in real time, where actions taken today that cannot be undone have unknowable consequences for the future. This position contains the essential Post Keynesian criticism of neoclassical equilibrium analysis: since adjustment processes necessitate change, and change can take place only in real time, by the time the logical process leading to equilibrium could work itself out, the conditions on which the equilibrium outcome was specified have all been altered: no deterministic outcome is possible: 'economic decisions are made by human beings facing an uncertain and unpredictable future while they are moving away from a fixed and *irreversible past*' (Davidson 1991, p. 32). For Keynes, neoclassical equilibrium analysis was just a 'pretty, polite technique which tries to deal with the present by abstracting from the fact that we know very little about the future' (Keynes 1936 [1987], p. 115). For some purposes Keynes did employ a concept of logical time, but such usage was confined to countering standard theory's arguments on its own terms or in establishing preliminary statements identifying various causal relations; this is of little interest in analysing his general theory, which is conducted in historical time (see Robinson 1980).

Keynes's position on money and uncertainty requires a theoretical stance on time, where economic *processes* occur in real time and within a distinct form of economic organization that cannot be analysed on the basis of universal laws deduced from a reductionist (individual agent) foundation. Production processes obviously occur through time, but this fact, while important for Keynes, was not the defining aspect of a monetary economy.

Production occurs in all forms of economic organization, but a monetary economy differs in its fundamental nature from non-monetary economies. In a monetary (capitalist) economy, the objective of production is to produce not goods, but money. In his early drafts of *The General Theory*, Keynes, following Marx, was very specific in his formulation of such an economy as M-C-M', where money is required to purchase inputs to produce commodities that are then sold for money. The objective, of course, is that the money at the end of the circuit (M') is greater than that at the beginning – a profit is made.

For Keynes and the Post Keynesians, such an economy is driven by aggregate spending. If current spending is limited to income received in the previous period, spending cannot increase beyond the level of that period – M' could not exceed M. As capitalist production is undertaken primarily on the expectation that M' will grow, such an economy requires a source of spending in excess of current income – debt (and its dialectical opposite, credit). Indeed, the production process in a monetary economy must begin with debt, because workers must be paid and capital goods purchased *before* income-yielding output is produced. Hence the owners of productive property must not only incur debt to allow production, but must also *hope* that sufficient spending will occur in the future so that M' exceeds M and debt can be cleared (or at least serviced). The capitalist market, then, is not a *device* to clear goods through changes in prices, but a *process* to clear debt. And, as a lender makes loans today on the promise of payment in the future, this process requires the creation of *dated* contracts; these in turn require the establishment of a unit of account that allows the recording of debt:

> A money of account comes into existence along with debts, which are contracts for deferred payment, and price lists, which are offers of contracts for sale or purchase. Such debts and price lists . . . can only be expressed in terms of a money of account.
> Money itself . . . derives its character from its relationship to the money of account, since the debts and prices must first have been expressed in terms of the latter. . . . Money proper . . . can only exist in relation to a money of account. (Keynes 1930 [1971], p. 3)

But, since the future cannot be known, it is impossible to make accurate predictions as to the outcome of any production-exchange process. Hence, in a monetary economy, production cannot be undertaken on the basis of a known, quantifiable (or even probabilistic) calculation, as is supposed in neoclassical models. 'Animal spirits' (or 'spontaneous optimism') drive investment and production in a world where historical time is of real importance and thus *fundamental* uncertainty is a fact of life.

In a monetary economy, the owners of productive property have obviously separated that property from the control of the larger community.

Since capitalists produce goods only in the expectation of future gain, the community cannot depend on such individuals for its economic well-being. Nor can the capitalist depend on the community should he or she encounter economic (financial) difficulties: the capitalist faces an uncertain future.

To protect themselves against the vagaries of this uncertain future, capitalists must accumulate stocks of wealth. These stocks will not be in the form of real goods (use values), for such forms of wealth are not readily convertible into other goods (they are not very liquid), and they entail large carrying costs. Thus, the capitalist will hold wealth in the form of money. Since this appears objectively irrational (one cannot 'eat' money), such actions can only be comprehended within an economic organization where time is important and the future is unknowable. '[*T*]*he importance of money essentially flows from its being a link between the present and the* (*uncertain*) *future*' (Keynes 1936 [1973], p. 293; emphasis in original).

For Keynes, then, historical time is one of the core features of his general theory. It is only through the inclusion of time that one can understand the uncertainty that is central to the decision-making process under capitalism, and it is only through an analysis of uncertainty that one can understand the nature of money. And money, of course, is the central characteristic of a monetary economy. In Hyman Minsky's succinct words, '[o]nce a financial perspective is adopted, time cannot be interpreted away as just adding additional commodities (Walrasian money) to the economy' (Minsky 1982, p. 62).

JOHN F. HENRY

Note Portions of this entry are based on J. Henry and L.R. Wray, *Economic Time*, Working Paper No. 255, New York: The Jerome Levy Economics Institute, 1998.

See also:

Agency; Equilibrium and Non-equilibrium; Keynes's *General Theory*; Non-ergodicity; Uncertainty; Walrasian Economics.

References

Davidson, Paul (1978), *Money and the Real World*, 2nd edition, New York: Wiley.
Davidson, Paul (1991), *Controversies in Post Keynesian Economics*, Aldershot: Edward Elgar.
Dow, Sheila (1996), *The Methodology of Macroeconomic Thought*, Cheltenham, UK and Northampton, MA, USA: Edward Elgar.
Dunn, Stephen (2001), 'Bounded rationality is not fundamental uncertainty: a Post Keynesian perspective', *Journal of Post Keynesian Economics*, **23** (4), 567–88.
Hicks, John R. (1939), *Value and Capital*, Oxford: Clarendon Press.
Keynes, John Maynard (1930 [1971]), *A Treatise on Money*, in *The Collected Writings of John Maynard Keynes*, Vol. 5, edited by D. Moggridge, London: Macmillan for the Royal Economic Society.
Keynes, John Maynard (1936 [1987]), *The General Theory of Employment, Interest and Money*.

Reprinted as *The Collected Writings of John Maynard Keynes*, Vol. 14, London: Macmillan for the Royal Economic Society.

Minsky, Hyman (1982), *Can 'It' Happen Again?*, Armonk, NY: M.E. Sharpe.

Robinson, Joan (1980), 'History vs. equilibrium', in J. Robinson, *Collected Economic Papers*, Vol. 5, Cambridge, MA: MIT Press, pp. 45–58.

Tobin Tax

In his 1972 Janeway lecture at Princeton, James Tobin (1974) proposed a tax on foreign exchange transactions as a way of limiting speculation, enhancing the efficacy of macroeconomic policy, and raising tax revenues (Davidson 1997 opposes this view). Keynes, in the *Treatise on Money* and in the *General Theory*, had already suggested that a tax on foreign lending to contain speculative capital movements might be necessary (see also Haq et al. 1996). Official interest in the Tobin tax has been repeatedly expressed. The United Nations Development Programme (1994) emphasized its potential for raising large amounts of money that could be used to finance development. The Tobin tax has been gaining popularity since then, and governments have either shown approval or willingness to discuss it.

In Arestis and Sawyer (1997) four sets of rationale are advanced in support of the Tobin Tax. In a world of floating exchange rates, the large volume of transactions is viewed as generating volatility in the exchange rate, with consequent detrimental effects on the real economies. The second rationale is simply its revenue potential. Tobin (1978) suggested it as a byproduct of a financial transaction tax, not as the main aim – a financial transaction tax of 0.05 per cent could have raised $150 billion a year over the 1995–2000 period. The third rationale concerns the possibility of enhancing the autonomy of national economic policy, and reducing the constraints on such policy imposed by financial markets. In this context a financial transaction tax increases the independence of policy makers by reducing foreign exchange rate volatility through hitting the most frequent transactors the hardest. The fourth is that this tax can potentially tackle the problems just alluded to more flexibly than the introduction of financial controls, especially quantitative exchange controls, which are usually viewed as rigid.

Three reasons for the increased interest in the Tobin tax are mentioned in Arestis and Sawyer (1997). The first is the growing volume of foreign exchange trading. The second reason is that a transactions tax is now seen as important not merely by policy makers and others concerned with foreign exchange market volatility, but also by those who attach significance to public financing of world development. The third reason is an increasing realization that foreign exchange markets do not operate in the efficient manner portrayed in the rational expectations literature. Foreign exchange markets suffer from asymmetric information, herd behaviour, moral hazard and from the possibility of multiple equilibria; the implication of all these is persistent misalignments and unstable exchange rate regimes.

One common argument raised against the Tobin tax relates to its possible distortionary effects. The argument is that such a tax leads in a competitive market to an equilibrium that involves a lower quantity of transactions, and fewer resources being allocated to that particular market. There are three points to be made in connection with this argument. First, the financial sector may at present be relatively lightly taxed, and the 'products' of the financial sector are generally not subject to either general sales or value-added taxes or to specific excise taxes and the like. This would mean that the imposition of a financial transaction tax might in effect be removing some distortions rather than imposing them. To the extent that this view is accepted, the introduction of a financial transaction tax would help to reduce the distortionary effect of the tax system.

Second, the distortionary nature of a tax arises from some potentially beneficial trades not taking place that would otherwise have happened. This leads to the question of whether there are gains from the current volume of exchange transactions, which would not arise with a substantially smaller volume. Some further doubt is cast on the distortionary argument by the observation that while the two parties to a foreign exchange trade may believe that they will gain from the trade (through a favourable price movement), both cannot do so, that is it is a zero-sum game.

Third, the analysis of distortions is an equilibrium one, and it is equilibrium trades which are discouraged. But there is a sense in which much of the trading in currency markets is disequilibrium trading in terms of seeking to take advantage of price changes. Thus the conventional analysis of distortions does not apply to this situation, and if it is the case that the amount of 'noise trading' is excessive, then a tax is beneficial rather than distortionary.

Assuming that the tax was fully passed on to consumers, it is clear that there could be a substantial impact on the volume of international trade (Davidson 1997). However, a rather low rate of taxation and the tax being absorbed by producers rather than passed on to consumers are distinct possibilities. In evaluating the overall balance of effects of a financial transaction tax on international trade, due consideration would need to be given to the effects of reduced volume of exchange transactions, of reduced volatility, enhanced independence of national economic policies and the probable stimulus to world-wide aggregate demand. These latter factors would stimulate international trade, and the overall net effect of such a tax on international trade cannot readily be predicted.

It is expected that the introduction of a Tobin tax would be a major economic and political development. At the same time it would have to be introduced on a 'big bang' basis, for otherwise foreign exchange dealings would quickly move to those countries that were not applying the tax.

It is also expected that a financial transaction tax would have a significant impact on world-wide aggregate demand. Besides the obvious point that the aggregate demand effects will depend on the use to which the tax revenue is put, it is quite reasonable to assume that a financial transaction tax would be levied on those with a low propensity to spend, and the redistribution would be towards those with a much higher propensity to spend. Hence aggregate demand may well increase. This would be an additional effect to the enhanced capability of national governments to pursue economic policies that stimulate a higher level of demand. Furthermore, to the extent to which the tax revenue does not lead (at the national and/or international level) to increased government expenditure, there would obviously be some reduction in budget deficits. Some would argue that the reduction in budget deficits would lead to a reduction in interest rates, with some stimulus to investment.

The appropriate definition of the transaction should be as follows: any transaction that involves the exchange of a financial asset denominated in one currency for a financial asset denominated in another currency. This was Tobin's initial suggestion when he wrote:

> [T]he tax would apply to all purchases of financial instruments denominated in another currency – from currency and coin to equity securities. It would have to apply ... to all payments in one currency for goods, services, and real assets sold by a resident of another currency area. I don't intend to add even a small barrier to trade. But I see off-hand no other way to prevent financial transactions disguised as trade. (Tobin 1978, p. 159)

A number of proposals have been put forward on the way to distribute the tax proceeds (see United Nations Development Programme 1994). To the extent that it is the International Monetary Fund (IMF) or World Bank which are the intermediate recipients, a further proposal may be to enhance the lending capabilities of these institutions especially to the Third World countries, which could embrace development and anti-pollution projects. The workings of the tax could be reinforced by making the administration of a Tobin tax a condition of membership of the IMF. It should be conceded, though, that this may not be sufficient to prevent the growth of offshore dealings. This is so since a small country would have very little to gain from membership of the IMF as compared with the potential revenue as the location of offshore financial markets.

There is widespread agreement that the tax would have to be implemented on a coordinated international basis. It may not be necessary for there to be full agreement over the tax rate, though there would be strong pressures towards a degree of uniformity (and probably a requirement for a minimum rate to avoid competitive undercutting of the tax rate between countries). It is clear that there would be very considerable differences in the amount of tax collected in each country. Part of the international agreement could clearly be that a proportion of the tax collected be paid over to an international body and/or used for agreed development and environmental purposes. The obvious difficulty which arises here is obtaining international agreement over the introduction and the rate of the tax when the revenue from the tax would be so unequally distributed across countries (and to the extent to which countries fear that their financial centres would be reduced in size, the costs also unequally distributed). Furthermore, a substantial retention of revenue at the national level obviously reduces the funds available for international development and global environmental purposes. It should also be expected that the economic and political influence of the financial markets would be much reduced; indeed the imposition of such a tax would be a clear signal that the influence of the financial sector was in decline. The point should be made, though, that the high-yield UK securities transaction tax, known as stamp duty, has been maintained in one of the most sophisticated financial markets. It has not obviously met with any serious opposition from these sophisticated financial markets, nor have there been cries of tax evasion in a market where players are most likely to find mechanisms to evade such a tax.

Most advocates of a financial transaction tax recognize that it would have to be 'universal and uniform'. This requirement may well be the most important practical obstacle to the implementation of such a tax. It would clearly require the cooperation of all countries with significant foreign exchange dealings within their borders, although there would be incentives for countries to apply a lower tax rate within their jurisdiction. Given the IMF's considerable expertise in international financial markets, it would be in a good position to undertake such a task. Furthermore, recognition of the IMF's central objectives of the promotion of international monetary cooperation, to maintain exchange rate stability and orderly exchange arrangements among its members, substantially strengthens the argument that the IMF should play a central role in its implementation.

A Tobin tax is expected to diminish the volatility of exchange markets and raise in revenue substantial sums of taxation. Its introduction could face political problems; and yet it has been gaining popularity, including with the Commission of the European Union. It might be more appropriate to use the Tobin tax as one of several policy instruments to combat speculation on the world's foreign exchanges, and to finance development.

PHILIP ARESTIS

See also:
Development Finance; Economic Policy; Exchange Rates; Globalization; International Economics.

References
Arestis, P. and M. Sawyer (1997), 'How many cheers for the Tobin financial transaction tax?', *Cambridge Journal of Economics*, **21** (6), 753–68.
Davidson, P. (1997), 'Are grains of sand in the wheels of international finance sufficient to do the job when boulders are often required?', *Economic Journal*, **107** (442), 671–86.
Haq, M., I. Kaul and I. Grunberg (eds) (1996), *The Tobin Tax: Coping with Financial Volatility*, Oxford: Oxford University Press.
Tobin, J. (1974), 'The new economics one decade older', *The Eliot Janeway Lectures on Historical Economics in Honour of Joseph Schumpeter, 1972*, Princeton: Princeton University Press.
Tobin, J. (1978), 'A proposal for international monetary reform', *Eastern Economic Journal*, **4** (3–4), 153–9. Reprinted in J. Tobin, *Essays in Economics: Theory and Policy*, Cambridge, MA: MIT Press, 1982, pp. 488–94.
United Nations Development Programme (1994), *Human Development Report 1994*, New York and Oxford: Oxford University Press.

Transition Economies

The term 'transition economy' can, in general, be applied to any economy moving from one dominating mechanism for coordinating its economy to another. However, since 1989 the term has been applied specifically to the post-communist, centrally planned economies of Central and Eastern Europe. Before 1989, these economies were, to a greater or lesser extent, characterized by a high degree of administrative planning, absence of the market mechanism in the allocation of resources, and a relative scarcity of consumer goods as compared to the advanced Western industrialized economies.

The appearance of various inefficiencies and distortions put pressure for some sort of change in the way these economies functioned. This pressure began intensifying after the 1970s, when the area's previously high growth rates could no longer be maintained. Since then, and up to the time of writing, although most of these economies have professed a commitment to adopting the market mechanism and the incentive of the profit motive as the only way to improve their economic performance, the record of achievement is mixed. 'Ten years after the breakup of the Soviet System, what is perhaps most striking about the European and Central Asia (ECA) region is its diversity. A decade ago, all countries in the region seemed to face similar challenges of transition from a planned centralized system to a market economy' ('Europe and Central Asia: Introduction', World Bank 2000, p. 63).

The explanation for this diversity can best be explained in terms of the presence or absence of those supportive, usually non-economic, institutions that make market mechanisms work, and market-oriented behaviour feasible. Hence, those Eastern European economies such as Hungary, Poland, the Czech Republic and Slovenia, which had already more diverse economic structures, have fared better in the post-1989 years, while others, most notably the Russian Federation and Ukraine, have experienced negative growth over much of this period, and are struggling to regain levels of gross domestic product reached before the Soviet collapse (ignoring for the moment the question of the reliability of pre-1989 economic statistics).

In response to an emerging recognition of various economic problems connected with their poor economic performance, some of the socialist economies had already begun to reduce the role of bureaucratic decision making, starting in the 1980s. Originally, in the inter-war period, bureaucratic planning had been instituted as a way to jump-start the industrialization process; after the Second World War, it was extended to the countries falling within the Soviet sphere of influence. Some of the characteristics of these economies were as follows.

Planners gave preference to the production of investment and intermediate goods, and energy production, because they aimed to catch up to the Western industrialized economies as fast as possible. Enterprises were operating entities but not decision-making units, being responsible only for fulfilling the plan's targets with the resources allocated to them. Planning was taut, targets were set high, all resources were fully employed, and there was little slack. A price system existed, but as an accounting device rather than as an incentive or allocative mechanism; firms did not need to respond to financial incentives. At first, prices were more or less in accordance with resource (opportunity) costs, but diverged considerably over time: planners were slow to respond to changing supply conditions or wanted to manipulate the numbers for various political purposes. The result was prices that were out of alignment with both opportunity costs and world prices for similar items.

Various distortions and imbalances appeared, but the structure and functioning of these economies prevented their elimination. Because enterprises were subject to a soft budget constraint – meaning that they could manipulate external financing and/or negotiate taxes, grants and credit in order to avoid bankruptcy indefinitely – there were no penalties for failure (Kornai 1980). Hence even though shortages and bottlenecks were common, and investment plans to eliminate them were therefore justified, they could not be fulfilled because of resource limitations. One example was the ubiquitous existence of queues, evidence of shortages of consumer goods. In other words, these economies were high investment, resource-constrained economies, rather than (effective) demand-constrained economies, as Western capitalist market economies are. However, innovative responses were not forthcoming, because enterprises, which had to deal with the problems, were not decision-making units, and enterprise managers responded to political, not economic, stimuli. In any event, enterprises had no incentive to respond innovatively, for fear that plan targets would be revised upwards.

Whether or not the changes that were already beginning to take place would have eventually resulted in more effective economic performance became an irrelevant issue following the events of 1989–90. At that time, the collapse of communist-dominated governments across the region initiated both political and economic changes – towards the adoption of democratic political processes and the market mechanism.

Economic advisers to many of the new governments favoured a three-prong approach to economic restructuring: eliminate planning in favour of a market mechanism; privatize productive assets to replace government ownership; and rely on a price system to coordinate economic activity so that financial incentives replace quantitative targets. While recognizing that there could be some short-term costs of adjustment – for example, a rise in unemployment as enterprises got rid of excess workers, or balance of payments deficits as Western imports poured in following the opening up of these economies – advisers recommended speed, the so-called 'shock therapy' approach.

The assumption that markets are the best mechanism for coordinating economic activity underlay these recommendations. In turn, this assumption underlies the standard model that focuses on self-interested individuals making rational choices so as to maximize utility/income/welfare/profits. In the transition economies, enterprises will have a crucial role to play in both generating and responding to price signals because they will become financially self-sufficient and therefore subject to a hard budget constraint with real penalties for failure, rather than simply carrying out the central bureaucracy's orders.

Unfortunately, and partly in explanation of the problems facing the transition economies since then, marketization is not a universal solution. Because the standard model was devised with the already-mature market capitalist economies in mind, it assumed that all the necessary institutions and behaviour patterns that make the price system work were in place. Such assumptions cannot be made in the transition economies; instead, an approach that takes into account their history, culture, institutional development and values is called for. This alternative approach also recognizes that it takes a long time for these supportive institutions to take root.

For example, private ownership of productive resources will only produce socially favourable results if a legal system specifying property rights, and the rights *and responsibilities* associated with them, is in place. In these countries, the necessary legal changes are still being put into place (and in some cases, required a first step of legitimizing the very concept of private property). Enterprises can only respond to financial incentives if there is a well-developed financial system: banks and other financial intermediaries to replace the government's role as finance provider. This further requires the establishment of more mechanisms to enforce accountability, including proper accounting procedures, bankruptcy laws and so on. Using prices presumes not only that there is some way of estimating the relation between opportunity costs and market prices, but also that there is a monetary institution capable of ensuring adequate liquidity in the system. Replacing planning with the market mechanism assumes that behaviour patterns are appropriate, and economic agents will respond in the right way: for example, that enterprise owners and managers have the specific knowledge and training to respond to price signals, and that the incentive system does in fact harmonize the actions of consumers, employees and managers in an acceptable way. But desired behaviour patterns are not inherent but learned, so that the mechanisms necessary for teaching and learning them have to be put into place.

Of particular importance to the transition economies is reworking the role of the state. Market democracies rely on a strong effective state in order to work as well as they do: to provide necessary infrastructure, guarantee property rights, provide a monetary system . . . the list could go on. Also, because of the absence of an automatic self-correcting mechanism in a capitalist market economy, there is an important role for government to ameliorate market failures and maintain the level of effective demand as a growth-enhancing policy. This is vital once the dynamic role of (privately generated) investment in a world of uncertainty, and in an uncertain *global* economy, is recognized.

In general, the transition economies have more to do than simply replace bureaucratic decision making and material balances planning with the profit motive, private property and the market mechanism. They also have to put into place all the institutions and processes that make a private enterprise economy function, as well as those that are needed for when it fails to function properly.

Policy options compatible with a Post Keynesian approach start from the (often difficult) realization that improved economic functioning depends on effective operations in many different areas. It is not simply a question of removing bureaucratic intervention and leaving markets alone so that the price system can work its magic.

Certain key elements of policy can be distinguished. First, the necessary legal, social, political and economic institutional arrangements that coordinate and promote correct economic behaviour should be put into place. Those with a special impact on economic activity include finance-granting institutions, with some sort of control in order to determine that an adequate amount of liquidity exists. Money and monetary institutions are definitely not neutral, and do influence economic activity.

Second, those elements contributing to effective behaviour patterns should be developed. These include the different levels of formal and informal educational institutions, information gathering, analysis and dispersion, and control and accountability mechanisms (including accounting rules and procedures).

Third, specific economic policy options need to be developed because a market system does not automatically correct its failures. Hence mechanisms to maintain aggregate demand and employment at appropriate levels, and to stabilize prices, are needed. Also, the dynamic aspects of economic growth and development are too important to be left to chance or opportunism. This requires giving attention to investment – its level and distribution – in order to promote growth in the face of an uncertain future. Also appropriate here would be a social safety net, not only to provide income security for its traditional clientele – the retired, sick, or destitute, for example – but also to encourage risk-taking and innovative behaviour by cushioning the hardships of failure.

Clearly, many other specific aspects of policy could be identified and described. What is important is the flexibility that comes with the recognition that each society has its own past, present and future, and that the goal of a pluralist, democratic market system will not be reached through a rigid commitment to a single official blueprint.

CHRISTINE RIDER

See also:
Economic Policy; Institutionalism; Socialism; Third Way.

References
Kornai, J. (1980), *The Economics of Shortage*, Amsterdam: North-Holland.
Rider, Christine (1993), 'The pricing problems of Eastern Europe', in Ingrid Rima (ed.), *The Political Economy of Global Restructuring*, Vol. I, Aldershot: Edward Elgar, pp. 86–99.
Rider, Christine (1996), 'Ethical policy making in the transition economies', in Edward J. O'Boyle (ed.), *Social Economics: Premises, Findings and Policies*, London and New York: Routledge, pp. 178–90.
Rosser, J. Barkley Jr. and Marina V. Rosser (1996), *Comparative Economics in a Transforming World Economy*, Chicago: Irwin.
World Bank (2000), *Annual Report 2000*, International Bank for Reconstruction and Development, Oxford: Oxford University Press.

Traverse

The traverse defines the movement of the economy outside equilibrium. It plays a particularly important role in Post Keynesian theory, as most Post Keynesian economists have serious doubts about the relevance and usefulness of equilibrium analysis.

Economics and political economy have almost always relied on some concept of equilibrium as a central organizing concept. A major methodological difference between different schools of thought has been the operational significance that each ascribed to that concept. For some economists, the concept of equilibrium is important for organizing ideas, and as an idealized point of reference. Others see it as being descriptive, with actual economies showing strong tendencies towards equilibrium, which might be achievable except for constant shocks. However, despite the importance of the concept of equilibrium, little was usually said about the process whereby the economy achieved it. For equilibrium to serve the function which economists have for so long assigned to it, there must be forces pushing the economy towards equilibrium, and the path the economy takes towards that equilibrium, that is, its adjustment path, must not influence the equilibrium to which it is tending. In the absence of these conditions, analysis of equilibria, independent of the 'traverse' become pointless. Hicks, who first introduced the term 'traverse' into economics, characterized it as 'the path which will be followed when the steady state is subjected to some kind of disturbance' (Hicks 1973, p. 81). In other words, the traverse describes the economy's dynamic out-of-equilibrium adjustment path in historical time. The importance of historical time is its uni-direction, time can only move forward, with the link between time periods given by the stock of capital inherited from the past, and the expectations embodied in it (Robinson 1974; Setterfield 1995). Although initially the traverse was used to describe the path between equilibria, later the traverse itself was seen to be the end of the story. Post Keynesian economists, among other heterodox economists (especially evolutionary and institutional economists), have been vocal about the fruitlessness of studying the equilibrium properties of an economic system without considering the question of whether the economy will actually get there. In other words, they have voiced their doubts about the comparative static method which dominates modern economics. More pointedly, Joan Robinson often criticized the separation of equilibrium analysis from the analysis of the traverse, as she believed that the actual equilibrium which an economy achieves (if it is capable of achieving one) will be vitally dependent on the path it takes, so that equilibrium would always be path-dependent (Robinson 1974).

The traverse is of relevance both to economists who deny that the economy is attracted to any equilibrium, as well as to those who accept that the economy will tend towards equilibrium, but argue that the final equilibrium position is path-determined, in the sense associated with hysteresis where current outcomes are determined by past values. Hicks and Lowe undertook detailed analysis of the adjustment paths economies take outside equilibrium. They considered the question of whether the market would send the correct signals to allow the structure of production to adjust as a response to a shock. 'The necessary *adjustment path* requires both *time* and *costs*, and faces difficulties which arise from disproportions between sectors and misleading market signals' (Hagemann 1992, p. 235 italics in original).

Hicks's initial analysis of the traverse utilizes a two-sector, fixed-coefficients model making use of the methods of the classical economists, with similarities to Piero Sraffa's model. In a two-sector model the one capital good can freely be moved between the capital- and consumption-goods sectors. Without the complications implied by structural disproportionalities, Hicks concludes that a full-employment path to equilibrium is only possible if the consumption-goods sector is more mechanized than the capital-goods sector. Even if this condition is fulfilled, a full-employment traverse is not guaranteed but must satisfy a series of technologically determined conditions with respect to the man/machine ratios in the two sectors. Hicks reaches the important conclusion that 'smooth adjustment may not be possible', with prices providing inappropriate guides to decision makers (Hicks 1965). In his later work, Hicks moved away from the 'classical' traverse, and attempted to analyse the traverse within a hybrid neoclassical/Austrian framework. In order to get a unique and unambiguous period of production, he resorted to the uninteresting case of the 'simple profile', for reasons related to the capital controversies. Unfortunately, this becomes essentially a one-commodity model, and is not, therefore, particularly enlightening. In any case, the neo-Austrian model cannot incorporate a specific machine-goods sector, or adequately treat fixed capital (Hagemann 1992), and so abstracts from the main problems. This attempt by Hicks to analyse the traverse within a neoclassical framework may be contrasted with the efforts of Kalecki and Lowe, and illustrates the difficulty of using the neoclassical approach to meaningfully discuss disequilibrium phenomena (Lavoie and Ramirez-Gaston 1977).

Lowe, in a return to the concerns of classical economics, sees the main problem of economics as the description of the 'path of economic growth' (Lowe 1976), which is not normally of the steady-state equilibrium type. He specifically analyses the traverse, and concentrates on the implications of structural change. For this reason, he focuses on the nature of changes in the structure of production and on intersectoral relations, in a manner reminiscent of the classical economists. To examine this problem, Lowe developed a three-sector model which incorporated not only the concept of historical time but also two important aspects of production; the specificity of capital goods and the importance of reproduction, which is necessary for the incorporation of intersectoral relations. Specificity is dealt with by differentiating two subsectors of the capital-goods sector. In the first subsector, capital goods are produced which can either reproduce themselves or produce capital goods for the consumption-goods sector. Although, at this stage, there is no distinction between the capital goods, specificity becomes important when the capital goods produced in this sector are installed, as on installation they lose their generality and, in an irreversible process, become specific to the production of capital goods for the consumption-goods sector. These capital goods may be considered a separate branch of production. The capital-good output of this sector is installed in the consumption-goods sector to produce consumption goods.

Lowe uses this model to examine the nature of the traverse. From an initial stationary state, the implications for the traverse of changes and restrictions on variables are analysed. The model is used to consider the structural changes within the capital-goods sector which are necessary to facilitate, for example, changes in technology and in the rate of growth of the labour force, and their implications for intersectoral relations.

An important conclusion to emerge is Lowe's demonstration that, although there may very well be a traverse which leads to a new full-employment steady state, it is unlikely to be achieved within a decentralized market system. This, in part, results from the market transmitting the 'wrong' signals in terms of the optimal structure of production and intersectoral flows.

While the Hicks/Lowe traverse analysis concentrates on the supply-side questions of the responses of the structure of production, Kalecki's emphasis was on the demand side. For Kalecki, the structure of demand was the key to the adjustment process, with the essence of the problem being what happens to the composition of demand as a result of the changes in the distribution of income during the cycle. As a result, although Kalecki, like Lowe, disaggregated the economy into three sectors, the disaggregation served different purposes. For Kalecki the division of the economy into a capital-goods sector and two consumption-goods sectors, differentiating workers' consumption from that of capitalists, was the result of his emphasis on the problems associated with realization in the form of effective demand.

He did, however, share Lowe's concern with reproduction and with intersectoral relations, but concentrated on flows of commodities and of incomes between sectors. Kalecki saw the main determinant of income and growth in mature capitalist economies as being the level of effective demand. Crucial to this was the dual role of investment, which, on the one hand was part of effective demand (so that the higher the level of investment, the greater the level of employment in that period), while on the other, it contributed to the creation of extra capacity (so that the higher the level of investment, the larger would be the problem with achieving full employment in subsequent periods). This 'paradox', according to Kalecki, struck at the heart of the capitalist system: 'The tragedy of investment is that it causes crisis because it is useful. Doubtless many people will consider this theory paradoxical. But it is not the theory which is paradoxical, but its subject – the capitalist economy' (Kalecki 1990–97, I, p. 318).

Although Kalecki concentrated on the role of effective demand in his analysis of capitalist economies, in his work on socialist economies the structure of production, rather than effective demand, was seen as the important constraint on economic activity. Here he came much closer to the traverse analysis of Hicks and Lowe, and in many ways their efforts are complementary. In a capitalist economy, a reduction in investment causes a reduction in profits which feeds through to a multiplied reduction in income and aggregate demand. Kalecki contrasts this with the effects of a reduction in investment in a socialist economy, where he argues there need be no problem with effective demand:

> The workers released from the production of investment goods would be employed in the consumption goods industries. The increased supply of these goods would be absorbed by means of a reduction in their prices. Since profits of the socialist industries would be equal to investment, prices would have to be reduced to the point where the decline in profits would be equal to the value of the fall in investment. (Kalecki 1990–97, II, pp. 254–5)

In his analysis of 'the structure of investment in socialist economies', he acknowledged the possibility of short-run problems in adjustment caused by capacity bottlenecks, in the sense of too much (or too little) capacity in the capital-goods sector. It is here that Kalecki's work touches on issues raised by Hicks and Lowe. Using a two-sector model, and differentiating investment in the capital-goods sector from aggregate investment, he showed that changes in the growth rate of the economy will necessitate deviations between the growth rate of investment and that of the economy, during the transition period. However, 'there exists a ceiling to the deviation of the rate of growth of investment from that of national income which is determined by the productive capacity of the investment sector' (Kalecki 1990–97, IV, p. 102).

Kalecki's two-sector model suffers from its inability sufficiently to disaggregate the structure of the investment-goods sector. This is of particular importance when the problem is that of differential growth rates between the consumption- and investment-goods sectors, with investment goods being provided to both sectors. It is here that Lowe's model can supplement Kalecki's discussion of structural problems, as well as showing the difficulty of getting rid of excess capacity.

There are many other examples of traverse analysis in economic theory. The literature on path-dependency, hysteresis, cumulative causation and lock-in are some examples. The general conclusion of this literature is that, without serious analysis of the traverse, all economic theory utilizing some concept of equilibrium (including the long-run equilibrium analysis of the Sraffians) is vacuous. Without some demonstration that there are forces in the economy which push it to equilibrium, without influencing the position to which the economy is gravitating, it is difficult to foresee any useful role for such equilibrium theory. However, such a demonstration is unlikely, as 'without a visible hand, the invisible hand is likely to guide us on to the wrong path; this is perhaps the most important conclusion from the analysis of the traverse' (Halevi and Kriesler 1992, p. 233)

PETER KRIESLER

See also:

Dynamics; Expectations; Growth Theory; Kaleckian Economics; Sraffian Economics; Time in Economic Theory.

References

Hagemann, H. (1992), 'Traverse analysis in a post-classical model', in J. Halevi, D. Laibman and E. Nell (eds), *Beyond the Steady State: A Revival of Growth Theory*, Basingstoke: Macmillan, pp. 235–63.
Halevi, J. and P. Kriesler (1992), 'An introduction to the traverse in economic theory', in J. Halevi, D. Laibman and E. Nell (eds), *Beyond the Steady State: A Revival of Growth Theory*, Basingstoke: Macmillan, pp. 225–34.
Hicks, J.R. (1965), *Capital and Growth*, Oxford: Oxford University Press.
Hicks, J.R. (1973), *Capital and Time: a Neo-Austrian Theory*, Oxford: Clarendon Press.
Kalecki, M. (1990–97), *Collected Works of Michał Kalecki*, Oxford: Clarendon Press.
Lavoie, M. and P. Ramirez-Gaston (1997), 'Traverse in a two-sector Kaleckian model of growth with target-return pricing', *Manchester School*, **65** (2), 145–69.
Lowe, A. (1976), *The Path of Economic Growth*, Cambridge: Cambridge University Press.
Robinson, J. (1974), 'History versus equilibrium', in J. Robinson, *Collected Economic Papers*, Vol. V, Oxford: Blackwell, 1979, pp. 48–58.
Setterfield, M. (1995), 'Historical time and economic theory', *Review of Political Economy*, **7** (1), 1–27.

Treatise on Probability

The *Treatise on Probability* (Keynes 1921) is J.M. Keynes's main philosophical work. The book had a long gestation period. The key idea was advanced in an undergraduate paper of 1904, before being expanded into a dissertation, awarded in 1909, for a fellowship at King's College, Cambridge. Publication was envisaged shortly thereafter, but extensive revisions and the First World War delayed its appearance until 1921. At the time, it established Keynes as a leading authority in the philosophy of probability, the ongoing interest in the work being indicated by at least six reprints (1929, 1943, 1948, 1952, 1957 and 1963). Its influence continues nowadays, but in a weaker vein.

It is not a mathematical treatise on the probability calculus but a wide-ranging philosophical work which could easily have been entitled *Treatise on Reason* or *Treatise on Logic*. In general terms, its significance is threefold. Firstly, it is a pioneering work advancing the earliest systematic exposition of the logical theory of probability, and its differences from rival theories (on which, see Weatherford 1982). Second, this theory of probability forms part of a broader theory of rational belief and action under uncertainty. Third, Keynes's philosophizing across a range of topics throws light on various aspects of his thinking in economic theory, economic policy, politics and the arts.

Keynes began his analysis of probability and rational belief with a question. How are we to understand the large class of arguments encountered in many spheres of life that we regard as rational in some sense and yet we know are non-conclusive (or non-deductive)? His answer was that rationality implies a connection with logic, and non-conclusiveness implies a connection with probability. The synthesis of these two ideas led to his conception of probability as a general theory of logic, the subject matter of which was rational but non-conclusive argument. Traditional or deductive logic was embraced by the general theory as a special case.

Every argument, whether non-conclusive or conclusive, proceeds from a set of premises, h, to a conclusion, a. Probability, in Keynes's theory, is concerned with the relation between the two propositions, h and a. In the general (non-conclusive) case, h lends some support to a but not complete or conclusive support; that is, the premises partly entail the conclusion, but are insufficient for complete entailment. Keynes postulated that the relation between h and a is a logical relation, which he called the 'probability-relation'. It is a relation of partial support or entailment which, in his view, belongs as much to logic as does the complete entailment of deductive logic. The distinctive symbol Keynes adopted for probability is a/h, read as the probability of a on premises h, this symbol emphasizing the data dependence of probability.

The connection between probability and rational belief was made as follows. Assuming that h were true and that a deductively followed from h, then the probability of a on h would be unity ($a/h = 1$) and it would be rational to believe *a* with complete certainty. However, if *h* were true and only gave partial support to *a*, the probability of *a* on *h* would be less than unity (*a/h* <1) and it would only be rational to believe *a* with a degree of certainty, this degree of certainty being given by the probability. If, for example, it has been raining for a week and no information indicates a cessation in the next few days, the probability of the proposition, 'it will rain tomorrow', will be high, and it will be rational to believe this proposition to a high degree, though not with complete certainty since it cannot be deduced from the available information. Notice that rationality of belief in *a* is not tied to the truth of *a*. The fact that *a* might later turn out to be false does not mean it was irrational, on the available evidence, to believe *a* to some degree in the first place.

Keynes's logical probability-relations express three aspects of arguments – degrees of partial inference (the extent to which *a* may be inferred from *h*), degrees of rational belief (the extent to which it is rational to believe *a*, given *h*), and degrees of certainty. The limits at either end of these degrees are the probabilities of unity and zero, both of which are given by deductive logic. Unit probability corresponds to full entailment and complete certainty. If *a* is fully entailed by *h*, then $a/h = 1$. Zero probability corresponds to contradiction or logical impossibility. If $-a$ is the contradictory of *a*, then $a/h = 0$ means $-a/h = 1$, that is, *h* fully entails the contradictory of *a*, so that *a* is impossible and requires complete disbelief. Bounded by these two extremes ($0 \leq a/h \leq 1$) is the densely populated universe of Keynes's probability-relations.

Such probabilities are always objective and never subjective. Their objectivity derives from their status as relations of logic. Between any pair of propositions, *a* and *h*, the logical relation is unique and fixed independently of personal opinion or psychological belief. Probabilities are thus members of an immutable, non-natural realm of logical relations transcending human subjectivity.

Knowledge of logical relations is arrived at by intellectual intuition, that is, by careful reflection on the support *h* gives to *a*, or by mental insight into the realm of logical relations. However, since mental ability varies across individuals and history, not all logical relations will be known to all individuals at all times. Depending on our powers of logical insight, some probabilities will be known and some unknown.

The measurement of probabilities is an intriguing aspect of Keynes's theory. While other theories reduce probabilities to numerical (and hence universally comparable) form, Keynes's ordering of the probability space is far more complex. Three types of comparative relations are postulated:

1. *Cardinal comparison*, which generates the relatively minor class of numerical probabilities. These only exist under the restrictive condition

of equiprobability, which is established by careful use of the 'principle of indifference'.
2. *Ordinal comparison*, which generates the much bigger class of non-numerical probabilities. This class consists of many separate, incommensurable series whereby probabilities belonging to the same series are comparable in terms of greater or lesser, but probabilities belonging to different series are generally incapable of being compared in magnitude.
3. *Non-comparability*, which typically exists between numerical and non-numerical probabilities, and between non-numerical probabilities in different series.

Such heterogeneity in the ordering relations between probabilities greatly restricts the scope of the probability calculus.

Keynes proposed that a second, independent variable, called 'the weight of argument', is also relevant to rational belief under uncertainty. Weight is positively associated with the data, h. It provides a measure of the 'well-foundedness' of non-conclusive argument and hence of the confidence that may be placed in the argument. Arguments of high weight are based on much information, are well founded and hence merit high degrees of confidence, regardless of whether their probability is high or low. Arguments of low weight rest on little information, are poorly founded and deserve low degrees of confidence even if their probability is high. All other things being equal, rational agents should choose the argument with the greatest weight.

After outlining the fundamental ideas in Part I of the book, Keynes extended the discussion to associated issues in the remaining four parts. In Part II, he undertook the necessary task of deriving the probability calculus. Using definitions and axioms based on probability as the relation, a/h, he first arrived at the theorems of deductive logic, and then turned to probable inference to derive the theorems of the addition and multiplication of probabilities and of inverse probability.

In Part III, Keynes observed that logicians had not offered satisfactory accounts of the processes of induction that lay behind numerous arguments. Believing that every inductive argument was probabilistic in nature, he sought to explore the analysis and logical justification of induction. His procedure was, first, to dissect inductive methods; second, to isolate the fundamental assumption(s) on which induction rested; and, third, to inspect these assumption(s) for their truth or self-evidence without resorting to appeals to experience, which would involve circularity. The main assumption he saw underpinning induction was the principle of limited independent variety, which essentially says that the variety of the universe is limited because it derives from a finite number of independent generators. He then cautiously suggested that this principle was self-evidently true, thereby accepting the existence of synthetic *a priori* knowledge which, along with the role of intuition in his theories of probability and ethics, places the epistemology of his philosophical work in the rationalist camp.

In keeping with much philosophy of the time, Keynes's treatment of chance and randomness in Part IV is based on determinism. On this view, chance, randomness or indeterminateness are not objective or inherent characteristics of the universe, but are purely subjective phenomena deriving from human ignorance. It is our lack of knowledge of the relevant causal order which leads us to say that certain events are due to chance or are random occurrences, when actually they are the product of causal influences of which we are currently ignorant.

Also in Part IV, Keynes addressed the vital question of 'what ought we to do?', but in only one chapter. His answer, which combined his logical theory of probability with the ethics of G.E. Moore, may be described as a probabilistic form of consequentialism. On this view, rational or right action is that which is judged to produce the greatest amount of probable goodness on the whole, appropriate attention being paid to weight and moral risk. Broadly speaking, the assessment of an action involves a listing of its possible consequences and a means of combining the probabilities and values of these consequences into probable goodness on the whole. When numerical magnitudes can be ascribed to probabilities and values the procedure is straightforward, but, when probabilities and/or values are non-numerical in nature, Keynes appealed to direct judgement or intuition as the means by which we arrive at the probable goodness of the whole. If such judgement was not within our power, he accepted the matter as indeterminate. In such cases, suggestions were made that reason can turn to second-best options such as conventions, rules and caprice.

The concept of moral risk directs attention to the probability of failure or non-occurrence. It is most relevant to extreme cases where probable values derive from a combination of very low probabilities and very large gains. Even if the probable value is acceptable, the probability of failure is very high, as is the probability of losing the money or effort wagered on the outcome. If this loss would have catastrophic effects, rational individuals should be prudent and pursue actions with lower risks of loss. One should not bet all one's wealth on a horse race; winning might produce enormous gain, but losing would result in pauperism.

In the final part, Keynes investigated the logical basis of statistical inference. He analysed the Law of Large Numbers, the theorems of Bernoulli, Poisson and Chebyshev, Laplace's rule of succession, and the methods of Lexis, before concluding, all too briefly, with an outline of a constructive theory. His object was to uncover and discredit invalid inferences and to clarify and support valid inferences, his guiding principle throughout being that logic was the master and mathematics the servant. What drew his censure, here and in relation to mathematical methods generally, was loose thinking and inappropriate application, not valid and logically consistent use.

Questions naturally arise as to the existence of connections between Keynes's philosophical thought and his non-philosophical thought in areas such as economics, politics and the arts. Of central importance is the relationship between his major philosophical work (the *Treatise on Probability*, hereafter the *Treatise*) and his major economic work, *The General Theory of Employment, Interest and Money*. Some of the key issues discussed have been whether substantial connections exist between: (i) the treatment of probability and uncertainty in the *Treatise* and the treatment of uncertainty and expectations in the *General Theory*; (ii) the non-neoclassical rationality of the *Treatise* and the non-neoclassical treatment of agent behaviour in the *General Theory*; (iii) the epistemology of the *Treatise* and his epistemological remarks in the *General Theory* and elsewhere; (iv) the approach taken to quantitative matters and formalism in the *Treatise* and his comments on mathematical methods in economics and econometrics in other writings; and (v) the ethics and theory of right action of the *Treatise*, and his thoughts on political philosophy and party politics in other works.

Such questions have generated considerable controversy. Some writers argue that various strong threads of continuity exist between the conceptual framework of the *Treatise* and major themes in Keynes's other thought. Others claim that his philosophical thinking changed significantly after 1921, thereby creating serious discontinuities between the *Treatise* and the *General Theory*. Debate has arisen over whether he remained an adherent of the logical theory of probability, or was converted shortly afterwards to Frank Ramsey's subjectivist theory. Discussion also surrounds rationality, irrationality and Freudian influences in his thought. For two views, out of the many available, on the relations between Keynes's philosophy and his other writings, see Carabelli (1988) and O'Donnell (1989).

ROD O'DONNELL

See also:

Agency; Econometrics; Expectations; Keynes's *General Theory*; Uncertainty.

References

Carabelli, A.M. (1988), *On Keynes's Method*, London: Macmillan.
Keynes, J.M. (1921), *A Treatise on Probability*, London: Macmillan. Republished in 1973 (with different pagination) as Volume VIII of *The Collected Writings of John Maynard Keynes*, London: Macmillan.

O'Donnell, R.M. (1989), *Keynes: Philosophy, Economics and Politics. The Philosophical Foundations of Keynes's Thought and their Influence on his Economics and Politics*, London: Macmillan.

Weatherford, R. (1982), *Philosophical Foundations of Probability Theory*, London: Routledge & Kegan Paul.

Uncertainty

Economics texts commonly define a situation of *risk* as one in which an individual with a decision to make is able to assign numerical probabilities to all outcomes that could possibly follow from that decision. If probabilities cannot be assigned, a situation of *uncertainty* is then said to obtain. These texts characteristically focus their attentions on the 'risk' situation thus specified: having defined uncertainty, they simply ignore it. Some mainstream theorists take a different tack and assume that economic agents can *always* identify, and assign probabilities to, the whole range of possible future 'states of the world'. This group has no need to make a distinction between risk and uncertainty: for them, uncertainty itself is inherently quantifiable.

The passion for numerical probability shown by mainstream economists is no accident. For their central concept of 'rational' optimizing choice, developed under assumptions of perfect knowledge, can seem somewhat irrelevant to the real world, where certainty is never obtainable. However, if knowledge of probabilities attaching to alternative possible future scenarios is assumed to be available, then (statistically) expected values can be calculated. These can, in turn, provide a basis for a theory of optimal decisions in a world in which perfect knowledge is lacking. In this way, many orthodox economists believe they have remedied a major perceived deficiency in their theoretical apparatus.

For Post Keynesian economists, in contrast, the future is characterized by *fundamental uncertainty*. They take their cue from Keynes, who rejected the possibility of a theory of optimal choice under uncertainty, observing that 'human decisions affecting the future ... cannot depend on strict mathematical expectation, since the basis for making such calculations does not exist' (Keynes 1936, pp. 162–3). Drawing primarily on the work of Paul Davidson, the discussion which follows tries to explain the concept of fundamental uncertainty in broad terms and to show why it occupies such an important place in Post Keynesian economic theory. As a first step, it is appropriate to review some important concepts developed by George Shackle, since his theories have been a major influence on the way Post Keynesian economists in general think about uncertainty and on Davidson's ideas on the subject in particular.

Any 'question about the future' represents what Shackle (1968 [1955], p. 63) calls an *experiment*. He defines a *divisible* experiment as one consisting of 'a series of trials all in some sense alike and each important only as it contributes to the total result of the series' (p. 64). For instance, a firm might regard any sale to a prospective customer as a *trial*. Its sales 'experiment' would then be a divisible one, if (as is likely) its management were primarily interested in the total revenue generated by its sales effort and not in the outcome of its dealings with any specific customer.

Shackle accepts that it might in principle be possible to calculate numerical probabilities in divisible experiments, provided that frequency distributions could be derived from '"suitably uniform" circumstances and a "large" number of [past] repetitions' (p. 4). His point, however, is to challenge what that would achieve. For, suppose our firm *could* draw up reliable frequency data from individual customer records and so meet these preconditions for calculating numerical probabilities. Its total monthly sales revenue could then be forecast with considerable accuracy and could not be described as being a matter over which its management was in any real sense uncertain. Thus, Shackle argues, a situation in which numerical probabilities *could* be calculated 'has nothing whatever to do with ignorance or uncertainty: it is knowledge' (p. 4). His argument implies that the orthodox economists whose approach was outlined above delude themselves in imagining they have developed theories that have anything to do with real uncertainty.

An even more potent concept developed by Shackle is that of the *crucial experiment*. This he explains as follows:

> An experiment can be such that . . . the making of it will radically alter the situation . . . so that it will subsequently be impossible . . . to perform another experiment of a relevantly similar kind. Napoleon could not repeat the battle of Waterloo a hundred times in the hope that, in a certain proportion of cases, the Prussians would arrive too late. His decision to fight on the field of Waterloo was what I call a crucial experiment . . . Had he won, repetition would . . . have been unnecessary; when he lost, repetition was impossible. (Shackle 1968 [1955], p. 25)

Shackle's main point is not that the 'average' outcome of a large number of 'similar' experiments is hypothetical when the experiment is crucial. Rather, it is that any such average is *of no interest* to the crucial experimenter, because the latter is never going to be in a position to offset a poor outcome now with better ones later. Shackle's position can perhaps be summarized as follows: when numerical probability calculations are relevant, the situation is not uncertain; when the situation *is* uncertain, they are not relevant.

Shackle insisted that 'The difficulty of obtaining reliable frequency ratios is the lesser strand of my argument' (1968, p. 4). Although drawing on Shackle's concepts, Davidson's efforts have, however, been directed at showing just how serious that 'difficulty' is. Now Keynes (1973 [1921], p. 468) castigated the 'Professors of probability (who are) often and justly derided for arguing as if nature were an urn containing black and white balls in fixed proportions'. Nevertheless, Davidson insists that the conceptions of these professors' modern-day counterparts must be used if the case against them is to be demonstrated. To follow Davidson's analysis it is therefore helpful to begin by considering what the world would be like if nature *were* akin to Keynes's urn.

The outcome of any drawing from the urn will be a *stochastic* (random) event, so that we can possibly think of a series of outcomes in a succession of drawings as resulting from a stochastic *process*. Furthermore, if these drawings take place at consecutive points in time, they will yield a *time series*, from which an average outcome, a *time average*, can be calculated. This series could be infinite. It is not so easy to conceive of all possible outcomes of a drawing at a *single* point in time as existing simultaneously in a universe or *ensemble* (Davidson 1982–83, p. 189) of alternative 'logical' worlds. However, having made this conceptual leap, we can grasp the idea of a *space average*, the mean value taken by a (finite or infinite) set of such drawings (ibid.).

On this basis, we can begin to understand the following definition of an *ergodic process*, Davidson's formal equivalent to nature's urn: 'If the stochastic process is *ergodic*, then for an infinite realization [that is, set of drawings from the urn], the time and space averages will coincide. For finite realizations . . . the space and time averages tend to converge' (Davidson 1994, p. 90; see also Davidson 1982–83, p. 185). The importance of this concept in Davidson's work is measured by the frequency with which more or less this same terse definition is restated in his writings. It is the basis on which he asserts the existence of what he calls the *ergodic axiom*, the assumption that economic events are broadly governed by ergodic processes. This axiom, he suggests, is the ultimate logical foundation of orthodox theorizing (Davidson 1994, pp. 89–90; 1996, p. 494). For the convergence of averages in an ergodic system implies that, over a long enough period of time, events will tend to follow repetitive patterns, and it is central to Davidson's argument that just this kind of conception lies behind the orthodox belief in an inherent tendency in market economies towards a long-run (full-employment) equilibrium (Davidson 1996, p. 496).

Of course, Davidson's purpose in highlighting the importance to orthodox theory of an ergodic axiom is only to demonstrate that belief in it is untenable. This he seeks to do on both empirical and logical grounds. Now, simply stated, a time series is stationary if all observations that go to make it up are drawn from distributions with the same mean and variance, and his empirical objection is that real-world time-series data often fail to exhibit evidence of stationarity. As he points out, non-stationarity is, formally, a sufficient condition for non-ergodicity (ibid., pp. 494–5).

Davidson's logical objection is perhaps the more fundamental. He observes, referring to Shackle's concept, that 'When agents make *crucial decisions*, they necessarily destroy any ergodic processes that may have hitherto existed' (Davidson 1982–83, p. 192). Furthermore, if crucial decisions are 'all pervasive' (Shackle 1968 [1955], p. 63) or even just 'very common' (Davidson 1982–83, p. 192), then the economy as a whole will be in a state of constant change as economic agents continually alter the pre-existing state of things by taking them. That will in turn represent 'a sufficient condition for a non-ergodic world' (ibid.; see also Davidson 1996, pp. 497, 500). In that world, decision makers will typically operate in an environment of fundamental uncertainty, since it will be impossible to base a whole range of significant economic decisions on forecasts derived from past data.

The significance of this analysis for Post Keynesian theory is immense. For, as Davidson (1994, pp. 93–4; 1996, pp. 501, 506) insists:

1. individuals will exhibit long-term liquidity preference only under conditions of fundamental uncertainty;
2. the Post Keynesian contention that money is not neutral even in the long run assumes the possibility of long-term liquidity preference;
3. the Post Keynesian critique of the notion that market economies have an automatic tendency towards full-employment equilibrium is based on a denial of the neutrality of money; and
4. Post Keynesian policy analysis, with its emphasis on government intervention and the need for protective institutions, arises out of that critique.

As has been shown, the essential premise of the first of this argument's four steps is the proposition that the crucial experiment is, at the very least, a 'common' phenomenon in the economic sphere. But if 'crucialness' is important in the real world, why do orthodox theorists fail even to acknowledge it as a possibility? The answer would seem to be that, conceiving nature as an urn like Keynes's professors of probability, they cannot do so. For that would be tantamount to accepting that the proportions of black and white balls in the urn could be changed by human decisions and would make it impossible to view cause and effect simply in terms of the operation of stochastic processes.

The idea of a stochastic process, it is reasonable to argue, implies a metaphysical view of the world that is at odds with human experience. This is because:

> the existence of a process implies that the outcome today stands at the end, in real time, of a chain of causation and may be different from what it was yesterday because of prior changes somewhere along the length of that causal chain.

Processes are in reality the polar opposite of repeated drawings from some eternally subsisting distribution. In other words, in place of a genuine process there is, within the stochastic scheme of things, only the isolated, accidental outcome, dissociated from any determining cause/effect relationship with anything that has gone before. (Glickman 1997–98, p. 262)

Davidson has noted that 'If observed economic events are not the result of stochastic processes then objective probability structures do not even fleetingly exist' (1994, p. 90). The historical/causal conception of a process just outlined offers a realistic alternative account of how economic events are determined that can help us understand *why* uncertainty is fundamental in economics.

MURRAY GLICKMAN

See also:

Agency; Expectations; Keynes's *General Theory*; Liquidity Preference; Non-ergodicity; *Treatise on Probability*.

References

Davidson, P. (1982–83), 'Rational expectations: a fallacious foundation for studying crucial decision-making processes', *Journal of Post Keynesian Economics*, **5** (2), 182–97.
Davidson, P. (1994), *Post Keynesian Macroeconomic Theory*, Aldershot: Edward Elgar.
Davidson, P. (1996), 'Reality and economic theory', *Journal of Post Keynesian Economics*, **18** (4), 479–508.
Glickman, M. (1997–98), 'A Post Keynesian refutation of Modigliani–Miller on capital structure', *Journal of Post Keynesian Economics*, **20** (2), 251–74.
Keynes, J.M. (1936), *The General Theory of Employment, Interest and Money*, London: Macmillan.
Keynes, J.M. (1973 [1921]), *A Treatise on Probability*, reprinted as *The Collected Writings of John Maynard Keynes*, Vol. VIII, edited by D.E. Moggridge, London: Macmillan for the Royal Economic Society.
Shackle, G.L.S. (1968 [1955]), *Uncertainty in Economics*, Cambridge: Cambridge University Press.

Underconsumption

Although Keynes wrote about underconsumption at some length, the term is seldom used these days by Post Keynesians. Some of the central issues continue to resonate, however, in discussions of economic growth and the relationship between wages and employment.

Keynes devoted chapter 23 of the *General Theory* to 'Notes on Mercantilism, the usury laws, stamped money and theories of under-consumption', revealing considerable sympathy for seventeenth- and eighteenth-century work on the dangers of excessive saving. He also quoted Thomas Malthus and provided a critical commentary on such later underconsumptionists as

J.A. Hobson and Major C.H. Douglas. The 'primary evil' identified by these writers, Keynes concluded, was 'a propensity to save in conditions of full employment more than the equivalent of the capital which is required, thus preventing full employment except when there is a mistake of foresight' (Keynes 1936, pp. 367–8). By 'the capital that is required' he seems to have meant the addition to the capital stock needed to cater for the increase in output as a whole (not just consumption goods), while 'the mistake in foresight' referred to the belief of Hobson and other underconsumptionists that unemployment would normally result unless entrepreneurs wrongly invested more than was justified by this requirement.

In chapter 22, 'Notes on the trade cycle', Keynes declared his support for 'all sorts of policies for increasing the propensity to consume' (ibid., p. 325), and offered a numerical example to illustrate what might be required:

> [If] the average level of output of to-day is 15 per cent. below what it would be with continuous full employment, and if 10 per cent. of this output represents net investment and 90 per cent. of it consumption – if, furthermore, net investment would have to rise 50 per cent. in order to secure full employment, with the existing propensity to consume, so that with full employment output would rise from 100 to 115, consumption from 90 to 100 and net investment from 10 to 15: – then we might aim, perhaps, at so modifying the propensity to consume that with full employment consumption would rise from 90 to 103 and net investment from 10 to 12. (ibid., pp. 325–6)

Quite how this was to be achieved, Keynes did not say. The earliest underconsumptionists had called for a larger share of national income to go to the idle rich, who could be relied upon not to save very much of it. Subsequently, liberal and socialist writers urged redistribution in favour of the poor, on the grounds that the propensity to save out of wages and salaries was considerably higher than that out of profits (and rents).

This is where Keynes – or at least his left-wing supporters – met Marx. The brief references to Marxism in the *General Theory* are disparaging, though in a 1933 draft Keynes had been much less critical. There was in fact a long tradition of underconsumptionism in the Marxian literature on economic crises and – not surprisingly – it featured prominently in analyses of the Great Depression by socialist theorists like Otto Bauer, Natalie Moszkowska and Eugen Varga. The inexorable tendency of capitalist production, they argued, was towards an increase in the rate of exploitation, and hence in the share of profits in net output. This had become even more pronounced in the latest, monopoly stage of capitalism, which was dominated by what Paul Baran and Paul Sweezy termed 'the law of the rising surplus'. The decline in the wage share had rendered the system liable to crises of overaccumulation, with the capital stock growing more rapidly than was warranted by the increase in consumption. Thus, even if higher saving were to stimulate higher investment, the situation was inherently unsustainable. Any boom would end in a severe cyclical downturn, or perhaps (in the most dramatic versions of the argument) in the complete breakdown of the system. The maturity of capitalism was therefore synonymous with stagnation, according to the Austrian 'left Keynesian' Josef Steindl (King 2002, chapter 2).

Of all Keynes's close allies, it was Joan Robinson who was most receptive to these ideas. While she criticized Marx for trying to work out a theory of crisis in which Say's Law continued to hold, she also saw considerable merit in his reproduction models. They could be used, Robinson suggested, as the basis for a theory in which

> consumption by the workers is limited by their poverty, while consumption by the capitalists is limited by the greed for capital which causes them to accumulate wealth rather than to enjoy luxury. The demand for consumption goods (the product of group II) is thus restricted. But if the output of the consumption-goods industries is limited by the market, the demand for capital goods (group I) is in turn restricted, for the constant capital of the consumption-good industries will not expand fast enough to absorb the potential output of the capital-good industries. Thus the distribution of income, between wages and surplus, is such as to set up a chronic tendency for a lack of balance between the two groups of industries. (Robinson 1942, p. 49)

In this interpretation Robinson was heavily influenced by Michał Kalecki who, though not himself an underconsumptionist, had absorbed the closely related work of Mikhail Tugan-Baranovsky and Rosa Luxemburg while still a young man in Poland. In a celebrated passage Kalecki wrote of 'the tragedy of investment', which adds both to effective demand and to the capital stock, simultaneously stimulating growth and undermining it (Kalecki 1939 [1991], p. 284).

In formal terms, there are certain similarities between models of underconsumption and the accelerator principle that is central to Harrod–Domar growth theory, itself a major influence on Post Keynesian thinking about economic growth. It is significant that both Roy Harrod and Evsey Domar acknowledged their debt to Hobson. 'Keynes analysed what happened when savings (of the preceding period) are not invested', Domar wrote. 'Hobson, on the other hand, went a step further and stated the problem in this form: suppose savings are invested. Will the new plants be able to dispose of their products? Such a statement of the problem was not, as Keynes thought, a mistake. It was a statement of a different, and possibly also a deeper problem' (Domar 1957, p. 52). Some intricate analytical issues are involved here, in particular the precise specification of the accelerator principle (does investment depend on the rate of increase in consumption or the rate of increase in total output?), and the relationship between underconsumption and what has been termed the 'underinvestment' theory that is implicit in the Harrod–Domar model (Schneider 1996, pp. 77–83).

If growth theory is one area in which underconsumptionist thinking continues to influence Post Keynesian macroeconomics, the other is wage and employment theory. Sidney Weintraub (1956) approached this question from the perspective of Keynes's aggregate supply–aggregate demand analysis. An increase in the general level of money wages would shift the aggregate supply curve upwards, by increasing firms' costs of production, and would therefore tend to reduce employment. But it might also shift the aggregate demand curve up, through increasing consumption by wage earners; alternatively, it could reduce aggregate demand by depressing the marginal efficiency of capital and discouraging investment. Weintraub distinguished three possibilities: the classical case, where employment falls as money wages rise; what he termed the Keynesian case, where shifts in aggregate supply and aggregate demand cancel each other out; and the underconsumptionist case, where employment increases as money wages rise.

While Weintraub focused on money wages, Amit Bhaduri and Stephen Marglin (1990) provided a formal analysis of the effects on aggregate demand of an exogenous change in the *real* wage. They distinguished 'stagnationist' and 'exhilarationist' regimes, the former (which corresponds to the classic underconsumptionist position) prevailing when investment responds weakly to a reduction in profitability while consumption increases substantially if real wages rise. The case for the stagnationists, they argued, is stronger in the context of a closed economy than in an open economy, where effective demand can be increased by a currency devaluation that lowers the real wage.

The policy issues that are involved here are evidently very important, and potentially very divisive. Kalecki angrily criticized those self-proclaimed 'workers' friends' who urged trade unions to accept money-wage reductions in the interests of increased employment (Kalecki 1939 [1991], p. 318), although this did not make him an advocate of wage inflation as the route to full employment. Instead he suggested that higher money wages were likely to generate price inflation, leaving *real* wages – and real consumption – unchanged. Only a reduction in the product market and labour market power of the capitalists, Kalecki concluded, would permanently raise real wages and reduce the share of profits in national income.

Is it possible that both workers and capitalists might gain from an increase in real wages that increases effective demand, thereby raising capacity utilization and increasing total profits? Bhaduri and Marglin contrast the social democratic ideology of economic cooperation between the classes with the conservative (and Marxian!) view that conflict over income distribution is inescapable in any capitalist economy. In their model the values of the parameters determine precisely when cooperation will give way to conflict, and it proves impossible to establish an unambiguous association between the stagnationist regime and class cooperation on the one hand, and the exhilarationist regime and class conflict on the other (Bhaduri and Marglin 1990, Figure 3, p. 389).

The evidence on the relationship between real wages and aggregate employment is also rather mixed. In the late 1930s Keynes was convinced by 'friendly critics', among them Kalecki, John Dunlop and Lorie Tarshis, that increased employment was associated with higher, not lower, real wages. More recent research suggests that he (and they) may well have been mistaken. Lavoie (1996–97) defends Kalecki, arguing that an increase in the 'base' real wage paid to 'fixed' (or core) employees does indeed generate greater employment. But the *average* real wage falls due to a rise in the proportion of low-paid peripheral (temporary or 'variable') workers. Empirically no less than theoretically, underconsumption remains one of the more contentious questions in Post Keynesian economics.

J.E. KING

See also:

Growth and Income Distribution; Growth Theory; Income Distribution; Kaleckian Economics; Saving; Wages and Labour Markets.

References

Bhaduri, A. and S. Marglin (1990), 'Unemployment and the real wage: the economic basis for contesting political ideologies', *Cambridge Journal of Economics*, **14** (4), 375–93.
Domar, E.S. (1957), 'Expansion and employment', *American Economic Review*, **47** (1), 34–55.
Kalecki, M. (1939 [1991]), *Essays in the Theory of Economic Fluctuations*, London: Allen & Unwin; reprinted in *Collected Works of Michał Kalecki*, Vol. I, Oxford: Clarendon Press.
Keynes, J.M. (1936), *The General Theory of Employment, Interest and Money*, London: Macmillan.
King, J.E. (2002), *A History of Post Keynesian Economics Since 1936*, Cheltenham, UK and Northampton, MA, USA: Edward Elgar.
Lavoie, M. (1996–97), 'Real wages, employment structure, and the aggregate demand curve in a Post Keynesian short-run model', *Journal of Post Keynesian Economics*, **19** (2), 275–88.
Robinson, J. (1942), *An Essay on Marxian Economics*, London: Macmillan.
Schneider, M.P. (1996), *J.A. Hobson*, London: Macmillan.
Weintraub, S. (1956), 'A macroeconomic approach to the theory of wages', *American Economic Review*, **46** (5), 835–56.

Unemployment

In capitalist economies, individuals and families are largely responsible for providing for their own well-being. In all industrialized and many developing economies, most workers do not have the means of production to provide for their own subsistence, but rather must obtain the means of purchase and means of payment (money) necessary for buying the means of subsistence by selling their labour power in the market. In addition, the requirement that taxes be paid in government currency means that even those possessing the means of production to provide for their own subsistence nevertheless must usually enter the labour market to obtain that which is necessary to settle their tax obligations.

Unemployment, the failure to obtain employment that earns wages or salaries paid in money, thus has a dire impact on the jobless, and is also associated with tremendous social and economic costs for society as a whole. Whereas, in neoclassical economics, market systems possess an inherent tendency to full employment, in Post Keynesian economics unemployment is seen as a normal feature of capitalist economies. The *effective demand problem* means that capitalist economies have trouble *attaining* full employment, while the *structural change problem* means that capitalist economies have trouble *maintaining* full employment, even if it could be attained. In addition, some Post Keynesians – echoing Marx – have identified the *functionality* of unemployment, which presents obstacles to Post Keynesian economic policies to eliminate unemployment. Nevertheless, Post Keynesian economics does suggest policies that might assist capitalist economies in attaining and maintaining full employment, without resulting in other macroeconomic problems, such as inflation.

Unemployment has tremendous social and economic costs (see, for example, Piachaud 1997). Unemployment causes permanent losses of output of goods and services. The unemployed are faced with financial insecurity, resulting in poverty and indebtedness. Certain kinds of criminal activity are directly related to unemployment. Many studies have linked unemployment to family disruption, suicide, ill health (physical and mental), drug addiction, homelessness, malnutrition, poor prenatal care, school dropouts, racial and ethnic antagonism, and other social problems (see, for example, Jahoda 1982). Unemployment also differentially affects certain sectors of the population, so that disadvantaged minorities, those with little education, and youth, for example, can suffer from rates of unemployment two to ten times the overall rate.

Unemployment can also destabilize business expectations, as fears of low demand cool private investment. Related to this, unemployment can also lead to technological stagnation. If, as Marx and others suggest, high levels of employment stimulate technical innovation, unemployment would be associated with less innovation. Firms with high and stable levels of demand have the resources and the incentive to support high-tech development; with high unemployment and thus cheap labour, firms lack the resources and the incentive to retool. It has also been shown that unemployment leads to deterioration in labour skills. All of this suggests that unemployment may lead to lower productivity growth.

Unemployment is the direct and indirect cause of many social and economic problems. It can also lead to political instability. Since Keynes, Post Keynesians have dedicated significant attention to the problems of unemployment. Since unemployment is the cause of so much social and human misery, it is of great interest whether capitalist economies tend to full employment or whether unemployment is a normal feature of capitalism, and thus a target for government intervention.

In neoclassical economics, market systems tend to utilize all resources fully, including labour. Perfectly flexible wages, prices and interest rates constitute the self-adjusting mechanism that will tend to eliminate unemployed resources in the long run. In the neoclassical version of Say's Law, if there is unemployment wages will adjust to increase labour demand, and interest rates will adjust to ensure that the excess of aggregate income over aggregate consumption at the full-employment level of output will be invested. There is no *involuntary* unemployment in the long run, unless there are market imperfections such as 'sticky' wages, government interference, or other institutional rigidities (for example, unions). For neoclassical economics, if there is unemployment, government should stay out and let the market correct itself; if there are market imperfections, government may promote conditions under which the self-adjusting mechanism works most smoothly, for example, deregulation, anti-trust and so on.

In *The General Theory of Employment, Interest and Money*, Keynes overthrew Say's Law and demonstrated the possibility and the likelihood that market systems do not tend to fully utilize resources, even under competitive conditions, due to insufficient effective demand. Keynes criticized the neoclassical theory of saving and investment, arguing that traditional loanable funds theory holds income constant when looking at savings and abstracts from expectations when analysing investment. If aggregate saving is primarily a function of income, not interest rates, and investment is determined by the expected profitability of investors and lending institutions, then saving does not determine investment through variations in the rate of interest, and the economy does not automatically tend to full employment. Instead private investment determines savings through changes in income, but there is no reason to expect that the full-employment level of investment will always be undertaken. Keynes's analysis takes place in historical rather than notional (or logical time). The past is unchangeable and the future is unknown and unknowable. Money must be understood as an institution for dealing with radical uncertainty. The result is that capitalist economies tend to operate with excess capacity and unemployment. It is therefore unlikely for a capitalist economy, on its own, to attain full employment.

But capitalist economies have problems maintaining full employment, even if it could be attained, due to ongoing structural and technological change, such as changes in labour supply and the supply of natural resources, labour- and capital-displacing technical change, and changes in the composition of final demand. An economy running at full capacity and full employment would be unable to respond to such changes, and sectoral imbalance is here added to aggregate imbalance as a further cause of unemployment. Bottlenecks and rigidities mean that full employment is likely to be inflationary. Structural change will soon result in unemployment, as technology displaces workers in one sector and fails to absorb them in another, the formation of real capital fails to keep up with the pace of a growing labour supply, or declining demand in one sector fails to be offset by demand for new products. Works such as Pasinetti (1981) and Lowe (1976) offer structural models that demonstrate the great unlikelihood of capitalist economies maintaining full employment, even if it could be attained.

The effective demand and the structural change problems are economic causes of unemployment. But Post Keynesians such as Michał Kalecki have noted that there may also be political obstacles to full employment. Since unemployment in Keynes is a negative byproduct of capitalism, it is viewed as serving no purpose in the capitalist system and so is clearly undesirable for all. Kalecki, Josef Steindl and others, however, have highlighted that unemployment may be functional in capitalism, an insight that is drawn from Marx's analysis of the reserve army of labour.

In Marx, unemployment serves several functions. First, it provides the system with a pool of available labour from which to draw when the pace of accumulation increases. Second, unemployment serves to discipline workers, who may not fear being laid off in an environment of full employment. Third, unemployment holds down wages, since one of the ways in which unemployment disciplines workers is to decrease their bargaining power and thus keep wages from rising. Thus, in this view, unemployment is not only a natural byproduct of capitalism, it is essential to its smooth operation.

Marx postulated a number of different components of the reserve army of labour. The 'latent reserve' includes those currently outside of the market system, either performing unpaid household labour or eking out a meagre subsistence in the periphery of Third World economies. The 'stagnant reserve' includes those who are almost never employed, boom or bust. Members of the 'floating reserve' alternate between employment and unemployment, with the ups and downs of the business cycle. 'Paupers' is the term Marx used to identify those who are now often referred to as the 'underclass'. Recently, it has been suggested that changes in global capitalism have rendered some of these components no longer functional. This has resulted in an environment conducive to policies that may promote the elimination of the emerging 'surplus population' with scary genocidal and racist connotations (Darity 1999).

Policies to address unemployment must recognize both the effective demand and the structural change problems, as well as the functionality of unemployment and the emergence of a hard-core, 'unemployable' sector no longer functioning as a reserve army. Traditional Keynesian policies initially attempted to stimulate aggregate demand through fiscal and monetary policies. Stimulating the private sector to full employment may address the aggregate demand problem but not the structural change problem. In fact, since the structural change problem emerges most forcefully at higher levels of capacity utilization and employment, stimulating private sector demand may increase the structural change problem. Some Post Keynesians would utilize incomes policies to deal with some of the symptoms. Other routes would include promoting public works and the 'socialization of investment'. These latter approaches, if designed correctly, may be more effective than conventional fiscal stimulus in dealing with the structural change problem. In the framework of a capitalist economy, full employment requires a policy – or a set of policies – that can increase effective demand without bringing on structural rigidity and that can eliminate unemployment while finding some institutional mechanism for dealing with the functionality question.

Recently Post Keynesians have suggested that such a policy is available in the form of a kind of permanent Works Progress Administration (Wray 1998). Hyman Minsky (1986) referred to this as government as 'employer of last resort'. Under such a policy, the government would provide a public service employment (PSE) job to anyone ready and willing to work. As the economy expands (contracts), the private sector demand for labour would increase (decrease), and the PSE sector would shrink (grow). PSE workers would be employed in all kinds of social and public services that would benefit the community. Elimination of long periods of unemployment would preserve and potentially enhance labour productivity. The social and economic costs of unemployment due to income insecurity and poverty would decline, and society would experience a significant benefit in the form of less crime and other social problems associated with unemployment. The effective demand problem would be solved by maintaining aggregate income at high levels, but the PSE approach, unlike traditional demand stimulus, would address the structural change problem as well (Forstater 1998). Instead of workers alternating between employment and unemployment, sectoral and aggregate change would only alter the proportion of private and public sector employment. PSE also can address environmental problems. Stimulating the private sector to full employment would surely result in greater pollution and exhaustible resource utilization, while PSE activities may be designed to pollute less and use less fossil fuel.

Unemployment is at the root of many of the economic and social problems of capitalism. Some would argue that, instead of tinkering with capitalism, a new economic system should be sought in which the right to a job as put forward in the United Nations Universal Declaration of Human Rights is realized. Perhaps in a post-capitalist society the employment–money link will be severed and a new mode of social and economic organization will make unemployment extinct and irrelevant. Until such a time, however, there is no reason not to go immediately to full employment with a guaranteed public service job for anyone ready and willing to work.

MATHEW FORSTATER

See also:

Economic Policy; Effective Demand; Employment; Full Employment; Kaleckian Economics; Keynes's *General Theory*; Say's Law; Wages and Labour Markets.

References

Darity, Jr., William A. (1999), 'Who loses from unemployment?', *Journal of Economic Issues*, **33** (2), 491–6.
Forstater, Mathew (1998), 'Flexible full employment: structural implications of discretionary public sector employment', *Journal of Economic Issues*, **32** (2), 557–63.
Jahoda, Marie (1982), *Employment and Unemployment: A Social–Psychological Analysis*, Cambridge: Cambridge University Press.
Lowe, Adolph (1976), *The Path of Economic Growth*, Cambridge: Cambridge University Press.
Minsky, Hyman P. (1986), *Stabilizing an Unstable Economy*, New Haven: Yale University Press.
Pasinetti, Luigi (1981), *Structural Change and Economic Growth*, Cambridge: Cambridge University Press.
Piachaud, David (1997), 'A price worth paying? The costs of unemployment', in J. Philpott (ed.), *Working for Full Employment*, London: Routledge, pp. 49–62.
Wray, L. Randall (1998), *Understanding Modern Money: The Key to Full Employment and Price Stability*, Cheltenham, UK and Northampton, MA, USA: Edward Elgar.

Wages and Labour Markets

To most mainstream economists, the market for labour services is comparable to that for any other commodity. In accordance with individualistic methodology, neoclassical economists posit many buyers (demand) and sellers (supply), and wages are the price signals that pull together these economic agents within a labour market setting whose two presumed functions are allocation and clearance. As long as there are no obstacles to individual agents' hedonistic pursuit of gain, wages fulfil their primary allocative function across markets by directing labour services to their most productive use with the establishment of appropriate compensating differentials. In the absence of institutional constraints, wages are assumed to perform well their crucial market-clearing function by means of price adjustment. In particular, movements in real wages would guarantee that the aggregate labour market comes to rest either at full employment or at some natural level of unemployment whose magnitude is believed to depend on the degree of market imperfections that prevent labour market flexibility. The orthodox conclusion, usually in the form of policy prescriptions, is that, to preserve its self-correcting properties, the labour market must be designed by the state in such a way as to eliminate all institutional features that hinder market clearance and, more precisely, limit downward wage adjustment, such as trade unions, minimum wages and transfers to the unemployed. While some neoclassical economists, especially of the New Keynesian variety, have come to recognize that this peculiar conception of the labour market is somewhat problematic and have pointed to the latter's unique characteristic as a 'social institution' with features quite distinct from the market for other commodities, all point to nominal and real wage stickiness in the light of aggregate demand shocks as the principal explanation for the existence of unemployment.

Keynes and Post Keynesians completely reject this neoclassical depiction of an equilibrating labour market with self-adjusting characteristics. First, Post Keynesians agree with other critics of orthodoxy for whom a labour service cannot be conceived as just another commodity. As pointed out elsewhere (Seccareccia 1991), labour services have little in common with most commodities, whether they be consumption or capital goods, to which the standard tools of supply/demand are indiscriminately applied. Since it cannot be stored, a labour service is a particular flow variable which, if left unused, is lost for ever (Eichner 1979). Being instantaneously perishable, the neoclassical price-auction model becomes highly inappropriate. In fact, the self-equilibrating role that inter-temporal arbitrage is supposed to play in commodity markets is not only entirely absent in the market for labour services but, because of the presence of hysteresis, may actually work against the type of labour arbitrage analysed, for instance, by New Classical theorists of the real business cycle. This is because, in addition to the complete loss of the current flow of labour services, unemployment also causes the deterioration of skills, thereby making both workers and firms even more anxious to contract during the current period.

Second, it has been recognized since Alfred Marshall that one cannot separate the labour service from the particular human being who offers it. In opposition to the Walrasian price-auction model of the labour market that presumes no prior relationship existing between buyers and sellers, the money-wage bargain actually takes place in a social and historical setting in which the relationship between employers and employees is an ongoing one. Hence, the form of market coordination in line with the Post Keynesian perspective is that which accounts for the operation of customary practices and social norms in regulating the level of money wages and their structure across sectors. Compatible with the institutionalist labour market paradigm (Gimble 1991), money contracts may be considerably insulated from market forces and reflect primarily bargaining power and the normative pressures arising from custom and workers' beliefs as to what constitutes fairness in the determination of wages.

Third, and perhaps most importantly, the whole notion of a distinct aggregate labour market analysed in isolation must be abandoned in favour of a more organic approach grounded on the principle of effective demand. Unlike the market for other commodities, changes in the price of labour, the average real wage, have both supply and aggregate demand effects which impact on firms' employment decisions. This is because wages are not merely an element of a firm's cost. Through their impact on a community's consumption, wages also directly influence aggregate demand. Hence, as Keynes had made very clear, a 'reduction in money-wages will have no lasting tendency to increase employment except by virtue of its repercussions either on the propensity to consume for the community as a whole, or on the schedule of the marginal efficiencies of capital, or on the rate of interest' (Keynes 1936, p. 262). It is the demand-side effects of wage changes that really matter to Post Keynesians, and these effects would normally work in the opposite direction to what is generally theorized by neoclassical theory. Moreover, a cut in wages may also further compound these contractionary aggregate demand outcomes, which cannot be averted in a world of endogenous money via Pigovian wealth effects, because of the negative expectations of future market conditions (Deprez 1996). Consequently, following Michał Kalecki, Post Keynesians generally surmise a positively sloped aggregate demand curve for labour in the real wage/employment space because of significant feedback effects via aggregate demand or, in some cases, they suppose no relation whatsoever between real wages and employment (King 2001, p. 71).

Although rejecting the neoclassical notion of an aggregate labour market, Post Keynesians point to the overwhelming significance of demand, both the level and structure of aggregate demand, in conditioning employment. While the aggregate level of demand sets the macroeconomic constraints on the utilization of labour, it is the dual structure of product markets in industrial economies traditionally typified by a core oligopolistic sector and a more peripheral competitive sector that defines the precise segmentation of labour demand (Appelbaum 1979).

Following the work of institutionalist economists, the dominant oligopolistic sector is composed of megacorps (domestic or transnational) which, because of their larger size, are commonly distinguished by more capital-intensive methods of production, and faced with a more stable demand especially for skilled labour and a relatively better paid and more unionized labour force. Indeed, technological requirements in the primary segment call for more highly-skilled workers with firm-specific training, necessitating low labour turnover or employment variability. One crucial feature of the primary sector is the existence of internal labour markets that regulate internal mobility and promotion and are characterized by more rigid and hierarchical wage structures patterned along formal seniority ladders. Such internal labour markets are assumed to be largely insulated from the external labour market, except at the ports of entry via external job clusters and wage contours. Internal labour markets meet a number of employer objectives, of which the most important is to guarantee that skills are transmitted vertically across seniority districts so as to minimize the cost of on-the-job training while, at the same time, bringing about a more efficient mutual supervision of workers once on the job. However, in response to other competing corporate objectives, a wide diversity of internal labour market systems can subsist that are more or less insulated from the external labour market (Grimshaw and Rubery 1998).

Although the primary sector can itself be subdivided into upper and lower tiers, depending on such factors as the degree of capital intensity and stable demand patterns, this sector must be formally distinguished from the secondary sector. The latter, instead, normally comprises smaller, more competitive firms, specialized in more labour-intensive activities and associated with lower wages and much greater employment flexibility. Indeed, even where there are large corporations, as in some of the personal services industries, work units tend to be small and isolated and thus, for instance, create barriers to unionization. The relative absence of structured internal labour markets in the secondary sector, however, is explained primarily by firms' need for lower-skilled employment, thereby entailing higher labour turnover and greater sensitivity of wages to external demand pressures.

Given this particular fragmentation of demand, it follows that labour supply for each segment is rooted in different social stratifications that are perpetuated by the dynamic interaction between job characteristics and social affiliation – a process termed by Eichner (1979) as 'human developmental' or 'anthropogenic'. Unlike neoclassical theory which presents the labour supply decision within a static model of rational choice, Post Keynesians focus on labour supply as an outcome of the cumulative acquisition of competencies, attitudes and habits that have been moulded by workers' social affiliations and subcultures. Although habits and affiliations can be changed by formal education and on-the-job training, the labour market tends generally to preserve distinct social strata of non-competing groups.

While Post Keynesians recognize that wages may be affected by short-run demand/supply considerations, wages are not the result of an optimizing process whose purpose is to allocate labour to its most productive employment, as emphasized by neoclassical theory. As was well understood by both classical writers and Marx, workers are the only input in production who must provide for their own sustenance and social regeneration. Therefore, relative real wages have little to do with specific marginal products but reflect, instead, the social reproduction needs to maintain hierarchies within firms that have been sanctioned socially by force of custom; this is dubbed by Rubery (1997) the social cohesion/social stratification function of wages. Once a particular wage structure has evolved historically, customary norms lead to a process of calcification of these wage differentials that generally can withstand market pressures and, hence, exhibit a high level of empirical stability. Keynes, himself, had recognized the significance of this institutional stickiness of wage differentials in the *General Theory* when he attributed to workers the primary concern of protecting their relative wages. Only during periods of acute crisis would such ossified wage structures succumb to management pressures and result in new precedent-setting wage relativities.

In much the same way, the aggregate level of the money wage can essentially be considered a historical datum, serving as the calculable starting point for actual bargaining between workers and employers. Given its ubiquity, the aggregate money wage presents itself as the anchor on which the actual level of nominal values in the entire system depends. The aggregate level of the real wage, on the other hand, is not such an arbitrary standard, but represents primarily forces at work in the product market, especially firms' degree of monopoly in the primary sector. Unlike changes in the money wage that would have their greatest influence on nominal magnitudes, movements in the real wage would affect employment via their consequences for aggregate effective demand. Through their feedback on the pattern of spending, real-wage movements play a key role in the determination of overall employment, as well as its allocation between the primary and secondary sectors of the labour market. Accordingly, high real-wage growth would engender a virtuous cycle of prosperity as well as an increase in the share of the primary sector of the labour market – a scenario characteristic of much of the early post-1945 golden age of Western capitalism. Conversely, a fall in the real wage, associated with a concomitant rise in the Kaleckian degree of monopoly, would generate a vicious cycle characterized by a growing problem of effective demand and a proliferation of low-wage jobs in the secondary sector of the labour market.

MARIO SECCARECCIA

See also:

Effective Demand; Employment; Institutionalism; Marginalism; New Keynesian Economics; Unemployment.

References

Appelbaum, E. (1979), 'The labor market', in A.S. Eichner (ed.), *A Guide to Post-Keynesian Economics*, White Plains, NY: M.E. Sharpe, pp. 100–119.
Deprez, J. (1996), 'Davidson on the labour market in a monetary production economy', in P. Arestis (ed.), *Keynes, Money and the Open Economy: Essays in Honour of Paul Davidson*, Vol. 1, Cheltenham, UK: Edward Elgar, pp. 123–43.
Eichner, A.S. (1979), 'An "anthropogenic" approach to labor economics', *Eastern Economic Journal*, **5** (3), 349–66.
Gimble, D.E. (1991), 'Institutionalist labor market theory and the Veblenian dichotomy', *Journal of Economic Issues*, **25** (3), 625–48.
Grimshaw, D. and J. Rubery (1998), 'Integrating the internal and external labour markets', *Cambridge Journal of Economics*, **22** (2), 199–220.
Keynes, J.M. (1936), *The General Theory of Employment, Interest and Money*, London: Macmillan.
King, J.E. (2001), 'Labor and unemployment', in R.P.F. Holt and S. Pressman (eds), *A New Guide to Post Keynesian Economics*, London and New York: Routledge, pp. 65–78.
Rubery, J. (1997), 'Wages and the labour market', *British Journal of Industrial Relations*, **35** (3), 337–66.
Seccareccia, M. (1991), 'An alternative to labour-market orthodoxy: the Post-Keynesian/institutionalist policy view', *Review of Political Economy*, **3** (1), 43–61.

Walrasian Economics

Walrasian economics originated in the work of Léon Walras (1874 [1926]) and was one of several neoclassical approaches emerging from the marginal revolution in the late nineteenth century. Its hallmark was the focus on the interrelations of markets and their simultaneous, or general, equilibrium.

Walrasianism was, therefore, distinct from Marshallian neoclassicism, which sought analytic devices to neutralize interdependencies so as to allow partial equilibrium analysis of particular sectors of the economy. And it was different, too, from the neoclassicism of J.B. Clark, who resorted to extensive aggregation to avoid the complexities resulting from interdependence. Since Walras's early formulation, his general equilibrium theory has been increasingly refined, and it became the dominant form of orthodoxy during the twentieth century, only recently being somewhat displaced by game theory.

The neoclassical quality of Walrasian economics is evident in the derivation of agents' choices, or supplies and demands, from particular types of maximization. It is assumed that each consumer's domain of choice (commodity space), preferences (typically represented as a utility function) and assets (labour capacities, physical possessions and financial securities), and each producer's technology (input–output combinations) are exogenously specified, and economic interaction takes place only through competitive markets. Every consumer is depicted as maximizing utility subject to a budget constraint, and every producer maximizes profit constrained only by technology. A set of prices that allows these optimizations to be realized simultaneously, so making demands and supplies compatible, and markets clear, is a Walrasian equilibrium.

Two varieties of Walrasian economics can be distinguished: Arrow–Debreu intertemporal equilibrium theory and temporary equilibrium analysis. They differ in their treatment of time: that is, in how agents relate to the future. The Arrow–Debreu version classifies commodities not only by their physical properties and locational attributes, but also by their date of availability and the 'state of the world', which specifies the corresponding values of variables that were previously uncertain. The rationale for this is straightforward. All of these characteristics can affect utilities and profits, and therefore demands and supplies. For example, consumers' preferences are generally sensitive to a commodity's physical properties and the location where consumption occurs, as well as embodying time preferences and attitudes towards risk. But the implications of conceptualizing commodities in this fourfold way are dramatic. When coupled to the usual assumption that agents can completely rank consumption bundles and input–output combinations, it means that there will be a single decision date for all agents and a comprehensive set of futures markets and contingent commodity, or insurance, markets. Agents will form supplies and demands for every date and for every contingency, and will determine all of their choices in the very first period.

Walrasian temporary equilibrium theory implicitly recognizes the unreasonableness of assuming that agents have complete rankings of commodity bundles. Instead, they are likely to be uncertain as to what commodities and technologies will be available in the future and what their preferences will be, as well as the exact composition and value of their assets. And typically they will encounter transaction costs that are especially high for trading in futures markets and contingent commodities. Thus markets will be incomplete, and at least some trading will take place sequentially. An Arrow–Debreu equilibrium will be impossible, and any equilibrium will be 'temporary'. J.R. Hicks (1946) formalizes the matter as follows. There are a number of periods and, at the beginning of each, spot markets exist together with *some* futures markets and contingent commodity markets. Agents can trade on the markets that exist, and will do so on the basis of expectations about future prices for commodities that are not presently tradable. Equilibrium is defined only in terms of clearance on those markets that exist, and these are not comprehensive. At the beginning of the next period, markets reopen, and new trading can occur on spot markets and newly available markets for forward contracts. Expectations formed at the beginning of the first period may turn out to be incorrect, and will be revised, so that market prices in the second period will reflect new expectations. At the start of the third period markets reopen again. And so on. The economy thus moves in a sequence of temporary equilibria.

The causation structure of both types of Walrasian theory is clear-cut. The equilibrium values of the endogenous variables (prices and quantities traded) are determined by the exogenously specified preferences, asset endowments, technologies, optimizing behaviours and agents' expectation formation rules. The endogenous variables, prices and quantities are, of course, the microeconomic components of the macroeconomic variables. The time path of these aggregates can be very complex in both forms of Walrasian model. They certainly need not result in the steady states of Robert Solow's growth model. The causal fundamentals would have to take very special forms for this to occur. However, no matter how complicated, equilibria will always involve market clearance, so there will be no involuntarily unemployed labour or underutilized productive capacity in the Keynesian sense of these terms. (There can be excess supplies in Walrasian equilibria, providing there is free disposal, but they will correspond to zero prices.)

Five problems have been examined in both types of Walrasian theory. First, under what conditions do equilibria exist? Second, when will the economy be stable, in the sense of disequilibrium proving transitory? Third, what are the efficiency properties of equilibria? Fourth, what circumstances will guarantee a unique equilibrium, and, fifth, generate definite comparative static results? Overall, coordination through prices as depicted by Walrasianism is shown to be a delicate matter. Very restrictive assumptions are required to ensure existence, stability, efficiency, uniqueness and definite comparative statics. For example, take the existence question, that is, the problem of determining what types of consumers' preferences, producers' technologies, asset distributions and expectation formation mechanisms will ensure that there is a vector of prices that will clear all markets simultaneously. Since Walrasianism is essentially a set of propositions about the properties of equilibria, the significance of the problem is difficult to exaggerate. But the assumptions required to guarantee existence are stringent. In particular, they must ensure that demands and supplies vary *continuously* with prices. Further restrictive assumptions are required to guarantee that, if equilibrium exists, it is unique, and stable, and that parameter shifts engender definite changes in endogenous variables. This has led some eminent orthodox theorists to suggest that Walrasianism is *not* the route to proceed along in analysing real economies, or, alternatively, that it should quickly lead into a more secure path (Arrow and Hahn 1971).

Such caution is notably absent from orthodox macroeconomics, whether monetarist, New Classical, or real business cycle theory. Here actual economies are modelled as oscillating between two types of Walrasian temporary equilibrium, those with rational expectations and those deviating from rational expectations. The deviations may be the result of monetary or real shocks, and are regarded as quickly self-correcting. Walrasian equilibria thus prevail continuously and are each treated as unique, stable and exhibiting definite comparative statics. Since it is difficult to justify any of this in terms of the theorems proved by Walrasian theorists, orthodox macro economists usually take refuge within the confines of Milton Friedman's instrumentalist methodology to justify their extreme modelling simplifications, most notably their resort to heroic aggregation, where markets are reduced to a very small number and where there is a single economic agent with well-behaved preferences and constraints. In such a context, the problems of existence, stability and efficiency are much reduced, and unambiguous comparative static results are easier to generate.

Beginning in the 1960s, some Keynesians insightfully exposed the key assumption guaranteeing market clearance as a property of equilibria in Walrasian theory. Clower (1965) and Leijonhuvud (1968) argued that this resulted from treating agents as formulating their demands and supplies in the belief that they can always trade whatever quantities they desire, providing only that they deliver equivalents in exchange. This seems innocuous, but is in fact crucial, as can be appreciated by considering a Walrasian disequilibrium. Obviously, in such a situation not all agents' choices can be realized simultaneously, and some will be rationed if trades actually occur. Then it is not unreasonable to imagine that this rationing will affect choices. For example, a consumer who is quantity constrained in the sale of labour and expects this to continue at future dates will not necessarily alter the supply of labour from that resulting from a Walrasian maximization of utility, but will probably reduce consumption demands, thereby contributing to an effective demand deficiency. A producer who is quantity rationed in the sale of output, and expects this to continue at future dates, will not necessarily reduce the supply of output below the Walrasian level, but is likely to reduce demand for labour inputs, again contributing to a shortfall in demand. Agents' supplies and demands will not, therefore, be correctly specified by Walrasian theory, and their equilibration may involve significant deviations from market clearance. If a new equilibrium occurs it can be Keynesian, in the sense of there being excess supplies of commodities, including the involuntary unemployment of labour, without the corresponding prices being zero. Furthermore, disequilibria will exhibit multiplier processes, which are wholly absent from Walrasian economics.

Post Keynesians have been very much more critical of the entire Walrasian edifice, including all notions of optimization and equilibrium. Radical uncertainty, it is claimed, is not only something irreducible to a probabilistic calculus; it cannot be sensibly treated as affecting only the way expectations are formed. Instead, it will result in behaviour that cannot be modelled as maximization subject to constraints. And the institutional structure in which decisions occur will also be significantly affected, particularly in the monetary and financial sectors. The historical processes consequent upon both are unlikely to be representable as equilibria because – speaking in Walrasian terms – the determinants of equilibria will undergo change in the process itself. Thus 'the notion of general equilibrium is irrelevant to a world of ignorance and uncertainty, where irreversible decisions must be taken in calendar time and equilibrium states are (if indeed they are attained) invariably path dependent' (King 1995, p. 245).

M.C. Howard

See also:

Bastard Keynesianism; Equilibrium and Non-Equilibrium; Marginalism; Say's Law.

References

Arrow, K.J. and F.H. Hahn (1971), *General Competitive Analysis*, Edinburgh: Oliver & Boyd.
Clower, R.W. (1965), 'The Keynesian counter-revolution: a theoretical appraisal', in F.H. Hahn and F. Brechling (eds), *The Theory of Interest Rates*, London: Macmillan, pp. 103–25.
Hicks, J.R. (1946), *Value and Capital*, Oxford: Oxford University Press.
King, J.E. (1995), *Conversations with Post Keynesians*, London: Macmillan.
Leijonhuvud, A. (1968), *On Keynesian Economics and the Economics of Keynes*, Oxford: Oxford University Press.
Walras, L. (1874), *Elements of Pure Economics*, Edition Définitive, 1926, London: Allen & Unwin, 1954.

Name index

Akerlof, G. 113
Anderson, W.L. 229
Arestis, P. 14, 85, 96, 116, 158, 217, 346–50
Arrow, K.J. 385–6
Asimakopulos, A. 306–7, 328
Atkinson, A.B. 46, 328
Azariadis, C. 113

Bagehot, W. 57
Baily, M.N. 113
Baran, P.A. 195, 371
Barro, R.J. 271
Bauer, O. 371
Bausor, R. 130
Bell, S. 242–8
Bellamy, E. 317
Bellofiore, R. 60
Beveridge, W.H. 155, 157, 269
Bhaduri, A. 173, 373
Bhaskar, R. 82–3
Blair, T. 338
Blanchard, O. 113, 114, 233, 278
Blatt, J. 178
Blecker, R. 200–205
Bloch, H. 249–52
Böhm-Bawerk, E. von 5
Bowles, S. 182
Brid, J.C.M. 175
Brown, A. 82–6
Brumberg, R. 73
Bunting, D. 72–7
Burbidge, J. 328

Carabelli, A. 160, 364
Carvalho, F. 57–60
Cencini, A. 60
Chamberlin, E.H. 222
Champernowne, D. 46
Chandler, A. 167
Chiarella, C. 95, 179
Chick, V. 28, 59, 268, 290
Clark, J.B. 296, 385
Clinton, W.J. 338
Clower, R.W. 387

Coddington, A. 159–60
Colander, D. 188
Cornwall, J. 94–5, 322–7
Cornwall, W. 94–5, 275–80
Courvisanos, J. 191–6
Crafts, N. 19
Cross, R. 94
Crotty, J.R. 254

Davidson, P.
 on axiom of gross substitution 70, 233
 on Austrian economics 6–8
 on balance-of-payments-constrained growth 19
 on central banks 59
 on critical realism 85
 on effective demand 229–37, 253, 255
 on employment 255
 on ergodicity 97, 159–60, 236–7, 280–83, 368–70
 on finance 28, 89, 208, 247
 on international finance 33, 134–5, 204, 260, 346
 on investment 207–8
 and *Journal of Post Keynesian Economics* 215–18
 on Keynes's *General Theory* 229–37, 269
 on methodology 85, 96
 on money 93, 94, 198, 233–4, 236, 247, 369
 on the multiplier 268–9
 on New Keynesian economics 230, 233
 on rational expectations 280
 on Say's Law 230–35
 on the Tobin tax 346
 on uncertainty 266–70
Day, R. 95
Deane, P. 50
Debreu, G. 385–6
Delli Gatti, D. 94–5
Dixon, R.J. 174

389

Name index

Dobb, M.H. 47, 50, 212
Domar, E.S. 135, 269, 372–3
Douglas, C.H. 371
Dow, A. 247
Dow, S.C. 11–15, 22–3, 78, 81, 96–7, 247
Downward, P. 96–101, 252
Duesenberry, J. 207–8
Dunlop, J.T. 374
Dunn, S.P. 280–84
Dutt, A.K. 189, 289–93
Dymski, G. 256

Eatwell, J. 322
Edgeworth, F.Y. 162
Eichner, A.S. 68, 96, 167, 218, 383
Eisner, R. 153
Engels, F. 314

Fazzari, S. 208, 252–7
Feynman, R.P. 11–12
Fine, B. 51–7
Fischer, S. 276
Fisher, I. 146, 187, 206, 229
Fitzgibbons, A. 160, 271–5
Flaschel, P. 95, 179
Foley, D.K. 94
Fontana, G. 60, 237–41
Forstater, M. 374–9
Franke, R. 95
Freeman, C. 192
Friedman, M. 27, 73, 156, 187, 221, 259, 271–2, 387
Frisch, R. 39
Fusfeld, D. 217

Galbraith, J.K. 216–17
Gallegatti, M. 95
Garegnani, P. 93
Garretson, H. 256
Georgescu-Roegen, N. 70
Gerrard, B. 159–64
Giddens, A. 338
Gintis, H. 182
Glickman, M. 366–70
Gnos, C. 60
Godley, W. 38
Gomulka, S. 193, 330
Goodhart, C.A.E. 262

Goodwin, R.M. 40–41, 49, 95, 176, 178, 185
Graziani, A. 60, 142–5
Grossman, H. 226

Haavelmo, T. 98
Hahn, F.H. 234
Halevi, J. 92
Hall, R.L. 251
Hansen, A.H. 25
Harcourt, G.C. 29, 44–51, 192, 216
Harvey, J.T. 131–5
Harrod, R.F. 17, 19, 25, 40, 47, 49, 92, 135, 170–74, 176, 212, 250, 372–3
Hawtrey, R.G. 339
Hayek, F. von 5–9, 92, 221–2
Heilbroner, R. 217
Hendry, D. 98
Henry, J.F. 341–6
Hewitson, G. 20–24
Hicks, J.R. 17, 25, 222, 223, 276, 283, 284, 342, 355–8, 386
Hicks, U. 221
Hitch, C.J. 251
Hobson, J.A. 371–2
Hodgson, G.M. 4–5
Howard, M.C. 384–8
Howells, P. 257–61
Hudson, J. 112–17
Hume, D. 202
Hymer, S. 167

Jevons, W.S. 216, 249
Jorgenson, D. 252, 255

Kahn, R.F. 47, 48–9, 211, 216, 221, 230, 266, 304
Kahnemann, D. 132
Kaldor, N.
  on business cycles 40
  on capital theory 49
  on central banks 58–9
  on cumulative causation 94, 174
  economics of 221–6
  on equilibrium 222
  on expectations 135, 138
  on growth theory 49, 92, 125–6, 171–2, 176–7, 223–5
  on income distribution 171–2, 177, 183–4, 223–4

on innovation 193
on money 58–9, 264
on the multiplier 306–7
on speculation 138
on taxation 222–3
Kalecki, M.
  on budget deficits 34–7
  on business cycles 39, 41, 93, 193, 329
  on economic growth 92–3, 102, 193–4, 330, 357–8, 372
  on economic policy 101–2
  economics of 226–9
  on government spending 35–7
  on income distribution 49, 173, 183, 226–7, 329, 373–4
  on innovation 191–4, 209
  on investment 205–9
  and Joan Robinson 212
  microeconomics of 106, 109, 183, 251, 290–91
  on monopoly capital 227–8
  and paradox of costs 173
  on political business cycles 41, 151, 157, 377
  and the principle of increasing risk 146, 207
  on profits 148, 226–7, 296–7
  on the rate of interest 228–9
  on socialism 227, 358
  on the traverse 356–8
  on uncertainty 228
  on underconsumption 372
  on wages 373–4, 381
Katzner, D.W. 126–31, 217
Keen, S. 95, 175–80
Kenyon, P. 192
King, J.E. 370–74
Kirzner, I. 5, 7
Kiyotaki, N. 113
Klein, L. 227, 281
Knapp, G.F. 263
Knight, F.H. 283, 296
Kornai, J. 178
Kotlikoff, L. 328
Kregel, J.A. 59, 94, 135, 139, 177, 247
Kriesler, P. 92, 251, 355–9
Krugman, P. 19
Kurz, H.D. 93
Kuznets, S. 230

Lachmann, L. 5, 7
Lancaster, K. 69
Lange, O. 25
Laramie, A.J. 328–32
Lavoie, M. 22, 60, 69–72, 80, 92, 193, 246–7, 374
Lawson, T. 13, 82–5, 96, 160, 282
Leamer, E. 99
Lee, F.S. 218, 251, 285–9
Le Guin, U. 317
Leijonhufvud, A. 27, 230, 387
Lekachman, R. 153
Lerner, A.P. 102, 149, 151, 188, 216, 222, 251
Lodewijks, J. 24–30
López, G.J. 34–8
Lotka, A. 178
Lowe, A. 356–9, 377
Lucas, R.E. 27, 253, 271
Lutz, M.A. 69
Lux, K. 69
Luxemburg, R. 191, 226, 372

Machlup, F. 5, 249, 251
Mair, D. 328–32
Malthus, T.R. 44, 154, 304, 309, 311, 370
Mankiw, N.G. 29, 113
Marcuzzo, M.C. 211–215
Marglin, S. 373
Marshall, A. 44–5, 50, 94, 106, 110, 211, 214, 216, 249, 290, 295, 341, 381
Marx, K.
  on business cycles 41, 154, 178
  and the Cambridge economic tradition 49
  and classical political economy 319
  and growth theory 116, 178, 213, 269
  influence on Joan Robinson 212, 214, 372
  and the monetary theory of production 264, 311, 344
  and the rate of interest 302
  and Say's Law 309, 311–12
  on technical progress 170, 213
  on underconsumption 371–2
  on unemployment 41, 116, 154, 377

Marx, K. (*continued*)
  and value theory 56
  on wages 383
Matthews, R.C.O. 50
Matzner, E. 337–41
McCombie, J.S.L. 15–20, 175
McGregor, P. 18
McKenna, E.J. 1–5
McKinnon, R. 87, 89
Meade, J.E. 25, 46, 47–8, 306
Mearman, A. 98–100
Medio, A. 95
Menger, C. 5–6, 249
Messori, M. 60
Milberg, W. 165–70
Milgate, M. 322
Miliband, R. 314
Mill, J. 309
Mill, J.S. 216, 309
Minsky, H.P.
  on banking 22–4, 148
  on budget deficits 37, 147
  on business cycles 40, 81, 94, 146–7, 219
  on central banks 59
  on disequilibrium 28
  on economic growth 179
  on economic policy 37, 147–8, 378
  on employer of last resort policy 37, 378
  on expectations 135, 136–8
  on financial fragility 24, 78, 88, 145–9, 219
  on the financial instability hypothesis 145–9
  on investment 136–8, 207–8, 255–6
  on money 345
Mises, L. von 5, 6
Mitchell, W.F. 153–9
Modigliani, F. 25, 73, 173, 252, 255
Mongiovi, G. 312–22
Moore, B.J. 21, 59, 117–21, 246–7, 264, 267
Morgenstern, O. 5
Moszkowska, N. 371
Mott, T. 92, 205–10
Mundell, R. 262
Musgrave, R.A. 328
Muth, J. 273
Myrdal, G. 217, 222

Nell, E.J. 68, 93, 176, 178
Nevile, J.F. 149–53
Newton, I. 11

O'Donnell, R.M. 160, 359–65
O'Hara, P.A. 215–20
Ohlin, B. 242
Okun, A. 276, 333

Palley, T. 181–6
Panico, C. 170–75, 321
Pareto, V. 249
Parguez, A. 60
Parkin, M. 113
Parsons, S.D. 5–10, 85
Pasinetti, L.L. 49–50, 68, 93, 111–12, 171, 176–7, 183–4, 377
Patinkin, D. 230, 269
Perez, C. 192
Peterson, W. 217
Petty, W. 153
Phelps, E.S. 113, 156, 276
Pigou, A.C. 46, 211, 222
Pivetti, M. 299–303, 321
Pollin, R. 304–9
Popper, K. 213
Poulon, F. 60
Pressman, S. 196–200
Puu, T. 95

Ramsey, F. 162, 364
Realfonzo, R. 60–65
Reddaway, W.B. 25
Ricardo, D. 47, 50, 55, 202, 212–13, 214, 217, 294, 297, 300, 304, 309–11, 319
Rider, C. 350–54
Robbins, L. 221
Robertson, D.H. 46, 60, 142, 242, 249
Robinson, E.A.G. 47
Robinson, J.
  on Bastard Keynesianism 25
  on business cycles 40
  on capital theory 51, 95, 181–2, 213, 250
  on comparative advantage 167
  on economic growth 49–50, 176–7, 212–13, 250, 355, 372
  economics of 211–15
  on equilibrium 214

Name index 393

on expectations 135
on imperfect competition 47
on inflation 187–8
influence of Kalecki on 49, 212, 227, 372
on methodology 213–14, 268
on the 'new mercantilism' 201–2
on the rate of interest 300
on time in economic theory 92, 95, 214, 355
on underconsumption 372
Rochon, L.-P. 60, 145–9
Roemer, J.E. 182
Romer, D. 92
Rosser, J. Barkley, Jr. 92–5, 218
Rotenberg, J. 113
Rowthorn, R.E. 189

Sadigh, E. 60
Salter, W.E.G. 192
Salvadori, N. 93
Samuels, W.J. 217
Samuelson, P.A. 25–7, 29, 40, 171, 261, 280
Sardoni, C. 309–13
Sargent, T. 271
Savage, L. 282, 283
Sawyer, M.C. 92, 101–5, 158, 218, 346
Say, J.-B. 154, 309–11
Schmitt, B. 60, 267
Schmoller, G. 5
Schmookler, J. 193
Schumpeter, J.A. 5, 60, 62, 95, 114, 191, 192, 238, 297
Seccareccia, M. 380–84
Seidman, L.S. 332–8
Semmler, W. 95
Setterfield, M. 94, 105–12
Shackle, G.L.S. 5, 28, 129, 135, 159–60, 217, 281, 283, 298, 366–7, 369
Shapiro, C. 113
Shapiro, N. 65–7, 218
Shaw, E.S. 47
Sherman, H.J. 313–18
Shove, G. 47
Silverberg, G. 95
Sismondi, J.C.L. Simonde de 154, 309
Skidelsky, R. 199
Skott, P. 38–43, 80, 94

Slutsky, E. 39
Smith, A. 94, 170, 202, 213, 214, 309–10, 319
Smithin, J. 94, 186–91
Solow, R.M. 27, 29, 92, 113, 171, 213, 281, 296, 386
Sraffa, P.
  on capital theory 51, 55–6, 171, 213, 318
  and classical political economy 214, 302, 319, 356
  economics of 318–22
  and effective demand 319–20
  and growth theory 178
  on income distribution 182, 318–19, 321–2
  and Joan Robinson 211, 213–14
  on money 321–2
  and Post Keynesian economics 93, 319–21
  on the rate of interest 173, 302–3, 321
  on the rate of profit 173, 182
  on the theory of production 295, 356
Stalin, J.V. 317
Steedman, I. 172
Steindl, J. 37, 92, 173, 195–6, 209, 228, 372, 377
Sterman, J. 95
Stiglitz, J.E. 77, 328
Stohs, M. 11
Stone, R. 44
Studart, R. 87–91
Summers, L. 114, 328
Swales, K. 18
Swan, T. 92
Sweezy, P.M. 195, 228, 371

Taylor, J.B. 121, 187, 259, 276
Thirlwall, A.P. 16, 174–5, 217, 221–6
Thornton, W. 242
Tinbergen, J. 27
Tobin, J. 29, 333, 346, 348
Toporowski, J. 226–9
Trigg, A.B. 265–70
Tugan-Baranovsky, M. 226, 372
Tversky, A. 132
Tymoigne, E. 135–41

Urban, F.M. 162

Van Ees, H. 256
Varga, E. 371
Variato, A.M. 256
Veblen, T. 116, 197
Vernengo, M. 30–34
Vernon, R. 204
Vickers, D. 217
Volterra, V. 178

Wallace, N. 271
Wallich, H. 188, 333
Walras, L. 249, 384
Walters, B. 85
Watts, M.J. 153–9
Webster, E. 294–8

Weintraub, S. 25, 27, 188, 215–16, 218, 333–7, 373
Weiss, A. 77
White, H.D. 31
Wicksell, K. 60, 187, 301
Wieser, F. von 5
Wimsatt, W.C. 11
Winnett, A. 121–6
Wolfson, M.H. 77–82
Worswick, G.D.N. 227
Wray, L.R. 37, 102, 247, 261–5

Yellen, J. 113
Young, A.A. 94, 221
Young, D. 85

Zannoni, D. 1–5

Subject index

Absolute advantage 203
Accelerator principle 207, 372
Accumulation of capital *see* growth
Accumulation of Capital, by Joan Robinson 212–13
Administered pricing *see* mark-up pricing; oligopoly
A General Theory of the Price Level, by Sidney Weintraub 333
Agency 1–5, 97, 125, 132–3, 196–7, 252, 254–5, 281–2, 284, 364, 384–5
Aggregate supply and demand model 27–8, 105–12, 135–41, 230–35, 291, 373
Animal spirits 39, 42, 141, 163, 198, 209, 235, 254, 274, 344
Asset prices 147, 340
Asymmetric information 23, 77, 79, 87, 114, 230, 256, 279, 347
Atomism 13, 96–7, 162
Austrian economics 5–10, 84, 221, 283, 297, 356

Babylonian methodology 11–15, 85, 96–7
Balance-of-payments-constrained growth 15–20, 94, 104, 150–52, 158, 174–5, 204–5, 225
Banana parable, of J.M. Keynes 240
Bandwagon effects 133
Banking
 circuit theorists on 61–4, 267–8
 credit rationing by 78–82
 and development finance 88, 90
 and endogenous money 118–21
 and interest rates 119–21, 247
 Keynes on 58, 142–4, 240, 307
 main entry 20–24
 Minsky on 146
 and the theory of money 263–4
 see also central banking; money
Barter 262, 310–11
 see also neutrality of money
Bastard Keynesianism 24–30, 292

 see also neoclassical economics; neoclassical synthesis
Beveridge Report 222
Borrower's risk 78, 138–9, 207
Bretton Woods 30–34, 48, 102, 134, 166, 202, 204
Budget deficits 28–9, 34–8, 102, 147, 149–53, 158, 273, 331, 348
Business cycles
 banks and 23
 dynamics of 92–5
 globalization and 166, 169
 growth and 95, 176, 178
 Kaldor on 222
 Kalecki on 226–7, 229
 Keynes on 23, 238–41
 main entry 38–43
 Minsky on 145–8, 219, 229

Cambridge circus 211
Cambridge controversies *see* capital theory
Cambridge economic tradition 44–51, 51–7, 84–5
Cambridge equation 171–2
Cambridge Journal of Economics 215
Capacity utilization 173–4
Capital accumulation *see* growth
Capital markets 87–91
Capital movements, international 31–2, 42, 131–5, 165–6, 201–4, 346–9
Capital theory
 Cambridge critique of 49, 93, 181, 209
 and environmental economics 124–5
 and income distribution 181–2
 Joan Robinson on 181, 213, 250
 main entry 51–7
 neoclassical 171, 281–2, 296–7
 Sraffa on 171, 293, 318–22
Capitalism's Inflation and Unemployment Crisis, by Sidney Weintraub 334–6

396 Subject index

Central banks
  and endogenous money 118, 120, 264
  and interest rates 21, 108, 120, 257, 264
  and international finance 103
  Keynes on 307
  as lender of last resort 24
  main entry 57–60
  Marshall on 45
  Minsky on 147
  see also monetary policy; Taylor rule
Chaos theory 42, 282
Choice of technique 51–6
Circuit theory 61–5, 119, 264, 267
Class conflict 171, 184–5, 373–4
Classical dichotomy 153, 258
  see also neutrality of money; Say's Law
'Classical economics', J.M. Keynes on 232–7
Classical political economy 44, 72, 170–74, 212, 271, 289, 300, 302, 309–11, 319, 356–7 *see also* Marxian economics; post-classical economics; Sraffian economics
Classical Keynesianism, by Sidney Weintraub 336
Closed-system thinking 12–13, 83–4, 96, 282
Cobweb theorem 225
Co-integration 281
Cold War 30
Commodity money 117, 261, 263
Communism 350–54
Comparative advantage 203
Competition 65–7, 167–9
Complex dynamics 94–5, 177, 179
Conflict theory of inflation 189–90, 219
Consumer theory 68–72, 73, 197
Consumption 72–7, 197, 370–74
Conventions 2–3, 13, 23, 68, 80, 133, 140–41, 163, 254, 312
Costs 285–8, 294–5, 300–302
Cost-plus pricing *see* mark-ups; oligopoly; pricing and prices
Cost-push inflation 33, 93, 188–90
  see also tax-based incomes policy; wages policy

Credit money 21–2, 117–21, 264
Credit rationing 20, 22–3, 63, 78–82, 91, 120, 279
Crises *see* business cycles
Critical realism 13, 82–6, 96–7, 100
Crowding-out 36, 149–50
Cumulative causation 174, 217, 359

Debt 15, 22–4, 64, 146–8, 152–8, 344
Debt deflation theory of crises 147, 229
Deficits *see* budget deficits
Degree of monopoly 173, 183, 251, 329, 383–4
Demand, consumer 68–72
Demand-pull inflation 189–90
Demi-regs 83–4
Democracy 313–17
Depreciation 304–5, 329
Deregulation 337–8, 376
Development economics 227, 315
Development finance 87–91
Dictatorship 313–17
Disequilibrium 28, 123, 151–2, 355–9, 387–8
  see also equilibrium; history and equilibrium
Distribution *see* income distribution
Dual labour markets 382–4
Dualism, philosophical 13–14
Dynamics 92–5, 128–30, 171, 175–80, 212
  see also business cycles; growth; traverse

Econometrics 17–18, 27, 96–101, 114–15, 281, 364
Economic growth *see* growth
Economic Philosophy, by Joan Robinson 213–14
Economic policy
  Austrians on 8–9
  and economic development 91
  and environmental issues 122
  and employment 155–8, 375, 378–9, 380
  institutionalists on 179–200
  international aspects 134–5, 167, 201–5

Journal of Post Keynesian Economics
and 219
Kaldor on 172
Kalecki on 34–8
Keynes on 45, 48, 240–41
main entry 101–5
Minsky on 146–7
New Classical economists on 271–5
New Keynesians on 28, 276
and saving 308
and stagflation 325–7
and transition economies 354
uncertainty and 369
and unemployment 375, 378–9
see also fiscal policy; monetary policy; taxation; tax-based incomes policy; Third Way; Tobin tax; wages policy
Economics, by Paul Samuelson 26
Economics of Imperfect Competition, by Joan Robinson 47, 211, 222
Effective demand
and cumulative causation 217
and growth 178
Kalecki on 358
Keynes on 31, 136, 138–9, 162, 231, 236–7, 250
main entry 105–112
and microfoundations 255
and production 292–3
Sraffa and 319–20
and the Third Way 340
in transition economies 353
and unemployment 116, 269, 292–3, 375–7, 381
see also Keynes's *General Theory*; Say's Law
Efficiency wage theory 113–14, 276–7, 292
Emergent properties 4
Employer of last resort, state as 37, 102, 157–8, 378
Employment 105–10, 112–17, 136–9, 153–9, 373–4, 374–8, 380–84
see also labour market; unemployment; wages
Endogenous growth theory 56, 92, 94, 125, 224
Endogenous money
banks and 20

Dow on 78–9
and fiscal policy 150
Kalecki on 228
Keynes on 28, 246–7
main entry 117–21
and monetary policy 257
and monetary theory 264–5
and the rate of interest 108, 302, 321
see also circuit theory; horizontalism
Entrepreneur economy 88
Entrepreneurs 7–8, 62, 134–41, 144, 239–40, 296–7
Environmental economics 72, 117–21
Equality 313, 316–17
Equilibrium and non-equilibrium
Davidson on 28, 369
and fiscal policy 151–2
Harrod on 177
Hicks on 356, 386
Joan Robinson on 159, 212–14, 355
Kaldor on 94, 177, 222–3
Kalecki on 357–9
Keynes on 136, 163–4, 250
in labour market 250
Lowe on 356–8
main entry 126–31
Marshall on 45
Minsky on 28
in Sraffian economics 359
and time 213–14, 342–3
temporary 386–8
and Tobin tax 347
in Walrasian economics 385–8
Ergodicity 97, 140, 233–5, 280–84, 368–9
Essay on Marxian Economics, by Joan Robinson 212
Essays in the Theory of Employment, by Joan Robinson 213
Essays in the Theory of Economic Growth, by Joan Robinson 212
Ethics and economics 364–5
Excess capacity 178
see also capacity utilization
Exchange rates 15–17, 30–34, 102–3, 120, 131–5, 151, 158, 166, 201–4, 260, 349

Expectations
  asymmetric 79
  Austrian economists on 6–7, 103
  and credit rationing 78–9, 81
  Davidson on 280–81
  and equilibrium 127
  and exchange rates 132–3
  and financial fragility 78
  and investment 205–6
  Kalecki on 228
  Keynes on 161, 163, 244–6, 290
  and liquidity preference 244–6
  and Lucas critique 253
  main entry 134–41
  in neoclassical economics 253–4, 342
  rational 253–4, 273–4, 280, 284
  and stagflation 386–7
  see also New Classical economics; uncertainty
Exploitation 182
Export-led growth 174, 202
Export multiplier 17–19
Externalities 123

Fiat money 117, 263
Finance 132, 142–9, 208, 255–6, 267, 295, 306–8, 346–9
Finance motive for holding money 62, 142–5, 247
Financial crises 81, 216, 219
Financial fragility 78, 91, 146
Financial innovation 187
Financial instability hypothesis 40–41, 88–91, 145–9
Fiscal policy
  and Bastard Keynesians 26, 28
  Chick on 28
  and economic policy 101–2
  Godley on 38
  and inflation 32
  institutional economists on 199–200
  Kaldor on 174
  Kalecki on 34, 35–7, 328–32
  main entry 149–53
  Minsky on 37, 147
  and the multiplier 265–6
  in New Classical economics 272–3
  and socialism 317
  Steindl on 37–8
  see also budget deficits; taxation
Forced saving 239
Foreign direct investment 167–8
Formalism in economics 41–2, 46, 364
  see also econometrics
France 60
Free trade 167, 201, 214
Full-cost principle 251–2
  see also mark-ups; pricing and prices
Full employment
  Davidson on 369
  and employer of last resort 378
  and fiscal policy 101–5, 149, 151
  globalization and 166–7
  Hicks on 356
  and inflation 102
  Joan Robinson on 212
  Kaldor on 177
  Kalecki on 36–7, 101, 151, 377
  Keynes on 101, 166, 246, 376–7
  Lowe on 356–7, 377
  main entry 153–9
  and monetary policy 257–8
  and the multiplier 269
  in neoclassical economics 26, 242, 250, 380
  and the traverse 356–7
  see also effective demand; Say's Law; unemployment
Functional finance 102, 149
Fundamentalist Keynesians 159–64
Funding 88–9

Game theory 385
General equilibrium theory 123, 261, 342, 384–8
General Theory of Employment, Interest and Money, by J.M. Keynes
  borrowers' and lenders' risk in 78, 138–9
  on expectations 135, 138, 163
  on full employment 169, 250
  on income distribution 169
  on investment 205–6, 217–18, 290, 306, 319
  Joan Robinson on 211
  on the labour market 250

Subject index 399

on liquidity preference 246–7
main entry 229–37
and the monetary theory of production 344
on money 142–4, 246–7
and non-ergodicity 283
on the rate of interest 246–7, 301, 307
on saving 306–7
on Say's Law 311
on speculation 346
Sraffa on 319–20
and *Treatise on Money* 238, 241
on uncertainty 159–60, 162–3, 217–18
and wages 319–20
German historical school of economics 283
Gibson paradox 300
Globalization 165–70, 338–9
Golden age 30, 32–3, 49, 176–7, 213, 323–6
Government expenditure 34–8, 149–53, 265–6, 317
see also fiscal policy
Government policy *see* economic policy
Great Depression 147, 154, 170, 178–9, 242, 371
Growth and income distribution 170–75, 177, 223–4
Growth, economic
balance of payments and 15–20, 94, 104, 174–5
endogenous 15
Harrod on 17, 47, 49, 269, 372–3
and income distribution 170–75
Joan Robinson on 212–13
Kaldor on 49, 171–2, 174, 223–5
Kalecki on 93, 104, 358–9, 372
main entry 175–80
neoclassical theory of 16, 54–5, 125–6
neo-Ricardian theory of 174
Pasinetti on 93, 171–2
Steindl on 209
see also dynamics

History versus equilibrium 212–13, 281, 341–5, 355–9

Holism 2
Horizontalism 21–3, 59, 78–9, 121, 264–5
Human rights 379
Hysteresis 113–15, 137, 359, 381

Imperfect competition 211–12, 222, 255, 277
see also degree of monopoly; monopoly; oligopoly
Income distribution
in classical political economy 300, 302–3, 318–19
and fiscal policy 152
and growth 170–75
Kaldor on 171–2, 223–4
Kalecki on 202–3
Keynes on 239
main entry 181–6
monetary policy and 259
neoclassical theory of 51–7
and socialism 313–16
Sraffa on 318–19
and underconsumption 370–74
Implicit contracts 113
Income and substitution effects 71–2
Incomes policy *see* wages policy
Inequality 338, 340
Inflation
Austrian economists on 7
and the balance of payments 151
and economic policy 103–4, 151, 258–60
main entry 186–91
and monetary policy 258–60
and social conflict 32–3, 218–19, 325–6, 373
and stagflation 322–7
Weintraub on 218, 333–6, 373
see also monetarism; Phillips curve; Quantity Theory; stagflation; wages policy
Inflexible prices and wages 275–9, 287–8, 292–3
Innovation 67, 125, 178, 191–6, 209, 213
see also technical progress
Insider–outsider theory 115–16, 292
Institutionalism 68, 145, 196–200, 217, 283, 355, 381–2

400 *Subject index*

Institutions 1–2, 6, 13, 196–200, 351–4, 380–84
Instrumentalism 387
Internal labour markets 382
Interest, theory of
  see liquidity preference; money; rate of interest
International economics 30–34, 131–5, 165–70, 200–205, 346–9
  see also balance-of-payments-constrained growth; Bretton Woods; exchange rates; free trade; globalization
International Monetary Clearing Union (IMCU) 204
International Monetary Fund 169, 339, 348–9
International monetary system 30–34, 131–5, 260
Introduction to the Theory of Employment, by Joan Robinson 211
Investment
  and competition 66
  and development finance 88
  and economic policy 102, 150
  and effective demand 107–8
  and expectations 136–8
  and finance 88, 144
  and growth 93
  and interest rates 150, 228–9, 242, 246, 301
  Joan Robinson on 173
  Kaldor on 173, 183, 306–7
  Kalecki on 36, 173, 183, 228–9
  Keynes on 48, 136, 162–3, 235, 239–40, 246, 301, 307, 372, 376
  main entry 205–210
  Minsky on 136–8, 255–6
  and the multiplier 266–9
  neoclassical theory of 255–6
  and profits 294–8
  and saving 107–8, 242, 306–7, 372–3
  and uncertainty 217–18
  and underconsumption 372–3
IS–LM model 25–9, 265, 313
Italy 60

Japan 18, 19
Joan Robinson's economics 211–15

Job guarantee *see* Employer of last resort
Journal of Economic Issues 334
Journal of Post Keynesian Economics 96, 215–20

Kaldorian economics 221–6
Kaleckian economics 226–9
Keynesian cross diagram 25–7
Keynes's *General Theory* 229–37
  see also General Theory of Employment, Interest and Money
Keynes's *Treatise on Money* 237–41
  see also Treatise on Money

Labour market
  and effective demand 109–10
  and employment 112–17
  and income distribution 102–5
  Keynes on 254–5, 319–20
  in neoclassical economics 276–7
  and stagflation 326
  and unemployment 374–8
  and wages 380–84
  see also employment; full employment; trade unions; unemployment; wages
Labour theory of value 56, 212
Lender of last resort 24, 57–9, 146
Lender's risk 78, 138–9, 207
Lexicographic preferences 70
Liability management 20–21
Liquidity preference
  and banks 21, 23–4
  Davidson on 369
  and effective demand 108, 312–13
  Keynes on 233–4, 265, 312–13
  main entry 242–8
  and rate of interest 184
Liquidity trap 313
Loanable funds theory of interest 22, 29, 148, 162, 242–3, 245, 376
Long-period analysis 44–5, 47, 112, 212, 214, 320–21
Long waves 38, 41
Lucas critique 253, 256

Marginal productivity theory 5–6, 63, 113–14, 181–2, 185, 213, 296–7, 321

Marginalism 249–52, 300, 384
Market socialism 315–16
Mark-up pricing 61, 63, 67, 92, 120, 168, 183, 188, 201–3, 218, 227, 285–8, 291, 330–32, 334
Marshall–Lerner condition 17
Marshall Plan 30
Marshallian economics 44–5, 319–20, 385
Marxian economics 92–3, 154, 182, 184, 212, 228, 289, 371–2
Materialism 3–4
Mathematical methods in economics 364
Megacorp 168
Menu costs 278
Methodological individualism 2, 6, 8, 61
Methodology 46–7, 96–101, 112, 126–31, 159, 252–3, 271, 321, 387
Microfoundations 61, 74, 106, 109–10, 234, 252–7
Monetarism 156–7, 187, 189, 259, 271, 275
  see also Quantity Theory
Monetary circuit, theory of 61–5, 119
Monetary policy
  and banks 21
  Bastard Keynesians and 26, 28
  and endogenous money 117–21, 265
  and fiscal policy 150
  and inflation 187, 333
  Kaldor on 172
  Keynes on 240, 246
  main entry 257–61
  neoclassical economics on 187, 300–302
  in New Classical economics 271–5
  and rate of interest 300–302, 321
  see also central banks; inflation; interest rates; Quantity Theory; Taylor rule
Monetary theory of production 60, 88, 136, 179, 216, 233, 238, 262, 264, 311–12, 344
Money
  Cambridge economists on 44–50
  circuit theory of 60–64, 267
  Davidson on 57
  and equilibrium 128–9
  and finance motive 142–4
  Kaldor on 58–9
  Keynes on 142–4, 198, 233–6, 237–41, 242–7, 311–12, 343–5
  Lavoie on 246–7
  main entry 261–5
  Moore on 59, 117–21, 246–7
  and the multiplier 267
  and Say's Law 310–12
  Wray on 247, 261–5
  see also endogenous money; liquidity preference; monetary policy; neutrality of money; rate of interest
Monopolistic competition *see* degree of monopoly; imperfect competition; oligopoly
Monopoly 47, 92, 296–8
  see also degree of monopoly; imperfect competition; oligopoly
Monopoly capitalism 228, 371
Multiplier 17–19, 35, 48, 144, 230, 265–70, 304, 306–7, 388

NAIRU (Non-accelerating inflation rate of unemployment) 156–7, 279, 324
  see also natural rate of unemployment
National debt 36
Natural rate of interest 187, 190, 240, 301
Natural rate of unemployment 103, 113, 114, 156, 190, 272, 324, 380
  see also labour market; unemployment
Neoclassical economics
  Austrian economics and 4
  and capital theory 51–6
  and consumer theory 73–7
  and economic methodology 96–7
  and environmental economics 121–3
  and fiscal policy 149
  and growth theory 92, 94, 176, 223
  and income distribution 181–2, 185
  Joan Robinson on 25
  and labour markets 380–81, 383
  and microfoundations 252–6
  and production 289, 292
  and the rate of interest 300–301

Neoclassical economics (*continued*)
and Say's Law 312–13
Sraffa on 47
and taxation 328, 331
and time in economic theory 341–3
and uncertainty 364
see also general equilibrium theory; IS–LM model; marginalism; neoclassical synthesis; Walrasian economics
Neoclassical synthesis 25–9, 292, 301, 313, 320
Neo-Keynesian economics 157, 173
Neoliberalism 31, 165, 308, 337–41
Neo-Ricardian economics 55, 84, 93, 122–3, 174, 182, 293
see also Sraffian economics
Neutrality of money 6, 19, 63, 186, 233, 236, 238, 282, 284, 321–2, 369
New Classical economics 29, 233, 252–3, 271–3, 276–7, 283, 381
New Keynesian economics 29, 77, 87, 89, 145, 230, 233, 256, 275, 275–80, 283, 292, 380
New mercantilism 201–2, 214
Non-equilibrium 126–31, 355–9, 388
Non-ergodicity 1–2, 8, 72, 97, 140, 159–60, 217–18, 233–7, 254, 256, 280–84, 368–9
Normal cost 285–6, 299
Normal profits 296–7, 300–302

Oligopoly 19, 65–7, 209, 291, 382
see also degree of monopoly; imperfect competition; mark-up pricing
Open-system thinking 12–14, 82–4, 96–7, 167–8, 193, 202–3, 252, 283
see also critical realism
Organicism 14, 96–7, 128, 162
Outsourcing 168–9

Paradox of costs 173
Paradox of debt 22
Paradox of thrift 173, 306
Pasinetti theorem 171
Path dependency 355–6, 359, 388
see also history versus equilibrium; hysteresis

Perfect competition 65–7, 168, 181, 183
Permanent income hypothesis 73
Phillips curve 27, 42, 156–7, 189–90, 272, 318–19, 322–5, 334
Philosophy 11–15, 46, 82–6, 96–7, 99–100, 160, 162, 360–64
see also methodology
Planning 313–16, 350–52
Pluralism 14
Poland 226–7
Political business cycle 41
Policy *see* economic policy
Power 183
Predator-prey models 178
Pre-Keynesian economics 156, 292, 306
see also neoclassical economics
Pricing and prices 19, 46–7, 65–7, 123–4, 168, 227, 250, 275–7, 285–91, 299, 351–2
see also inflation; mark-up pricing
Principle of increasing risk 146–7
Principles of Economics, by Alfred Marshall 249
Principles of Economics, by David Ricardo 212, 249
Privatization 352–4
Probability 160–61, 280, 360–64, 366–70
Procedural rationality 68
Product cycle theory 204
Production 61–3, 122–6, 167–8, 289–93
Production functions 51, 54, 181–2, 213, 296–7
see also capital theory
Production of Commodities By Means Of Commodities, by Piero Sraffa 47, 50, 171, 173–4, 213–14
see also Sraffian economics
Productivity growth 66, 174, 224–5, 375
Profit, rate of *see* rate of profit
Profits
and budget deficits 35–6
in circuit theory 63
in classical political economy 319
Kaldor on 171–3, 183–4, 223–4
Kalecki on 35–6, 226–7, 329–30

Keynes on 239
main entry 294–8
and taxation 329–30
see also rate of profit
Propensity to consume 72–6, 107, 183–5, 197, 237, 329, 371
Propensity to save 246, 371
Pseudo-production function 213
Psychology and economics 132–3, 223–4
Public employment 37, 102, 157–8, 378–9
Public works 35

Quantity Theory of money 45, 48, 58, 117, 186–7, 238, 242, 246, 333
see also monetarism
Quarterly Journal of Economics 159, 171

Radcliffe Committee 172
Rate of interest
in circuit theory 64
in 'classical' economics 310–11, 376
and credit rationing 81
and fiscal policy 150
Friedman on 271–2
Kaldor on 58–9
Kalecki on 58–9
Keynes on 108, 184, 225–9, 240, 242–7, 265, 307, 312, 376
main entry 299–303
and monetary policy 257–60, 265
Moore on 21–2, 58–9
in neoclassical theory 21–2, 120–21, 124, 187, 310–11, 376
Pasinetti on 184
and profits 295
Sraffa on 321
see also credit rationing; interest; IS–LM model; liquidity preference; liquidity trap
Rate of profit 173, 177, 184–5, 212–13, 293, 297, 300, 302, 319
Rational expectations 103, 132, 233, 253–4, 258, 273, 280–81, 284, 307, 387
see also New Classical Economics

Rationalism 8, 11, 363
Rationality 68, 271–5, 276, 282, 342–3, 360, 362–3, 366
Realism 2, 6, 82–6
see also critical realism
Rent 249
Reswitching of techniques 52–3, 55, 213
Rhetoric 98
Ricardian equivalence 272–3
Risk 78, 138–9, 207, 296, 366
see also principle of increasing risk; uncertainty
Russia 169, 314–15, 351

Saving
and development finance 88
and economic policy 102
and effective demand 108, 234–6, 246, 269, 312
and investment 93, 108, 239–40, 312, 372, 376
Keynes on 234–6, 239–40, 242, 246, 312, 376
main entry 304–9
and the multiplier 266–7
and underconsumption 371–4
Say's Law
Bastard Keynesianism and 29
and full employment 134–5, 154
Joan Robinson on 372
Keynes on 109, 162, 230–33, 376
main entry 309–13
and neoclassical theory 131–2
New Classical economics and 272
New Keynesian economics and 29
and saving 304
Segmented labour markets 382–4
Shock therapy 352
Short-period analysis 44–8
Social democracy 337–41, 373
Socialism 227, 229, 313–18, 337, 350–54, 358
see also Marxian economics
Soviet Union 314–15, 337, 341, 373
Speculation 30–32, 90, 138–9, 143, 146, 168, 202, 207, 222, 244–5, 346, 349
Speculative demand for money 143, 243–6

404 Subject index

Sraffian economics 55–6, 72, 216, 269–70, 318–22, 356, 359
   see also classical political economy; neo-Ricardian economics
Stagflation 2, 7, 216, 322–7, 332,
   see also inflation; unemployment
Stagnation 209, 228, 372–3
State theory of money 262–3
Structural change 93–4, 178, 377–8
Subcontracting 168
Subjectivism 160, 182
   see also Austrian economics
Substitution 69, 71, 104, 233–6
Supply-side economics 331
Surplus, economic 49–50, 153, 270, 295, 319–20, 371
   see also Marxian economics; Sraffian economics
Sustainability 125–6

Target rate of return pricing 286
Taxation 172, 222–3, 262–3, 317, 328–32
   see also budget deficits; fiscal policy; tax-based incomes policy; Tobin tax
Tax-based incomes policy (TIP) 103, 151, 188, 332–8
   see also wages policy
Taylor rule of monetary policy 121, 187, 259
Technical progress 54, 95, 176–7, 213, 375–7
   see also innovation
Technical progress function 224
Technology gap 203–4
Temporary equilibrium 385–6
Third Way 337–41
Thirlwall's law 16, 18, 94, 217
Time in economic theory 2, 6, 44–5, 108, 127–9, 163, 214, 284, 341–6
   see also expectations; history and equilibrium; hysteresis; uncertainty
Time-dependence see hysteresis
Tobin tax 103, 346–9
Trade, theory of 167, 200–205
Trade cycles see business cycles
Trade unions 115–16, 185, 188, 277, 373, 376, 380, 382

Transition economies 350–54
Transnational corporations 168
Traverse 355–9
   see also history and equilibrium; time in economic theory
Treasury view 304
Treatise on Money, by J.M. Keynes 35, 47, 54, 60, 79, 88, 205–6, 211, 237–41, 247, 261
Treatise on Probability, by J.M. Keynes 160, 162–3, 359–65
Trieste summer school 320
Twin deficits 149–51

Uncertainty
   in Austrian economics 6–9, 13
   and credit rationing 77
   Davidson on 6–9, 13, 280, 342
   and economic policy 103
   and effective demand 108
   and environmental economics 124–5
   and equilibrium 128
   and exchange rates 133
   and investment 207, 209, 217–18, 290, 295–6
   Kalecki on 228
   Keynes on 159–64, 207, 234–5, 271, 280, 312–13, 343–4, 364
   main entry 366–70
   and New Classical economics 274
   and neoclassical economics 254, 256, 321
   Sraffa on 321
   and Walrasian economics 388
   see also expectations; principle of increasing risk
Underconsumption 370–74
Unemployment
   and competition 65
   Davidson on 198
   economic policy and 103–4, 155–6, 259
   and inflation 41, 103, 156, 322–7
   Keynes on 47–8, 162–3, 230, 234, 241, 265
   main entry 374–9
   Marx on 154
   monetary policy and 159
   New Keynesian economics on 29
   wage rigidity and 113

Walrasian economics and 386, 388
see also employment; full employment; NAIRU; natural rate of unemployment; Phillips curve; stagflation
United Nations Development Programme (UNDP) 346, 348

Velocity of circulation of money 272, 334
Verdoorn's Law 224

Wage differentials 383
Wage-cost mark-up 188, 218, 334–6
Wages and labour markets 380–84
see also employment; full employment
Wages, money
and employment 185, 250, 292–3, 373
and inflation 188–9, 325–6, 334–5
main entry 380–84
in New Keynesian economics 275–7
and real wages 250
rigidity of 113, 275–7
see also labour market; Phillips curve; Pigou effect; tax-based incomes policy; trade unions; wages policy
Wages, real
conflict over 189, 302, 325–6, 373–4
and effective demand 254–5, 373
and employment 109, 113–15, 181–2, 185, 311, 374
and growth 173, 185
Kalecki on 331, 373–4
Keynes on 254–5
main entry 380–84
Marx on 377
and money wages 250
and the rate of interest 300, 302
Ricardo on 297
Sraffa on 319
see also efficiency wages; marginal productivity
Wages policy 103, 151, 157, 188, 332–7
see also inflation; tax-based incomes policy
Walrasian economics 26, 342, 345, 381, 384–8
see also general equilibrium theory; IS–LM model; neoclassical economics; neoclassical synthesis
Washington consensus 337–41
Weight of argument 161, 163
Welfare economics 122–6
Welfare state 337–41, 354
World Bank 348
World Trade Organisation 341

Yugoslavia 316